DYNAMICS

of

GROUPS AT WORK

By HERBERT A. THELEN

DYNAMICS
of
GROUPS AT WORK

THE UNIVERSITY OF CHICAGO PRESS

CHICAGO AND LONDON

ISBN: 0-226-79473-3 (clothbound); 0-226-79474-1 (paperbound)

THE UNIVERSITY OF CHICAGO PRESS, CHICAGO 60637
The University of Chicago Press, Ltd., London

Preface to the Phoenix Edition

The reissue of a book in the gay and soaring guise of Phoenix is one of those ceremonial occasions calling for a few words from the author. It is an opportunity to reintroduce a work to a world which is not quite the same as it was eight years ago. The Cold War is eight years older; the Organization Man has been discovered; somehow national life has fewer degrees of freedom; the educational pendulum has swung from a humanistic goal toward the goal of providing manpower; political overtones are found in more and more varieties of decisions. These developments do not change the dynamics of human behavior, but they do alter the kind of significance one finds in an account of human behavior.

This book, with its underlying respect for individual orientations and feelings and its assumption that wisdom is an emergent thing to be developed through give-and-take discussion in the service of shared purposes, is more revolutionary today than it was eight years ago. The message that social processes appropriate to human nature can result in creative solutions and in the adaptive maintenance of groups, communities, and societies seems more obscure than it did—and is, therefore, more worth asserting. The fact that, when all is said and done, life is the experiencing of and by real persons creating real events together needs to be reaffirmed as an antidote to the attitude that bureaucratic policy, centralized power, and expert opinion have a kind of monolithic life of their own quite apart from people.

This book presents social process as the means by which individuals cope with their problems and as the instrument through which societies and groups try to legislate á better state of affairs. This generalization is, in fact, true. And we propose that the understanding of this truth will lead to better action and to more significant lives.

HERBERT A. THELEN

Preface

The face-to-face group working on a problem is the meeting ground of individual personality and society. It is in the group that personality is modified and socialized; and it is through the workings of groups that society is changed and adapted to its times. These two processes are not separate; they are merely two aspects of the same phenomenon. Moreover, they are necessary to each other: without social purposes shared with others there would be no basis for the give-and-take through which the individual develops his capabilities, and without the differences among individual personalities there would be no basis for the creation of new and better solutions to the problems of living.

Both the relationships between these two processes and the slanting of group experience toward personal growth or social purposes differ from group to group and are determined by leadership. Effective leadership depends on understanding these two processes, and it facilitates both. It recognizes that every group has purposes to be achieved, that it has problems of organizing itself and utilizing the resources of its members to achieve these purposes, and that its members have problems of assimilating their experiences in the group within their own private worlds. The goal of effective leadership is to encourage behaviors that contribute simultaneously to the solution of these fundamental problems.

These, then, are the matters with which this book is concerned, and two kinds of approach are used. The first is "practical." It assumes that basic principles and understandings can be found from the analysis of successful practice in such areas as citizen participation, classroom teaching, in-service professional training, administration and management, human relations training, and public meetings. Part I devotes one chapter to each of these technologies. Each chapter pays particular attention to the things that "stand out" most. Thus, the distinctive feature of citizen programs is that participation is voluntary; of classroom teaching, that it demands so many roles of the teacher and is concerned with so wide an array of student needs; of in-service training, that it changes the character of an institution through individual growth; of administration and management, that it involves the exercise of power; of human relations training, that it is based on the continual diagnosis of emotion; of public meetings, that they represent a patterning of activities in a sequence to achieve carefully defined and limited goals.

Behind these differences, however, are fundamental similarities. Part II is concerned with concepts useful in thinking about group activity regardless of its social purposes or particular clientele. The six chapters of Part II present a development of ideas beginning with the meaning for individuals of group membership and then considering in turn the processes of experiencing by individuals, the kinds of facts with which a group operates, the nature of group control, the problems of leadership, and, finally, the community as the context for group activity. It is in this part that we attempt to weave together many ideas from the social sciences.

To aid the reader in seeing how the material in the various chapters fits together, we have included in each chapter references to other parts of the book that are particularly revealing by way of illustration, amplification, or explanation. An annotated list of selected readings is given at the end of this book.

The background of this book can perhaps be seen in the acknowledgments made below. I owe a great deal to a great many people: to Professor Lawrence F. Foster (supervisor of practice teaching, Education Department, University of California), for showing me that teaching is a continuous adventure, challenging one's faculties of creativity and objectivity; to the late Professor E. D. Eastman (Chemistry Department, University of California) for understanding of the scientific method of inquiry as guided by human imagination; to Dean R. W. Tyler (Social Sciences Division, University of Chicago) for his insistence on operationality as the sine qua non of meaning in ideas; to Professor Carl Rogers (Department of Psychology, University of Chicago) and Dr. Helmut Baum (associate psychiatrist, Division of Neuropsychiatry, Michael Reese Hospital) for insights into the central importance and dynamics of man's subjective life; to the writings of Kurt Lewin and John Dewey for understanding of the basic approach to human behavior—as interactions participated in by the whole person; to the writings of Dr. W. R. Bion for a psychiatric approach to the group as a whole; to the late Tom Wright (Chicago Commission on Human Relations) for his brilliant insights into the social meaning of urban group activity.

I am indebted to many people and groups for making possible the wide range of research and practical experience on which this work is based: to the Chairman of the Department of Education, Maurice Seay (University of Chicago); to Howard Page and Joan Criswell of the Human Relations and Morale Division, Office of Naval Research, for support of theoretical and methodological investigations; to the Education Directorate, Human Resources Research Institute at Air University, for opportunity for applied research with learning groups; to the Wieboldt Foundation for support of community action research; to the National Training Laboratory for Group Development for induction into, and experience with, human relations training; to the Chicago Commission on Human Relations for partnership in our citizen action workshops; and, finally, to a large number of classes, citizens' organizations, professional conferences, and research project seminars for the opportunity to work with them in exploring better methods of group operation.

Lastly, I wish to acknowledge with deepest gratitude the emotional support, stimulation, and inspiration of my research students and associates; my professional colleagues Hugh Coffey, John R. P. French, Don Nylen, Freed Bales, Alvin Zander, Ron Lippitt, Floyd Reeves, Bruno Bettelheim, Leland Bradford, Helen Jennings, Fritz Redl, Kenneth Benne, Ted Newcomb; my journalistic mentors, Stuart and Marian Chase; my indefatigable secretary, Mrs. Pearl Bunton; and, above all, my wife, Leonora Elizabeth Thelen.

HERBERT A. THELEN

HUMAN DYNAMICS LABORATORY
DEPARTMENT OF EDUCATION
UNIVERSITY OF CHICAGO

Contents

PART I. SIX TECHNOLOGIES

PART II. EXPLANATIONS

SELECTED READINGS

INDEX

PART I

SIX TECHNOLOGIES

A PRELIMINARY NOTE

A technology is a set of principles useful to bring about change toward desired ends. One distinguishing feature of a particular technology, then, is its target for change—the individuals, groups, or objective conditions which it is designed to alter.

The right to influence others is founded upon some kind of authority, and this is best symbolized in the leadership of the group trying to promote change. A second difference among technologies, then, is the source of the authority of leadership.

A third difference is the role of the member in the group trying to produce and maintain changes. This is defined by the expectations he and the other members hold for his performance and action.

A fourth difference is in the method of group control employed. In each situation there will be a distribution of emphases on problem-solving, on maintenance of the change-group, or on problems of individuals within the group.

A fifth difference is in the relationships between the group promoting change and the other groups with which it communicates; and the ways of communication also vary.

We shall begin each of the next six chapters with a brief comment on the nature of the technology and shall then characterize it with respect to each of the five features noted above. It is hoped that these introductory statements will facilitate comparisons among the technologies as here presented. We shall close each of the next six chapters with further identification of some of the theoretical problems behind the practices described, and we shall indicate sections in Part II which are particularly relevant to these problems.

CHAPTER 1

When citizens get together and share ideas and feelings, they tend to shake off their apathy and become ready for work. When they deal with problems they feel strongly about—in their own neighborhoods—they improve the community and learn what it means to be citizens. The whole political and friendship climate changes. But for success there must be proper leadership and training and the support of a parent organization.

DISTINCTIVE FEATURES

Participation in the program of citizen action is voluntary, and this means that the authority of leadership is the shared and mobilized optimism, determination—or possibly resentment—of the citizens. The primary target of change is a set of community standards. These are standards which sanction inactivity, exploitation, and the every-man-for-himself attitude. The change required is an awakened and maintained social consciousness and conscience. The role of members in the organization is defined by the expectations that they will take care of their own social and financial investments, come to meetings, recruit others, work in committees and projects agreed upon by their group, and, possibly, undergo training for leadership. The method of control of meetings is through the development of group commitment to particular projects, and then satisfaction of the demands of these projects; behavior is relevant and useful when it contributes to getting the job done, and it is hindering or nonuseful to the extent that it is a response to ideological, class, or racial factors. The neighborhood group communicates with city officials directly, receives services from a central parent organization, and joins with other neighborhood groups on large-area projects. Unofficial communication to other organizations to which neighbors also belong is through the initiative of individuals.

Rebuilding the Community through Citizen Action

There is only one phenomenon quite as spectacular in its own weird way as the rapid growth of a city, and that is its decline. It is a quiet, spotty, unnoticed decay, neighborhood by neighborhood. Hoopla and excitement attend the opening of the new chrome and glass-incased high school in the currently "nice" part of town; but the overcrowded, beat-up old pride of the eighties on the "wrong" side of the tracks does not even get a decent burial.

A large part of many big cities is middle-aged—neither very "nice" nor very "wrong." These parts, serene and stable to the eye, represent a state of balance between forces of growth and of decay. A school fight every decade, a trickle of ritualistic gossip about the neighbors, an occasional new wing for the hospital, a sudden meteoric business success or failure, the hearings when the transit company replaces streetcars with busses, the annual three-day merchants' shopping event—this is the life of the neighborhood. Dull and comfortable.

It does not take much to put such a neighborhood on the skids. A new superhighway, prosperity, plant shutdowns, influx of population to the city, opening of suburbs, depression, shortage of construction materials, political administration of city services— any or all of these factors can tip the scales in favor of deterioration and blight. World War II, with its massive dislocations, brought to many cities unprecedented prosperity and widespread ruin. The prosperous moved on and out, but the ruined neighborhoods remained.

Accompanying and supporting and causing physical change is social change. Deterioration of a community is not only a matter of crumbling bricks and insecure fences; it is a matter of crumbling morale and insecure people. Maintenance of a community

3

is maintenance of civic consciousness; both must be fed by continual positive communication, planning, and action. These things require the participation of citizens. When citizens lose interest, the balance between growth and decay loses its dynamics, its resilience and restoring force. It no longer can reestablish itself in the face of inevitable changes in the neighborhood.

This chapter presents an exciting story of citizen participation in a community that had one foot on the skids. Through this story we shall investigate the dynamics of action and social problem-solving, and we shall see, on a community-wide scale, the application of the same principles that govern operation in face-to-face groups.

We begin in Chicago in the year 1950.

THE COURSE OF URBAN DETERIORATION[1]

World War II created a vast number of jobs in Chicago's industry. Labor was attracted from all over the country, but especially from the South. During the decade beginning in 1940, there was an increase of 42 per cent among the nonwhite population in Chicago. The construction of houses and other dwelling units did not keep pace with the increase of population, and the resulting shortage of housing became Chicago's number one problem. Two-thirds of the new dwelling units created between 1940 and 1950 failed to meet minimum legal standards of quality. Overcrowding developed and, with it, the decline of morale and communication among neighbors.

The population increases strained the available city services to the utmost. The conditions accompanying overcrowding aggravated still further the problems of maintaining police, fire, and health protection. The average cost of maintenance per citizen increased far beyond what the city budget provided. Many areas were slighted altogether by one or another of the city's services.

1. The next several pages come from a speech more or less as delivered to the Chicago Chapter of the International Society for General Semantics, March 27, 1953. See "Shall We Sit Idly By?" *Etc.*, Vol. XI, No. 1 (fall, 1953). H. A. Thelen and B. B. Sarchet, *Neighbors in Action*, Human Dynamics Laboratory, University of Chicago, 1954, is a considerably expanded discussion of these ideas and practices.

After the United States Supreme Court ruled that bailiffs of federal courts could not be used to enforce restrictive covenants, people began to react not only to the grim facts but also to all sorts of racial fears and fantasies. In some neighborhoods there was panic or rioting when the first Negroes moved in. As residents fled, their places were taken by Negroes, whose need for housing was most desperate—and who were willing to make desperate bargains for property. In some areas, the Negro in-migration took over one block after another, thus in effect simply extending the "black belt."

SOCIAL DISORGANIZATION

The skyrocketing prices of property, the limitation by rent control of income from property, the pressure for housing of any kind—these caused individuals in all parts of the city to decide to sublet or to create new, smaller units in their buildings. In many cases this decision ushered into neighborhoods a hitherto unfamiliar kind of person: the rooming-house tenant. With increased mixing of apartments, rooming-houses, kitchenette flats, and single-family residents came greater mixing of people who differed in their class levels, social backgrounds, values, and ways of life. And these changes were most visible when the incomers were Negroes.

The mixing of class and of caste resulted not only in the breakdown of communication on the block but also in the feeling that communication would now be impossible. Neighbors were no longer seen as people one could identify with; the sense of common cause was lost. People felt more and more reluctant to talk with the neighbors, and their concerns accordingly turned inward on themselves rather than being directed outward as in the past. The deterioration of the physical community seemed to create only personal problems for individual residents, rather than problems for the block or the community as a whole to deal with.[2]

2. It is true, however, that some neighborhoods contained many groups with regular meetings. But these were nonaction groups which provided, perhaps, some feeling of escape from the frustrations of the role of citizen. They contributed very little to the rectification of conditions or to the adjustment of individuals to the conditions.

The feeling of apathy and frustration of neighbors was assimilated into "official" attitudes toward neighborhoods where changes were occurring. There was increasing reluctance of city servants to meet the needs of these areas—and this added fuel to the flames of resentment and frustration. The result was, in effect, that all the usual channels by which citizens normally can get at least some action were gradually blocked off.

Finally, as if to complete this sorry picture of disorganization, there was flight; people moved out, sometimes in blind panic and sometimes to find the better living their war prosperity made possible. In either case, the flight was by people who had enough money to flee; and these people tended to belong to the group which had provided leadership and vigilance in the past. Thus flight was not only the symbol of panic and of defeat in the face of anxiety, but it was also the creator of a vacuum in the power structure of the city. And there was no lack of people ready and able to turn civic disorder into personal wealth. Most notable was the alliance between crime and politics: during the decade it changed from a hothouse plant, delicately and blushingly nurtured by a few, into a rank prairie weed, openly and knowingly nurtured by the many.

PERSONAL DISORGANIZATION

Most citizens were part, parcel, and carrier of the social disorganization. They felt lonely, isolated, cut off from the group. Some felt that they had been singled out for special persecution. Feelings of helplessness became widespread, and, with these feelings, came a stifling blanket of fears. It was, for example, not uncommon for people to be afraid at night to put their autos in the garages on the alley. Along with fear came anxiety and anger at feeling fearful. Out of this arose interpretations that were mostly projections of hostility onto convenient target groups (scapegoats): the Negroes, the cops, the landlords, yes, and even the Democrats.

The fears were expressed in rumors of all sorts; nothing was too silly to be handed on: "the Urban League has a million dollars to break white blocks for Negro occupancy"; "the syndicate wants to convert all the big homes in the Fourth Ward into rooming-houses." Fears and anxieties snowballed because there were no channels for constructive action to relieve frustration. Apathy and defeatism set in, and, with these, hypocrisy and guilt feelings. When one is lonely he thinks it is his own fault; he blames himself and at the same time tries to put up a front both to himself and to the "group," which, he does not realize, exists no longer. These conditions were clearly revealed, for instance, in an interview with a lovely lady who said that she had lived in the neighborhood all her life and intended to finish her days there. In the midst of this painted picture of security and comfort a man in overalls interrupted by ringing the doorbell. He said, "I'm from Ace Moving Company. Is this the house where I am to pick up the furniture?" People would protest they were going to stay in the neighborhood and they loved it—right up to the point where they melted away into the night.

The over-all interpretation of all these things is that individual behavior became more and more determined by self-concern. It expressed reaction to anxiety insufficiently controlled by contact with the world of objective social facts.

Facing Facts

By November, 1949, the flight of people along Drexel Avenue where the Negroes had moved in threatened serious depletion of the congregations of certain churches. At their request, Tom Wright, director of the Chicago Commission on Human Relations, began preliminary discussions with the Social Order Committee of the 57th Street Meeting of Friends. These led to a meeting of forty concerned citizens from various organizations in the Hyde Park–Kenwood area.[3] The meeting was stormy, and it faced some very sobering facts: (1) that sociologists and planners predicted that the area would be a slum in ten years; (2) that nobody knew of any examples of a community which, when once started on the path of deterioration, had worked its

3. On the South Side: Forty-seventh to Fifty-ninth Streets, Cottage Grove Avenue to Lake Michigan. This was the nucleus of the Hyde Park–Kenwood Community Conference; and the examples used in this chapter all come from the experiences of the Conference. I have been concerned from the beginning in the development of the block program. Another account is by Stuart Chase, in *Reader's Digest*, May, 1953.

way back out; (3) that a whole dynamic pattern of forces toward deterioration was practically unopposed, and that the reversal of these forces would require all-out action on a staggering array of fronts.

The group also saw that there were logically just three alternatives: (1) that citizens could flee from the area, leaving it to exploiters and opportunists to profit from social deterioration; (2) that the group could sit tight and do nothing on the grounds that the problems were too big or that they did not have the required resources; (3) that the group could start to work.

I think that this group recognized that going to work did not necessarily mean success, but that successful or not they must try. Following this feeling of commitment, the group planned a program and talked about what it could do, rather than what it could not do, to get started. Half of the resulting program would be concerned with the pinpointing of specific objectives: enforcing the law, bettering the schools, getting recreation facilities, establishing relations with the building commissioner's office, planning for future development, running a survey of the area to find the extent of deterioration, and so on. As each of these objectives became clarified, working committees would have to be recruited and set up, and they would have to become influential in mobilizing pressures strategically to get decisions changed or improved for the benefit of the community.

It was seen that the second half of the program would need to be concerned with what sometimes has been called the grass roots aspects. Basically, the origin of this part of the program was the realization, in general terms, that no one group of forty dedicated individuals could possibly provide the man-hours, skill, and energy required to reverse the whole pattern of social action in the community. A veritable army, co-ordinated and energetic, would be required.

It was recognized that the area was unstable in the sense that its ultimate fate was in doubt. In such communities, the positive forces of growth appear to have been halted, but deterioration has not yet progressed to the point of slum conditions. For slum conditions, incidentally, there is a pat answer: bring in the bulldozer and knock everything down, relocate the citizens, build new buildings, then move some of the people back in. This area had not run down that far. It was seen that progress or deterioration in the area would depend upon the cumulative wisdom of the thousands of decisions made by citizens every day. Some of the individual activities which would forecast the community's future were:

1. Decisions about how extensively and how adequately to keep up property.

2. Decisions about the use to which property will be put, particularly with respect to the type of dwelling units and number of people living in each.

3. Initiation of actions and follow-up requests for city services.

4. Participation in neighborhood conversation to share ideas of the standards to be maintained.

5. Expression of attitudes of friendliness or indifference or hostility which foster concern for the welfare of all or which indicate only concern for one's self.

6. Maintenance of an attitude of objectivity toward rumors: the tendency to make objective inquiry and the feeling of trusting other people's common sense, so that one does not rush off always believing the worst.

Since these and many other everyday behaviors of citizens were seen to determine the fate of the community, it was necessary to try to reach everybody under conditions which would result in the most intelligent behavior possible.

Following this analysis of what would be required to stop deterioration and rebuild the community, the initial group of forty citizens talked with officers of existing improvement and planning councils and associations. None were ready to spearhead the immense effort that would be required.

A new organization, the Hyde Park–Kenwood Community Conference, was formed. It set up working committees to study problems of law enforcement, schools, recreation, planning, zoning, and the like. The Conference also created the program of "block organization," through which it hoped to enlist every citizen into a massive, co-ordinated, and self-disciplined movement to halt deterioration and to rebuild the community.

Before finally adopting the program of block organization, the

Conference decided to try the idea of neighborly meetings in one block first. A certain block on Drexel Avenue held the first meeting in January, 1950; it illustrates many of the principles and characteristics of subsequent block meetings.[4]

As it turned out, this block meeting was planned at a strategic time—when rumors were sweeping the block that a house was about to be sold to exploiters who would pack a Negro family into each room. People were concerned, and they knew that each of the others was concerned; there was something to discuss, no question about that! As soon as the rumors swept the block, four people put their houses up for sale.

Everybody in a row of fifteen owner-occupied houses was invited to the meeting by a small planning group of four. These four personally visited the families with whom they were already acquainted—it was easier that way. As the people came into the house, it was clear that they had different expectations, ranging from the notion that we were met to consider strategies to keep the Negroes out to the feeling that we ought to invite Negroes in and turn the neighborhood into an interracial paradise. These attitudes were expressed fairly readily by people in small discussion groups which had formed before the meeting started.

After about twenty minutes, the feeling arose that we should get started, and there were many glances toward the chairman and host. An old man about eighty climbed up on the stair landing and opened the meeting with this gem: "What do you want me to tell you about those damn niggers?" There was a decidedly awkward pause. The leader replied that while listening to the informal conversations before the meeting opened he had discovered that we had a wide range of feelings about Negroes among us, and he suggested that we might as well accept this as a fact about ourselves about which we could do nothing. He pointed out, however, that Negroes had bought the apartment building across the street and he felt that the block faced certain objective possibilities:

1. It could form a pitchfork mob to try to drive the Negroes out.
2. It could attempt to ignore them.

4. The following account is from H. A. Thelen, "Social Process versus Community Deterioration," *Group Psychotherapy*, IV (December, 1951), 209–10.

3. It could attempt to establish communication with them with the idea of explaining the block's determination to prevent physical deterioration and to make the block a pleasant place in which to live.

Posed in this way, looking toward alternative possibilities for action growing out of a real situation, the group quickly decided to begin talking to people. A committee, combining the features of investigating team and friendship group, was appointed to go calling on the new neighbors. The Negroes, fortunately, could see the committee's embarrassment and were mature enough to help them establish communication. The fact that members of the committee did not have strong feelings either way about Negroes undoubtedly made matters easier.

Three other actions were taken at the first meeting; and the second meeting started with a report of these actions, the introduction of new people, and the setting-up of an agenda consisting of the things people on the block thought were problems to be looked into.

As the neighbors left the first meeting they felt considerable relief from anxiety. The meeting had not yet done anything very important by way of taking action but the neighbors had found out something that they knew intellectually but could never have really felt if they had not been called together to enter into action. They had found out that there were a lot of people just as concerned and just as frustrated as they were. Instead of feeling that "everybody else is perfectly able to cope with the situation, but I am not," the individual found that everybody was equally unable to cope with the situation, so that the feeling of inadequacy dissolved and was replaced by the much more objective perception that the group as a whole had problems. Thus the feeling of being out of the group, of being a helpless spectator on the sidelines—feelings which had led individuals to turn inwardly on themselves and feel lonely—these were replaced by a complete reversal of the relationship to the group. The group of neighbors was felt now to be supportive; one was no longer alone. Under these conditions of establishment of communication and support the individual could feel free to act intelligently rather than out of anxiety.

The restoration of communication thus grew around the need

for reducing anxiety, but it continued as a new pattern on the block. The neighbors had become acquainted at the block meeting, and each day, as they passed up and down the block, they would greet each other. The network of communication on the block was reinforced and grew because it became a part of the way of life on the block.

The reduction of anxiety freed the group for active problem-solving efforts. To feel better was nice—and the neighbors openly acknowledged it. But they also saw that improvement of the neighborhood requires people to take action; feeling good makes action possible, but does not, by itself, rebuild the block.

Thus there arose spontaneously from the meeting a demand for subcommittees to get busy. The group identified a wide range of practical problems: the moving of abandoned cars, the installing of porch lights to dispel darkness, the prompt reporting of movements of materials into houses so that the plans for conversions could be checked, the development of tot-lot and recreational space, the collective buying and sharing of garden implements. Working committees arose from volunteers who felt strongly about one or another of these problems. And committee action, supported, encouraged, and supervised by the block group, resulted in positive acts of neighborhood improvement.

The actions resulting from working together had their effect on the physical community. In addition, during the processes of co-operation, neighbors began to make some highly significant personal discoveries about themselves and each other. They learned that the things they used to worry about don't need to matter. A Negro worker or a low-income renter can have just as useful ideas, make as many phone calls, dig out just as valuable facts, and be just as helpful as anyone else. Through these discoveries, the neighborhood as a community of people became stabilized. The block began to feel like home; life on the block acquired new richness of meaning and satisfaction. The neighbors learned that the physical and social communities are inextricably linked: actions are taken to maintain and improve the physical community, but it is the way in which neighbors participate to take action that maintains and improves the social community.

With the first successful actions, the neighbors began to think of themselves as a group. They gave their group a name, an identity. They developed loyalty to the group, and standards of upkeep which strengthened their individual desires to keep their own houses in order. The group found the language in which to state its goals, and it began to take a long look outside itself at the city government. As time went on and other neighborhood groups developed under the leadership of the Conference, loyalty spread from the block to the community, and, through the central Conference organization, community feelings and pressures began to be felt in many offices of the city hall. The local organizations, which had not been ready for action in the beginning, began, one by one, to respond to the new attitudes of the citizens, and to add their efforts to the program. At the end of four years, it is literally true that practically every major institution of the community is actively participating in the total program.

Events in the Hyde Park–Kenwood community have amply demonstrated the importance for community betterment of massive, creative participation by the citizenry.

We will, in the remainder of this chapter, try to transfer to more general terms and for use in other areas, some of the experience gained in the Hyde Park–Kenwood Community Conference program in Chicago.

PRINCIPLES OF THE BLOCK PROGRAMS

PROBLEMS FOR BLOCKS TO WORK ON

It is clear that there are certain kinds of problems that every block needs to work on. There are, in addition, many types of projects which seem to be congenial to certain blocks but not necessarily to others.

Thus, the problems all blocks must be concerned with include:

1. Setting up block standards, for example, of quality for dwelling units, or of behavior that the block expects from its residents. In the development of such standards through discussion and in participation in them, a coercive group force arises which prevents many selfish impulses from finding expression.

2. The range of city services available to citizens for maintaining and servicing the neighborhood. Continual alertness in

checking these and, if necessary, complaining about their inadequacy might be thought of as vigilance functions. The most important of these from a community standpoint are probably those centering around the reporting of suspected illegal conversions and the reporting of crime.

3. The typical type of improvement project—putting in tot-lots, installing lights, planting flowers, and so on—has been discussed above.

In addition to these three basic kinds of effort some of the following types of projects have been undertaken:

4. Joining with other blocks on an area job, such as cleaning up the length of a business street or digging out all the fireplugs in the area when they become covered with snow.

5. Collective private enterprises, such as equipping a shop or running of hobby nights and sharing of tools.

6. Recreational or social activities, such as parties, square dancing, and poker festivals to raise money for tot-lots and the like.

7. Educational programs, featuring speakers who can tell the neighbors what they can do to make their homes less attractive to burglars, what to do about auto larcenies, or how to have a beautiful lawn.

PRINCIPLES OF BLOCK LEADERSHIP

In conducting meetings to attain these objectives, a number of important principles have been identified. These have become, in effect, the bases for the training of leadership. Let us take a look at some of these principles, not necessarily arranged in order of importance.

1. *Participation depends on reward.*—For the neighbors to remain involved and interested over a long period of time, they must receive rewards at a sufficient rate. The two kinds of rewards possible are *gratification* of individual need for such things as dominance, friendship, intimacy with certain people, opportunity to test ideas, and so forth; and *satisfaction* with group accomplishment of tasks. Particularly at the beginning it is evident that the reward for task accomplishment will not be sufficiently great and frequent to avoid discouragement and to maintain in-

volvement. Therefore, the meetings by design should be given a quasi-social character so that through parties, the sharing of hobbies and games, and informal conversation of all sorts people can obtain rewards over and above the rewards of work.

2. *The block works on "felt" problems.*—The only matters on which people will expend energy are these which they feel are problems, things about which people have feelings which they must deal with. Therefore, the survey of problems suggested by members is the starting event of the meetings, so that the group will not inadvertently commit itself to action along lines nobody will be motivated to carry through.

3. *Leadership is by team.*—The kind of leadership required encourages free expression of feelings and opinions, sifts these to help diagnose problems realistically, and guides the group into action. This requires a range of skill greater than most men can provide. A leadership team is therefore far more effective than a single leader: it will make a more objective analysis of how the last meeting went and it will have more information and understanding to use in planning and conducting the next meeting. The team concept also includes getting the help one needs from anyone who can supply it.

4. *Movement spreads through friends.*—A component of the initial attitudes of people in disorganized areas is the feeling of lack of trust; they are suspicious of each other. Meetings can be organized most successfully when friends call on friends so that the initial hurdle of distrust does not have to be overcome.

5. *Membership is based on willingness to work, not on ideology.*— The basis of participation in block meetings is merely that one lives on the block. There is no test of ideology because it is not what people say they believe that is important so much as their willingness to work on problems. As long as there is willingness to work on problems, ideological differences can be settled or avoided. Moreover, the people who are out of sympathy with the movement are very likely to be the ones whose actions are most damaging to the block; therefore, special effort is put forth to have them participate in the meetings.

6. *Discussion focuses on concrete problems.*—Arguing about "ideologies," making grand generalizations which take in all the

territory from here to Alaska—these behaviors are gratifying to some individuals, but they are irrelevant to the action part of the block meeting. When the group is trying to select problems, define them, and work on them, it gathers steam and enthusiasm through being able to see more and more clearly what the problem is and what acts will be appropriate. In short, the discussion marches along and leads to action when arguments are settled and generalizations are tested by getting concrete—talking about particular times, places, peoples, and behaviors. The first requirement for carrying the discussion beyond its initial questions is the production of the necessary facts, either from informed people at the meeting or through the efforts of a committee between meetings.

In general, it is assumed that people will hold different opinions about Negroes, city offices, liberals, real estate agents, etc. These differences of opinion can be accepted as differences of opinion rather than as the start of a battle. Decisions for action are sound when they are based on relevant facts, not on opinions, and the number of facts needed is the number required to make a confident choice among the suggested actions. Whatever one's opinions, attitudes, or ideology, he is pretty likely to join with his neighbors to get a wrecked jalopy off the street, a rat colony discouraged, or a new landlord indoctrinated.

7. *All decisions are subject to revision as a result of taking action.*— A "good" decision results in action which remedies the situation. A "bad" decision results in action which makes people even more uncomfortable, apathetic, or frustrated. It is possible for a group to make the wisest decision of which it is capable and then find that when it acts on the decision matters get worse. The value of a decision cannot be known at the time the decision is made; it can be known only through study of what happens during action.

Thus it is possible—although it has not yet happened in our community—that a block might, after sober discussion, decide to sell property only to white people. If this is a "bad" decision for that block to make, then acting on the decision should produce evidence that the situation on the block has been made worse. We should expect people to discover such things as feelings of guilt, of fear of being called into court, of loss of self-respect, and of weakness. The decision would hang like a heavy cloud over the block; spontaneity of discussion would be reduced, and every time a Negro walked down the street people would have uncomfortable feelings. Needless to say, there would be a greater wish to flee the neighborhood, and a developing mistrust of the suddenly increased protestations that people are going to stay. This is, of course, an extreme example, but it is an instructive one because it reminds us that the evidence to be taken into account must include information about how people feel. In any case, decisions should always be kept open for review as evidence accumulates, understanding that behavior depends more on how people feel than on what people say. The example is instructive also because it indicates rather clearly why some property owners' associations have typically contributed to the deterioration of the community.

8. *Each block group determines its own autonomy.*—The fact is that the existence, success, and prospects of most block groups are in no small measure owing to the efforts of the Conference organization. Block groups, however, react in different ways to this fact. Some will deny it; others will accept it gladly and look to the parent organization for much help; still others will feel little concern one way or the other. Some block groups develop jealous loyalty to themselves; others, to the community. In any case, the way a block group feels toward the parent organization changes from time to time. Generally, as the group matures, it tends to be able to be loyal not only to itself but to the parent organization and to any other group perceived to be working for the community.

Members of the block group are likely to differ in their knowledge about and attitude toward the parent organization. If the block leaders received help from the Conference to get started, they are likely to belong to the Conference, and to feel they ought to try to get all the neighbors to belong also. Further, the block group receives services from the parent group, which also helps make the local efforts "add up" through the development of other groups which can reinforce each other's demands. But for most leaders there is considerable embarrassment in asking their neighbors to contribute to some other organization. Block groups are likely to be involved in projects which need money from the neighbors, and to advocate diverting potential contributions to an outside group has some of the feeling of embezzlement. Moreover, leaders hesitate (and rightly) to do anything that will give the impression that membership in the parent organization is a necessary condition for participating in block activities. It seems clear from experience that block groups cannot alone finance the parent organization, and that the people most able and ready to contribute to the parent organization are likely *not* to be the ones most active in block groups. Block leaders can help the general fund-raising activities such as theater parties, community fairs, and rummage sales.

IMPLEMENTING THE PROGRAM OF PARTICIPATION BY CITIZENS

The difference between an occasional meeting on one block and a vigorous widespread program of citizen activity is a matter of services helpfully rendered. Potential leaders must be found and recruited, advice and training must be given to those needing it, the community must be informed as to what is going on, action channels to the city hall must be opened and maintained, new methods for dealing with the wide vista of community problems must be continually developed and pooled, encouragement must be maintained for all workers, a place must be found for everyone to help, and competent professional help must be enlisted and made available to all.

The list of facilitating services is long and demanding. And no less demanding is the spirit of co-operation which must be consistently maintained in the offering of all services, and, indeed, throughout all communications with everyone in the community. It is not always easy to put problem-solving ahead of prestige; to refer decisions to the good of all rather than to the need for organizational power; to welcome all who will help regardless of personality, beliefs, or vested interests; to accept help of people on their own terms rather than on your terms; to regard attacks by organizations and individuals as a sign that efforts to co-operate must be redoubled, rather than as the signal for counterattack; to confine publicity stories to the records of accomplishments for the community, even in the face of requests from the papers for "news"; to develop and make room for new leadership at the top, and to allow those who want retirement to pass on to their new opportunities; always to stand ready to interpret any part of the program to anyone who asks—for whatever reason; to resist the temptation to overload a willing volunteer or one's friends with chores; constantly and forever to concentrate on improving the ongoing processes of problem-solving rather than to go around taking a stand on every attractive issue or campaigning for one's own solutions to problems.

The principles and attitudes which govern the friendly meeting of neighbors on the block must also govern the entire community enterprise. The social and neighborly situation of the block meeting is the model for the organization as a whole. Executive secretaries who love to give orders, nonworking boards of directors, jealous and ego-inflated working committees, chronic advice givers, dogmatic idealists—these have no place in the setup. The pitfalls are greatest at the level of over-all organization because the status rewards are greatest and because the contact with the community problems is most remote. The organizational leaders do not directly experience the conditions they are trying to alleviate; they know of slums through the testimony of others, but they do not know slums. It is always someone else whose experience tests the wisdom of actions by the board.

Finally, the central organization has a complicated problem of working methods to clarify for itself: one co-operates with others in his group or in his community, but one makes a show of power to groups outside the community. Within the council chambers of the city, one more neighborhood organization is always just a group that wants something for itself, and its chances for success are proportional to the pressure the organization is perceived as controlling. But the same pressure ideology—epitomized by the business deal—that works when groups are in competition with each other is fatal to the development of a program of voluntary participation.

The importance of co-operative attitudes is so great that one almost hesitates to discuss specific techniques of operation. A co-operative group with poor techniques will develop the tools it needs; a nonco-operative spirit, manifesting itself through the most up-to-the-minute techniques that can be devised, still adds up to exactly nothing of long-range significance. On the other hand, a preaching of attitudes is not likely to change attitudes either. Understanding and practice and objective study of results are the ways to the learning we all need for effective community work. The following discussion of the facilitating services required for development and maintenance of the action program can suggest techniques that have been found useful under at least some conditions. And we can try, in discussing these, to spell out some of the meanings of the co-operative method of community problem-solving.

DEVELOPING LEADERSHIP

RECRUITMENT

There seems to be no systematic and certain way to locate and recruit leaders, possibly because there are so many different possible motivations for becoming a leader. Recruitment is an everlasting job for everyone concerned with the program. Finding leaders can have much the same zest as hunting big game, although in some respects the rules are different.

Several neighbors on a block can usually put their heads together and suggest possible leaders. Many a leader has been nominated at a bridge party, baseball game, local supermarket, and husbands' night at the PTA. Anyone who shows leadership talent in the Rotary Club, Scouts, rummage sale, or anywhere else can be marked down as a candidate for a cozy interview. A person who calls up to ask questions or make complaints is displaying that rare jewel, initiative, and should be followed up. A properly planned community meeting, with a sober discussion of community problems, can end with everyone being asked to fill in a card indicating the ways he can help. Certain categories of people, such as housewives whose youngest child has just entered school, and who have had jobs working with people, may be appropriate material for leadership in some communities. Librarians, ministers, doctors, and others can be more useful informants if they are given a general description of the sort of person sought.

Whatever the method of identifying likely people to contact, the next step is to present them with information in such a way that they can make a wise decision about their own participation. The most common mistakes are probably presentation of the wrong sorts of information, and presentation of too little information. A leader can hardly make a realistic decision until he has decided that the problems to be solved are important to him, the amount of time and skill required are within his reach, and the rewards he hopes to get for serving as leader are attainable. In general, the potential leader should be able to visualize the sort of meetings he will help lead, should talk with other leaders, and should attend at least one training session or neighborhood meeting so that he will know what to do and whether he can do it.

Whatever information the potential leader has is never adequate to guarantee to him that he will get what he wants from the experience of leading. Volunteering for anything always involves taking a calculated risk. Most people make up for their lack of information by putting their trust in another person. It follows from this that it is decidedly worth while to pay attention to the selection of the director or block leader who should talk with or sponsor the candidate.

TRAINING

Most people know by now that running meetings successfully is a somewhat more complicated art than falling off a log. Adequate information, creative knowledge of techniques, and appropriate attitudes are all required. The maintenance and spread of the action program is directly proportional to the quality and effectiveness of the training program.

In general, the training program must satisfy two requirements: first, it must get specific help to leaders at the times they need it and in such a way that they can learn from it; and second, it must establish the role of leader as a valued, continuously supported part of the organization. The training program does much to create a leader group which, in some ways, has the characteristics of a profession. The leaders know each other, feel loyal to the group of leaders, recognize certain minimum skill requirements, stand for a set of attitudes—ethics—and have concern for the over-all improvement of leadership in the organization. Training can be provided in a variety of ways, both formal and informal.

1. *The community clinic.*—This can be developed as the only regularly scheduled, carefully planned public meeting of the parent organization with special effort exerted to get potential and new block leaders to attend. The various features of the agenda reflect some important principles or conditions of training.

The meeting is started with a welcome and a statement of objectives of the program designed to communicate confidence in significant goals. A report from the executive secretary of the parent organization, summarizing actions and events significant to the community, is intended to give people some idea of the range of resources available to block groups and to increase their identification with and understanding of the over-all program.

The third event is informal reporting by block leaders of meetings they have had since the last clinic, telling of problems considered, actions taken, the feelings and hopes of citizens. These reports help people see that the meetings are practical and accomplish results and let them feel the enthusiasm and delight of other leaders, showing leadership as a route to social approval and reward.

Following these reports, the group divides into smaller interest groups to study the various skill problems of calling and conducting meetings, gathering information, and so on. The clinic meeting closes with a report from each skill group as to what problems they have worked on and what bright ideas they wish to pass on to the others.

2. *The training seminar.*—A beginning leadership group has to learn how to organize itself to put on mass meetings and use other recruitment devices, to discover and maintain needed communication with other parts of the organization. It has to understand its own attitudes toward other groups in the community, and it needs to learn the experimental approach to problem-solving, with its emphasis upon firsthand experience and doing things for one's self. The attitudes learned by this executive group pretty

much determine the attitudes of the action people throughout the community.

A training seminar, run with competent professional consultation, is a rapid and effective means to meet these needs for this group. Meeting every week or two for at least eight sessions, and relying heavily on experience-sharing as the people start trying to get blocks going, it develops a strong sense of groupness and dedication, and results in many policy suggestions to the organization's board of directors. The members of the seminar work on their own blocks, and, as the movement grows, take over the administrative problems of the block action program. Representatives of other committees of the parent organization are invited to the seminar so that its developing body of policy can remain coherent.

3. *Congress of block leaders.*—If all block leaders meet together about once a month to share problems and program ideas and responsibilities, they tend to remain active and to contribute to the storehouse of useful suggestions. A congress of leaders may itself have working committees, with specific functions to work on and continuously keep in the awareness of the larger group. They may, for example, concern themselves with the dissemination of program ideas, solicitation of memberships, organization of community clinics, etc. Through these working committees, training for leadership at the organizational level is provided, sharply differentiating the training function of the congress from that of the clinic.

4. *Individual consultation.*—Group training methods can never fully deal with the private doubts and tentative insights of the trainee; it takes an understanding individual to do this. Moreover, in the group methods, the trainee can never get enough information and advice based on specific facts about his own block. Through discussion with someone who can help him sift his perceptions and see which ones make the most difference, the embryo leader can be helped to make realistic and confidence-giving plans. Experienced group leaders very commonly fail to realize the extent of the help they must stand ready to give to the new leader. One result of experience is that we can formulate for ourselves concise formulas and instructions, but

we fail to realize that the meaning of these paradigms and prov-
erbs is in the context of our extensive experience. A variety of
individuals—the officers of the parent organization, the experienced block leaders, interested professionals from schools and
universities and public agencies, and so on—should, as leaders,
stand ready to work with novices.

5. *Local summer workshop.*—The developing principles and
techniques of community participation represent the application
of a rapidly developing body of knowledge in the social sciences to a major social problem. It is clear that both scientists
and community practitioners have much to learn from each
other, and that the problems of community action provide an
ideal focus for bringing these groups together. It is also clear that
promising social inventions like the block participation program
should be adaptable to other blocks, and that the general
methodology of the Conference should provide stimulation and
inspiration to churches, youth houses, industries, agencies, and
other groups whose functioning depends on their dynamic relationships to the community.

In the specific case on which this chapter is based, the Human
Dynamics Laboratory of the University of Chicago and the Chicago Commission on Human Relations, with some assistance from
the National Training Laboratory in Group Development, in-
augurated in 1951 annual three-week workshops in the community. At the present writing, the evidence from the first workshop is encouraging. Two neighborhood organizations in other
parts of the city have taken a new lease on life—along conference
lines. The training in face-to-face group operation and urban
sociology has markedly influenced programs of several agencies.
The participants from the workshop have been meeting once a
month to keep alive the communication and mutual supportiveness developed during the summer.

While there are many practical difficulties involved in getting
agencies and organizations to assign their leaders to a three-
week training period, the notion is gradually developing that
community leadership in agencies and organizations is a growing profession. Groups are learning that training is a good investment. In the first nine months following the workshop we

can estimate conservatively that fifty citizens groups got started, all directly traceable to training given during the summer.

FACILITATING SERVICES

The potential effectiveness of a citizen group is determined by the number and quality of the action channels available to it. As co-operative relationships are established with each city office in turn, the possibilities for successful block action increase by just that much. As the legal panel, working with the zoning and housing committees, establishes relations with judges as "friends of the court," the blocks on which housing cases arise can provide more and more effective testimony about the prevailing housing standards to be maintained on the block. As the Conference board joins with other organizations in the city to demand a shake-up in the police department, the block group is encouraged to document and report local instances of misfeasance or faulty enforcement. Similarly, with the real estate, recreation, public schools, and lighting committees.

The pattern is clear and the moral inescapable. Working groups in the community in or out of the Conference can add endlessly to the potential power of the grass roots movement IF there is two-way communication. Moreover, two-way communication keeps the working committees spurred on to greater activity and accomplishment. Probably the most common source of the frustration felt by all too many working groups and social agencies is the feeling that nobody has any expectations for them. And the occupational disease of executive secretaries is the feeling of isolation; they talk to themselves for a while, then fall silent.

Two-way communication is possible under just one set of conditions: both parties have purposes in common and recognize the need for each other. This is the essence of the co-operative relationship. The job of a community conference is clear. It is to facilitate and develop co-operation among all the elements in the community, to align the various forces going our way into one vast drive for betterment. The novel thing about the conference is that it defines and demonstrates an important new social role: that of teacher of methods in community co-operation.

SIGNIFICANCE AND ACCOMPLISHMENTS OF THE PROGRAM
OF CITIZEN PARTICIPATION

1. The Community Conference program of the South Side of Chicago has, in a three-year period, been adapted to six other communities in the city. In each case, there has been the initial hue and cry that city dwellers cannot get together on neighborly lines. In each case, as the program started rolling, leadership has been found and blocks have started on the long road from incipient deterioration toward stabilization and recovery. Over two hundred citizen groups are now meeting in Chicago on an average of once a month. In the Conference area, about 2 per cent of the population has attended one or more block meetings.

The spread has been almost entirely the results of voluntary, lay leadership, and it has been most rapid in the areas which had greatest anxiety, usually about (*a*) the in-migration of Negroes; (*b*) the economic problems of keeping up neighborhoods composed of beautiful "white elephant" houses; or (*c*) the neighborhoods where there is greatest concern over crime.

It is interesting to compare this urban movement with the Rochdale (England) co-operative movement, which subsequently spread to Nova Scotia, Denmark, Jamaica, Michigan, and Ohio. The co-operative movement started with economically depressed industrial workers, and its original purpose was to provide food more cheaply. The personal economic base remains, and the movement has caught on most effectively in rural areas, with co-operative self-help as the theme. The conference movement had for its driving force the unrest and anxieties of urban dwellers caught in a period of uncontrolled industrial expansion. The average citizen became submerged; he lost his voice, and with it, to all intents and purposes, he lost his prerogatives as a citizen.

In both movements, however, the individual has found himself by recognizing his interdependence with others in a narrow geographic area. In both cases, the focus of communication is objectively defined problems which are important to the participants. In both cases, the program has been conceived as partly educational. And in both cases, consultative and organizing help has been available through church, government, or university.

The first accomplishment, then, is the fact that needs of citizens are being met, and the evidence is the growth and spread of the movement through voluntary action.

2. The experience of each new conference is that it takes a substantial amount of time and a large number of followed-up demands on the city hall to get for the neighborhoods the city services they should have. In each case, however, the attitude of downtown has gradually changed, and demands for maintenance of services are now met almost routinely. The demonstration of the effectiveness of continually applied, nonhostile demands as a way of getting civic services is a second major accomplishment.

3. There are, in most neighborhoods, other organizations already in existence when the conference begins. The first effort is to try to work through these organizations rather than to start a new one. The typical result has been that none of the other organizations is ready to move along the necessary problem-solving lines. As the program gets going, however, it is usual for the other organizations to become much more active. In effect, the new conference group sets the pace for other groups. In some cases, the renewed activity seems to be an expression of competitiveness; in other cases, of guilt. There may be a renewed optimism and encouragement acquired from people who belong to both groups.

In any case, whatever the reason, the development of the conference, with its co-operative attitudes, results in a parallel re-activation of other groups, and thus vastly increases the total effort going into community problem-solving.

4. There is no question that many neighborhoods with active block organizations have improved physically and have stabilized themselves psychologically. Illegal conversions have been stopped, panic flight no longer happens, and people are investing money in their homes. There is a clear determination to stay on the block, and a feeling that the remaining problems can be solved, and that it is rewarding to try to solve them.

Organized blocks are gradually being recognized as a social fact to be taken into account by real estate operators, housing speculators, and mortgage-loan groups. The average civic spoiler is ambivalent, and his exploitative tactics are often at least partly an expression of insecurities that have little to do with the need for money. The organized block has an effect on such people. The standard of maintenance and the optimistic determination of the group reinforces the positive sides of ambivalence. Thus, most real estate firms do not really set out to wreck a neighborhood; they know that the ruination of housing through speculative exploitation is also, in the long run, the ruination of their own business. Similarly, the mortage-loan people, who, mostly on the basis of racial stereotypes, refuse to loan money on houses in areas where Negroes are moving in, know underneath that such tactics contribute to the creeping blight that eventually destroys their own opportunity to invest their money. Both groups can be influenced by home owners *en masse*.

The psychological stabilization of a neighborhood through meeting the needs of residents develops a positive force which can be applied through organization to the target groups contributing most to decay.

5. Speaking personally, as a methodologist in the field of social action, the block action program outlined in this chapter presents to me three highly exciting demonstrations.

The first demonstration is that there is a vast, almost limitless source of power that can be tapped for the improvement of the community. The source of this power is the individual's need for security and for an adequate way of life. The manifestation of this power is through constructive community activity. And the results of this power are an improvement of conditions which release more activity to improve conditions further. The dynamic of the power is in the processes of re-education and training; a conscious utilization of experience to make the next effort more effective; a renewal of the idea of co-operative self-help. The block program seems to me to be the refutation of the notion that the answer to community problems is the bulldozer, the government planners, or the big life insurance project. These last resorts are just that—the final, desperate effort to buy back, at terrific expense, something that could have been maintained and conserved through maintenance of neighborly interaction.

The second demonstration for me has been the gradual definition of the role of the citizen in urban society. It is a much larger role than merely that of putting a ballot in the box every couple of years. The citizen role is not only a political act, it is an aspect of the role of father, husband, consumer, hobbyist, club member, and resident. And it is not separate from these things. The actions and expressed attitudes of each one of us have implications for the community. In the small town we all know that there is "feedback," that our acts come home to roost. In the city, we do not get "feedback"; the influence of our acts is hard to trace; it spreads outward like the ripples on a pond, and dissipates itself in many tiny unknowable ways. In a neighborhood, particularly one with well-defined geographic boundaries and with good communication among the neighbors, we are more likely to get "feedback," and we learn from experience that interdependence exists and that we are a part of it. And thus we have consciousness of our citizenship role.

So far as I know there is no place where the citizen role in this sense is taught. It probably cannot be taught effectively apart from its proper context of co-operative action. The block program, it seems to me, can be regarded as a vast adult education program directed to learning of the operational meanings of democracy.

The third major demonstration, and one which we shall point to again and again in many situations, is that there is a close relationship between the concepts of scientific method and democracy. Avoiding for the moment the arguments about what democracy is, still one is impressed by a number of parallels. Thus the scientific requirement of objectivity as the evaluating and testing of competent witness is also the reason in the block group for expecting all the members to help in defining the problems to be tackled. The scientific effort to test hypotheses without inquiring into their origin in creative thought is closely akin to the block group's problem of weighing opinions in the light of factual evidence rather than personal status. The scientific concept that an idea is "truthful" if it can be used to predict what will happen is brother to the block group's testing of action plans by assessing the results of the first step before planning subsequent steps.

It is my belief that these and other parallels are by no means accidental, and I see these notions, along with characteristics shared by many religious creeds, as evidence that man through various avenues of interpretation of experience is gradually beginning to nail down a basic methodology of human interaction and, with this, the possibilities of a better world for us all.

The problem of the neighborhood group versus the central parent organization involves divided loyalty, the dynamics of which are discussed on pages 231–35. Growth of the citizen group over time will probably generally follow the model given on pages 360–65. The way the neighborhood group operates to reduce racial conflict is examined on pages 349–56. Appropriate attitudes of leadership are described on pages 284–89, and, by implication, in the discussion of two points of view on pages 103–8. Chapter 11 is entirely concerned with problems of leadership.

CHAPTER 2

Classroom teaching is whatever the teacher does in the classroom. He must find ways to keep defined school problems in front of the class, to help the children organize their efforts to attack these problems, and to arrange opportunities for them to obtain insight as to what it all means to themselves.

The teacher guides the class by shifting his own role experimentally in response to his diagnosis of the kind of experience the class needs and is ready for.

DISTINCTIVE FEATURES

In the classroom, the authority of leadership is conferred on the teacher by the community. It is further enhanced by the fact that he is an adult and has special, recognized, and valued competence in the group. The primary target of classroom instruction is the capability of the students, which is to be modified in accordance with particular educational objectives. Secondary targets include parental attitudes toward the school and the children. The role of the student is determined by the will of the teacher—with some qualification by the standards of the peer and family groups to which the student belongs. The method of classroom control is dictated by the teacher's understanding of the conditions required for learning and his ideas as to how these conditions are to be achieved. There may be in addition rules of politeness, courtesy, or other school-sanctioned limits to behavior. The classroom group per se has no direct formalized relationships to other groups, although the teacher represents its needs to service functionaries, and the children act unofficially as ambassadors to family, club, and other groups in the community. The parent-teacher relationships may be formal and group-provided or informal and selective. The principal is typically the spokesman for the school, including the classrooms.

Educating Children through Need-meeting Activity

THE ARGUMENT AND THE PROBLEM

It is good practice, if you will forgive a bit of "pedagese," to start with the learners where they are. What are their problems, what are they ready for, what are their capacities and needs?

In education generally, it seems to me that where we teacher-learners are is in the middle of an argument; our problem is to restate the argument in such a way that we can settle it; and what we are ready for is to try to understand what we know about learning wherever it occurs and to see what the implications are for classroom situations. We shall then, depending on our needs and capacities, be in a position to modify classroom experiences for the better.

The first thing that ought to be said about the argument is that it is not just an educational argument; it has been going on in one way or another for as long as there has been a society of men. It is in educational circles, however, that the argument perhaps finds its most direct and hottest expression, partly because "educating" youngsters is safely remote from what we adults do, partly because the classroom is played upon by every segment of community opinion, and partly because everyone has spent at least a few years in school and therefore has a backlog of school experience in terms of which the big issues can be explored.

The second thing that ought to be said about educational argument is that it is contributed to by philosophers, psychologists, teachers, politicians, welfare workers, sociologists, manufacturers, educators, journalists, judges; and that somehow, out of the welter of many voices and many points of view, there has emerged a first-class list of "either-ors." In other words, the battle lines seem to have been drawn, and the resulting unreasonableness and heat underscore the point that we have here no mere argument

33

about education but rather a basic conflict cutting across all aspects of society.

We shall, however, attempt to consider the argument simply in its relevance to classroom teaching, even though we shall need to range far beyond the classroom to find the light we need.

The most simple expression of the argument is through a sampling of the conflicts it contains. Stated as either-ors, we have:

Individual	versus	society
Child-centered	versus	subject-centered
Guidance	versus	instruction
Discussion	versus	lecture
Pupil planning	versus	teacher planning
Intrinsic motivation	versus	extrinsic motivation
Insight learning	versus	drill and practice
Growth	versus	achievement
Firsthand experience	versus	vicarious experience
Freedom	versus	dominance
Democratic	versus	authoritarian
Subjective world	versus	objective world
Spontaneity	versus	conformity

The terms on the left-hand side of all these "versuses" fit into a pattern; see if you recognize this theme song:

"I want my child to be treated as an *individual* by teachers who *center* their attention on the *children* and see themselves essentially as *guides*. Children are capable of *planning* and *discussing* their experiences, of being *guided from within*. The important thing is understanding and *insight* that leads to *growth*. I want them through *firsthand experience* to learn the meaning of *freedom*, to understand and be committed to a *democratic* way of life. But, above all, I want them to be adequate people, with a rich and ennobling *subjective inner life;* only thus can they achieve the creative *spontaneity* which is man's most precious attribute."

But the terms on the right-hand side cannot be ignored; here is another theme song:

The teacher is an instrument of *society* and he is hired primarily because of his mastery of the sciences and the arts as arranged in *school subjects*. His job is to give *instruction* and to communicate not single interesting facts but rather ideas organized in meaningful relationship to each other, as in a *lecture*. The *teacher* knows the material to be covered, and it is his responsibility *to plan* in such a way that it will be covered. The teacher knows that getting ahead in this world requires ability to meet the *demands of the community*, and that only through *drill and practice* can school *achievement* become part of one's habit pattern. Many of the important things in life were discovered by others and are learned through *vicarious experience dominated* by these great *authorities*. The child is free to think as he wishes, but in the *objective world* of action he must *conform* to the standards of the community."

It is interesting to note the grammar of these theme songs. The first makes use of the words "I want"—it is a statement of wishes and values. The second song uses the word "is"—it is a statement of facts. (Not all of them are correct, incidentally.)

This observation makes clear why the argument has existed so long and also why it is not a real argument at all. The confusion lies in the assumption that stating values (first song, "I want . . .") immediately implies specific instructional procedures, which it does not; and in the assumption that stating social facts (second song, "The teacher is . . .") immediately implies specific instructional procedures, which it does not. From these two assumptions then follows a lot of discussion and taking sides about what ought to be done in the classroom. Actually, of course, there is no argument between facts and values, between what is and what we want. There is, however, a gap and a question: Taking the facts into account, how do we get what we want; how do we move from where we are to where we want to be?

This is a question of method of instruction. And the method can be created only by considering both the facts and the values. It cannot be deduced from one or the other alone. Let us note that the little phrase "how do we get what we want?" requires two kinds of thinking: first, what is the nature of the means by which we get what we want, and, second, what kinds of changes are to be brought about by these means? In other words, what does a class look like when it is learning, and what changes in behavior occur as a result of learning? The teacher's image of what a class looks like when it is learning determines his behavior while teaching. The teacher's idea of what changes in behavior are required determines his construction of examinations and his assignment of grades to students. The two questions together determine his planning of instructional activities.

THE PICTURE IN OUR MINDS

As one watches different classrooms, he notes that each teacher has a style of his own. He is quite consistent in the way he operates: the amount of challenge to the class, the depth or superficiality of his comments, the feelings about his job. It is as if he had a model in mind and operated consistently to make the classroom conform to this model; it represents the teacher's idea of what the classroom should be like. When the classroom situation deviates from this image, the teacher then tries to rectify matters by taking action: making more of an explanation, reassigning working partners, bringing in a personal experience to increase interest, stopping talking so that the students have a chance, and so on. The teacher's model summarizes for him the principles of learning; his action is taken to maintain the model, using principles of educational method as his guide.

Let us look at a number of models which teachers have used.

MODEL 1: SOCRATIC DISCUSSION

The image is of a wise, somewhat crusty philosopher getting into arguments with more naive people. The issues discussed are known to both Socrates and the other party, and both have adequate factual knowledge for the discussion. Socrates shows the other up by pointing to inconsistencies in his logic. The arguments are primarily to clarify concepts and values.

As applied to classrooms, this type of discussion is an aid to the assimilation of ideas. *After* the children have learned some facts and had some experiences together, the teacher-Socrates can challenge the class and test their conclusions. The teacher has a central role, and the discussion has much of the emotionality of argumentation.

MODEL 2: THE TOWN MEETING

The image is of a group of citizens whose lives are interdependent meeting together to decide on courses of action required to solve problems. These problems are objectively defined in terms of acts of God, services needed, demands to be met. The group draws on the experiences, feelings, and thoughts of each other, and the method is co-operative. The leader is a moderator rather than an expert. The most appropriate action is decided by vote of the majority.

As applied to classrooms, this type of discussion best fits teacher-class planning of activity, in which the task is to decide how to organize to carry out specified learning activities. Some differences between class and town hall, however, are that the neighbors immediately recognize the problem to be solved as important, whereas the students do not; the action to be selected makes a financial or status or other difference to all the citizens, whereas there are fewer "real" consequences for the students; the citizens are competent to testify because they have all experienced the problem, whereas the students do not have such backing of relevant experience; the moderator is simply looking for the most complete consensus he can get, whereas the teacher must also give information and the results of his past experience.

MODEL 3: APPRENTICESHIP

The image is of a young person's life being "taken over" by an older one. The apprentice learns a trade, how to behave in the social-class level of his chosen occupation, how to be a parent in the family, and so on. The master is teacher, father, friend, colleague, and boss. Psychologically, the apprentice identifies himself with and imitates the master: he is there to learn how to be like the master and to live like him.

Some of the dynamics of apprenticeship apply in the classroom. The student does identify himself with the teacher, and he learns many attitudes in imitation of the teacher. And many teachers, basically, attempt to make the student over into their own image (as they perceive it). Much of the master's warmth and concern for the welfare of the apprentice is appropriate for the teacher also. In many universities today, training for the Ph.D. has considerable resemblance to apprenticeship experience.

MODEL 4: BOSS-EMPLOYEE, OR ARMY MODEL

The image here is of a person who has higher status and also the power to reward or punish, telling others what to do and how to do it, then seeing that it gets done, and, finally, evaluating how good a job he thinks it is. It is not necessary that the relationship be harsh or unfriendly, but it is necessary that there be considerable acceptance of many kinds of dependency by the subordinate. The rather small minority of people who thrive best as dependents may be quite creative in this situation.

This is probably the most prevalent model of the classroom, although there is wide variation in the extent to which the model is "softened up" by procedures for taking account of what the students feel about the teacher's demands. In other words, the teacher has to modify the image in the direction of more attention to pupil motivation and interest. This image is realistic for skill learnings like typing in which the requirement is to practice objectively described behaviors until a clearly defined level of performance is reached. It is also realistic with respect to a class working on a project involving physical work laid out according to plan.

MODEL 5: THE BUSINESS DEAL

The image is of one person with money (or some other inducement) making a bargain for the services of someone else. Thus one might pay a cabinetmaker to build him a chair. He would discuss specifications for the object, be available for making some decisions as the work progressed, and would finally decide whether to accept or reject the object.

This is essentially the "contract plan," in which the teacher makes the best deal he can with each individual workman (student) and consults with him as the work proceeds. The advantage of this model is that the child assumes a high degree of responsibility and the contract can be written to fit reasonable expectations of him. The disadvantages are that the teacher has to supervise a wide variety of different jobs, and the social factor and possibilities of learning better through working together are either denied or ignored.

MODEL 6: THE GOOD OLD TEAM

The image is of a group of players listening to the coach between quarters of the football game. This is followed by inspired playing which defeats the opposing team. The coach's objective is to get better playing, and almost any devices of persuasion or threats or promises that will produce high-level performance are accepted as legitimate.

This is an unrealistic model for the classroom, although its use is sometimes encouraged. The coach is working for a quick spurt rather than for long-range effects; there has to be an "enemy" team to compete with; the product to be evaluated is a score run-up by the group, rather than individual achievement; the team players are required to submerge all but very limited aspects of their individuality as completely as possible; and finally, the team is primarily an instrument for expressing the will of the coach. Few of these characteristics can really be found in the teacher-pupil relationship.

MODEL 7: THE GUIDED TOUR

The image here is of a group of interested children following closely behind a mature guide as he leads them through the jungle, brewery, courthouse, or wherever. From time to time he calls their attention to objects he wants to tell them about, and he gives them information, stories, and opinions. He also answers questions. He maintains order and sees to it that the number of children who arrive home equals the number who set out in the morning. He may or may not plan with them certain questions or major categories of information the field trip is supposed to answer.

The acceptance by the teacher of the fact that he has been "over the field" before and has much to tell should be realistic. His personal enthusiasm and ability to "let the class see for itself" help motivate the children and arouse their interest. The experience of learning names for objects is a rather small intellectual task, and usually is inadequate to absorb the class's energies. The guided tour (e.g., survey course) is a quick way to cultural ornamentation but the "knowledge" learned may be unrelated to possibilities of personal use.

The fact that so many models or analogies are possible under-scores the complexity of classroom teaching. The fact that there may be particular times when each of these models is most ap-propriate points to the vast array of roles in which the teacher must act at different times. Even within the space of a very few minutes, the teacher may have to show considerable flexibility. He may speak as a representative of the group or culture he grew up in, act as social analyst to help the class evaluate the opinions he expresses, give expert answers or facts about subject matter or school rules, consult with the class on how to proceed to next steps, act as counselor to some child needing help, act as symbol for parent, sweetheart, or generalized adult authority in the eyes of children "working on" such problems.[1]

Actually, however, nobody has an unlimited repertoire of roles. In general, the attractiveness for a particular teacher of the model he has adopted or worked out lies partly in the fact that it enables him "to play the role" which is most congenial to himself. The teacher's identifications with business, sport, gov-ernment, wisdom—these are expressed through his playing, in effect, the role of businessman, coach, moderator, Socrates. Each of these occupations also is characteristic of a social class posi-tion in the community, and the wish we all have for belonging to some particular class enters into the choice. We could guess that in communities where the teacher's position has little pres-tige, where control is in the hands of groups who have little com-munication with the school, the teacher would feel strongly the pull of some class and occupation group other than his own. The place in the teacher's life where he is free to act out his wishes of belonging to another group is the classroom, because there the teacher has sufficient power and control to mold its culture to almost any shape he desires.

Models like the above help the teacher define the working re-lationship between himself and his class. They serve to clarify the role of the teacher: his power, his concerns, his style of teaching. The roles of the students are not differentiated in these models—

1. Thelen and Tyler, "Implications for Improving Instruction in the High School," chap. 12, *Learning and Instruction*, 49th Yearbook, National Society for the Study of Education, 1950.

all the students are expected to behave alike in ways which enable the teacher to enforce *his* role.

The view of teaching implied by the existence of these models is realistic, but it is also inadequate. It is realistic in recognizing that the only behavior under the direct control of the teacher is his own; and the teacher, by virtue of the authority of his position, age, and professional competence has the power to determine his behavior pretty much apart from consideration of student needs. The models also realistically recognize that the roles possible to the students depend upon the role that the teacher chooses to play. In effect, the freedom of students is with respect to whatever functions the teacher does not pre-empt for himself. These two basic principles provide us with clues for understanding how the teacher consciously and by design alters the activities in the classroom.

The inadequacy of the models becomes apparent with the realization that they only illuminate half the problem of method. The models make clear what is expected of teacher and students once the teacher's role is decided. They do not, however, give any basis for determining the appropriate role of the teacher, and they start from the needs of the teacher rather than from an analysis of the requirements of learning situations. Effective thinking about the design and control of educative activity must begin with the question "What sort of participatory role must students have, to learn what they need to learn and are supposed to learn?" Only after this question has been answered quite apart from any consideration of the teacher's needs can we begin to see the sort of role the teacher must play if student experience is to be educative. The most significant quality of a good teacher is that he is able to meet his own needs through playing the roles required to make activities educative for students.

The question of the sort of role-participation required for learning by the students is complicated by the facts that different kinds of learning require different roles, and that learning experience is complex, involving thoughts, feelings, actions, emotions, and desires. To give students the kinds of experiences they need demands from us first that we understand the nature of classroom experience. What, then, are the facts?

THE FACTS IN THE CASE

What I am about to describe as an accurate picture of the state of affairs in the classroom would, I think, be agreed to by many competent students of education who are concerned with the social-psychological factors which influence learning. Nonetheless, these comments, if they are to fit the "typical" classroom, must be generalizations, and, as such, I shall submit them as hypotheses which are suggestive and probably correct, but which have not been rigorously, i.e., competently, demonstrated.

The first important facts represent a set of rules that the child has to accept. He didn't make them, and in most communities he has no effective way of rebelling against or changing them.

The basic rule is that the child must go to school. Other rules are that he must accept as teachers the people he is assigned to; that he must accept the other pupils as fellow-members of the classroom group; that he must learn whatever he is told to learn up to some minimum level of competence as given by the authorities.

The facts are legislated. They could be changed by the proper authorities, but they operate like laws; in fact, in most states there *are* laws governing many of these requirements. For many students, these rules are so fully accepted that their existence as limits to behavior is very rarely felt; for others, the whole school experience is colored by the existence of the rules. These students are like the man who loves to speed on a Sunday outing. He is so concerned with lawmen that he misses the scenery—and pays an occasional fine.

A second important set of facts represents description of the child's firsthand experience. The most fundamental thing about classroom experience is that it is social; it is a continual set of interactions with other people. I call this the most fundamental thing because there is no escape; the demands are there, and they must be met. You can ignore what a dead author has left behind on a printed page, but you cannot ignore the youngster behind you snapping with a rubber band. You can know that a story about how Horatius held the bridge is just a story; but teacher holding the class after school is no mere journalistic creation.

These interactions are most fundamental for another reason: they make a difference in the learning process. I do not now remember who and what was involved in 1066, but my interactions with Miss Burke still color my feelings and attitudes about Latin. I have forgotten most of the formulas in statistics that I learned in summer school; but I married a girl I met in that class. No matter how deeply immersed in play the nursery school's four-year-olds may be, every time the door opens every head turns toward it to see if Mike, the bully, has arrived. One girl in my present seminar never participates except immediately after another girl has spoken; one boy in the group says very little when I, the teacher, am present; but when I am absent he says many good things to the group. Social interactions set the conditions under which learning occurs.

These interactions are most fundamental for still another reason: they involve direct feedback. If Willy hits Mary in class, he can't just pretend that it did not happen. He has to face a return behavior from Mary, the teacher, or another child. If Willy reads into O. Henry's story "The Ransom of Red Chief" the principle that a boy who is naughty enough can control the adults in his life, nothing happens. There is no direct test of his belief until he starts acting toward people as if he believed it, and by then, his citing of O. Henry as his authority will be pooh-poohed as a "rationalization." I still do not know whether the lesson from college ROTC was (a) that with proper equipment and skill we can beat the enemy, or (b) that war is futile because the other side can manufacture equipment, strategies, and soldiers too. There was never any occasion in ROTC to test which of these morals made most sense, and I sometimes still wonder what was intended. But there was plenty of opportunity for an immediate test of the idea that, while a cat can sneer at a king, a private had better not sneer at a major. When I taught high-school physics, I had two beginning classes which, as far as I could tell, were composed of children who were equally bright, had equal social standing in the community, and, on individual interview, expressed the same range of interest in physics. Yet teaching one class was like pulling teeth and teaching the other was like singing around the piano. In one class, I had the immediate response of apathy to everything I did; in the other class, the feedback was of challenging questions and meaningful ideas for the group to pursue.

Every one of these illustrations points to the compelling nature of interactions with other people in the classroom. The highest priority needs of students are to find their places in the group, to work through their anxieties about their competences, to adjust to authority, to explore and define their growing social capacities. These needs determine much of the quality of classroom experience, and they color the meanings of the subject matter learned. Good school achievement is usually the socially approved way of getting commendation from other people, or the way of withdrawing from social interaction, or the victory one gets from successful competition, or all of these. It is part of a socially determined pattern, produced through interaction with other people in and out of the classroom. Most school learning is partly a means to some other end.

A third set of important facts helps us to assess the probable meaningfulness of classroom experience over and beyond its social implications. There are two conditions under which ideas are meaningful. First, they have been connected through direct experience to real feelings so that they have color and richness; and, second, they have been assimilated into the student's fund of previously learned ideas so that they serve as doorways to whole structures of thought. But thoughts without organization and without associated feeling are basically nonsense; they have little usefulness of any kind to their host.

Ask any six people what they visualize when you say, "Columbus discovered America in 1492," or what you should do now that you know that the density of lead is 11.35 (11.35 *what*, for Heaven's sake!). What comes into your mind when I say that "frustration leads to aggression," or when I quote that dear old chestnut of the child-development courses: "Ontogeny recapitulates phylogeny" (or is it the other way around?)? I just opened a book I studied in anatomy, and I am trying to figure out why I once underlined in red the following: "The nuclei or centers of several cranial nerves lie in the gray matter of the medulla immediately under the floor of the fourth ventricle." I have, of course, taken these ideas out of context, and that is my point: out of context they are dream stuff. But in what context did they have reality and meaning?

One kind of meaning is "developmental." At one stage of life, Columbus represents high adventure, and studying about him can be gratifying. A few years later, Columbus can be pretty dull. Another kind of meaning comes with problem-solving. The figure for the density of lead could make sense if I were building a model boat and wanted to know the dimensions of an appropriately weighted lead keel. Of course, if I just imagined I was building a boat, the fact would be only academic and it wouldn't matter whether lead's density is 4.5, 11.35, or 26. In either case, however, the context is that of a practical problem to be solved.

Thus learning is useful or real if it makes a difference or helps solve a problem—in other words, if it has a meaningful context in purposive experience. The "problem" may be one of taking action, organizing ideas within a consistent framework, getting out of emotional conflict, and so on. But for an idea to be useful there must be not only a use for it; in addition, the idea must be usable. Thus we all have uses for ideas about democracy, but many of our notions about democracy are not usable. They are either high-sounding phrases which, on examination, are either meaningless or else mean something other than what they sound as if they ought to mean; or they are misunderstood assertions such as "all men are created equal," which, if taken literally, would refute the known facts of biology and psychology. The test of the usability of an idea is that when one operates in accordance with it, the results have the expected consequences

The facts about classroom experience are, in brief:

1. Classroom experience occurs in classrooms set up and operated by authorities for children who have to participate.

2. The firsthand tested experience of the child is one of interaction with other people.

3. On top of this experience is grafted a great deal of "school subject content" which may or may not have any reality and meaning for the child, depending on the conditions under which it is taught.

THE THREE BASIC ASPECTS OF THE TEACHING
AND LEARNING EXPERIENCE

"Teaching method" is the set of policies used by the teacher to guide or control activity in the classroom. Control is exercised through the fact that the teacher is the "authority" in the sense that nothing can be planned without his acquiescence or permission. Under proper conditions, the teacher exercises this control through continuous definition of purposes and expectations rather than through threat of punishment. The matters for which the teacher assumes responsibility include the particular school achievements to be striven for, the ways of working together, and some of the kinds of socially authorized meanings of the experiences of children. The way the control is exercised—the feelings responded to and the timing of the response—determines both the fruitfulness of the immediate activity and the motivation for future learning. By influencing the children's participation in immediate activity, the teacher determines what they have a chance to learn; and the quality of reward or punishment in his relationship to the children determines their taste for further activity along the same lines. The acts by which a teacher controls the situation and, through this, the participation of the children have both long- and short-range effects.

As we now examine the three facts about classroom experience in the light of the foregoing facts about teacher control, we shall see that the quality of the total classroom experience is woven from three distinguishable but ever present aspects of all activity.

The first fact of classroom experience, that "classrooms [are] set up and operated by authorities for children who have to participate" tells us that the community expects teachers to teach. And teaching is, in this context, the "transmission of the funded capital of human experience"—an elegant way of saying that the preservation of the community requires everyone to know some things that have been learned by other men. But the first fact alone, that authorities determine subject matter, does not tell *how* to teach. In general terms, at least, the answer is perfectly clear: the "funded capital of human experience" is more successfully transmitted through a goal-seeking type of experience than through a formally organized passing-on of information "from the notes of the instructor to the notes of the student without passing through the mind of either." It is certainly well established that content is better retained and creatively used when it is learned in response to a sense of problem than when it is simply passively absorbed.

We may, therefore, think of control of the conscious goal-seeking or problem-solving aspects of experience as one basic function of teaching. And we can see that the objective sciences and technologies, with their easy-to-obtain data and their possibilities of incontrovertible proof of propositions, offer the opportunity *par excellence* for demonstrating to children the methods, meanings, and satisfactions of problem solving. We conclude that one requirement of teaching method is that it must enable the teacher to accept contributions from children within a framework of problem-solving. Chapter 1, dealing with community problem-solving, delineates many of the attitudes the teacher needs in order to facilitate learning of school subjects.

Our second fact presented above, that "the firsthand tested experience of the child is one of interaction with other people," also has implications for teaching method. The social interactions of the classroom appear to be viewed in different ways. To some, they are distracting occurrences to be suppressed in the service of orderliness, discipline, or learning. To others, they are the most important expressions of individual personality, and they should therefore be encouraged and, in some magical way, guided and controlled. Our point of view is that through social interaction, conversation, and expression of feeling the group exerts its influence on the individual and the individual on the group; the problem of control is not to prevent these kinds of influencings but to try to obtain a quality of influencing that improves learning.

A genuine learning situation is one which involves the emotions of the learner; the social conditions in the group determine whether the necessary emotionality will be facilitating, distracting, or inhibiting of learning. Successful methods of teaching do control emotional phenomena or "group process" in such a way that learning is better motivated, challenge is greatest, and accomplishment is the goal of the group.

Control of social interaction—of side-conversations, of expression of opinion, of relaxation into humorous episodes, of work stoppage—is legitimately for one purpose: to increase learning. It is by now quite clear that the appropriate qualities of informality, concentration, rigorousness, and expressiveness differ from activity to activity, depending upon purpose. A freewheeling "bright-idea" session is far different from a careful attempt to deduce courses of action from explicitly stated principles. The amount of frustration and difficulty that can be tolerated and worked through depends very much on the extent to which people can share with each other their feelings about the situation. It follows, then, that there cannot be any one specific model for social interaction; the quality of interaction is good when it is appropriate to the task and to the purposes. Without a clearly defined achievement task, there is no precise way to judge the appropriateness of social interaction.

It is true, of course, that there are some limits. Murder is not admissible regardless of the learning task. Licentious activities which place a burden of guilt on students should not be allowed to occur, regardless of the state of definition of the achievement problems. Aside from the prevention of events that are bad from a mental hygiene standpoint, there are no criteria to be applied to social interaction beyond the requirements of behavior appropriate to the learning task. Thus the notion that a classroom should always give the appearance of "co-operation" and "shipboard intimacy" implies that these conditions are in themselves good, quite apart from what people learn under these conditions. Actually, when dealing with ideas, learning probably occurs under conditions of conflict over ideas, accompanied by sharing of feelings about common purposes, and subconscious agreement that hostility is not meant personally. If a teacher likes an orderly, quiet classroom, there is only one legitimate way to obtain it: make the work so interesting and challenging and need-meeting that the students naturally work in an orderly and absorbed way. It is probable, however, that such periods of orderliness will be interspersed with periods of give-and-take, during which students are preparing for the more studious activity.

Just as students need to learn the discipline of problem-solving so they can know how to participate for school achievement, they also need to learn the discipline of group management and organization so they can deal with their problems of security, belongingness, and individuality within the classroom group. The social sciences—sociology, civics, history, psychology, anthropology—should be taught in such a way as to illuminate these matters.

The second aspect of experience to be guided, controlled, and understood by adequate teaching method is social interaction. It is required that the teacher be able to diagnose from the contributions of the children the appropriateness to learning of the particular state of social interaction, and that he then be able to steer the classroom experience as a result of such diagnosis. Chapter 5, dealing with human relations training, shows what is involved in these skills.

The third fact is that " 'school subject content' . . . may or may not have any reality and meaning for the child, depending on the conditions under which it is taught." This statement asks us to recognize the ultimate fact about classroom instruction: that its purpose is to enrich the lives and capacities of all of the students. The aspects of experience important here are the self-discovering and reality-testing parts. The quality of these experiences probably determines whether knowledge is for power or merely for social ornamentation, whether it is an instrument for creativity or simply more material for the dead files.

The development of these experiences is referred to in various ways: the development of an effective personality, the development of personal objectivity, the learning of appropriate personal-social attitudes, the integration of thought and feeling, the gaining of personal security, the getting in touch with reality. However it may be referred to, the kind of experience required is clear: one must have opportunity, with appropriate guidance, to reflect upon and understand his own reactions to immediate experience. And the most useful content of experience from which to start in such a discussion is the feelings the individual is aware of having had. To explain our feelings we must study our participation within a total framework of self-knowledge. Gradually we learn to use this knowledge to help decide in each new situation how to participate, i.e., what behaviors to present to the group.

The method of teaching should enable the student to relate the personal meaning of his experience to his individual behavior and to ascertain the appropriateness of his behavior both for himself and for others. If Jack wants affection but all his behaviors antagonize people, then he needs some personal re-education. If Joe distorts all experience to prove over and over to himself that getting ahead is primarily a matter of "pull" and favoritism, then Joe needs to reinterpret his own experience along more realistic lines.

The fundamental point is that the quality of the inner subjective world, created by each individual and used by him to guide his impulses into behavior, is the heart of the educative process. It is not enough to say that "every individual is free to think as he pleases" any more than it is appropriate to try to mold individual thinking into the teacher's pattern. But if an individual reacts unrealistically, then his inner world needs modification; his concepts and theories, whatever they are, are inadequate.

The third aspect of experiencing to be guided and controlled by the method of teaching is the connecting of problem-solving and social participation to the private inner subjective world of the individual. This is the process of finding meaning in experience, of understanding, experimenting with, and modifying one's orientation to the world in the light of new learning. The arts, particularly literary and dramatic, have a contribution to make to the student's understanding of this aspect of experiencing.

We conclude that the method of teaching guides three basic aspects of experiencing: conscious goal-seeking or problem-solving, group process, and individual meaning. Instead of being "society-centered," or "subject-centered," or "group-centered," or "child-centered," respectively, the teacher needs to be *reality-centered*. He must determine his behavior in such a way that all three aspects of experiencing fit together and enrich the education of the child.

How is this to be done?

THE METHOD IN OPERATION

We have suggested that, within a classroom learning activity, energy goes into three types of processes: (1) working with school subject matter, preferably within the context of problem-solving; (2) organizing social relations to maintain greatest support for and participation in learning activities; and (3) discovering, formulating, and testing meanings of experience for one's self. We shall refer to these three types of processes as three aspects of classroom experiencing. We believe that these three aspects provide the functional framework for learning, and that at any time, as needed, any aspect may become the central object of attention, the central organizing principle for learning experience.

The problems we are confronted with in implementing these ideas in the classroom may be identified as follows:

1. How can the understanding of these three aspects in their relationships to learning become part of the classroom culture?

2. How can the teacher and class diagnose which aspect should be central to activity at any given time?

3. How can shifts in focus on the three aspects be accomplished without producing ambiguity and confusion?

4. How can needed activities of the three types be created?

5. How can the class be organized to carry out the needed types of activity?

PROBLEM 1. HOW CAN THE UNDERSTANDING OF THESE THREE ASPECTS IN THEIR RELATIONSHIPS TO LEARNING BECOME PART OF THE CLASSROOM CULTURE?

The assumption behind this question is that the class and teacher, in so far as they operate together, do so on the basis of shared expectancies about what is important, necessary, desirable, and possible. Among the shared expectancies and agreements, which constitute the culture of the group, are: (*a*) that the course is concerned with problems of school achievement; (*b*) that in working on these problems it will be necessary to pay attention to the part played by the teacher and by the students, and that these role-definitions may change from activity to activity;

and (c) that the conclusions individuals are drawing about themselves, the others, and the work need to be understood, tested, and used as data in planning activities.

Ultimately, of course, such understandings should be part of the total school culture, and at such a time they will be acted upon as a matter of course. Assuming, however, that these expectancies are not yet institutionalized in the school, the teacher has the problem of getting them incorporated into the group culture. The simplest way to accomplish this is for the teacher to act as if he believed them and to make clear to the group why he proposes each activity he does. Thus it is easy for the teacher to say, for example, "It seems to me that we have talked about a lot of factors that influence public opinion at election time and I believe we ought now to think about which ones would influence each of us, and why. I propose, therefore, that we break up into twosomes, and each of you can try to persuade the other to vote for, let us say, Mr. Smith for mayor. Use all the appeals we have been talking about. Then you can discuss which appeals seemed to work and why you thought so. After we have done this, we can compare notes in the class as a whole." Thus the teacher could move from the level of general group discussion of objective facts about elections to the level of individual feelings, resistances, and needs.

Such simple explanations not only instruct the group well enough so that it can carry out the activity; they also, if consistently offered and discussed as necessary, rather rapidly lead to the development of expectancies for the three types of basic experience.

Questions that the class needs to understand as part of the various basic experiences are:

For problem-solving:
What is the nature of the problem?
What factors are involved in a specific instance of the problem?
What will have to happen if the problem is to be solved?
What are the ways of getting these things to happen?
How can we judge which suggested way is the best in our situation?
How can we test whether the way we select really is effective?
How can we explain why it worked the way it did?
Etc.

For group membership and management:

What kinds of ideas or facts do we need now?

How shall we organize ourselves to get these needed ideas?

How can we put these ideas together to guide the group?

What provision do we need for special roles: chairman, secretary, blackboard-writer, messenger, boss, etc.

What factors stood in our way of working efficiently?

How does our job today (e.g., reporting facts dug out of books) differ from our job yesterday (e.g., defining the task).

Etc.

For individual meaning:

What disagreements do you have with these conclusions?

What would you do differently as a result of knowing about . . . ?

What other interpretations do you think other people might make of (this information)?

What parts of our (discussion, project, experiment, etc.) seemed most interesting to you? Why?

What things made it (easy) (hard) to participate in the (discussion, etc.)?

Who do you think would find this (information, principle, attitude, etc.) important, and why?

Etc.

The teacher, by asking such questions and helping the group answer and discuss them, gradually establishes the expectancies of the group for the range of qualities of experience required. The best sign of group growth and development of the group culture is that the students themselves begin to pose these questions at the appropriate times. Approval should be given for such efforts and suggestions, so that paying attention to the process of learning becomes in itself a source of reward for the students. The greatest reward, however, probably is not the teacher's expressed approval, except when the class is still new. The greatest reward comes when the class adequately discusses the suggestions and plans its activities as a result of the answers it gets to its own questions.

PROBLEM 2. HOW CAN THE TEACHER AND CLASS DIAGNOSE
WHICH ASPECT SHOULD BE CENTRAL TO ACTIVITY
AT ANY GIVEN TIME?

The basic method of guiding a classroom group is through diagnosis of the problems and need which the group is expressing as it works. Advance thinking can be helpful, too. A good lesson plan, made the night before, may imply shrewd guesses about developing needs. Thus, if the class is shown a movie which is predicted by the teacher to be highly stimulating, then the teacher is likely to plan a discussion period organized in such a way that the children can express their feelings of enthusiasm, their bright ideas, their identifications with people or problems shown in the picture. Such planning represents the process of "prediction of need"; it is a kind of "diagnosis-in-advance." And, if the children actually are stimulated as anticipated, then the teacher can stay with his plan; but of course he should also have planned what to do in case they were not.

The implications of diagnosis-as-you-go are two: first, running diagnosis is required to assure the teacher that the plan should in fact be followed or to show him that it should be modified; and second, since the plan can never indicate all the details about what is to be done and how, decisions will have to be made on the spot as a result of diagnosis with the class of "where they are." This latter type of planning is essential because it provides for the conscious collection of data and the clarification of next steps.

The purpose of diagnosis is to enable psychologically sound or realistic choices to be made. The responsibility for securing wise choices—that is, choices which result in educative activity—is the teacher's. Many decisions should be made by the teacher alone. In other cases, the teacher may present alternatives for the class to discuss and choose from. Or the teacher may give information from which the class can formulate alternatives and make its choices. Finally, the teacher may suggest that the class is at a "choice-point," and then leave both the decision and the processes of reaching the decision to the class.

The process of diagnosis is both evaluative and explanatory. The teacher is concerned with how well the class is doing, and this is made known to him by the feelings which arise in his automatic and often subconscious application of criteria for good operation. Thus the teacher generally can "feel" whether or not the class is interested in its task. He then checks his feelings by noting signs of attentiveness, ease of distraction, pace of work, the trivial or helpful nature of comments, and the like.

When the class falls short of the teacher's criteria, it is a sign to him that there is some problem to be diagnosed and dealt with. Thus, if the conversation does not seem to be "adding up" and no one is able to summarize the discussion, the teacher may realize that the problem the group is working on is not clearly enough defined; or that the role of the group member is ambiguous, so that the children do not really know what sort of contribution is appropriate; or that some other, more compelling problem is distracting them, so that they cannot concentrate on the task. The kinds of questions listed above under Problem 1 may now be asked in an effort to clarify the difficulty. It may be found necessary to change the focus from attempted problem solving to discovery by each individual of how he feels about the task, so that the group can "get its bearings" and redefine the task in more significant terms.

It is not unusual, for example, for a discussion of a selected problem gradually to lose force because the group needs to change its focus. An initially interesting discussion in civics about how laws are made may have been interesting chiefly as a way of testing whether other people in the class had the feeling that laws are frequently unfair. If the teacher sees that this feeling is shared by the group, and that the discussion is becoming slow and uneasy, he may be justified in surmising that the class really is concerned about the teacher's own rules in the classroom. He may test this notion by interjecting some remark to the effect that as a teacher he has to make rules from time to time, and that it isn't always easy to make fair rules. A response of dead silence, too enthusiastic picking up of the discussion, hasty reassurance that his rules are fine, or too rapid effort to change the subject might seem to the teacher to bear out his diagnosis. In that case, he could propose a shift in the activity, presumably to discussion by smaller groups, since the reactions indicated a reluctance to discuss the problem in the large group of which the teacher is a member. On the other hand, if the class readily falls in with the teacher's suggestion, he could propose a role-played scene in which someone (a boss, for example) hands down rules to his workers, and then the workers discuss the rules among themselves. Class discussion of the way the workers reacted to the boss's edicts would be pretty likely to indicate more clearly where the trouble with the teacher's rules lay.

Thus diagnosis of shifting needs of the group may require modification of activity. The occasional need for emotional catharsis by a classroom group can be accepted by the teacher who, if he has rapport with the group, may even share the feeling. But it does not follow that it is educative or even helpful to the group simply to translate their needs into action without any thought about it. Thus an uncontrolled, emotionalized period of semi-riot, for example, may express a need for catharsis, and it may be better for the group than inhibition of emotional expression; but for educational need-meeting experience there must also be thoughtful discussion of what the feelings are, where they come from, and what sorts of problems this implies. The part the teacher contributes, that the class cannot, is the understanding of *how* needs can be channeled through educative experience rather than just allowed to "blow off."

Teachers learn to diagnose the educational effectiveness of activity and to shift its focus as needed. Thus, when a discussion becomes too academic, interest can often be regained by inviting personal reactions to the material being discussed. When the class seems apathetic and inhibited, the teacher may try to put into words some fear or worry that may be troubling the group, and thus free the group to consider its concerns more objectively. When students are confused or frustrated, it may help to redefine the achievement problem. Personal opinions, tumbling out irresponsibly, may call for some thinking together about the kinds of contributions needed. Too much dependency on the teacher for suggestions may often be overcome by dividing the class into working committees.

PROBLEM 3. HOW CAN SHIFTS OF FOCUS ON THE THREE ASPECTS
BE ACCOMPLISHED WITHOUT PRODUCING AMBIGUITY
AND CONFUSION?

The machinery through which the teacher harnesses the classroom energy into educative work is a set of understandings about how to shift the basic focus of activity in response to diagnosed needs for control.

To comprehend its activities as it shifts from one kind of focus to another, the class needs to have consciousness of itself as a group of individuals trying to work and learn together. The reason for shifting focus is that the group *needs* to do so; and it needs to do so because it has run into a problem which it cannot solve under its present mode of operation.

The first requirement for avoiding confusion, then, is to know why the change is made. This explanation does not need to be a deep, clinical one; it merely involves explicit recognition that the way things are organized now does not give us the chance to really do what we most need to do—or are, in fact, actually trying inefficiently to do. If people are exchanging personal experiences, which are only loosely relevant to the discussion task, the teacher may find it better to figure out how this can be done more efficiently than to worry about how to prevent or stop it. Presumably there is a reason why the discussion has turned to experience swapping. If the teacher knew the reason, he might then approach the real problem more forthrightly.

The simplest type of explanation is, in effect, description of what the group is doing. "We started out to talk about how Hopi children are brought up, but we seem more interested now in talking about what part our own relatives have in *our* bringing up. Why don't we make this our question for the next little while and give everyone a chance to contribute his experience along these lines?" The assumption is that when the group leaves the task and gets involved in another task, it may be appropriate to clarify the new task and accept it as legitimate. Such switches in topic may appear at first to be digressions, but can often be used for contrast or illustration or as the basis of broader generalization. And the fact that they are entered into spontaneously may mean that somehow they are needed to maintain the group as an interactive organism.

A more diagnostic type of explanation is interpretative rather than descriptive. In the case above, for example, one might notice that the spontaneous digression carried with it the quality of complaint: "We don't have it as good as the Hopi children, whose relatives are indulgent and give them more attention than ours give to us." The interpretation might be something like this:

"The last several comments suggest that we are aware of differences between Hopi and American communities with regard to the relationships between children and their relatives." This interpretation then could lead to several follow-up questions for focusing discussion more explicitly: "What do we see the major differences to be?" or "What conditions in Hopi communities might account for these differences?" or "What seem to us to be advantages and disadvantages of the Hopi way as compared to ours?" Thus the purpose of this type of interpretation is to recognize the need for working through the feelings indicated by complaining, and to channel such feelings into relevant school achievement.

If the quality of complaint (to continue with our illustration) were intense, as though the class were really envious of the Hopi children, one might decide that this feeling should be made explicit for what it is rather than simply worked through by recasting the learning problem. In this case, after pointing out the awareness of difference between Hopi and American child-relative relationships, the teacher might decide not to raise questions but rather to set up an activity to make the feeling more explicit. He could propose that the class set up two sets of skits which would reveal their perceptions of differences between Hopi and American ways of dealing with the same situation: scene one might show a child in some naughtiness, such as taking a toy away from a younger brother; scene two might show what the parents would do in this situation; scene three might show what the relatives would do. Following the two sets of scenes, discussion would center about how the child felt in the two cultures, and why all the participants reacted as they did.

A more evaluative type of explanation is to point out the discrepancy between what the group is doing and what it said it was going to do. The purpose here is to get a redefinition of the problem or to get back on the track if the digression represents avoidance rather than reformulation of the problem in more meaningful terms. Such comments as, "We started out to see how many different ways we could find to account for the relationship between mother's brother and child in Hopi communities, and we seem to have lost sight of this task for the present. Have we gone as far as we can on that task? Or shall we get back to it?" Whichever is done is, at least, explicit, so that the students know what type of contribution is appropriate.

The answer to the question of how to avoid ambiguity and confusion when activity is shifted from one focus to another is simply that the teacher makes sure that the students have a satisfactory explanation. A satisfactory explanation represents the state of affairs honestly, points the way to activity seen as more appropriate or gratifying than what the group is doing now, and is understandable to the children: neither too deep, complex, nor vague.

Explanations for changes in activity are not fully understood at the time they are given because they represent untested anticipations of experience. To some extent, then, students have to trust the teacher. The meaning of the explanation becomes clearer, however, as the activity proceeds, and during this process it may be necessary to provide clarification of the relationship between the activity and the plan. Such necessities make themselves known through difficulties of participation or frustrations about what to do next.

Finally, the need for explanation and the satisfactoriness of an explanation are both determined by diagnosis. The behavior to be diagnosed is the expressed feelings of reluctance, frustration, conflict, tentativeness, anxiety, and the like. Every time an activity is changed it is important to provide a kind of reasonable objectivity which makes the expression of such feelings possible. The simplest way to provide such conditions is to explain candidly (leaving out unnecessary threat—or guilt-producing comments) what the activity is about and why it seems necessary. The simplest way to know how to make such statements in such a way that the class can understand them is to get some discussion by the students first, so that one can see how they view what they are doing and how they feel about it.

PROBLEM 4. HOW DOES THE TEACHER GUIDE THE CREATION OF NEEDED ACTIVITIES?

The teacher controls the learning situation by controlling his own role, and his role is different in different types of activity.

With regard to school achievement problems, the teacher is

essentially the leader whose primary loyalty is to the community. He is the boss, and his power is actually less open to question than is the power of the business or factory boss. Because his power is unquestioned, he can afford to be co-operative and friendly. He knows he can get his way with regard to what is to be studied, so he has nothing to lose by talking it over with the children and explaining and developing the logic of the choices of topics.

With regard to the group requirement for organization of effort, differentiation of roles, enforcement of its expectations for itself, development of its natural leadership and the like, the teacher's role is basically consultative. He cannot decide who the natural leaders are to be, but he can help those who are capable of leadership at each time to discover such roles for themselves. He cannot legislate the degree of commitment the group will find toward the achievement tasks, but he can give them a chance to explore the question and develop a group standard about it. He cannot force the group to express creative, personally significant ideas, but he can help them see that such ideas are useful to the group and that they are rewarded when they are expressed.

With regard to the individuals' requirements of personal gratification of their own unique needs, the teacher again provides conditions and opportunities, but he does not demand any particular learning or behavior. As a matter of fact, he seldom has enough relevant information about the children's internal problems to make much of a guess about what will be upsetting, significant, threatening, stimulating, or bothersome to individuals, although he can usually anticipate such reactions from the class as a whole with considerable accuracy. The kind of opportunity required here is for personal interaction between teacher and individual student, or among small groups of friends (under more limited conditions). The teacher's role is that of counselor, and it is not a "put-on" role. It is a side of the teacher which is less evident and available to the students at some times than at others. But it truly represents the teacher's real personality in his relations to individual students.

The appropriate activity, then, is whatever results from the teacher playing the proper role at the proper time; its creation is a natural process of interaction, of living together. The only behavior the teacher can control directly is his own, and he does this through diagnosing the class need and then shifting himself into the type of role needed from him to enable the class to meet its need. The members of the class must then shift their roles to accommodate to the teacher; but if his diagnosis and operation is correct, the class will have high motivation and involvement in making the shifts in their own roles. If they are unable to accommodate to the teacher's change, then he would be advised to reconsider his diagnosis, timing, or skills.

In actual practice, the teacher tests whether to shift his role by tentative probing, by beginning to act in the new role and assessing the class's reaction. If they accept the new role, immediately shift their own participation to maintain interaction, and start moving effectively, then the teacher knows that his diagnosis was correct. As soon as the class has operated on the new basis long enough that it can be clearly seen that the shift has occurred, then the teacher may raise the question of proceeding along the same lines, but more efficiently.

Thus, "readiness" is not something to discuss, but rather to act. The evidence that the group is ready for a change of activity is that, given the chance, it changes its activity. On the other hand, the efficiency of activity depends upon the explicitness with which the member role, during the activity, is visualized by the children. Such explicitness is achieved by talking about the activity: by planning together. But effective planning is possible only when the group is committed, and knows that it is committed, to stated goals. Changes in the way of working demonstrate to the class that they have a new commitment to "something"; and their diagnosis of the new things they are doing tells them what the "something" is. At this point, planning activity more directly to achieve the goal becomes not only reasonable but inevitable. Planning is complete when each individual has a clear picture of what sort of participation is required from him and also when he is motivated to accept the challenge to produce the needed types of behaviors—in other words, when he is ready to experiment with his own role, his own ideas and feelings.

PROBLEM 5. HOW CAN THE CLASS BE ORGANIZED TO
CARRY OUT THE NEEDED ACTIVITIES?

This is the problem of what things need to be taken into account during planning, and how this is to be done.

The class and teacher take direct and explicit account of the objective requirements—of what must be done to solve the problem. The students, as individuals, are affected by their perception of opportunity to meet certain personal needs; this is their vested interest.

Instrumental to these considerations is the central concern over who should work with whom, and under what conditions. One way to think of the question of how to organize effort is in these terms: How can the people who will stimulate the best in each other, who possess among themselves the needed resources to avoid frustration and to keep their groups going, who have with each other the kind of relationship which best promotes exploration of personal meanings and, therefore, the internalization of experience—how can these people be put together, and under what circumstances should they be put together?

There are some general principles that are relevant to this problem:

1. Subgroups composed of friends are likely to have more energy to spend in participating.

2. Groups composed of friends are more likely to deal with whatever problem they need to, whether it is centered around school achievement or not.

3. Individuals, when among friends, can express their real feelings easier, and are threatened less and supported more by the others.

The use of friends is advocated when the going is tough, as in diagnosing what is wrong, or in creating a wide range of ideas, or in working under pressure.

On the other hand, there is another side of the question, indicated by the following generalizations:

1. When members of the group get into conflict everyone tends to get involved rapidly (as in a debate situation, for example).

2. People need challenge and stimulation to cause them to think through their ideas.

3. When a person is undecided about some issue, it helps to let him see people who are committed to the two sides of the problem "fight it out."

The use of groups with some possibilities of clash is advocated in situations which require aggression and where taking things for granted might jeopardize success. Thus, after a tentative plan has been formulated, its possible bugs are more likely to be found by its opponents than by its friends.

The amount of clash that can be tolerated depends upon the possibilities of channeling aggression into work. If the job is clearly defined so that everyone can tell what is relevant, then aggression can be channeled by the group.

The size of the subgroup and its relation to the total group both affect participation by individuals:

1. The smaller the learning committee, the more time is available for each person to test his ideas directly through overt participation.

2. The smaller the learning committee, the less clearly defined the problem has to be for them to be able to work on it.

3. The smaller the learning committee, the greater pressure each individual feels to participate, and the more visible is his nonparticipation.

4. The smaller the working committee, the easier it is to express intimate thoughts and feelings.

5. The smaller the working committee, the less are its potential resources, but the greater is its motivation.

6. The smaller the working committee, the greater the influence of each individual, including the "blockers" and "wreckers."

7. The clearer the expectations of the total group for a given product, the harder the working committee will work to produce it.

8. The status of the working committee within the total group is of no direct significance, but the desires of the subgroup for mobility and improvement of status are significant motivating or blocking factors.

In general, the simplest way to express what is required to organize subgroups for *most* achievement related tasks is: that the members be well enough acquainted that they can communicate fairly readily; that there be enough range of temperament that they challenge each other; that they have among them enough skills of group process (socialization skills) that they can work together; that they have enough resources and enthusiasm for the achievement problem that they keep going on; and that they have a secure enough role in the total group that they do not waste much energy comparing themselves to or belittling the other subgroups. And finally, that the difficult children are in groups that can handle them, either by containment, giving of security, or meeting them on their own terms.[2]

The different subgroups may or may not be given the same assignment:

1. The problem of steering the group is aided best by having several subgroups working on the same assignment, followed by total group debate about differences in the subgroup findings.

2. The problem of extending the range of experience to increase its significance is probably best dealt with by having the subgroups working on different but complementary assignments.

3. The greatest account of individual differences can be taken by having students choose their subgroups on the basis of interest in the topic assigned to that subgroup. But such choosing should not be permitted until there has been adequate discussion in the total group of what is expected with respect to each interest-task.

The strategy of breaking down the achievement of purposes into specific problems to be assigned to subgroups is decided by: the extent to which the subgroup experience is to be the basis for deciding on next purposes of the total group, the extent to which the subgroup is primarily to help the individuals find more of a place for themselves, and the extent to which the product of the subgroups, when put together, "closes out" the unit.

The total group can delegate particular functions to working committees:

1. Working committees, set up after short preliminary discussion, are used to give each person a better opportunity to find out what he thinks and feels through informal discussion in a con-

2. H. A. Thelen, "Group Dynamics in Instruction: The Principle of Least Group Size," *School Review* (March, 1949), pp. 139–48.

genial group. Reporting, in this case, is of whatever any individual wishes to report.

2. Working committees, set up to produce plans, hypotheses, or analyses, have the job also of preparing a formal set of conclusions. These may be reported back in a panel discussion composed of representatives of each working committee.

3. Working committees, set up to extend the range of experience of the class, have the task of "walking" the total group through a brief recapitulation of their own experiences. They can do this best by some variant of a developmental discussion, planned by the committee and directed by it.

4. Whatever the assignment of the working committee, it must also identify and lay before the total group any reservations, or problems, or needs of the group in order to clarify the purposes, directions, or means used in the total group working together.

5. Working committees can be set up completely informally to make whatever use of a period of free time they wish. This is primarily for individuals to express their ideas and feelings, following a significant amount of study and experience with a unit. Their only responsibility in this case is to indicate what use they made of the time so that their new readiness for learning can be assessed as a basis for further planning. A steering committee, made up of leaders of the working committees, can make a preliminary diagnosis of possible new directions and present them to the class as a series of alternative proposals.

6. Working committees, delegations from working committees, or individuals may bring to the teacher any question they wish for clarification. The teacher can use such questions to decide what the problem is, who is involved in it, and what further checking he ought to do, either to ameliorate conditions or to capitalize on the issue for the good of the class.

The generalizations simply spell out the fact that no matter what the assigned focus of the working committee is, attention must always be paid to the objective achievement problem, the problems of social co-operation, and the typical needs or problems of individuals.

The teacher's job is to be helpful at all times. The following suggestions may be useful to him:

1. The teacher prevents the waste of effort on planning activities outside the competence of the group by telling them, as needed, the limits within which they may work. Thus a teacher should not allow a working committee to operate on the fantasy that it can make decisions for the total group.

2. The teacher attempts to understand the problems as they are seen by the children, and he helps them deal with these problems primarily by helping them take into account the factors of which they are unaware, and by redefining the task in such a way that they can deal with it.

3. The teacher joins working committees as a consultant only when asked, and he clarifies his own role with the committee before proceeding to offer advice or suggestions.

4. In follow-up discussions with the total group, the teacher acknowledges the contributions of the working committees, and helps them report such parts of their experience as the teacher feels will be helpful to the total group.

5. The teacher, particularly on long assignments, keeps track of the progress of the working committees, preferably through short questionnaires filled out by each person at the end of each working period.

6. The teacher encourages working committees to make use of each other as resources during working periods, by arranging joint meetings or visitation among committees.

7. At all times, the teacher is concerned with maintaining work as a learning experience. He can do this to the extent that the children themselves want to learn, and he does it by challenging them to create new solutions and to deal maturely with all suggestions.

8. After making recommendations to a group, the teacher then withdraws from the group so they can make their own decision. The teacher, however, does not abdicate responsibility for seeing to it that the decisions of working committees are properly tested against reality by the committees before they have committed themselves to a good deal of effort which can only end in failure.

9. Such disciplining as a working committee needs is adminis-

tered by the teacher through redefinition of the requirements of the task and of the expectancies of the total group for a useful subgroup product. He may need to shift students from one group to another in order to get each student into a group in which he accepts the challenge to work constructively.

10. The teacher is always ready to represent the group to the outside world if their work takes them out of the classroom into the school or community. But his representation is mostly in affirming to others the need of the children to communicate with them. It is up to the children to represent their own needs or wishes, in their own way.

11. In so far as possible, the teacher helps the children find resources other than himself for work on objectively defined problems. On the other hand, he is also concerned that the children gain help from these resources commensurate with the effort expended. He avoids sending them on wild-goose chases, and he answers simple, direct questions if they can be answered without consideration of a broad context of facts or experiences. He helps them clarify their questions in such a way that the available resources can be helpful.

RECAPITULATION

The foregoing discussion endeavors to spell out the following basic assumptions about classroom learning:

1. The purpose of the classroom is to change people as a result of their own experiences.

2. Experiencing is an active process of working with others for common goals. In the classroom these goals are related to school achievement.

3. Experience is educative to the extent that it involves thinking about what one is doing, why he is doing it, and the general significance, usefulness, and applicability of the methods he is using in doing it.

4. The control of learning is through the use of consciousness. While all experience may produce changes in a student, the part that is educative is the part that is understood through conscious thought processes.

5. Utilization of consciousness to guide experience, and to im-

prove the constructiveness of subsequent experience, requires that experience be seen as inquiry; and this includes such functions as explanation, experimentation, and test of the consequences of behavior.

6. The guidance of education requires that teachers strive at all times for the needed and, therefore, appropriate distribution of energy into these objectives: the defined and required school achievement, co-operation within the group, and the formulation of individualized meanings of experiences. Inquiry is directed to all three of these objectives.

For elaboration of the kinds of facts with which teachers deal, see chapter 9. Some obstacles to learning are considered from the social standpoint in chapter 7, and from the psychological standpoint in chapter 8. Chapter 1 indicates by analogy the nature of motivated participation in projects, and chapter 5 exposes in detail how a group is steered in response to its relatively deep needs. Administrative Propositions I and II, on pages 114–26, are highly relevant to setting up and controlling subgroup activity within the classroom.

CHAPTER 3

The improvement of performance by professionals is self-stimulated. Teachers, nurses, engineers, lawyers, have to train themselves on the job. This requires opportunity, under group-supportive conditions, for studying their own professional skills.

But the efforts toward self-improvement of small groups within an institution succeed only if there is an over-all program which involves working with other groups in the community.

DISTINCTIVE FEATURES

In the plan here discussed, the motivation of the teachers for self-training is a combination of professional drives, desires for gratification in small groups, loyalty to the faculty and desire for advancement, and expectations of citizens with whom the teacher co-operates. The authority of leadership is the combination of these commitments, and is delegated to teachers chosen by their peers. The primary targets of change are teaching methods, to be improved, and school programs and curricula to be advanced. Secondary targets are youth-serving agencies in the community, businessmen, and others co-operating in the training of students. The role expectations of faculty members are: initiative in working on teaching problems in their small groups, co-operation with certain citizens in giving training, and participation in professional discussion within the total faculty group. The method of control is through organized faculty leadership, which plans and executes agenda in accordance with the canvassed interests of the faculty. The relationships with other groups include co-operation of individual teachers with citizens, two-way conversation with the school administration, and individual and small-group participation in out-of-school training classes, workshops, and the like.

Developing the School through Faculty Self-training

71

View X: "The supervisor used to come snooping around my class, but I cured him. How? It's easy! I just turned the class over to him. Boy, did he fall for it!"

View XI: "If I get put on one more faculty committee I'll scream."

View XII: "Well, you know where *that* idea came from, don't you? It's that English Department trying to build up its position."

View XIII: "You know, he was caught writing a letter while his class was working in the laboratory. . . . The new crop of teachers just docsn't have the old professional discipline."

View XIV: "I so admire the way you teach. . . . I hope after I get the house fixed up a little better we can get together and really *talk*."

View XV: Add a few of your own.

It seems fair to say that a school can be a pretty complicated institution. The problem of being a professional person without the status of a professional; the fear of being misunderstood by the parents if anything is said that they don't agree with; the nuisance of being saddled with blue forms, pink forms, reports, societies, PTA meetings, room meetings; the diplomacy required to thread one's way through the maze of cliques; the confusion between one's desires to try new things and yet not be seen by the others as a threat to them—these are no mean problems.

On top of all these matters, as a sort of last straw in many schools, is a half-hearted effort to "improve the ·instructional program."

It is easy to be critical, particularly if you have to sit through department meetings when you know you should be preparing the next day's work. It is easy to be bored if you are an old-timer getting acquainted with one more freshly scrubbed new principal. It is easy to be discouraged if everyone else leaves promptly with the closing bell so they can work in their gardens. It is convenient to be dependent if the principal throws his weight around.

Given the complicated, busy confusion of the school, and the typical overloading of work onto the staff, and the difficulty of finding energy for long-range concerns when forced to meet the deadline of a new class lesson every fifty minutes—given all these things, it is clear that the in-service training program cannot be just one more task piled on top of teaching: it must be a part of operation, part of the way of life in the school; and it must be continuously rewarding and adaptable to individual teachers; yet—it must add up to a better school program.

The purpose of this chapter is to analyze what is involved in in-service training, to make explicit some of the major principles guiding in-service training, and to suggest a concrete plan. We shall discuss the problem in terms of schools, but the same general principles and many characteristics of the plan would fit hospitals, engineering firms, large libraries, and other professional institutions. The plan has been tried in part, in various ways, but never in its entirety. It cannot be offered as a blueprint, but it may be a model against which present practice can be examined and improved. The plan will be developed step by step and will be organized around a series of assumptions.

DEFINITION OF AIM

Instruction occurs in classrooms and its effectiveness depends upon the teacher. The teacher guides instruction by what he says and does; by the ideas, wishes, attitudes, feelings, and values he communicates to the class. Those which he communicates outside the classroom to other teachers or to parents or in written articles affect the class's learning indirectly—if at all. The quality of learning by the class is determined to a very large extent by the classroom performance of the teacher. The creation of effective performance is a continuous production job which is affected by fatigue, skill, imagination, insight, anxiety, possibilities of reward, personal needs, and many other factors. But the central fact that must never be forgotten is that all efforts to improve instruction succeed or fail by the criterion of better performance by teachers in their classrooms.

THE OBJECTIVES OF IN-SERVICE TRAINING

Teaching is what the teacher does. To change teaching means that the teacher himself must, in some respects at least, change. And only the teacher can change the teacher.

Not all changes are equally possible or equally desirable. The most appropriate changes for any teacher are toward improved ability to cope with the problems of educating children—that is, of giving instruction more creatively and more realistically.

Coping with a situation is actually coping with one's self in a situation. And, more precisely, it is coping with one's feelings as he interacts in a situation. This may be done in a number of ways. The teacher can pretend, against all evidence, that certain feelings do not exist. He can deny feelings of inadequacy with respect to his rapport with children. Or, he can recognize the feelings, try to understand them, and then consciously set about to acquire the information, emotional orientation, or skill required to do better next time, i.e., to feel more satisfied with his improved operation. Feelings can also be fought, projected on others, run away from, and so on.

The changes that a teacher can be motivated to produce through training experience are the ones he wants and which are not surrounded by feelings of threat, coercion, fear, or other blocking emotions. These appropriate, desirable changes will differ from one teacher to another. The training objectives for each teacher should be formulated from interpretations of feelings he is aware of in the classroom. Since interpretation of one's feelings is a personal matter, it is clear that, for training to succeed, the teacher must be deeply involved in it; training for the total creative act of educating children is not a matter of gimmicks or superficial knowledge—it is a matter of integrated changes within one's total self.

RESISTANCE TO CHANGE

To understand the conditions required for training, we might profitably start with the question: Why haven't the needed changes happened? If these changes are really profitable to the teacher to make, and, in fact, even necessary to individual functioning, what stands in the way of their occurring spontaneously?

We assume that the reason needed changes have not occurred is that there are blockages, or obstacles to change. These barriers may operate to prevent awareness of the relevant feelings, or diagnosis of the particular types of problems encountered by the teacher, or the formulation of new alternatives and experimentation in new ways. Thus, for example: in some schools, when the teacher feels that he does not like certain pupils, he also feels threatened because of a group standard that "we are all unprejudiced here"; in others, the school's strong insistence on a "good solid academic program," and the greater prestige of academic teachers, could make him hesitate a long time before diagnosing that the content he is supposed to teach is simply unsuitable to the needs of his pupils; and experimentation with teacher-pupil planning can be suicidal in any school which goes on the basic assumption (whether it admits it or not) that all children are alike and teacher, by definition, always knows best.

In addition to such faculty-maintained group standards, designed, by defining the acceptable orthodoxy, to preserve one from discomfort, there are many more important possible barriers within the self:

1. A person may need to maintain illusions of expertness or infallibility, and to do this, he may rationalize failure as success. "Well, the class sure got into a mess today, just as I predicted it would"; or "We didn't get anywhere on the lesson, but we had a good experience together."

2. A person may also feel that the job is too big, too demanding: he simply cannot muster the energy required to tackle it. Thus: "To move into the project method is really asking me to prepare ten different lessons each day for each class." "To give students more freedom of choice would really require that I change my whole method of teaching." "How can I get permission to experiment with those new workbooks now that the official textbook list has been turned in?"

3. A person knows subconsciously that any significant change in himself as a teacher also means a change in his role or position in the total faculty. Thus a professional person is almost inevitably an advocate of his own methods; he is expected to "represent his professional point of view" to his colleagues. He can fear new learning because it changes his role in the group: others have to accommodate to it through revision of their expectations. Thus a teacher who has been seen as the leader of the academic subject-matter crowd might find it difficult to contemplate giving up the rewards of this role for the frustrations of a neophyte in the child-

centered approach. A teacher who was safely pegged by the faculty as a rather ineffective academician suddenly became a severe threat to her colleagues when she introduced role-playing into her classroom. A science teacher who went away to a workshop and returned as an expert on evaluation suddenly found himself snowed under with a new testing program.

Changes in competence mean changes in what a teacher is perceived as advocating, as being able to do, and as wanting to push others into doing. He can fear upsetting expectations of others, threatening others, or being given new responsibility.

4. Another kind of resistance to change comes from the fear of ambiguity or lack of guideposts. To experiment with new ways always means to strike out into the unknown. The teacher may not have confidence that his past experience and old habits can be relied on: he is "on his own."

It is commonly accepted that people have a vested interest in their professional practices. What we need to see is that this is a *total* vested interest, not only in the ways of doing things but also in one's position in the group, his confidence in himself, his ways of regarding the world, and his image of himself as a special kind of person. And this total vested interest means that resistance to change is inevitable—even with regard to changes that one knows might represent real improvement.

With regard to self-changes, the typical state of affairs, at least initially, is ambivalence. We have impulses to change, to try new things; but at the same time we have impulses to go back to the safe and certain and easy and rewarding. People cover up or deny ambivalence through such means as too much enthusiasm, too much dependence on the literally interpreted word of a new authority, overassertive attempts to persuade others, increased hostility to the people still doing things the old way, and the like. The most significant problem of changing is the problem of dealing with ambivalence with regard to the changes about to be produced.

A person who is ambivalent needs to resolve the ambivalence. A person who is ambivalent with regard to learning needs to resolve the ambivalence in favor of, rather than against, learning.

THE NEED FOR GROUP SUPPORT

Resolution of ambivalence is facilitated by working in the right kind of small group. The "right kind" is one in which a participant can express his feelings of doubt, hostility, excitement. It is one whose other members can give him reasonably accurate perceptions of his work. It is one with the group goal of improvement. It is a group of friendly well-motivated colleagues who feel that they are mutually benefited by working together.

Such a group supports a member in many ways: It enables him to face feelings which he could not otherwise face, through his discovery that others feel the same way. It encourages him to produce, so that he will have something to talk about and be rewarded for. It helps him face the total group by backing up his opinions or at least by helping him get a fair hearing. And its other members articulate openly the sides of the conflict he has not yet been able to formulate in words for himself.[1]

The first organizational principle of in-service training is to get each person into a small, supportive group in which the member's responsibility is to help the others.

Such groups can help some people merely by talking. But for any direct effectiveness, they must actually know at first hand how their members perform. In other words, these small groups need to have the opportunity to watch their members' work from time to time—and possibly to help carry out new kinds of activity. The ideal would be realized when a teacher, about to try out a new activity, could get the help of the others in planning it, could get their observations and reactions to the procedure as actually tried, and could then discuss it with them.

The small group could begin simply by having the members observe each other in a period of regular work. Discussion would be for the purpose of diagnosis and for comparing notes on the shared experience. This is a quick way to get into communication and develop common assumptions about what the members

1. Bruno Bettelheim and M. E. Sylvester, "Therapeutic Influence of the Group upon the Individual," *American Journal of Orthopsychiatry*, XXVII (October, 1947). The kind of group we envision has many characteristics of a psyche-group. See also Helen H. Jennings, *Sociometry of Leadership* (Sociometry Monograph No. 14 [New York: Beacon House, 1947]).

are looking for or working toward. For such operation during the working day, the school administrator will have to co-operate. He may need to provide a substitute teacher from time to time, mobilize parents in the community to help with classes temporarily left by their teachers, or sanction arrangements for handling classes together every so often.

ADDITIONAL RESOURCES FOR SMALL TRAINING GROUPS

Most of us working with people in groups would improve remarkably if we could suddenly understand all that we know. In other words, very few of us, including teachers, are limited by lack of resources as much as by the unavailability of the resources we have.

Nevertheless, the small training groups will need help from time to time. The difficulty may be in their own processes of operation, it may be a lack of knowledge of available techniques or materials, or it may be simply a lack of confidence in their own new planning operations. Effort on the part of the administrator to have resources made specially available is reassuring, too, provided the principal does not insist that his resource people be used.

There are few communities in which the schools have made serious efforts to catalogue the resources and consultant help that would be readily accessible to teachers and students. Schools could have lists of citizens who are willing and, in fact, eager to make their past experience in teaching available. There are, in most communities, people competently trained in human psychology and with experience in consulting with business and other institutions. There are people who have had illuminating adventures, or who are knowledgeable about workshop techniques (useful in classrooms), or who know visiting dignitaries well enough to get them out to help a school. There might be a nearby university which would be willing to exchange its help to the school for opportunity to study the school's program.

The productivity of the small groups will be affected very much by the availability of a wide range of resources. And when the small group is too insecure ever to use outside help, then it needs consultation to improve its own internal functioning.

The generosity of the administrator in seeing to it that many resource people are available is largely canceled out if the administrator cannot also see to it that the use of the resource people is initiated by the small group, and that the resource person is used by the training group in its own way. In other words, to give help you really have to give the help. To accomplish this, a small faculty committee might be put in charge of the resource pool, and it could provide the necessary information to the small training groups to use in whatever way they wished— within faculty-decided policies for communicating with non-school personnel.

THE ROLE OF THE TOTAL FACULTY

It is probably safe to guess that if we were to select all the instances of real growth of teachers on their jobs we would find that in one way or another they had found themselves other persons who could give them the sort of support we have been advocating. In other words, we believe that the small training group must be operating informally wherever one finds the kind of improvement which in-service training ought to be creating. It may operate in a clandestine way and out of school hours in the unfavorable social climate of some schools, or it may be easily visible at a quick glance.

Our planning so far, then, has merely been directed to make explicitly effective a set of necessary processes that go on anyway. The next step is to get larger numbers of people into such relationships, and to produce the kind of incentive and school climate in which, after a time, the small training group becomes an expected and automatic part of the school way of life. This requires certain conditions in the faculty seen in its entirety as a total group.

One of the required conditions is that the prestige system in the total faculty group be based on contribution to the instructional excellence of the school. Past teaching experience, courses taken during the summer, number of years of college work completed, personality, contacts with the right people, and other such factors will probably always have some place in the initial hiring of teachers. But their prestige and pay, once they are hired, should

depend only on merit: how well they teach and what they contribute to the teaching of others. The faculty must accept as its
major purpose the improvement of its teaching.

A second required condition is that the faculty accept the notion that the end of good teaching can be achieved by a variety
of means. There is no one right way to teach, although for any
particular teacher in a specified classroom situation there is
probably one best thing to do. A faculty concerned with improvement of teaching will encourage development of a variety
of methods, rather than demanding conformity to one method.
And it will then study these various methods in an effort to see
what is common among them, what is different, what method
seems to work best under what conditions, and so on. In other
words, the other half of the proposition that responsible diversity should be encouraged is that there must also be provision for
assimilation.

Diversity is important as the way to encourage development of
good ideas and special insights on the part of each teacher. But
the school gets maximum profit when it arranges for communication and deliberation on these unique contributions. The
simplest communication is through demonstration lessons taught
to student volunteers before the total faculty. The most efficient
way to make sure that time is well utilized on such occasions is
by having a steering committee, perhaps with a consultant to
assist it, sift the various available possibilities for demonstration and select the ones offering the most illuminating contrasts,
or the most stimulus value, or the greatest modifiability to fit a
range of subjects. An effective steering committe will recognize
that the other side of the program of small training groups is the
total faculty group as audience, encourager, setter of expectancies, challenger, and resource pool. The total group must strive
for standards of tolerance of differences in means along with continual reinforcement of the over-all goals.

The dynamics of the total faculty meetings will be a benign
type of competition among the small training groups. This is
guaranteed to the extent that status depends upon productivity
of the small groups, so that the interpersonal motivating factor
will be the desire of each to contribute more to the total meeting

than the others. The difference between this kind of competition and that between teams is that the aim is to contribute to all rather than to destroy the opponents. The steering committee must be given the responsibility of seeing to it that the rules of competition are fair, opportunities are equal, and rewards are distributed according to contribution. A simple way to achieve this is to have on the steering committee representatives of all the small training groups. These people will help test and check the proposed agendas for faculty meetings.

THE ROLE OF THE PRINCIPAL

The principal is a key figure in in-service training—regardless of what he does about it. By virtue of his position, he has legal responsibility for developing adequate instruction in his school. And he is usually expected by the community to be the spokes-man for the school as well as the translator of the community's wishes into school practice.

Within the school, the principal recommends the hiring and firing of teachers, determines their work loads, opens or shuts doors to professional advancement. It is not surprising that the morale of teachers, their creativity, and their dedications to their classrooms are much influenced by their perceptions and inter-pretations of the attitudes and acts of the principal. For an in-service training program to succeed, the principal must believe in it, express enthusiasm for it, and have a well-defined and ac-cepted role in it.

Defining and fulfilling this role is a difficult business because in many ways the appropriate role in the in-service enterprise is in conflict with the role of administrator and public relations man.

Thus the principal is a facilitator to the in-service program. Essentially he provides services to the teacher group. The teach-ers are the ones in this situation who must wield the authority and assume the responsibilities. This state of affairs contrasts sharply with the boss-employee relationships typical of action in administrative and public-relations capacities. In these func-tions, the principal speaks (or should speak) with authority and with full assumption of responsibility. The simple but complicating fact of the matter is that it is not easy to keep distinct two roles which differ so drastically in the way one exercises his authority. The man who hires and fires and is responsible for the teachers' welfare may find it difficult to have faith in their leadership with respect to instructional matters.

The facilitator also works within a different orientation than does the administrator. The facilitator is concerned with the processes of working, and accepts the notion that, so long as the processes are sound, the results will be good. He cannot be sure of what will have been accomplished by next June; he has to believe that whatever does eventuate is sufficient and appropriate. But in his role as administrator, the principal would know that this point of view is suicidal: deadlines must be met, reports prepared, definite promises fulfilled.

The difference is between participation in essentially creative, experimental activity as distinguished from routine or maintenance activity.

At the level of personal relations, too, there are differences. As facilitator, the principal must be equally available and emotionally supportive to all the teachers as they strike out into new realms of experiencing. Trying new ways of doing things is an anxious business. If the principal himself, as administrator, is anxious about the program, he will be of little help to the teachers. Some of the anxieties on both sides are related to the "payoff" value of new efforts; others are related to the problem of adjusting to new prestige and status relationships. The lines of communication on the organization chart of the school are unlikely to be the actual needed lines of communication within the in-service program.

What all this adds up to is the conclusion that determination of the principal's role, like that of each teacher, does not depend simply on the way the individual happens to feel about it. The roles in some respects must be worked out and defined as the enterprise gets under way. Several formal considerations are suggestive. The fact that the principal is spokesman for the school means that the teachers should insist on his being in a role which keeps him informed as to what the teachers are trying to do and what their intentions are. Otherwise, his interpretations to the community may involve illusions about the school which solidify in public expectations and which the teachers feel forced to try to meet—even though they consider them unwarranted.

The fact that the steering committee and the principal are both concerned with the development of the program as a whole suggests that they should have a close relationship. The fact that the principal, in his administrative capacity, can do much to implement the needs which he, as facilitator, can see, suggests that he might well be the executive secretary to the steering committee. Not all principals would be temperamentally able to act in this capacity, however, and in any case it is perfectly proper for the principal and steering committee to experiment to find the best way to define his participation.

The Need for School-wide Programs

We noted that a basic dynamic for training would be benign competition among the small training groups. We saw that the total faculty meetings had, among other purposes, the control of the rules for competing, the bestowal of rewards (e.g., increased status in the group), and, through the steering committee, the provision of services needed by the training groups. All this was seen as necessary to make effective the work of the training groups.

What, however, is to make the total faculty effective as a group? For example, why should *it* develop the set of standards and expectations of creativity, tolerance of new ideas, reflection on and utilization of suggestions? What is to prevent the small group competing in not-so-benign ways for the purpose of taking over the faculty leadership?

If the total faculty group is only a convenience to spur the small training groups, then each training group will expect to use the faculty for testing its ideas and rewarding them. In the absence of any controls, the temptation will be to assume that the best test of quality is influence, and the best test of excellence of ideas is counting the number of teachers who vote for adopting the new gimmick throughout the school. This is, of course, nonsense.

The point is that testing of ideas and acceptance of contribution and insight is not possible except when the total group, as a group, has a purpose of its own over and above the stimulation of members to improve their own skills. What sort of problem—and purpose—can the faculty (as a total professional group) legitimately have? Let us look at some of the possible answers which have been assumed in various schools:

1. The chief problem of the faculty is to educate the children of the community.

Comment: More accurately, the chief job of the teacher is to teach his classes. But one hundred teachers, each teaching his own classes, constitute collective, not group, action. Most schools are actually buildings in which each teacher, with whatever help he needs from the services of the administration and maintenance staffs, does whatever job of teaching he can. It is roughly similar to a hospital clinic except that the "patients" are involuntary groups of children rather than single individuals. Education of children is a job for the school as an institutionalized collection of teachers; it is not a job of the faculty as a group.

2. The purposes for which the faculty acts as a group are to increase wages and get better contracts. Preservation of academic freedom, planning better public relations for a school bond campaign, and the like, are other examples of the same sort.

Comment: These are illustrations of problems tackled by the faculty as a group, and all professional groups engage in such protective activities on behalf of their profession. But the skills required for such activities are not the ones required for teaching, so that contributions of the small training groups are irrelevant to such problems. Ideas created or discovered in the in-service training program cannot therefore be tested against the demands of such problems.

3. The purposes for which the faculty acts as a group are to plan better curricula for the students.

Comment: Meetings for this purpose would probably be along departmental or grade lines, rather than total faculty lines. Such problems *do* provide the *raison d'être* for department meetings because the department bands together to meet demands from the outside. For example, there may be a demand that certain courses be taught, made by the school (principal) presumably acting on behalf of the board, which in turn acts on behalf of the community. Thus planning the various curricula, playground supervision, study halls, after-school programs, etc., are all in response to demands originated from outside the teacher, and the groups for whom meeting these demands is a problem are composed of the people who have to do the work. The faculty as a whole may act in an advisory capacity and as a pool for recruiting manpower, but neither of these functions provides criteria relevant for testing ideas from the in-service program.

4. The purpose of professional faculty meetings is to hear and discuss good ideas about how to teach.

Comment: This is a popular fallacy. It is true, for example, that stimulating ideas from important people from universities or elsewhere can be discussed with pleasure and profit. A few individuals might be induced to try out a new idea, or to feel superior to it, or to reject it flatly; and in so far as this is of value to the individuals, it may be of value to the school. But a more common consequence, however, would be to stir up anxieties on the part of teachers who are not as adequate as the more psychologically sophisticated teachers attending the lecture. Other effects—with respect to a matter like discipline—are likely to include furnishing the "student-centered" teachers ammunition for further battling with the "community-centered," "subject-centered," "reality-centered," or, possibly, "self-centered" factions.

If there are committees working to produce new ideas about school problems, they may present reports to the faculty. These, of course, will be voted acceptance if the principal says the right things about them; otherwise, they will result in nothing because only the people who worked out the ideas have any particular insight or commitment to them. If the report is by one training group, and everyone else is in other training groups, then we can expect the discussion to be primarily the acting-out of the intergroup competition. There could be conflict or withdrawal from the discussion, and ideas might be stimulated. But the ideas will not be realistically tested in their own right because it is the subgroup itself which is on trial, not its ideas. This is the problem which opened this section, and led us into the discussion.

5. The purpose of the faculty meeting as a total group is to consider how better to use the entire community for educative purposes.

Comment: Yes.

To use the community for educational purposes requires collaboration by the faculty with many other groups, businesses, and welfare organizations. Through the processes of collaboration, the faculty can develop meaningful professional relationships with the adult community. And, as these relationships develop, so also do public expectations for the role of faculty member, going beyond the role of caring for children and keeping parents satisfied. The school can move from the occupation of governess within the family of community institutions to the role of active collaborator in solving, through education, community youth problems.

Specifically, the role of a group in the community depends upon the social transactions into which the group enters. The following sorts of collaboration are suggested by way of illustration:

1. Collaboration with merchants and consumers to provide better consumer education
2. Collaboration with civic leaders to devise classroom experience to reduce racial tension
3. Collaboration with parents to evaluate and improve the school's contributions to better living in the family
4. Collaboration with agencies and employers to provide a work-experience program which complements course work in the school
5. Collaboration with a university to aid in the preparation of teachers

The faculty operates in two distinguishable ways within the collaborative relationship. First, it shares in diagnosing problems as they exist in the community, and it trains students in how to behave in their immediate problematic contacts with buying, prejudice, family discipline, etc. These training experiences presumably are set up within the school curriculum, and only a few teachers are actively engaged in direct training with respect to any one type of problem.

Secondly, the faculty has the responsibility of educating children, not just training them, and the entire faculty is involved in this. Thus, with regard to consumer education, for example, the home economics and science teachers may offer to the students training through direct acting-out experiences as young consumers. But the entire faculty is concerned in the development of an understanding of economic interdependence, long- versus short-range values, the nature of wealth, attitudes against waste, appreciation of good design, and the like.

The central curricular problem in most schools is to relate their training functions, which are assigned to different courses and teachers, to their educational functions, which are the province of all. It is no solution to the problem to attempt to squeeze the educational functions into general education, college preparatory, or academic courses; and the training functions into vocational, nonacademic, or professional courses. The most pressing needs of students are to live successfully in a community run by adults, and these needs are satisfied by training through firsthand experiences provided by school and community together. But in the training process, needs arise in the student for understandings and knowledge, for assimilating his experience into his personal scheme of things. These are needs for finding meaning in the relationships between himself and the world, and, by extension, in the world outside his immediate experience. The meeting of these needs is what we mean by "education."

From this analysis, we see that various teachers need to get cooperation from groups and individuals in the community to set up needed training activities, and that the faculty as a whole needs to be concerned with discovering and sharing methods for making these activities educational. We can also see that the results of the faculty's experiences should be communicated or fed back to the various community groups so that they can make such changes as will lead to a more healthy life for youngsters. Thus, we arrive at three possible and complementary roles for the schools as institutions within the community: (1) as collaborators with others in setting up and supervising training experiences; (2) as professional educators working among themselves to improve methods for the simultaneous training and education of children; and (3) as consultants to the collaborating agencies, on aspects of their functioning related to the welfare of students.

The role of collaborator gives individual teachers their place in the community. The professional educator role gives the faculty group as a whole its place among other groups in the community. And the consultative role, usually, but not necessarily, exercised through school officials as representatives of the school, gives the school as an institution its place in the community.

Professional in-service training represents the development of the faculty into the professional educator group. But motivation for this development comes from interactions between the faculty and the outside; motivation depends upon the experiences of teachers in the community and upon the possibilities of reward available to teachers for co-operating in training and for contributing to the consultant role. Aside from its importance to students, the notion of school-wide programming around the problem of how to use the entire community for educational purposes results in demands and expectations from the community. These outside demands require policies and agreements within the total faculty, but it is the small training groups which create the necessary insights and do the necessary preliminary testing and the ultimate implementation of policy. And the need for school-wide policy becomes translated into discipline and encouragement of contributions from the small training groups.

WHERE THE PROGRAM MIGHT LEAD

The small training groups will be in a position to discover a number of helpful administrative revisions. Thus, it may be found that longer periods are needed to enable the class to plan an activity and carry it through on the same day. Or needs for a broader range of resource materials to replace the single textbook may be seen as desirable. Or the new role of volunteer assistant teacher may be discovered and spelled out, with the consequent recruitment and training of citizens interested in such experience.

The faculty may wish to revise sizes of classes, too. If teachers learn to make much use of discussion, they will wish smaller classes. On the other hand, if they make more use of subgroupings, they may wish larger classes so that there is better opportunity to control the composition of the subgroups.

An additional type of outcome is the diagnosis of further types of experience needed by the faculty. Thus teachers may, after a period of deliberation and thinking together, realize common needs for better training in particular areas, such as discussion leadership and group management. This could lead to a series of faculty workshops, with the help of outside consultant-trainers. The faculty might discover that its greatest concern at some point is to talk over its programs with citizens, and this could lead to the setting up of joint faculty-parent-citizen workshops, meeting on several evenings during the week or on week ends.

If new instructional methods are formulated and consistently used in some classes, the faculty may wish for a careful study of new methods, and it may see a university as helping in this. Similarly, the small training groups will have functioning problems of their own, which could lead to the use of a consultant to talk with some of these groups.

The faculty is likely to feel itself pulled together by its newly found common enterprise, and it may wish to plan a few social events to capitalize on the need-satisfying possibilities of the new closeness and interest in each other as people.

All of these recommendations require collaboration with the school administration.

SOME QUESTIONS AND ANSWERS

1. Does the plan call for forcing every member of the faculty to work in small groups with other members? What if a teacher doesn't want to?

Comment: People cannot be forced to work in the kind of creative relationship required for training, and there are some teachers (and others) who do not work well in this type of small group relationship. They need time to see how it works out with others, and they may need special help or training, as in a summer workshop. In general, the safest principle is to start with the groups that are interested, let them report to the total faculty, and back them up. Motivation is strengthened by the expression of enthusiasm and sympathy for those in the groups, and by understanding of the doubts of those who hold back.

As the program moves along, a group standard and expectation of effective small-group participation will develop, and it will tend to bring in others. If this standard is uncongenial to certain teachers, they may leave. But they obviously must not be fired or driven out: that may be threatening to the ones left behind.

2. Won't the program produce extra difficulties in scheduling classes so that certain teachers have the same period free to work together?

Comment: Yes. This will require administrative ingenuity. If the principal cannot see how to manage it, he should ask the small groups themselves to make suggestions. Finding time for the small groups to meet, and making decisions about how often they should meet, is actually the responsibility of the small group itself. It is up to the administrator to make such arrangements as are possible to help. In those cases where nothing can be done, except perhaps to meet on the teachers' own time, such a decision should be reached jointly by the principal and the teachers concerned.

3. Doesn't this plan assume many more resources than most schools now have?

Comment: No. The plan attempts to make much more effective use of what have always been and always will be the school's most important resource: the teachers. It attempts to develop these resources further, and to make them available to each other. Additional resources are by no means necessary, though there is no doubt that it would be nice to have them from time to time.

4. Do you think that all principals could set up this kind of program and run it successfully?

Comment: Probably not.

5. It seems to me that in a city with several schools, if one school tried this, and it worked, all the teachers would want to come to that school. Wouldn't this disrupt the system?

Comment: Possibly. If the scheme is found to work in one school, then it should be adopted and adapted by other schools throughout the system. Schools which have, through the years, developed firm defenses against new ideas and ways of working might have to be considerably shaken up through transfer of personnel. In this case, the amount of disruption would depend upon the extent to which the community is behind the plan, the extent to which displaced people can be relocated in jobs suitable to their talents, and the rapidity with which early experiences with the new plan are rewarding to participants.

6. Won't such a plan upset the relationships among teachers in the school?

Comment: Indeed yes. Every major change in group activity calls for a reshuffling of status positions. But in so far as prestige has been dependent on worth-while contributions to professional growth, it will not be upset. This would merely provide another route to recognition. In so far as the bases of prestige are reversed or toppled, then the status pattern will change markedly.

7. How can such a plan be set up in a school which has no faculty meetings and no established pattern of working together?

Comment: In most schools where these conditions exist, it is probable that the principal would have to initiate the plan. But the principal does not have to offer the plan "cold." It could be preceded by several faculty meetings devoted to the making of a census of problems the teachers see, or the obstacles to better teaching. The dimensions of these problems or obstacles could be discussed for clarification. Decisive action by the principal to clear away one or more obstacles identified by the faculty will do more to promote the program than any amount of his talking. After the development of initial rapport and trust, the principal and a temporary faculty steering committee can decide on the best means for launching the plan.

SUMMARY OF THE PLAN OF IN-SERVICE TRAINING

We should hardly expect the details of the plan as implemented in different schools to be alike. But we would expect that in one way or another every successful program would meet at least the following specifications:

Specification 1: Improvement of teaching calls for improved performance of teachers in the classroom.

Specification 2: Only the teacher can change the performance of the teacher.

Specification 3: To do this, he requires the emotional support and technical help of a small, friendly group of colleagues (the small training group).

Specification 4: Resources will be needed and should be available to the small training groups.

Specification 5: The total faculty group, with the help of a steering committee, provides the members for the groups, creates expectancy for performance, and assimilates the results of the training groups' experience.

Specification 6: To do this, the total faculty must itself be a group with shared purposes and outside demands or expectancies to be met.

Specification 7: The "outside" must be composed, for this purpose, of responsible citizens representing the community as a whole, or defined groups such as parents, merchants, civic leaders, etc.

Specification 8: Teachers must maintain interactive contact with the outside, so as to get necessary feedback for the faculty as a whole.

Specification 9: As the program rolls along, the faculty must be able to identify its shared needs for further training and make use of faculty-wide workshops and other devices to meet these needs.

All the above specifications and the suggested plan itself (with slight changes in wording) can be seen to apply to in-service training in hospitals, engineering firms, libraries, and other institutions.

The kinds of policies and conclusions about teaching methods with which teachers will be concerned during in-service training are suggested in chapter 2 and in the pages indicated in the note at the end of that chapter. The problem of building the school as a small community is illuminated on pages 337–41, and the nature of the diversity of faculty attitudes and needs is analogous to the picture presented on pages 341–45. For the planning of effective faculty meetings, the techniques presented on pages 180–217 are suggestive.

CHAPTER 4

For maximum productivity, the individual must have sufficient autonomy that he can be self-directing in his job. This autonomy is based on a thorough understanding of the job and its relation to the work of others. By organizing jobs within co-operative teams responsible for blocks of interlocking functions, individual autonomy, self-direction, and satisfaction can be greatly extended.

The authority of power is used to secure the required communication among the co-operative groups—to insure co-ordination of their activities within the over-all design for production.

DISTINCTIVE FEATURES

Leadership authority exerted on groups *is dependent upon the power of superior position in the vertical hierarchy. Leadership authority exerted upon* individuals *originates in the need of working groups to be governed; and the agent of leadership is usually the boss or other designated official. The primary target of change is defined by institutional purposes, from the processing of raw material in factories to the promotion of research by foundations. Secondary targets of change include the competence and productivity of workers, and the efficiency of communication within the organization. Members of the organization are expected to conform to demands for co-operation in achieving organizational purposes, in return for which they are expected to initiate demands for improvement of their own welfare. The method of control is through feedback of information on productivity, information about changes in the environment that affect operation, and supervision of performance. The relationship between groups arranged "vertically" in the organizational chart is through pressures, both up and down; between groups arranged "horizontally," it is co-operative. Communication with other groups in the community is through spokesmen or officially appointed representatives.*

Administration and Management: Group Responsibility and Individual Autonomy

Administrators, managers, and supervisors—like other leaders —are concerned with simultaneous work on three kinds of problems: the task or job functions, the problems of organizing for work, and the problems of individual need-meeting to maintain motivation.

The unique features to be considered in this chapter are *vertical organization* as a way of defining performance expectancies, and *power* as a basis for leadership authority. By virtue of his power alone a boss can overcome resistance to participation by his subordinates. This is not true of community work, in which citizens participate voluntarily, nor of school classrooms in which the student has to attend but does not have to learn.

After considering the nature and types of authority and getting acquainted with a couple of administrators, we shall examine a number of typical conflicts in administration. Then we shall offer two propositions which we think may point the way to considerable improvement of many administration and management situations.

THE CONCEPT OF AUTHORITY

The work of the world is done through the co-ordinated efforts of many people. With respect to some kinds of work, co-ordination is through common adherence to an ideal, a point of view, and a goal. Thus at the beginning of World War II, physical scientists all over the world were building on each other's discoveries to erect the formidable theories of atomic science. The efforts of each man were co-ordinated with those of others through his own processes of reflection and assimilation of ideas. Each man worked at his job because he was interested in it, and the recognition he could get from himself and from his colleagues was his reward. Such leadership functions as "speaking" for a school of thought, convening occasional meetings, and publishing

95

learned journals arose naturally and spontaneously. Efforts to speed up production or to meet deadlines were not part of the picture; it was assumed that findings would become useful in their own good time, and that efforts to hurry the process would be disastrous or wasteful.

Co-ordination of effort through shared ideas and ideals is characteristic of many of the noncommercialized aspects of life. Hobbyists have their shared delights in solving problems and their shared goals of perfection when it comes to model railroading, petunia raising, and wood carving. The ideals of perfection and competition are sufficiently generally understood and shared that people know how to participate in amateur athletics. During the first stages of any club or movement or revolution, activity is coordinated through shared social purposes; it is only as the central organizing clique begins to take in members that bylaws are introduced. (The principle that development of hierarchical organization *follows* definition of tasks is discussed in chapter 12.)

In general, co-ordination through shared ideas is possible for those endeavors in which each man fully comprehends the scope of the problems and is competent to weigh, assess, and assimilate the contributions of all other participants.

American technical and productive genius expresses itself in our ability to specialize and to break down complicated operations into simple, easily learned tasks. A factory employing thousands of workers may contain but a handful of men who fully understand the product being manufactured and the details of the manufacturing process. Moreover, men work mostly at one aspect or another of each manufactured item, and no one worker could possibly decide for himself how hard he must work to keep the whole sequence of operations running smoothly. Co-ordination of effort in this kind of situation obviously cannot be left to the voluntary independent decision of each individual.

In such cases, *organization* is introduced. One basic feature of organization is its provision of well-defined *expectancies* as to the behavior of each person. These expectancies can be astonishingly detailed and precise, as in a military post in which both social and professional communications are decided as much by the rank-structure as by the nature of the problems to be solved. But

there are certain kinds of expectation that must be maintained
and defined in all organizations: who can hire and fire whom;
what are reasons for dismissal and for promotion; who are one's
superiors, peers, and inferiors; what are the required communications from and to each person.

A second basic feature of organization is *power*. Designated individuals have power over other individuals. This power may be
wielded flagrantly or unobtrusively; it may be great or little; it
may be with respect to many parts of the job or to only a few.
But whatever the exercise or perception people have of power, the
fact remains that it is our superiors, not our inferiors or peers, who
determine our prospects on the job. In any organization, then, we
have two goals: to satisfy the requirements of our job as defined
to us, and to please our superiors. In "good" organizations the
same behaviors satisfy both conditions.

In general, co-ordination through organization is required for
those endeavors in which each man deals with only a part of the
product, an aspect of manufacture, a phase of development. Only
the men at the top comprehend the total design of the enterprise,
and the others *must* rely on the insights and comprehensions of
these men for guidance in making many of their own decisions.

Co-ordination of effort solely through shared ideas, on the one
hand, and solely through organization, on the other, seldom exists
in actual practice. In every job, the worker's actions arise out of
two sorts of decisions: genuine decisions made by the worker on
the basis of his understanding of acceptable and shared ideas; and
deduced or enforced decisions representing implementation of
instructions or policies given to the worker by others from whom
influence is accepted.

From the standpoint of each individual, these methods of co-
ordination are different ways of achieving the same goal: confident knowledge of what to do, when to do it, how to do it, and
with whom to do it. When the individual has full knowledge of
the total enterprise and when he himself builds a complete product or work of art, he has his greatest freedom and greatest
autonomy. He can arrange his own hours of work, set his own
standards of performance, communicate when and if he wants
to—provided he accepts the authority of the ideals he shares with

his community. Whenever he is perplexed as to what to do, he turns to further study leading to reaffirmation of these ideals as the means for resolving his doubts and settling his questions. What we mean by "self-direction" is that to a high degree the authority for one's behavior is one's own understanding of ideas and one's commitment to ideals shared with others.

When the individual comprehends only a fragment of the total enterprise, he depends less on the authority of his own knowledge and more on the authority of other individuals. These others tell him what he needs to know as a basis for whatever decisions his job requires him to make. If the decision involves merely a simple choice between two definite alternatives—e.g., whether to push the red button or the black button on the machine—then, he simply needs to know the appropriate cues for choosing one or the other. The greater the number of available alternatives and the less repetitive the operations on the job, the more insight he must have and the greater the autonomy he needs. If his job requires no decisions at all from him, then his required autonomy is zero.

There is seldom a lack of people willing to tell him what he needs to know. A worker has his own ideas, his colleagues have their interpretations—often different ones—and the boss has his ideas. It is reasonable to assume that each would-be authority is competent with respect to some things, and incompetent with respect to others. The ideal would be that each person would supplement his fragmentary knowledge by getting competent advice or help in finding out each of the things he needed to know. But how is an individual to tell who is competent to give advice in the fields wherein he is ignorant? And who is to advise him where to seek advice in each of these fields? And is it not important that the same interpretations and advice be given to everyone concerned with the same problems?

These questions lead us to consider the functioning of power in the organization. The situation can be put in these terms: "My superior is the person of whom I ask advice. He is the person from whom I accept commands. Because he understands not only my fragment of the total enterprise but also all the other fragments co-ordinate with mine, he has more competence than anyone on my level. And because he supervises all of us, we all get substantially the same set of facts when we go to our boss; hence my work is co-ordinated with that of my colleagues. Moreover, when it comes to decisions about how we at the same level are to work together, the boss gets us all together: he delegates his authority to the group." These statements sound reasonable. They ought to be true. Can they be made true?

There are two ways of making the statements true. The first is to select and train men to wield the kinds of authority their work requires them to exercise, and the second is to invest them with power.

The exercise of power lies in the control of communication. The man with power can enforce his decisions as to who talks to whom about what. The fact that my superior has power over me means that I shall go to him for the things he says I must go to him for. The fact that he has power over me, however, does not automatically insure that he is wiser than I or my colleagues, even though with respect to some matters he ought to be. Under proper conditions, the superior knows the limits of his competence, and his exercise of power is not to set himself up as *the* authority for all matters, but rather to insure that his subordinates make use of the *appropriate* authorities, whoever and wherever they may be.

In other words, power can be authoritarian or it can be facilitative. The former is primarily directed to preservation of power as an end in itself; the latter is directed to getting the job done.

So far we have been contending that action is determined and justified on the basis of some relevant authority. We have talked about the authority of ideas and the authority of position. We have said that the former governs those acts over which an individual has autonomy, and the latter governs those acts which lie outside his autonomy. We have also said that authority of position, based on power, should be used to help subordinates locate the particular authority most appropriate for their problems. But what are the types of authority, and what is the domain over which each is valid?

THE TYPES OF AUTHORITY

Faced with the need to choose among alternative courses of action, to what kinds of authority might one resort?

1. *Dedication.*—When one is dedicated to a goal, the choice among alternative courses of action is a matter of deciding which leads most effectively toward the goal. One's goal dedication is his authority.

2. *Experimentation.*—Choice is made tentatively, and a first action step is taken. Next steps depend upon the results of the first step. The authority is in the empirically appraised nature of the situation as discovered through the first step.

3. *Revelation.*—Choice is based on a dream or "authoritative" advice given by a palmist, numerologist, financial column, friend, etc. Since the advice-giver has a minimum of relevant information to take into account about the particular organizational situation, the basis of his authority is the faith of the advice-seeker in the adviser's hunches or intuition or susceptibility to revelation.

4. *Social standards.*—That alternative is chosen which calls for behavior deemed most acceptable to some group to which one belongs. In any group, an individual does some things but not others, and in the organizational situation, he may try to maintain a code of ethics derived for use by some other group in connection with problems of its own. The authority is a code of ethics which represents the bases of belonging to the group.

5. *Organizational policy.*—Here an ethical position is directly inferable from policies that were made to fit the operating realities of the organization on some previous occasion. The authority is faith in a series of past conclusions about similar situations.

6. *Position.*—Decisions based on concern over one's position are likely to be punitive or aggrandizing. When one feels secure in his position, he is able to distinguish between the functions of his office and the symbols and gestures of its power. The authority, when decisions are based on position, is fear.

7. *Technical expert.*—The man who has had a great deal of experience with the kind of problem under consideration may have valuable notions about what can be done. The authority is prestige based on demonstrated competence.

8. *Personal.*—The personality of a "natural leader" evokes a warm response; he is felt to be talking sense. The authority is in one's wish to identify with, and depend on, someone for help.

9. *Alter ego.*—The assistant-to-the-president and the office "wife" achieve, through identification with a superior, some skill in representing his ways of thinking, and they give substantially the same advice he would. The authority here is that of power transmitted through the power person's alter ego.

ORGANIZATIONAL PROBLEMS

Human relations problems in organizations are likely to be posed by the "top" people. The coldness of a department head, for example, presents the rest of the department with anxieties and inhibitions in their friendship relations. A dogmatic boss sets the stage for undercover revolt and a desire to outmaneuver him by his men. A hesitant or reluctant administrator engenders in workers much anxious conflict over their own roles in the organization. These phenomena are reactions by subordinates to the way their superiors relate to them. The existence of bad feelings within the superior is in itself evidence that he has false expectations about the relationship. False expectations by the top level present subordinates with a prediction of failure, and this strains the relationship further. The existence of false or inappropriate expectations indicates that false prophets have been used—i.e., wrong, inadequate, or inappropriate authority.

The existence of *confused* expectations, in which nobody knows what to expect from himself or anybody else, is an even more serious problem, for it indicates a confusion of the relationships between power and authority. And without clarity in these matters there is no machinery for dealing with any other problem.

The central importance of these propositions is demonstrated by the fact that the "Commandments of Good Organization" are concerned in one way or another with these matters:

1. Define responsibilities.
2. Always give authority with responsibility.
3. Never change job responsibilities without informing all concerned.
4. No man should have more than one boss.
5. Never give orders to another boss's subordinates.
6. Always criticize subordinates in private.

7. Settle promptly every dispute over authority or responsibility.
8. A boss's boss should always approve promotions, raises, and disciplinary actions.
9. Never ask a subordinate to criticize his boss.
10. Give every executive enough help to let him check on the quality of his own work.[1]

When definitions of authority and responsibility are not clear and appropriate to functions, it is necessary for individuals to take matters into their own hands. Each tries in his own way to deal with confusion and demoralization. The situation becomes dominated by a philosophy of "every man for himself," grafted on top of the official but unworkable table of organization. The result is burgeoning of the unofficial and frequently unacknowledged real power structure, as illustrated in the following engaging account of goings-on at Turbid Manufacturing Company.

"Turbid's aggressive managers, however, pay scant attention to jurisdictional distinctions. The industrial relations department's authority, for instance, completely overlaps the personnel department because of (1) the president's enthusiasm for industrial relations, and (2) the emphasis is on public relations in the public utterances of Turbid's dominant board member. Similarly, Turbid's finance chief has so much drag with the president that his department cuts right across all decisions handed down the line of command. The dotted circle (in Turbid's Organizational Chart) symbolizes the post held by the fun-loving brother of Turbid's president, who is incapable of managerial functioning, and dangles—the fruit of nepotism. The president is surrounded by committees, one so dominant it can give orders down the line, as well as advice to him. His young 'assistant to' in his confidential status colors much of what the boss hears from the twelve executives who jealously insist on reporting directly to the chief."[2]

If management is to function effectively it must function openly and in an orderly way. If there is to be an informal system of communication outside of the official system, then a vast amount of energy will go into office politics, and decisions will be power

1. Perrin Stryker, "Can Management Be Managed?" *Fortune*, XLVIII, No. 1 (July, 1953), 138. Quoted by permission.
2. *Ibid.*, p. 101.

plays rather than problem solutions. But the kind of orderliness and predictability required for honest relationships up and down the hierarchy is based upon the clarity and appropriateness to functioning of authority and responsibility.

One major result of improper or confused selection of authority and the relationship between authority and power is administrative ulcers. The administrator is extremely vulnerable to confusion in authority because he plays a number of different roles. Thus he is (*a*) petitioner on behalf of his men to the group above; (*b*) designated leader of his subordinates; (*c*) a subordinate to the levels above him; (*d*) consultant to his men on interpersonal process problems, and so on. If the complex of leadership expectations is unclear, the administrator may find himself unable to bring all these roles into relationship within his personality.

THE ADMINISTRATIVE PERSONALITY

The manager, functioning to co-ordinate operational efforts; the administrator, functioning to form policy and facilitate long-range welfare; the supervisor, functioning to improve efficiency of the men—all these are wielders of power. The quality of each person's need, use, and wish for power, and his fantasies about destructive and constructive possibilities of power enter very decisively into his predispositions for and objectivity about the different sorts of authority to be favored.

Let us quote soliloquies of two hypothetical administrators in order to get some feeling for the orientation of their ways of life around concepts of power and its uses.

One point of view.—"I worked hard to get into my present position of power. The fact that I succeeded is prima-facie evidence of my superiority. To get where I am meant that I had to see facts straight and realistically. It meant being able to assume responsibility and deliver the goods. When I make a decision it is probably better than the decision that could be made by the people I boss. If they could make better decisions, they would be my bosses. I go around with other people like myself, and we tend to run things, both in the plant and in the community, although we delegate a lot of the community running to our wives. We married women who, by and large, would be assets to us in the community, and we're a pretty decent set of people, if I do say so.

"We think well of the people who work for us, and we know that they must be kept reasonably happy and secure and satisfied. When outsiders come in and stir up trouble we resent it because we are always willing to meet the employees halfway and there's no sense in trying to do things by violence when peaceful means are available. Our competitors, too, we respect. There's plenty of room for competing companies, and their advertising budgets, added to ours, increases the public's demand for our products. And we work together to head off unfavorable legislation. Of course, we are not in business for our health, and any time we can run a competitor to the wall it is our obligation to the stockholders to do so. Everyone in business knows this, and he accepts these rules as part of the game when he goes into business. We neither ask nor give any quarter.

"My personal life? What does that matter to you? Well, sure, I suppose you might say that my group pretty well controls the investment of money in our town. It's a fine town, and our company, through providing jobs all these years, and through taxes and voluntary contributions, has done a lot to make it a *great* town. Look at the way our population has grown! You know, a high percentage of these new people—fine people, too—came to town to work in our company. No, I don't know where they live —over on the South Side, I expect. Yes, I have heard that the housing over there is pretty bad, but I guess it's at least as good as the people are used to, or they wouldn't live there. Every man to his deserts, I say."

Another point of view.—"Sure, I worked hard to get where I am. My wife tells me I'm sort of compulsively ambitious, and maybe I am. All I know about that is I like to get ahead. I enjoy prestige and being listened to. I guess I'm personally sort of competitive. Of course, I'll admit I got some good breaks. When I first came to the plant I was pretty green, and old 'Doc' Saunders sort of took me in hand. I owe a lot to him. And I owe a lot to the other fellows on the bench alongside me, although I didn't realize it at the time. Our first boss was pretty rough, and we used to have to calm each other down every so often. When we found out we all hated him it made things easier, and we learned how to handle him. And he gave us a square deal when it came time for promotions.

"Ever since then I've sort of had the habit of listening to what people say. When I make a decision it is usually a pretty good one, but the reason is that I know my men and how they look at things. They make a good team. Of course, I have to lay down the law every so often, and sometimes they get mad about it, but we generally talk it through. You know, when I finally got up into this high-level bracket, I palled around at the country club with the other execs, and I still do. But I get tired of doing everything with the same people, and I've recently gotten out the old fishing tackle. I found a local group of anglers—the Isaak Walton Association—and the leader of the group is one of our foremen. We've had some pretty fine trips, too, although my wife is suspicious of them.

"Are our workmen happy? Golly, I woudn't know how to answer that. What I mean is that that's really up to them. Every so often an organizer comes around the plant, and I always try to be sure that he gets a fair hearing if a group of the men are interested in what he has to say. One fellow made a lot of headway telling them they were being exploited; so I suggested they appoint a committee and go over our books with the auditor. No, that wasn't my idea. It was tried in another company in the East somewhere, and the workers decided not to ask for the raise. In our case, we figured out with them what would be fair wages, and we made some adjustments. That committee really impressed our management board, and they have consulted with us about a lot of things since. I don't know whether they will formalize it as the nucleus for a union or not. I have offered to see what can be done to get them good training in union management if they want to try it.

"Sure, we have problems. Our expansion during the war brought in a lot of new people, and it's been hard to find places for them to live. We don't think it's up to the company to provide them housing—we see it as a problem for the entire community, and we have been putting money and staff time into a new civic organization to study what to do. It's discouraging, though. That

South Side housing just isn't good enough for our new laborers. Sure, its as good as they were used to where they came from, but everyone lived that way there. They're not living there now, they're living here, and our community has a higher standard of living. We'll have to see what can be done about it."

These two points of view are admittedly extreme, although I have actually known men who held them. The two men represented in these interviews have different concepts of the sources of their success, different ways of relating themselves to other people, different concepts of the autonomy of their companies, different perspectives on plant operation.

It would be a mistake to dismiss this pattern of differences with some phrase such as "Oh, that's just the way people are!" It is true that there is a relationship between a man's personality and the beliefs he holds. But these beliefs and ways of working come from living in our culture, which offers both the alternatives given above.

In a situation where such divergent ways of life are available —a matter of choice, so to speak, of each individual—we need to find some way to make the choice, not "once and for all" but creatively, in terms of the requirements of each situation. The way of life we need is illuminated by principles and understandings: it is the method of intelligence—relevant facts plus appropriate interpretation and decision. These conditions are not easy to achieve because the culturally induced administrative confusion extends to methods of thinking.

Methods of thinking in administration are based on concepts of authority. Thus, the man who sees himself as the authority, who uses only his own experience as the basis of decision, tends to set up his own private theories of administration, and these are generally not very well articulated simply because they are private. Such explanations as he makes for his policies often strike the outsider as rationalizations, and these policies may be quite inconsistent from one situation to the next. Thus, one can hold the policy that promotion is based on merit in one case, that it is based on need in another case, and that it is for the good of the group to kick the man upstairs in still another case. To the outsider, this adds up to three ways of explaining rather personal prejudices. The person who bases his action primarily on his own experience, interpreted by his own private theories, also tends to limit the range of his experience. He surrounds himself with yes men, which means that he uses other people simply for the reassurance that he is adequate. In effect, such people talk to themselves because they are basically afraid to talk with others. Their approach to management is likely to be in terms of pressure.

The man who believes that the source of authority is the experience of all those concerned in the operations he governs, has to make his methods explicit so that others can give him relevant information. In the process of this communication, his theories get tested and ironed out, and they become part of the rationale of the group rather than his private property. Such a man tends to surround himself with those people who are most competent to help with respect to each major kind of problem. This kind of administrator admits to himself that he is not the most competent person to decide everything, and he learns how to use the competence of others. When he gets differing advice from competent people, he makes the decision tentatively and with some provision for testing and revising in the light of experience.

Such an administrator can add to the skills that got him to the top in the first place additional skills in dealing with groups through the use of an open-minded experimental approach—he grows on the job. There are times when he acts alone on his hunches, but these are either emergencies or familiar situations. He tends to look far enough ahead that things can be checked before they reach a crisis stage, and he tends to develop through experience shared with others new areas of judgment in which his competence is clearly that of the expert. The methods favored by this administrator are those of co-operation.

In comparing our two prototypes, the first man appears to solve problems in whatever way protects or enhances his own position or, by extension, that of his own group. The second man simply tends to solve problems. Such personal vested interest as he has is a partiality for use of the experimental method. This amounts to the conviction that the "right" decision is obtained by "right" methods of decision-making, rather than by having some absolute "rightness" in itself.

Either of these men is probably a better administrator than the one who simply withdraws from the job of administering. Such a person, for example, is likely to act only when he has to, and then in desperation. Desperate decisions are also expedient and unpredictable, so those around such an administrator never know what to expect. We have many examples of this kind of administration given by such city officials as police chiefs, housing commissioners, and mayors who tend to let things slide until a newspaper or some citizen group sets up a clamor and then crack down hard—but only on those most obviously vulnerable. People who "make an example" of occasional incidents, or who plead that every decision is just a matter of opinion, or who listen to everybody without any estimates of their competence, or who judge everything on the basis of personality, or who seem uncommitted to any goals—such people fit this image.

In social terms, the basic conflict of administration, then, is that there is available in our culture a variety of fundamentally conflicting ways of approaching the problems of authority and power, and that to some extent most of us are either unable to act at all or act out of confusion among these conflicting ways.

Typical Problems of Administrators

The administrator, in one way or another, has to come to terms with the following conflicts:

1. Divided Loyalty

When his men express resentment at some new ruling from above, foreman Jackson defends the company. When the division chief complains about occasional lapses in productivity of his men, Jackson defends his men. He now has the uncomfortable feeling that the men think of him as a "company prig" and that the division chief, his boss, thinks of him as being "touchy."

Analysis.—The key word is "defend." The need to defend implies the feeling that an attack is going on, and this implies lack of co-operation between levels, as well as lack of acceptance of the normal gripes that men at one level usually have about men at another level. Jackson's attitude should be that he can help determine the facts, not that he must defend. It may be that he finds it hard to identify or "belong" in the two groups, or that he feels he must select one or the other for his primary loyalty. His indecision is probably uncomfortable to him and angers him. In this case, his defense of the group under attack may serve to reassure him that he feels warmth rather than hostility toward the groups.

Suggestions.—Set up a meeting of Jackson, his men, some other foreman, and Jackson's boss. Let them talk out the problems of what each expects of the other and what criteria of judgment are being used by people at each level in assessing their subordinates. The hope is that this kind of frank and specific talking will increase Jackson's security and belongingness, and will also bring the groups closer together in a reaffirmation of joint purposes.

2. WORK VERSUS AFFECTION

A principal makes it a point to report to meetings of his teachers the latest recommendations and actions of the school board. But he never reports back anything critical of the teachers or the school. He also works long hours on weekends collecting information for reports rather than asking for help from teachers.

Analysis.—This sort of "protectiveness"—which seems more like a fear of imposing on the teachers—is unfortunate, because it makes an additional demand on the principal's time and energy. He not only has the job of running the school, but also of continually reassuring himself that he is giving no cause for dislike.

Suggestions.—His anxiety is probably well communicated, and this is at least one probable cause for his being disliked. He should concentrate on his job of running the school, and pay no attention to whether he is liked or not except in so far as such feelings become forces affecting the school program. He might, for example, get himself a small executive committee from the teachers to talk over the various matters of which teachers should be informed and to decide what recommendations should be made.

3. DELEGATION OF RESPONSIBILITY

In many organizations, the job of the assistant or junior levels is the most difficult, because of the unwillingness of the superiors to delegate definite responsibilities. The juniors have little to do, but they hesitate to ask the chief for work because he gets angry when they do.

Analysis.—Such bosses usually are frightened men, rather than hogs for work. They feel that sharing responsibility also means sharing power, and this is intolerable, either because they feel they do not have enough for themselves or because they fear the use of the shared power against them. By doing all the work, probably better than his subordinates could, the boss reassures himself that he really is entitled to his power—even though he cannot accept or use it intelligently.

Suggestions.—Some superior could point out to the boss that the group standard in the plant is to delegate responsibilities, that this is expected and proper. He could also suggest a self-survey, to discover how present personnel are utilized, and could suggest a discussion between the boss and his assistants to work out an understanding of their several tasks. In these discussions, every effort should be made to reassure the boss that he has earned his power.

4. FINDING OUT "THE TRUTH"

The reaction of the leader to the various categories of information offered by his men will, in the long run, determine the nature of bottom-to-top communication. Most men realize that some things have to be reported upward, and some other things should not be mentioned; they also are aware of an in-between category of relevant information not directly about the jobs but which illuminates what is going on. The problem is to get appropriate communication upward: and this means adequate information undistorted by the personal concerns of the reporter.

Analysis.—Communication upward depends on threat, opportunity, and reward. If information is invited only as a prelude to punishing a culprit or assigning extra work, then distortion of information and reluctance of most men to communicate can be expected. If the only opportunity to communicate is at social functions or during minutes stolen from work, then some men will not initiate communication. If the boss listens gladly to information from some people but brushes off others, then only certain men will have an incentive to volunteer information—and they are likely to be hated by their fellows.

Suggestions.—The routinizing of channels for information-gathering should be discussed with all the people involved in the operation—i.e., with everyone in a position to collect needed information. Agreements are needed on "who communicates what to whom and when." If there are kinds of information the boss cannot accept objectively, then these should be passed to someone else with whom the boss can share responsibility for action. A training session may be set up to help all concerned understand the sorts of information which will be most useful for the improvement of operation.

5. WHEN IS A FRIEND?

The man with enough power to smooth the way for others, but whose power is not enough to take him out of social contact with his subordinates, is likely to find that he has many "friends." And he may feel (properly) that his attractiveness to all these people is not solely due to his personal charm. He will also find that many of his former friends no longer seek him out if he is promoted, and he may assume that they are jealous of him. In any case, the man with power is like a debutante with a two-million-dollar inheritance: neither can ever really be sure of the motivations of their "friends."

Analysis.—The merging or confusing of a man's private world (friendships) with his public world (job) can lead to problems of partisanship and double standards. When the boss cannot separate the two worlds—so that he judges technical skill by the warmth of a smile—there is considerable anxiety aroused in all because the rules for job and pay competition are now obscured by caprice. The informal structure of the organization loses its legitimate adjustive and ameliorative functions and becomes decisive with regard to jobs.

Suggestions.—The formal work structure should be kept separate from the informal interpersonal structure. To keep them separate requires provision within the formal structure for all the work-required types of communication. A further useful policy may be to achieve more remoteness from the social needs of the men by assigning responsibilities to groups rather than to individuals. This would require the primary social interactions of the men to remain among themselves rather than with the boss; but it would leave the door open for necessary discussion of job-related matters with the boss. (This is, in effect, the "project" method of organization.)

6. "NOBLESSE OBLIGE" VERSUS "CHANNELS"

This is a conflict not only with reference to the way people work together, but also to the way they feel about each other, and the extent to which they identify with each other. The "stickler for form" makes everyone fill out all slips in quadruplicate, as a general principle, and he also usually questions the right of others to make requests of him. He simply does not trust others, and he does not trust himself either; which is why he hides behind his tablets and rubber stamps. At the opposite end of the scale is the expansive fellow who will give anybody anything; he seldom has any records to show who now has possession of the calculator or the last annual report or the model of the proposed new product.

Analysis.—These are caricatures of two conditions: first, that channels and procedures exist and are needed for the orderly operation of an organization; and second, that formal communication through channels is basically facilitative of informal agreements reached earlier and noted in private memoranda. Both types of communication are needed, but they operate on very different assumptions. The informal agreement can be used under certain conditions: the participants trust each other, their verbal agreement is as good as a contract; the participants probably identify with each other as members of the same class or social group, and they have enough power to impose their judgments on the "channels," so that clerks are recording-instruments rather than policy-makers. But in the absence of these conditions for informality, the clerks are likely to take over.

Suggestions.—The *sine qua non* for mutual trust is that people have facts rather than fantasies about each other's work in relation to their own. This is accomplished through advisory boards which hear about project plans, successes, and failures. Outside friendships and social functions can help, of course, but they should not be required; they can be carried to the point of unwarranted interference in private lives.

7. LONG-RANGE VERSUS SHORT-RANGE IMPLICATIONS

Administrative behavior has two kinds of consequences. First, as action, it brings about some sort of immediate change; and second, the attitude communicated with the action may reinforce or change relations among people. This latter change carries with it the probability of changes in motivation, readiness, trust, confidence, and the like. The feelings going with administrative action, then, bring about changes the implications of which are long range. Every administrator knows that many of his acts imply relative judgments about the men he judges to be helpful for various purposes, those he sees as co-operative, those whose ideas he most wants, and so on. Similarly, punitive measures are at least as important for their effects on the group as they are for correcting an individual.

Analysis.—There are many times when "doing it one's self," or picking out a pleasant youngster for a task ordinarily done by one of the older people, or making a casual remark in front of a group instead of in the office would be easy and natural to do. But those behaviors, inevitably related to personal problems, are likely to be interpreted differently by every spectator, and even the simplest nonwork gesture of an administrator can be the topic of considerable speculation.

Suggestions.—Action should be governed by two sets of criteria, not one. The first set defines what it is hoped the action will accomplish. The second set defines the characteristics of action: the right of the agent to take action, the amount of consultation with those affected by it, the use during its consideration of existing groups whose jurisdiction can be extended, etc. Finally, each discussion of action also should be partly a training session for setting conditions favorable to the growth and long-range strength of the groups.

Two Central Propositions

One implication of the above discussion is that administrative behavior is perceived and reacted to by many people; and that the behaviors of the administrator are themselves affected by the perceptions and feelings of those about him.

This leads to the suggestion that administration and management may be thought of as *functions* arising within the organization, rather than merely as roles played by a handful of people. Our first proposition, then, is: Proposition I: Not all systems or organizations are equally susceptible to administration or management. The one best administered in the long run is the one in which the power of position is least often exercised, individuals have belongingness in groups to which responsibilities are assigned, and the autonomy of each individual is agreed upon in group discussion in which he participates.

This proposition implies in effect that a vast percentage of the industrial work of the nation is poorly organized. It seems to me that this is indeed the case. The fragmentation of complex manufacturing arts into sequences of simple repetitive operations has gone so far that many workers are mere machines, living in a state of suspended animation during the day and living as persons only after work hours are over. We seem to have sacrificed creativity for productivity; and worth-while living for a high standard of living. But, in the light of Proposition I, this is not unalterable.

Take the case of a punch press operator, assigned to a machine eight hours a day, five days a week. How can our talk of group discussion and individual autonomy affect him?

One suggestion is that possibly a man should not be assigned to a punch press eight hours a day, five days a week. The reasoning of this chapter would suggest that *a group of men should be assigned to a group of operations*, and they should decide among themselves how to man the machines.

The cluster of operations assigned to each group should be visibly interrelated in the product. Thus, if Jim forms the aluminum, Joe drills holes in it, Jerry inserts the waggobbles into the holes, Jack tightens them in place, and Jacqueline tests them to be sure they operate—then this much of an assembly enables all five workers to see their work in relation to each of the other four. Their work has meaning with respect to other work, and they have a place with respect to other people who share the same purpose. And their team can have relationships to other teams.

Suppose there are 40 of each of the punch presses, drill presses, waggobble bins, tightening wrenches, and inspecting instruments. Suppose one person is assigned to each. This makes 200 workers. Suppose there is a foreman for every 20 workers. Our proposal would be that each foreman plus 20 workers constitute a group. This group would be given the responsibility of organizing itself into 4 teams of 5 persons each to turn out subassemblies.

They could form their teams in any way they wanted to, and divide up the five jobs among the five team members in any way the team desired. Rotation would be possible at will,[3] and so would reconstitution of the teams. The group of four teams could work out its own plan for breaking in new workers.

Under these conditions, the job itself would have far more meaning, more challenge, and more reward. The robot concept of workers would pass from the scene. And each person would have a clearly defined part in certain decisions relevant to his work. Thus his individuality would be enhanced and his autonomy increased.

There are further implications, too: Instead of the personnel department's trying to select each individual for one rigidly described "slot," it would be possible to accommodate a wider range of temperaments in the team groups. Thus the team idea makes it easier to use whatever workers are available at the time they are needed.

It will take ingenuity to redesign plant layouts and job coordination to make use of these principles. Some unit operations

3. The following item appeared in the business section of *Newsweek* on March 22, 1954, under the heading "How They Got More Done": "While the boss was away, some factory workers in Endicott, N.Y., switched jobs, just to break up the boredom. Result: it turned out to be just what the doctor ordered. By the time the switch was discovered, the men were all doing so much better that the boss decided to rotate jobs in his department—at an International Business Machines plant—as a matter of policy. That was a year ago. Since then manufacturing costs in the department have dropped about 19 per cent. If nobody gets bored by the routine of rotation, everything will be dandy." Comment: If the boss maintains the kind of relationship that allows this spontaneous action of the workers to occur, he will keep production up. If he imposes rotation as a gimmick, the effect will be only temporary.

are faster than others. One man might service several teams. The continual challenge is to maintain the basic psychological conditions through whatever adaptations of the simple model are required.

In general, Proposition I calls for explicit effort to develop worker groups. By and large, workers *are* in groups which strongly affect their productivity already, so that we are advocating making conscious use of a situation that already exists. The evidence for the assertion that worker groups exist anyway is the fact of interdependence: what one man does influences others, and vice versa.

There are different degrees and qualities of such horizontal interdependence:

1. The interdependence may be as *members of a team in competition* with other teams. *Examples:* A team tending a blast furnace; a small in-service training group within a school; subgroups of different academic specialties within a university department. In these cases, each member of the team has somewhat different responsibilities, and each other person is affected by the manner in which he does his job.

2. The interdependence may be in the *setting of standards* governing essentially parallel activity. *Examples:* Pieceworkers all doing the same job will gradually arrive at coercive standards of production; regardless of individual skill and apparent motivation, all the workers turn out finished pieces at approximately the same rate. Salesmen in widely separated territories tend to have common standards of honesty and diligence. In a university, there tend to be group standards for research productivity; in a school, for concern over children; in a factory, over waste, workmanship, quality and kind of supervision, and so on.

These standards usually express the feeling of the group toward its job. A major factor influencing them is the shared feeling about the people who control the job. Interaction with the superior may be private and separate among individual workers, but they find ways to compare notes and to set up standards for their own "protection" in the face of demands seen as coming from the boss—whether he is a foreman, plant manager, or the executive head of a corporation.

3. The interdependence within the group may be through its power to *regulate the pressure of its own work*. *Examples:* Initiating an active faculty committee results in a general increase in responsibility; a bottleneck on the production line reduces the rate of work all down the line; the acceptance of money by the directors of an organization means that more work must be turned out by operating personnel. The interdependence here is essentially sequential: the effects of events at some one place may gradually fan out through the entire institution. These changes can often be anticipated, and can be a source of concern long before they become real. The best example of this situation is probably a change in top leadership, but the place where the accommodations are successively made is within each horizontal level.

Thus, we note that people within a given level may be in face-to-face contact, finding that the way in which they operate is dependent upon each other's actions; or they may simply share the same ideas about themselves and the "proper" rate of production, a common perception of the boss, the general expectancy of fair or capricious treatment, and the like. Finally, they may be affected by fluctuations in operations prior to their own, and these may be fluctuations in the flow of materials, rumors, or rewards.

Our first assumption, then, is that because of these interdependences within each horizontal level, we may think of the workers within each level as constituting a "group." Each group has a designated "leader." Each group meets demands from "above," and the experience of each group contributes to policy which affects the nature of those demands.

Assuming that we now have defined each job in such a way that one can have significant experience through his work, and that we have done this through the creation of worker groups, then our next problem is to co-ordinate these groups of workers within the hierarchical situation. We note that the group has a boss or supervisor, who provides leadership to the group, and who also communicates between the group and the other superior and inferior groups. It is almost inevitable that the administrator finds himself caught in a conflict among his various roles, and that conflict would be greatest when he is wielding administrative power. Thus, consider the situation when the boss brings to his group a new set of demands or regulations from "upstairs":

1. Demands from "upstairs" are *pressures* on the group from a superior or dominant group. These pressures may be seen as reasonable or not, but the group must meet them.

2. The group meets these pressures by mobilizing its resources, as if against a common "enemy." The process of pulling together is one of co-operation.

3. The job of the boss as leader is to help the group co-operate efficiently to deal with the pressures.

4. In dynamic terms, the basic conflict of the administrator is a real one: he is seen as putting pressure on *at the same time* that he must also help the group co-operate to meet the pressure. He is essentially "enemy" and "leader against the enemy" at the same time. The administrator thus finds himself in a very difficult role conflict.

There are several ways to deal with the conflict. One is to deny one or the other of the roles. Thus, the administrator or supervisor can say that his job is to tell his men what to do. He includes, in the definition of the demand, instructions of how to meet the demand. In other words, he squeezes out the place of co-operation among the men, and establishes basically a one-to-one relationship between each man and himself. This, of course, loses the resources of the group, removes a number of important interpersonal types of gratification and involvement, and may set the men competitively against each other.

The administrator can also deny the other role, that of communicating demands to the group. He cannot, of course, fail to transmit demands, but he can fail to communicate them. Thus, he can post a memorandum on the bulletin board rather than talk directly to the men. In this case, he knows what the demands are, but the group actually discovers them to be only barriers to operation: it is as though a new "house rule" were suddenly invoked against them every time they got rolling. The group can never define the extent of its autonomy under such conditions. It would be justified in gradually sinking into a state of dependency and apathy as a way of avoiding the continual disappointments of being constantly interfered with. The point is that demands from "upstairs" actually become part of the facts, the "given's," with which a group must operate. These facts should be told them.

A common way in which administrators react to conflict in their role is to muddle things up—to exert pressure at times and to co-operate at times, without understanding when and how to do which. Possibly a basic cause of such muddling is the administrator's inability to distinguish a demand from "upstairs" from his own demands upon the group. An administrator whose security depends mostly on feeling that he is a part of the "upstairs" group identifies with it, and, therefore, feels that all his pronouncements to his men have the official backing of his superior group. Another administrator may learn that demands from "upstairs" have to be obeyed by his men, whereas things they see only as his personal demands do not; therefore, he may be tempted to imply constantly that what he wants is really a part of the demands from "upstairs." Some administrators act as if the group should arrive by themselves at a formulation of the demands from "upstairs" by some process of spontaneous generation. A final example of muddling is the administrator who swings like a weather vane from pressure tactics to co-operative tactics in an effort to keep everyone happy. This kind of oscillation is easy because the group, too, is subject to the cultural confusion between pressure and co-operation, and from time to time they will make a strong bid for one or the other.

The sequence of thought leading to Proposition II is as follows:

1. Demands from above are made on each group and its leader together. The leader and his group together then face the problem of meeting the demands. This means that the leader, in all his working with his group, never is placed in the position of the demander or "enemy."

2. The demand is made by someone superior to the leader in a meeting with the group. This superior stays around long enough to be sure that the demands are clearly understood. The leader is likely to mediate between the group and the superior: his job is to help the group ask the questions necessary for clarification.

3. Since all demands originate from outside the group, they

can be translated objectively into problems for the group as a whole to solve. The existence of problems to be solved (or changes to be made) provides the necessary focus and discipline for group discussion, and the group has sufficient autonomy to deal with the problem.

4. Since the demand is made by the superior, he is also the person responsible for evaluation of results. It is up to him to decide (preferably with the group's help) just how the evaluation is to be done. He may delegate some of the procedures to the group or to the leader, but he must keep the responsibility.

5. Because the group's leader now has a clearly co-operative role in his group, he is able more accurately to carry the group's thinking "upstairs," and thus is able to help his group exert an influence toward a more realistic formulation of the demands which it receives.

6. Because each man has contact not only with his *immediate* superior but also with higher-ups, he has less feeling of isolation, better understanding of the total operation, and an opportunity to assess the implications of his relation to his leader.

It is clear, in summary, that the intention here is to purify roles so as to avoid ambiguity and confusion. Proposition II may be stated: Each administrator in the heirarchy has three roles, but they operate in defined ways on different occasions. Thus: (*a*) Each man is a *member* of a group, working co-operatively with its leader, to meet work demands from "upstairs" and to formulate policy for the group below. (*b*) Each man is the *leader* of his group of subordinates, and has the responsibility for maintaining conditions of co-operation within the group, for transmitting relevant experience of the group upward, and for transmitting work demands downward. (*c*) Each man is a *transmitter of demands* (superior) to the groups led by his subordinates. His job is to make sure that the demands are understood as problems to be solved by his subordinates' groups; and to check on and evaluate the results of their efforts.

SOME QUESTIONS AND ANSWERS

1. Are you seriously suggesting that the administrator should attend meetings of groups led by his own subordinates?

Comment: Yes, when it is necessary to transmit a demand from "above."

2. Suppose a department manager is responsible for eight subdivisions, and each of these has an average of six sections. Should the manager attend meetings of all forty-eight groups?

Comment: That would be nice, but it may be impractical. If so, the following suggestions might be weighed:

a) He could consider talking to some of the subdivisional sections together. This would succeed to the extent that the same demand, presented in the same way, was equally appropriate to the sections. What he loses by this arrangement is some of the freedom to talk with the men in each section.

b) He could, possibly, send someone in his place. If, for example, he has an assistant who is known to be able to speak for him, this functionary could be sent. What he loses by this arrangement is the opportunity for his men to identify with him as representative to them of "top-level" thinking. The men get less gratification, and may have less motivation to deal with the demand.

c) He could relay the demand through small committees sent by several section groups to talk with him. Thus, one good meeting with sixty representatives might serve to bring the demand to twenty groups. What is lost by this arrangement is the objectivity with which the demand will be presented to the group, and there may be difficulties in clarifying the demand further when the men ask questions.

d) He could write a letter to each of the men, explaining the demand and requesting them to discuss it as a group. In this case, however, he should also be prepared to talk with those who may wish conversation with him; otherwise the communication is just "one-way" and motivation may be low.

e) He might call for some reorganization, on the grounds that eight subdivisions are too many for one man to control.

3. Wouldn't this plan mean that everyone would spend all his time in conferences? When would the work get done?

Comment: There are several relevant considerations here:

a) The "proper" division of time between "working" and

"conferencing" is that division which leads to satisfactory productivity. If another half-hour of talking results in more than half-an-hour's worth of additional production, then the time is well spent. A pointless conference, or one with bad leadership may be a waste of time. All such a failure shows, however, is that someone needs more training.

b) After getting the plan in operation, the need for conferences should decrease quite considerably. Increased co-operation between the boss and his men means more individual initiative, more incentive for men to work things out for themselves rather than to depend on the boss or on a meeting. A co-operative group is one which supports and challenges individual activity and growth; a group which serves as a crutch to lean on or as a pool in which to submerge one's individuality is coercive, not co-operative. As long as the problem to be solved is central, the group spends its time in effective work, whether it be at the conference table or at one's desk. And, by seeing the problem as a whole before beginning work, the men know to whom to go for what further discussion; it is not necessary to call a conference to talk about things that Joe and Mike can take care of in a twenty-minute chat by themselves.

c) At first, time will need to be spent at the conferences defining everyone's role in connection with each new problem. After a while, expectancies will develop, and the roles will be defined much more quickly in connection with new tasks. The groups, under competent leaders, will pick up considerable efficiency in translating demands into problems. They may also earmark certain kinds of demands to be delegated routinely to certain individuals or to "working committees." All delegated activity should, however, be reported to the total group from time to time, and, very probably, the "working committees" should be reconstituted with some frequency.

Two Applications to Administrative Problems

Our proposal is that work in an organizational setting is best produced by small groups which provide scope for significant experience. The internal basis of co-ordination of effort can be found in common ideas and purposes shared among the members. Data gleaned from operating experience are transmitted to superior groups, considered along with other data, and then sent back down in the form of demands or assignments. The demand is made on the group and its leader together. This protects the autonomy of the members and leads to co-operation between group and leaders.

The following represent applications of certain aspects of the model:

1. *Mr. Smith cuts the budget*

Mr. Smith is head of the dormitories at Grip College. Word came down from the business manager that he must operate next year with 10 per cent less funds than he did this year. Smith saw how to cut 4 per cent without hurting the services for which he was responsible. In desperation, he decided to ask his staff to help. He called them together and explained the problem. He was asked to read the letter from the business manager, in which the cut was requested. He read this to the group and they then started making suggestions. No one suggestion represented a major saving, but the staff reapportioned some of its duties so that two men who were leaving would not have to be replaced; they decided to let the students run the snack bar instead of hiring help; and they thought up an altogether new idea: that the students might organize to put on social events on a profit-sharing basis with the dormitory.

Mr. Smith, as spokesman for his staff, came to a meeting between his staff and the dormitory student committee. He presented the suggestion about social events (e.g., he "demanded" that the group consider the suggestion). He then left, and the group considered the plan, finally agreeing on a modified form of it for Mr. Smith to take "higher up" for necessary facilitating policy.

Through these means, Smith saved the college 12 per cent of the usual budget for his operation.[4]

Comment: This illustration fits the model fairly well. The business manager, Mr. Smith's boss, was represented by a letter instead of appearing in person. The business manager lost the op-

4. Related to me by Mr. Smith.

portunity to get suggestions about economizing in other parts of the college, apparently assuming that one can have ideas only about his own little corner.

Mr. Smith's staff, facing the outside demand together, was able to find answers of which Smith alone had not thought, and which he would have thought unacceptable to his staff if he *had* thought of them.

Smith, by presenting the suggestion to the students himself, freed his staff to discuss the matter effectively and without feeling tied to their own vested interests.

2. *General Smith investigates the black market*

General Smith, commanding officer in a corner of the European Theater, heard rumors of black market operations involving the theft of goods from his post and their subsequent possession by "natives." He called in three of his immediate subordinates and told them to bring him the facts "by next week at 2 o'clock." At report time, the subordinates, who had told *their* subordinates to snoop around and interview people, had the names of three malefactors on the base to report. They also had the names of fifty citizens seen with the goods.

The general guessed from the way the reports were made to him that his subordinates were covering up something. He decided to investigate personally.

His subordinates and *their* subordinates received invitations to "come to the game room of the officers club next Wednesday." The invitations were signed by the general. All those invited canceled their other plans and came. The general opened the affair by saying: "Gentlemen, tonight we have the opportunity for a bit of man-to-man talk. I am going to take off all this 'hardware' and pitch it on the table." He peeled off his brass insignia, with a flourish. "I suggest," he continued, "that each of you pitch yours on the table, too." The others followed his suggestion. They had mixed feelings, of apprehension at the unexpected, and of pleasure at the closer identification with the general.

After all were seated again, the general said: "Gentlemen, what are the facts about the black market?"

There was a long silence, during which several men exchanged uneasy glances.

Lt. Jack spoke up: "Do you ever go by the corner of East and Hollyhock?"

The general: "I could."

(*Silence*)

Capt. Tom: "I suppose the stuff gets stored temporarily in warehouses."

The discussion developed in hypothetical language: the men appeared to be planning how to carry out the black market operation instead of talking about actual events. At one point, Lt. Jack said: "If I were the head operator, I'd probably try to get information from someone like the supply officer—even if I had to pay for it." Lt. Jack was the supply officer. The general said: "I suppose the head of the supply depot could refuse to give further useful information, couldn't he?" "Yes," replied Lt. Jack. At no point did anyone have to name names. When it was clear who knew the names, the general gave these people the task of drawing up recommendations for a procedure to learn the names of those people whose initiative kept the business going.

Within five days the black market operation was completely destroyed, and new security provisions, planned in part by men who had connived in the operation, were set up.[5]

Comment: At first glance, one might suppose that this problem was solved by extra-administrative or informal means. But do not be fooled by the stripping off of the insignia. Shedding the "brass" did not mean shedding rank. But it did mean shedding many of the *distractions caused by rank.*

The "problem" as defined by the general was to stop the black market operation and to do what he could to prevent further resumption of the illegal enterprise. He acted on the hunch that these men could stop it, and, with their knowledge and experience, would know how to prevent similar developments in the future. The general may or may not have had any intention of taking punitive action when the meeting began, but he al-

5. I have heard three versions of this story, but am not able to document it. It is a useful story for our purposes, true or not.

lowed each person the opportunity to make such restitution as he could by helping the group more or less anonymously.

By acting informally, without the "hardware," the boss communicated the idea to these men that they were, in effect, his partners—that he accepted them as people, not as cells in the table of organization. He was inviting them to help solve a problem; he was not telling them to answer his questions—or else. His manner put the whole investigation under the rule of *noblesse oblige*, rather than the "big stick." And the group accepted the challenge to act maturely. The general's authority was inherent in his functional relationships to his men—that is not something that he could "put on" every morning with a clean tunic—and this episode probably reinforced his actual authority.

The general made his demands on the two levels just beneath him. These two levels constituted a group, and they quickly set up the group standard of hypothetical discussion. The general was wise enough to let them handle it that way: he wanted to solve a problem, and he knew that they knew that they were not going to leave the room until the general was satisfied. Therefore, the "Old Man," having given them the responsibility and knowing they could not evade it, could afford to relax and let them edge up to the problem in whatever way they could.

RECAPITULATION AND SUMMARY

1. Responsibilities are assigned to small groups whose members co-operate to define the roles of each individual, to train themselves, to induct new members, etc. These small groups have sufficient autonomy to carry out their responsibilities and, also, for their members to meet many personal-social needs in the process. Belongingness in the group gives each person security and emotional support, so that there is minimum need for the self-oriented anxious behaviors so troublesome in administration.

2. The groups meet as they need to, for the accomplishment of various phases of problem-solving: exploration of the problem, planning of individual responsibilities for taking action, and evaluation of results. No man ever acts alone except on behalf of his group.

3. Groups may be recomposed so that the most appropriate

people are working on each problem. Continuous-production groups would presumably make adjustments for turnover and compatibility; problem-solving groups may be *ad hoc* working committees which exist only during the life of the particular problem.

4. Recommendations are formulated during the working of a group and are transmitted by the leader, serving as spokesman, to the group above. Then this receiving group, working co-operatively, translates these (and other recommendations) into policy and into demands to be transmitted downward.

5. Demands are formulated by each group in the vertical hierarchy for transmission by its leader to the group below. This "receiving" group, working co-operatively, translates the demand into problems of changing operation or of finding specific unique solutions. Furthermore, demands may be *initiated* by recommendations coming up from below.

6. The transmission of demands and recommendations up and down the vertical hierarchy constitutes *pressure*, applied through spokesmen, onto the group above or below. The working-out of problems and the taking of action in the horizontal levels constitutes *co-operation*, with the immediate superior serving as leader. The two forms of communication are separated. These two basic modes of operation remain unentangled and unambiguously applicable in their proper situations.

Further discussion of basic principles is offered on pages 181–91. Thirty-four specific empirical generalizations, of considerable help to people concerned with the organization of work for specific purposes, are presented on pages 62–68. Chapter 7 may be useful in understanding the basic nature of loyalty problems, and chapter 12 points to the important relationships, too often ignored by administrators, between organizations and their surrounding community. The principles listed on pages 14–18 apply very well to creative meetings at the staff level, and the principles of group control, pages 284–89, are relevant to understanding the problems of participation by individuals within the organization.

CHAPTER 5

To train people in the skills of group leadership and membership, one must study their behavior in group situations. The trainer's function is to keep the requirements the group needs to meet clearly before it; but he also safeguards the right and opportunity of each individual to experiment with new ways of co-operating to meet the requirements. Thus the "situation" is permissive for the individual, but the "problem" is clearly defined for the group.

DISTINCTIVE FEATURES

The authority by virtue of which the trainer operates is the trainee's trust in and dependence on him. The method of control of the group is through trainer-planned or trainer-approved agreements about activities planned to satisfy the diagnosed needs of the group. The primary target of change is the trainee's competence as a participant in groups; the secondary target is the groups to which the trainees will return after training. The role of the member is defined by the expectation that he will experiment with new behaviors, be loyal to the group, and try, on occasion, to produce behaviors needed by the group. The communication between the training group and other groups is highly individual and unofficial; it ranges from individual resolutions to behave differently in a "back home" group to the utilization of others for "blowing off steam," discussing the training experience, and receiving emotional support from one's own organizations.

Training for Group Participation
The Laboratory Method[1]

During the past decade, an interest in and an extension of the notion that the effectiveness of groups depends to a great extent upon the ways in which they operate has been rapidly gaining force. While personalities, techniques, experience, cultural backgrounds, and education of the participants in groups are important, the fact remains that effectiveness in the use of these resources is largely determined by the individual characteristics of the situation in which they are to be used. And this situation is basically one of interaction among people.

It is possible, for example, for a group whose members are mostly educated, well adjusted, and knowledgeable to get no-

1. The writing of this chapter, and the research mentioned in it, were facilitated by a contract with The Human Relations and Morale Division of the U.S. Office of Naval Research.

The concept of "laboratory method of training" has been developed through the years since 1945 by a number of research men generally identified with the Group Dynamics movement. The core ideas were proposed by the late Kurt Lewin and his followers at the Research Center for Group Dynamics. This group, with the collaboration of the Department of Adult Education, National Education Association, has been the core for operating the National Training Laboratory at Bethel, Maine, which began in the summer of 1947.

Since 1948, the National Training Laboratory has been operated by a Policy and Planning Committee, consisting of men from the original two groups, plus eleven major universities. I joined this group in 1948, and through the years since then have been deeply concerned with the "laboratory method."

During the summer of 1952, at least eight different workshops, run by as many other groups, made use of some modification of the "laboratory method" as a major part of their training programs. The same basic ideas have been modified and applied to three-day conferences, institutes, and even single meetings.

The method of training requires a great deal of insight and skill on the part of the trainer. Each trainer has his own concept of the method, and there has never been (so far as I know) any complete statement of the method. This chapter represents my attempt to formulate such a statement. In doing this, I am speaking out of my own experiences; this is not an official statement from the National Training Laboratory.

where: consider many school faculty meetings. It is possible for administrators marvellously trained to be unable somehow to run successful staff meetings. It is possible for members of a community council, highly successful as leaders in their own organizations, to be unable to work together. It is possible for people trained in research and loaded with information about what happens in groups to be unable to contribute effectively to groups of which they are a part. It is even possible for a group, highly successful in planning policy for its organization's executive secretary, to fail miserably when its co-operation with other groups is required.

The point is that successful group operation is a matter of taking into account not only the characteristics of individuals but also the nature of the problem, the limitations of time and freedom of action imposed by the institution or community, and such "group" factors as morale, expectations, power fantasies, status in the community, and conceptions of the kind of group the members think it is. All these factors come together to determine the quality of experience the group will have, or, to put it in other words, the nature of the "group processes."

The laboratory method of training provides a situation in which group processes can be observed and studied. The objectives are to train members to recognize when these group processes are appropriate to the group task, what the consequences of different sorts of processes are, how members contribute to determine the nature of the processes, how leaders effect these processes, how a group whose processes are inappropriate may be helped to improve. The task of the trainer in such groups is to see to it that the group has significant experiences in trying to work together, and that conditions are such that people can learn from these experiences. Thus, for example, allowing the group to "flounder around" for six meetings may be giving them a significant experience, but it is one from which the group's members learn little about group process; and what they do learn can seldom consciously be used to guide subsequent membership experience. Or, the trainer can see to it that the group is exposed to a great deal of information about groups, but the information may not be sufficiently related to the members' own deep experiencing for it to have meaning for their subsequent activities. The problems of maintaining a useful balance between feeling, thinking, and doing; between trainer, group, and individual control of behavior; between individual and group goals; between inferring principles from experience and applying known principles to guide new experience; between problem-solving directed toward stated goals and problem-solving related to the resolution of anxiety—all of these problems must be dealt with by the group under the supervision of the trainer.

The purpose of this chapter is to clarify what is involved in the laboratory method of training, and to formulate what appear to us to be basic assumptions and principles used by the trainer. We shall begin with the assumptions on which the laboratory method is based, and will then present a case study of a training group with some interpretations made by the trainer to guide his working with the group. We shall next indicate the sorts of changes produced by the training experience. Finally, we shall summarize the principles used by the trainer to guide the group at all times.

Basic Principles of the Laboratory Method

1. The aim of training is (a) to help people learn how to behave in groups in such a way that the groups solve the problems for which they were assembled and (b) to insure that individuals have a meaningful, rewarding, and need-meeting experience. When both these conditions are present simultaneously the individual is challenged and rewarded for creativity and insights, and the decisions reached by the group are wiser than those any one person could reach by himself. Thus, we might say briefly that the aim of training is simultaneously to help other groups become more effective instruments for social action, on the one hand, and, on the other, to help individuals to grow and learn.

2. In order to accomplish this aim, the trainer ideally should work with the actual groups whose efficiency is to be improved. This would mean that he serve as a roving, "nomadic" consultant, and it would require the dedication of parts of group meetings to training. Actually, however, this is impractical: there are too many groups and too few trainers; furthermore, many of the groups most in need of training either would not acknowledge the

fact, or if they did, could not find the time or money to use the training consultant.

It is practical, however, to set up special training groups to which one or several members of the groups needing improvement could come. In this case, the aim of training is to help some members learn how to train their own groups. This is a difficult job because it means that these members must learn not only how to contribute more effectively as group members but also how consciously to influence the underlying psychological conditions and assumptions on which their group is operating. To do this beneficially means that they must not only be able to diagnose the existing situation in their group; they must also have an image of more desirable conditions and know how to work toward them. Fortunately most groups can accept help if it is given unobtrusively and with the interests of the group at heart, and the member-trainer is likely to find others in his group working with him. If he does not find that his efforts are actually helpful, the chances are that his motives for helping the group are mixed up with less desirable motives—to cut down the designated leader, or to promote some particular course of action, or to satisfy personal needs in ways which disturb the group. It follows that the member of the training group, then, must learn not only about group operation but also about himself—or at least about those aspects of himself which affect his interactions in the group.

3. It is because of this last requirement that training is sometimes thought of as a type of therapy. Conceived in this way, the theory of training would be primarily a theory about the ways in which people can be released from the neuroses which block their operation in groups. Emphasis would be placed on interpersonal relations and the group would be used both to provide a range of personalities for each member to interact with and as a supportive instrument to reinforce the individual's efforts to change —as, for example, in Alcoholics Anonymous. The reader will see that the laboratory method to be spelled out here requires enough understanding of the therapeutic method that conditions harmful to mental health and emotional growth can be avoided; but the laboratory method tends to conceive of training as a learning experience rather than a therapy experience, and the necessary

understandings are drawn from a much wider range of sciences. The laboratory method uses interpersonal interaction and group supportiveness, but it places these within the context of a group consciously trying to solve problems rather than dealing with them without relation to problem-solving.

4. The image of "effective operation," which produces wise decisions and individual growth, is an image of a desired state of affairs continuously prevailing. This image is characterized in different ways by different schools of thought about training. Some folks think of it as "democratic"; some prefer the term "group-centered," "co-operative," or "healthy." If we were to choose a single term, it would be "reality-based." Group operation is sound and therefore effective when it is "in contact with reality." This means such things as these: the immediate tasks of the group are within its competence, with the potentials and opportunities it has; the responsibilities the group assumes are proper to its position in the community or institution; the activities of the group represent direct working toward its goals, rather than indirect ways of building fantasies or attacking concealed enemies; the kind of participation required from members is well enough defined that all know how to participate, and the ones who have something to offer do participate; the tasks of the group are such that everyone there has a reason for being there—or else the composition of the group is determined by the kinds of resources needed for the defined task.

Since the group itself changes through learning, and since the nature of its problems changes continually, it follows that the image we are describing cannot be put in terms of some particular style of leadership, some particular level of peacefulness or avoidance of conflict, some one pitch of morale or enthusiasm. To maintain contact with things as they are requires adaptability, change, and flexibility of operation. It requires the continuous exercise of choice among alternative behaviors.

5. The means by which the group maintains contact with reality through the exercise of choice is determined by its method of operation. By "method" we mean a consistent way of approaching, thinking about, and determining its own behavior. Methods include reliance on the judgment of the leader, imitation of what

other groups have done in situations believed to be similar, analysis of the effects of past performance, and the like. In general, however, the only method man has for maintaining contact with reality is the scientific method, with its basic emphasis upon learning from the study of his own tested experience. In the case of a group, the experience most relied upon is that of the group itself, because so many of the realities to be taken into account are facts about the group as an on-going organism actively related to the larger community.

Labeling a method merely provides a name by which to call it. Labels tend to gather around themselves facts and feelings present in the situation in which the label was applied or is most used. The label "scientific method" evokes a variety of images: perhaps you see a scientist in a white coat squinting into a microscope, or maybe fifteen rats bumping into the walls of a maze, or possibly some character ringing the doorbell and than asking a lot of odd questions. In the case of a group, scientific method implies several important understandings: that the only way a group can discover its strengths and weaknesses is to tackle a defined problem and study what happens; that planning for group activities is a process of adding details as the group proceeds, rather than a process of producing detailed blueprints in advance; that whatever happens has perfectly natural causes, and that if we had enough of the "right kind" of relevant information we could explain it; that there is continuity throughout the life of a group, and one thing leads to another; that the *ultimate* test of an idea is what happens when it is put into effect, not whether it fits into a particular "ideology"; that the proper function of knowledge is to enable us to figure out a course of action in whose "rightness" we can have enough confidence to take action in such a way that its effect can be interpreted.

The method of learning in the training group is through conscious use of the experimental method under conditions "safe" enough that one can think objectively. And the problems to which it is applied are the problems the group is ready to deal with. Finally, the means by which the group learns about unrecognized factors that must be taken into account is through comparison of one situation with another. In particular, the group needs to contrast periods of work with periods of nonwork; periods of frustration with periods of high morale; periods having one kind of leadership with periods having some other kind. Thus, the factors that make a difference—in other words the "real" factors—are uncovered so they can be dealt with and understood.

6. The decision to regard training as a supervised experience in using the experimental method requires the assumption that at all times the group is working on some problem or is trying to overcome some barrier between itself and its goals. The "theory" which the training group learns is fundamentally a set of ideas about the sorts of conditions which imply various specific sorts of problems in a group. The "technology" which the training group learns is fundamentally a set of ideas about the ways of organizing group effort which will be useful to resolve such problems.

Initially, the training group is likely to think of problems in such terms as these: "The goals weren't clear"; "The leader was too autocratic"; "We didn't have enough time"; "We weren't interested in the topic." As training goes on, problems are more likely to be stated in such terms as these: "The needed roles were not defined well enough for us to know how to participate"; "The anxiety of the leader prevented his understanding what the members were trying to tell him"; "We did not know how the others felt, so our attempts to solve the stated problems were really ineffective efforts to share feelings"; "We engaged in academic debate because the real problem was too threatening," etc. Initially, the training group's ideas of technology pretty well collapse into this question: "What techniques can a group use and when should it use them?" As training goes on, the technological questions become: "What are the demands this problem makes on the group?" "Where are we going to find, or how are we going to develop, the skills needed to meet these demands?" "In what order should the various required activities be arranged for maximum participation and efficiency?"

Two general trends are noted: first, the tendency to move from superficial "interest" or "behavioral" (e.g., "he done wrong") definitions of group problems, which imply that everything is done consciously and intentionally by individuals, to definitions of problems in terms of basic feelings, motivations, conflicts, and anxieties which stand in the way of direct group goal achievement; second, a movement away from a tendency to act everything out, with no awareness of what the group is doing, to a tendency to think through the requirements of problems and then to create procedures most likely to meet these requirements.

The purpose of all experience during training is to contribute to the continuous development of greater awareness of what the group's problems are, what behaviors are required in the group to solve these problems, and how effort can be organized in such a way that individuals can present these required behaviors to the group.

7. During training, the group changes as a result of learning. The amount and kinds of change depend upon what is learned and how it is learned. A classroom group, for example, learns to talk more intelligently about social problems or about chemistry; it learns to solve objectively defined problems in arithmetic or composition with greater skill; and it learns to respond emotionally to many stimuli (e.g., in the arts) that previously left it unmoved. But it may remain just as dependent on the teacher for telling it what problems it is to study next, what skills it needs to develop, how it is to organize for study. In other words, the group may show little if any growth as a group, even though there may be considerable development of ease and satisfaction among the students if they have the chance to interact with each other rather than only with the teacher. In contrast, the training group shows very great growth and change because everything it learns rises out of its problems of operation and has implications for what it is to do differently.

It is for this reason that the trainer of the group may consider his major objective to be to "help the group grow." Among the signs of growth, of the development of power to use the experimental method, are: increasing self-direction; increasing efficiency of working; increasing ability to cope with frustration; increasing skill in avoiding realistically anticipated failure; increasing ability to channel spontaneously expressed emotion into work; increasing flexibility in designing plans to fit changed situations; increasing rapidity in recovering from emotionally destructive periods; increasing meeting of individual needs within group problem-solving activities; an increasing tendency to define group problems realistically and in fundamental or dynamic terms— e.g., in terms of what is "really" going on.

Halting of growth, or regression to earlier stages, is taken as evidence that the group has some problem of which it is probably not aware and on which it needs to work.

It is interesting that it is the group that grows. Individuals change their roles, their reactions, and their understandings, and the changes are organized around, and occur because of, their own individual needs. Individuals may arrive at quite different ways of explaining what is happening in the group, and they may change their ways of responding to each other. But they do not all change in the same direction or to the same extent. They develop, if anything, more rather than less individuality—because there is great freedom to try out new behaviors and attitudes. They learn how to act, each in his own way, to change the group situation to give themselves more opportunity to *be* themselves. In the process, they discover a great deal about the "selves" they are—or, more accurately, the selves they *can* be in a supportive but demanding situation.

The growth of a group requires a much wider range of contributions than any one person can supply. Needed contributions at the skill level include such things as setting the problem, clarifying ideas, finding common assumptions behind several ideas, summarizing, stimulating interest, compromising, suggesting hypotheses, generalizing, etc. These contributions must be made under a variety of emotional conditions: when the group feels dependent, aggressive, hostile, peaceful, withdrawn, uneasy, "warm," under pressure, sociable. Furthermore, these contributions must be made to a variety of topics: the styles of leadership, the nature of interpersonal identification, the concept of work, the idea of productivity. Any one person will find that he has competence with respect to certain skills under particular emotional conditions and with respect to a particular range of topics. Although topic and skill demands have some effect on participation, the most important determining factor is the emotional state of the group. Some people participate most easily when the group is dependent on the leader, or when it is fighting the leader, or when everyone is angry or when peace descends. Others may be made anxious or even become immobilized under each of these conditions. Yet the group as a whole works under all these conditions, works through a wide range of problems. And with each "working-through," the group develops greater strength, greater ability to tolerate frustration, and to progress along the various other dimensions of growth listed above.

8. Group growth, although not directly related to the growth of each individual, is, however, in the last analysis, dependent upon the kinds of people in the group. The basic emotional dynamics of the group is a working-out of the changing strains in the network of relationships among the members and trainer. For example, if everyone in the group were thoroughly content to be forever dependent on the trainer for all decisions, the trainer would find it very difficult to teach the group much about the nature of dependency, its uses, forms, and causes. Training is much easier when some people in the group are satisfied with being dependent and others react against the feeling of dependency. Under these conditions the trainer can help the group see that some of its conflict centers around the finding of an appropriate balance between dependency and resistance to dependency, and activities can be set up to discover or test ideas about the effects and control of dependency relationships. The curriculum of the training group is ultimately determined and limited by the composition of the group.

Thus each group "writes its own history." These histories are not entirely unique because most of us were raised in similar cultures. We subscribe to many of the same ideals and are troubled by many of the same value conflicts, even though we may react differently to these conflicts. It is a fairly safe prediction that at some time or another, and to some extent, every training group will get into the culturally induced problems of dependence versus independence, individuality versus conformity, freedom of expression versus inhibition of emotion, competition versus co-operation.

The problem of composing a group for the most effective training is not a simple one. The ability of the trainer is far more often the limiting factor than is the composition of the group. Probably the only reason to keep someone out of this kind of training program would be that he needs therapy instead. In other words, some individuals are not ready for such an experience, and no good is served by putting them through it. The more critical problem is to secure a neat balance among the various kinds of temperaments or emotional predispositions or character structures.

9. All of the above discussion implies that the trainer deals with the group as a whole. The trainer is concerned about whether processes going on in the group are growth-producing in the various senses indicated above. He believes that each individual has a great opportunity to learn things that are necessary and meaningful for him to learn, and he notices changes—sometimes very remarkable changes—in the performance of individuals in the group. In general, what the trainer using the laboratory method does not know (at least in 1953) is, from some standpoints, the most important thing of all: does change in individual performance represent merely an intelligent adaptation to the changes in the group as a whole, or does it mean a whole new integration of personality such that the individual will inevitably perform differently from now on? Follow-up studies to date indicate that both possibilities exist.

Thus, some individuals become "good group members" because that is expected, and because they have to make some changes in order to continue to participate in the group. But when they return to their "back home" groups, the power of adaptation remains, and they rapidly adjust to the prevailing conditions: it is as if they had not had the training experience at all. Fortunately, these individuals are rare. On the other hand, there are people whose apparent learnings and changes during training seem to carry over into subsequent group experience. Instead of adjusting to the norms of the group (no matter what the norms are) they make a two-way adaptation in which they both fit into the group and change it at the same time.

It seems reasonable to suppose that the training will be transferred to new situations to the extent that:

1. The individual has a realistic understanding of what is happening, particularly to him, during training.

2. This understanding is related by him to a wide variety of past experiences—that is, it gives him insights which enable him to understand other experiences he has had.

3. The individual experiences a substantial reduction of anxiety about the roles he plays and thus develops a greater feeling of adequacy.

4. The individual achieves commitment to a valid image of the kinds of processes characteristic of effective group functioning.

It seems clear that the laboratory method of training should be backed up by a program of individual (or possibly small group) interviewing, to give greater opportunity for each person to understand and study his own reactions to the group experience. A study now in progress should tell us whether this deduction is correct.

Up to this point, we have tried to give some characterization of the laboratory method of training—how it conceives the job of training, and the principles on which it operates. We wish now to present, rather briefly, a case study of one training group so that the reader can see what actually goes on; and then we will try to point out principles by which the trainer can continuously guide his own participation.

THE LABORATORY METHOD IN OPERATION: A CASE STUDY

This is a brief presentation of some of the events transpiring during a training course offered to graduate students. The course consisted of ten three-hour weekly meetings[2] with the trainer and, in addition, probably a like amount of time spent outside the meetings in informal groups discussing the class events. The class contained 25 people (the usual class contains 12–18 people), of widely different ages and experience. The trainer, here referred to as Jim,[3] had an assistant, Jane,[4] who participated little during the

2. More commonly, such groups have met every day for three weeks, as at the National Training Laboratory, Bethel, Maine.

3. For other news of Jim (he calls himself "Tom," here) see the National Training Laboratory in Group Development, *Bulletin No. 3* (1948), pp. 16–34. This gives "Jim's" perceptions of his first training group. For another group trained by Jim (Tom), see Stuart Chase, *Roads to Agreement* (New York: Harper & Bros., 1951), pp. 88–92.

4. Jane was Dr. Dorothy Stock, a project director in the Human Dynamics Laboratory.

meetings but helped Jim analyze and plan between meetings. This particular case is cited because it represented the most conscious effort so far to put the principles enunciated in this chapter into practice. Interpretations are put in italics to distinguish them from the descriptive comments.

MEETING I

Jim took the first 15 minutes to have people put their names on large cards and to make the usual remarks about objectives and method. (*Jim did not expect the remarks to mean much at this point, but he wished to satisfy initial expectations and to anticipate some of the feelings he knew would arise from time to time.*) The group had nothing to say when Jim was finished and he went on to suggest an activity to start with. (*They could not tell what the remarks were going to mean in terms of operation, and they did not know Jim and each other well enough to risk questions. They accepted the ritual and were not disturbed.*)

The suggested activity involved forming three subgroups, working for 14 minutes, re-forming new subgroups, working another 14 minutes, and then, for the third time, forming new subgroups. Jim gave them a question to discuss: What problems do you think we will encounter in attempting to use the experimental method? He also suggested that they might wish to contrast their experiences in the three subgroups. (*Jim knew that to get acquainted involves working together, not talking about yourself when it is not clear what sort of thing should be revealed. He gave the group members a question so that they would have some common starting point and goal for talking together. He posed the question in terms of difficulties in order to make possible expression of any negative feelings people might have. He put them in subgroups but did not participate himself so that they could talk more freely, and so that they would have an experience on their own, albeit a protected one. He had them move through three subgroups so that they would have the experience of getting acquainted three different times under somewhat different conditions. The 14-minute period was chosen as being long enough to avoid the frustration of not talking and short enough to prevent serious work on the assigned problems. He felt that neither of these would be desired at this point in the group's history: frustration would not be instructive, and the problem was not "real" enough to justify serious effort.*)

The subgroups fell to work with ease. While they were talking, Jim circulated around and tried to decide what differences the people would probably be aware of (and able to discuss) among their first, second, and third groups. When the whole group got together, they were polled as to how they would rank the three subgroups with respect to a number of kinds of feelings. (*Jim wanted some objective data on the blackboard so that there would always be a clear content to deal with if the group wished to use it; he also wanted the polling to occur so the members could see the extent to which others felt the same way they did; he further wanted to start right in using data and showing that such data can be interpreted usefully.*) The members thought their first subgroup stayed most closely to the assigned problem, was most aware of Jim's presence in the room, and was the one in which they felt most self-conscious. The discussion in the last group was seen as more personal, more oriented to problems of how the group was doing, was least "groupy," and for this group the time passed slowest.

Jim said the group could discuss anything of interest to them about their experiences in the three groups, and that the data on the board might help suggest hypotheses about group operation. The discussion was "free" (*much "freer" than under such instructions as "Discuss anything you want to"*); the data were referred to several times when the discussion needed a fresh topic, and the group made some effort to draw conclusions from the data. The greatest amount of feeling, however, expressed concern about the freedom with which one should express feeling, whether an individual can "be himself," how far he must knuckle under to the group, and notions about the effects of expressed hostility on other people. Jim stayed out of the discussion except to clarify some rather vague statements from time to time; he also came in at one point to "protect" an individual whose comments, he felt, would turn the group against that individual. (*The "protection" took the form of indicating to the group how to react to the remarks, rather than of talking at all about the individual who made them.*)

Most of the discussion was quite satisfying to the people, and the content was pretty much of their own choosing. The trainer, however, made all the decisions required to set up the activities. (*He had decided that the group should get into activity to provide an ex-*

perience to discuss, rather than that it should spend all its time—probably fruitlessly—talking about possible activities.)

The last hour was devoted to answering a self-perception questionnaire to help Jim's research program.

The first hour of the second meeting was set up as a "free" discussion, going on with the things the group had started at the end of the last meeting. The trainer stayed out, so that the group could get a clearer image of its strengths and weaknesses—an accurate image of itself. (*Jim usually saw himself as providing definitions within which the group could work, but not as influencing how the group worked, since that was the basic thing to be discovered and studied.*) The problems of individuality and freedom of expression were the centers of group concern. *The discussion also showed a wish on the part of some to "go deeper" in revealing their concerns, coupled with a tendency to cover up if anyone pushed them about these concerns.*

Jim gave everyone a questionnaire to fill out to get reactions to the "free" discussion, and again the answers were polled and listed on the board. There was a short discussion of the reactions, and most interest settled on the "roles people played" during the discussion: the blocker, conciliator, nonparticipant, etc. (*This seemed to confirm Jim's belief that during the first meeting or two, the major concern of people in training groups is to find a comfortable and socially approved role they can play; or, to put it more clearly, to find out how they can participate and what kinds of participation will be rewarded.*)

The last 30 minutes was spent in the subgroups' trying to use the data on the board in order to plan an activity for the next group meeting. The subgroups did not finish their plans, but Jim stopped them five minutes before the end of the period to have them report progress to each other. All the groups were concerned with the effects of different kinds of member roles. In addition, each plan showed some level of concern about group leadership—a new element that had not arisen explicitly in the total group. (*Jim felt that the group was not anxious about his leadership because they were working well under it; so he interpreted the concern to indicate recognition of the fact that member roles cannot be defined until assumptions about leadership and authority have been clarified.*)

MEETING III

Jim and Jane did a great deal of thinking before the third meeting. They had observed that one of the subgroups was a cohesive group of minority-group members whose culture was decidedly authoritarian and competitive. Jane had prepared an analysis of the research questionnaire given at the first meeting, and it was evident that there was a definite split in the group about whether individuals should feel free to express aggression and compete with each other and the leader, or whether everyone should work for harmony and avoid expressing strong feelings. (*It was felt that this fundamental difference in emotional orientation would have to be settled before people could participate in any very gratifying way; and that until it could be settled, the group would go round and round on the question. It was also felt that the group could not yet tackle so threatening a problem, and that the concern over kinds of member roles was an off-target way of edging into the problem.*) Jane and Jim saw two alternatives: first, they could encourage the group to think that the problem really was one of "how to define the role of the group member"; and this would logically result in a long list of "characteristics of the good group member." Second, some means might be found to so reduce the threat connected with this problem that it could safely be recognized and dealt with. In view of the fact that the conflict evidently was, at least in part, a conflict between subcultures within the total group, the trainers decided to reduce the threat by helping the group discover that people behave the way they do, not only because of their personalities (*which is the belief that made the problem threatening*) but also because of the cultures in which they grow up (*and they cannot be blamed for them*). It was further decided to try to help the group see that the problem was one of group standards—a concern of the total group—rather than a problem primarily for each individual to deal with on his own (*in order to reduce the threat further*).

Accordingly, Jim pointed out at the beginning of the third meeting that the group had three plans from the earlier activity of the three subgroups, and it now had the problem of combining these plans or of creating a single new one. He suggested that the processes involved in reaching the final plan were well worth study, and that he had a scheme for simultaneously arriving at a single plan and also studying some of the member roles involved in so doing. He outlined his proposal, and the group agreed to try it. (*What else could they do? It should be noted that the group had not openly recognized its deeper problem; it was concerned with member roles seen at the level of how people act.*)

Jim's proposed activity involved several steps; first, the three planning subgroups would meet long enough to sharpen their plans and get them clearly in mind. Second, two members from each of the subgroups would represent their subgroups in a conference to decide on the best plan for the total group while the rest of the subgroup members would observe, presumably from the standpoint of their own groups. In addition, Jim selected from each subgroup a person with some experience in group observation to be part of a three-man team to observe, presumably without subgroup bias. Third, Jim gave out questionnaires after the conference to enable the three subgroups, the observers, and the participants to indicate some of their reactions to the conference. Fourth, the answers worked out by the three subgroups were put on the board as the basis of discussion, with the observers and participants also contributing their opinions at will.

The plan was carried out. The conference discussion was vigorous and much feeling was expressed. The two representatives from the "minority" subcommittee fought hard to get their plan accepted without change. The representatives from another subgroup pushed for compromise; those from the third committee were not clear on the details of the plan their subgroup had proposed, and they tried to find common elements in the three plans. All the rest of the group responded openly to the various expressions of aggression and the efforts to compromise.

With the observations of the three subgroups summarized on the board, the whole group then spent the remaining hour in a rather penetrating sharing of feelings and ideas about the conference. There were some short flights into abstract questions (e.g., "What is 'structure' and how is it determined?"). Two people had been seen as "leaders" during the six-man conference. One of them was dominating, and drove for acceptance of his group's plan; the other was much more gentle, and tried to clarify feelings and discover areas of agreement. Jim entered into the discussion actively in an effort to interpret some of the things the group saw. Thus it was seen that the two leaders were leaders because each validly represented a side of the conflict within the total group between competition and dominance versus co-operation and sharing. In effect, these two were spokesmen for different sides of the group's feeling. It was seen, further, that these two "leaders" also were much reinforced by the very different positions taken by their own subgroups in this matter. And it was clear that people behaved the way they did not just because of their personalities but also because of their loyalty to other groups and to the ways of working in these other groups.

There was no resolution of the basic problem which had arisen implicitly in so many different forms. However, the realization that a problem existed was expressed in many individual statements.

(*The trainers felt that the meeting resulted in a greatly increased freedom to express significant individual concerns, and, along with this feeling, that there was a considerable increase in cohesiveness or groupness. People had expressed their own concerns and had obtained reactions from the group; the group was achieving more meaning for the members as a field in which individual needs might be met.*)

MEETING IV

Because the trainers did not know the extent to which the previous discussion had prepared the group to deal with its basic problem (of competition versus co-operation), they decided to start the group with a continuation of the discussion from the last meeting. The group talked for an hour in a more or less desultory fashion, and except for a few comments, never reached the level of penetration of the last meeting. (*The feeling aroused by the six-man "conference" had been drained off during the week.*) Toward the end of the first hour, Jim suggested that the group list the questions it now had in mind. Twelve questions were suggested, and all but two were requests for advice about how to keep a group working, how to minimize the effects of conflicting loyalties to other groups, what to do when things get "emotional," etc.

During the break for coffee, the trainers had a whispered consultation, and decided to take the calculated risk of confronting the group with the problem of its basic conflict. Accordingly, after the break, Jim openly said that he and Jane had been in consultation and that they had decided to suggest that Jane begin the new session by giving some impressions of the preceding discussion. *(It was decided to have Jane do this because if the group was not ready for the interpretation it would be likely temporarily to reject the interpreter along with the interpretation; and to reject Jim at this point would hurt the group too much, since it had not yet developed enough natural leadership to carry on alone.)* Jane pointed out what was clearly evident in the questions written on the board: that the group was seeking some means to control individual participation so that its conflict could not come out into the open; the group was anxious about the conflict, and was hunting for techniques to handle it rather than trying to understand and resolve it. Jim later added the opinion that techniques might be resorted to in some kinds of groups, but that in the training group the goal is understanding and resolution. The question was: "How ready was the group at this point to approach its conflict directly?"

(This confrontation by means of an apparently reasonable interpretation of data on the blackboard in front of them could not be denied. But it could be resisted; and this would be shown by the discussion's going off onto other topics, by discussing the bases of interpretation, or by asking the trainer to tell them what to do next or even to give his judgment about how freely emotion should be openly expressed. The trainers felt that it must be left completely up to the group to decide whether, or how deeply, to go into the problem which they could no longer overlook. Therefore, the trainers stayed out of the ensuing discussion until the very end.)

The first comments following the interpretation were individually concerned denials that anyone ever had hostile feelings, confessions of fear of expressing one's self freely, requests to return to the problem of the leader's role, and the like. *(In effect, the group experienced a mild shock, and the discussion had, for a few minutes, an every-man-for-himself quality.)* The group, then, under the emerging leadership of one or two people, began to ask what activity it could plan to study these emotional phenomena in an effort to understand them. Several ideas were suggested, and then Jim was asked point-blank to be a resource person and suggest an activity. Jim hesitated, and then said that if this question had been put to him because of the group's emotional dependency he did not want to answer it; but if the question merely meant that the group now was emotionally committed to the goal of working on the problem, then he would be happy to offer suggestions—he then offered three alternative suggestions for activity. After some discussion, the group decided on one of them, and laid plans for beginning work on it at the next meeting.

(*The trainers felt pleased with the meeting. They saw that the group had not run away from the problem, that the decision had been its own, and that the group's own leadership had begun to emerge. The trainers believed what they had seen, but still had some question as to the depth of the commitment and the extent to which the group had made it in order to avoid the pressure of the "authoritative" interpretation.*)

MEETING V

Jim opened the meeting by asking someone to recall for the group what the plan was. (*This was a test of commitment: If the plan had been made merely to escape the stress caused by the interpretation, then it was likely that no one would remember the plan very accurately. If, on the other hand, the plan had been an object of concern in its own right, then the group would remember it and forge ahead to complete its details and put it into operation.*)

The plan was quickly recalled by several members of the group, and at Jim's question as to what further details needed to be decided to put the plan in operation, the group quickly made several decisions. The plan was to break into five subgroups and have each subgroup decide on an "emotional role" to be played by one of the members. Each subgroup would then select one of its number and coach him on how to play the role. The roles decided on in the various subgroups included: a stereotypic "nondirective" person; a hostile person with feelings of always being "left out"; a person who cannot stand conflict and tries to conciliate; an assertive, unconflicted "strong" personality; and a person who believes in rationality "no matter what."

The five role-players discussed the question of how many more meetings the training group would have (beyond the minimum scheduled meetings). The scene was quite hilarious at points, and everyone had a good time. The scene went on for twenty minutes, and three of the players obviously enjoyed their own expression of very aggressive feelings.

After the coffee break, Jim took over, very much as a teacher might, to guide the group through the analysis of the emotional phenomena they had seen. (*Jim felt that the analysis of emotional dynamics is potentially dangerous because of possible exploitation for so many individual needs; he was determined that the analysis be objective and not become the vehicle for expressing feelings against others.*) He explained that talking about the emotional expressions of individuals should be done with some safeguards, that the roles might or might not represent the "real person" acting these, and that it was better to assume that it was all acting guided by the briefings given in the subgroups. Jim then went to the board and listed the following headings: "What We Saw" and "Speculative Interpretations." He then asked who the group wanted to start with; they named a person, and the analysis began. Jim carefully maintained a clear distinction between "fact" and "guess," and kept the discussion on each person going until the group had produced several alternative interpretations. (*This was done to make it impossible for the group to think they had really identified the role and the person.*) Then the role-player was asked to react to the group's speculations: he could reject all of them, support one or more, or add other ideas of his own. (*This was done primarily to allow the role-players to work through any uncomfortable feelings the group diagnosis may have produced—they could have the last word in a designedly open field.*)

This meeting was highly gratifying to all concerned. Individuals got out of it a good deal of relief for their own anxieties—at least as related to the training group situation—and the group as a whole felt "strong" and ready for anything. People stayed around for half an hour after the meeting, talking excitedly in small groups, and the typical feeling was probably best expressed by one person in response to the comment, "Gee, we didn't make any plans for next time!" The reply was: "We don't need to!"

MEETING VI

During the week between meetings, Jim did little thinking about the group. He had shared in the general feeling of strength and relief, which may have been heightened for him because of his recognition that he had taken a chance in confronting the group during Meeting IV. In effect, there were forces in the situation and in Jim that made him tend to overestimate the strength of the group: with part of his being, Jim wanted to believe that the group was now full grown, capable of solving all their problems on their own and without his help. On the other hand, Jim also knew that this belief was 'not realistic; that it could not be realistic. And, Jim wanted to believe that the group needed his help. If they did not need his help, then he would have no role, no place in the group, and, at a time when the group has become cohesive and rewarding, it is bitter to feel not needed. These attitudes, and Jim's real ambivalence of feelings about the group, are, of course, "unprofessional"; they are reflections of problems in Jim. Jim lost sight of his job as trainer and became concerned about himself, and this stood in the way of his being objective and helpful to the group.

Meeting VI, then, presents the picture of a group trying to identify a new problem to work on, and for which to plan activity, at the same time that they are struggling with the anxieties communicated by their leader; and, because they are the leader's anxieties, he is unable to help them—they have to operate in the face of confused emotions about their leadership. One can see that the problem for the group would have to be the nature of leadership and the relations between leader and group. (This is a legitimate problem, and one that nearly all training groups need to deal with. But it is unnecessarily difficult to study the problem when the question of leadership revolves around the trainer. It is much better to have the problem arise in terms of conflict within the group, rather than between the group and the trainer. When the conflict arises out of the efforts to establish and develop the group's natural leadership, the trainer can help by clarifying feelings well enough that the problem can be seen and worked out before the emotional intensity and frustration become so great as to disrupt work. Much uncontrolled frustration and depression present the group with a major problem, and any way out will be sought—even having a wild party. This is all very interesting and absorbing, but it makes practically no contribution to the goals of training.)

Jim opened the meeting by telling the group that it appeared to have completed (to the extent that it needed to, at this time) the working out of the anxiety problems associated with the expression of feelings. He went on to suggest that the group had pre-sumably developed considerable strength in the process, but that it would have to wait to see what happened to be really sure of this. He then proposed that the group's task now was to plan its next activity; and he said he felt that the group could do this pretty much on its own, with his participation only as a resource person.

(*Jim's comments, and the way he made them, communicated to the group the double feelings both that Jim had confidence in them and that he did not have; that he would help them, but only on his own terms. It should be noted, too, that the task of the group, to plan a new direction based on a new analysis of problems—and following a very successful day which they could hardly repeat—was a larger task than any so far tackled by the group alone; and everyone knew it.*)

The group discussed plans in an unfocused and desultory fashion for about an hour. Many insightful contributions were made, but they were not picked up and reacted to. There was growing bewilderment and increasingly strong efforts by individuals to help the group; as these efforts increased and failed, uneasiness and frustration grew.

(*The group was struggling with the experience of an emotionally confused and ambiguous relationship with the trainer. They did not know whether they were being rejected or not, and for the first 20 minutes of the discussion there was no awareness even that there was a problem of this sort. There was probably some resistance to admitting the possibility. It is probable that a clear rejection by the leader, particularly if he had then walked out, would have been easier to deal with.*)

The break for coffee was an explosion of the total group into smaller fragments. (*There was a great load of feeling to share, but it could not be shared in the total group.*) During the break, Jim tried to collect his wits. He could see quite clearly what had happened. At the reality level, he saw that his judgment had not been mis-taken: he had correctly judged the group's emotional unity re-sulting from the last meeting. But he had been completely blind to the fact that they did not have the skills required for complex problem-solving without his help. He put it to himself that he had gotten into the trap of confusing the emotional conditions present for growth with the ability to perform; he had felt the motivation and overlooked the lack of ability; the group did not have any secure, consciously applicable set of agreements on how to operate by themselves, and there was no independent natural leadership ready to take over. Many individuals were trying to fill the vacuum produced by Jim's abdication, but until the group accepted the fact of his abdication they could not accept the efforts to fill the vacuum. And Jim had not clearly abdicated.

After the coffee break, Jim suddenly came in strongly in an effort "to help the group understand what was going on." What the group perceived was an unaccountable change in Jim's role, and a violation of the definition he himself had given. (*The problem began to be acted out as a difference of opinion between those who had tried to take responsibility earlier and now felt that responsibility was being withdrawn from them by Jim, and those who wanted Jim to "take over" and pull them out of the difficulty. Neither group was happy about this and because of Jim's ambiguity and, now, his inconsistency, the problem could not be discussed.*) Several approaches, which probably would have been useful if there had not been the underlying unresolved problem of the group's relationship to Jim, were attempted. Thus, at one point, the group listed hypotheses on the board to account for their troubles, without a word about leadership. From time to time individuals would try to test one or another hypothesis, or to suggest procedures by which the group could test them. There were one or two efforts to state the problem directly in the form: "We don't know whether to trust Jim or not because he is inconsistent." At this point, Jim explained his incorrect diagnosis, but this added fuel to the anger of those who still felt that had they been given a little more time and less interference by Jim, they could have led the group out of its difficulty.

(*It seems clear that Jim's second diagnosis was correct. The strong efforts of individuals to provide leadership, and even the depth of the group's frustration showed that it wanted to tackle the problem, rather than to run away from it; this also showed that the group had high expectations for itself. On the other hand, the fact that the group could not make use of some very good suggestions indicates that the group had little technical competence as a group in analyzing problems and building on contributions; they could not use work as the way out of frustration. The development of the needed competence was blocked by the fact that the emotional confusion was in the area of leadership. And the lack of competence was what made Jim's behavior and attitudes such critically aggravating factors.*)

MEETING VII

Jim opened the meeting with the suggestion that probably a lot of "outside conversations" had gone on since the last meeting, and possibly it would help the group to form subgroups and exchange ideas. He called this quite frankly a "fishing expedition." (*The trainers were now convinced that the group would not be able to move until there had been a sharing of feelings among the members so that individual feeling, differently mobilized in each person, could be found acceptable, and, through this, the group's anxieties reduced to the point where work could begin.*) The group accepted the suggestion, and five subgroups formed. Discussions seemed subdued. Each subgroup reported to the total group, and each report showed a different way of reacting to the group's problems. The differences in the reports were closely related to differences in the personnel of the subgroups. The reports consisted of:

1. An analysis of the problems of last time.
2. A statement of principles so far learned plus suggestions of problems to be investigated.
3. A list of questions apparently related to the problem of control of the group.
4. A plea for help.
5. A listing of member "roles" needed for the group to progress.

(*Behind these reports were various assumptions about how to perceive the group's difficulties. Thus, report 1 assumes that the trouble is in the nature of the interaction among members, group, and trainer; report 2 assumes that the trouble is lack of ability to apply knowledge; report 3 assumes the problem to be one of leadership; report 4 assumes that the group is too "weak" to solve its problems; and report 5 assumes that the problem is that individuals do not know how to behave. All of the reports had some element of truth in them, but none really got down to the basic problem: the need for sharing feeling, reducing anxiety, and resolving the emotional ambiguities in the relationship between group and trainer.*)

The reports were given in a "dead-pan" manner, and there were no reactions to them. The fishing expedition was a failure. Presumably the same factors which had prevented the emergence of natural leadership among individuals were also working to prevent any subgroup from making a bid for leadership.

After desultory conversation in the group, Jim decided to try to get the group into contact with reality. He pointed out that one thing many of the remarks seemed to be saying is that the group is in a state of confusion; he asked whether everyone felt that to be true. There was general agreement, shown in nodding of heads and other gestures of recognition. The group did not pick this up so, a few minutes later, Jim plunged in again, reminded them of the agreement about confusion, and said that the way out of confusion was through clarification: what were the questions needing to be clarified? Several questions were asked, and Jim wrote them on the board. Out of six questions, five dealt with Jim's role, and his hopes, consistencies, and feelings about the group.

Jim felt that the group, concerned over its mixed feelings with regard to its own leadership, was projecting the entire problem onto Jim as the symbol of leadership. However, he also felt that to some extent the questions were realistic, since Jim's troublesome behavior had precipitated (but not created) the present circumstances. Jim, therefore, decided to answer the questions. He spoke primarily of his conception of his role of trainer, and tried to define it as something different from the role of leader, so as to once and for all open the way for the group's leadership to emerge. Jim also explained why he had shifted roles during the last meeting. At this point Jim's anxieties were back under control, and the communication was very relieving to the group. There was a feeling that the relationship between Jim and the group was now patched up. (*Probably if this could have happened at the middle of the last meeting, it would have been completely effective. By now, however, there was the additional anxiety problem of the relationships between each individual and the group—anxieties which arose in response to the frustration the individuals had experienced in trying unsuccessfully to fill the leadership vacuum.*)

Jim's comments cleared the way for an unconflicted competition for leadership. He had said in effect that he did not wish to be leader, and that he would support the group's efforts to provide its own leadership. Individuals and, later on, cliques began to make strong efforts to get various plans accepted in the group.

None of these sorties was successful; each would gather momentum until the plan was revealed clearly enough that action could be taken. Then it would die, and the group would start talking about its need for control, for more enlightened membership behavior, for a definition of its long-range objectives. At one point toward the end of the meeting, the group was swept by a contagion of self-doubt, and there was some effort to pretend that the whole experience to date had been a failure. Jim tried to get behind one plan, and his support was no more successful than anyone else's had been.

(*It seems probable that a rather interesting shift had occurred in the form of the problem. At first, the problem had been felt as a competition for leadership, imbedded in anxieties about taking over responsibility, in a situation whose requirements for the taking of responsibility were not clear. Now, following Jim's comments, it became a tug of war between the desire to work and the desire to do something else, the nature of which was not at all clear to the group. The conflict was between those who were ready to work, to go ahead to make plans and carry them through, and those who were not ready for work. This appears to mean that Jim's comments had "freed" those individuals whose anxieties had mobilized around the question of leadership; but those whose anxieties were mobilized around feelings of personal inadequacy, or around their relationships to the group as a whole, still had this higher-priority problem to resolve. And, since these latter types of problems took a different form in each person, it was not possible to bring them into group awareness and give them clear definition.*)

In talking about it afterward, Jim and Jane decided that the group would not be able to go to work until there had been enough sharing of feeling for individuals to recognize that others had the same sense of discomfort that they did, the same problems of relating to the total group. (*If people could discover that these feelings were shared, they would then feel that the group was behind them in their efforts to work problems through. It seemed to Jim and Jane that the problem of definition of member role, which had been shelved while the group devoted almost two meetings to the problem of their fears of emotional expression, had now returned full force under the provocation of the more specific difficulties about leadership.*)

The trainers were undecided as to how to get this sharing of feeling to occur. They had used the fishing expedition in a vain hope that the subgroups would provide the needed permissive situation. They could see that no individual by himself could change the situation to one in which the need could be met—after all, many people had tried without success. The trainers finally felt that the best solution was to have a planning committee that would meet outside the group, returning to it with enough feeling of adequacy that its members could work in concert to keep the group working on a task. The task would provide enough clarity of purpose and definition of member role that people would be able to participate; and, if the need for sharing feeling really existed, it could occur. But no such committee had been provided for.

MEETING VIII

The day after Meeting VII, Tom, one of the members of the group, called on Jim. He said that he was very worried about the group, and that a lot of other members were, too; that they were engaging in endless inconclusive conversations in the dormitories and coffee shops; that possibly a group on the outside, if they knew Jim was behind them, might be able to come up with a plan which could be presented to the total group; and that such a "committee" could also work for the plan and increase its chances of success. However, Tom expressed considerable anxiety that this might seem, to the rest of the group, to be an unwarranted attempt at imposition by a minority. Jim told Tom to go ahead, although he also agreed that people's anxieties over their own roles might well be projected into the charge that the outside group was trying to "run things." Tom was troubled at the thought of leading such an expedition, but after finding that Jim was able to accept his hostility (expressed under the guise of reporting to Jim a couple of scurrilous and false rumors about him), he felt better about going ahead.

Tom opened the eighth meeting with a long, sober, introspective analysis of the feelings members had had in and out of the group since the trouble began. This was not easy for Tom, and he communicated a good deal of anxiety about the report he was making. The guilt felt by the committee in operating apart from the total group was clearly communicated. The germ of an idea for a plan was also presented, but not as something the committee felt strongly about.

The first reactions to Tom's report were highly individualistic. They ranged from deep resentment to gratitude, from wishing to deal with the report to wishing to ignore it completely. The members of Tom's committee operated very effectively and securely to keep the group pointed toward either of two tasks:

a) reacting to the statements of feeling that had been presented, or
b) working toward the development of a plan for action

(*Jim felt that the particular comments made by individuals represented their ways of reacting to their confrontation with reality; in other words, Tom's comments were recognized as valid, even though there were differences among individuals in their readiness to deal with awareness. If this were true, Jim felt, the group would need to break into more permissive subgroups so that individuals would have a better chance to work through the problems that this awareness had brought.*)

One member of the committee suggested that the group break into subgroups. No reason was given, although the committee's rather vague plan had involved breaking into subgroups. The suggestion was taken up immediately. There then remained the problem of deciding what the subgroup task would be. This was settled in a very few minutes in a way which took account of three major suggestions made by the group: one subgroup to work on goals, another on methodology, and a third on how to integrate subgroup thinking into the total group.

(*At this point, Jim knew that the group would pull itself out of its frustration. The fact that the decision could be made so readily showed that Tom's report had, as hoped, restored the feeling of "togetherness," that anxieties about feelings were now reduced by the recognition that individuals "were not alone." The fact that the question of what to discuss could be settled so quickly showed that it was a relatively unimportant question— the topic was the excuse, not the goal, for doing what everyone felt needed to be done. The fact that the subgroups, for the first time, had different tasks and that these were along the lines of expressed interest showed the extent to which the group was willing to accept individual differences, and that this probably meant an acceptance of the group's own natural leadership.*)

The groups promptly settled down to their tasks, allowing

themselves half an hour. The discussion was sober, and participation was well distributed. The groups kept to their work, with little digression into individual emotional expression. (*This worried Jim and led him to wonder if the groups were not really fleeing from the need to work through individual problems; but it soon became apparent from the wide range of suggestions in each group that individual emotionality was being integrated into work, rather than evaded. It also became apparent that it was not so necessary to deal directly with individual's anxieties (as would be done in therapy) as to re-establish for each individual the feeling of place and "belongingness" in the group. This was best done through co-operation in work rather than through expressions of individually centered emotion*).

The subgroups worked for the full half-hour. Each subgroup kept track of the time, and each subgroup, without prodding, took the initiative in preparing, as a group, its report. Coffee was ready by the time the first subgroup had completed its task; it broke up for coffee, but the others kept working until they felt satisfied with their reports. (*These actions were felt by Jim to indicate that the subgroups were demonstrating a high degree of maturity, as groups. Jim wondered what would happen when the reports were presented. If the breaking into subgroups had been done in the spirit of running away from the frustrations of the total group, Jim expected evidence of intersubgroup hostility to appear in the reporting; if, however, the subgroups formed out of an understood and direct need of the total group, Jim would expect the reports to be straightforward, objective, and useful to the total group. The sense of responsibility shown by the subgroups toward the total group was reassuring and led Jim to feel that the total group would be able to incorporate and assimilate this strength into its own operation*.)

The subgroup reports showed a high quality of thinking, and enough comprehensiveness to indicate that everyone in the subgroup had contributed, and that they had worked together effectively to clarify each other's thinking. The group was pleased with the reports, which seemed to be providing a consensus rather than provoking argument. It was as if the group was speaking in three different voices through the subgroups, rather than listening in parliamentary fashion to the reports of three working committees.

One of the reports outlined a four-step plan for next action, and this was accepted as a good plan. The first step was to ask Jim for his analysis of the growth of the group; next, to study this interpretation as the basis for making the principles of group operation more explicit; next, to set up some "back home" situations in which to test the principles; and, finally, to review various techniques of group work and discuss the sorts of situations in which they would be useful.

During the last few minutes, the group was reminded of the questionnaires (a repeat of the one used the first meeting) to be taken next time. The group quickly decided to come a half-hour early so as not to take too much time from the meeting.

The group took time to compare its feelings now with its feelings at the beginning of the meeting. The initial feelings of anxiety seemed very far away and, to some extent, unaccountable, as if the group was trying to forget the emotional travail as quickly as possible. The present feeling of well-being and adequacy was shared by all and could not be missed.

(*Looking back on the day, Jim and Jane felt that Tom's subgroup had been largely responsible for the remarkable recovery of the group. They analyzed the effects of the subgroup as follows:*

1. *It relieved some of the anxieties other subgroups had felt in meeting outside the total group, even though some resentment was stirred up in people who had consciously repressed, in the interests of "group unity," the impulse to report the deliberations of "their" subgroups.*
2. *It spoke for the feelings of most individuals in the group. The introspective analysis of feeling, and the anxieties that went with the analysis, rang a bell for most of the group. They recognized Tom's feelings as their own, and they identified with his anxieties in bringing these feelings out into the open. As the group listened in almost breathless silence, they knew that they, through Tom, were sharing with each other.*
3. *The members of the subgroup acted as a team to provide the leadership which the total group had needed so sorely.*
4. *The leadership was provided in such a way that anxieties over natural leadership were reduced rather than increased. The team gave the others a model— it removed the last doubts that members could provide acceptable leadership to the group.*
5. *It is possible, also, that in some inexplicit and subconscious way the total group recognized that all the members would have to have some of the same quality of experience that the members of Tom's subgroup had had. The ease*

with which the subgroup members assumed leadership promised a reward for others who would follow in their footsteps. And the contributions of Tom's committee very much reduced the ground that subsequent subgroups would have to cover.

Jim decided that to all intents and purposes the course was now over. In trying to guess what would happen next, he conceded that there would be much interest in his report next time, but he felt it unlikely that the group would "pick it up" and discuss it very much. Jim asked himself what possibilities remained for the group:

a) It had satisfactorily dealt with the major group problem of the last three weeks.

b) It had no demands (e.g., for action) from the "outside" that it had to meet.

c) The most likely possibility seemed to be that it could now become an instrument for individual need-meeting. The individual needs would be mobilized by the fact that the network of interpersonal relationships involved a feeling of "closeness" among members—an opportunity for intimacy, perhaps; and this would be a problem for some and a challenge to others.

Jim felt that the interest in his interpretations—really a request for him to "tell all"—was made possible by this new feeling of closeness; that it was an act through which Jim, in giving up to the group his special knowledge or secrets, would now become one of them, a member on equal terms with the others. But Jim also felt that the present well-being of the group would make possible considerable objectivity in thinking about their past experience; and that they were in a position to assimilate and understand the meaning of many ideas which previously would have eluded them. But the question was, would they be motivated to learn?

MEETING IX

Some people arrived a half-hour early, as planned. Others arrived at the usual time, and a few were late. They filled in the research questionnaire—the same one used during the first meeting.

The group was eager to get started listening to Jim's interpretations, and impatience was felt by some toward the slowpokes. Jim and Jane had had their material dittoed in two documents: one, a descriptive log of the meetings; the other, their interpretations. The group decided to read the log first, and then have Jim hit the high spots of the interpretations. Then, they could read the detailed interpretations with a better idea of the major themes to look for.

When they had completed their reading, Jim gave a 20-minute, off-the-cuff set of impressions. He organized his statements around the theme of group growth, and tried to indicate the way in which the various events contributed to the development of the group. He was candid about his part in the difficulties during Meetings VI and VII, but he focused on their growth-stimulating aspects rather than on the feelings of discouragement. (*From the comments that followed, Jim judged that the notion that a group can grow even while frustrated and discouraged was a new revelation to some and of resentful contention for others. The questions asked of Jim were not taken up by other members, and this confirmed Jim's hunch that the completion of his report might usher in a period of essentially individually oriented need-meeting.*)

The coffee break took longer than usual, and discussion was happy and animated. A few individuals compared notes with others; they were concerned with reactions of which Jim's report had reminded them; two other knots of people seemed to be discussing existentialism and dog raising.

There was much good-humored resistance to coming back to the meeting table for the last half-hour. There was certainly no sense of urgent business to be done. The group was not in the mood to work; equally, it was not in the mood to undertake the slight amount of work required to agree explicitly not to work. What the members did, then, was to listen for about twenty minutes to a rather abstract conversation by four members. But eventually there arose the realization that this was no good either: they were being denied the gratifications of the coffee buzz groups and were not getting the satisfactions of group accomplishment. Two private conversations were going on quietly. (*The fact that the "pairers" felt that the group would permit this has special significance as evidence of the close interpersonal feeling in the group.*)

One person called for clarification of goals so that all could participate, and the group fell into a review of the next steps of the plan—presumably to be carried out next time. Jim pointed out that the effort to arrive at "principles" would be unrewarding except in so far as individuals could clarify ideas important to themselves. He also said that he believed that probably each individual had one or two questions he would like to have cleared up at the next (and last) meeting, and he suggested that the group begin the next meeting by compiling these questions, and then talk directly about them. No decision was reached regarding Jim's suggestions.

(*Jim felt that he, as trainer, probably should have called the group's attention to the fact that the last half-hour's work was not really work. But then he felt, why bother? He had rather enjoyed, as a new member, participating in the group's enjoyment of itself.*)

During the week preceding the tenth (and last) meeting, each individual began to try to adjust in his own fashion to the ending of the group. One person called a meeting to study one of Jim's articles; presumably those who attended wanted to prepare themselves to make the most of their last opportunity to learn from Jim. Another began reading everything he could in an effort to understand the rather dramatic changes that had occurred in his relations with some teen-age groups he was supervising; he also found an opportunity to tell Jim about these changes. Rumors came back to Jim that a movement was under way to request an eleventh meeting—and possibly more.

(*It seemed to Jim that the character of the group's outside activities had changed. Previously, individuals had banded together in unfocused bull-sessions for the purpose of dealing with rather diffuse feelings. Now, there was a direction in the activities, and the direction depended upon the individual. It was as if each person was trying, in a work-oriented way, to do whatever he had to do to adjust to the termination of the group. Jim felt that many individuals would have different wishes about how time should be used at the last meeting.*

When Jim thought in terms of the group as a whole, he felt that certain points were relevant, even though he was not altogether clear as to how these fitted together: first, the group had no compelling emotional conflict or anxiety which they would be motivated to deal with. Second, the group could not accept "just doing nothing" (e.g., turn the meeting into a social one) because this would be a serious violation of its concept of itself as a group that "grows." To not work would be too threatening. Third, although the group seemed secure and adequate, there would still be a wish to avoid the difficulties of a completely unstructured or ambiguously defined situation; the individuals would probably desire to work on their last day, but not to be frustrated by the work. This seemed to indicate reflective work rather than work on group process. Fourth, reflective work was also in line with the group's expressed wish to formulate principles. In other words, although the group had achieved emotional "closure" at the end of Meeting VIII, it still had to sort out its thoughts before it could achieve a sense of intellectual completion. Fifth, there was a feeling of interpersonal warmth in the group, a strong sense that individuals (whatever their personal motives might be) do "speak for the group." Sixth, Jim felt that there was little or no anxiety about leadership in the group: any leadership that could help to get the job done would be acceptable.)

MEETING X

Jim opened the final meeting. He said that probably there were various different things that people wished to see done before the course was over. He suggested that these wishes could be the basis of an agenda; he then asked the group for them, and wrote the different requests on the board.

There were eight requests, and they fell into three categories:

1. Reporting on the research and on a meeting some members had had the previous night.
2. Sharing ideas about what the experience had meant to them.
3. Clarifying further ideas about emotionality, work, growth, and applications of these ideas to other groups.

The categories were quickly agreed to. Jim felt that if the reports came first they might contribute information useful for the subsequent discussion, and he arranged the categories accordingly. (*He also felt, but did not say, that the group could use the individual reports to help discover how to delimit the discussion of principles.*)

The first report, on the research, was "followed up" into implications for what sort of leader would be most effective for what sort of group. The second report, on the previous night's meeting of 11 members of the group, dwelt mostly on the process problems encountered and solved by the subgroup. It was reassuring to the class. The success of the subgroup, rather than being a threat to the others, was shared by the others—it was their success, too. To get ready for reporting on "what the experience meant to me," Jim suggested that people write their reports first, and then select the one or two most interesting points to tell the group. He also said he would like the written statements for his own use in studying the group. Assent was expressed by a few people, and paper was passed out. The writing went on for 20 minutes; then Jim called a halt. (*The group's hard working on this self-analytic task reinforced Jim's feeling that members would have a heightened concern over themselves and would behave individualistically in seeking their conclusions from the experience.*)

The writing done, the group decided to "go around the table" to hear from each person—provided it did not take longer than 15 or 20 minutes. The group seemed "uninvolved"—neither eager nor denying. The reports began. The third speaker said the experience was a failure. (No reply beyond a murmuring.) Another speaker said his whole pattern of behavior had changed. (No reply.) Ideas, conclusions, unresolved questions—all were expressed; and without replies. There was attentiveness without tension, receptiveness without reaction, thoughtfulness without expression. It was as if each person were listening, not to someone else, but to himself; no shocks, no surprises, but quiet, steady interest, as in listening to music. The speakers were objective and controlled, but they also expressed feeling about what they were reporting—no confessions, no testimonials, no effort to "have the last word," no saying of one thing but meaning another, simply sober, shared introspection.

The coffee break lasted 20 minutes, and was spent in quiet conversation.

Toward the end of the break, Jim and two others sat down at the table. The others remained in conversation a few minutes longer. Then, as if a signal had been given, they all quickly sat down. Picking from among the topics on the board, Jim suggested that the most useful to start with might be "The Signs and Symptoms of a Group at Work." Ten different suggestions were made, and it was seen that these formed a pattern. The group saw that "work" could be toward stated "achievement" goals or on unstated but shared problems of their own processes. Forty-five minutes later the discussion shifted from the subject of group phenomena to the problem of leader-behavior in increasing the efficiency of group operation. A central theme of the entire discussion—of the group's life together—was the relationship between emotion and work. The meeting ended on time with a statement by Jim summarizing the last topic discussed and also stating some of his convictions about the relationships between group and leader self-confidence.

Jim had been actively participating, and had given freely and easily of his ideas. Discussion drew many illustrations from the life of the group together. The period was one of very high-level work, and retained the quality of internal communication: the feeling that every speaker somehow was speaking for all. According to comments later, many members achieved a feeling of "closure"—things "fell into place"; and there was considerable consciousness of the fact that much of the meaningfulness of the discussion came from the long experience together, and from the readiness and need for final understanding.

GROWTH PHASES AND TRAINING

This case study presents three major phases, and the ways of working in each phase reveal different degrees of fidelity to the principles on which the laboratory method is based.

The first phase, Meetings I through V, shows a conscious and successful application of training principles. The group developed a number of skills, worked through a basic and universal emotional problem, and had considerable awareness of what it was doing most of the time. The experiences were reflected on and reasonably well understood. Presumably the learning would have implications for succeeding participation in other groups. There was, on the whole, sufficient clarity in the situation that there could be maintained a balance between emotion and reflection such that these two levels of experiencing could be integrated (e.g., could interact with each other to produce meaningful, unconflicted understanding).

The second phase, Meetings VI through VIII, presents a different picture. It was a successful growth experience, but an ineffective training experience. The failure of training stems from the fact that the group was not sufficiently able to clarify to itself what was going on. The situation was too confused for cause-and-effect relationships to emerge in consciousness, and the emotional problems were so disturbing that calm reflection was impossible. The group was preoccupied with its own emotionality, it was unable to make use of individual insights, and it was swept from time to time by waves of emotional contagion.

During Meeting VIII, the group made a spectacular recovery from the frustrations of Meetings VI and VII. This was the wish of the group, and it succeeded—and this is also the meaning of the meeting: a working out of frustration. But the group was probably little aware of what was going on. One notes, for example, that the subgroup reports, which were felt to represent high-level thinking, did not offer any analysis. Principles, yes, but these were things the experience reminded them of—not pinpointed diagnostic understandings of emotional dynamics. And the content of the reports was lost for the most part in the feeling of gratification that swept through the group as it listened.

From the experiences of the second phase, one may doubt that much was learned that could later guide the operation of the members in subsequent groups.

The third phase, Meetings IX and X, would, one might suppose, represent the golden opportunity for objective thinking and consolidation of ideas—for thinking back over the preceding experience and seeing it "whole"; or for sober analysis of the differences between this training situation and other, more typical group situations.

Meeting X pretty well satisfies these expectations. It would be rated as a valuable day of training.

Meeting IX appears to have made little contribution to training. Jim's report was enjoyed as an assurance to the group that Jim was now a member, that the group had not wasted its time during Meetings VI and VII, that what happened to the group was understandable and not uncommon. In effect, it probably contributed to the group's concept of itself as a mature group, but not to the understanding of dynamics of group operation.

It should be noted that other evaluations of this case study could be made from other points of view. It is possible that many trainers would regard the second phase not as the worst but as the best, because of the intensity of feeling and the consequently greater possibilities of emotional (and subconscious) reorganization within individuals. A therapist called in during the second phase might well have turned it to good account. And even within the framework of the method as we have presented it, the training would have been much better in the second phase if there had been individual counseling available outside the group. Such possibilities of supportive training-help need more consideration and experimental study.

WHAT DID THEY LEARN?

The target of training is, of course, the individual members of the group. The final criterion of successful training is that the people significantly improve their performance in subsequent groups. To appraise this would require careful observation of their behavior in these other groups both before and after training. In the case presented here, the graduate students in the group did not come as representatives of particular groups in need of help. They were primarily concerned with the course as a sort of professional and research training: to fit them for foreseen but generally undefined co-operative working situations.

We have three kinds of evidence to consider in assessing the training in this group. First, there were noticeable changes in the way some people participated. These changes were generally toward better control and the channeling of disruptive impulses into work—a change toward constructive rather than destructive expression of emotion. In addition, noticeable changes in skill occurred: there were attempts to apply the skills of diagnosis, decision-making, and the like at more appropriate times. Second, the research questionnaires filled out during the first and ninth meetings (actually a sorting of 90 items of self-descriptions of role in groups) make possible a rather precise estimate of change in the way individuals felt they related themselves to the group. The particular questionnaire in this study was designed to show rather basic aspects of emotional orientation to the group and to its problems of reconciling work and emotional needs. Third, there were the written statements prepared by each member during the tenth meeting. These statements give evidence of the extent to which the members thought they had changed. The members were free to write on any aspects of change they wished, and this has the advantage of showing what each person thought was important; it has, however, the disadvantage of not allowing systematic comparisons with respect to any specific changes.

The trainers studied the data rather carefully and feel that the following estimates of change during training are reasonably accurate, and that if they are in error the direction of error is toward overconservativeness. In other words, the following judgments probably underestimate the effects of training rather than overstate them.

Here is the way the trainers see it:

Of 23 people from whom data were collected (out of 25 in the group):

7 people changed their behavior in the group, were aware of changes in their behavior, and had a good understanding of their participation in the group.

3 additional people changed their behavior in the group and were aware of the changes, but did not demonstrate any very adequate understanding of why these changes had occurred or what they meant for future participation.

4 additional people changed their behaviors in the group to some extent, indicated no awareness of these changes, but demonstrated considerable insight into the principles of group operation and individual participation.

The trainers felt that the training had been effective for these fourteen people, and that the first seven had profited most markedly.

8 people showed little change, and little awareness of change; the principles they learned were stated academically: they were not "internalized" enough, presumably, to guide future participation. The changes were in the direction of talking about group process a bit more glibly, but not toward better participation.

1 person, mostly nonparticipant, ended the course full of concern over one general problem involved in his own participation. He appeared to have learned very little and to have had his anxieties aroused, although not to a disruptive level of intensity.

The trainers felt that these nine people had had the least "readiness" for the experience, had learned least, and changed least; and they certainly had participated least.

Analysis of the research questionnaires generally confirmed the impressions that the members and trainers had of the changes in members. The correlation of pre-training and post-training questionnaires is higher—showing less change—for the last nine than for the first fourteen people classified above. The nine who did not profit so much tended to be more "rigid." They tended to be disturbed by emotional expression, and they tended to be "out of step" with the greater aggressiveness and outgoingness character- istic of the rest of the group. They tended to be more resistant and in two cases there was some threat involved in acknowledging their need for training.

Of the nine who got least out of the experience, the trainers felt that five would have profited greatly from individual counsel- ing along with the training in the group; and that the three who changed but did not know it might have achieved awareness through such "outside interviews."

It is interesting to note that the course was very differently re- acted to by different members. For three or four of them it ap- peared to serve as a rather limited but effective therapy. Their friends and colleagues noted that these people expressed more warmth and spontaneity in their relationships: it was as if they had gained in acceptance of themselves and others. On the other hand, the eight "academicians" reacted to the experience pretty much in classroom terms: as a cognitive experience but not one with much emotional pull or meaning for them.

HOW THE TRAINER OPERATES

The role of the trainer is central. It requires considerable intel- lectual activity at all times to know how to stay out of the discus- sion at some points and how to come in at others. The trainer understands his job when in each situation he can consciously formulate several alternative things he might do, and can self- confidently select one as the most appropriate. In addition, he then must study the effects of the alternative selected as a key to further insights about the state of affairs in the group. The goal of the trainer is "to work himself out of a job" through helping the group take over as many of his initial roles as possible.

There are, however, two kinds of functions which probably become more firmly located in the trainer as time goes on. One of these is the provision of emotional support to the efforts of the group to experiment and learn. The group is able clearly to dis- tinguish friendly encouragement to its own development of strength from efforts to take over or "do it for" the group. There is no sense in withdrawing friendly encouragement unless the trainer thinks the group ought to spend the rest of its time working through the feelings of being rejected by the person who is supposed to help them. Under proper training conditions, the group will tell the trainer when it feels that he is being too active; but the group finds it extremely difficult to tell him when he is being nonsupportive.

I make a point of this because it seems to me that a great deal of malpractice at the present time is due to the trainer's inability to distinguish feelings from actions. Some trainers do not know how to withdraw from action without also rejecting the group. Along with this confusion usually goes some feeling of guilt in the trainer's mind at doing *anything* for the group. He feels, somehow, that to be helpful he must show that he has no faith in the group; otherwise, he suspects his own motives. The realistic faith of the trainer is that the group will make the most out of any situation he helps set up; but there is also the understanding that no group can make much out of confused situations—unless they are set up consciously as objects for study and reflection.

Besides the function of continual encouragement to the group's efforts to develop competence and understanding, the trainer has a second function, which probably becomes more pronounced as the group grows. This is the teaching function. The trainer is the purveyor to the group of a set of scientifically based understandings about experimental method as applied to group problem-solving. In addition, he must teach the group many concepts about group process that are necessary for understanding. As the group works through vital experiences together it is more and more able to assimilate information and ideas from the social sciences, and it has more and more need for conceptualizing its own experience. The trainer who does not know how to supply needed conceptual resources should learn to do so; no good is served by pretending that important concepts, developed through years of scientific study, will be germinated spontaneously by a group in the space of a few meetings.

The problem of functions served by the trainer is also the problem of desired versus undesired qualities of dependency. The trainer must learn to distinguish among the various aspects and conditions of dependency. Acceptance of certain forms of dependency on him is part and parcel of the dynamics of training, because the group's trust in the trainer is actually the source of his ability to train. In every situation, some aspects of the trainer's relation to the group involve its dependency upon him, and he must accept some of this dependency as legitimate and desirable. There are other aspects that are acceptable initially but will disappear as the group develops its own resources. Finally, there are some kinds of dependency to which the group can resort under stress as one of several ways of avoiding the responsibilities that it must take on. Even these efforts toward greater dependency should not be fought by the trainer; rather, he should help the group to see what they are doing and then encourage them to find more growth-producing ways of dealing with such situations.

Let us now try to spell out more specifically the central targets of the trainer's conscious concern during group meetings.[5]

1. *The balance between work and emotion.*—At all times the trainer is interested in the "way things are going." His basic characterization is in terms of the balance between "work" and "emotionality." He is continually comparing conditions in the group with his model of work. Group work can be seen and felt. It can also be recognized by a variety of criteria. Thus, people, when the group is working, listen to each other. The comments of each individual show that he heard and understood the previous comments, and that he understood from them what the speaker meant, not what he wanted to imagine the speaker meant. Further, people seem to know how to contribute the sort of comment which is needed. In other words, there is a clear understanding of the member role, even though it may not have been discussed. Also, there is a sense of "getting some place," a sense of purpose and movement. The goal may or may not be defined; at times it would be very difficult for the group to put its purpose in words. But there is a shared feeling about the need for the discussion, and an acceptance by everyone of that need—whatever it is. When the group is working, individuals feel free to say what they want

5. The reader is again reminded that different trainers formulate the bases of their operation in different ways.

to; they do not want to say things that are off the subject, and they freely say whatever they think is pertinent. There is a sense of leisure and relaxation, coupled with the kind of excitement that goes with significant experiences when the group is working.

The trainer knows that groups do not achieve this kind of work immediately, but he and the members themselves can tell when the group is moving toward this quality of experience and when it is moving away from it.

The trainer assumes that the reasons why the group falls short of this image is that it has problems which stand in the way and which it cannot understand explicitly, even though it may be aware of its strong feelings about them. The trainer assumes that the group is always working on some problem concerning the relationship of its members, of defining goals or roles, of dealing with individual needs, or trying to avoid anxieties or other pains that go with new insights, etc.

The signs of lost effort include: trivial conversation, apathy, unusual politeness, incoherence, too much regard for the feelings of others, too rapid talking, talking at cross purposes, individually oriented confessions, hostility greater than the situation calls for, efforts to find out what the leader wants, making long lists on the blackboard, looking up past history of the group—and a host of other symptoms of avoidance, resistance, disorganization, attack, and disintegration.

2. *The trainer helps set conditions.*—The trainer distinguishes between "doing" and "thinking" activities. It is understood that the group is to plan and carry out activities and to reflect upon the results. During the planning and reflecting stages, the trainer intervenes to test the realism and feasibility of plans, and the validity and implications of conclusions. He serves as a resource person to make the planning and reflecting effective. But in the carrying out of a plan—such as role-playing several styles of leadership, or having working subgroups, or interviewing each other, or having "free discussion"—the leader does not intervene. The purpose of these activities is to provide information about the group's strengths and weaknesses, or to share feeling more directly, or to give individuals greater scope to "act out" feelings by providing temporary escape from the difficulties of having to try

to be a group member. In connection with the "doing" activities, the trainer is concerned that the purpose of the activity be clear enough that the information, recorded during the activity or obtained by testimony of observers and participants immediately afterward, can be interpreted. In these "acting out" or "doing" activities, nonwork conditions can be looked at safely because, after all, the activities were planned to demonstrate nonwork conditions; the hostility or dependence or other expressed feelings required by the activity were under control even though they may have been expressed in an excessive manner.

The trainer is likely to be most active during the shift from "doing" to "thinking," and vice versa. Thus, for example, when work orientation gets lost during a thinking activity—and the group knows instinctively when it happens—there begins to be a push for action. The trainer tries at this point to get planning which will make the difference between an escape into doing as compared to an orderly retreat into doing for the sake of providing useful diagnostic information.

On the other hand, when the group has been acting out its conflicts through an unfocused bull-session, anxieties have been mounting; the group may hope that by continuing to flounder it will somehow come up with a resolution of its emotional problems (which are responsible for the ambiguity and, therefore, the floundering) but it knows that usually it will not. Under these conditions, the trainer may call for a thinking period to look back at "what we have been doing." The purpose, of course, is to provide a structured work task which can pull the group back together, and to work toward the development of competence and readiness to deal with anxiety. And the work task is to diagnose the problem.

The point is, simply, that the trainer is aware of two fundamentally different sorts of activity, and is concerned to get a strategic alternation of these two types.

3. *The trainer speaks to the group.*—His remarks about individuals are confined to behavior presented by design during "acting out" periods, when their purpose is to demonstrate interpersonal dynamics. The trainer, during work periods, is constantly pulling the group together by seeing all problems as group problems.

Thus, the behavior of a deviate individual is per se no problem; the problem is that the group does not know how to respond to particular types of communications. Anger or bullying of individuals is seen not as a response to the individual, but as a response to the members' own anxieties, set off by the more or less accidental behavior of the deviate. In the same way, during a work situation, deviate behavior that is disturbing must nonetheless be seen as "speaking for the group." Otherwise, why is the group upset by it? Thus, even the most obtrusive individual behavior is seen by the trainer as arising out of the group situation that all helped create, and as important only because of the feelings it mobilizes in the group as a whole.

4. *The trainer helps the group understand.*—The steering of the group into needed activities can be done through two kinds of interpretation: one is in terms of learning theory; the other is in terms of psychiatric theory. Both are based on diagnosis of the state of relationship between work and emotionality in the group.

Learning theory is useful for planning: e.g., "We have just been formulating a lot of ideas about how the leader influences the group, and it now seems to me that the logical next step is to set up a situation in which we can see these behaviors and find out if they have the effects we think they will." The concepts here are that ideas need to be assimilated through the experiences of applying them; that learning is a kind of inquiring based on problem-solving models.

Psychiatric theory is useful for diagnosis: e.g., "We seem generally agreed that we saw Richard and Henry as leaders, that they were in a sense spokesmen for the group; but they appeared to be in competition with each other, which suggests that the group as a whole has mixed feelings about the problem." The concepts here are not so much concerned with the way in which learning takes place as with describing the dynamics of the situation.

Either type of interpretation can be used at certain times. The most successful type is usually not recognized by the group as an interpretation at all. This happens when the group sees that the trainer is merely summarizing several contributions which have already been made; he is building onto the group's own sensitivities, the group is "ready" for the interpretation, and the interpretation calls little attention to itself. The kind of diagnosis that is noticed as such is the one for which the group is not "ready." The objection frequently voiced against diagnosis or interpretation is probably an objection to poor timing, or to the unconscious hostility that a person whose timing is poor would presumably have.

Another method of steering the group—particularly in early stages when it has not yet developed a rationale for interpretation, or agreements on procedure, or a sharing of feeling about leadership, etc.—is simply to suggest what seems appropriate and to ask for permission to give it a try.

5. *The trainer helps the group "grow."*—The trainer may believe he sees what needs to be done next, or the diagnosis which should be made. How shall he decide whether to speak up? There are several general policies that need to be considered.

The first notion is that an insight achieved by the trainer at a particular time may occur to someone else at the same time, so perhaps the trainer should wait.

The second notion is that the trainer should enter the discussion only when he knows what he is doing and why: this cuts down an astonishing number of impulses to talk.

The third notion is that the trainer must forever be helping the group to take such responsibility for itself as it is ready for, and this means standing aside enough to let the group experiment with new skills, including ones for which they have in the past looked to the trainer.

The fourth notion is that the training value of the experience must be protected. For example, if the group is all set to role-play a scene and several individuals start a big argument over "whether role-playing is valid," the trainer has to decide whether the resistance to role-playing means that the plan to role-play needs further discussion, or whether to go ahead on the grounds that the factors expressed as resistance to role-playing will come out much better in the scene itself. Usually the latter is the case, and the subsequent discussion adds insight in a way that dealing with the resistance directly could not. The trainer's suggestion to "wait and see" often enables the group to move into action and collect data rather than to spend its time endlessly and fruitlessly in "planning." In the same vein are the unrealistic requests for certainty: the group can be delayed indefinitely because it is not "really sure" that it wants to move. In such a case it can be pointed out that nobody can be sure until the results are in.

6. *The trainer knows his limitations.*—Every trainer has certain blind spots or certain emotional conditions in which he cannot help the group. In such cases he can explain what is called for and ask if someone will take a shot at it. Thus, when a group gets into a discussion whose real purpose, hidden or explicit, is to clarify feelings about leadership, a trainer who cannot help getting defensive under such conditions can simply state that for private reasons he feels incompetent to help and that perhaps the group had better name a chairman pro tem. Of course, if the group has already developed its natural leadership, no explanation of trainer silence is necessary unless asked for.

7. *The trainer does not try to be a "member."*—The trainer needs to realize that he is not a group member. His job is to deal with the group, not with individuals. Thus, for example, a good deal of member behavior originates in the need to find a position in the group and to deal with feelings about certain members. This should not be the source of the trainer's behavior. He does not need to establish his position because it is defined from the very start, and he does not need to be concerned over his relationship to individuals because he is stimulated only by conditions within the total group. He must be sufficiently free of personal entanglements to respond to the interactions between members, but his behavior is expressed toward the whole group.

When the trainer himself enters into debate, he is in the difficult position of trying to support a position as a group member and trying to help the group respond to the conflict which he himself is helping to produce. In effect he is trying to be a protagonist in and a commentator on the battle at one and the same time. This is an impossible position, and it is inevitably the difficulty trainers with "messages" get into. The job of the trainer is to help the group deal with the problems it encounters, but he should not be seen as part of the problems.

The rigor with which this criterion is applied diminishes as the group grows. Particularly after the group's own leadership has emerged, the trainer is seen primarily as a consultant rather than a leader, and he may now safely enjoy *some* of the gratifications of membership in the group.

Perhaps the simplest way to recapitulate the principles and major features of the laboratory method of training would be to quote the remarks with which Jim intends to begin his next training group:

"We begin here as a collection of individuals. Perhaps a few of us know some things about each other, but by and large we do not know each other's attitudes, skills, beliefs, purposes, etc., with regard to questions of leadership and participation in groups.

"During our time together we shall change from a collection to a group. We shall do this as a result of our efforts to solve problems together. The problems we shall work on will be the things we feel are problems; in other words, they will have to do with difficulties we encounter. As we work through our own problems of operation we will grow as a group; to the extent that in this process we understand what is going on we will have a learning experience which should lead to more effective participation in other groups.

"As trainer to the group, my job will be three-fold: first, to help the group have significant experiences together; second, to help the group understand what is happening during these experiences; and third, to help the group relate these ideas about its own experience to a general methodology for group problem-solving.

"Practically all my remarks will be addressed to the group and will be about the group—as if it were a single, albeit complex, organism. At first, I shall make definite suggestions to, and demands on, the group for certain types of activities. As the group learns to use the methodology of group problem-solving, it will begin to make these demands on itself. Basically, however, the demands we make will all serve two purposes: first, to keep the group in contact with reality, through collecting and interpreting information about its performance; and, second, to safeguard conditions in such a way that valid conclusions can be drawn from our experiences and that people will know in general how to participate when they wish to.

"Our theorizing will tend to be mostly about the processes of group work. We shall live our own history, but we can expect to have to deal with problems of freedom versus inhibition of emotional expression, the individual versus the group, natural versus designated leadership, and conflicts, possibly, between the subcultures we represent. In working through these problems, we shall learn to use two sets of concepts:

a) concepts of relationships between emotional and work processes
b) concepts of experimental method as applied to problem-solving by the group

"*In our working through these matters, I shall not tell anyone what to do, but I shall continually help the group see what needs to be done.* It will be up to each person to decide whether, how, and when to participate in the work of the group. He may share with the group his problems of participation to the extent that he wishes to. I hope that people will experiment with their own roles, and that each person will take the opportunity to test the sort of contributions he can make under various conditions.

"Many of you will feel a need to discuss your own participation and the meaning of your experience either with one of the trainers or with other members of the group. Such discussion can make a valuable contribution to your maximum utilization of this training experience."

More details about techniques for holding meetings which may be useful to trainers are given on pages 180–217. Chapters 7 and 8 present background for the understanding of some commonly observed difficulties of trainees. Pages 349–56 indicate conditions for resolving conflict between training and "back home" groups. The group case study, pages 322–26, is taken from a training group and illuminates the kind of decision process in which the trainer is continually involved. Some kinds of anxieties of which trainers need to be aware are described on pages 313–22. The discussion of steering the group through control of the trainer's role, pages 59–62, and of diagnosis and interpretation, pages 53–59, is directly applicable to the training situation.

CHAPTER 6

The effective meeting is planned according to the same principles that are central in all technologies for organizing human effort. In addition, a variety of techniques, useful for particular purposes, are available. The aim is to create a psychologically effective sequence of activities through which the specific aims of the meeting will be achieved.

DISTINCTIVE FEATURES

The authority of leadership in the public meeting is delegated by the audience through the act of attending, and it is reinforced by the expectancy that whoever calls the meeting will take charge. The primary target of change is either knowledge, attitudes, or readiness for action by the audience; secondary targets may be conditions to be changed, actions to be taken, memberships or finances to be secured for the host organization. The role of the audience is indicated by the leadership at the meetings, and the method of control is through the direction of activities planned in advance.

The relationship of the meeting to other groups is generally through actions of individuals in the audience who may be persuaded to try to influence organizations to which they belong.

Effective Meetings: Principles and Procedures

BASIC PRINCIPLES OF SOCIAL TECHNOLOGY

The aim of science is to describe nature and its laws. The aim of technology is to state policies by which man can control nature for stated ends. Technology is the set of ideas man uses in acting out his needs and in satisfying his purposes. As science develops and nature is understood better, technology also changes.

Thus in the days when it was "science" to assume that the gods who affect men also control stars, the technology of predicting the success of men's enterprises was based on interpreting the movements of stars. As science changed, and men and stars were seen to be independent in their actions, the technology also changed.

At the present time, science in the field of human relations and social action has developed a great deal further than have our technologies for affecting action in valid ways. The preceding parts of this book attempt to show the sort of technologies toward which science in these areas is leading us. We have discussed technological considerations with respect to community action, in-service training, classroom instruction, administration and management, and human relations training. These are, in effect, technologies in five areas of application of the science of human dynamics, by which we mean a coherent body of relevant principles drawn from hitherto "different" social sciences. Are these technologies different? In what respects are they alike? Is there a basic technology of social action?

There are certain principles which appear to be common to these technologies and, we suspect, to all technologies of social action and learning. It is our purpose to formulate four basic principles, which we think are clearly entitled to first place among all technologies of social action.

PRINCIPLE 1: THE PRINCIPLE OF EXTERNAL DEMAND

In a group, the behavior of each person affects and is affected by the behaviors of the others. The power of a group depends upon the extent to which the mutual influencing of members' behaviors is helpful. For members to facilitate each other's efforts, they must share some of the same ideas and feelings about the goal and about what is required to reach the goal. For effective co-operation among members, the most important feeling to be shared is that of "a job to be done."

The development of this feeling usually signals a change from vague longing to acceptance of demands or requirements that the group is prepared to meet. It is as if some "outsider" (the problem) had to be dealt with on its *own* terms—the actions to be taken are seen to stem from the nature of the problem itself rather than from the whim of the leader, the urgings of a consultant, or the wish to identify with action taken elsewhere. In other words, the conditions to be changed are formulated and possible actions are discussed objectively as though they existed apart from the members of the group—even though the problem could not exist if the members of the group had not had private feelings and concerns about it.

What we mean by saying that "a group has formulated a set of purposes," is that it has defined and accepted a set of demands which it will try to meet. It is in this sense that purposes are "externalized" as demands.

Basically, there are three ways in which demands can be externalized:

1. Orders from a "higher" authority which has power to reward and punish. Demands of this sort are "pressures," and the group has to devote energy and time to change its way of operation in order to meet these pressures. These pressures may be seen as reasonable or not. They are "reasonable" if the group "sees where they come from"—in other words, if they are seen as arising out of the requirements of the "situation."

2. Changed conditions in the environment, which call for adjustment by the group. The university budget cut, which affects each department; the burning down of Farmer Smith's silo; the passing of tax legislation; the rising cost of material and labor—all these things are not seen as being caused by the group, but the group has to take them into account in its own planning and operation. Such "outside" factors make themselves known as difficulties in maintaining the established way of doing things.

3. Projection of internal needs as a set of external relations to be changed. One is uncomfortable and he does something about it. To do something in any rational way requires that one think about why he is uncomfortable and what things he can change so that he will feel better. This is the classic concept of need-meeting.

Groups do the same thing. The typical citizen improvement group meets to "improve the community." The goal is stated very broadly to provide a large enough umbrella for many different people. The process of narrowing purposes and defining specific jobs is basically the problem of focusing feeling and diagnosing what changes can be made to provide greatest relief and satisfaction. Meeting of need has the quality both of learning and of taking action, because changes and insights happen within one's self (learning) and because these changes and insights are stimulated by what one does in relation to the environment (action).

In the applications presented so far, the "external demands" are of various sorts:

In classroom learning, the external demands are the requirements of a learning activity. The work of the group is to carry through activities in which their experiences will result in "significant" learning. But you do not plan significant learning, you plan activity. The teacher makes the demand that the class participate in such activities. The more effective the teaching situation, the more the response of the class is to the activity demand rather than the teacher demand, since only the former is educative.

In the laboratory training group, the external demand is the required roles that must be produced by the group. The trainer's job is to clarify "what is needed" to get out of confusion, to have useful shared experience, and the like. The group's job is to figure out how to supply "what is needed," and in this process, its members learn not only how to diagnose needs but also the experimental method as applied to groups participating in social action, a variety of skills of leadership and membership, and, probably, some useful insights about themselves as personalities.

In the management situation, the external demand is the pressures from above and from below. Any order from above has to be considered and dealt with simply because it came from above. An appropriate order represents to subordinates a kind of external demand which they can easily identify with their own purposes as well.

In the in-service training program, the external demand is the changing of the faculty's perception of its place in the community through improvement of instruction. The all-school program, which provides the basis for controlling intergroup competition (of the training groups) and channeling it constructively, is primarily one through which the school acts interdependently with other groups in the community. The community becomes a vast consumer-audience which, however, cannot sit entirely on the side lines. Members of the community work with the school; thus there is some "reality" of relationship between school and community. One is not free to think anything he wishes without any check on the process. Professional "improvement" is the legitimate basis for improved school "position" within the family of community groups.

In the community action situation, the external demand is the obligation to take action to improve one's community. It is the feeling of pressure to "get something done" which causes action to start on one's doorstep: problems at home are understood and can be worked on. The demands are seen as arising from objective problems: one works on housing, education, job opportunity —not on race relations or ideologies per se. These latter problems are dealt with as factors affecting the former, but they cannot be dealt with alone and by themselves through processes of co-operation.

In all of the above situations, there are, of course, many kinds of external demands at work. We have merely attempted to show the unique or most characteristic demand for each application area.

The meaning of the "principle of external demands" as part of a technology of social learning and action is that provision must be made to facilitate:

1. The formulation of group purposes in such a way that they are felt as demands from the outside made on the group as a whole.
2. The development of group leadership and control in its most basic terms: as the means through which the group co-ordinates individual effort to meet the external demands.

PRINCIPLE 2: THE PRINCIPLE OF RESPONSIBILITY
ASSIGNED TO GROUPS

For human beings to be able to co-ordinate their efforts, they must know "what to expect" from each other. The things we expect from each other as a result of discussion and agreement are the "responsibilities" of particular individuals. That is, each individual is responsible for doing something—for carrying out action of some particular type under some set of conditions; in other words, "responsibility" is for implementing policy. Since creativity and initiative are required, there must be sufficient freedom and autonomy for the individual so that he can act. Thus goes the orthodox argument.

So long as the work gets done satisfactorily, the above set of concepts—which may be summed up in the admonition, "Find the right man for the job, be sure he knows what's wanted, and then turn him loose"—are adequate. When, however, the work is not getting done properly, we discover that there are certain difficulties in operating with these concepts.

The most serious difficulty is that individual actions are seldom actions of single individuals; they are, rather, interactions or co-actions of two or more people. Most acts of problem-solving in social spheres are acts of communication; and what breaks down, typically, is the process of communication. If the process of communication conformed to the simple model of A talking while B listens, followed by B talking while A listens, then we might be able to see action as simply the exercise of responsibility by individuals. The fact is, however, that what A says depends on how B listens; A gets continual feedback of cues from B, and A modifies his message as he interprets B's cues. Communication, then, is more fruitfully viewed as a process within a group; in this case consisting of at least A and B.

In broad terms, the social action and implementation of policy is dependent on group standards of performance and quality, and it is through these standards that the particular capabilities of each individual for resistance, objectivity, creativity, and determination are selected and reinforced. This leads us to the conclusion that responsibilities are in fact located in groups, wherever they may be represented on a table of organization.

A second argument for the principle that responsibilities should be assigned to groups rather than to individuals is that, under these conditions, the job is defined as including a range of social interaction with peers, and this means that there is enhanced opportunity for meeting "unofficial" but highly motivating needs of individuals. The range of needs that can be met in a co-operative work situation is considerably greater than the range possible in a solitary repetitive task situation.

A third argument is that groups, under proper conditions of leadership, will make wiser decisions about matters within their competence than will any individual.

The principle of responsibility assigned to groups stands for the following included ideas:

1. Demands are felt to be on the group as a whole, rather than on one individual, although one individual may have the special role of speaking *for* the group to others.
2. The group meets the external demand through defining its meaning to the members, diagnosing and formulating problems, deciding how to tackle the problems, assigning special functions to the individuals who carry them through, and the like. In other words, the group *co-operates* to meet external demands.
3. The data required for operation by the group come from its own experience, not from the experience of only one person or from the experience of some other group. Working co-operatively is a matter of taking the relevant social facts into account. It is necessary to consider facts about the operation not just of one's self but of others, and this concern implies responsibility for all the group.
4. For a group to be "responsible" means that it is responsible *to* somebody, as well as *for* something. The responsible group has an audience which is concerned with its performance, and which is likely to be associated in the group's mind with the external demands. It is to this "audience" that the group reports its progress, and it is to this audience that the group probably looks for such outside support as it needs.
5. Individuals do, of course, have responsibilities. But these are not for implementing policy or for problem-solving action per se. The responsibility of each individual is for his own co-operation and participation to further the progress of the group toward its goals. He

acts with reference to the group both when he is physically present in group discussion and when he is acting "on his own" outside the group.

PRINCIPLE 3: THE PRINCIPLE OF INDIVIDUAL CHALLENGE
IN THE LEAST-SIZED GROUP

The central assumption of this principle is that the quality of performance depends on how one is motivated to perform, and that it is possible to compose groups in such a way that motivation is high. Such groups are the "*smallest groups in which it is possible to have represented at a functional level all the social and achievement skills required for the particular required activity.*"[1]

In general, the way to increase motivation is to help people find a wider range of "rewards" for working. This is done by defining roles in such a way that each person is, and feels he is, necessary to the group; each person has opportunity to grow on the job; each person feels secure and able to do his job.

1. All too often people know that if they just "sit tight," someone else will do their job. The way to avoid this is to avoid overlapping of functions and duplications of roles.

2. All too often people find it hard to break into a discussion, and so they withdraw. Thus they miss out on the testing of ideas so essential to learning. The solution to this is to have the group as small as possible, so that each person can have more of the group's time.

3. A small group also makes the nonparticipant more visible, and may lead him, when he does not know what the problem is, to inquire of the others so that he can see how to break in.

4. In a small group each person tends to feel a greater share of the responsibility for meeting the demand. This means that he also expects a greater percentage of whatever approval or punishment follows from the group effort.

5. A small group also can operate at a level of greater intimacy, and this means greater involvement of the members in the process of the group, and a wider range of possible need-meeting, extending into the personal domain.

6. A small group can work more informally because it does not

1. H. A. Thelen, "Group Dynamics in Instruction: The Principle of Least Group Size," *School Review* (March, 1949), p. 142.

have to make all rules and purposes explicit: people communicate more easily. This means greater relaxation, greater tolerance of individual effort, better morale, and more freedom to experiment.

7. The small group, as a subdivision of a larger group, also is likely to help its members adapt to the larger group. This is the place for tussling with the problems that cannot be discussed in the larger group; and such discussion should do much to help the larger group.

In general, if groups are composed in such a way that each person can have a larger "place" he will tend to try to move into this place. In effect, he accepts the challenge. The administrative and leadership problem is to see how to compose groups in such a way that the "place" people need is also the "place" people will have if they accept the work challenge.

PRINCIPLE 4: THE PRINCIPLE OF STEERING BY CONSEQUENCES

Our first three principles recognize the nature of a problem, the nature of interdependence of effort, and the importance that the meanings of work have for individuals. Thus are represented the social-objective, group, and individual "levels" of human effort.

Our basic assumption so far is that the purpose of a technology is to set conditions such that what happens is what is wanted and needed. We get co-operation by setting up a situation in which co-operation is the natural and effective thing to do—we never demand co-operation. We get individual motivation by setting up a situation such that individuals want to strive—we do not tell them to strive. We get good leadership by setting up situations in such a way that the group as a whole is challenged—under these conditions leadership will be forthcoming.

The technologist is a person who sets conditions. He manipulates the situation, but he does not manipulate people. A successful technologist manipulates the objective situation in such a way that people find it to their advantage to act in the way the technologist believes they should in order to meet their needs. An unsuccessful technologist manipulates the situation, finds that individuals do not know what to do or else simply reject the situation; he then tries to put on pressure, set up a system of rewards and punishments that are really not part of the job, etc.

Now actually what we are looking for is a technology that proceeds at all times with the best possible guesses and which provides for its own corrections in each situation. It is not a "correction" to make the monstrous or undignified seem respectable; a "correction" rather extends the scope of legitimate motivation and the reward to the individual for participating.

The principle by which this continuous correction or "steering" is accomplished is the Principle of Steering by Consequences. It might be called the Principle of Feedback, but I have chosen to use language which implies that conscious thought is involved in steering a group.

The principle includes at least the following associated ideas:

1. Most goals are reached by a sequence of identifiable acts, and each is the result of a process of weighing and selecting among alternatives.
2. Since the acts are related as a sequence in time, it follows that each act changes the situation in which the next act is performed.
3. Thus, the consequences of each act need to be taken into account in determining the next act.

There are two interesting implications of this logic:

1. The effort should be to take each action in such a way that it yields a maximum of information about the situation (so the next act can be planned more wisely).
2. This in turn means that taking of action becomes an application of the experimental method (of action research—to which much attention is devoted in chapters 10 and 11).

The meaning of this principle in a technology of social action and learning is that:

1. Jobs should be divided into small units so that problem-solving is actually a defined sequence of identifiable subactions.

2. The purpose of each subaction must be clearly seen, so that its consequences can be appraised (as to the extent to which it satisfies its purposes).

3. Deliberation is required following each act and before deciding on the next.

4. Part of taking action is planning on how to collect the data

required to evaluate the action, and how to use these data when they are in.

5. The entire range of consequences should be taken into account following each act. The range is implied in the above three principles: What do the consequences of this act tell us about the nature of our problem or of the external demands? What are the consequences in terms of our own division of functions and our definition of group responsibility? How do people now feel with regard to the challenge of the next step, their readiness to undertake it, their feelings of confidence about it, their possibilities of reward for trying?

6. The actions of a group have consequences for other groups as well. Consequences ramify like the spreading circular ripples on a pond. This means that other groups need to be classified according to a communication schedule: To what groups should what sort of experience be reported? And what groups are in a position, in view of their purposes, to collect useful information for my group?

Back of these principles is a deep commitment to what seem to be the scientific facts in the case: that men are interdependent. The only sense in which one acts alone is physical: some things are done in private. But the group mediates between the individual and the world of life and experience. A man's ideas of what is, what is good, what is possible, what is allowable, what is desirable—are all partly determined by the groups to which he belongs.

This whole book attempts to answer the question: How can we take account of the facts of social interdependence to live better lives? I should say that this is the major problem being formulated in politics—institutional, domestic, and international—since 1914. The principles discussed above are shorthand ways of summarizing some of the cores of ideas which are elaborated over and over in this book.

We believe that we cannot change facts: men work hardest to meet their own needs; a group which is new gets easily confused about its job; there are some kinds of decisions that a group simply has to make for itself. What we can do is to accept these things as true about ourselves, and then organize ourselves in such a way that we work *with* rather than against nature. If men work to meet their needs, then we should figure out how to set up situations in such a way that that is possible. If a new group gets confused easily, then we should pay careful attention to making facts and problems clear, small enough to be attacked, and unconfused by extraneous expression of anxiety that has nothing to do with the job. If there are some decisions the group has to make for itself, then the first task is to try to recognize such occasions when they arise.

These, then, are the technological goals.

TECHNIQUES FOR BETTER OPERATION

There are, to a person used only to the parliamentary, program-planning type of operation, an astonishing array of "new ways" in which groups can work. Role-playing, buzz groups, panels, problem census, listening teams, interviewing, polling, demonstrations, even silence periods—these terms have become part of the conversation of the group leader. And rightly so: in any art—and leadership is an art as well as a science—there is plenty of room for the creative use of new devices. We have probably just begun to scratch the surface of the mine of useful ideas for working better in groups.

There is, however, a body of past experience from summer workshops and conferences, that leads me to put in a word of caution: a technique is in itself neither good nor bad, but it can be used effectively, with little consequence, or disastrously. Role-playing out of place can be gruesome; buzz grouping when there is nothing to talk about is downright embarrassing; discussion by a panel of "experts" who have had no experience relevant to the needs of the group is simply maddening; problem censuses before people feel able to formulate their "real problems" stick them with goals they will reject later; audience listening teams with no opportunity to report back get angry, and so on. I should say that these new techniques should not be assimilated as part of the orthodoxy of a new religion, and they should not stand for "group dynamics."

If you have a job to do and know what the job is, you are then ready to talk about techniques. The critical technical questions are:

1. What is the main thing this technique should accomplish?

2. Under what conditions does it work that way?

3. What are the other things it does, too, that may not be desirable?

4. What part of the technique is "given" and what things about it are modified in accordance with each particular situation?

We shall present these techniques in the form of a set of models or snapshots of groups in action. We shall then show some of the large number of modifications possible for adapting these basic models to special conditions or needs. And we shall use the discussion as an excuse also to make a number of observations about group behavior and leadership in general.

MODEL TECHNIQUE NO. 1: ROLE-PLAYING

To the best of my knowledge, the technique of role-playing, which children employ entirely spontaneously, was adapted to use of adults by Dr. J. L. Moreno, of the Psychodramatic Institute in New York. He worked out two quite different models, which he called "psychodrama" and "sociodrama." With each of these models, he developed a rather complete and detailed rationale and language. Psychodrama, according to Moreno, is a scheme for giving individual therapy through acting-out rather than talking-out procedures. It should only be used by a skilled and adequately trained therapist, and it has no place in this discussion.

Sociodrama, on the other hand, is one form of what has loosely become known as role-playing. In general, sociodrama is for the purpose of testing ideas in advance of putting them into effect in a "real" situation. It is, then, a means for *rehearsing* action and, through subsequent diagnosis of the action, identifying various factors that enter into the situation. Sociodrama is often used in this way in laboratory training groups.[2]

All the uses of role-playing have this in common:

1. The situation to be enacted is a dramatic one, with a begin-

2. Anyone interested in these dramatic devices would find it well worth his while to visit the Psychodramatic Institute during one of the public performances of psychodrama or sociodrama.

ning, middle, and end. It is not a sugar-coated panel discussion: there is a problematic situation, with suspense and point.

2. There is no script, written line by line. The skit is developed from a consideration of the nature of each of the characters in the scene, their attitudes toward each other, toward the problem, and toward various factors entering into the problem. In effect, then, the plot is what you get when people of different sorts are thrown into a situation together. It is dramatic to the extent that these people, in their different roles, come into conflict with each other or develop some other quality of personal relationship.

From here on, the basic scheme may be modified for a variety of purposes.

Purpose 1.—To "warm up" an audience; to get "involvement."

This is a complex business. It involves such things as: (*a*) "giving" everyone a chance to share feeling with the rest of the audience—which occurs when they experience the same dramatic reactions together, much as in a regular theater; (*b*) expressing a wide range of feelings about the problem involved, so that everyone will feel freer to express the way *he* feels; (*c*) obtaining everyone's immediate interest, without a good many boring preliminaries; (*d*) communicating problems directly rather than merely characterizing them in descriptive language; (*e*) providing everyone a common place from which to start, and a "safe," because fictional, situation to talk about.

All these ends can be accomplished through role-playing if it is carefully planned and developed for these purposes. Ordinarily it can be most useful in such situations as a group of citizens meeting to consider for the first time the problems of their community. In chapter 1 this use was discussed. The procedures usually include the following steps:

1. Since this activity comes first on a program (after a decent word or two of introduction), it must be prepared in advance, presumably by a planning committee.

2. After deciding on the objectives of the meeting, the committee considers a wide range of situations which are familiar in the everyday experience of the audience, and which show the problems or issues in a reasonably direct way. One, or preferably several members of the planning committee, take responsibility

from here on. They begin by getting from the other members suggestions of people who might enjoy role-playing.

3. The potential role-players are gathered, and the purposes of the program and its various parts are explained. They are then presented with suggestions for situations, and begin to add their own. They are encouraged to think in terms of the sort of part or character they would each like to play. After some discussion of this sort, they usually arrive at the definition of a situation they like.

4. The casting begins, usually with the group as a whole throwing in suggestions as to the attitudes and feelings of the various characters. (What would our "tough administrator" feel when someone came in with this request? How does he feel about his subordinates? What are his pet peeves, his enthusiasms, etc.?) After a considerable number of "bright ideas" are in the open, people begin to see the roles they would like, and they also begin to nudge each other into them.

There needs to be some control over the casting process. People should not be chosen on the basis of friendship, or real-life position, or status. They should be chosen because the part is meaningful to them: they have confronted such situations often, and have genuine feelings about it. And people who cannot talk above a whisper, or who freeze in audience situations, or who want to act just to prove to themselves that they can, should not be invited to this meeting at all. The control over casting is, when necessary, the responsibility of the people setting up the scene. If possible they should be tactful; if not, they will have to be blunt. Such bluntness is usually acceptable as long as it is clear that the leader is talking out of concern for the job rather than out of personal anxiety.

5. The development of the skit begins. It is played through several times, and everyone makes suggestions to sharpen its impact. The temptation to load the scene with a "message" or with the point of view the planning committee may want the audience to adopt must be sternly resisted. This role-playing is for honest stimulation, not for persuasion.

6. The polishing-up process is completed. Here there are a variety of possible procedures. Some people like to establish an

order of speaking, and to decide what issues will be introduced when, and by whom. Others prefer not to decide such matters explicitly. A great deal depends upon the confidence and experience of the players. But it should be understood that this use of role-playing is a planned communication, worked up in detail and in advance; it is not a spontaneous let's-see-what-will-happen sort of activity. It may seem spontaneous, as any good play does, but this is the result of feeling the role as it is played, not the result of creating it fresh the first time. Because it is worked up by the participants themselves, it should suit their talents, and should have the kind of spontaneity we mean by the word "naturalness."

7. A day or two before the meeting, the skit should be rehearsed in the auditorium that will be used for the meeting, entrances and exits smoothed out, voice-carrying abilities tested, and the whole thing timed.

The exact forms which such skits can take are dictated by the specific circumstances in which they are used. For example, a three-day conference on school administration might be started with a few scenes in which an administrator is portrayed trying to "handle" a variety of typical problems. Possibly he could handle each situation twice, by method A and by method B, in which A is "typical" and B is "good," or in which both A and B have some "good" aspects and some "bad" aspects. Or, if a faculty steering committee wanted to launch the in-service program described in chapter 2, it might start with a classroom incident showing some teacher-pupil planning, and then follow this by scenes showing "students" from the class talking about it outside, the teacher talking about it to two other teachers, and one of the students telling his parents about it at supper.

Or, for a final and more difficult example, suppose a local League of Women Voters wants to present a program on taxation. It might start with a role-played skit of one of those family conferences in which the adolescent daughter wants a new party dress, which leads papa into giving a practical lesson on economics, from which the group gets into the business of taxation and looks for all the ways they pay taxes—and ends with the positive question of what all our taxes pay for. The difficulty of these scenes is that taxation is not in itself a dramatic subject: the drama has to come in the building up and reduction of conflict between the players, and the tax business is grafted on. But it still can make the point that we are affected by taxation, and that is a fair way to begin.[3]

This kind of role-playing is most effective when the problem is one which is controversial or threatening, so that it is hard to discuss. By simply portraying it as accurately as possible, it is possible to avoid the need to characterize it, and thus avoid as well the implied evaluations connoted in practically all use of language.

Purpose 2.—To help communicate a specific problem so people will have something "real" to talk about as the basis for discovering their own problems.

When a group of people are working toward better methods of dealing with various kinds of situations, it is almost inevitable that at some point they will get off into "experience swapping": "You know, I was in a situation like that last week. His secretary said he was out, but I didn't believe her, so I began making friends with her to prove I wasn't really out to hurt anyone, and then she. . . ." At this point, the chairman could say, "Why don't you show us, Mr. Brown? Anyone in the group look to you like the secretary you are talking about? Miss Jackson? Why not take her in the hall and give her enough facts to go on, and while you are doing that we can try to make some guesses as to what you will say and how she will answer you." Then they come back and, in effect, show the group what Mr. Brown is talking about— but they show it more as it actually might happen and less in the way Mr. Brown wants them to think it happened. It is more "real," and a much better starting point for insights, than the merely verbal description of the same events.

For setting a problem which is to be analyzed and discussed, one wants a spontaneous performance. The hesitations and embarrassments and fishing-for-words and windy excursions are all evidence to be considered in trying to understanding the dynamics of the situation. In fact, without these, the group may find it hard to get started in a discussion.

3. I am indebted to a local League group for this suggestion—they said it worked pretty well.

Following the scene sketched above, Mr. Brown should be given first innings because it was *his* experience, and he may feel that Miss Jackson did not do justice to it. It is only fair to let him tell how the *real* situation was actually far more successful, and how it was different from this scene. After that, the group will probably decide to discuss the scene anyway, not as Mr. Brown's actual experience, but as an event of interest in its own right. Thus it is removed from Brown's bailiwick, and he can enter into the discussion nondefensively. In the discussion, the kinds of questions most likely to be of value are such matters as: "Where did Mr. Brown seem to be making most headway, and least headway?" "How did the secretary, as portrayed by Miss Jackson, seem to react to his proposals?" "What assumptions did Mr. Brown seem to be making about the relationships between himself, the secretary, and her boss?"

Out of such questions, there emerges a variety of answers. And THIS is the real problem: to explain or reconcile or reduce the conflict implied by these different perceptions of the group. The next step should be the setting up of a variety of hypotheses to be studied and tested.

Another very similar use of role-playing to this, is in diagnosis of the problems the group is facing in its own operation as a group. Situations useful for this involve, usually, a leader (present or absent in the scene), members who do not get along, and several who do. For example, several teachers arrive at the night school building and find the door locked. They fall into discussion about the principal while waiting for him to appear and unlock the door.

In this situation, the attitudes of the members toward their leader will almost certainly be projected into the scene, as will some of the conflicts over leadership which the group may be having. The critical point in the discussion afterward is when somebody says: "I wonder if these 'teachers' weren't also saying some of the things we feel about our own leadership?" The most difficult problem in this diagnostic use of role-playing is to know how and when to make the transition from play-acting to the actual group. The most common mistake is for the leader to be too eager, putting everyone on the defensive by presenting an interpretation before the group is "ready" for it. The best suggestion is simply that if the group is "ready" someone else will think of the question all by himself.

Purpose 3.—To test various ways of dealing with a problem situation.

This is the commonest and, in many ways, the most generally successful use of role-playing. It is also closest in its details to sociodrama.

After a problem is defined, the group sets up a number of different portrayals of how it might be handled. Usually all the elements remain the same except for the central character who is trying to deal with the situation.

A good example of this use was in a foremen training institute. A question arose as to the difficulty of handling infractions of rules without jeopardizing good long-term relations with the men. The foremen had been forced to come to this "training session"; and were not at all sure they needed training. But when the foremen were invited to suggest a tough situation of this sort, they got a good deal of satisfaction out of posing the following problem:

"One of the best spray-painters in the division is caught smoking for the third time. There is a rule: 'Three times and you're out.' The man is a Negro, and tends to feel that white foremen are against him. He has a good record, except for the smoking, and is due for promotion soon. Everyone knows he should be promoted. You are the foreman. What would you do?"

One of the foremen was picked by the group to play the worker. Three others said they would show ways of dealing with the situation. Each of the foremen tried his luck. Two of them offered the man all sorts of fatherly advice and tried to appeal to his better nature. The third one fired him, and then explained what he would have to do to get back on the payroll, and how he might go about saving some of his past performance record if he did come back. The group finally saw that this was actually the only alternative they had.

A fourth man spoke up: he would like to show another way to handle such a scene. Invited to go ahead, he walked up to the "worker," grabbed him by the shirt front, said, "Smoking again!" smashed his cigar in his face and threw him out, to the accompaniment of obscenity and profanity on both sides. The group reacted vigorously and hilariously. Without attempting to explain the dynamics at this point, we can at least predict that from this point on the training session was not only not resisted, it was enthusiastically entered into. Both sides had been faced, and the reservations were gone.

In general, the chief procedures in this use of role-playing are:

1. Pick a typical, familiar, and problematic situation.
2. Demonstrate different ways of dealing with it, without trying to make one "bad" and another "good."
3. Prepare the audience to look for differences in the way the characters act (descriptive) and how they feel (inference, usually).
4. "Cut" each scene as soon as it has made its point or presented an adequate sample of behavior.
5. Discuss the scenes, writing on the blackboard the group's answers to the questions.
6. Check the various ideas as to how the characters felt against the testimony of the characters themselves.
7. Go from this point into discussion of the different assumptions on which action was based, or into generalizations that may be true of other situations "like" these, or into incidents in the history of the group that come to mind, or into possible explanations of why people react the way they were portrayed.

Purpose 4.—To develop "sensitivity."

It is possible to "plant" into a scene rather subtle factors which the group needs practice in working with.

For example: A surprising number of situations involve someone trying to get someone else to do something: give money, sign a petition, write a letter, serve on a board, buy a product or service, come to a meeting, pay a bill, etc. In a fair percentage of cases, the person being worked on does not comply. He gives reasons such as lack of time, lack of money, prior contribution of effort or of funds, or, possibly, lack of concern or interest. Often these actually are his reasons, but in many cases one may correctly feel that they are not his real reasons. It is thus important to learn to be sensitive to what the other fellow is really saying, underneath his excuses, and such sensitivity can be developed or aided by role-playing.

For a demonstration, pairs of people go out of the room to prepare scenes. In each scene, one person is trying to get the other to do something, and the other is resisting. In resisting, he is told to give one set of reasons but actually to be dead set against the proposal for some deeper, possibly irrational reason, such as lack of trust in the demander, jealousy of the demander's status, objections to the morals of the group the demander represents, basic unwillingness to give except as a means to personal power, some hidden but treasured slight stored up over the years, etc.

The discussion following these scenes needs to be handled with care because the group can say deeply anxiety-arousing things when it is hunting around for a "deep" interpretation. If the trainer gets satisfaction out of dissecting personalities, he should not try this technique. A good example of its proper use is given in connection with Meeting V, chapter 5.

It probably should be pointed out, to keep the record straight, that this kind of use should *not* give people the idea that they are going to be able to overcome deep resistances; it serves merely to help them understand better the dynamics of interpersonal relations.

Other uses of role-playing are legion:

1. In role-reversal, the scene is played twice, with the protagonists taking each other's roles the second time. Typical situations: conflict between worker and foreman, parent and child, white and Negro.

2. "Alter egos" may be provided as auxiliary characters who "reveal" private unexpressed thoughts of the actors. Typical situations: one man refuses to help another; this person feels fearful, hesitant, angry—but denies that he does.

3. "Consultants" may be provided to advise an actor as to what he should do next at various choice-points within the scene. Action is stopped or "frozen" while the actor discusses with his consultants. Typical situation: four consultants giving advice from four different points of view to a "leader" trying to run a difficult staff meeting.

4. The audience may be used as consultants who watch a scene, then form buzz groups to diagnose how the situation could have been played better. The "leader" is briefed by a representative from each of the consultant groups, and then replays the

scene trying consciously to take the suggestions into account. Typical situation: demonstration and training activity for a "leadership conference."

In conclusion, we should like to remind the reader that the chief precaution for handling discussion subsequent to role-playing sessions is always and forever to maintain the attitude that we have in front of us a sample of behavior to look at, but we are not competent to judge whether it is at all typical of the actual personalities of the role-players. Such speculations must be ruled out. And second, it is good policy to follow the group's lead in the discussion. If members get into a discussion of "deep" factors that may be involved, one can keep the discussion "safe" by turning it onto the question of: "What further evidence would one need to decide among these hunches?" If the group wants to discuss the scene at a seemingly superficial level, that is their privilege and probably is evidence that they are not yet ready to go deeper. Such evidence should be respected.[4]

MODEL TECHNIQUE NO. 2: BUZZ SESSIONS

The technique of "buzz groups" appears to have been invented by Dr. Donald Phillips at Michigan State University. The "Phillips 66" technique is one of breaking the large audience into small groups of six members each, having them introduce themselves to each other, and then talk for six minutes to find answers to some questions assigned to the whole audience. One of the six people acts as chairman and another as recorder; the latter reports back to the total group the deliberations of his buzz group.

There seems to be little reason for insisting that each group must contain exactly six people: this merely complicates setting up the groups. The time of six minutes also seems arbitrary: it should depend on how big or how interesting or intriguing the question is, how much people have to say about it, and how much digression they need, etc. In general, the simplest way to tell when the group discussion has gone on long enough is to ask several groups how much more time they need after they have gotten well started. An alternative is to wait until a drop in noise volume

4. The journal *Group Psychotherapy* (New York: Beacon Press) contains many articles about the uses of sociodrama and psychodrama.

shows either that the groups have nothing more to say or that they are now soberly trying to work on the problem (as distinguished from a sharing of off-the-cuff reactions). For working toward serious solutions, more formal working committees should be used, with planning for adequate resources.

The buzz-group technique has changed many meetings from passive listening seances into active, alert, and action-oriented sessions. The technique properly used can accomplish a great deal in moving the group toward purposive activity. It is highly flexible and easy to use. Let us describe the steps in a typical buzz-group situation, and then show some of the many ways the technique has been found useful.

1. First, the entire audience must be instructed very clearly about (*a*) what it is to discuss, and (*b*) what and how it is to report back to the total group.

a) The matter to be discussed should be something the audience needs and is ready to discuss. There is implied, then, a warming-up activity, such as role-playing, to get the audience "ready" to talk, and to give them some immediate experience as a point of departure for their discussion. The question may then be formulated in such terms as: What are all the things you see which might be done to improve our neighborhood? What additional examples of this sort of thing have happened to you? What might the leader do differently to improve the situation we just saw? What do you suggest as steps we must take to solve this problem? What questions shall we address to our resource person? Which of these suggested topics do you think, after preliminary discussion, is the most appropriate for us to start work on? What instructions would you like to give to our delegate before he goes to that council meeting? (It helps to write the questions on a large blackboard visible to all.)

b) The definition of the product to be brought back to the total group also can be varied: "Let's just see how many different ideas we can get from all the buzz groups"; or: Prepare one person from each group to be part of a panel to discuss in front of the group all the most important suggestions emerging from his buzz group; or: "Let's use the buzz groups as an opportunity for each person to try out his ideas in a small group, and then, if he would like to report the ideas to the total group, he will have his chance."

2. The audience is given good reasons for discussing in smaller groups. The best reason is probably the "real" one: "There are so many of us that it will be hard for us all to be heard." The audience, therefore, may properly be urged to work out a two-stage process in which everyone has his say to a few others, with each small group summarizing its findings and reporting them to the total group. Or it might be pointed out that for a controversial subject, it would probably be a good idea for each person to have a chance to rehearse his arguments in a small, informal group before presenting them to the total audience. Or again, it can be made clear that by dividing into thirty groups, thirty people can talk at a time instead of just one, which means thirty times as much discussion and, therefore, many more useful ideas.

3. If there are special roles, such as chairman or recorder for the buzz groups, the audience should be reminded of this by the director of the meeting.

4. The audience is then instructed in the most convenient way to break up into groups: for instance, everyone in the odd rows can stand up, turn his chair around to face the row behind, and then sit down. Then the audience can divide into groups of not more than eight or ten, and start discussing. The director acts with confidence as though this were the most natural thing in the world.

5. As the buzz groups begin, the director wanders around and listens to conversations from each group; he may decide that the question is not clear enough, and interrupt the proceedings long enough to restate the problem. He should also be sure that nobody is left out of a group unless he wants to be left out. But in general, the director should not participate in the buzz-group deliberations because the object is to get the *group* into discussion, not the director.

6. The director judges when the discussion is beginning to wear thin, or be repetitious, or lack interest. He may then call out a two-minute warning, and finally terminate the buzzing.

7. The total group is reconvened, and the reporting-back procedure is started.

This procedure implies the kinds of opportunities provided through buzz sessions. First, the groups are small, the people have been introduced, and the director is on the other side of the room. These factors combine to make possible a relatively free or candid expression of individual feeling, such as may be needed after an exciting or emotion-arousing presentation. When used for this purpose, adding a chairman and recorder vitiates some of the freedom by restoring these notes of formality; these roles may not be desirable.

Second, the fact that the buzz groups are unsupervised by the director or anyone else in charge means that they have to take responsibility for their own operation. In effect, leadership is transferred from the "officials" to the people themselves. This is desirable for such functions as deciding what the meeting should talk about, letting each individual discover the extent to which he is interested in proposed actions, appraising the organization's program, discussing recommendations, etc.

Thus the buzz group offers a natural and useful transition from the listening situation to the decision of each individual to act. It is an intermediate step in the movement of responsibility from the officials to the small groups to the individuals. It is this dynamic which causes meetings sometimes to change their whole action orientation as a result of the informal small-group discussions. What happens is that each individual suddenly finds that he has the role of an active participant at the meeting: his action later is merely further active participation required to get closure in the role begun in the buzz group.

Third, the fact that a lot of talking goes on at once means that surveys and polls can be taken very rapidly. The situation becomes one in which one person in each group (the recorder) interviews the other members and lists the different ideas or suggestions they have. The various recorder's lists, particularly if they are made by recording each different idea on a separate 3- by 5-inch card, can be quickly shuffled, classified, and reported back to the total meeting.

The fact that there is opportunity for a lot of talking in an informal setting also means that people have a chance to rehearse their ideas or practice skills in a reasonably nonthreatening situation. Thus buzz groups can be set up as practice sessions for recording, observing, leading, summarizing, etc.

With this much general overview of the procedures involved, we may now examine a number of suggestive uses of the technique.

Example 1.—To get a meeting started on significant problems, with the members assuming considerable responsibility.

A student club which was limping along with no very clear or significant objectives, invited Professor Thomas to tell them about "The Student's Role in Curriculum Decisions." Thomas guessed that this topic implied a wish for more active participation in determination of the graduate school program, and he decided to act on that hunch. The meeting was scheduled in an informal social room within one of the academic buildings.

Thomas arrived ten minutes early, and a few of the students were already occupying easy chairs and not talking to each other. Acting on impulse, Thomas took the bull by the horns. He walked over to the student nearest the door, introduced himself, and said: "Let's pull your chair over here. I want you to meet some more nice people." The move was made, and Thomas introduced the first student to the second and third. Then he said: "I understand that I am expected to open the meeting in fifteen or twenty minutes. When I do, I shall start by asking the group: 'What sort of things that students do probably have an influence on our graduate courses?' Why don't you three sort of discuss this question now so you'll have some good suggestions we can start with?"

The indefatigable Thomas then moved on to the next student and repeated the performance. By the time he got halfway around the room, setting up buzz groups as he went, most of the chairs were taken, so he then gave his instructions to all the others: to introduce themselves and get started on his question.

At 8:15 the groups were still going strong, so Thomas gave them another fifteen minutes, called the meeting to order, and asked his question. The answers came quick and fast. The meeting retained its steam to the very end, and its final outcome was a decision that each student would observe in the next several meetings of one of his classes the kinds of questions raised by students during discussion periods, and the kinds of answers given by the teacher. They would then compare notes at the next club meeting and try to see what sort of assumptions the teachers' answers seemed to imply about the needs of the students asking the questions.

Comment: Thomas, of course, had the advantage of being used to having students act on his suggestions, and this gave him confidence enough to experiment. The students, too, he could count on as being rather starved for social interaction—why else would they stick with an ineffectual club program? His hunch was that along with this starvation for social relations there would also be a feeling of lack of "place" in the graduate school; and that if this were so there might be a good deal of energy available for taking some sort of action.

This meeting revived the club for a period of several months. It then subsided into its former lethargy, presumably because its need was satisfied by the making of a gesture or because it lacked the leadership skill required to build on its own experiences. Several of the club members enrolled the following quarter in one of Thomas' classes.[5]

Example 2.—To set up the agenda for a meaningful learning experience.

One evening at 7:30 P.M., "Red" Fredericks phoned Mr. Garth at home. He explained that he was running a series of lectures for home economics teachers on eight successive Wednesday nights, and that the speaker for tonight, who was flying down from Minneapolis, had been grounded in Milwaukee, and would be at least an hour late. In the meanwhile, the teachers were pouring in; what should he do?

Garth told "Red" to tell the teachers just what had happened, and suggest to them that since they were all familiar with the problems the speaker was going to talk about, they might gather in small groups to formulate the questions around which they would like to have the speaker organize his presentation. "Red" doubted that it would work, in view of the inexperience of the teachers in such situations but, faced with the alternative of an hour of tedious waiting, tried it anyway. The only demurral actually offered by the teachers was that possibly the speaker would

5. This incident was reported to me by Professor Thomas and several students.

not like having questions made up for him. "Red" took a chance and said he was certain that this particular speaker would be delighted to be able to talk to questions he could be sure the audience cared about.

The buzz groups went to work in some embarrassment, but quickly warmed up, because the problems were familiar and challenging. The teachers exchanged some of their own experiences, and were quite reluctant to come back together to list their questions on the board. "Red" thought fast, and asked the groups simply to put the questions on cards and give them to him; thus they could keep on talking. By the time the speaker arrived, the questions had been sorted and arranged in a pile in order of their popularity, as shown by the number of groups asking each.

The speaker was delighted. He thumbed through the questions quickly, estimated the amount of time he could allot for each, and then proceeded to give an excellent performance, for he was sure of his audience's interest, and their responsiveness was most rewarding to him.[6]

Comment: Sometimes an airline and an act of God conspire to make clear the difference between speaker as "stimulator" and speaker as resource person.

Example 3.—To overcome a feeling of helplessness or apathy, and to redirect a group toward action.

Overcoming feelings of defeatism is something that one seldom can manage by himself, and yet which no one else can manage for him. We have seen the process occur many, many times during "buzz sessions" within large community meetings, and the meeting described at the end of chapter 1 shows this use of buzz sessions.

The people in the audience are first given a chance, through role-played problems, to acknowledge to themselves that the staged problems are theirs as well. This recognition is facilitated by the reactions of the rest of the audience; it is easier to admit things everyone else is admitting. The second part of the program gives the "facts," and this information acts in two ways:

1. It shows how large, serious, and difficult of solution the

6. Reported to me by both "Red" and Garth.

problems are—which may increase resentment and frustration; and

2. Because the problems become much more sharply defined, it increases a feeling of confidence in the possibility of doing something. In effect, the information shows the targets against which energy needs to be directed, and this knowledge makes more energy available to be directed.

The buzz sessions are given the question: What specific things can be done about the situation causing concern? After the chairs are rearranged and people have introduced themselves, the conversation becomes lively. The first subject of discussion almost invariably involves things people feel angry about, and not the assigned question. These things usually include community conditions (overcrowding), personal complaints ("How the neighbors' kids tear up my petunias"), and anecdotes ("How I tried to do something about it but nobody would help"). All this, and more besides, finds expression *before* the groups can start thinking constructively about specific behaviors or plans.

When they finally get going on what can be done, the list grows rapidly, with plenty of excursions into side issues. When the groups reconvene and share their lists with others, there is great social reinforcement and strengthening of the forward-looking attitude, and the reorientation from defeatism to optimistic determination is largely accomplished.

Comment: This illustration reveals the peculiar and unique usefulness of the buzz session: to provide opportunity to "blow off" enough steam that one can get to work—or, to be more precise about it, to give people a chance to reduce some of their anxieties so that they can direct energy into trying to better the situation.

The kind of transition described above would be most unlikely to occur under the guiding hand of the chairman and within the total group. But it is a kind of transition people in general try to make, for it is driven by the need for adequacy. The usual groupings which arise spontaneously after the boss dismisses a staff meeting, or following a meeting where the PTA chairman acted arbitrarily—these informal "gripe groups" help individuals meet needs to reduce their anxieties. Having a meaningful work question and knowing that a report is expected enables people in small groups to discipline their cathartic expression and rather rapidly turn energy into constructive channels.

Example 4.—To test a set of ideas, and to increase communication between speaker and audience.

A simple but effective illustration of buzz sessions in this connection is described by Stuart Chase in *Roads to Agreement*.[7] The audience of about 310 people was divided into six sections, and each section given an assignment *before* Chase began his lecture. The "external" demands were to improve *Roads to Agreement*, then being written, and to improve training methods used at Bethel and "back home" by the delegates. The six specific assignments were:

"Group 1 was to listen for implications in the lecture which might prove useful to Bethel.

"Group 2 was to listen for ideas which the speaker should elaborate later, things he had slurred over. . . .

"Group 3 was to listen for high points of the talk, and later emphasize them to the audience.

"Group 4 was to think about additional data for possible inclusion in Chase's book.

"Group 5 was to listen to his description of areas of human conflict and see what areas could be added.

"Group 6 was to concentrate on suggestions for making the book more readable. . . ."[8]

For these demands to be met, it was clear that Chase would have to make clear the purposes of the book, summarize its contents, and read the group a sample sufficiently long that they could get valid impressions of the style of the book. And it was clear that the audience would have to listen, not just give stereotypic responses.

After the speech, each of the six sections of the audience was divided further into three or four buzz groups to discuss its assignment. Spokesmen from all the buzz groups within each section met together to prepare a report for their section, and the six final reports were presented to the entire group. These six reports took as much time as Chase's initial speech.

7. New York: Harper & Bros., 1951, pp. 93–96.
8. *Ibid.*, p. 94.

Comment: Was the purpose really satisfied? Was communication increased between speaker and audience by reducing the subconscious resistances on both sides to communication? Chase says of his feelings during the lecture: "The audience gave me a different feeling from any I had ever encountered. The words did not bounce back as they often do from a bored or indifferent aggregation; they went home, but I was not entertaining anybody. The words went home but were turned around and examined before being taken in. The audience was listening as I never have been listened to from a platform—not agreeing, not disagreeing, neither hostile nor especially friendly, weighing and thinking."[9] And the audience, on questionnaires filled in after the meeting, indicated clearly a feeling that the experience had significance for them.

The usual speaker-audience situation is one in which the audience is trying to take from the speaker something of himself: his ideas or wisdom. Possession of these ideas, however, is what gives the speaker his prestige and power. To what extent this results in speakers not really wanting to "give," one cannot be sure. It is clear, however, that the situation recognizes only one direction of demand, from audience to speaker; the demands the speaker makes on the audience for respect, warmth, adulation, or audible approval are not explicitly facilitated and are often not even admitted.

The simplest way to change the speaker situation from one of conflict to one of at least partial co-operation is to arrange matters in such a way that speaker and audience together face a set of externalized demands. Thus an externalized demand could be to improve the speaker's speech—as if it were, as presented, a committee report to be modified by the whole meeting before final adoption. Another externalized demand could be to evaluate the group's present practices in view of a set of ideas presented by the speaker. In either case, speaker and audience have a reason and a way to collaborate, and this greatly facilitates communication.

9. *Ibid.*, pp. 94–95.

MODEL TECHNIQUE NO. 3: PANEL DISCUSSION

The panel discussion is a conversation among several people, held in front of a larger group. It is one of the most abused techniques; but it can be extremely effective—provided it is properly planned and guided. There are a variety of reasons why people might make use of a panel discussion. We shall list some of these reasons, good and bad, and discuss their implications. Then we shall try to suggest how to set up and use the panel discussion technique.

Reason 1.—"Let's have naturalness and spontaneity—it gets people more interested." This is the watchword on the radio round tables and panels. When a panel *does* have spontaneity and interest—which is rather seldom—it is because it is carefully planned and rehearsed.

The notion that a panel is easy to use because "all you have to do is get a few quick-on-the-draw speakers together" results merely in a number of quick-on-the-draw speakers sitting around and talking. They may or may not say anything worth hearing or relevant to the program topic. Not having any clear idea of what to talk about, they will probably end with experience-swapping or abstractions.

Naturalness and spontaneity are the result of careful organization of topics to be discussed, definition of the point of view or role of each of the panelists, and a moderator whose main job is to help the audience and the panel know at all times just what is being discussed and where it fits into the over-all discussion.

Reason 2.—A panel makes possible the discussion of the topic from several different points of view, and, when these get into conflict, the audience gets drawn into the discussion.

A panel provides for several different points of view only if the members *have* different points of view and if the moderator makes sure that each person in turn offers his comments on the same topic. As any mediator or leader knows, conflict growing out of different points of view usually disappears when the discussants agree to talk about particular cases; to maintain conflict usually means to maintain high-level abstraction.

The conflict—the struggle between giants—which was counted

on to get people worked up, also is likely to disappear for another reason: it is bad manners to fight in public. The panelists who get into violent dispute in front of the group may actually arouse the audience's interest, but the interest will be in the personalities of the protagonists, not in the merits of the argument.

If all that is wanted is a good conflict, why not just set up a well-planned debate, in which conflict is controlled and expected, and let it go at that?

Reason 3.—Dividing up the presentation makes it less of a burden on any one person.

This is correct, and the result is a series of short speeches. This is not a discussion, and is not a panel discussion, either.

Reason 4.—A panel discussion is a good way to start discussion from the floor.

This is true when the panel discussion is planned to open up issues, sharpen questions, present ideas in a stimulating and colorful way, etc. But the panel can also kill questioning. Here are some effective discussion-stopping techniques I have seen panels use (not usually on purpose):

1. Overwhelm the audience with its vast experience, prestige, subtlety, or cleverness.

2. Exhaust the topic, giving clear and satisfactory answers to all the questions likely to occur to anyone.

3. Bore the audience so thoroughly that anyone asking a question and thus starting the panel going again will be seen by the rest of the audience as a candidate for tarring and feathering.

4. Become so cozy with each other that the audience feel like intruders and wonder if they should not just tiptoe out.

Reason 5.—A panel of well-known speakers draws a bigger crowd than does a lecture by one man.

It depends on the man.

These considerations lead to the following suggestions for setting up a panel discussion:

1. Decide what the program is about, what it is hoped will be accomplished through the program, and what sequence of parts or activities will be needed to accomplish its purposes. After this

is done, the requirements the panel discussion is to meet will be evident.

2. Consider the range of kinds of people or roles required on the panel: a civic leader, a housewife, a welfare worker, a policeman, etc.

3. Decide who to invite to be on the panel in each category, and explore with them how they would fit in and what they think they could do to help. If the exploration is reassuring, invite them to serve. If not, invite them to suggest someone else "to take their place."

4. Get the panel together for a rehearsal, and let the moderator summarize the main outline of the discussion. The panel can discuss the outline, correct it, reorganize it, and block out in general each person's approach to each point. The panel members also can decide what, if any, signals to use to get the moderator to call on them.

5. Have the moderator prepare a final outline, which will then be duplicated and sent to the others on the panel. He should probably indicate the approximate distribution of time among the topics.

6. At the meeting, have the chairman introduce the moderator (if they are separate individuals), who in turn defines the problem the panel is to tackle and then introduces the others. As the discussion proceeds, the moderator restates the questions, makes sure the points agreed upon are made, and summarizes at the end of each section of discussion. The summary should probably end with a question or two (preferably written on a blackboard) that will stimulate the audience.

7. Summarize at the end in such a way that the audience is clear as to just where the panel is leaving the major problem.

8. Have the chairman introduce the next activity, which may be one or more of the following:

a) Invite questions from the floor to the panel, in a discussion led by the moderator; or

b) Divide into buzz groups to react to the questions and then report back; or

c) Divide into discussion groups for prolonged discussion. Each discussion group may take a few of the questions, and the audience can subdivide according to interest in the questions.

d) Ask for additional questions to be added to the list the panel identified, and then use a rapid voting procedure to discover the priority of interest in the questions—in effect this amounts to making up the agenda for the remaining discussion.

Example.—To open up a big problem.

The most successful panel discussion I have seen was planned by the steps outlined above. It had to do with neighborhood conservation, and the speakers represented each of the major types of organizations or agencies interested in this problem. The outline of topics was logical:

a) What are the evidences that the neighborhood is deteriorating?
b) What are the forces contributing to deterioration?
c) What are the major ways to fight deterioration?
d) Which of these ways are now being tried, and by whom?
e) What specific things ought to be done right now, and later?

Not all the speakers contributed to all the questions. In so far as possible, they made their points by citing clear-cut illustrations from the experiences of their own agencies. The moderator stated each question, and tried to make it clear and challenging. He summarized frequently, and he sometimes made positive evaluations of the impact of the speaker's organization with respect to particular forms of action.

The next planned activity was to be buzz groupings, but the audience upset this by firing in questions and offering comments the minute the panel discussion was over. The moderator turned over some of the questions to other members of the audience whom he knew had relevant experience to contribute. For two questions, which were matters of fact the panel could not answer, the moderator asked if anyone in the audience knew the answer (and found people who did). The panel also participated in asking questions of each other and of the audience. The discussion shifted from audience to moderator to panel to audience; it became, toward the end, simply a free discussion with the moderator summarizing from time to time, and the people calling on each other.

The meeting ended forty minutes overtime when the moderator said it was almost time to go home. The chairman, capitalizing on the great interest of the group, suggested that a number of people might volunteer to become a committee to plan a follow-up meeting (which had not been anticipated). Twelve volunteers came forward, set a date for their meeting, and the chairman adjourned the session. It was another hour before everyone finally left.

Some other uses of panel discussion: panels can be used after presentations of buzz-group thinking to comment interpretatively on the various suggestions, highlighting the most significant suggestions, relating them to each other, and otherwise clarifying and organizing the ideas from all the groups. Even in an ordinary discussion situation, a panel of two observers can sometimes be used to summarize the discussion as a basis for helping the group see where to go next in the discussion. Or a panel of two or three resource people can be provided to be called on by the group at any point at which they need technical information.

MODEL TECHNIQUE NO. 4: THE GROUP INTERVIEW

This technique deserves more use than it currently gets. The group interview fits very well into problem-solving meetings of any sort; and it probably provides for the most effective use of resource people.

The group interview is simply a situation in which one person, the interviewer, asks questions of several others. He ordinarily has a list of questions developed by the group or by a planning committee, and he usually asks the same question of each interviewee in turn. A useful "house rule" for the interviewees is that they should respond to the questions only with ideas that have not already been given. To give all the interviewees equal visibility and status, the interviewer begins each round with a different interviewee.

Example.—Reporting buzz-group ideas.

The problem of presenting to the total group the results of discussion in fifteen buzz groups can be a time-consuming and boring process. Group interviewing is especially useful as a way of not only presenting the thinking of the buzz groups but also for organizing their reports and appraising the importance of their suggestions. It works like this:

The reporter from each of the buzz groups comes to the front and sits down. His job is to represent the *thinking* of his particular buzz group. The interviewer may use the list of questions assigned to the buzz groups (if there was one) as an interview schedule, or may simply ask each reporter for the most significant idea his group thought of. By a show of hands among the reporters, the popularity and acceptability of each idea can be tested. The more important ideas are written on the blackboard, both for future reference and to maintain a sense of constructive effort. Up to five questions can be handled with as many as twelve reporters without loss of interest among the larger group.

Other uses of group interviewing: Plans can be tested economically by interviewing a panel of selected people who are competent with respect to the plan under consideration; for example, a new personnel policy for use in a hospital can be examined by a panel composed of a doctor, a supervisor, a nurse, an aide, a service man, etc. Broad objectives such as "community improvement" can be broken down into component problems of the sort a club or class can deal with through the use of experts who thoroughly understand such problems, interviewed by a person who is thoroughly familiar with the resources of his group.

FURTHER NOTIONS FOR GROUP MEETINGS

Throughout this book there are numerous additional techniques suggested for a variety of other purposes. Chapter 11 is meant to help in the actual leading of discussion, as is also chapter 2. In general, we reiterate: the proper technique is one created to fit the requirements of the situation. The creative process is, however, helped by a background of knowledge and experience and ideas of what to look for, and images of what goes on, during discussion. The practical aim of this first part of the book has been to derive policies and principles for guiding operation in a variety of areas of social learning and action. These principles plus the concrete illustrations and models will, we hope, help equip the leader or planning committee with the analytical tools and insights they need.[10]

The chief omission of this chapter—and a critical one—is the recognition that a meeting is only one episode in the life of a group or community. Understanding the relevant social context of meetings is basic to proper diagnosis of objectives and to effective follow-up. The preceding five chapters develop a variety of contexts and show the kinds of backgrounds and motivations of which the planners of meetings ought to be aware. In addition, chairmen will find the content of chapters 10 and 11 pertinent to successful operation.

10. The reader is strongly urged to become familiar with *Adult Leadership*, a journal issued monthly by the Adult Education Association of the United States of America, 743 N. Wabash Ave., Chicago, Ill. Selected practical articles in this magazine could well be the subject of intensive study by small groups of leaders of all kinds of groups.

EXPLANATIONS: A PRELIMINARY NOTE

Behind every technology, every policy decision—indeed, every behavior— is a set of understandings of the nature of the processes one is dealing with. These understandings may be explicit or implicit, clear or vague, narrow in scope or comprehensive in insight. It is the purpose of Part II to present the range and kind of understandings that I believe are required for creative action.

Such a presentation involves a selection of ideas from the broad field of the social sciences, decisions about their effective organization, and policies for deciding in each case how "deep" to go. The central criterion I have used in making these judgments is the probable usefulness of the material for illumination and explanation of the technologies in Part I. It is my hope that the technologies will make the explanations more meaningful, and that the latter material will free the practitioner or technologist for experimentation leading to better technologies.

The development of Part II is based on several propositions: that the needs of individuals cause them to participate in groups; that the group as an organism exists to satisfy the purposes for which it was gathered together; that the group is influenced by the standards of the environing community and that actions taken by the group influence the community; and, finally, that through experiences in the groups of the community the individual develops and changes his pattern of needs. Thus the line of reasoning comes full circle.

More specifically, chapter 7 proposes that much of a person's behavior as a group member stems from his needs to work out his relationships to various groups and to resolve conflicts arising from the different approaches offered by different groups to the same problems of living. In chapter 8 we point out that the individual deals with these problems through processes of feel-

ing, thinking, and doing; and that the particular balance among these processes is characteristic of his personality and is learned through experiences with other people. In chapter 9 we look at the various sorts of realities with which experience deals and which we attempt to control through consciously applied methods. Chapter 10 explains the development of the group itself as a whole—a miniature society with its own standards of behavior, needs, and policies for controlling itself. In chapter 11 we discuss leadership as the means through which the group guides the creation of its culture, the attainment of its purposes, and the satisfaction of needs of individuals. We also examine some of the typical problems of leaders. In chapter 12 we attempt to make clear the notion that the operation of a group is not just a matter of the kinds of members and the competence of the leader; it is also a reflection of social conditions within the larger community. We indicate how groups contribute to the development of the community and to the state of intergroup relations.

Reference is made at appropriate points to earlier pages in which are explained or illustrated specific matters in further detail.

CHAPTER 7

We meet our needs as members of groups, and the ways we behave are the ways that we have learned in such groups. When confronted with alternative action possibilities, as in solving any genuine problem, the different possibilities are weighed partly in terms of their acceptability to our past groups—as we see them.

Social problem-solving requires the sorting out of "overlapping group memberships" and the selection of behavior in terms of the needs of the present "real" situation.

Membership: The Groups Within

INTRODUCTION

It is a matter of common observation that individuals differ in their approach to people and problems—and to life in general. We use words like "optimistic," "cheerful," "suspicious," "wrapped up in himself," "driving," "lazy." We think of some people as being out-going, making friends easily, enjoying being with people and feeling free to make demands upon them. We may think of others as being withdrawn, reflective, finding it hard to ask or receive favors. These and many other characteristics of personality are developed through experiencing. The equipment or tendencies one inherits biologically and culturally are continually undergoing modification through communication and interaction with other people. The classic studies of the differences in personalities of identical twins reared in different family environments; the studies of the change in such a relatively stable property as the I.Q. as a result of changing the social environment; the fact that people can be redirected through therapy of various sorts—such studies support our belief that people may be affected in fundamental ways by the nature of their relationships with other people.

As observers and students of human behavior, we find certain directions of change or areas of concern which most people have in common. Thus most people want approval from others; they have a hunger for "belonging" to an identifiable group; they need to feel that they can be themselves—that they can express feelings spontaneously without fear of punishment. Various students of these problems cast the list of "needs" in different forms, but most students do act as if such needs exist. And in studying individual-group relationships, there is general agreement that part of an individual's energy during any meeting of persons goes into trying to meet these private needs as they exist in himself.

We believe that people learn the ways they can use to meet needs, and that they learn these ways through group experience. But the ways in which past groups, imaginary groups, and absent groups operate in influencing behavior need to be understood better than they are at present.

As one moves into detailed study of particular situations, it becomes clear that different things in a situation are seen as problems for different people. Thus, whatever kind of leadership a group has, there are likely to be some people who accept it and work with it, and there are likely to be some others who feel uncomfortable and who spend a good deal of energy "working on" it. These latter people may attack the leadership, may try to form cliques outside the group to act as pressure blocs, may withdraw from participation, and the like. We need explanations for these things—a way to understand them so that we can deal with them more effectively.

There is also the question of direction and growth. We know that groups and people may change as a result of working together; are there certain directions of change, certain goals toward which change tends? If there are, we need to understand these tendencies and take them into account. The more we can make use of them, the greater our results will be. When we work against "natural tendencies" we have to use much more energy to solve problems because we find everyone subconsciously resisting the ways of working. The final result of working against the group is that leadership has to use more policing, it has to give up its objectives, or it has to be sabotaged or overthrown.

To discuss and learn about these problems, we need to have concepts and ideas to work with. And we need to organize these concepts not as isolated ideas but as working tools which complement and supplement each other. I propose the concept of "membership" as one of the principal tools, central to thinking about the problems indicated above. The rest of this chapter will try to develop some of the meanings associated with this concept.

We shall begin with the classic picture of how social needs develop and how, through experience with other people, the individual learns to behave. We shall think of his characteristic tendencies toward certain patterns of behavior as his "personality." Next we shall consider how tensions are created within a person as a result of conflicting demands made on him by different groups in his past or present experience. In our speculations, we shall pursue this matter into the mind of the person, and will advance the thesis that much of the determination of individual behavior is through decisions reached by his own ad hoc "internal committee." Finally, we shall suggest the directions in which individuals and groups tend to change over a period of time. At this point we shall have the opportunity to summarize the rest of the material, and to see more clearly how these problems relate to each other.

THE CLASSIC PICTURE OF THE DEVELOPMENT OF PERSONALITY THROUGH SOCIAL EXPERIENCE

As a starting point we may begin with the baby. He is hungry, therefore restless. He makes a lot of motions, including vocal ones. Mother comes with the bottle. This happens many times, and he learns that yelling brings mother, even when he is not hungry, and that mothers are useful to reduce boredom, as well as to provide for material wants. He can do little for himself; he is dependent on others for nearly everything. He learns that every need-meeting activity involves a stronger person. He learns that this stronger person is not entirely reliable, that she may deny him at times, that she can even punish. He begins to work out ways of increasing the probability that this person will respond as he needs. Thus subconsciously he becomes a social strategist, and in many cases exerts real leadership (or even tyranny) over the household. The important thing for us to note is that even the simplest material problem of the baby has social overtones; co-operation is involved.

After a while, the human being learns to direct effort to provide and maintain the conditions under which his needs can be met; this becomes in itself a secondary or instrumental need, but it is just as real and more pervasive than most other needs. The problems of co-operation or competition, dependence or independence or interdependence arise as problems of ways of working to solve the problems of hunger, housing, group morale, etc. The attitudes, theories, and skills which one forms and uses to deal with people become, in effect, a world-view, and the key to prediction of one's behavior.

People differ in their availability for interaction. Strangers are mostly not available. As acquaintance deepens, the breadth and depth of communication possibilities increase. People who have significant usefulness for each other tend to hold many beliefs, attitudes, and notions in common. They are likely to subscribe to a set of common purposes; and the existence of shared purposes gives them the right to make demands on each other.

When two or more people have the sort of communality described above, we think of them as constituting a "group." The quality of a person's possible interactions, his gratifications and satisfactions, depends upon his position—central or peripheral—in the group. The extent of his affiliation determines his opportunity to meet needs, e.g., to compare ideas with other people, to be stimulated or challenged, to unleash energy of others in his own behalf. In any particular group, the quality of each individual's affiliation is known, not always consciously. The group learns to act as if it differentiated roles; it comes to expect, under certain conditions, that Joe will plunge in with new ideas, that Mary will be concerned about the nonparticipants, that Jack will be sensitive to the "democraticness" of procedures used, that Ida will waste time and block action, and so on.

The development of such expectancies operates to give the group the security of being able to anticipate and ward off interpersonal problems it cannot solve. When a member tries to change his pattern of behavior, he may meet resistance from the group because he is upsetting their ability to predict his behavior and to know how to respond to it.

The amount of motivation one has depends a good deal on the amount of reward one thinks one can get. The fellow who thinks that whatever he does will not influence the group may either become a nonparticipant or he may fight the group. To get the approval which reassures one and increases the desire to participate and tackle problems, one must know how the member role is defined—what will be judged relevant or irrelevant—and what standards of performance will be applied—what will be judged helpful or destructive. Just as groups develop expectations through which roles are stabilized, so they develop standards for judging quality and, eventually, for acceptance and rejection of members.

It is as if a set of agreements is reached in the group, and each member is party to these agreements, and controlled by them in his opportunities and his rewards. The group may respond to violation of the agreements either with punishment of the "criminal" or with reconsideration of the rules to see why they were broken. The latter method, itself reached by agreement, is the way the group can continue to exist in the face of changes external to itself but reflected by members. The former method, of punishment, is unhealthy, and, in the long run, self-defeating.

It is to the interests of all members continually to be ready to modify their agreements. The member behavior most significant in this adjustive process is expression of feeling. A member communicates his reactions to the group's expectancies for roles, its ways of working, and its values, by the emotion-carrying elements in his statements. Thus, in a training group recently, we found that over a course of fifteen meetings every other statement (on the average) had some recognizable feeling in it. Feelings represent the members' evaluation of the situation, and they have to be taken into account as data needed to understand and improve the situation.

The word "climate" is used to speak about the state of affairs in the group with respect to dealing with feelings. A "free" climate is characterized by two properties: first, there are agreed-upon limits to expression, but within these limits anything can be expressed without fear of reprisal. Second, there is analysis of expressed feelings as important contributions to be reflected upon and understood. The group in which there is freedom to fight but not to work is one in which anything can be said but nothing can be reflected upon. The climate is one of license, not of freedom. Individuals do not grow in such a group.

The most common feeling to be expressed and dealt with is aggression. Without aggression there is slavish dependence, "drifting with the tide." Every new gain in maturity has to be fought for, and every planned change requires aggression to carry it out. One of the most serious problems in thinking about socialization is the tendency to equate aggression with hostility, resulting in rejection or guilt about both.

The rules of operation one learns in a face-to-face group are the most real ones. These rules for working together and for expressing one's self become generalized in the individual's value-attitude system, and these rules plus his learned reactions to them describe his personality. Even when a person is alone, he tends to think and act in accordance with these learned agreements, the culture of the group. (The soliloquies of two executives [pages 103–8] imply numerous relationships among past experiences in groups, attitudes and values, and personality.)

Thus runs the classical picture of the development of social personality, of one's own way of life. The "group" is seen as the frame of reference and the environment in which the individual moves; and "membership" describes the quality of the relationship between the individual and the group. What, specifically do we mean by a "group" and by "membership"?

Definitions of "Group" and "Membership"

Man lives in a complex world. He relates himself in different ways under different conditions to various parts or aspects of his world. He differentiates among objects, both material and abstract in nature, and different objects have different meanings for him in various situations. The meanings people have for him and the way he relates to them are important objects of inquiry because men are interdependent; all men are involved somehow in everything man does.

In immediate experience, at any one time, only a relatively small number of people are involved with a person. We use the word "group" to indicate these people. Depending on the act and the situation, the group not only contains different people, but the relationships among them are different. And the variety of relationships among people involved together in a situation is so extensive that we have to conclude that "groupness" is a general impression, not a specific characteristic. It is not helpful to try to mark some amount or kind of "groupness" as typical of a "group," nor to say that any lesser amount of "groupness" may characterize a "collection" but not a "group." In other words, the dichotomy "group–not group" is of little value.

We form our impressions of "groupness" from a large number of specific properties of the collection. Here are some of the properties that people have in mind when they talk about "groups":

1. The membership can be defined. We know who is in the group, either by name or by definition of the kind of person who belongs. Thus we know the names of those at a party. This group is defined easily, its size is known to the member. On the other hand, in a national organization to which we pay dues, we may not know its size, but we have an image of the "sort" of person who belongs. And when we send in dues or run for office or take on any other responsibility on behalf of the association, this image of the other members affects our behavior.

2. The members think of themselves as constituting a group. There is a shared image of the collection; this image marks it off from other collections. To paraphrase an old quip, a group is a bunch of people who think they are a group.

3. There is a sense of shared purpose among members. The members can state some "reasons" for their being a group, and the reasons include a concept of something striven for, some advantage to be gained through mutual effort. (There is often a distinction between the reasons members give, and the reasons a student of the group might think were more important. In other words, there are not only consciously but also subconsciously understood aspects of the group *raison d'être*.)

4. There is a feeling of greater ease of communication among members than between members and nonmembers. There is a feeling of greater intimacy and of preference for others within the group.

5. One has a sense of approval or disapproval for himself and his actions, receiving feedback from others in the group. One takes this information into account in determining subsequent behavior.

6. One feels an obligation to respond to the behavior of others in the group. The embarrassment most people feel during a

silence in a group probably contains feelings of frustration at not knowing how to respond. (There may be some feeling of personal inadequacy—one cannot carry out his felt obligation to respond.)

7. A member has expectations for certain ways of behaving in the various situations in which the group finds itself. He is aware of performance standards, and of limits to expression; of criteria of relevance which he can use to control and direct his behavior in such a way that he can obtain reward for participating.

8. There are leadership policies and roles. There is a recognition of the need to co-ordinate effort efficiently, to maintain the conditions required for problem-solving. Policies are formed at some level of explicitness about how the group is to guide itself. There is agreement on what sort of authority will ultimately guide decision-making.

9. There emerges a status system, a hierarchy of worth of individuals to the group. In a mature group, this hierarchy is based on demonstrated ability to contribute to the group—to further its interests, either within it or in its behalf. In an immature group, this hierarchy may be based on such factors as social class, wealth, occupation, age, number of children, years of experience, etc. But the hierarchy exists, and members have clear ideas of where they fit along the scale.

Different students emphasize different dimensions from the list above; and the list can be written in different ways. Basically, we may think of "groupness" as an over-all impression of the extent of involvement people have with each other, of the ways they can interact with each other, and of the methods of control of behavior they accept for each other and for themselves. No two groups are alike in the various dimensions indicated above. There may be considerable "involvement" but very inadequate leadership. There may be a well-shared set of purposes unaccompanied by much differentiation among member roles. There are vast differences in the patterning of these dimensions in "autocratic," "democratic," and "lassez-faire" groups.

One can think of groups arising out of social conditions, such as contiguity or the need to solve problems; chapter 1 presents a perfect example. One may also think that groups arise out of the need for membership—out of the need to have people available for interaction, the need for feelings of significance and influence, the need for expressing feeling and getting the reactions of others to it as a way to self-understanding. The laboratory group (chapter 5) exemplifies these processes.

In any case, membership is the perception by the individual of the quality of his relationships to the group. The broadest concept of membership would be the individual's perceptions of his role in the human race. Membership is a feeling which integrates the individual's feelings and ideas about his participation with others.

If a person belonged only to one group, or if all groups were alike (making them one group in effect), then life would be much less complicated than it is at present. But what happens when an individual belongs simultaneously to several groups, and his behavior represents an acting-out of his memberships in two or more groups at the same time? For this is the state of affairs in our situation today, when our communities are divided, and the various groups which exist are heterogeneous.

TYPES OF REFERENCE GROUPS

What different sorts of groups are these, in which an individual may hold membership, and to which he may address his behavior?

First, of course, there is the actual group of people he is meeting with in a given time and place. This is the only group he can really interact with, test ideas, appraise himself, and learn from. Only in the actual group can one have new experience, new raw materials for reflection and challenge. In any actual group, however, there are differences in member role, and in the extent to which different people matter to each other. In any meeting, we tend to address our remarks to a few individuals, for these are the ones whose reactions we trust or are worried about. In a group of twenty people or so, the effective group for each of us is probably not much larger than eight. This effective group, different for each member, may change its composition from time to time; but whatever its composition, it represents to us the total group. We have the feeling that we can influence the total group through these people. They are, in a sense, gatekeepers to our influence and to the exertion of our rights of membership.

Second, there is the group we represent. We are sent as its official representative (or we think we are so sent), and it is expected of us that we shall speak for our group. We represent its wishes, its membership and power, its ideas about how to proceed. We fight for these things and, in so doing, we feel that we are fighting for our group. Thus we have vested interests.

A second origin of the vested interest is almost the opposite. We may quite unnecessarily defend our group with a sort of blind loyalty, and it is possible that the motivation for this stems from feelings of lack of membership. We are worried about our place in the group and we therefore defend the group to assure ourselves that we belong—that there is something there to defend.

In either case, however, the person reacts both to the actual group and to the vested interest group as it is carried about in his mind. If he is anxious about his membership in this group, the actual group may experience considerable difficulty in working with him. When a person comes as an appointed representative, he owes it to himself to find out what problems the group he represents consider only tentatively settled in their minds, what problems he is not to accept suggestions about, and, finally, what actions his group wants taken in case of head-on collision with the actual group.

A third type of group to which people refer their behavior might be characterized as the abstracted group or the "relic" group. This is a faceless group, which the individual probably could not identify at all accurately. The people, roles, and actions have dropped out of memory; all that is left is coercive belief. The public in the phrase "public opinion" is an abstracted group. So is the "community" for most people; so are the "nation," the "church," the "scientists," etc.

The most usual relic of the abstracted group is the value system, remembered long after times, places, circumstances, and individuals are forgotten. In our quest for authority and certainty we often carry over to the actual group the values and attitudes that made sense for some previous group; we hope that they will guide us out of the perplexities of the present group. When values abstracted from these forgotten groups or cultures come into conflict with the evaluative criteria of a current actual group, the former had better be examined carefully to see if there is enough similarity of circumstance that they can be accepted as the "absolutes" one wishes they were.

A fourth type of group under whose influence one may act in an actual group is the "hangover" group. Basically this is a group similar to the family in which one had membership problems and anxieties which are still not relieved. The unresolved anxieties arising from sibling rivalry in the family may rise again in any situation of working with peers. When this happens, a person re-acts to his peers in the actual group as if they were brothers and sisters from long ago or far away. Many problems of leadership probably are not legitimately problems in the actual group but are hung-over problems from unsatisfied relationships with father or mother or priest or people in authority. Anxieties connected with an unsatisfied craving for leadership in one group may be translated into tremendous and inappropriate striving for or avoidance of leadership in another group. It is as if a person were always working out the same plot in all his memberships; as if he were in the inexorable grip of problems which would not let him go. Group therapists are particularly concerned with seeing how an actual group can help individuals understand these peripheral motivations in their behavior.

A fifth type is the fantasied or constructed group. It probably operates more when the individual is alone than when he is in an actual group. Still, even in an actual group, a person will some-times withdraw into fantasies in which he is getting from a con-structed group the responses he cannot get from an actual group. There are descriptions of the child, punished by the teacher, who then daydreams about how sorry everybody will be when he gets drowned rescuing the fair-haired daughter of the superintendent from the mill pond; one may also at such times have dreams of glory in which one receives ovations from large and conveniently vague crowds; destruction and death plots can also be used.

For our purposes, however, the most interesting constructed groups are those produced to give one emotional support. An imagined audience can be used to provide one with authority against the actual group—to help sustain a course of action which is unpopular (or which it is feared will be unpopular). If a person has read a lawbook he may develop for himself and the group the fantasy that he is now representing the "legal point of view." Consultants called into schools are often seduced into thinking they represent a group of gray-bearded professors of education. A member addressing the actual group or a teacher giving a lecture may be addressing some other group not actually present. "Talking over our heads" is a common way in which the audience recognizes this. They read into it snobbishness, exhibitionism, and the like; but it may merely be that the lecturer got his wires crossed and is using the platform to defend his thesis from the criticism of a lot of absent or even nonexistent critics.

In any case, when a person does not accept the actual group and address his behavior to it, he will use some other group or mixture of groups, even if they have to be specially constructed for the occasion. Such groups are clearly and consciously seen by some people; with others, these extra groups remain in the subconscious.

It will be our postulate that in any perplexing situation in the actual group, it is as if there were other groups overlapping. In other words, the problem for the member is partly one of dealing with conflict among or anxiety about his memberships. Behaviors that enhance membership in one group are felt to lead to rejection in other groups. Any choice of behavior thus is to some extent felt to be a choice among groups.

Roger Barker gives an excellent picture of the possible overlapping groups operating in a teaching situation:

Teachers must be highly sensitive to the changing demands of many relatively independent groups: their classes, their colleagues, their administrators, their communities. Because of their exposed and dependent position, the behavior of teachers is very sensitive to these simultaneously acting, but independent and often conflicting influences. Consider some concrete determinants of the teacher's behavior in the classroom. First of all, there is the classroom situation: the attitude of the pupils, the requirements of the lesson, and the teacher's intentions and ideals with respect to it. At the same time, the teacher's behavior is to some extent determined by the facts of the larger school administration: perhaps an uncertainty as to the attitude of the administration toward his work, a feeling of frustration, failure, and abuse because a colleague has received an "unwarranted" salary increase, or a feeling of futility over the small prospect of professional advancement. There is also the community situation which the teacher cannot escape and to which he is particularly sensitive: limitations upon his personal freedom in some political, social and economic spheres, and coercion in others.[1]

We seem to be on safe ground so far in recognizing that an individual is influenced by groups other than those "actually" present. This is another way of saying that people can be in conflict and can have anxieties about it—they can feel pressures and doubts—and that we look to previous social experience as somehow involved in these perplexities.

The technologies presented in Part I grapple with these problems. Thus, with respect to racial matters, the neighborhood group, chapter 1, provides a test of attitudes frequently formed in fantasied groups. The teacher in chapter 2 deals with roles of children which are maintained in actual peer and family groups. In chapter 3, the small training group bridges between vested interests of the teacher in his classroom and in his total faculty. A major problem of chapter 4 is to avoid overlapping of the demanding groups "above" and "below" with co-operating groups at the same level.

Accepting the notion that people do find themselves in situations which fall under the jurisdiction of overlapping groups, the next question follows: What goes on within the individual, and how is his behavior affected?

A Tentative Picture of the Effect of Overlapping Groups on Behavior

Our job at this point is to construct a bridge of explanation that will connect two sorts of information. On the one hand, we have the notion that in problematic situations an individual is under the influence of two or more groups whose requirements for membership are felt by him to be incompatible. On the other hand, we have generally accepted observations of the variety of ways in which an individual can behave when he is in doubt: he may "withdraw" from the situation, in which case he becomes nonparticipant so far as the business of the group is concerned;

[1] Roger G. Barker, "Difficulties of Communication between Educators and Psychologists: Some Speculations," *Journal of Educational Psychology*, September, 1942, pp. 416–26.

he may fight any of a number of possible targets as a means to defining limits more clearly—the leader, the group, himself, the problem, the possibilities of solution; he may become dependent in the sense that he gives up his own rights to take initiative and tries to find someone to follow; he may flee to a high level of generality or into telling stories, swapping experience, splitting hairs, or arguing procedures; etc. What we are looking for at this point is some way to predict from the nature of the pressures on a person in a perplexing situation what behavior he will present to the group. Or we may turn the question around and ask what information, from observations of a person's behavior, we can get about the pressures he is under.

The groups that overlap at any particular time are the ones which have meaning of some sort for us in the particular situation. They are groups with which we identify; we have some quality of membership in them. In each of these groups our behavior as members is different. You behave differently in a staff meeting than in your family. As a Scout leader your role is clearly distinguishable from your role as a fourth hand at bridge. We are, on different occasions, different people. And we are different in just the ways we have to be different to maintain the kind of membership we need in the various groups we are party to. When groups overlap in our minds we become, in effect, several different people at the same time.

There is a struggle within us among our various selves—the different people we are as members in each of the groups which somehow are felt to be pertinent to a given situation. In effect, our behavior is decided by what goes on around an internal "conference table." If we can bring all our selves to agreement, we proceed fairly directly and easily. If we cannot, our behavior depends upon the dynamics of the conference within. Thus if the "Scout Master" in us wants to give advice, the "psychologist" in us wants to reflect the other fellow's feeling, the "judge" in us wants to punish—if these others all stick to their line there is no decision, and we may have to withdraw momentarily from the group, or strike out at it, or find ourselves defending an ill-advised position reflecting that group pressure which is momentarily dominant within us.

The notions presented above may be summarized as follows:

cues in any actual situation remind us of groups in which we are anxious about our membership role. Our reactions to the present group become contaminated with anxieties about ourselves in relation to other groups. The different selves we have in those other groups come into conflict. The interaction among these selves decides how we shall behave—with confidence, hostility, ease, creativity. It is thus that internal conflict can be seen as conflict in membership roles, and that whatever decision is reached enhances membership in some groups at the expense of membership in others. The stress and strain of conflict becomes the pain of losing approval and affiliation and other need-satisfactions in some groups while gaining these things in other groups. The decision is likely to express our judgment of which changes in membership will be least painful or most rewarding.

This viewpoint has interesting implications. Thus as group members, we may see a person's opinions as more than merely a response to the "actual" situation; therefore, before accepting an opinion we would wish to test it against the facts of the actual situation. Or in therapy, for instance, when an individual is in conflict it might be profitable to inquire after the other people to whom the patient feels his behavior makes a difference. One can see, too, the problem presented to pupils when the climate differs from classroom to classroom, or from school to home.

This picture also points to the problems of heterogeneity among groups in our society. The wish for a society in which the major values (or requirements for membership in groups) are consistent is a wish for less conflict in people. A homogeneous society seems an impractical hope, and it would be undesirable in any case. But there is one important possibility which is the central thesis of this work: that in groups which customarily test ideas against the facts—of both ideas and feelings—people can learn ways to integrate these inner selves. They can learn to react to situations as they are; they can learn to use past experience for wisdom and guidance, without interference.

Social Goals and Membership

People live together, they need each other, they are influenced by each other—in short, they are interdependent. Interdependence is a mixture of dependence and independence. The quality of membership in the group defines the nature of the mixture; it decides the relative degrees of independence and dependence, and also the things for which a person depends on the group and the things for which the group depends on him. Membership is the right to influence; it is also the agreement to accept influence. Obviously, the more fully involved one is in group membership the greater are both the privileges and the responsibilities—the more meaningful and significant is the relationship. Full membership is a means to enable one to meet his needs more effectively (or change them to needs that can be met).

But the type of group makes a difference. Groups which are oriented toward the goals of their members and test all ideas against what they are trying to accomplish, tend to seek stability in the understanding of basic principles. Events are seen as representing the operation of understood "laws." Because these "laws" are understood, it is possible to predict what will happen next. With the ability to predict and anticipate comes freedom, by which we mean the possibilities of deciding behavior intelligently and to our advantage. Here all things can be tested and, if necessary, changed, even the requirements of membership. Membership is referred to the situation as it exists and to the authority of group experience.

It seems clear that there will be little conflict among memberships in such groups. When conflict does arise, one knows what to do because the group agreements include provision for testing and modifying the membership role. We shall refer to this type of group as "purpose-oriented."

On the other hand, some groups appear to be oriented toward the maintenance of preconceived ideas. Their basis of performance and stability is ritual, custom, and preservation of the power structure. Events are seen as unpredictable and as threatening, because new ways have to be found to deal with them, and there is no means for discovering new ways with confidence. Reliance is on a higher authority—sometimes mystically revealed. Judgments are not tested against the facts of group life. The group always has to guess because it not only does not have the relevant facts to go on, it does not even know the categories of facts it ought to have. Membership roles are rigidly defined and enforced through coercive expectations. All members are expected to accept a common ideology, and unorthodox views are resisted. Such rules as the group makes explicit to itself govern procedures rather than methods of working. We shall refer to this type of group as "procedure-oriented."

The individual whose major social training and experience is in the purpose-oriented group will be able to accommodate subsequently to the wide variety of groups in our heterogeneous society. Social training in the procedure-oriented type of group will tend to block effectiveness in subsequent group experience.

Some Comments on This Chapter

Our basic objective is to understand how people work together, why difficulties arise, how to avoid or remove them. There are two very different aspects to the problem. One whole side of the matter stems from the facts about human relations—the conditions under which people can participate in social experiences, the nature of the participation, the immediate and long-range obstacles to it, and the values and costs of various patterns of participation. The other side of the matter is the fact that society is faced with such "objective" problems as housing, food distribution, lack of parking space, supervision of city officials, etc. In any real situation, both the human relations problems and the objective problems must be dealt with simultaneously.

This chapter has said nothing about "objective" problem-solving, and it has said nothing very directly translatable into action about human relations problem-solving. We have tried to show that the individual has a "place" in groups, that he fits into and is part of a larger social structure. We have also implied that the social structure to which he responds is the social structure as seen and experienced by the individual. This social structure is "subjective" in the sense that it differs for different people. From the concept of overlapping group memberships, we have pointed to a major source of the "human relations" problems in group operation. We have also implied that these problems of individuals do not arise from wilfulness, obstinacy, or stupidity per se, but are due to his experiences in a community. We can see that people can be awkward in handling these conflicts and the anxieties over their conflicts, and as we go on we want to indicate some understandings that may be helpful in this regard. We have also implied that groups can operate in such a way that the individual is not so often or deeply trapped by membership conflicts.

The reader may wonder just how literally the notion of an "internal conference" is meant. What are these other selves, and how do they interact? The answer is that this is a theory of functioning—it is *as if* some such process went on. It is by no means meant to be a description of verified phenomena. Such a description, if made in psychological terms, would go heavily into impulses, their blockage, reinforcement, and control. In physiological terms, it would go into the matter of the behavior of the nervous system. It seems most helpful in this context to think of the individual as a "black box." Knowing something about what goes into it and about what comes out of it, we then try to guess at the sort of thing going on inside. If we are successful, we can use this information to predict what will come out from our knowledge of what goes in, and vice versa. This particular concept of the internal conference appeals to me because I see public behavior as coextensive with private behavior; and not radically different from it. How much of public behavior is merely "acting out" the things in one's mind? It seems to me that the relationship between a person's thoughts and feelings and what he does in a group is so close that we are entitled to think that the two sorts of phenomena are fundamentally similar. In such a case either could be modified by experience with the other; and I think this happens.

To what extent do the matters discussed here belong to "consciousness" and to "unconsciousness" of the person? There may be some feeling that the more "conscious" these things are, the more readily they can be controlled and worked with. Clearly, there are differences from one person to the next and from one situation to the next. There may be some minimum level of conscious diagnosis that must go on before a person can proceed effectively to deal with his problems of membership. Certainly one of the major policies of trainers in human relations is to make it possible for such inexplicitly understood factors to emerge into consciousness so they can be dealt with at a more overt level.

Another basic question: To what extent is behavior a matter of "free choice" by the individual, and to what extent is it determined by such factors as his membership in groups? We do not expect to settle this question, but we are certainly investigating it in various ways throughout this work. At the present stage of the discussion, we should like to call attention to two sorts of relevant observations. The first is that it is possible to generalize about how people will behave. For example, if we know that Tony is the son of an Italian immigrant who worked in a vineyard in Italy and now lives in the "Italian" section of a large city, we might expect from this alone that Tony will be caught between the transplanted Italian society and the urban American society. We expect him to have difficulties in moving from one to the other, or of maintaining loyalty and relationships to both. If he is an adolescent, we expect him to be torn in his choice of friendships, and to be very sensitive to "stereotypic" remarks made by his "American" friends. Simply because of his membership conflicts, we may expect such things as extra self-assertiveness, defensiveness or rebelliousness directed at the Italian group, efforts to copy the mannerisms of some "American" adolescent, and the like. The fact that such expectations are generally held by the people with whom he comes in contact will tend to make them come true. Much work on caste and class characteristics of various ethnic groups in American society has led to many generalizations of this sort. We may as well accept the fact that there is to some extent a cultural determinism in individual behavior.

On the other hand, we may observe a second adolescent, Gino, ostensibly from the identical cultural situation, who seems to function in a way vastly different from Tony. The latter becomes "Americanized" with very little apparent conflict, and gets along well in other groups; Gino seems to get caught in a shadowland of dubious fringe groups, projects his troubles on everyone else, and becomes a victim for every demagogue who comes along. This, too, can be predicted, but to do so requires a great deal more information about the relationships between the parents and the children, about such biological matters as energy output, and about such psychological matters as his fantasies and the subjective meanings for him of his experience. The latter type of information is protected by custom. We tend to feel that it is an "invasion of privacy" to try to find out these things.

The matter at present can be left somewhat as follows: Behavioral norms or expectancies for groups of people exist. To assert that any particular individual does, must, or should act in accordance with these norms is to engage in a kind of stereotyping which may be harmful because it prevents our seeing and reacting to the individual as he "really" is. But knowledge of norms and personality dynamics should not be resented, because we all use them intuitively. The problem is to learn our facts more accurately, and then to train ourselves to use such knowledge more appropriately. At most, all that can be predicted in advance is the existence of certain tendencies to react to types of situations (described in general terms) in certain types of ways. A specific reaction usually cannot be predicted accurately except by an observer or member of the group, and then only in the moment just before the behavior occurs.

The conclusion to the question of free will versus determinism is thus that there are broadly stated limits within which individuals can be seen to operate; but there is room within these limits for unpredicted, original, self-expressive behavior. A person can be himself, self-determining and creative, but to be so he must understand and accept his memberships in a variety of groups.

This chapter begins with the individual as the locus of tendencies to behave in the host of social groups in which he is involved. Several chapters hence, after considering many more factors and concepts, we will complete the circle by returning to the individual as the means for building communities. We will at that point try to show that the fact of overlapping memberships is not merely a source of problems for the individual, but also offers the most promising possibilities for building the kind of world we want.

CHAPTER 8

Awareness and interpretation of our own feelings in a situation is the starting point for defining the problems we have to solve. Thinking about the problem is a process of rehearsing possible actions in our minds. The "best" solution is based on all the necessary data in the problematic situation, and it represents the application of open-minded experimental attitudes.

A problem is "solved" when serenity of feeling returns and new insights have been fitted into our scheme of things. Both we and the situation undergo changes, and these changes give rise to new problems.

Integration: Evaluating and Acting

INTRODUCTION

We have suggested that in any given situation, a person may find himself confronted with problems of divided loyalty, expectations about how to behave that are carried over from some past group but which he fears are not appropriate in the present group, anxieties about himself in similar situations in the past, and the like. In other words, the person is played upon by many forces which are mobilized by cues in the present situation.

These ideas deal essentially with the *structure* of the pressures to which one is subject. But these concepts do not give us much insight into what the individual will do, what changes will occur, and how these changes are going to be brought about. Concepts of this sort refer to "process"; processes result in change of structure, and without ideas of structure we have no way of describing such changes.

The primary concept needed for an understanding of behaving as a process is that of purpose. We do not "understand" behavior until we can assign it a purpose, conscious or unconscious. The purpose we have talked about so far is to resolve conflicts in one's memberships and to reduce anxieties associated with these conflicts. We are postulating the idea that when a person has such anxieties about his membership, he will behave in a way which, from his point of view, will reduce these anxieties—either by testing them and finding them unnecessary, or by learning to live with them, or by sharing them with others, or in some other way.

A second concept needed for a consideration of the process of change is that of problem-solving. Whenever a structure needs to be altered, there must be some reason why it has not already automatically changed and this ordinarily involves the notion of an obstacle that must be overcome. The obstacle must be diagnosed; plans for overcoming it must be laid, alternatives weighed, action taken and continuously tested as the process of change continues. This series of steps, when rigorously undertaken, is "action research"; in all problematic situations similar steps go on with more or less consciousness and formality. This abstract series of steps provides us with a model with which to compare actual behavior. It is a model deriving from a conception of behavior as purposive, rather than as a simple set of conditioned responses to situations over which no control is possible.

From observation of people, one soon learns that there are vast differences among individuals and among groups with regard to the extent to which problem-solving is conscious, and therefore with regard to the possibility of learning problem-solving methods and applying them with increasing efficiency and productivity.

Some people and groups are conscious of objective barriers only, and try to deal with them as if there were no other problems involved. The notion that a research worker in social science is himself not involved as a person is in accord with this pathetic fallacy; the very choice of a problem for research necessarily signifies his involvement in the situation. The notion that the group observer can "stay out" of the group's activity is equally mistaken. On the other hand, some people and groups seem almost entirely concerned with anxiety problems, with their own selves. One hears people insisting that a group must develop "as a group" before it can be expected to deal with objective problems. The main outcome of such efforts is probably to increase anxiety further by making everyone self-conscious.

These lopsided approaches differ in the types or aspects of group process to which attention is given. Those who try to deal with group problem-solving as if its content were entirely objective tend to pay attention to the "logical" processes of interpreting information. They typically make the mistake of confusing the formal steps, which in our culture we accept as the ways to demonstrate or prove already known theses, with the steps through which a group has to go in its own sometimes blundering way in order to arrive at the conclusions or decisions. What is forgotten, typically, is that feelings exist, have to be taken into account, and actually are the bases in experience for knowing which steps the group must take and in what order.

On the other hand, those who see problem-solving primarily as the development of "groupness," or as the solving of interpersonal problems among the members, tend to pay considerable attention to "permissiveness" and expression of feeling. They get feeling "out in the open" and shared—and this is certainly helpful. But it is not enough. There is no way to know how to proceed unless there are objective requirements to serve as the basis for testing and interpreting feeling. A clear example is the so-called "race problem." No community has ever yet solved the problem of interracial anxiety by approaching it directly; what is required, rather, is a type of experience through which people learn to deal with the anxieties surrounding their notions of "race." But this experience has to be provided with regard to problems such as housing, employment, wage levels, educational opportunity, hospital care, and other objectively defined concerns. It is only in these objective problems that unequivocal facts can be obtained and therefore that the success or failure of policy can be demonstrated clearly. The use of this principle is demonstrated in chapter 1.

We shall begin in this chapter with the postulate that the fundamental problems people have to solve arise from membership conflicts and anxieties. We shall then approach the processes of solution with our model of problem-solving: diagnosis, interpretation, planning, acting, obtaining feedback, modifying plans and actions, and so on. We shall look at these steps as processes of feeling, thinking, and acting. We shall be concerned with the balance among these processes, and the control of this balance. And we shall use the term "integration" to describe the effectiveness and appropriateness of the principles by which a person or group appears to control this balance of processes.

FEELING

Feeling is a state of affairs within a person or group, evoked by situations or parts of situations. Feelings cannot be expressed by words; we can talk *about* them, but we cannot talk *them*. On the other hand, we can communicate to others how we feel. We do it partly through the nonspecific content of our talk—not through the idea we wish to express but through the way we express it: the tone of voice, the inflections, the tempo of speech. We also use formal elements of speech: the elaborateness of our phrases, the shock we convey through bluntness, the associations of feelings with which people invest particular words, etc. In general, any departure of our behavior from what people think a problem requires is likely to be interpreted as an indication of feelings. Such indications we may refer to as the "affect" of statements.

Feelings are, of course, communicated by many behaviors other than speech. Speaking happens to be particularly useful to communicate them, perhaps because the tiny muscles of the vocal cords are extremely sensitive to changes in tension within the body and respond in audible ways that are detectable. But posture, expression, gesturing—all these movements, and particularly the involuntary ones, communicate to others how we feel. Or at least they communicate the fact that our feelings have changed.

In a group, we note many ways in which people respond to such communication. A change of seating from one meeting to the next often confirms our impressions of change of friendship feelings among members. Verbal responses may include attacking, reassuring, changing the subject, or asking for clarification. Responses may be further expressions of the same feeling, or of some other feeling. They may somehow take account of the mood of the group as a whole during a fairly long period, or they may seem to arise from a single comment by one person.

In general, an expression of feeling engenders further feeling in others, and their responses are actually stimulated by their own feelings. Thus when a person attacks: "I just don't think we are getting anywhere; I don't know what we are trying to do, and I don't think anyone else does either," his action may evoke different feelings among the various members of his group. One person responds as if this were an attack on the group or on the leader; he feels defensive. Another person may respond to the feeling of frustration which he hears in the statement; he may add to it: "Amen, brother." Or he may respond to the feeling of frustration with some diagnostic comment: "It seems to me that we are all pretty frustrated at the moment." Another person may counterattack: "I'd like to refer you to the purposes we stated and wrote on the board at the last meeting." Still another, who has been actively participating, may feel discouraged and fall silent. These responses give us some clues as to the way in which feelings affect the group. Fundamentally, expressed feelings are responded to as if they were evaluations. Different people may view such expressions as evaluative of different things: the leader, the group, the problem, the activity, the speaker, other individuals, other groups.

Feelings themselves are nonspecific; they are involuntary, overall responses. They signal to us that we like or dislike the way things are going; that we anticipate success or failure; that we are comfortable or uncomfortable; that we feel relaxed and adequate or tense and inadequate in the situation; that we sense danger or haven; that we are in conflict or at peace; that we have anxiety or are undisturbed. If we are unaware of these signals, if we do not know how we feel, we tend to "act out" the feelings; in one way or another we express them to the group. If they arise primarily from the events in the life of the actual group, such expression is probably helpful. But if they arise from other sources, not in the experience of the rest of the group, then a direct expression may be troublesome.

For example, if the group has learned that I become aggressive whenever the goals of the group are unclear, then they can use my expression of aggressive feelings as a barometer to indicate the possibility that further goal clarification may be needed. On the other hand, if my aggression during a particular meeting is due to the fact that earlier in the day I had an argument during which I handled myself badly, the group, not knowing the source of my anger, will be at a loss to know how to respond to it. It then constitutes an additional and unnecessary problem for the group to deal with.

When we are aware of our feelings, we may respond to them in three ways. One way is to deny them, to pretend they do not exist or to attribute them to others. Thus people who cannot accept their own feelings of hostility are likely to say that *they* are not hostile but that everyone else is. This is called projection. It is a subconscious rationalization of one's own feelings which he dare not acknowledge in consciousness: "If everyone is hostile to me then I am justified in being hostile myself, even though I deny to you that I feel hostile." If a person does not have open this projective way of accepting feelings he refuses to acknowledge, he is likely to feel anxious and probably guilty. He may withdraw, lash out at others, change the subject, etc. None of these devices are helpful to the group.

A second way to deal with our awareness of how we feel is to accept the fact that we feel as we do and then try to interpret this fact as a guide to action. Thus a person who recognizes that he feels hostile may try to explain to himself why this is so. Through watching what is happening to the group each time he has these hostile feelings he may discover that he feels this way every time a particular person speaks, or whenever a stereotypic statement is made about his religious group, or whenever the group loses its sense of direction. He may then decide to report to the group the results of his insight: that he is unclear about the direction in which the group is going, or that he wonders whether particular kinds of statements are realistic, etc.

A first way of reacting to one's feeling is to "act it out"; the second is to interpret it and report his diagnosis of group malfunctioning to be corrected. The third way is somewhere between the first two. It is to report objectively how one feels. Thus he might say in a reasonably pleasant but sincere way: "I feel unhappy at the turn our discussion has taken." Such statements invite others to indicate whether they share the feeling; if they do, it may be worth taking time for everyone to help diagnose the group experiences causing this "unhappiness." Often sharing the knowledge that we all feel anxious by itself reduces anxiety enough to let the group move ahead.

Common knowledge of generally shared feelings in the group is extremely important information. It is essential to get and interpret this information if the group is to select its activities in a way that is maximally productive. But feelings do not have to be ascertained and interpreted every hour on the hour. As long as everyone who has a contribution to make is making it, as new ideas are coming up, as people are listening to each other and building on each other's ideas—there is no need to be concerned about feelings. High morale is readily shared. But when things go sour, when the discussion drags, when there is little feeling of growth of insight, when there is much unnecessary dependence on the leader, then ascertaining the feelings which are shared may give the data needed to rectify the situation.

It should be evident that the unbridled, disorderly, acting-out of feeling is by itself of little value. Catharsis alone does not help.

THINKING AND ACTING

We do not respond to everything about us. We take action only on the things about which we have feelings. Of course, if we like our feelings, we will want to maintain the situation, rather than change it. But when our feelings are painful—more painful than the discomfort of taking action—we are likely to move if we can see something to do. The demagogue operates in essentially this type of situation: he shows people the easy way out of the uncomfortableness of their feelings. The more persuasive he is in discounting what is really involved in the action—its long-range costs, for example—the greater the danger in following him.

There is a more healthy basis for taking action: this is to search for greater reward rather than to search for the avoidance of discomfort. Training groups frequently operate in this way. During their periods of high morale and productiveness, individuals feel more rewarded for participation, and the group goal becomes identified with having more such periods. To reach this goal, the group members must analyze the differences between the desired situation and the more usual one of lower efficiency. If they can recognize this difference, they can then alter their policies of operation in an effort to reach the goal. In more general terms: the nature of group goals involves a state of being which has been experienced and of which the group wants more. If a group has never experienced a really productive period, there is no assurance that the goal of productiveness is appropriate or attainable. The basis for confidence in goals is the group's own experience, not the promises of a leader whose ways of knowing are not available to the group.

In general, a diagnosis of our feelings with regard to our problem is the starting point for intelligent behavior. Knowledge of the sorts of situations which gave rise in the past to the feelings in question is helpful in making the diagnosis. This is an intellectual operation. It involves comparing the facts about a present situation with the facts about other experienced situations, with an eye to seeing the similarities and differences between the two.

Following diagnosis, in the problem-solving process, there comes a fascinating process of rehearsal of action. Planning action is in many ways similar to the writing of a play. The kinds of roles needed—characterizations—must be considered; the plot line—the strategic sequence of required action—becomes clearer; the dialogue is written and tested for validity against the group's intuitions from past experience. The conversation is likely to move from the hypothetical level ("If such and such were to occur, one could then do such and such") to the level of immediate readiness for action ("I think we ought to start by doing so and so").

Emotionally, at least, the problem is solved at the point where people can see what the next step is going to be. Action is the acting out of that which has been rehearsed in the mind. While action is being taken, additional feelings arise, and the next step is planned in response to the new definition of the problem that has thus become possible. Problems are never really solved in any conclusive or absolute sense. They are merely reformulated in such a way that action can be taken. In the process, however, the environment gets changed and attitudes are altered.

In this view, thinking is vicarious anticipatory action. People react to the imagined action with feeling, and at the point where there is a sufficient shared feeling of confidence in the group, action can be taken. This confidence emerges when people can visualize clearly what is to be done, and when they feel it is the "right" thing to do. For confidence to be highest, the group sets up criteria which the action is to satisfy and then considers a number of alternative plans, selecting the one that meets the criteria best. And the more "operational" the plan—the more easily translatable into imagined action—the easier it is to visualize and test it against the criteria. Acting out alternative plans through role-playing (spontaneous dramatic situations which contain the elements of the problem to be solved) is often helpful in appraising a suggested course of action. Guidance may be obtained from various sources—accepted practices, analysis in terms of values involved, use of experts, dry runs—all these may be used to help examine proposed plans for action.

During this group job of planning action, what sort of thinking is the individual member doing? Fundamentally, he is trying to work out existing membership problems and, probably, attempting to influence the group in such a way that additional membership problems do not arise for him. Thus he has a vested interest in the direction of action upon which the group decides. He knows that after all the talking is over, he will be committed to do something, to play some role, and he prefers that this action be congenial and rewarding to himself.

The group member, then, is thinking about the strategy for solving the problem, but, at the same time, he is concerned that the strategy selected should make sense in terms of his own needs. He must be realistically concerned with such problems as the amount of frustration he will probably encounter in relation to the amount he can tolerate easily, the perceptions he thinks others will have of him if he undertakes the particular job suggested, the future opportunities which will be opened to him by participation in action, etc. By and large, members do not discuss such problems with the group, not wishing to expose their membership problems to others. In a sense, then, each member has his own "hidden agenda" in a meeting.

We see now the importance of the objective problem facing the group. With all members having their own hidden agendas to work on, there must be some sort of reality outside the group, some purpose over and above the concerns of each individual to which attention can be directed. The objective problem makes communication possible, it gives people something about which to share feeling, it gives them a focus which is not more favorable toward one individual than another. Without it there would be no basis for differentiating roles, for settling leadership competition, for organizing effort. There would be no criteria for testing ideas, and the group would end in nothing but a series of divisive moves for individual power.

During discussion of the objective problem, members project their own general concerns onto the outside reality. A person concerned about himself in relation to leadership in the group may be the one to ask who is going to be in charge of the project. One who is divided in loyalty between this group and another one may be the one to inquire about the philosophical assumptions behind the action to be taken—particularly with regard to the ethics of the situation. A member who is worried about lack of time may be the one to insist on a careful analysis of the job requirements for getting the proposed action accomplished. One with a problem of "feeling left out" all the time may ask what communication must be provided for among workers while they are taking action. All these are important and useful questions, growing out of the sensitivity of individual members to the particular factors which they emphasize during problem-solving. But these individual motivations are not the real concern of the group, which is to interpret queries within the body of decisions that need to be made. By the time answers have been found to some questions, others have been tabled, and still others determined to be irrelevant, each individual should not only feel secure in going along but should also have a clear idea of his role and where he fits into the process.

The ingredients of problem-solving are the processes through which members try to deal with their problems, which, of course, include their involvements in the objective problems. With the large array of member-concerns to be expressed and dealt with, it is clear that there must be some means of controlling contributions and, particularly, the timing of contributions. The more complete an image the group has of the structure of a problem, of the wide range of types of ideas required, the more readily it can control the offering of the various contributions. It is worth paying explicit attention in a group to developing a common "frame of reference" or "set" toward problem-solving. We shall see that the control of contributions in such a way that they add up efficiently into a group product is the function of leadership, and we shall have more to say about that later.

But for the time being, let me point out that the group operates as if it had some set of ideas about how to solve problems, about the larger purposes it is to achieve. The work is done by individuals, but within the framework of agreements and understandings about the nature of problem-solving. And let us also note two further points about this agreed-upon approach to problem-solving: first, that this becomes the code or set of beliefs the group lives by, and it gets incorporated into the individual's ideas of what the group stands for; and second, the more thoroughly this code is understood by the individual the more responsibility he can take for self-discipline, for making his contributions in a way that helps the group most directly but at the same time gives him maximum opportunity to meet his own needs.

INTEGRATION

In the last chapter I referred to integration as a state of affairs in which one's various "selves" were in harmony and mutually reinforcing. Under such conditions, committment to action is greatest, and the action itself is most direct. We might refer to this as structural integration.

The processes by which membership problems can be solved involves the achievement of structural integration. In this section we shall examine the relationships between the two major types of process—evaluation and action; we shall see that these both occur in sequence or combination, and we shall consider the nature of the relationships between them as likely to lead toward or away from structural integration. Thus, some behaviors, involving a particular combination of evaluation and action, may result in better integration; other behaviors may lead in the opposite direction.

From the standpoint of our model of problem-solving, ideally, at least, every "unpleasant" feeling would lead to the need for action; and every action undertaken would result in a new evaluation of the changed situation. The relationships between acting and evaluating would be seen as sequential and as guided by the need to reduce anxiety over overlapping memberships. In this ideal picture, a very small feeling could result in a new act which would engender more feelings and actions. One would be busy indeed!

Actually, the tension associated with "unpleasant" feelings has to be sufficiently great and sufficiently recognized that the person is "ready" to do something to reduce it. Some people appear to be able to tolerate a good deal of tension before they take action; others seem to translate most feelings of discomfort directly into action. Some people seem to have to carry a planned action through to completion before they allow themselves to be aware of the feelings produced during action; others appear to start modifying their action as soon as it starts, using the feelings discovered in the process of acting as the basis for steering their behavior. Then again, there are those whose tensions toward action appear to be reduced simply through the mental rehearsal stage; their need to know that they can handle situations is satisfied by the visualization of a possible plan of action. There are also those who need actually to take every planned action as a way, perhaps, of convincing themselves of their own adequacy; and these people may resist any plan which makes unusual demands on them.

The feeling of adequacy, that a person may live serenely in the various groups he belongs to, is probably an expression of confidence that he can find the action-channels he needs to reduce anxieties should they arise. He feels sure that he will not be "trapped" in intergroup or membership problems, and thus need not fear participation in the host of varieties of social relationships. There is only one way in which such adequacy can be learned and accepted: through finding out from experience that these self-attitudes are realistic. Action is an individual's means of testing his own attitudes about himself. Only action evokes responses by others, and only action (or public behavior) has consequences that can be appraised.

From the standpoint of the group member, participation is experimentation. He decides more or less consciously which behaviors to submit to the group, and pays attention to the feelings engendered in himself by the responses the group makes. One of the usual conclusions to be drawn from the experiment is a notion of "place," of the quality of membership in the actual group. In this sense, every group we operate in is a laboratory in which we test ideas about ourselves and our relationships to others.

There are two extreme modes of experimentation by group

members, corresponding roughly to inductive and deductive methods. These methods are most clearly recognizable in the early life of the group. One is to "dive in": to make comments testing the leadership's permissiveness, the boundaries to expression of ideas and feelings. The member in effect tries out the roles he would like best, to see if he can establish himself in them. The second extreme method is to sit back and watch what happens to the fellows who dive in. From the way the leadership responds to them, one learns how to relate to leadership. The active people are watched closely. If a conflict develops over methods of leadership, the watcher identifies with both protagonists, for they are apt to represent different sides of his own confusion or ambivalence.

The two methods are likely to be used by different types of members. We expect rash behavior from aggressive and counterdependent people—people who cannot tolerate the idea that they must depend on anyone. We expect the "safer" method to be employed by more dependent people. Dependency and counterdependency, of course, are learned from previous experience; they reflect the qualities of membership which one has developed as most suitable to meet needs in other groups.

These differences in approach illustrate differences in the principles with which people appear to operate in their search for integration of experience. The watcher tends to be critical. He responds to the actions of others. He tends, often, to have his greatest facility with data that others have produced and "processed" for him. His evaluations are primarily of the feelings expressed by others, and he may actually be more aware of them than of his own feelings—or at least he "feels" safer in reacting to others' feelings than to his own. He may deny his own feelings because he cannot accept them, and may be "blocked" until the permissiveness of the group is so well established that he need not fear punishment or reprisal for his feelings. The "plunger" makes less subtle evaluations—he accepts opposition at first hand—and takes action more easily. He represents the opposite situation to the watcher: a person who is relatively more sensitive to and aware of his own feelings than the feelings of others.

The kind of member experimentation which is of greatest help to the group stems from an easy relationship to the problem and to the people in the group. Such a member is not anxious, and seems to act spontaneously rather than compulsively (like the plungers) or with inhibition (like the watchers). His spontaneity reflects an "inner freedom" which comes from acceptance of the limits, on the one hand, and lack of fear of his own feelings, on the other. One might expect a considerable amount of self-discipline in the spontaneous person: the problem-solving methods are understood so fully that behavior is automatically relevant to problem-solving and therefore can be expressed easily. With this sort of self-discipline, action-channels are available, and he does not get "tied up" within himself as a result of frustration. His energy goes to the problem rather than being expended internally in fantasies, bottled emotions, and monumental evasions of feelings and inhibitions of impulses.

Thus various people appear to follow different principles of experiencing and reacting. These different principles result at any given time in a particular kind and quality of integration, each with characteristic amounts of spontaneity, peace, ease, inhibition, anxiety, or tension. With each pattern of integration, there is a characteristic evaluation-action pattern, and its characteristics become the foundations of the ability to solve problems. These patterns are made known to the observer as different ways of conducting the experimental inquiry through which the member solves his membership problems, within the framework of the objective problem-solving of the group.

ADAPTATION

Social learnings are determined by the social aspects of experiencing. The face-to-face group is the most effective laboratory for social learning because there is immediate response to one's behavior, and cause-effect relations are therefore readily established. In every group, there are agreements and rules. And there is also a group-sanctioned set of explanations about why these rules are necessary, under what conditions they hold in force, and how they may be changed.

From the standpoint of the individual's need to grow and develop, two questions need to be asked: Does life under these rules have enough scope for me to experiment? How valid are our explanations of the rules? If there is sufficient opportunity and validity, then living in the group increases the possibilities of adaptation in other situations, of meeting life as it comes. If there is not sufficient scope, or if the group explanations are unsound—as when authoritarian dictates are sought and accepted without question—then experience in the group is teaching the individual things that will make his adaptations in other situations more difficult.

The "purpose-oriented" group referred to in the preceding chapter is likely to be an environment in which means to adaptation can be learned. The "procedure-oriented" group has false bases for adaptation; it teaches a rationale which, when it is tried in other groups, will result in frustration and member conflict.

The purpose-oriented group is one which is realistically in touch with the situation; the procedure-oriented group is not. Being "in touch" means producing behaviors appropriate to the demands of a situation; and this requires accurate appraisal of the elements that can be changed by means available to the group and of the limitations that, for the time being at least, have to be accepted.

Adaptation is thus both an individual and a group affair. The individual adapts to the group—accepting some things and changing others. But *through* this adaptation—not apart from it—the individual also adapts to the larger world for which his group provides the necessary experience.

The concepts of thinking, acting, and feeling, and of integration and adaptation, were basic tools used in designing the technologies in Part I. Throughout the case study in chapter 5, these concepts are used explicitly and openly by the group as an aid to its training. The skill of the teacher in planning classroom activities that will meet the needs of his children depends upon his recognition of these processes going on within the children. The success of the neighborhood groups in chapter 1 and the productive working groups in chapter 4 is determined by the extent of their vested interest in purpose rather than in procedure. The ability to guess correctly the balance between evaluative and acting responses of audiences is fundamental to the strategic use of the techniques of chapter 6.

These considerations are important because they are a part of the realities with which a group must deal—in one way or another.

CHAPTER 9

A group is influenced by and must take account of the laws of nature, the laws and customs of groups in the community, the unique way of life of the group itself, and the meanings and needs of its individual members.

This is a highly complex process and it requires continuous awareness of the relationships between achievement and process problems.

Reality: Factors in the Problem-Situation

INTRODUCTION

The basic principle for the guidance of human behavior is the "reality principle." This principle states that there are facts which need to be taken into account; there is a prior reality—a set of existing conditions independent of the will of a person or group—within which one must operate. When a person tries to act as if these conditions do not exist, or as if they were different than they are, his action is aggravating to the problem-situation rather than constructive; it makes bigger problems out of little ones; it jeopardizes immediate goal achievement; and, through thwarting the potential for individual and group growth, it may curtail long-range possibilities.

In practice, the meaning of the reality principle is that some possible behaviors and actions are "appropriate" and "realistic"; others are not. One way to describe the task of a group is "the production of behavior appropriate to the situation." It is clear that to pursue the matter further, we must know how to define the situation, the factors one must know immediately to take action, and the factors which can safely be left to discover themselves as action unfolds.

"Appropriate behavior" is achieved through the exercise of choice, and this is done by selecting from among possible alternatives. The exercise of choice is creative with regard to formulating alternatives; it is judgmental with regard to the selection of a particular alternative that is most appropriate—i.e., most capable of realization in the existing situation.

Some choice-points are crucial. In these the consequences of choosing one alternative rather than another may be long-range and conclusive, because the range of alternatives for future choices is drastically reduced by the specific action undertaken. On the other hand, there are choices in which the particular alternative selected is of little importance, where all that is required is that some decision be made. An example of this is the selection of a person to be chairman in a meeting of a mature group. If all the alternatives satisfy the best criteria the group can formulate, then it makes little difference which of these alternatives is selected. Certainly the history of the group will depend upon the choice made, but no group can do more than make the best choice it can at the time.

As a rule, effective group operation and productivity is possible only when the group is aware of its crucial choice-points, is creative in formulating alternatives, and is able to select with confidence one alternative as most appropriate.

In this chapter, we wish to consider the realities of the group-in-a-situation. We wish first to see what sort of ideas have to be taken into account; to do this we shall consider several different sorts of "realities." We shall pay some attention to thinking about the extent to which each sort of reality is coercive, and the extent to which it can be changed. We then wish to consider the variety of changes necessary in situations, and to point out the kinds of things groups have to make choices about and take action on.

Types of Realities

We have considerable confidence, in the absence of any contradictory experience, that things dropped will fall; that the sun will rise at the prescribed time; that dry coal will burn if heated to its kindling temperature in a proper supply of air; that an airplane will rise faster if it takes off into the wind rather than with the wind. We accept such statements as "facts," presumably proof against human tampering or vested interest. They are also generalizations, not depending for their truth upon some special combination of circumstances. They are also bases of prediction as to what I can safely expect: that if I do so and so, such and such consequences will follow. And finally, they can be tested and found "true" by people of different races, creeds, political beliefs, and intelligence.

Although these statements are made by men, we tend to act as if men only "discovered" the laws, and we attribute the laws to the nature of the physical world, not to the nature of men. We also think of these statements as being able to "stand alone"; they require very little in the way of supporting assumptions. Possibly they refer to situations so deeply understood and familiar that the supporting assumptions can be taken for granted. Thus we regard the physical world as one vast self-consistent system: the universe. All parts of this system work on the same principles, so that study of any one part helps us understand better the operation of the whole.

This physical world extends, in our thinking at least, some distance into the organic biological world. Physiology, for example, is the study of physical and chemical aspects of living beings. Those aspects of life in which we feel most certain of our understanding are the ones to which we can apply the concepts of physical science. Where such concepts cannot be used, biological science employs the idea of probability. Probability statements are true for groups, but cannot be used to make certain predictions about any individual or event. We can know, for example, that 25 per cent of the offspring of a blue-eyed father and one type of brown-eyed mother will have blue eyes. But we cannot relate blue eyes to birth-order, sex, month of conception, or any other characteristic which distinguishes one child from another. All we can really say is that so far as any particular child is concerned, he has one chance in four of having blue eyes. In the same way, the actuarial tables tell us what chance the "average" man of sixty has to live to be sixty-one; but who is "average"?

By and large, the principles and facts of biology are comments about the way in which large homogeneous collections of individuals interact with the physical world. The variability of interaction is all attributed to the living creatures, rather than to caprice in the world of rocks and stars. And "proof" in biology is the verification that in a given percentage of instances certain physical and chemical aspects of living things will have a predicted composition, size, energy content, structure, or other objectively measurable characteristic.

There is another class of statement about the physical and biological worlds. These are definitional and they specify relationships among various properties or characteristics. An object which displays some of the characteristics will have the other associated properties as well. Thus objects which, on the basis of simple tests, are classified as "living things" can be counted on to take in materials, give out other materials, and be changed in the process. They have a course of growth, they have the property of irritability, they reproduce their kind. These statements are descriptive and they are true of objects selected to fit the description.

Classification can be based upon properties either of structure or of process. Thus plants are often characterized by physical characteristics, through the sense of sight alone. On the other hand, diseases can be classified by symptoms, which in turn are interpreted as evidence of what is going on in the body. The former is a "static," the latter a "dynamic," basis of classification. By way of illustration, the definition of an electron has both aspects: it is defined both in terms of its material structure and in terms of the possible ways it can interact with other forms of matter.

For the most part, such definitional statements are comments about functions or kinds of reactions, by which we can recognize the species or processes we wish to define. These statements are tools for thinking. They are meant to be used to solve problems; to help determine our conduct in problematic situations more wisely. If a human being inevitably performs certain functions, then it is *as if* he needs to do these things. Carrying out the functions is interpreted by us as motivated, purposive behavior. This feeling in us is reinforced by the observation that these functions can be carried out under the most adverse circumstances. If you plant seeds in a dark closet, the resulting plant is taller and more slender than one which grew in the sunlight—almost as if it were "trying" to grow out of the dark into the light, which somehow is "known" to be there.

We have, then, the notions of a physical world; of living things interacting with this world; of certain defining and characteristic kinds of interaction or functioning; of some hypothetical purpose or need to carry out these functions. We note that the "facts" are of different sorts: the physical facts give us a material frame of reference, the properties of which are stability, consistency, and generality; the biological "facts" are probable descriptions of related functions; and finally the interpretation of need gives us concepts of tendencies which "must be realized" and which have to be accepted as forces to be dealt with, whether or not we like them.

Turning to human beings, it is clear that they can help each other or hinder each other in meeting their "natural" needs. As communication and transportation developed, as exchange systems came into being, as one man became able to command more than one man's worth of energy, human organization developed. Simple biological needs originally required for their fulfilment a social organization no more complicated than the family, in which individual roles were determined by sex, strength, and age. But with newer technological developments, these simple needs began to manifest themselves through elaborate means, whose various aspects seemed increasingly unrelated to the simple drives. With them came control systems for the regulation of individual behavior and for the limitation of individual power. Maintenance of the control systems became a social end in itself.

The "facts" in the area of social reality are, first, statements about the agreements men live by—customs, laws, procedures, doctrines, status systems; and second, statements about the conditions under which these agreements obtain, who holds them, how they are to be changed. These agreements operate at all levels of explicitness, from written laws with elaborate machinery of enforcement to unwritten "rules of the game" which make possible social mobility, change of social structure, and adaptation of the group to its environment. They describe control systems of particular cultures or institutions of particular people at a particular period and place.

But such social-cultural realities are less coercive than physical and biological realities. There is more fluidity, confusion, and anxiety; less can be taken for granted. There is less universality and less consistency, as any examination by the bylaws or legal code of an old group will quickly reveal. Social reality is "legislated" by men, and there is considerable consciousness in this process. What men can arrange, men can change—provided they have the necessary agreements upon means and methods. It is our thesis that only as men learn the necessary methods can changes be brought about to enable them to find and maintain an effective adaptation to their physical, biological, and social realities.

Our technologies can and should be examined from this broad point of view. Thus the citizen participation program described in chapter 1 was created as a means to help the community face the facts about its own changing character. The notion discussed in chapter 3, that for successful in-service training the school must have direct relations with the community, can be seen as an effort to build communication in the faculty around the processes of adaptation to some reality more significant and reliable than the usual set of institutional and administrative rules. The educational importance of "learning by doing" is not so much that activity is desirable per se as that through activity one perforce comes in contact with physical, biological, and social realities about which one can then develop a stable view of the world.

It is within these realities that a face-to-face group proceeds to develop its own particular culture, its own view of reality as it is to be perceived and operated upon.

REALITIES WITHIN THE FACE-TO-FACE GROUP

In the last two chapters I have tried to indicate the genesis of the kinds of problems of individuals in groups. We begged the question of how consciously or unconsciously these problems would be worked on. Judging by the fact that so much of "human relations" training acts to make aware to the group things that are blocking it in ways only vaguely felt, there must be a considerable content and activity in the unconscious. We wish to consider this possibility further in connection with face-to-face groups, and add to our list two additional kinds of reality which are crucial to group operation and which are commonly ignored.

The first has already been given sufficient attention in the first two chapters. It is the subjective reality of the individual's world. This world is not merely of interest to the psychologist: it is actually the direct context of all acts, since there are no acts except those of individuals. We have spoken sufficiently for the time being of the individual's need to keep this private house in order; and of his need, therefore, to influence the group's definition of the membership role in such a way that his need-meeting skills also help the group.

There is a second type of subjective reality in groups, and we want to discuss it, although we feel less sure of its operation. This has been called the "group unconscious," or the "collective unconscious," or the "group mentality."

In chapter 7, we mentioned the concept of internalized groups. Although every individual is influenced by somewhat different internalized groups, it is likely that all individuals have experienced the same types of problems. Problems, particularly those invested with anxiety, are easy to communicate, to share, to know that they are shared. Assuming the universality of anxiety-problems, the fact that they can be mobilized by cues, and the possibility that such feelings are readily shared, we may be a little closer to an explanation of some difficult-to-describe periods in group life. These are periods which have the quality of sibling rivalry, of adolescent ambivalence between dependence and independence, of seemingly "self-destructive" tendencies, of sudden group "insights" which crystallize apparently within the space of a few minutes. These phenomena are difficult to explain solely in terms of strictly individual problems and needs. It is as if certain cues in the actual situation mobilized the same set of feelings in most members, as though a process of remembering were occurring, and as though the individuals were remembering the same things, the same threats, the same barriers to forward action.

As applied to groups, Bion has developed this theme in the concept of a subconscious "group mentality," which he opposes to consciously guided group achievement.[1] In the group mentality there is a shared agreement to avoid certain tasks, a resistance to allowing certain problems to become explicit. There is a conspiracy of shared emotionality which reinforces that side of all of the members' ambivalences which is resistant to "work." The resistance is easily felt, and it expresses itself in many ways. Periods during which the group mentality is in force are characterized by apathy; "running away from work" into storytelling, jok-

1. W. R. Bion, "Experiences in Groups. I" and "Experiences in Groups. II," *Human Relations*, I, No. 3, 314–20, and No. 4, 487–96.

ing, theorizing, making long lists on the blackboard, breaking up into private conversations, sudden hostility toward the leader, quarreling, and the like. Such emotional periods represent a state of affairs to which every individual, according to Bion, is a party. Applying the principle that to understand behavior is to know its purpose, it is as if the group as a whole has a "hidden agenda," a secret task into which its energy is flowing. Chapter 5 is centrally concerned with the diagnosis and development of awareness of hidden agendas in a training group.

If we judge what is real by what makes a difference, then the group mentality and the individual subjective worlds are the most real of all. For these are the spheres in which feelings, tensions, and impulses to action arise. Objective problems have a lesser reality, one derived from our need to do something to relieve tensions which arose in the other spheres during past actions. The formulation in explicit language of a problem is a process of abstraction from action to thought; and thoughts about a problem have less emotional significance than do impulses during problematic situations.

Compared to the basic emotional dynamics of the group, as represented in the feelings of individuals for or against one another, the objective problems are unreal. They provide escape from emotional travail into socially meaningful fantasy. This fantasy takes the form of a rehearsal of possible actions; and these actions, when achieved, become part of objective social reality.

The realities, which to a large extent determine what happens in a group, are at two levels of influence and are dynamically related. The reality of the objective problem is an interpretation of the relations of the group to its outside world. In this interpretation are incorporated the patterns of factors from the physical, biological, and social worlds described in the preceding section. The job of solving the problem is one of arriving at a solution which is appropriate, in terms of the sorts of facts belonging to these reality spheres. These are facts which can be obtained by measurement, polling, observation—by experimentation and statistics. They are capable of logical and rational manipulation. The problem is safe because the factors involved are part of the common community domain; they are not vested interests of individuals in the group, and objectivity is easy to achieve. Solutions to objective problems have the highest material reality. The results are incontrovertible, and the changes brought about get incorporated into the objective realities of men. These problems we shall call the "achievement problems" of the group.

But there is greater reality in the world of desire and fear of the individual and group unconscious. Problems of this sort make more difference to the group, require more energy to deal with, are more challenging to leadership, require greater self-discipline among members, and produce a greater reward for participation. Problems at this level we shall refer to as "process problems." The motivation to solve achievement problems is a reflection of the need to resolve process problems which originate in or between the actual group and other internalized groups. The obstacles to achievement problem-solving are due to one's inability to find behaviors which simultaneously satisfy both sorts of problem-solving demands. In such a case, the energy goes into the process problem because of its more compelling anxieties, and the objective problem is left untouched. We are forced to recognize that seemingly nonproductive periods of flight and emotionality exist for a reason, and that our job is to find the reason, even though it may require the help of a theory about transactions within the individual and group unconscious.

The simplest way to understand nonproductive periods is through studying the relationships between the process and achievement problems. The demands of the achievement problem come from the relatively stable and objective physical, biological, and social worlds. They provide a clear frame of reference for understanding the public meanings of behavior. We observe the group working on achievement problems. If the activity is inefficient or nonproductive, we look for process problems which would account for the trouble. Through attempts to explain these inferred process problems, we arrive at our theories about the subconscious reality worlds of the individuals and the group. If action taken on the strength of these theories rectifies the problems, then we assume that the theories were correct (pp. 51–61 discuss the method as applied to classroom teaching). Note that I am advocating here the use of the biological model set up earlier: just as we know the properties of living things by studying their interactions with the physical world, so we know the process problems of a group by studying its behaviors in working on achievement problems.

In general, then, it is the relationship between process and achievement problem-solving that we need to watch and understand. While both may be studied separately as well, the choice of the one deserving attention, the kind of attention, and analysis which is appropriate are things we learn from the relationships between the two. It is in the light of this biological model that we distrust group therapies which purport to deal only with the process problems, and planners who think planning for physical objectives is all that is required. What is needed is not a complete blueprint for the solution of one kind of problem or the other, but rather a set of policies for deciding how next to proceed under every possible type of relationship between the two.

The basic problem of the *group*, then, is to develop a rationale for dealing simultaneously with problems on both levels of reality; the basic concern of the *individual* is to deal with his own subjective world; and the basic concern of the community is to establish an environment for the various groups sufficiently stable for them to be able to formulate realistic objective problems and carry the solutions into socially significant action. But these latter concerns are by-products of the former, not separate enterprises.

The conclusion we draw from the above is that the group's major task is to steer and control its behaviors, and that it needs a methodology for doing this. The particular procedures employed in a particular case should represent applications of this methodology to the realities of the situation. This application is achieved through the process of continual decision among alternatives for dealing with the various emerging and changing relationships between process and achievement problems. We wish in the next two chapters to deal with methodology and policies for controlling group process—the function of leadership.

CHAPTER 10

As a group works, it develops its own way of life, its own culture. This culture is a set of agreements by means of which the group as a whole appears to co-ordinate the effort and contributions of individuals. When the agreements are appropriate to the task, the group is effective.

We here spell out thirteen basic principles which underlie the operation of successful groups. Then we see some of the processes by which the group disciplines itself to enforce or change its culture.

Control: Developing the Group Culture

INTRODUCTION

As can be seen from the preceding three chapters, group operation is a highly complex business. Every group, even at its first meeting, has a long and manifold past, extending through the history of its members. Every group is part of a larger scene, and is continually receiving pressure from and exerting pressures on a vast number of other groups. Every group is a microcosm of the prevailing culture, and, at the same time, is a unique event.

The purpose of this chapter is to take a large conceptual step: from description of what goes on in groups (chapters 7, 8, 9) to the concept of leadership as the intelligent control of group activity. This will enable us in the next chapter to deal directly with the problems and policies of leadership. Another way to describe what we wish to do is to say that we shall attempt to bridge the gap between the science of group interaction and the technology of groups as social instruments.

Technology is the putting of science to work for conscious, human ends. It accepts scientific knowledge as the portrayal of the processes that go on. Among these processes are some which tend to move in the direction of the ends desired. Some of the other processes are seen as moving toward undesired ends, or away from the desired ends. The job of the technologist is to find the means to increase the rate of the processes going toward desired ends and to slow down or inhibit the processes going against them. But he has to begin with an understanding of the processes he has to deal with, and with some notion of their relative driving force. Above all, he must be able to distinguish processes that cannot happen from those that can be made to happen.

We cannot, in social science, expect for a long time to reach anything like the precision of scientific application that the chemical engineer, for example, reaches with his science of thermodynamics. There are fundamental differences, too, in approach. The chemical engineer is essentially a dominating manipulator, bending to his will a mass of chemicals. The social engineer or administrator working with people is dealing with a very different sort of entity. Manipulation, bending people to one's own will against their wishes, has been thoroughly tried at many times and places in man's history, and it does not work—at least not for long. By adding to his team the propagandist, with his arts of persuasion, the manipulator can go farther and last longer, but he can never get the kind of efficiency of which man is capable. He ultimately has to rely on force, on a terrific expenditure of energy which may well exceed what he can get from the group.

I am thoroughly convinced that the group itself has to be the engineer. It has to make its own applications of scientific knowledge to its own situation. Utilization of scientific knowledge for better group operation is not so much an engineering matter as it is a training problem. The "expert" is not the leader or manipulator of the group; he is the consultant or trainer. This is why we find over and over again, from case histories of groups that developed into effective instruments, that there was an unusual awareness of their own processes; that in these groups a significant common element was a continual effort to make explicit in the group the things the group was feeling and doing. It is only by making conscious to members the state of affairs in the group that intelligence can be effectively and systematically applied.

This chapter will describe the kinds of things of which groups need to be conscious in their own operation if they expect to learn to solve their problems more efficiently.

In meetings there are at least four distinguishable types of legitimate and inevitable problems facing groups all the time: (*a*) the publicly stated problem the group was brought together to solve; (*b*) the hidden problems of dealing with shared anxieties which usually are not explicitly formulated (problems within the "group mentality"); (*c*) individual efforts to achieve publicly stated ends (getting ideas to "take home" to another group, or learning something, or making a contribution to a worthy project); and (*d*) individuals' efforts to deal with their own hidden problems of membership anxiety and self-integration and adaptation.

The group must determine what provision, if any, needs to be made in order that each of these types of problem-solving go on. It must also control its activity in such a way that the energy going into each of the four types helps the group move toward its goals. But what are these goals?

The typical action group sees problem-solving of type *a* as its goal; some human relations trainers concentrate on type *b;* type *c* is typical of most workshops and "educational" enterprises; and group therapists are likely to strive for type *d*. There is no objection to selecting one particular type of goal to define success —unless it causes us to resist giving the necessary consideration to the other three types. Groups are well advised to acknowledge the "completeness" of people, the fact that significant achievement by human beings requires an engagement of thoughts, emotions, and actions, and that there must be sufficient scope for all these kinds of behavior in their proper and necessary integrative relationships.

Effective group operation requires conscious co-ordination and control of the four types of problem-solving; and this is not automatically achieved. The possibility of achievement is even affected by some decisions which are typically made before the meeting starts: Who will be members of the group? How shall the task be defined initially? What time limits or other pressures on our deliberations do we accept?

Control is also exerted in the opening remarks; in fact, some research workers have felt that the whole course of a meeting is determined by the events of the first few minutes. The particular reality factors to which the group's attention is directed in the opening remarks can make a vast difference in the proportions of the four types of problem-solving. Thus it may be "realistic" to want much overt participation (at least in some kinds of meetings), but calling people's attention to this at the beginning is likely to raise the amount of energy going into problem-solving of type *b*—dealing with hidden shared anxieties—at the expense of the others.

In general, we usually think of control as exerted continuously during the meeting. The conditions we are trying to safeguard through this control of process are, typically, stated in the following ways: (*a*) to keep the discussion "group-centered," so that it is of interest to all and so all can participate; (*b*) to safeguard ease of expression so members can say what they really think; (*c*) to keep the discussion at a sufficiently "practical" level that everyone can visualize what is being talked about; and (*d*) to maintain sufficient "sensitivity" to what happens that participants take account of each other's wishes and keep everyone interested and motivated.

In developing our notions about the control system and how it operates, we shall begin with the concept of "work" and its relationships to the four types of problems. Then we shall discuss productivity (actual goal achievement) as depending upon the creation of the appropriate balance between work and nonwork in all activity. Next we shall state a variety of principles of control, and this will lead into a portrayal of a number of different ways in which control is exerted.

Conditions Required for Work in the Group

Both for practical and theoretical reasons, it is useful to distinguish work from other kinds of activity. At the visceral level, we can tell immediately when a group is "working well" or "not getting anywhere." Ordinarily, work is a kind of activity in which we feel that people are "pulling together." There is a feel of co-operation about it, a voluntary, high-morale aspect.

It is evident that for this kind of work to go on, there must be publicly stated and generally shared goals. Of the four types of problem-solving listed above, types *a* and *c*, group and individual efforts to achieve publicly understood goals, are most likely to be involved when we feel that the group is "working." A characteristic of work toward stated goals is that it is easy to see what is happening. A host of decisions have to be made, but they are made openly, and people know that they are being made. They furnish precedents for future decision-situations. The decision-making processes during work contribute to the body of agreements that constitute the "culture" of the group.

The "work" involved in problem-solving activity directed to hidden problems of the individual and the group (types *b* and *d*) is mostly in the subconscious. We shall not consider such ac-

tivity to be work, preferring to reserve this term for purposive
goal-directed behavior in which an obstacle to the goal is overcome by conscious effort. We may, however, refer to the hidden
agenda as problem-solving, because as observers we can fairly well
predict behavior on the theory that the individual or group acts
as if guided by a particular purpose—even though this purpose is
subconsciously held.

For any but the most impulsive behavior in the group, there is,
on the part of the individual, some conscious perception that he
can and wants to contribute to problem-solving of public types
a and/or *c*. He has motivation, and he is conscious that he has
it. He is "involved" in the work of the group and wants it to "go
well" so that his opportunity to participate will be protected. The
publicly accepted problem gives him a basis for communication
with others and for knowing how to act and choose appropriate
behavior. Moreover, when his behavior contributes to the public
goals, he is rewarded by the group's expressed approval or—and
this is a higher compliment—by their making insightful use of
the contribution.

At the same time, however, according to chapter 7, the need
which has the highest priority for an individual or group is for
problem-solving of the private sort to reduce anxieties to tolerable
levels. The source of anxiety is in the quality of relationships with
other people, even though anxiety can be mobilized by cues associated with objective problem-solving processes. Anxiety enters
into objective problem-solving only to the extent that it is "contaminated" with problems of human relationship. When we say,
for example, that "Mr. Smith committed suicide because he lost
his money and felt himself to be a failure," we are probably only
half-right. Success and failure are group determined. The unfortunate Smith's despondency was primarily, we would guess, over
the feeling that people would look down on him or "sympathize"
with him; that he "couldn't take it" any more. The problem-
solving at which he failed was only partially of type *c*, his own
efforts to reach a possibly stated goal. The significant difficulty
was with type *d*, his own anxieties about himself. Had he been
able to deal with the imagined problems of his relationship to
other people, loss of money would be merely annoying or uncom-

fortable; but it would hardly produce anxiety at such a level of intensity that it had to be removed at its source.

The fact that there is most need "to do something to relieve the situation" at times when there is anxiety; and the fact that anxiety is primarily concern over relationship problems; and the fact that no two individuals have the same relationship problems —these, when added up, lead us to the conclusion that if people behave similarly in a group, they do so for different reasons. They have a common understanding that some particular behavior is possible and is relevant to public goals. In general, however, members do not behave identically. They have "readiness" for differeat behaviors at any given time; and there are times when some members are not really "ready" for any overt participation. And, given the same goal, they are almost certain to approach it in somewhat different ways.

Control and co-ordination of individual contributions occur through the public meanings of behavior to the group. For the individual producing the behavior, there are, in addition, meanings known only to him. Private meanings may be insights newly achieved, reassurances that an individual can meet competition, feelings that he really demolished another's silly argument, sudden realization of possibilities for friendship with another member, etc. Or, members can be gratified with the behaviors of others in the group as well as their own. They can be reassured that they are smarter or that someone really understands their point of view, or they may be glad someone finally "told off" the leader, etc.

These nonwork gratifications are characteristic of the bull-session, of private problem-solving, and of periods of emotionality. When the work-type problem focus becomes too dim, or too uninteresting, too much of a detour to more basic need-meeting, private problem-solving activity becomes greater. There is more emotionality, and the content of discussion may appear to be any set of ideas that can serve as a vehicle for communicating feeling. The group seems to be trying to maintain itself, its mutual involvement, its rate of reward, through recourse to less obvious, private problem-solving. If the group does not feel free enough to engage in such activity, or if there actually are not, for the time being, any sufficiently strong tensions, then the group may fill in the vacuum with academic argument. Sometimes it can be quite convincing, too.

In the second meeting of one training group, the leader decided to withdraw temporarily. The group members did not know why he did this, and did not feel free enough to ask. Reasonably, they started talking about the "problems of this group." But there were not enough prior agreements for the diagnosis of their group problems, and they had not yet had enough experience together to find much data for evidence.

The leader was not surprised to find them speculating about their problems with very little basis in fact. But as the conversation went on, the leader began to detect something else (later verified through interviews): the group did not feel much concerned over its own problem of withdrawal by the leader; the group did not yet mean enough to them for such details to matter. What was "really" happening was that they were simply trying to maintain their involvement in the group; they found interaction more gratifying than the embarrassment of sitting quietly. It was as if there was a particular rate of reward they were trying to establish and maintain. They did it by talking about problems, and since they had little to go on in the actual group, they drew on problems from their various internalized groups. Thus it happened that the leader listened to a learned discussion of such questions as: Are we too dependent on the leader? Does a person have to give up his independence to work in a group? Aren't we just competing with each other? The problems were those from the prevailing culture, and they were simply advanced to fill the gap.

I cite this illustration to indicate the very real drive to maintain the group through maintaining interaction; and I am also warning against the dangers of taking too seriously what people say about group problems in such nonwork situations. It is almost impossible to diagnose group problems accurately unless there is an accepted work task; only then does one have immediately useful mental images against which to contrast and interpret the behavior of the group.

To summarize: one can usually count on a group doing *some-*

thing, but co-ordination comes primarily through the work components of the group's total activity. One can also count on individuals having some readiness to participate, but the readiness is greater when there is a work job to be done because then the member role is more readily definable and individuals know how to behave. When the group is working, one finds the following by-products: first, the problem is being continuously reformulated and redefined as new meanings are consciously explored by the group; second, the culture of the group is developing, efficiency is increasing, the group is acquiring technical skills; and third, the feelings of membership in the group are increasing; the group develops more meaning for the individual, and he will work harder and take more risks to keep it going.

GROUP PRODUCTIVITY

Productivity is a concept of the amount and quality of desired change produced through group experience. The kind we refer to as "learning" means change in the way of behaving, presumably reflecting a new attitude, insight, degree of skill, etc. This sort of alteration has continuing long-range effects, and it occurs to people and groups. The productivity of classroom activity is ordinarily judged by the amount of change it produces in the pupils. But there are other types of changes that could be considered in measuring productivity: changes in the teacher, changes in the "maturity" or efficiency of operation of the class, changes in parental attitudes brought about by pupils as a result of experiences in the classroom. Let us look at three distinguishable types of stable changes which can be used to assess the productivity of group activity.

First, there is the amount of change during a period of time in the group itself. Any learned, stable change in a group would be evident as an alteration in its ability to solve problems, make decisions, meet individual needs of the members, encourage or inhibit the formation of cliques, etc. The change would be maintained as such in the "culture" of the group, the set of agreements through which the group controls its own operation. The characteristic change of the culture of a group is developmental—not from one rule to another, but from no rule to some rule. More agreements are constantly being achieved within broad policies. Thus, if a group has a "set" toward encouraging members to participate in its leadership, the cultural shift is likely to be the development of the agreements necessary to implement this policy. The agreements will be in the form of decisions about whether or not there will be a chairman, under what conditions, how selected, how recalled, how his duties are to be defined, the sort of supportive behavior expected of the others. Through experience, the group spells out in practical language the "meaning" of its beliefs about method, authority, justice, and other values. The "spelling out" is done in the development of habits and practices which are thereafter automatically used in the relevant situations.

Besides a change toward greater specificity, the culture of a group can also alter in its basic value patterns. Typically, for example, the orientation of a training group changes from dependency on the leader to dependency on itself for procedural suggestion, from reliance on the authority of the leader to reliance on the authority of its own experience.

A second way to think about productivity of group experience is in terms of the amount of change it has produced during a period of time in the behavior of other groups. This amounts to an assessment of the influence of the activities of one group on the activities of adjacent groups. For such an influence to have long-range effects, some learning, some change in the control system, must have occurred in the influenced group. Community councils, human relations commissions, and *ad hoc* citizens groups attempt to bring about changes in other groups, in their practices, attitudes, skills, officer personnel, etc. We shall present the thesis later that this kind of change can be brought about only through the agency of people who have "membership" both in the influence group and in the influenced group. We might refer to this kind of productivity as the rate of change of the community in which the group operates.

A third kind of productivity through learning can be seen in the rate of change of the subjective internalized community of the individual. Thus, as learnings occur in the actual group, one's memberships in other groups are also affected. The productivity of a therapy group's activities might be considered as the rate of rearrangement of the individual's pattern of overlapping memberships, toward a state of lessened conflict or anxiety. In so far as any group participation has therapeutic effects, one can think of its productivity partly in these terms.

In summary.—Any experience can be seen as a pattern of four types of problem-solving endeavors: of these, two types can be referred to as "work," as "achievement problem-solving," or as "culture-building." The other two types are referred to as "nonwork," "process problem-solving," or as the operation of "group mentality." The productivity of group activity depends upon the manner in which these kinds of endeavors are controlled. A productive activity is one from which the group learns to control its next activity, so that it will be productive of further change in the group toward still more productive activity. Productivity is determined by the group's control system.

In Part I we have seen, either directly or by implication, a number of concepts of productivity. In the case of citizen action, productivity is primarily change of social and physical conditions in the community, and, secondarily, change within participating individuals. Productivity of in-service training presents exactly the reverse situation. Administrators are concerned with changes in working groups and in the relations among them. In the classroom, changes within students and teacher should both be appraised. Productivity in laboratory training involves changes in individuals and also in the culture of the training group.

Principles Underlying the Control of the Group

There are different assumptions about what it is that is to be controlled. A theoretician might ask: "Is a group more than the sum of its parts? Does it have properties over and above the pooled characteristics of its members?" A student of the group might ask: "Should I be looking at individuals or at the group as a whole?" A leader might ask himself: "Is my job to encourage participation of each individual, or is my job to pay attention to keeping the problem clearly defined?" The socially mobile member might ask himself: "Is it all right for me to sit next to Joe and get in a word with him now and then, or will this be resented?"

All of these questions betray the same underlying perplexity: Is the group an organic whole, made up of parts, to be sure, but basically organized as one unit; or is the group really just a lot of people reacting to each other in their own ways?

But this is not a real problem. The group is not "really" one or the other. For some purposes, such as ours when we want to talk about the "control system of the group," we find it useful to think of the group as a whole. For other purposes, such as predicting the role an individual will play in a meeting, it is more useful to think of that person as an individual and the group as his environment.

Our question then becomes: What perception of the group is most useful for a participant to have? What viewpoint, if held by the members, will result in the most productive experience for all? In the remainder of this section we wish to delineate the set of member beliefs or principles which seems to result in most effective group operation. These beliefs must rest on a basic assumption by each member that the group exists as a whole, and that every member represents that whole and partakes of it.

1. *Each individual statement, as soon as it is made, becomes the property of the group.*—"Jack's suggestion" is the "suggestion made by Jack," but Jack does not own it, and Jack does not have to defend it or prove it. It is up to the group to determine whether the suggestion is useful to itself, to test whether it is a good suggestion. On this matter, Jack himself is usually the best informant to the group; he knows most about his own suggestion and he can be used as a resource person to clarify his thought or explain its possible usefulness to the group. (For an illustration, see the case study, pp. 322–26.)

2. *Emotional expressions by individuals express the needs of the group.*—If Chris and Bud get into a scrap, everyone else appears to the others to be in it too. The chances are that the members, for one reason or another, are getting some gratification out of the fight. Therefore the fighters are expressing the need of the group at that time to fight. If a member steps in to try to stop the fight, he will

be seen as fighting, too. If a member sits by and does nothing, he will be seen as wanting the fight to occur. Emotionality is shared throughout the group, and the group responds selectively to those aspects of behavior that can be interpreted as contributing to it or being part of it. (This is the basic principle useful in steering the group. The case study in chapter 5 shows consistent use of this principle.)

3. *In all but extreme cases, problem people are to be considered group problems.*—The group does not "work on" individuals. If there is somebody in the group who disturbs everyone, and everyone knows it, the question is: "Why does this sort of behavior bother us; why can't we deal with it?" The question is not: "Why is Fred such a troublemaker?" In general, the group cannot expect to change a sick or disturbed person, but it can learn to handle the anxieties that such members mobilize in themselves. Singling out these people and giving them attention, teaches them that their disturbing behaviors will be rewarded. But if upsetting behavior is treated as a general, group problem, the "troublesome" person gets no attention at all as a person; he does get educative feedback as to the consequences of his behavior and how the group feels about it. In general, the group works only on group problems, not problems of individuals (see also "The Trainer Speaks to the Group," pp. 173–74).

4. *The question is not: "Is this behavior relevant to our problem?" but rather: "To what problem is this behavior relevant?"*—(And then: "How serious is this problem for us, and do we need to do anything about it?") All individual contributions are relevant. They arose from the situation of the group trying to do something, and they are entitled to consideration by everyone, since everyone contributed to the situation. (Meeting VIII, pp. 156–60, is a particularly clear illustration of the usefulness of this principle for diagnostic purposes.)

5. *A problem is whatever everybody feels to be a problem.*—All contributions are regarded as symptomatic of problems the group is working on or may need to work on. But no problem is accepted as one requiring action without some sort of reality test: either the group takes it up and begins working on it spontaneously, or they test to see whether it is generally felt to be a problem (see also the

discussion of "readiness," p. 61). And, of course, the group cannot and should not work on every problem; many lie outside the group's limits of operation, and many more can be endured—at least until demands of higher priority have been met.

6. *The group moves by consensus and agreement, not by taking sides in disputes.*—Minority-majority splits are generally over issues couched in global terms, rather than over concrete questions of what to do in a particular time and place. By and large, such big issues, about which no agreement is possible, are not actually used to split the group but rather to justify the fact that the group has already split. Under these conditions, the interests of the group are against finding agreement. (For a clear application, see the beginning events of the meeting described on pp. 10–12.)

7. *A decision has been reached whenever people feel sufficiently confident to act.*—The psychology of decision-making is concerned with understanding the data or concepts or preliminary experiences a group needs in order to have enough confidence or trust in itself and its suggestions to act. The most important foes of confidence are ambiguity, vagueness, and inability to assess the values and costs of alternatives. These are matters calling for more thinking, more data, more exploring of the obstacles individuals see. Steamroller tactics and persuasion are of no avail because they block the objective evaluation of consequences and the possibilities of correction if plans go awry. (General Smith showed considerable insight into this principle, see pp. 124–26.)

8. *Voting is never used to determine the right alternative, but it can be used to test confidence in a particular alternative.*—The use of voting implies a promise: we will not act unless everyone says he has confidence in the idea. In most situations, this is a more rigorous requirement than is necessary, and it is unrealistic to expect people to commit themselves in advance to something they have not yet experienced. With regard to agendas, for example, it is frequently wiser for the leader merely to ask permission from the group and then proceed if there are no objections (provided the situation is one in which it would be possible to voice an objection). This involves risk; but a group is justified in taking a risk if it has some recourse should its judgment turn out to be poor. (For amplification, see pp. 306–7.)

9. *Whenever the group does not know what it is doing, it ought to stop and find out.*—This does *not* mean that the group ought to argue over its objectives, but rather that it ought to describe to itself what it is doing. In unclear situations, there is actually discrimination against the participation of some members. When a person knows what the group is doing, then he also knows how to participate, and if he does not participate, it is reasonable to assume that he has nothing to contribute. But when a person does not know what the group is doing, he does not know how to participate, and he is blocked. Therefore, with every change in the nature of the group's activity, it is well to be sure the member roles are redefined. (Meeting IV, pages 146–48, shows an application of this principle.)

10. *All seriously intended contributions are to be responded to.*—The group understands that contributions are not only supposed to be helpful to the group, but that they also express some need of the individual to test his interpretation of the situation. Failure to respond to contributions is thus an act of discrimination against the person. If the contribution seems of no value, it is better to admit an inability to see its implications for the group than to ignore it. In general the climate of the group should be sufficiently objective and purpose-oriented that ideas out of which the group can extract no good can be rejected without rejection of the person. This is an important requirement for learning (see also the discussion of reality testing, pp. 49–50).

11. *No individual can speak for the group; the group speaks for itself.*— Each individual is a piece of the group, and he can be a spokesman for that piece. He can honestly report how he feels and what he thinks, and the group knows how to interpret such information. He can also give his impressions of the group as a whole. But no man really knows how others think and feel, and if he misrepresents them, they are entitled to defend themselves. The problem then becomes an undesirable interpersonal squabble. Members may respond to each other and the leader in various ways, but not as authoritative spokesmen for the group. (Tom's soliloquy, pp. 156–58, is an excellent illustration of what members can do.)

12. *There are individual differences, and people play different roles in*

each situation.—The way a person participates depends upon what opportunities for reward each individual perceives. Different individuals are rewarded by different kinds of participation because their needs are different and because the repertoire of roles each can fulfil is different. Those who have in their repertoire a role needed by the group are the ones who should be participants in each situation. If the group never engages in activity which needs their participation, then there is no reason for those persons being members of the group. The aim of the group should not be to get participation equally distributed among members. The aim should be to deal with its problems in a way sufficiently comprehensive that everyone can contribute if he wishes, and to see to it that there are no barriers in the group that would prevent needed contributions. (This principle is illustrated also in the discussion of resistance to change, pp. 74–76.)

13. *Every change in activity alters the prestige system and the opportunities for reward in the group.*—In general, a shift to a new activity will increase the reward possibilities for some members because they can contribute better to the new activity, and decrease them for others. Variety among activities gives more people a chance to find themselves and to achieve prestige. Although the selection of activities should be based on problem requirements, boredom and the need for change of pace should be recognized. (For further relationship with needs, see p. 253.)

The preceding statements cover a set of beliefs regarding the realities of group operation. The list can be written in other ways, and probably other lists would include more things or different things. The assumptions on which a group seems to operate reflect its control system; our list represents one such system. (It is applied to leadership problems on pp. 314–19, and to the experimental method of leadership on pp. 302–10.)

How the Control System Operates

In general, the co-ordination of human effort is obtained in one of two ways. The first is through the authority of shared ideas. The second is through the authority, backed by power, of a particular person or group. These are dealt with at length in chapter

4. The first is the ideal of democracy; the second is the ideal of autocracy.

This work is aimed at developing, in so far as possible, the democratic basis for co-ordination because it is the more effective. Beliefs such as those presented immediately above, if fully understood and acted upon by every member of a group, would provide for the greatest range of useful ideas and for their sharing throughout the group. Because each individual subscribed fully to the same minimum set of agreements, he would find his efforts joined with the efforts of others, so that his "power" would be co-extensive with the power of the entire group. He would be able to exert the most discerning initiative without having to clear his proposals with the group leadership. There would exist the maximum of freedom: the greatest scope of individual action coupled with the greatest security of group reinforcement.

I have been in groups that were reasonably close to this ideal. They were brought together for laboratory training in group operation. The individuals were highly motivated to try to reach this ideal; the twenty-four-hour-a-day culture of the environing workshop was set up to support it and to give individuals ample opportunity outside the group for reflection on what was happening in the group.

It has been interesting to discover, over the years, that this state of maturity does not mean complete "independence" in the traditional sense. A shared agreement or bargain is a social contract, a two-way street. It carries with it the implication that if in any situation I feel my action not to be in line with the policies I helped the group make, I am no longer "on my own." I must have further interaction with the group either to adjust my behavior to the spirit of the group agreements or to get an agreement within which my behavior is appropriate. Moreover, this is not strictly and exclusively an intellectual dependence; it is also an emotional one. To accept this kind of relationship to the group I also accept the idea that group policies under conditions of proper deliberation are "better" than those I would make by myself; that the experience of the group is a higher and more useful authority than the experience of any individual; that when I am in doubt as to my conduct, I can get from the group the interpretation or judgment that is in the best interests of all. The feeling that goes with the acceptance of these relationships is that of trust and of security based on trust.

Thus interdependence is always a blend of independence and dependence. The ideal is not to eliminate all dependency but to establish, protect, and maintain the quality of interdependence most appropriate for the welfare of all.

Typically, control systems in groups operate in several ways. The first is through determining the nature of responses to statements. This is the basic, continuous, pervasive operating reality of the group. *A* says something, *B* replies, *C* responds to *B*'s remark, or to a combination of *A*'s and *B*'s remarks. *A* says something more, and so on. Each response to a statement is the immediate stimulus for the next response. At the same time, every statement is a response to the general feeling of the group, to the individual's internalized anxieties, and the like.

From the group's shared agreements an individual deduces the limits within which he can choose among possible responses. The control system develops in the first place from the group's need for a stable environment—an environment in which it is possible to predict whether what one is about to do will be rewarded or punished. This possibility of predictability (and therefore of individual security) is increased as the group writes its unwritten laws of how to respond.

Suppose, for example, Al says: "Gosh, I think that decision we just made is all wrong." These replies might be made:

MARY (*with heat*): Well, this sure is a fine time to tell us that! If you didn't like what we were doing, why didn't you say something earlier?

or

MAC: I feel we won't really be sure whether its "right" or "wrong" until we have carried out the first step written there on the blackboard. In the meanwhile we all will need to be thinking about what data will be needed to assess it. Would this be a good thing to discuss now, to sort of warm up our further thinking along these lines? What do you think, Al?

or

TOM: You feel dissatisfied with the decision.

In the early meetings of a group it is to be expected that comments like Al's will evoke such different responses, and Al has no way of knowing the sort of response he will get. He does not know whether somebody will attack him, or try to use him as a responsible resource person to the group, or simply encourage him to reveal more feelings he may later regret having expressed. He also does not know how to respond further to the comments he receives, because he cannot be quite sure of the motives back of them. Mary, Mac, and Tom are operating with different and in some ways incompatible assumptions. The group will need at least to eliminate the incompatibility, if not the differences. And in doing so, a contribution will be made to the body of agreements through which the group controls itself.

The group control system is reasonably adequate when there is an understood rationale for responding to all sorts of remarks: the hypothetical suggestion, the call for action, the personal confession, the irrelevant flight, the attack, the complacent avoidance, scapegoating, diagnosing, experting, blocking, creating, etc. Of these various types of comments, the ones most requiring agreement are the emotional ones. In general, the responses should reflect the basic understanding that group deliberation is an inquiry leading to realistic decisions. The thirteen principles above specifically implement this point of view. In the case of Al's remark, the replies by Mary, Mac, and Tom might constructively follow any of the kinds of insights of the thirteen principles: (*a*) It *is* embarrassing when objection is raised immediately after a decision has been made. (*b*) It is possible that many others share Al's qualms. How about it? (*c*) Al's comment may not be a response to the decision so much as to the *way* it was made. (*d*) Al should be encouraged to state (as hypotheses to be tested by the group) his hunches as to why he thinks the decision is wrong. (*e*) It is important to weigh all valid objections carefully before taking action; but we cannot tell until we weigh them whether they are valid or not.

A second type of group control operation is in the responses not to a particular statement but to the group's general activity over a longer period of time. To some extent, of course, all responses are in part to the situation as a whole and in part to the last thing said. But there are certain kinds of statements which reveal that the member has been considering a much larger unit of group experience than merely the single statement. Thus control may be exercised through an attempt to state the "sense of the meeting." Whenever a person designated for that purpose believes that the group has reached consensus on some significant matter, he attempts to put it into words. If his statement is accepted, it becomes part of the realities with which the group consciously works.

A third control device, similarly operating in terms of larger units than the single statement, is the descriptive diagnosis. At times when the member feels that the group task or the member role is ambiguously defined, he may attempt to describe what he thinks the group is doing. Such a description attempts to relate the activity to prior planning; it raises by implication a question: Are we carrying out our plan or do we need further planning? If the plan is unclear or too general, the diagnosis may have to be based on individual rather than group data: "I am finding it hard to participate because I can't figure out the sort of contribution that would be appropriate at this time."

A fourth kind of control device is the use of a group "watchdog," possible when there has been prior identification by the group of behaviors it wishes to avoid. It can then agree that when these behaviors occur, the group's attention will be called to them, either by one person appointed for that purpose or by anyone in the group. In this case, the group is using explicit prior agreements to enforce certain restrictions on the behavior of members, in the interests of co-operation.

Another control device, the fifth, is the evaluation session in which the group simply takes time out to study how it has been operating. This provides a real opportunity to hammer out the agreements the group needs for its own operation, and it can also serve as a basis for planning next steps. But the purposes of the session must be made clear; otherwise it may become either a festival of politeness or a session wallowing in emotion.

The sixth control device operating over limited periods of time is an initial "structuring" of member roles for each activity. At the beginning of each new phase of problem-solving activity, time is spent to decide the sort of contribution which is most needed: shall it be personal experience, theories, questions, opinions? This is a useful device, because it calls for the explicit reaching of agreements, but, unlike the evaluation session, it calls for them before vested interests have become strong. The evaluation session develops agreements inductively, by reflection on immediate past experience; the prestructuring session develops agreements deductively, by applying general principles of group problem-solving to the anticipated immediate problem situation.

Finally, there can be simple advance decisions that provide the necessary control. In large public meetings, where the audience is not expected to share in determining the program, planning usually settles in advance most of the things about which agreements in a discussion group would ordinarily have to be made. The need for agreements about ways to participate is just exactly as great as the opportunity for overt participation. Suppose, for example, there is a mass meeting in which the only overt participation of the audience is in buzz groups, reporting, and filling out cards. The necessary rules for reporting and filling out cards are given by the chairman of the meeting, and his authority is acceptable in regard to those two functions. In the buzz groups, the members have to reach at least some implicit agreements, but their task is often a nonwork one, confined largely to the exchange of opinion, making no demands that people do not commonly encounter in our culture.

Some people believe that the adoption of Robert's *Rules of Order*, together with skill in using these rules, should provide adequate control. As a matter of practical fact, such adoption has advantages: first, the rules are familiar enough so that people know what to expect when they are used; second, the rules provide for a sequence of phases, so that they are at times helpful in keeping the discussion moving along toward conclusions; and third, they provide the authority for easy maintenance of order and respect for evidence. The disadvantages appear to be: first, that the rules are not of general usefulness for all tasks; their particular strength is when the task is one of legislation. They are less useful in action situations because the work is for the most part done in committees and the larger group may not become sufficiently involved in the problems of the committees to be committed emotionally to action. When the entire group is made a committee-of-the-whole, then there is a free discussion situation for which the rules give little guidance beyond the maintenance of order. A second disadvantage, at least theoretically, is the assumption that conclusions are reached through debate, with the chairman serving as referee. Energy may be diverted unnecessarily into factional quarrels, and the contributions of those people who cannot operate in a conflict situation will be lost. (This is discussed further in Case II, pp. 323–26.)

In general, however, the quality of work in groups is dependent much more on understandings and attitudes than it is on the particular set of procedures used for control. The best procedures are those that best reflect whatever understandings the group has, for under these conditions they can learn from experience how to do better. All methods of control imply the exercise of some form of authority (see chapter 4, pp. 99–101).

THE CONCEPT OF LEADERSHIP

Up to this point, I have deliberately avoided the appearance of any specific comment about leadership, but the avoidance is less real than apparent. We have been considering major aspects of group control, and leadership is the means for developing, maintaining, and modifying the group control system. It is a means, not an end; a function, not a person. But we customarily think of certain people in the group as having more responsibility than others for this function. In the next chapter we shall discuss these people, the problems they face, and the kinds of policies leaders need.

CHAPTER 11

Leadership is the set of functions through which the group co-ordinates the efforts of individuals. These efforts must result in satisfaction to the participants, as well as in help to the group in meeting its purposes. The demands on leadership are complex, and to define these demands and discover ways to meet them is essentially a job of inquiry.

The inquiry can and should be consciously guided by the experimental method. We spell out here some of the important implications of this notion, and we examine some of the common obstacles to experimental-minded leadership.

Leadership: Co-ordinating Effort toward Group Goals

INTRODUCTION

To understand group behavior, we assume that the group acts *as if* it operated within the spirit or letter of a set of agreements. At any moment in a particular group, for example, it may seem as if there are agreements that aggression must not be expressed against the leader; that the problem cannot be solved; that only people with high prestige in the group are to be listened to; that the greatest approval of the group will be given to a person who sees what action can be taken; that whenever the group gets into difficulty it wishes to break into smaller groups; that the group prefers to operate with parliamentary method; that all comments made by Jim are probably clever but erroneous; etc.

Further, it is *as if* these agreements are enforced. Violations are punished, efforts to change them are resisted; there may even be a search for ulterior motives on the part of anyone who tries to question or change the rules. These agreements may be subconscious in the sense that the group does not know it holds them, or quite explicitly debatable and reached through conscious decision-making processes. The agreements define the opportunities for participation: they set the limits to behavior by ruling out some behaviors as unacceptable, and at the same time they determine the opportunity for behaving within the limits by stipulating how the permitted behaviors are to be used (and through this, rewarded).

Group agreements have teeth in them. Their determination of what is possible, at what cost or with what reward, is the control of the group. Changing the agreements, hammering out new ones to fit the continual diagnosis of realities in the ever changing group-problem situation—this is the function of leadership. More precisely, leadership is a type of gate-keeping; it is the function of determining the susceptibility of agreements to modification, of determining the processes by which agreements can be reached or changed. The agreements most directly related to leadership are those about how the existing agreements are to be changed: under what conditions, through what kinds of representations based on what sorts of evidence, with what speed, with what degree of confidence. In other words, provision for leadership is also among the agreements of the group.

All groups have some sort of leadership, whether they know it or not. The amount of leadership is roughly proportional to the rate of change of agreements or group culture. "Good" leadership is indicated when the decisions and actions of a group become more and more in line with reality; and when there is minimum effort devoted to achieving this adaptation. We note the directional criterion: not all changes in the group control system signify good leadership; when the group operates with principles contradictory to those discussed in chapter 10, it is moving away from the realities of its situation. It is moving away from the conditions required for it to realize its purposes of obtaining maximum wisdom through maximum individual health and growth.

From the standpoint of the preceding chapters, we might think of the problems of leadership as those of taking action to resolve certain types of conflict:

First, there is the conflict between our subconscious wishes and desires and our stated purposes and conscious efforts to solve public problems. Thus the faculty group whose major wish is to avoid getting involved in additional work may, at the conscious level, be trying to set up new and demanding procedures to follow.

Second, there is the balance between acting and evaluating, as discussed in chapter 8. Our first impulse in replying to a critical statement is to regard it as an accusation: to respond to emotionalized evaluative statements with further evaluation of these statements rather than with a test of the truth of their allegations. Leadership determines the balance: whether emotional remarks are to be self-perpetuating in the group through the arousal of more emotion, or whether emotional remarks are to be taken as evidence of the need to think through a problem.

Third, there is the problem of freedom. In groups, this is the question of individual exploitation of the group versus group exploitation of the individual. The quality of leadership decides whether the group culture will be discriminatory, whether the rules will be determined by needs for limitations in the situation or by needs to suppress individuals. The most common type of discrimination in the group is against the members: it is the notion that leadership is privilege rather than hard work on behalf of the group.

A fourth type of co-ordination or resolution through leadership is the matter of finding and maintaining an appropriate but ever changing balance among the four types of problem-solving functions: process and achievement problem-solving by individuals and the group (see chapter 10).

To deal with all these problems at the same time requires a *method* of dealing with them. I shall point out that this is the experimental method. It shall be my general point of view that a group is successful to the extent that this method underlies its control system and is incorporated in the viscera and brain of the leadership, and of the members too.

The experimental method is based on two central assumptions: that useful behavior must be in line with reality; and that the way to resolve doubts is to take a first or pilot step and see what happens. Thus the "experimental" approach is to suggest a way to get the data needed to interpret reality, and it makes the collection of such data a part of action itself. There are certain deductions that follow from these ideas in the case of a group.

First, problem-solving involves continual exploration and reformulation. We cannot plan all action in advance because we cannot be certain of the factors which will be involved as we go on. Therefore we have to expect to discover some of the evidence necessary for planning action during the process of acting (and of rehearsing action in our minds). But to select from all the data of experiencing the particular facts that are relevant to the action is no easy matter. Selection criteria are needed, and these are set up through trial and error. The quest for relevance is an exploration of ideas about *if . . . then:* "If this really is an important factor, then the following things will happen. . . ." The exploration comes in studying a wide range of "this's" to find those yielding consequences which make a difference to the purposes of the group. It is because of this exploratory aspect of all action that the way we define our problems changes as we work on them; and it is for this reason that it is correct, in one sense, at least, to say that the problem never gets solved but only reformulated—even though the environment gets changed in the process.

Many of the objections to group working are due to the inability of some to tolerate the necessary uncertainty about future action. If the source of a person's confidence is that some future action is the only "right" action, then he is walking on thin ice indeed. Basically he is denying that it is possible and necessary to learn from experience; and he is further assuming that the situation is stable and unchanging between the present and some future time. The source of confidence we need is in *method;* in the faith (learned from experience) that exploration is not a sign of inefficiency or incompetence or ignorance but rather a sign of sophistication and deep understanding of the realities of human experience.

Leadership, then, guides the exploring process; it keeps its ambiguities to a minimum. It does this through proper assessment of the degree of confidence it is judicious to have with regard to all the agreements—achievement and process oriented—in the group culture.

Second, leadership guides the processes of interpreting and exploring reality, through its control of awareness of choice-points. One does not make conscious use of data except in answer to consciously formulated questions. These questions in a group can be couched in a variety of ways, but the part of a question that is useful is the part that states or implies a recognition that alternatives exist and must be formulated and weighed.

Awareness that a choice-point exists is reflected in differences of feeling about what the group is doing, that some members have severe reservations whereas others are enthusiastic. It is through the equal acceptance of the feelings of all members that the group becomes aware of the need to make a choice of action. Accepting differences in feelings is what we mean by "having respect for individuality." The group may ultimately decide that Henry's feelings are a less valid guide than Jim's, but it must take the feelings of both equally into account before arriving at this decision. This is done automatically when the group acts on the assumption that all expressions of feeling are symptomatic of group need; and when it assumes that all expressions by individuals become the property of the group.

An interpretation of equality among individuals which leads to the conclusion that everyone has equal skill, equal authority, equal wisdom, equal insight, actually shows very little respect for individuals. It results in what has come to be known as "the cesspool theory of group dynamics": that pooled ignorance is wisdom. It denies the fact that some people are brighter, work harder, have had more useful experience, etc., than others. In a group, equality exists in only one respect; the fact that all individual feelings are data which must be taken into account. But this principle is crucial.

A third deduction about leadership functioning follows from this last: that attention must be paid to finding and maintaining conditions such that each person who can make a contribution that the group needs will make it. This requires awareness of the different resources which people can bring to bear on the problems being studied by the group; and it requires defining the member role in each activity in such a way that the most useful people will feel most called upon to contribute. And the obverse also applies: individuals who are hard to understand, or who make contributions for such ulterior private purposes as punishing the group, should not be encouraged unless their contributions are obviously needed. One of the problems of leadership is to see that such people will learn that they do not have to punish the group; that they can get more reward and gratification by making helpful contributions rather than those which produce anxiety or waste time. Leadership then, is concerned with the discovery and co-ordination of member resources, on the assumption that individuals are not equal and that their differences are the group's most valuable asset.

This introductory section is, in a way, a review of some of the implications for leadership of the preceding chapters. It is also the statement of some of the key points in the reasoning behind the assumptions which are desirable for a group to act upon. The reader will see that the various items of group control presented in chapter 10, although presented simply as notions that have been found to work, can also be deduced from the concept that a group controls itself through application of the experimental method. It should also be clear that improvement of group functioning is not a matter of learning new tricks but of learning to use the experimental method consciously as the guide to behavior in the group-problem-reality situation.

In the next section, we wish to spell out in some detail how this experimental method of leadership works. Then, we will consider some common obstacles to use of the method, and try to indicate something of their nature and what to do about them. Following this, we will present a case study which illustrates many of these points, and next we will look at the question of leadership personnel. In the final section, we will comment on the relationship between the method of experimental leadership as advocated here and some other approaches which have been presented.

The Experimental Method in Operation

There are four major functions of the experimental method:[1]

SETTING CONDITIONS FOR EXPERIMENTATION BY MEMBERS

In any new group, there is initially a certain amount of jockeying for position among the members, who are trying to appraise one another. Each wants to know how he compares with the others, in respect to those qualities about which each is anxious. Each member wants to uncover the status system and, if possible, to influence it in his individual favor. Each needs to explore, to discover whether it is all right to talk freely, to express "real" feelings about the group and its tasks. Each member also forms affiliations with a few others and from this definite alignments emerge. And each needs to know what the leader is like—his strengths and his weaknesses—so that he can see how to relate to the leader. All of this is neither good nor bad; it is inevitable.

The leader knows that it is inevitable, and helps the process go on with least interference to group learning and problem-solving.

1. This material is taken in large part from Herbert A. Thelen, "The Experimental Method of Classroom Leadership," *Elementary School Journal*, October, 1952.

He can organize the work in such a way that people discuss problems with each other in small groups, so that increased participation in a wide range of roles gives them a chance to "know" each other, and the fact of a task to accomplish gives them a reason for interacting.[2] Or the members can be given the opportunity to tell of past relevant experiences. Or the leader can make listings of the problems individuals feel are important, as data to be considered.

Most usefully, the leader can make sure that every comment receives a constructive response. The easiest way to accept all comments is by seeing how they are related to the topic at hand, rather than to theories of individual personalities and background; this latter approach is difficult and in the long run, probably, inhibits free discussion. Comments from members may be seen as suggestions of facts which the group will need to consider later, guesses as to what might happen under certain conditions, diagnoses or requests for diagnoses of possible obstacles to the group, reflections of the value of a proposed course of action, and so on.

Because of his responsibility for progress, the leader cannot always merely characterize contributions in relation to the problem. He may have to protect the group from anxieties about time and energy requirements by immediate "corrective" action. Thus, if a member shows in his remark a fantastic notion of the amount of work the group can do, the leader may suggest that one thing the group will learn for itself is its own capacities. If the enthusiast suggests an outlandish project, the leader can express doubt that this particular project falls within the definition of the group's job, interesting though the proposal may seem.

Always and forever, the leader must avoid all general criticisms. His attitude is that any specific proposal may be unworkable (or impractical), but the fact that the proposal was suggested calls the group's attention to the need for better definition of the group's job. His principle always is that individuals are not to be criticized, and that seemingly useless behavior makes the group aware of some lack of clarity of its goals or ways of working.

Under these conditions, the leader maintains enough freedom

2. Thelen, "Group Dynamics in Instruction: The Principle of Least Group Size," *School Review*, March, 1949.

for experimentation so that individuals who need to experiment can do so. The experimentation referred to in this section is private, personal, and probably subconscious. It is directed to finding one's place and way of life in the group. The leader can safeguard conditions for this experimentation, but he cannot force people to experiment along some planned line. Individuals differ in their needs. Seeing to it that people can experiment if they want to, and protecting them from ridicule or loss of face or other effects that block learning from experimentation, is sufficient.

SETTING CRITERIA FOR KNOWING HOW TO PARTICIPATE

Exploration by group members helps them discover the behaviors for which they can or cannot get rewards. In the process, too, members hope to influence the group to like the things they like (and can supply) and to dislike the demands that they cannot meet. All of this can be looked upon as the development of expectations of each other, so that the group can know what to expect from each, and under what conditions.

But besides expectations based on acceptance of people as they are, there is also a need for judging the demands of the situation. Thus, during each stage of *planning* a project, any idea, however wild, should be encouraged and examined for some germinal grain of insight. Here the limits to expression of ideas and feelings are broad. But *after the group has decided* what projects to undertake, then wild ideas are merely time wasting and distracting, and probably are efforts to avoid the pain of work. At this point, the limits to expression of ideas must be narrower. One must stay on the point—or agree to change the point.

Many leaders recognize that the requirements of the situation change as the group moves forward on its task. The group knows this, too, but not so explicitly. It is very helpful to make clear these limits or demands, as the criteria that behavior must satisfy. This can be done routinely at the beginning of each new task, but additional comments will be required as needs for clarification reveal themselves. And the leader must be ready to discuss and modify, if necessary, any stated requirements over which concern is expressed either directly or indirectly.

Some examples from the classroom may make clear the nature of such statements, to help people know how to participate:

"Let's agree to devote the next 10 minutes to finding out what things in the film made the most impression on us" (Moving from a movie to the planning of subsequent work).

"This would be a good time for those who have actually taken a plane trip at night to tell us what it is like" (Trying to get better visualization of night flying as a possible plot situation for a play).

"I wonder if at this point we don't need to restrict our suggestions to the various soluble sulfates we might consider using" (Approaching the specific details of planning a chemical experiment).

"It seems to me that we have about said all that comes readily to mind about these proposed actions. Let's see if each person by now wants to go ahead on one or another of them, and, if not, what questions need to be answered before he can decide" (Testing commitment and diagnosing needed next steps).

"So far, our comments about yesterday's field trip all seem quite happy. I wonder if there aren't also some other feelings. I, for instance, felt quite uncomfortable at times, and even downright angry at some of Smith's statements" (Making it easier to say what is "really" felt so class can identify more significant problems to tackle).[3]

In communicating these requirements of the situation, a great deal depends upon how the leader talks and what attitudes he conveys. When leadership is successful, the group sees that these demands or limits come from the requirements of the situation, not from the leader as a person. The former feeling is encouraged by directness and casualness; the leader seems confident that the limits are reasonable, and that, if not, they can be reconsidered. The impression that the leader has ulterior, personal motives can be communicated by anxiety-expressing attitudes: apologies, expressions of nonspecific displeasure, tiresome explanations. These behaviors present the group with leader-anxiety as a problem to handle—an additional unnecessary and probably insuperable task.

3. For fuller exposition in a third-grade situation, see Thelen, "Social Environment and Problem-solving," *Progressive Education*, March, 1950.

GETTING GROUP AGREEMENT ON NEXT STEPS

In any group, people have an astonishing range of ideas about what makes sense in a particular situation. It is seldom that everyone really believes that any particular course of action is the best. It is unrealistic to demand commitment based on belief that any particular action is the "right" action. What agreements, then, can be made that will enable the group to act?

Assuming that people cannot fully agree on action, the group has two problems rather than one. To the problem of deciding on action there is added the problem of dealing with uncertainty and reservations about the action. Here the experimental method can break the deadlock. The group is asked, in effect, to realize that it has both problems, and then to discuss the alternative action proposals from the standpoint of the extent to which each will result in information that can clear up the confusion. Members must find that action which is informative to the group as well as useful in the situation.

In other words, when a group cannot agree confidently on particular steps, it can agree completely on its *lack* of confidence and then proceed to act to increase its confidence. The desired agreement, then, is on the method of operation, the way in which action will be taken. But it is healthy to have reservations about the action itself. No one can predict the consequences of any course with complete certainty, and it is foolish to pretend one can. Moreover, the reservations of others about the things of which one person is convinced force him to reconsider and organize his thoughts; in effect, they provide him with the need and opportunity to learn.

The leader allows himself to be put in a difficult position whenever he uses steam-roller tactics to secure a particular course of action. By doing this against the group's better judgment, he assumes full responsibility for the possible failure of action. The group members learn from this that it is all right for them not to take responsibility and that their own, often considerable, resources are not wanted. Moreover, if failure results, they learn that the leader is untrustworthy, and their motivation to participate in the next action sinks. Finally, the (often unconscious) resentment of the leader, which certainly is to be expected, is likely to sabotage the action so that it will be a failure.

On the other hand, the leader is often justified in demanding that *some* action be taken. Particularly in a training situation, the leader knows that some things cannot be learned unless one has firsthand experience with them. He also knows that if everyone experiences the same situation, the group will be able to talk together about it instead of past each other, which is usually the case when there has been no common experience from which to build.

In any case, the group can be seen as moving from decision to decision. The decisions should be about what to do and how to do it, but agreement is required only on the fact that this action will be useful to the group, not on the fact that it is the "right" action. 'Rightness" can be ascertained only through taking action and assessing the results.

The leader, then, is a methodologist, concerned with whether or not proposed action will be informative, and whether or not it can be carried out within the boundaries of the situation. His concern over its "rightness" is no greater than that of any other member of the group. To put it another way, the leader's job is to set and maintain the conditions required for the group's maximum intelligence to assert itself. If everyone leaves a meeting with the justifiable feeling that he could have reached a better decision in five minutes all by himself, then leadership has failed.

STEERING THE GROUP

By steering the group, I mean mobilizing its individual resources in such a way that it moves efficiently toward its goals. This is achieved by continual modification and redefinition of the immediate group-problem situation so that members are strongly motivated and the purposes of the group are satisfied. Steering is one of the responsibilities of leadership, whether by one man or by all the members.

We have developed a number of propositions which illuminate the nature of the problem.

First, we have seen that whatever the stated purposes, the

group is in fact working simultaneously on private and public, individual and group, problems (chapter 10).

Second, we have pointed out that the needs to deal with anxiety are compelling and will drain energy away from working toward the group's stated purposes (chapter 8).

Third, we have seen that anxiety is mobilized by ambivalence, ambiguity of and confusion over roles ("membership conflict," chapter 7), leader-member relations ("authority conflict," chapter 4), and intergroup relations ("status and value conflict," chapters 1, 7, and 12).

Fourth, we have proposed that the "reality factors" in problem-solving impose their own demands on the group (chapter 9).

Fifth, we have asserted that leadership uses concepts of the group-as-a-whole and continually attempts to diagnose behaviors of individuals as symptomatic of a state of affairs in the group-as-a-whole (chapter 10).

Sixth, we have postulated the idea that the state of affairs which leadership tries to maintain is one that will result in the creative contributions of all members (implicit throughout this book).

In practice, those concerned with steering the group continuously appraise each contribution in its context of preceding events, with the following questions in mind:

a) Does this contribution indicate anxieties which are blocking work toward the goal? If so, is this anxiety shared by many, or is it unique to the speaker? Can the anxiety be removed by clarifying our intentions, or the limits to our power, or the present state of commitment and responsibility required from us all?

b) How does this contribution relate to the steps of problem-solving? How may it be incorporated into the growing body of agreements or specifications accepted by the group as criteria or requirements of the problems to be solved?

c) What does this contribution tell us about the nature of needed activity? Should it be more problem centered, group centered, or individual centered? (More routine, reflective, emotion discovering, implication seeing.)

d) What kind of response does the contributor seek? What sort of reward does he want? Approval from the leader? Reply from certain members? Acknowledgment of his feelings? Clarification of his ideas? Invitation to explain more fully? Recognition of his status or worth?

e) What will be the effects on the group of satisfying the speaker's demands? What part of the demand, if satisfied, will reinforce or improve our ways of working? What part of the demand cannot be satisfied within the scope of our purposes and methods?

f) Would it be better strategy to try to deal with the demand immediately, to ignore it, or to incorporate it as part of the evidence for a change in direction to be proposed in the near future?

It may be helpful at this point to present a rather broad, more abstract view of the theoretical requirements of steering. We shall, in the case study later on in this chapter, illustrate its main features:

1. The group as a whole keeps, for the most part, on an "even keel." It strikes a continual balance between the expression of emotion and work. Emotional statements lead to testing with facts; factual statements call for assessment of their felt meanings. Both kinds of statements are needed, and a shift in kind occurs whenever an emotion has become recognized and shared and whenever an argument has reached tentative or speculative conclusions.

2. Each individual, however, is not on an "even keel." The fact that individuals are emotionally involved in the discussion means that they are being stimulated and challenged; personal needs arise, build up, and discharge tensions; opportunities for gratification open up. Desire and readiness to participate are a result of these processes.

3. The purpose of steering is to keep the group as a whole working on problems in a reasonably objective and rational way; and this is done through the strategic utilization of needs of individuals to participate in specific ways that will reduce their individual tensions. Steering seeks always for ways of channeling tensions into group work, not for ways of suppressing or denying tensions of individuals.

4. When the tensions of most members become very high or

very low, the group loses its focus on group purposes and shifts to individual private purposes. Under these conditions, the "climate" needs to shift toward greater informality, and this is brought about by reorganizing the group through the use of buzz sessions, role-playing, leader withdrawal, coffee breaks, etc. Under conditions of most efficient working, there is a wide range in the amount of tension felt by the various individuals at any one time.

In this theoretical view, then, steering deals fundamentally with work, emotionality, organization, and individual and group needs. It tries to relate these to continually clarified demands the group must meet to achieve its purposes.

The production of steering behaviors appropriate at all times to the state of affairs in the group is an artistic job. Leaders internalize the guiding principles and understandings so thoroughly that their leadership roles appear to be a spontaneous implementation of attitudes rather than the end product of a set of calculations. This sort of artistry is learned through reflection upon one's own experience. Chapter 3 makes explicit the institutional conditions required for self-training a faculty in a school; the underlying assumptions of the plan are appropriate to any self-training situation. (Striking similarities between the roles of leader and trainer can be seen by comparing the present discussion with that of the trainer's role, pp. 169–77.)

Symptoms of Breakdown in the Use of Experimental Method

Since effective problem-solving is an application of the experimental method, we should expect to find groups learning to use the method simply as a result of trying to work better. There are, however, a great many culturally sanctioned ways to avoid the method, a great many problems of individuals and groups that indicate the operation of negative forces. Let us examine some of the common devices which are violations of the experimental method, and then turn to some of the reasons why they are used.

We are grateful to Paul Diedrich for his delightful research into the matter, and we should like to present it in his own words:

Most educational discussions become, sooner or later, a desperate attempt to escape from the problem. This is often done clumsily, causing unnecessary embarrassment and leaving the group without the comfortable feeling of having disposed of the problem. A "cultural lag" is evident in this situation. Educational leaders have long since worked out an adequate battery of techniques for dodging the issue.

In the course of a misspent youth, the writer and his friends have sat at the feet of many eminent practitioners of this art and have compiled a list of their devices. The list, of course, is only tentative, partial, incomplete, a mere beginning, etc., but it should at least give group leaders a command of alternative modes of retreat, enabling them to withdraw their forces gracefully and to leave the problem baffled and helpless. In the interest of promoting the Christian spirit, we must dispense with acknowledging the sources of the following items. Additions to the list will be gratefully received.

1. Find a scape-goat and ride him. Teachers can always blame administrators, administrators can blame teachers, both can blame parents, and everyone can blame the social order.

2. Profess not to have *the* answer. This lets you out of having *any* answer.

3. Say that we must not move too rapidly. This avoids the necessity of getting started.

4. For every proposal set up an opposite and conclude that the "middle ground" (no motion whatever) represents the wisest course of action.

5. Point out that an attempt to reach a conclusion is only a futile "quest for certainty." Doubt and indecision "promote growth."

6. When in a tight place, say something which the group cannot understand.

7. Look slightly embarrassed when the problem is brought up. Hint that it is in bad taste or too elementary for mature consideration or that any discussion of it is likely to be misinterpreted by outsiders.

8. Say that the problem "cannot be separated" from other problems; therefore, no problem can be solved until all other problems have been solved.

9. Carry the problem into other fields; show that it exists everywhere, hence is of no concern.

10. Point out that those who see the problem do so by virtue of personality traits: e.g., they are unhappy and transfer their dissatisfaction to the area under discussion.

11. Ask what is meant by the question. When it is clarified, there will be no time left for the answer.

12. Discover that there are all sorts of "dangers" in any specific formulation of conclusions: dangers of exceeding authority or seeming to, of asserting more than is definitely known, of misinterpretation, misuse by uninformed teachers, criticism (and of course the danger of revealing that no one has a sound conclusion to offer).

13. Look for some remote philosophical basis for settling the problem, then a basis for that, then a basis for that, and so on back into Noah's Ark.

14. Retreat from the problem into endless discussion of various techniques for approaching it.

15. Put off recommendations until every related problem has been definitely settled by scientific research.

16. Retreat into general objectives on which everyone can agree but which suggest no content and no changes in the present program.

17. Find a face-saving verbal formula (like "in a Pickwickian sense") which means nothing but which everyone will accept because he can read into it his own interpretation. This is the highest art of the good administrator.

18. Rationalize the status quo with minor improvements.

19. Retreat into analogies and discuss them until everyone has forgotten the original problem.

20. The reverse of "begging the question." Begin with a problem like "What should be the content of our core course?" End with the conclusion that maybe we ought to have a core course.

21. Explain and clarify over and over again what you have already said.

22. As soon as any proposal is made, say that you have been doing it in your school for ten years, even though what you have been doing bears only the faintest resemblance to the proposal.

23. Appoint a committee.

24. Wait until some expert can be consulted.

25. Say, "That is not on the agenda; we'll take it up later." This may be extended *ad infinitum*.

26. Notice that the time is up. If other members of the group look surprised, list your engagements for the next two days.

27. Conclude that you have all clarified your thinking on the problem, even though no definite conclusions have been reached.

28. Point out that some of the greatest minds have struggled with this problem, implying that it does us credit to have even thought of it.

29. Say forcefully, "Do we really want this laid out cold for us?" Obviously we don't. Therefore, wet-nurse the problem.
30. Be thankful for the problem. It has stimulated our best thinking and has therefore contributed to our growth. It should get a medal.

Certainly with all these techniques, there is no excuse for awkwardness in problem-evasion.[4]

THE PROBLEM OF LEADER ANXIETY

Back of these devices there is anxiety—anxiety over the possibility of failure, over the maintenance of prestige by the leader, over the feeling that the group is incapable, over the ambiguities and lack of certainty that are so inevitably a part of discussions prior to decision. In many cases these anxieties are needless, and they can be dispelled by placing one's faith in tested methods, and in the ability of people to learn these methods. Lack of such faith creates an impossible position, in which one must either be an "autocrat" or a "manipulator."

We are convinced, as a result of much research as well as from generally agreed-upon observations that the behavior of the leader is of vast importance. It is of so great significance that part of the method of leadership we want is one that can reduce this influence, that can distribute the chores of leadership more broadly within the group. The leader who sees his role as a lonely one, who feels that the whole weight of the enterprise is on him, cannot afford to fail, even in situations that are "impossible." He sees the success of the group not really as the success of the group but as a tribute to himself; and the group never fails—it is he who fails, even though he may feel that it is the fault of the group that he failed.

Just as we see decision-making as the process of developing enough confidence to take action, so we see leadership as a set of behaviors guided by confidence in one's understanding of adequate methods, and by confidence in the skills of implementing these methods. There are many "personal problems" with which leaders must come to terms in one way or another. Knowing this, and having some notions of their solution, is helpful in dealing with them. If a leader burns up all his energy worrying about

4. Paul Diedrich, "How To Run Away from an Educational Problem," *Progressive Education*, Vol. XIX, No. 8 (March, 1942).

them, he not only will have little energy left to apply to the job of leadership, but he may also have distorted perceptions of what is going on, and of the group "realities."

I wish to mention here some problems of leadership and to suggest some helpful insights into the ways they can be dealt with. I shall not attempt a deep interpretation of the leader's feelings, but will try to show what guidance can be obtained from understanding the experimental method of leadership.

Case 1: "We are going to have democracy around here or I'll know the reason why." In these words we can sum up the attitude of thinly veiled directiveness used by teachers who want to force the students into agreement on plans.

Comment: There is great concern over "being democratic." It has become an emotional word used to connote approval rather than a defined criterion for appraising reality. Most of what people seem to mean by being "democratic" is already safeguarded in the formulation of the experimental method given above. Therefore the leader may safely spend his energy in leading rather than in worrying about whether he is meeting such additional and inadequately defined criteria.

There are certain stereotypes about "democracy" that can stand in the way, not only of experimental leadership, but also of democracy itself. One of these is the unrealistic view that participation should be evenly distributed all the time. Another is that there is only one "democratic style" of leadership, as, for example, that shown by the benevolent autocrat. It is useful to reject this view; leadership should be appropriate to the situation, and the experimental method is the only known means for securing appropriateness in any conscious and systematic fashion. There are times when it is appropriate to hold the group to its task. There are other times when the group can be encouraged to explore widely in an effort to help define its task. The help we need comes from understanding principles, such as those on pages 62–67. It only adds a needless anxiety burden when the former is called "autocratic" and the latter "democratic."

Case 2: "I wish I could say what I really feel." This is a common plaint of leaders after meetings.

Comment: It is true that a leader accepts a higher degree of responsibility and self-discipline than is required from the others in the group. He is in a position of greater influence, and his abuses of that position have graver consequences. On the other hand, it seems unreasonable to make the leader a second-class citizen, deprived of his rights, and depriving the group of the kinds of contributions expected of others. Under parliamentary procedure, when the chairman wants to enter into controversy, he hands the gavel temporarily to someone else. This is the key for solving the problem.

If the image of group problem-solving is one of a battle between opposing camps, then the chairman is required to be "neutral." But if the image is one of the collection of data which are accepted and judged as the property of the group, then the chairman can present his data, too. If the required data are opinions, then the leader may state his opinion. Any contribution which the group needs at a given point should be given by anyone with the ability to do so. The leader can usually present his opinions safely if a few others have been stated first, so that the group does not feel that the leader is trying to shift the activity into new directions simply out of self-interest. If he feels a need to alter the course of action, then he should make his wishes explicit and give the group a chance then or later to react to them. But the leader, like the administrator, needs to understand possible long-range consequences of his behavior (see p. 113).

Case 3: "Aren't there some other factors you should take into account?" This is a common device used by leaders to bring the group to a particular desired decision.

Comment: Inviting the group to guess what the leader has in mind is possibly a useful teaching device in situations in which the members acknowledge their job to be one of learning to think "like teacher." It turns the discussion into a game, and sometimes it is flattering to a class to feel that the teacher thinks it capable of thinking the problem through in the same way he does.

In adult groups, however, it seems a wiser policy for the leader to say what he has in mind, rather than to obtrude his own self into the discussion in this way. If the leader is afraid to make explicit suggestions because he feels the group may simply accept them without thought, then the problem might better be tackled as one of setting up conditions for thoughtfulness. A similar attitude is shown in a leader's tendency to respond only to suggestions he likes, or in his unwillingness to make clear the fact that plans have already been laid, or in his keeping silent at times when the group turns to him for advice. He will do better to explain why he does not want to participate rather than simply to ignore requests. Withholding relevant data from the group, or acting capriciously both tend to make the group dependent on the leader's criteria of judgment as the ones to be used. They remain in his mind rather than out in the open where everyone can help to apply or develop them. Members, too, can be less than candid—particularly around the boss (see pp. 110–11).

Case 4: "Are you with me?" This phrase recurred over and over again in a long rambling report delivered by an air force officer to a group of his fellows.

Comment: In this particular case, the other members of the group said they were following him, and he need not have worried. But in general, a leader should indeed worry about whether the group is "with" him if he goes too long without testing his performance against reality. A few good questions, or any kind of requirement for action, may be the means for testing, since, if the group is not following, they will not be able to answer the questions, and they will not know what action to take. The leader role, as distinguished from the resource-person role, can best be implemented by short, concise interventions, rather than by a rambling monologue with punctuations by the group. In a reporting situation the simplest principle seems to be to go ahead and give the report (being sure one knows what it is to be about) and then deal with questions or misunderstandings later. (The air force officer should study principles 1, 3, and 4, pp. 181–91.)

Case 5: "I have the feeling that Joe's unfavorable feelings are due to the fact that he is a newcomer to the neighborhood and hasn't had time yet to see what it is really like." Thus spoke the leader in one citizen block group during a meeting in his house.

Comment: This is, of course, a very mild interpretation compared to such remarks as "I think Joe is having trouble because he is all tied up in guilt feelings." We have already proposed that statements need testing rather than "psychologicizing." The leader should accept the fact that he is not a therapist and that, in any case, his comments are no way to give therapy. In a group, such interpretations are likely to be antitherapeutic, because they may arouse anxiety in others who fear they will be picked on next, or who feel sympathy for Joe which they cannot easily communicate in the face of the leader's example. It is not the group's concern to diagnose why individuals feel the way they do. It is its concern to know what feelings people have and use the fact that such feelings exist as symptomatic of conditions in the group that need to be made more explicit and studied. (Besides violating principles 2, 3, and 10, chapter 10, this leader has forgotten principle No. 6, p. 16.)

Case 6: "Boy, did I get a surprise! I thought I had Tom all set to raise the question about the Groober case, but he just sat tight." This is a comment from a leader to a friend after the meeting.

Comment: That's the trouble with "planted" questions; the leader cannot really count on their popping up "spontaneously" when they are wanted. It is better for the leader simply to tell the group that a rump session, over beer in the back yard, produced a few questions the group might need to consider. Then the leader is free to call on Tom directly for his question.

Many things which affect group meetings go on outside the meetings themselves. For every "official" planning session there may be several "unofficial" sessions. The leader should help the group adopt the attitude that such sessions may well uncover ideas the group needs, or make diagnoses of difficulties about which something can be done. A plan is not necessarily a better plan because it developed during the meeting, and people should feel free to meet outside and then should be invited to contribute their findings to the group. (Tom was caught in a divided loyalty situation; see pp. 235–37.)

Case 7: "Aren't we wasting a lot of time?" One leader injected this comment several times into a long, wandering discussion.

Comment: Passing over the rather tactless implication that the group is engaging in irresponsible discussion (that the leader himself is supposed to help to avoid), it is clear that this leader felt the pressure of time. Indeed, there are often situations in which time is inadequate to cover the agenda; but if the leadership is effective, then this shows only that the agenda is too long. When many decisions have to be made too rapidly, nobody has any confidence in the results, and such decisions often do not result in action.

Worry about "wasting time" almost always is a worry about something else, that could be approached in its own right. Impatience can be dealt with either by accepting what the group is doing as necessary, or by redefining the activity so that it will be more productive. Time pressure as such can be handled by whittling down the agenda, delegating some of it to a subcommittee— if a subcommittee can handle it—or agreeing to meet again to finish the work. Since it is not easy to know how far a group can get within a specified period of time, it should be understood that it will get as far as it can and report whatever accomplishment it has made. This is also a common problem for school principals (see pp. 81–83).

Case 8: "Now children, I hope you will love me." This was the opening statement of a student teacher who had finally, after observing the class for several weeks, gotten up the courage to begin trying to teach it.

Comment: There is nothing in the experimental method that tells whether the leader should be loved or not. Under conditions of sound leadership, the group experience is rewarding, and most individuals know whom to thank. If a group has a significant job to do over a long period of time, members begin to have more and more personal meaning for each other. They can share more ot their own ideas and inner thoughts within the context of problem-solving; they can learn to use their own resources more effectively. The problem for the leader is that sometimes he feels that he must choose between helping the group solve problems, on the one hand, and being "loved," on the other. Uncertainty about the group's affection may reflect the leader's own reservations about his planned course of action. If so, the group should be given an opportunity to accept or reject the plan, or at least to choose among the possible courses. In any case, the only anxieties a leader should share with the group are those concerned with problem-solving, not those concerned with his wish for affection or with other matters the group can do nothing about. (The administrator, p. 109, and the leader in Case I, p. 322, also had difficulties of this sort.)

By all odds, the most common source of anxiety for a leader is the expression of hostility toward him. It may therefore be worth while to investigate this phenomenon in some detail.

The leader is a visible person who is always seen as representing the demands of the institution. Whenever the group members become frustrated, regardless of the reason, they are likely to believe that it is the leader's fault. In many ways they will express hostility to him; and he has to be wise enough to realize that hostility is being directed at him as the target simply because they are unable to discover and define what they are *really* upset about. When group members need to express hostility and cannot focus the problem that gave rise to the hostility, they will find somebody to use as a scapegoat. Sometimes, of course, they scapegoat another group—Jews, Negroes, Catholics, etc.—this is most often the case when they fear the leader too much to express feeling against him. Scapegoating outsiders is an attempt to evade responsibility for one's own behavior by blaming others who are not involved. Scapegoating of a clique within the group is not uncommon; some leaders tacitly give approval to this.

The tendencies of a group to blame the leader and to be unable to tolerate frustration through development of a "wait and see" attitude can be upsetting to a leader. It arouses his anxieties and makes him doubt himself, and, when a person is insecure and unconfident, he tends to do stupid things. In general, there are two opposite sorts of traps into which anxious leaders fall: seduction and dictation. Thus, when a leader cannot see the group's hostility toward him objectively, he is likely to punish himself or to punish them. In the former case, he does so by accepting the notion that trouble *really* is his own fault, and he may begin to try to win the group over with blandishments, gold stars, outside conversation with group members, etc. He spends all his energy trying to be seen as a "nice guy"; in effect, he attempts to seduce the group. The trouble is, of course, first, that he is likely to be unsuccessful because he is overanxious, and this overanxiety is what he will communicate. Second, he has no energy left to lead the group toward the solution of its problem. Third, he makes it hard for the group to express its hostility toward him because it will feel guilty at kicking a man when he is down; the group members either have to suppress their hostility or direct it at some even sillier target.

The other trap, dictation, is even more familiar; particularly in situations where status hierarchies are well defined. As soon as the leader feels the group members are hostile, he begins to blame them and, in effect, treat them like wayward children. This does not work, because the group now has to spend its energy in an undercover effort to placate or sabotage the leader. It has nothing left with which to do its work.

But seduction and dictation are at least positive (even if misguided) efforts to do something about the situation. Another possible behavior is withdrawal. This is essentially running away from the situation because the leader cannot handle himself in it. In many areas of life this is not only permissible but intelligent, particularly if one knows he is running away and trains himself to meet the situation next time it occurs. But in a group leader, running away is not permissible, because it is his job to lead. The withdrawn leader is seen as sulking or anarchistic. Some leaders build up elaborate rationalizations for their withdrawal: it makes the group "freer," "gives the members a chance." Actually it does not do either; it only aggravates the group frustration and makes a bigger problem out of what may be only a little one.

In general, when a leader gets anxious about himself, he loses his objectivity, his ability to diagnose accurately in terms of the realities of the situation. He may have fantasies that the group has somehow "found out" something about him of which he is ashamed, or that it is punishing him for being a minority group member, or for being a teacher rather than a father, dentist, housewife, or whatever he would rather be.

These observations may serve to illustrate some useful principles:

First, the leader does not have to take responsibility for everything that happens. When all is said and done, responsibility belongs to the group, and the leader is merely its instrument. His job is to get responsibility shared, and he does this by helping the group learn and work with its own methodology of control. If the job is too big for the leader, he needs help and should get it; there should be a leadership team. (We shall discuss this later in this chapter.)

Second, the leader has only one purpose—to help the group. As long as this is clear (as shown by the fact that the group feels free to give him advice and criticism), then he can also meet some of his own needs without jeopardizing his usefulness as leader. Under conditions of mutual trust, leaders can express indignation, anger, enthusiasm, and the like. The group chimes in or simply waits for the interruption to finish. It is not the feeling expressed by the leader that adds to the group's burden: it is the anxieties about his feelings that become additional demands which the group usually cannot meet. Leader anxieties are harder to deal with than are member anxieties because the leader also controls the means the group can use. In the areas where the leader is anxious, he will not be able to help the group find these means.

Third, the leader has to accept his own skills and limitations as realities in the situation. More than others, he has to know the sorts of situations which cause him to become angry, for example, so that when he becomes angry he can tell what part of that feeling should be attributed to the situation, and what part to his own personality make-up. Only the former is of concern to the group. It is not always easy to accept one's own limitations, particularly when the group is dependent, because at these times the members try to get the leader to run the show; they may use flattery and other seductions and blandishments to do so. But if the leader does not know and accept his own limitations, he has plenty of opportunity to discover them. As a matter of fact, the most effective and rapid way to learn about group leadership is to try to act like a leader and then study what happens.

The Dynamics of Leadership—a Case in Point

After so much discussion of the experimental method and of the kinds of problems leaders face in using this method, it may be helpful to illustrate some of these notions in their practical setting, namely, the meeting of a group of people. The following case study takes a group up to a rather embarrassing position and then shows how two different leaders might deal with the situation, and what might happen as a result. Following the case study, we shall call attention to some of the points which, from the preceding discussion, appear to us to have considerable significance.[5]

Let us imagine a group of twelve people in its second meeting. We find the group trying to define its "goals." There has been a rapid interchange of opinion, and everyone who wanted to has spoken. No agreements have emerged, the group has already expressed all its ideas about goals, and people are perplexed and rapidly becoming frustrated about next steps. Not knowing what else to do, four individuals repeat their original suggestions. The repetition is more expanded, and the effort to persuade is increasingly evident. The individuals seem less tentative, and the proposals are offered with overtones of exasperation. They seem to be saying: "Look! We want to move on. We can move on if we can all agree on a statement. Here is a statement. It's a good statement. Let's not be stubborn."

Each of the four presentations is followed by uneasy silence, except that one person tries to make a joke after the second.

Let us now describe two different ways in which the situation drawn from a leadership training group could develop from this point:

Case I: An argument develops among the four proposers. The others look uncomfortable. Two members attempt to make peace by pointing to elements common to the proposals. They are rudely interrupted. There is an increasing number of glances at the leader. The leader finally, after clearing his throat several times, suggests tentatively that "it might be a good idea to see what is involved in these proposals." The argument takes a fresh turn. Someone asks the leader point-blank which he prefers, and

5. This case is taken from Thelen, "Basic Concepts in Human Dynamics," *Journal of the National Association of Deans of Women*, Vol. XV, No. 3 (March, 1952).

someone else answers that this is of no importance—the group must make its own decision. A member who has been quiet so far, but was chairman last meeting, takes the floor and tells a long personally oriented anecdote; this falls of its own weight and trails off into silence.

Somebody suggests (as someone inevitably does in such a situation), "Let's vote," and asks how many favor proposal one. He is shouted down but someone else takes it up and tries to get a vote on proposal two. A few people listen. Another member says with considerable force, "Let's start over."

One of the proposers, with a great deal of controlled heat, says that the group is behaving childishly, that the leader should have settled the debate, that since the leader didn't, he, the proposer, insists that the group consider his proposal. He urges that if anyone can give a valid objection to it, he should do so now, and that otherwise the proposal should be taken as accepted by the group.

There is excited muttering, out of which a few phrases can be heard. The group is demurring, but nobody comes forward. The proposer says his suggestion is the group's wish. "Next question is the way to implement it," he says. "Any ideas?" (He looks belligerently at each member of the group.) One member, faced with the real threat of action, says: "This is outrageous!" Another says: "Why don't you go home and sleep it off?" A third says: "Whatever happens suits me. I came here to observe group process, and I'm certainly seeing plenty."

The leader suggests appointing a committee composed of the four proposers and the two noisiest objectors to bring in a consolidated statement of goals for the next meeting. Nobody says anything, and the session is adjourned.

Case II: The leader steps in, after the four proposals, by pointing out that they do not seem to be something the group is able to deal with at this time; he feels this may indicate that the task is premature. He then asks why it is hard to deal with the proposals, and what might be done to make it easier. A couple of people try to state reasons, but have difficulty with introspection along these lines. One states that it is hard to find the words in so large a group.

The leader suggests breaking into groups of three to find the difficulty, with all the reasons given then to be listed on the board as a basis for possible decision. There is some hesitation, and someone says he doesn't like to break up the group. This is discussed for five minutes until a member says: "Look, I don't like to see us break up, but I don't think we will get anywhere this way, and I would be willing to try it as an experiment. If it doesn't work, we'll know better next time." Several people say: "Fair enough."

The threesomes form. They are slow to get started. They seem unsure of what they are supposed to do. Contributions tend to be autobiographic, and ease of discussion increases as they take cues from one another. After about ten minutes, someone in each threesome suggests that they ought to list the difficulties they see. A recorder is selected and, in effect, becomes chairman for the purpose of organizing a list.

When the total group reconvenes, it listens to the lists. Many specific suggestions are made, and each is accepted, rejected, or tabled until a later time. The group members finally conclude that what they really want is not a set of statements about goals, but rather some activity whose focus is *not* their own group. They suggest making observation forms for studying some other groups. This is not accepted, but it leads to the formulation of the criteria the desired activity should meet: that it be a shared experience, that it involve study of phenomena outside the group, and that it be directed to the question of what is the role of the member in some types of situations to be decided on the basis of interest.

The first ending portrays increasing frustration, loss of objectivity, undirected and uncontrolled emotional expression. It is as if the group were in the grip of powerful forces which drove it inexorably further into conditions nobody wanted. A host of new anxiety problems arose: the "weakness" of the leader, open competitiveness, feeling that voting for a proposal is really voting for a person, lack of clarity as to what a decision is, weakening of group self-confidence, member feelings that participation is inhibited, participant feelings that they are not doing justice to their own ideas, etc.

Yet something was going on. Much energy was being spent, but it dissipated itself within the system in the development of cliques and of hostility among them, in individual escape into destructive fantasies, in aggression ineffectually directed at the group. Bion would say that the "group mentality" was in control: the group acted as if its major purpose was to keep any decision from being made (see pp. 269–70).

The second ending portrays a group in control of itself, with willingness to act in spite of some reservations, and with an organization for work appropriate to the task. And no new anxiety problems were created. At all times during Case II, behavior was in response to stated problems rather than to hidden ones. Each person was responded to. The original problem was reformulated as a problem on which action could be taken. Moreover, the group "culture" was developing—i.e., the group was learning procedures which it could use from its own experience. The gratifications of success are reinforcing to such learnings.

In Case II, we see certain major principles in operation:

1. Correspondence is preserved between feeling and action through making explicit the facts about the state of affairs in the group; steering of the group proceeds from interpretation of these facts. There is continuous feedback.

2. An unanxious climate is maintained in the group so that individuals can think objectively. The leader is leader of the group and controller of group process in the name of the group; he is not leader or controller of the behavior of the individual members. This means that individuals are "free" to experiment; that whatever they do is taken as an expression of *group* need and therefore as something to be responded to in terms of an evaluation of the requirements of the group situation rather than in terms of evaluation of individual worth. More particularly, the individual contributions are examined at one level for suggestions about the group enterprise, and at another level for their reflection of the emotional state of affairs of the group.

3. The method of control is not through the opposition of individual wills or of the group's will against the individual, but rather through the opposition of emotion by thought. An emotional expression is accepted as a tentative diagnosis that calls for confirmation; this is secured from inferences about how effectively the group is working. And a proposal for action is seen as a

tentative emotional commitment which calls forth processes for ascertaining the degree to which feeling is shared. Leadership determines the magnitude of the excursions into these two phases. Poor leadership and irreversibility is characterized by one emotion calling forth another; by one action proposal unleashing a host of competing proposals. In short, emotionality in Case II is assimilated in thought and action; and action is built into the permanent dynamics of the group through its consequent emotional reorientation. Each is resisted by the other, and, through this, a delicate balance is maintained—a balance sensitive to all individual influences.

The Personnel of Leadership—the Leadership Team

On the whole, in the thinking of students of leadership the ideal of the one-man leader, the paterfamilias, is on the way out. There is some doubt that the monolithic leader, working out his lonely destiny entirely by himself, ever actually existed—or at least that he existed in the numbers claimed by some of our contemporary "rugged individualists." Generals had their confidants, politicians their wives, presidents their "kitchen cabinets."

At any rate, the present tendency is to think of leadership as a team operation; and to think that the various functions of leadership are distributed among selected individuals within the total group. There have been efforts to formulate the various roles that belong in a leadership team. The most widely tried team is the leader-observer-recorder combination, as used in subgroup meetings in large conferences. We do not feel that any final conclusions can yet be safely accepted about the composition of the team. We are more inclined to look for the criteria to be used in forming such teams in each different situation than we are to try to write the role specifications for all of them.

In this section, we wish to discuss a number of "team" relationships, and examine them in the light of what has been said above about the experimental method in leadership.

TEAM RELATIONSHIPS

1. *The confidant.*—The more complex, subtle, and demanding the leadership job, the more difficult it is for the leader, and the

more likely he is to suffer from anxiety and loss of objectivity. In general, the novice leader is also conscious of his difficulty in meeting a bewilderingly large set of criteria. These people need someone with whom they can communicate readily; someone who was at the meeting; someone who is not himself hurt by possible mistakes; someone who has a secure relationship to the leader and a desire to help.

This is the role of the confidant. He is there to be used, and his skills are the skills of listening, and of taking his cues from the anxiety problems of the leader. The confidant works with the leader outside of meetings, and helps him diagnose what was going on and what sorts of difficulties may be anticipated next time. He is a person on whom the leader can try out his "bright ideas" without committing himself fully to them. Basically, the confidant helps the leader deal with his confusions and thus frees the leader's intelligence to help the group. The confidant may have little to say during the meeting, and when he speaks it is likely to be simply as a member.

2. *The co-leader.*—This functionary operates during the meeting. His role appears mostly in groups whose objective is intellectual activity, unrelated to emotional reorientation or action. He may operate to "spell" the leader, to allow the leader to withdraw temporarily so that he can develop new arguments or prepare himself for the next major issue. He may operate as a sort of supermember, presumably identifying himself with the group and formulating some of the questions other members hesitate to ask. He could also have a group protective function, in that he would feel freer to demand more adequate explanations by the leader. And he could serve as a sparring partner, engaging in argument with the leader as a way of developing emotional involvement in the other members of the group.

The co-leadership situation is probably seldom one of equality of leadership. One of the two is bound to dominate, and this is workable provided the fact is accepted. There have been instances in which the group tended to see one leader as the acme of all virtues, and the other as a gruesome epitome of evil. Co-leaders can attempt to avoid either too unequal roles or a fight for leadership, by planning in advance what each will do. This works if the meeting goes as planned, but if it does not, both leaders are likely to run into the embarrassment of stepping into each other's preserves or otherwise violating their agreements.

The fact is that unless the hierarchy of designated authority is unambiguous, the group suffers. In cases of confused authority, no decisions can be reached because no one can be sure whose word, in case of doubt, is to be considered final. It is our impression that the concept of equal leadership as a goal is unrealistic and stultifying. The second person should be an assistant, or handyman, or apprentice, or anything else that accurately assists the role relationship.

3. The planning committee.—There are clear advantages to the leader in being able to discuss the last meeting with a small group and get their assistance in thinking about the next meeting. During the meeting, too, members of the planning committee can help in clarifying plans, explaining assumptions, keeping the group on the topic. Such a committee is most useful in situations where the leader can lay his cards on the table, and when full consideration of problems is desired.

The selection of the planning committee is of some importance. If the personnel rotates, there is less likelihood that it will be seen by the group as a bunch of leader-dominated henchmen; but there is then also the problem of working with an occasional hostile or uninvolved planner. The rotating committee is a good training device, particularly when the leader serves as a resource person to the committee and then does not have to feel wholly bound by their planning. In the training situation, the committee's functions are mostly diagnostic and advisory. The practice of composing the committee from all those with complaints works well if the group accepts its planning responsibility seriously and if the complaints are responses to the situation rather than projections onto the situation. It is not unusual to try to get all "the various points of view" represented on the committee.

Probably the best method of selection of members depends upon the specific functions of the planning committee. If it is required to work out proposals for the group, those who know and care most about the proposals may be most useful. It is thrown together simply as a way of getting the group out of frustration—

if the problems are dumped on the committee—then the most useful people are likely to be those who can tolerate frustration and who have some sense of humor. If it is to organize topics for discussion, then it should include people who know how to organize subject matter. And so on.

4. *The natural leaders.*—When a person from the "outside" is designated to serve as the leader of a group, he may need more support than can be secured without special provision. This is especially true, for example, in the case of a university consultant stepping into a group of foremen for the purpose of helping them see their need for training. Here the leader has everything against him—class, salary, education, inability to communicate, lack of membership or acceptance in the group.

The greater the gap between the leader or consultant and the others in the group, the more useful are the "natural leaders." These are people with influence; they are watched by the others to see what reactions they have. The group takes its cues from them. The leader is well advised to talk with them in advance, not as the basis for "manipulation" but as reality-testers of his plans and approach. In a word, they know the situation and he does not. The fact that their opinions are respected by the rest of the group is the evidence that they are actually in touch with group realities. If they support the outsider in the meeting it is because they think the group ought to do so, not because they "sold out" to the consultant (who usually has nothing to buy them with anyway).

The other advantage of working with the natural leaders is that they have contact with the group members outside of the meetings, and can continue to further the objectives in the absence of the leader or consultant. When one works outside the group with the natural leaders, one has the opportunity to keep the leadership where it belongs—in the group—and to define his role as adviser realistically. It is strange that teachers make so little use of the natural leadership within their classes.

5. *The functional team.*—There are two bases for a team of persons whose special skills are complementary. One basis is to help the leader, by dividing some functions of leadership among themselves. The other basis is to provide special "services" to the

group. The leader-observer-recorder team is more often not a team so much as a trio of service functionaries, acting independently of each other, but each giving assistance to the group. The leader is chairman, methodologist, and, frequently, resource person. The observer may be anything from a "depth analyst" to a watchdog on participation, interruption, or audibility. The recorder is the "group memory."

There are times when such a division of service roles is helpful and, in that event, the group should give thought to defining the roles and getting the most competent people into them. This is especially true of the observer, whose task is usually so poorly defined that his observations are of no help, and he has to fight to get a chance to give them. He should be selected only after the group has decided that a watchdog will be needed during some particular activity, to keep a check on simple overt behaviors such as interrupting, passing from one issue to another without decision, and the like.

A planning committee might feel that meetings would be more productive if there were more effort to formulate agreements as soon as they seemed imminent; if someone would summarize progress so that the group could maintain its perspective with regard to the business agenda; if someone more sensitive than the leader would make an effort to clarify emotionally tinged contributions which the leader seems unable to "understand." If such roles seem useful, the committee might then divide them up among themselves and try to perform them. No special co-ordination of these roles would be necessary. Each would be active when the occasion and need for it arose naturally during the meeting. In a training group, the committee might decide to discuss these roles with the group, let members know who is trying to deal with each function, and encourage others to practice the roles too.

The ideal team for leadership is the total group. Either each person can produce all the needed behaviors or else each knows the roles he can play, and among the group all needed roles are provided for. The more nearly this ideal is reached, the more efficient the operation. As a group goes on meeting, it normally tends toward this ideal, although few groups ever reach it.

One last important concept about designated leaders is the principle of noninterference. In a word, the *designated* leader operates only when needed. In a training group, which accepts its own development as a major objective, the trainer may stay out of the discussion completely for a period of time in order that the group can find out what its missing roles and needs are. In the case of a group that meets only once to consider a proposal, the leader is not so much concerned with helping the group understand its process problems—but quite the opposite; his job is to get the group over the agenda as smoothly as possible.

Thus the definition of the leadership role at any time has to be given in terms of the long- and short-range goals of the group, the realities of leader and member skills, and the requirements of the problem.

SUMMARY

There are several approaches to leadership. Some writers, like Cantor,[6] emphasize the threat-defense principle: good leadership provides a "climate" in which members of the group do not have to be continually on the defensive. Lee[7] emphasizes the approach of general semantics: good leadership clarifies relationships between words and the objects they represent, and distinguishes between people and the ideas they express. Bion[8] puts stress on leadership as the facilitation of group skill in diagnosing its own state of emotion. The usual military concept appears to be that logical analysis of the problem is the fundamental act of leadership. Leadership in the Quaker business meeting is concerned with the continuous effort to locate and test the "sense of the meeting."[9] Thelen and Tyler[10] see leadership as the business of maintaining harmony between the "process" and "achievement" problems of the class.

6. N. Cantor, *Learning through Discussion* (Buffalo 2: Human Relations for Industry, 1951).

7. Irving Lee, *How To Talk with People* (New York: Harper & Bros., 1952).

8. W. R. Bion, "Experiences in Groups. I–VI," *Human Relations*, Vol. I, No. 3, *et seq.*

9. Stuart Chase, *Roads to Agreement* (New York: Harper & Bros., 1951).

10. Herbert A. Thelen and Ralph W. Tyler, "Implications for Improving Instruction in the High School," chap. xii in *Learning and Instruction*, Part I of the 49th Yearbook of the National Society for the Study of Education.

These various approaches are not mutually exclusive. They merely represent somewhat different starting points in thinking about an obviously complex phenomenon. Basic to all of them, and to the procedures spelled out by the various authors, is some concept of the experimental method. We have, therefore, attempted to "get behind" these procedures to state directly at least a few ideas as to what this experimental method is.

Any change from one style or method of leadership to another requires, as Kurt Lewin pointed out, the "unfreezing" of old habits and the formation of new ones. It is a process of breaking loose from the traditions, stereotypes, role expectancies, and group sanctions which maintain the older habits, plus the development of new supportive mechanisms to reinforce redirected efforts.[11] Even when an individual teacher works by himself, his effort is essentially a social one.[12] This leads us back to the recognition that groups do not operate alone. They exist in a community, and the next chapter, which is also the last, will take us back to the community—not as a set of forces operating on individuals, but as the interactive environment of all groups.

11. Kurt Lewin and Paul Grabbe, "Conduct, Knowledge, and Acceptance of New Values," *Journal of Social Issues*, December, 1945.

12. Roger G. Barker, "Difficulties of Communication between Educators and Psychologists: Some Speculations," *Journal of Educational Psychology*, September, 1942.

CHAPTER 12

For a group-as-a-whole to exist, it must be interdependent with other groups in a larger community. Only thus can it have purposes of "acting on" a situation to change the situation. Groups arise through the coming together of "like-minded" individuals within the community, and their methods of operation are seriously affected by the over-all culture of the community. Conversely, whatever changes occur within the community come about through the changes within and between groups.

The fact that people belong to different groups for different purposes produces the situation of "overlapping group membership" within each individual; and this concept closes our circle of concepts and takes us back to chapter 7.

Community: The Context of Group Operation

INTRODUCTION

To develop a framework of ideas, one has to choose a starting point and then build the argument according to some more or less logical scheme. We chose as a starting point for Part II the existence of membership conflicts within individuals, for we saw such conflicts as the stuff from which most if not all social needs elaborate. We then inquired as to the ways in which individuals deal with such internal problems, and we suggested that behaviors of evaluating and acting (including thinking) serve as the means. We next recognized that not all behaviors are helpful; that there are realities in each situation that must be taken into account. Since knowledge of reality factors is obtained and tested through interaction with other people, we were led to the question of how individuals participate in groups and to the idea that groups provide for and control participation by means of shared ideas and attitudes. At this point, we presented a set of principles on which we believe successful groups base their behavior; in effect we spelled out a moral code for groups, even though we maintained that it was developed through study of group operation rather than by deduction solely from "larger" ethical principles. The fact of group self-control or discipline then led us to inquire how the group provides for these functions, and this resulted in our last chapter on use of the experimental method in leadership.

This development of ideas is required from certain hard facts about language; that only one idea can be presented at a time, and that ideas therefore have to be arranged in sequence. In experience, however, ideas do not come one at a time, but come imbedded in impressions. Thus, in a given group a person is almost simultaneously aware of, for example, one member's discomfort, the group's lack of clear goals, the fact that "we are behaving like children," and the pressure of time. Moreover, as a person reacts

335

in a group, he behaves as if he were influenced by many more factors than he is aware of: his rejection of the leader's authority, his own wish for status, his need to impress some other member, and, possibly, the fact that he is talking angrily.

These additional factors, not comprehended by any one person, may be in the awareness of others. After the meeting, for example, there is usually a wide range of perceptions and feelings about it (unless the group has been working productively on clear problems); different people see and respond to different things—cues and gestures and ideas which did not seem to exist for others.

All of these considerations can be boiled down to the primary fact that we are constantly dealing with part-whole relationships, rather than with simply interrelated units. Whatever "figure" we give attention to is created out of the larger pattern of "ground" conditions by our own processes of giving attention. Many people "see" only the leader, or the "problem," or themselves. All our approaches to thinking about human behavior are learned, selective, and limited, and this is why they aid thinking. No one can think about everything at once, even though his feelings may be widely responsive. Thinking about groups is a procedure of extracting from felt impressions useful ideas of directions, causality, or progress.

The chief difficulty of an approach necessarily limited to what we are aware of is not that the "wrong" parts will be looked at so much as that they will not be related to an adequate "whole." It is all too usual to regard groups as autonomous. This is a real delusion, much like trying to think of individuals apart from their relations to others. *In a word, to understand and improve group operation you have to see the group as part of a larger community.*

The fifth-grade English class, the Rotary Club, the Nathaniel Hawthorne garden section of the Coriolanus Club, the board of directors meeting—all these have their social meaning through their impact on the social and physical environment, even though the means of impact is through the group members. All are affected by a larger community and have much greater effectiveness when they can call these "outside" factors into account. Not only from a long-range social standpoint, but also from the standpoint of better day-by-day operations, many characteristics of the larger community make a real difference to what a group can do and the means by which it can do it.

The purpose of this chapter is to relate individuals and groups to the community, to fill in the larger "whole" against which the parts of the discussion so far presented are to be understood. In Part II, our first two chapters saw the individual as the whole within which various psychological behaviors could be examined; our next three chapters saw the group as a whole within which individual acts could be examined and determined. This chapter sees the community as the whole within which the groups are to be understood as parts.

We shall begin with a description of the community as an interwoven network of processes of communication and communion; next we shall look at groups as subcultures within the community, and then we shall examine the nature of intergroup conflict and the dynamics of resolving it through the operation of the "bridging group." We shall then study more explicitly the part played by the community in intergroup conflict. Against this background we shall develop a model of group-community development. Such a model is useful because the state of affairs in the community determines how far and in what ways groups can grow; and the means groups employ in their operation determine the state of affairs in the community. Finally, we shall develop a series of basic principles useful for realizing this model.

Basic Processes in the Community

A community may be thought of as having two simultaneous sorts of processes constantly going on. One kind of process, communication, is the influencing of one part by another. Some identified person says some describable thing to some other identifiable person. The network of communication channels, whether via engraved stationery or over the back fence, keeps the parts of the community in relationship to each other. The content may be knowledge others ought to have so as to plan their actions wisely; it may be attitudes expressed to others and tested against their reactions; it may be orders or instructions handed down within organized institutions.

A second kind of process, communion, is the sharing of feeling about commonly experienced problems, ideas, physical features, and incidents. The processes of communion relate each part of the community to the community as a whole, rather than to particular other parts. The kinds of experiences that are available to all include past historic events (battles, disasters, revelations to local prophets), shared aesthetic experiences (scenic views, pioneer or prestige houses, monuments), common social experience (the first families, the colorful characters, the tragic ones, and the strange ones), "literary" experience (legend, folklore, and local customs), and so on. The important thing to note about communion is that something *outside* the individual or group, and available to all individuals or groups, seems to focus reaction. It may be a view, a story, a stereotype of other communities, a civic problem, an anticipated hardship. It may exist "on the ground," like Seattle's view of Mt. Rainier, or the garden courts and ironwork balconies in New Orleans. On the other hand, it may be merely an idea, like the notion that "our troubles are caused by in-migration of foreigners," or the notion that our town is the "best little city north of the Smokies."

A stranger moving into the community is first admitted to communion with respect to the existing and obvious landmarks; he can guess with some accuracy which are objects of pride or melancholy and the communal meanings of these objects are easily shared. After he gets settled in his own house and job, the stranger next becomes aware, let us say, of the problems of bad streets, sordid taverns, individuals and groups which are discriminated against. He is advised to "take it easy" at this point of problem recognition, until he finds out what these conditions mean to the community—what the common interpretations are. He may discover that bad streets are maintained as a smug gesture of defiance against the "world outside"; that the rowdy life of the tavern is required as a horrible example to keep moral teaching alive; that discriminating against a particular group is the accepted channel for expression of hostilities arising from many sources that "cannot" be examined objectively. The stranger may find that these interpretations are carefully guarded, or he may find they are easy to discover; but he does not fully belong to the community until he knows these meanings, identifies with or against the values involved in them, and accepts their existence as part of the realities within which he must operate.

It is noteworthy that these processes of communion are most facilitated in a small town and, possibly, one with an open interest in its present state of affairs. When the town gets too big, there are too many local events for any of them to become a symbol incorporated into communal experience in any significant fashion. The communality in a big city tends to revolve around big physical objects such as a waterfront, or colorful or influential buccaneers of industry, graft, government, or society, or complex abstractions like rent control or "the crime syndicate." Things happen because "they" managed it so; but nobody knows who "they" are. And there is little you can do with a waterfront parkway except admire it and curse Sunday traffic; a big industrialist or labor leader is known only through the newspaper, and you either wish you were like him or are thankful that you are not; the "crime syndicate" is reacted to as a sinister force but it is not something I even imagine I can do anything about.

Under these metropolitan conditions, the formation of groups may serve a number of purposes. Thus we can see the informal tavern group as arising out of bewilderment and a need to escape a feeling of nonparticipation and lack of place in the functioning of the community. The ethnic group may maintain its customs and language, not so much because it feels that these are "better" but because they are shared and known to be shared, and provide the basis for a higher degree of communality than is possible in the sprawling city as a whole. The minority group may be created by stereotypes whose operation represents a sort of perverse effort on the part of the majority to find belongingness; majority people may not have very much sense of groupness with each other, but they can try to reassure themselves by pointing to minority groups that assuredly do not.

The citizen group is likely to have limited civic objectives like beautification or delinquency, because the whole is too staggering and unavailable for comprehension by the average member. Because of weak communion with comprehended civic realities, such groups may pick other groups rather than objective problems as their "enemies." The amount of hostility and anxiety between "do-good" organizations, the jealous protection of their jurisdictional rights, their feelings of guilt and sudden stirrings of activity when a more powerful group is rumored to be in formation—these are signs of the lack of common bases for communion. People in the same and in different groups cannot share feeling about problems because any identified problem is too insignificant and any significant problem is too complex.

Probably of all the groups in the city, communion is greatest in the neighborhood group, existing partly for individual welfare, partly for maintenance of property, partly to put pressure on city officials, and partly to educate and induct newcomers into the neighborhood. A badly run rooming house is not insignificant to the neighborhood, even though it is only a drop in the city-wide bucket. The moving-in of a new family can be noticed and discussed formally. People are known as people, and the consequences of what they do get back to them. In effect, there is neighborhood provided and maintained interaction among individuals; there is expectancy and opportunity to talk together which is not all a matter of initiative by individuals who are seen as deviates. "Belongingness" is automatic at the point of communion, of shared meanings of salient aspects of neighborhood life. There is no need to bother with membership rituals, initiation ceremonies, or common alliance against "others."

What I have called the "neighborhood group" is, in effect, what exists in the village. The major difference is that such groups in the large city do not have the freedom for decision and the autonomy of the village group. They work within a set of prescriptions resulting from city-wide systems of politics, education, sanitation, etc., and they have comparatively little freedom to change these things. The neighborhood group must perforce put more emphasis on amelioration and adjustment and less on the creation of new political or organizational forms.

Our picture of the community may be summed up as follows: First, each individual experiences more or less of the same events or problems and knows that he shares the meanings of these events with others. Second, individuals and groups form a network of communication and mutual influence, and every person has some place in this network. Third, the nature of the spontaneous informal groupings depends upon the amount and quality of communion possible and needed. Fourth, there is discernible in all organizational life the acting out by citizens of needs for relating themselves through the group to the larger community. The technology of chapter 1 exemplifies these propositions.

GROUPS AS SUBCULTURES

We see that in any community there are more or less commonly experienced and felt objects, customs, stories, personalities, and institutions. These remind people of physical, aesthetic, moral, administrative, and educational facts about what people believe, how they shall behave, what they shall call good, etc. In short, every community has its culture.

Each individual reacts to the various facets of this culture: its authority, its complexity, its confusion, its form, its ethical assumptions, its images of individual and collective goals. The reactions of individuals differ. Some—the "100 per centers"—believe that they accept the culture; and others see them as trying to maintain their notions of the culture against all doubters. The people we call "antisocial" appear to be in revolt against the parts which are perceived as exerting "authority" or curbs to individual impulses. These people may form gangs to continually test the ways in which the boundaries can be breached. Those who react to confusion may, in their quest for authoritative interpretations, attend Great Books classes or a church. Or they can join the National Guard, the "Y," or any other movement which provides for them the discipline and clarity of goals they cannot find in everyday living.

Thus, in a general way, we can say that individuals are concerned about different aspects of the culture; and that individuals with similar concerns tend to affiliate with each other and become a "group." As a group, they state their purposes by differentiating out of the community culture as a whole certain particular objects which best represent their concerns.

The school, for example, formulates its goals by identifying those individual behaviors through which the culture is maintained and improved, i.e., through whose learning individuals will develop their greatest potentialities. As more and more individual behaviors are found to influence the community, these become additional objectives of the school. Thus, to the school curriculum have been successively added natural science, commercial subjects, health, social science, and human relations. As complexity of living develops, more and more "private" behavior is examined for its consequences for the welfare of others. Those behaviors whose consequences are appraised as significant must then be made consonant with the community control system (culture), and the school, as the primary instrument provided for bringing about the socialization of youth, has another objective to add to its list.

In the same way, but more informally and voluntarily, the fraternal organization, club, action group, and others, pick out certain objectives which imply communion within the group, and imply the objects to be investigated, the means to be employed (study, action, entertainment), and the bases for belonging. In effect each group develops its own subculture. It may be an "improvement" on the prevailing culture, thus giving the members protection and peace—and substituting the group for the larger community. In this case, withdrawal from the community plus effort to maintain the organization at all costs may result. On the other hand, the group subculture may merely be a reinforcement and refinement of *avant guarde* or regressive tendencies within the larger culture. These may be illustrated respectively by a modern art society in which the members actually paint and experiment avocationally with new ideas, as compared to a juvenile "gang" or a modern art society in which members listen to lectures on "art" criticism. Or, as some psychiatrists suggest, the subcultures may simply protect and cultivate in pure forms certain basic emotional drives. Thus Bion proposes the army as the maintainer of "fight," the aristocracy as the maintainer of "pairing" (sexuality), and the church as the maintainer of "dependency," in their most direct expressions.

Because a group has to be able to define its purposes explicitly or implicitly, and in a way acceptable to its members, it follows that the purposes of a group are always limited to those things which are common or acceptable to many people rather than being extended across the whole gamut of needs of any individual. Thus it is that from the personal standpoint, groups become limited instruments, and one may need to belong to several groups to satisfy all of the needs active within him. This, then, sets the stage for chapter 7, and the problems of overlapping group membership.

We see that the function of a group in the community can be defined in terms of the needs, arising from individual-community interaction, that it is concerned with, and that the flavor of its subculture depends upon these concerns.

In fact, however, it is only "as if" a group has a concern over such facets of culture as authority, poverty, and so on. A "cultural facet" is nothing that can be seen, touched, tasted, or felt, as such. What is experienced are the daily contacts, conversations, and feelings we have in the situations of living. We do not usually think of ourselves as reacting to the "culture," because that is statistical abstraction. A more accurate statement about what is going on is to say that all individuals do form some "world-view," some picture of the general conditions under which they live, and they also learn and use certain interpretations as to why conditions are what they are, and whether this is pleasing, discouraging, challenging to action, and so on. This "world-view" is tested through daily experience. One acts as if his view were correct (since he has no other view to operate with), and then sees what happens as a result of his action. If the results are as anticipated, or are merely comfortable, no problem is raised, and the part of the world-view concerned in the action is strengthened. If the results are uncomfortable, a problem may arise; that of bringing one's private world-picture into enough relationship to "the way things are" that one can operate more directly and with greater reward.

The notion that groups or individuals have a concern over some facet of the culture is only a way of saying that there are certain problem themes that run through enough of their experiences that they need to do something about them. A problem is what somebody sees to be a problem, and in that sense, it is always a projection from within one's self to targets outside one's self. Thus, it is by no means unusual for "liberal" groups to see and attack as a problem the fact that many individuals are subjected to discrimination. But the means they use often curtail the rights of others, and one is justified, perhaps, in feeling that the reason discrimination was selected as the problem was concern over the hostilities of the group members themselves, coupled with a need for reassurance that they really are not hostile to others. "Discrimination" is a socially approved target which makes possible the identification of people against whom hostility can be safely directed.

I hasten to add that this is not "bad"—it just is. And I should point out that there are many other motivations for working against discrimination. The point is, first, that there are reasons why the particular people working on any problem are the ones to be working on it; and second, that the subculture of a group is the set of operating agreements erected to make possible the attack on problems which are personally important to the group members. In the example given, the experience of "working on" discrimination is motivated by the uneasiness one has that his "world-view" is inadequate in some areas that have to do with the experience and expression of hostility.

There are some classifications possible of group subcultures in terms of the "kinds of people" who belong and, by implication, the "kinds of needs" characteristic of each category of person. I refer to the concept of social class. For our purposes we may note that people have different living standards, opportunities, incomes, occupations, etc. We note further that some characteristics tend to be found together. Thus we associate in our minds such things as professional occupation, relatively high income, a home in a "nice" part of town, many years of education, expensive clothes, membership in exclusive clubs, support of charitable and artistic ventures, and so on. We note, too, that people tend to find their friends among others similarly "placed" and that clubs tend to draw more or less the same "kind" of people into membership. Associated with these patterns of living are also, in general, certain more fundamental characteristics: the way in which people control their aggressive and sex impulses, the amount of inner freedom and of guilt in individuals with respect to different things, the tendency to plan in long-range or in short-range terms, and the ability to tolerate frustration versus the need for immediate gratification.

When these patterns of behavior, attitudes, motives, and manners are arranged along a scale, there are usually found to be clusters with breaks between them. Each cluster along the scale is termed a distinguishable "class," and as many as nine "classes" have been discerned in one city.

Practically all societies have this kind of class stratification. They differ in the rights and privileges given to each class as compared to the others. They differ also in the ease of moving "up" or "down" from one class to another. We in America probably have the fewest legally and socially recognized differences in privilege among classes, and we certainly have the greatest amount of moving upward. Class characteristics are not inherent in people—they are learned in and out of school, and they are practiced in social experience. To move upward requires that one learn to behave like members of the next higher class.

The categorization by "class" is one of prestige, power, opportunity, and contribution. Classification is also possible using criteria of skin color, religious preference, occupational status, ancestry, taste in literature, hobbies, etc.

For our purposes, there are two major consequences of the fact that communities are stratified, or, to put it more dynamically, the fact that people's voluntary associations tend to be with others "like" themselves. The first consequence is that communication is relatively easy within a class, and relatively difficult between classes. Thus many a "community organization" ends up only with people from the same class level, talking to each other rather than to others whose co-operation is necessary to solve the problem. The second consequence is that under these typical conditions, the organization is likely to have only its own class view of community problems and to arrive at poor, or at least partial, solutions, because the problem was never really seen realistically as a whole.

INTERGROUP CONFLICT

Our image of the voluntary groupings in the community is as follows: First, that we should expect each group initially to be formed from people who can communicate readily together; and we suspect that, generally speaking, such people will have similar "cultural backgrounds" or ways of life. Second, we should expect each group to attract to it people who have similar fundamental concerns or targets of communion; these people acknowledge the same goals and ways of working. Third, as each group works, it develops its own picture of the community, defines civic problems from its own point of view, conducts its own investigations, biases its members in favor of its own viewpoints, identifies its "enemies," and demands loyalty from its members.

If the groups are all just "talk" groups, the only problems produced are within individuals who happen to belong to two groups with different viewpoints, as portrayed in chapter 7. But, if the groups are action groups, trying to change and improve the community, and if there is inadequate direct experience shared among the groups, then there is likely to be considerable conflict between them. Each group has planned its own strategy independently of the others, and it comes as a rude shock to discover a competitor operating on different or opposite assumptions. They cannot both be right. So it becomes necessary for each group to do one of several things: (*a*) discredit the other group as a way of "disposing" of its solutions; (*b*) pretend in public that the more different solutions the better, but in private go around with a worried frown; (*c*) reconsider its own ideas, probably tapping new resources that should have been used earlier; (*d*) merge with the other group; (*e*) put on a big campaign to establish its rights to the problem and thus squeeze out the other group.

An illustration may bring this down to earth a bit: Two groups were formed independently in different parts of the community, and both decided to take action in cases of illegal conversion of houses into smaller dwelling units.

The strategy of organization *A*, in part, included calling on the city building inspector's office, telling him of their concern, and asking him to send out inspectors to check on suspected construction. After several proddings, the inspectors would go out, and, in a fairly high percentage of cases, would report that the construction was legal. The secretary of group *A* would accept this verdict

—for a day—and then call back and suggest that another inspector go out because the neighbors just reported (let us say) that thirty-six telephones were being installed in the six-flat building. The secretary would further respectfully suggest that the inspector sent out this time should not be the one sent out the day before yesterday (so that the owner would at least have to pay graft all over again to the new inspector). This time the report would be honest. Any publicity from the group would give the inspector's office thanks for its splendid co-operation. After several months of this treatment, the reports were prompt and honest the first time, and the inspector's office acted promptly enough to curtail attempted violations before the construction had gone very far.

Group *B* followed a somewhat different strategy. The inspector would be called up and told point-blank to send a man out to inspect the property. After several days, during which nothing happened, the inspector would receive a bawling out for being so slow. After that, he would be "out" when group *B* was on the phone. Group *B*, then, through its president (a reasonably wealthy lawyer) took the city attorney out to lunch and complained about the inspector's office. The president also committed his organization to foot the bills necessary to prosecute the owner in court. The city attorney put pressure on the inspector's office, the construction was found to be illegal, and the group had to raise the money to prosecute the owner.

The same differences in tactics characterized the approaches of the two groups to the police captain, the alderman, and others. Three years later, we find group *A* still trying to co-operate with people, and group *B*, as the result of a "deal," merged with another organization which has relieved it of all responsibilities and functions. During the entire period, there was much rumor-mongering and bad feeling between the two organizations, and a great deal of time and energy wasted by both in verbal forays against the "enemy" group. And many citizens, living in the area served by both organizations, became disgusted with the whole thing, sat on their purses, and were "too busy" to participate in community improvement programs. I leave to the reader's imagination the plight of two men who were on the board of directors of both organizations. (The heads of groups *B* and *A* were probably similar to the two executives, pp. 103–8.)

In general, conflict between two organizations will probably be greatest under one or more of the following conditions:

a) The two groups have approximately equal power in the community.

b) The two groups have a small core of common values within their subcultures; that is, their psychological motivations are different.

c) Very few members of one group belong to the other.

d) Both groups are nonexperimental in their methods of operation, so that there is no means for reality-testing solutions.

e) Both groups fail to be aware of their own internal process problems; this implies that members have little security and the groups therefore tend readily to become touchy and defensive.

f) Both groups have inflated and unrealistic notions of their own power and prestige.

g) Both groups are competing for the same members and the same rewards.

h) The *raison d'être* in both groups is a need for protection against real or fancied aggression by others.

i) Neither group has defined its objective problems comprehensively; and, in particular, little attempt is made to relate long- and short-range goals.[1]

Intergroup conflict should not arise when both groups operate along the lines discussed in the preceding chapters, because—

a) each group would feel "secure" enough that it could communicate with the other;

b) both groups would be in communion with the same problem, which they could talk about together as a problem in its own right;

c) both groups would develop their strategies a step at a time on the basis of evaluation of each step and would use substantially similar realistic methods;

d) each group, through overlapping memberships, would

---

1. Adapted from Herbert A. Thelen, "Educational Dynamics: Theory and Research," *Journal of Social Issues*, VI, No. 2 (1950), 24.

know about the other's existence, and it would develop a working relationship to complement the other's resources; and

e) the groups would clarify their separate and joint spheres of action, and refer inquiries to whichever was appropriate.

It is only in a riot situation that intergroup conflict is actually an overt war between two groups. Intergroup conflict is the aggregate of behaviors of individuals who behave emotionally or unrealistically as a result of feeling trapped in the struggle. The struggle is, as a matter of fact, within themselves. (Compare with principle 6, p. 287, and also the discussion of vested interests, p. 232.)

We turn now to the dynamics of resolving intergroup conflict. We shall present the thesis that all successful methods boil down, fundamentally, to the operation of a "bridging" group.

Resolving Intergroup Conflict: A Model

The most commonly accepted examples of intergroup conflict represent one special case: when group *A* and group *B* are both easily identified and both maintain hostility toward each other. There is often a rationalization in the surrounding community that these two groups are "natural enemies." This amounts to saying that the state of conflict is either approved of or is deemed inevitable and "naturally" right even if morally awkward. Examples of accepted "natural" enemies are labor and management, whites and Negroes, haves and have-nots, young and old, fundamentalists and liberals. Needless to say, a climate of expectation of conflict not only tends to maintain conflict but also makes its reduction difficult, because the parties involved would have to re-establish their place in the community if the conflict were to disappear. Moreover, the community would be deprived of one of its emotionally involving "interests"; those people not in group *A* or *B*, who work on their own needs vicariously through unacknowledged identification with the conflict situation, would have to find some other situations on which to focus their fantasies. Almost everyone in the community shares the conflict between groups and contributes to the conflict climate, even though he maintains that he is not "personally" involved.

Experience has shown that in this special "natural enemy"

situation, there is a perfectly simple solution. All that is required is that members of groups *A* and *B* work together on some project in which *A*-ness and *B*-ness are irrelevant, but in which the efforts of members of both groups are required for success. Labor-management luncheon projects, Friends Service Committee week-end camps, Negro-and-white army and shop groups, parent-teacher workshops (not the usual PTA meetings)—these are types of "working together" in which the participants can and do, over a period of time, learn for themselves that in the situations in which they normally have contact, the "differences" between their groups do not have to matter. And, of course, it helps if there is community agreement "against" rather than "for" conflict. This may be one reason why there are so many reported instances of reduction of conflict among "natural enemy" groups of young people; none of the older people likes gang wars, even though they are probably carrying on precisely the same thing emotionally at the adult level.

Let us examine in detail what must happen for conflict to be reduced between groups *A* and *B:*

First, we must define the problem by locating the conflict. Groups *A* and *B* do not actually interact with each other as groups except in the situation of battle. The conflict is demonstrated by members of *A* and *B* in their behaviors toward each other and toward bystanders, under a variety of circumstances. The reduction of intergroup conflict, then, is something that has to happen to members of the two groups, and it will be easier or harder to achieve depending on the community's interest in having the conflict maintained or eradicated.

In the "work together" situation, members of *A* and *B* are brought together to work on some problem or toward some goal which is important to them. They thus form group *C*. While they are working on this problem, group *C* is the directly experienced group, the one in which the members get immediate, actual responses to whatever they say or do. Group *C* develops its own culture, its own agreements, leadership, and expectations of its members; it also develops its channels of reward and of gratification for individuals. It must, however, keep its activity separate from the activities of group *A* or *B*. That is, its goals must be defined in such a way that there is no jurisdictional overlap with *A* and *B*.

Jurisdictional overlap occurs in many groups, such as community councils, and this explains why community councils (made up of representatives of other groups) so frequently are both ineffectual themselves in problem-solving and unable to help the cause of interorganizational peace. Suppose, for example, that groups *A* and *B* are trying to get a new school building, and that *A* wants to run a survey to establish the population trends among school-agers, whereas *B* wants to make immediate demands on the school board. If representatives of *A* and *B* are called together in group *C* to consider what to do about overcrowding in schools, Member *A* will suggest and defend a survey as the first step, and Member *B* will call for action. They cannot do otherwise without being disloyal to their groups. Both representatives, along with the chairman in group *C*, will quickly see that there is need for the survey, and then for taking whatever action the survey shows is required. But the representatives will find it hard to admit this because they are expected to report back to their own groups, and neither is prepared willingly to explain that his plan, presented by the representative, was rejected. If there is already hard feeling between members of *A* and *B*, then it is impossible to vote for a plan offered by either group: the vote would be for the group and not for the realistic solution of the problem. Community councils are therefore well advised to define the member role as "consultant from" rather than "representative of" the group.

An example of the significant *C*-type group in which there is no jurisdictional overlap is the meeting of whites and Negroes on a city block to work for better lighting. Here the fact that one is white or Negro, or has strong feelings about the other race, is irrelevant, because there is no "white" or "Negro" solution to the problem. It may be difficult to listen to each other at first because of the intrusion of fears, but if lighting is important, under good leadership the people will soon get absorbed in the problem. Here nobody is "representing" his race, and there is no need to attack the other or defend his own; such activity is out of bounds and, as such, is either ruled out of order by the chairman, or simply ignored by all.

Assuming that members of *A* and *B* dislike each other simply because they are known to hold these memberships (that is, they are strongly prejudiced against each other), then the first discovery that must be made is that you can work with people you do not like, in a particular group *C* situation. It is trust, not liking, which is essential for co-operation. The feeling of trust does not necessarily have to include admiration for other's ideas, or feelings of "equality"; its positive component is communion with respect to the same goal, and its negative expression is lack of suspicion that the other fellow says what he does as a means of supporting his own group.

The second discovery is that members of the other group can be pried loose from their group. To put it in more prosaic language, members of the "other group," present in group *C*, do not fit their image or stereotype. The conclusion must be either that the stereotype is wrong or at least of only limited applicability, or that these particular people are not typical of their group. This discovery frees individuals to act in accordance with the feeling of trust. Active co-operation is not with the enemy, because the other fellow is not really the enemy. Therefore there is no disloyalty to the groups, and there is freedom to try for the rewards of spontaneous participation in group *C*.

As participation becomes more spontaneous, member behavior in group *C* gets freer and more revealing of self. Members of group *A* may casually refer to or quote other members of group *A* who may have useful ideas for the discussion. Members of group *B* may talk about their place (and, by extension, group *B*'s place) in the community. In the discussion of lighting, for example, this might come out in considering a plan for voluntary installation of lights by owners: A Negro might contrast the position of the Negro home owner with that of the white owner.

This is a significant landmark in the progress of the group. The members feel free to acknowledge their "outside" affiliations, and to feel this freedom means that they perceive that the others will accept these associations. In effect, there is suggested a broadened identification: the group *A* person who could identify with and interact with a member from group *B*—under the special circumstances of group *C*—can now identify with group *B* as a whole. This amounts to an acceptance of group *B* and this in turn means potential membership in group *B*, at least with respect to problem-solving of the type going on in group *C*. When people accept each other they accept each other's affiliations—which is why the engaged girl wants the prospective groom to visit her family. The feeling of potential membership in the "enemy" group is evidence that the enemy no longer exists. There is a feeling of escape from conflict, and, instead of feeling immobilized and blocked emotionally, one is now "free" to bring conscious and objective thinking to the task of understanding the conflict, appraising its causes, inevitability, and relevance. Presumably this phase should mean the end of emotionally contaminated panic behavior toward members of the other group.

During the meeting of group *C*, the members from *A* and *B* maintain some sort of psychological relationship with their own groups. Since the problem of group *C* is not directly the concern of group *A* and group *B*, the relationship is not through the feeling of need to defend solutions from one's own group. The major "cue" for activation of person *A*'s feelings about group *A* is the presence of people from group *B*. These people initially are symbols around which are mobilized within person *A* attitudes learned in group *A* toward group *B*. And these attitudes are found to be irrelevant in the group *C* situation.

As the meeting goes on, assuming that the problem-solving is successful, the member learns to *accept* the fact that these attitudes are irrelevant, and he can now participate more spontaneously because he does not have to use a lot of energy in keeping himself from making a blunder. It should be noted, however, that this learning may be temporary; it is maintained by the climate of group *C*. When person *A* goes back to group *A*, he may at first reinstate his earlier stereotyped attitudes toward group *B* because having such attitudes is part of what it means to be a member of group *A*. It is likely that people pass through a period of flip-flops: of feeling one way while in group *A* and another way while in group *C*.

This is the point of "acting out" ambivalence in feeling toward the other group. The violence that goes with prejudice is the effort to maintain and justify prejudice when one also feels that prejudice is unsound or bad. Most hostile behavior would not be necessary if one could be completely *sure* that the other group was worthless. So that we are brought to an important recognition: bad feeling between groups *A* and *B*, expressed through stereotypic reactions, is a means to an end, rather than the inevitable behavior of "natural enemies."

The next phase of reduction of intergroup conflict is brought about by the need for integration within the members of group *C*. They cannot indefinitely go on having opposite feelings in meetings of group *A* and of group *C*. Will they succumb to the prevailing hostile attitudes assumed toward group *B* in the culture of group *A?* Or will they simply leave group *A?*

The probability is that the member from group *A* will now begin in group *A* to try to change its feeling toward group *B*. This prediction is based on an important learning from group *C:* that members of group *B* are *not* necessarily all the bad things group *A* "says" that they are; and that one can work with them. In other words, experience in group *C* has enabled the group *A* person to reality-test the attitudes of his group which have been maintaining the conflict. And he has discovered that these attitudes make no sense as long as one puts the problem first, and all have a defined part in the problem-solving.

The likelihood that one person *can* change the culture of his group depends on a number of factors. If he is an influential person in the group, his arguments are more likely to get a serious hearing. If he attacks group *A*'s attitudes directly, with all the zeal of a new convert, he will, in effect, be invited to join group *B*, where he belongs. If he acts consistently to insist that the planning of group *A* stick to the problem to be solved, and that decisions be made realistically in terms of who is needed to help, rather than in terms of whom do we like, then he may have some effect. If several influential people from group *A* were also participants in group *C*, the chances for success are much greater. And finally, if group *C* is run with skilful leadership which gives the members a chance really to understand the assumptions on which they are operating—then success is even more likely.

Group *C* was set up as a "bridging" group between *A* and *B*.

It built a communication bridge and provided for communion over a problem lying "outside" the groups in conflict. For group *C* to be successful, it had to retrain members of *A* and *B:* first with respect to their attitudes toward each other, and second, and much more fundamentally, with respect to *methods of group operation.* In short, for group *C* to be successful, it must, through members from *A* and *B*, bring about changes in the ways those groups work. The change is away from concern over the group's "position" in the community toward concern over solving community problems; this is a change from the effort to legislate reality to the effort to operate realistically. And this means a change away from pressure tactics and demagoguery toward objective analysis, recognition and development of individual potential, and adoption of the experimental method as the means for keeping contact with community realities. And finally, under these conditions the individual achieves integration because he can live simultaneously in all the groups of which he is a member; he can move without member conflict from one group to another within his subjective world.

The salient features of the operation of the bridging group re:

1. Bringing about communication between members of the opposing groups under conditions such that neither has to "defend" his group.

2. Developing the bridging group itself into a strong one with its own culture and appeal to members.

3. Operating the bridging group as a training situation in which the members can learn the experimental method of group problem-solving.

4. Facilitating acceptance by members of each other and of the groups they represent.

5. Influencing the members of the home groups toward gradual change of their ways of operating, toward a more problem-reality oriented approach.

It is our belief that in every successful effort (such as that reported in chapter 1) at reducing intergroup conflict these steps can be discerned.

The Community's Part in Intergroup Conflict

The average community contains many groups, and to some extent they act as bridging groups for each other. If I am in group *A* and you in group *B*, but both of us are in the Men's Chowder-Tasters Society, the chances are that we will use this common group partially as a bridging group. Or we may have a close friend in common, and, through him, test our attitudes toward each other's group. Possibly the local newspaper, through editorials and news coverage, makes it easier for us to accept each other's groups.

It is through common approaches to groups and problems that the culture of the community develops. And it is at points of choice or conflict that the prevailing culture tips the scales one way or the other. I have indicated that community expectancy can be "for" or "against" conflict; it can be "for" or "against" experimentalism; "for" or "against" problem-solving rather than empire-building. These matters are determined by hundreds of seemingly unrelated acts performed, wittingly or not, by many people. Let us pick out a few of the acts that probably tip the scales against co-operative group action—the acts that show the existence of forces against the kind of group operation we advocate.

Acts against co-operative group action

1. *The reporting of news.*—Newsworthy events are ordinarily either sensational or significant or both. The tendencies to report incidents between individuals as if they were intergroup phenomena and to report group decisions and actions as if they were individual phenomena tip the scales negatively. The first tendency (e.g., to identify sex criminals as Negroes) is disappearing, but the latter tendency remains. Group meetings are reported primarily as the sounding board for comments by individuals with high prestige. "Names make news" but they may not have much relationship to what is actually going on. Back of every annual banquet with a name speaker there may be a far more important tale of average people banded together in common cause. Editors should recognize the significance of grass-roots

movements, of hard, unspectacular, volunteer citizen activity. Mass media can do a great deal to keep up morale, and to give organizations a sense of common cause; perhaps even to assist the co-ordination of efforts of various groups through well-placed editorials, and through serving a clearing-house function. Editorial policy, including news coverage policy, may reflect too much the particular class and other group affiliations of the editor. Like any teacher, the editor needs to know how well the attitudes of his group represent the community as a whole.

2. *The preaching of ideological exclusiveness.*—The most pervasive and widespread model for intergroup competitiveness is the system of churches, each supporting, sometimes defensively, its own brand of religion, including nonsectarianism. The notion that people should be segregated on the basis of belief has been the undoing of many citizen groups. It automatically excludes nonbelievers, who are just the ones who ought to be reached, and it invites status competition over whose interpretation of belief is to be considered authoritative. Too much energy is spent in arguing beliefs and prejudices. The more churches work together for civic betterment, not as individual churches but as a part of a citywide movement, the more likely they will be to involve new members and alleviate civic apathy by means of operating faith. When religious work is used to tear people apart, it tips the scales one way; were it used to pull the community together, it could be a powerful force for promoting a healthy community climate.

3. *The relations between citizens and officials.*—Policemen, firemen, health officials—all the official denizens of city hall and precinct —represent civic authority to the citizen. The kind of reception and follow-up of complaints and suggestions made by citizens may well have more to do with the state of citizen apathy than any other single factor. It is astonishing that so much of what is good and hopeful in the life of the community bypasses the whole political structure, even though civil servants are hired by the people for the express purpose of maintaining their welfare. There is hardly a major job in city hall that would not profit from the help of an advisory board of citizens, and it is all too rare that school improvement begins within the school. Very few citizens

feel close to the processes of civic decision-making, and therefore very few citizens discharge their civic duties with any other feeling than one of being imposed upon.

4. *The self-discipline of special interest groups.*—Taverns, stores, architects, landlords, transportation arrangements—all these and many more give the community its flavor. The institutions with which citizens have their daily contacts, and which rely for their support on community patronage and good will, could profit by taking the larger view, by thinking in terms of long-range consequences of promotion, merchandising, pricing, and favored-customer policies—not to mention such things as an ideal of service, promptness, and accommodation to unusual individual circumstance. Such proprietor groups might well get together, formulate joint problems, and work with citizens in thinking them through. Anything that improves one part of the community rapidly affects the community as a whole.

This listing is of course very incomplete. The operation of courts, industries, real estate and property management, mortgage policies, medical care, and so on, through all the complex facets of living—all these services communicate attitudes of respect for people or of denial of worth; of open-minded optimism or of closed-minded defeatism; of concern for all or of flinty self-interest; of entrenchment of power groups or of co-operation in common cause. And thus the community climate and culture is built; and it determines what is possible, what activities will be rewarded, what aspirations the community can have; whether people will live in serenity and at peace with themselves and each other. These things people learn.

The operation of the community culture is through the consistencies of biases and attitudes expressed by the many acts of everyday living. The acts of the "influence people" contribute most because they are visible and make a difference to the welfare of a large audience, and because they "set the standard" for others who aspire to influence.

I have chosen to deal at length with the community because it is the underlying substratum of learned reactions, which, in ways hidden from the group members, for the most part, enter into all phases of group operation. But the relationships are mutual: change of community attitude is also the result of learning, primarily through interaction between people in formal and informal meetings.

There is a type of subcommunity in which all the same dynamics are at work, but in a more readily controllable and ascertainable way. This is the institution: college, factory, large store, art center, hospital. The institution mediates between most formal groups and the larger community. Studies of institutions lead to one highly significant generalization: the attitudes and biases which pervade an institution—its culture—filter down from the top. These are transmitted either as learned reactions taken over by lower echelons, or as problem areas fraught with anxiety which give the institution its continuing self-obsessions and concerns. It is because of this fact that leaders need to assume considerable responsibility for attitude-communicating behavior. At the present time, for example, there is beginning to be interest in the problem of feedback: how to get evidence for decisions about internal policy, from reactions to previous behaviors up and down the hierarchy.

The operations of large institutions penetrate many more dimensions of community life, and do so more directly, than do groups. We have, on the one hand, the company town, like the army town; it is an extension of the company which gives the town culture its basic framework and direction. On the other hand, the company may be one of many industries which ignore the community and are largely unaware of the mutual interactions which so vitally affect costs, labor policy, training designs, and, probably, creativity in research and production methods. In either case the troubles within the large institution tend to be elaborated more generally in conflict with the surrounding community; and the methods used for dealing with intra-institutional conflict provide a model throughout the community for dealing with many other conflicts arising in a host of other enterprises. (Adoption by industries of proposition I, pp. 114–17, would set a desirable model for the community.)

GROUP GROWTH AND COMMUNITY DEVELOPMENT: A MODEL

The development and growth of a voluntary citizen organization demonstrates most clearly the mutual relationships between groups and community. We shall trace such an organization from its inception through the various stages of growth, and attempt, in the process, to point out some of the ways in which the group and community interact.

First, a movement or organization starts in the mind of some one person, more sensitive or socially conscious than others. He is aroused about some felt problems, such as delinquency, defeatism, or the schools; and he talks about this to the people with whom he can communicate best, his friends. If the issue is anxiety-producing he may talk about it under cover of some safe activity like a bridge game, to which he can escape if necessary. Finally, he finds one or more friends who respond by sharing similar feelings about the problem; he gains a cohort, and both are now reinforced in their feelings and begin to work rather vaguely toward the goal of taking action. The ease with which he finds cohorts, as well as the way he presents the problem to them, will be much affected by the amount of freedom of expression in the community, and particularly the quality of tolerance for the disgruntled and sensitive individual.

Second, the leadership clique develops from the first conversations, primarily through the induction of close friends. This group shares many social activities, and has considerable internal freedom for expression of their power fantasies, identifying target groups and "enemies," and talking over people who for one reason or another it will be "strategic" to involve next. The amount and quality of organization of the community helps the clique decide who is strategic, as it helps it decide how big the problem is. The more organized the community, the greater the ease of communication and involvement of others.

Third, as a result of their own conversations, backed up by discreet inquiries directed to "outsiders," a few strategic people are located and added to the group, probably under the guise of a quasi-social meeting. These new people are likely to belong to the same social class, and they are strategic because they have needed technical knowledge about the problem, are in a position to in-fluence large numbers of other people through their own organi-zations, or are officials who will have to take action later in con-nection with the problem. These "strategic" people are explored warily, and are flattered by being put in the role of consultants. The clique attempts to reality-test ideas, and to get half-promises of co-operation; but at the same time it retains power by offering to do all the work. Of course, some of the strategic people may at this point be admitted to the clique—after considerable testing of their amenability and value. Once more, the community culture enters. These strategic people are likely to be leaders; their re-actions show how large a "bite" on the problem can be taken in the first action step, and their attitudes, the realism of which is assured by their record of successful operation, point to the prob-able forces of resistance and facilitation that must be taken into account.

Fourth, two things happen simultaneously: the over-all plan begins to take shape, and, in the process, the functional roles of the clique and the strategy people begin to get defined. Through dis-cussion of objectives the individuals assess how meaningful the movement will be to them; through discussion of leadership roles, the people find out what sorts of gratifications they can get and what price in assumption of responsibility they will have to pay; through discussion of the groups to try to involve next, the new group develops its own self-image, as powerful or dependent, as active or as promoting the activity of others, and so forth. The group is likely to consider whether its proposed activities will raise or lower its position in public opinion.

All these decisions are conditioned by estimates about the ease of communication of objectives, the potentials for action believed to reside in other groups, the previous examples of success or fail-ure along similar lines. In addition, the grand plan itself, particu-larly with respect to its boldness and creativity, suggests quite clearly the freedom for daring or the habits of dependence which characterize groups in the community.

Fifth, the first action step is taken. Assuming that the group has decided to play a central action role, rather than merely to study the problem by inviting in prestige speakers or to turn it over to some existing agency, this step involves bringing in other people. Several important things happen at this point. For one thing, a set of bylaws is worked out to protect the clique leadership and to define the steps in the prestige hierarchy of the organization. This enables members to estimate the effort required for the rewards of "moving up." Second, the informal group of strategy people is formalized in the board of directors, made up of a mixture of experts (who become heads of working committees) and prestige people (who help with membership, fund raising, and public relations). Third, the leadership group hammers out its basic methodology of either co-operation or pressure.

If the group feels sufficient internal security, the policy is likely to be co-operation. There is likely to be a strong effort to find a place for everyone who wants to help, through description of a wide variety of adequately supervised and rewarded jobs. There will probably also be an effort to maintain continuous involvement in the membership, through the feedback of policy decisions and reporting of progress.

If the group does not feel secure, and is basically more concerned with the protection of its power strivings, the policy will be very different. The first action may be to hire an executive secretary responsible to what now becomes an inactive board of directors; this really means that the group remains dominated by the officers of the original clique, and the secretary is given all the routine work. The group tries to get members not so much to work as to swell the number of people the officers can say they represent when they make demands on officials and other groups. The test of membership is therefore not willingness to work but rather similarity of belief, of readiness to "go along" with actions taken by officers who can give the beliefs expression.

Here, as always, the decisions are made in terms of existing models in the community. If there are no generally accepted patterns of co-operation, there will be no co-operative models to consider or emulate.

Sixth, along with the first action step, "public opinion" begins to enter the picture concretely. The right of a group to talk within itself is accepted as part of the right of freedom of assembly. But when the group goes outside itself to influence others, then a host of perceptions arises. The nature of these perceptions again depends upon the stereotypes already existing in the community, and the interpretations made of the first action steps accurately reflect the state of intergroup communication. If the problem is one which lies within the jurisdiction of other groups, these may get defensive and hostile; they may get very active to allay their guilt feelings at having done little themselves. There may be whispering campaigns and smearing of the officers. There may be tentative proposals made from other groups, ranging from threats to offers of merger.

Seventh, as action goes forward, working alliances with other groups have to be developed. This is likely to involve a redefinition of the problem and of the jurisdictions of the interested parties. If the group tries to ignore other groups it will gradually find there are limits to its action and growth. It will not be able to reach new types of people, it will stop developing new techniques, it will become more conservative and tend to rest on its past accomplishments. The excitement goes and self-training stops. The group gets ready to attack any new group that tries to start work in the same problem area.

If, however, the group has developed enough security so that it now exists as an institution apart from the original officers, it can form relationships with other groups. This is a crucial point, involving acceptance by the community and by the group of the worth of its functions. There develops the expectation that people will join, work hard for a few years, and then go on, without prejudice, to other experiences. A sufficient body of tradition and stabilized policy grows so that the group is no longer vulnerable to threats. It can contemplate with equanimity considerable change in the means it uses to achieve its goals: and these have been whittled down and redefined as realistic aspirations.[2]

Eighth, the group takes its place in the network of community organizations. It may engage in joint fund-raising activity. There is referral of potential members from one group to another, depending on the kind of participation the prospective member wants. Mass meetings tend to be sponsored by at least two or-

2. Much of this section is built on presentations of Professor Martin Loeb to the Chicago Workshop in Community Human Relations, 1952.

ganizations, and interpretation of the work of the group puts it in the context of action by other groups as well.

I have to confess that I have yet to see this last step developed very far. But that does not deter me from going on to suggest a further logical development that would ideally follow, assuming that the group and the community were growing. This step would be a joint membership campaign, supervised by an interorganizational group. Through mass meetings and other publicity, people would be acquainted, first, with the needs of the community, second, with the kinds of actions required to meet these needs, and third, with the various organizations trying to take these actions. The aim would be to help each person in the community find his niche, through the kind of participation he most needed and could be rewarded for. This is clearly a goal for the community as a whole, not for any one organization. Other possible developments, such as community centers operated interorganizationally, and total campaigns for limited objectives, are consonant with this stage of development. The interorganizational group referred to here would be the community council, new style.

Ninth, as time goes on, the objectives and methods of the coordinated network of groups would become elaborated and assimilated into the culture of the community. Individual behaviors and decisions would tend to be in line with the program. What had been the action program of one group would become a community movement in which most of the relevant forces were aligned. The movement would, in effect, define a generally sanctioned way of life with respect to its broad objectives. City officials would gradually become the functionnaires for its implementation, and necessary guiding roles would be provided within the planned official structure of community maintenance.

The original groups continuously redefining specific goals, would have—and will always have—a place. It is that of the active social conscience, the prophet of change, the formulator of new values. And it is only through such groups that individual insight, sensitivity, and creativity can be utilized for the development of the "humane community" toward which man's nature (including the processes described so far) is driving him.

It seems reasonable to suppose that this image of group growth is also an image of how the community can be built: with adequate communication and communion, maintaining realistic organizational structure and opening up the widest opportunities for individual growth and development.

BASIC PRINCIPLES FOR GROUPS IN RELATION TO THE LARGER COMMUNITY

The development of groups is accompanied by the taking of action. The taking of action changes the community. All the groups affected by this action react to it. Under favorable conditions within the climate of the community, they then begin planning action together, and eventually co-operate in realistic community-wide programs. So goes our model. Our argument has been that the growth of any group, and, with it, the possibilities of community development, can be truncated at any point in this progress.

In this section we wish to single out in brief recapitulation the assumptions basic to group operation which we believe will enable this social process to reach completion:

First: Community problem-solving is put ahead of organizational power as the objective.

Second: Anyone who can help with the problem-solving is welcome, regardless of professed belief or our theories about his personality.

Third: Efforts are made to seek out and reach working agreements with other groups working for the same objectives.

Fourth: The group serves as a bridging group to reduce conflict among the other groups to which the members are loyal.

Fifth: The group adopts an experimental methodology, determining action at each step on the basis of evaluation of results of preceding steps.

Sixth: The group pays attention to self-training and to its own development so that leadership is strengthened, goals are kept realistic, individuals make satisfying contributions, and workable solutions to problems can be formulated explicitly and passed on to other groups and communities.

Seventh: The group collects adequate data about the problem: the attitudes of all those involved, the "real" reasons why its actions have the effects they do, the objective picture of progress made so far, the phase of the problem the community is most ready to tackle next.

Eighth: The group realistically appraises its own resources and skills, and gets professional help when needed.

Ninth: Throughout all action, the group defines its "enemy" as objectively defined conditions in need of change rather than in terms of individuals or other groups to be demolished.

This is the last list. As I bring this book to a close I turn back to its other lists:

8 principles for neighborhood leadership (pp. 14–18)
3 basic aspects of experience (pp. 46–50)
34 generalizations about organizing activities for specific purposes (pp. 62–67)
9 specifications for in-service training (pp. 91–92)
7 problems of administrators (pp. 108–13)
6 summarized principles for organizations (pp. 126–27)
7 principles for trainers in human relations (pp. 171–77)
4 basic principles for all technologies (pp. 181–90)
13 principles for control of the group (pp. 285–89)
4 major functions of leadership (pp. 302–10)
8 problems of leaders (pp. 314–19)

and now:

9 principles of relationship between groups and their communities

Twelve lists!

In the Preface, we said of the six technologies: "Behind these differences, however, are fundamental similarities." We now say: "Behind these twelve lists is one fundamental set of principles— the principles of human interaction." These are the principles we live by, and each of us must formulate them for himself in response to his own needs and in terms of his own experience. And we shall communicate them to each other through our actions, as we try, through understanding, to build our better worlds.

Selected Readings

On January 1, 1954, Hare and Strodtbeck released an authoritative listing of books and articles which describe or explain matters in face-to-face small groups.* They found 1382 of them, covering the period 1900–1954. There are many from which to choose!

Of the publications which have contributed most to the thinking in this book and which seem memorable to me, I suggest for additional reading, the following:

1. BETTELHEIM, BRUNO, and SYLVESTER, M. E. "Therapeutic Influence of the Group on the Individual," *American Journal of Orthopsychiatry*, XVII (October, 1947), 684–92.

Explains how emotional conflict, expressed openly between two members of a group, may assist another member to deal with similar conflict within himself. Suggests use of this principle to compose groups for maximum need-meeting and growth of the members.

2. BION, W. R. "Experiences in Groups. I" and "Experiences in Groups. II," *Human Relations*, I, No. 3 (1948), 314–20; and No. 4, 487–96.

In these articles, the first two of a series of seven, Bion presents assumptions central to our discussion: that the state of the group-as-a-whole depends upon the relationships between emotionality and work; and that individual behaviors are interpreted as expressing needs of the group-as-a-whole.

3. CHASE, STUART, in collaboration with MARIAN CHASE. *Roads to Agreement.* New York: Harper & Bros., 1951. Pp. 240.

Presents stimulating descriptions of different ways of working of successful groups. Excellent material on which to try out your generalizations.

4. DAVIS, ALLISON. *Social Class Influences on Learning.* Cambridge: Harvard University Press, 1948. Pp. 100.

The first forty-six pages present a concise summary of the concepts of social class and how class differences operate to produce differences in children.

* Fred L. Strodtbeck and A. Paul Hare, "Bibliography of Small Group Research," to appear during spring, 1954, in *Sociometry*.

5. DE HUSZAR, GEORGE. *Practical Applications of Democracy.* New York: Harper & Bros., 1945. Pp. 120.

On the assumption that the meaning of democracy is expressed in the ways people work together, the author has sought out and here presents democratically promising (and psychologically sound) innovations in ways of working in a variety of situations.

6. DEWEY, JOHN. *Experience and Education.* New York: Macmillan Co., 1939. Pp. 116.

The concept of interaction and the significance for education of individual-group relations are here presented by this psychologist's philosopher. Presents a lucid and concise discussion of authority, freedom, control, and other concepts central to our book.

7. FRENKEL-BRUNSWIK, ELSE. "A Study of Prejudice in Children," *Human Relations,* I, No. 3 (1948), 295–306.

Prejudice is here seen as one part of a patterning of needs, approaches to problems, and personality. Makes clear the central importance of the way people accommodate to authority.

8. HILLIARD, A. L. *The Forms of Value.* New York: Columbia University Press, 1950. Pp. 330.

Adds considerably to our understanding of the nature of goals through scholarly and systematic analysis of values and their influence on behavior.

9. JENNINGS, HELEN HALL. *Sociometry of Leadership.* (Sociometry Monograph No. 14.) New York: Beacon House, 1947. Pp. 28.

Explains the psychology of socio-groups and of psyche-groups and the different needs they serve. A classic study which supports the notion that task-oriented groups must, at times, recognize emotional phenomena.

10. LEWIN, KURT, and GRABBE, PAUL. "Conduct, Knowledge, and Acceptance of New Values," *Journal of Social Issues,* V (December, 1945), 53–64.

A penetrating analysis of the way change is produced, particularly in organizations.

11. REDL, FRITZ. "Resistance in Therapy Groups," *Human Relations,* I, No. 3 (1948), 307–13.

An illuminating diagnostic picture of the psychology of individual change at various stages of relationship between individual member and group leader.

Index

STAR TREK®

STRANGE NEW WORLDS

9

STAR TREK®

STRANGE NEW WORLDS

9

Edited by
Dean Wesley Smith
with **Elisa J. Kassin** and **Paula M. Block**

Based upon
Star Trek® and *Star Trek: The Next Generation*®
created by Gene Roddenberry,
Star Trek: Deep Space Nine® created by
Rick Berman & Michael Piller,
Star Trek: Voyager® created by
Rick Berman, Michael Piller & Jeri Taylor, and
Star Trek: Enterprise® created by
Rick Berman & Brannon Braga

POCKET BOOKS
New York London Toronto Sydney

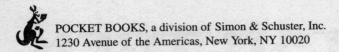

POCKET BOOKS, a division of Simon & Schuster, Inc.
1230 Avenue of the Americas, New York, NY 10020

This book is published by Pocket Books, a division of Simon & Schuster, Inc., under exclusive license from CBS Studios Inc.

Library of Congress Cataloging-in-Publication Data
    Star trek. Strange new worlds 9 / edited by Dean Wesley Smith, with Elisa J. Kassin, and Paula M. Block.
        p.   cm.
        1. Interplanetary voyages—Fiction. 2. Space ships—Fiction. 3. Star Trek fiction. 4. Science fiction, American.   I. Title: Strange new worlds 9.
    II. Title: Strange new worlds nine. III. Smith, Dean Wesley. IV. Kassin, Elisa J. V. Block, Paula M.
    PS648.S3S65966 2006
    813'.0876208—dc22   2006041618

ISBN-13: 978-1-4165-2048-1
ISBN-10:   1-4165-2048-1

This Pocket Books trade paperback edition August 2006

10   9   8   7   6   5   4   3   2   1

For information regarding special discounts for bulk purchases, please contact Simon & Schuster Special Sales at 1-800-456-6798 or business@simonandschuster.com.

Contents

STAR TREK®

STAR TREK THE NEXT GENERATION®

Contents

STAR TREK
DEEP SPACE NINE®

STAR TREK
VOYAGER®

— STAR TREK —
ENTERPRISE

Contents

SPECULATIONS

Introduction

Dean Wesley Smith

After I turned in my selections of wonderful stories for Elisa and Paula to judge for this year's anthology, Elisa and I were discussing ideas for my introduction. She suggested that maybe I should talk about the fortieth anniversary of *Star Trek: The Original Series*.

My initial reaction was: *Forty years? Wow. That's fantastic!*

Then a second thought came to mind. *That's not possible. I'm not that old*.

But I am. I can recall every Friday evening during my high school years. I would always be home to watch *Star Trek*. (Okay, that should give you a pretty good idea of what my social life was like when I was a teenager, but let's not go there.) Suffice it to say, *Star Trek* was an important element in my life during those years.

In hindsight, I realize that the reason I would insist on watching the show every week was clear: I didn't like being where I was during those high school years. What kid really does? *Star Trek* gave me an escape, in much the same fashion as the shelves and shelves of Andre Norton, Edgar Rice Burroughs, and Robert Heinlein books in my basement bedroom. *Star Trek* and all of those other books took me out of that house—out of that teenage life that everybody hates—to strange new places, distant planets, and awesome adventures. Science fiction, with its wonderful worlds, futures, and messages of hope, was what I turned to for a few hours of not thinking about the world around me. More importantly, though, it let me believe that a better future was possible.

Remember the world in which *Star Trek* was born? The cities of this country were going up in flames, and bombs were going off so often that only the regional ones were reported. Martin Luther King, Jr., and Bobby Kennedy were shot. Nixon was elected to his first term. And the war just kept getting bigger and bigger. I believed from almost the moment I understood what Vietnam was about that I would be drafted, when I got out of high school. To me, it also meant that I would eventually be shot at and maybe killed.

That I would be drafted in the fall of 1969 seemed inevitable. It was a fact that all guys thought about a great deal in those days. We didn't talk about it much, though. It was just too scary to talk about.

I was one of those who didn't believe the war was right, but I also didn't believe in copping out by cutting and running. So there I was, stuck in a life I didn't much like, with a future of war and likely death facing me.

So, you can see why I made it home every Friday night to watch the original *Star Trek*. And I have a pretty good memory of writing a letter when they tried to cancel the show in 1968.

I can't imagine what I would have thought if some time traveler had walked up to me during those years and said, "In forty years, you will have managed to stay out of Vietnam. You will have written over twenty *Star Trek* novels, edited several *Star Trek* anthologies for new writers, and written a few *Star Trek* scripts." I'm sure I would have just laughed. Being a part, even a minor part, of such a unique show would never have crossed my mind in 1966.

About thirteen years ago, my wife and I got the chance to join in creating some of this wonderful universe, and we jumped at it. Writing under the name Sandy Schofield, we wrote *Star Trek: Deep Space Nine: The Big Game*. Suddenly, I was a *Star Trek* writer. And it's such a high for me that I get to give new writers out there the same chance.

In nine volumes, there have been almost two hundred new *Star Trek* stories. Over one hundred different writers have joined in inventing *Star Trek, the Next Generation, Deep Space Nine, Voyager,* and *Enterprise*. I'm sure every one of them, since they are all fans, can talk about the influence *Star Trek,* in every incarnation, had in their lives, just as I can. The shows, now shown in syndication, continue to influence future generations as well.

With the world becoming a little rougher than it has been the last few decades, we now need the wonderful vision of the future that *Star Trek* brings us even more. We need the escape, the hope, and the belief that mankind goes forward.

At the moment, we only have the books and games that can bring *Star Trek* and its hope and vision to all of us. You hold it in your hand. You are the cutting edge of *Star Trek*—written by the fans, people like you and me, who love this universe almost more than our real one.

For forty exceptional years, *Star Trek* has given us all a look ahead, a wonderful escape into a great universe. So sit back, turn off the news, and let a few of your fellow fans take you away on twenty-three wonderful trips into the future. You won't want to come home.

STAR TREK®

Gone Native

John Coffren

"No, no, no. This simply won't do."

The creature deftly shuffled his papers with hook-clawed appendages in a swirl of activity as the multitasking arms wrote, turned papers over, absently scratched behind his blowhole, brought a drink up to his beak, and restlessly tapped the wooden table we both sat at.

My own hands were rough; callused and worn from the winter harvest and appeared quite fragile compared with his rubbery tentacles. I turned my attention to the golden rows of quadrotriticale whipping in the afternoon breeze.

"I don't want the report on seedless, waterless crops, the reclamation of plasma-polluted soil and other such wastes of my valuable time. Where is your forward command center? Why has the Klingon Empire been left intact? What happened to establishing a military presence beyond this meaningless speck of dust with zero tactical importance? You should have pushed clear across to the

Delta Quadrant by now. You've had more than sufficient time to accomplish your mission. In short, what have you and your agents been doing for the past three hundred years?"

I decide to answer his question with another question.

"You received the Federation's proposal welcoming us to this region of space?"

"Oh, they sued for peace. Excellent, we'll set up interim camps and disposal facilities in central locations: Alpha Proxima Two, Arvada Three and Ivor Prime."

"You mistake their meaning," I said.

"Did you say something, Rojan?"

The language barrier was twice as thick as deuterium. I remained silent for a time. My gaze drifted back to the upper fields where a curl of smoke wafted from the wreckage of Prefect Tamar's ship. His vessel, like mine before, sustained critical damage after crossing the galactic divide. He put down not fifty meters from the original landing site.

"I believe the Romulans are best suited of the locals to help us process the Federation worlds and races," he said.

I laughed. I could barely understand half of what he was saying. It had been a long time since I heard so much of the mother tongue spoken to me at once.

What I could gather from this alienspeak pointed to questions of a military nature. This centipod before me knew nothing of combat. I could tell just by looking at him.

He had all one hundred of his tentacles intact. Any soldier worth his monthly stipend is missing five, ten, arms at least.

I used to be like him. So full of pomp and ceremony that I couldn't see past my own uniform. I stood up and dusted off my coveralls.

"My fields need tending," I said. "We can talk after supper. My wife sets a fine table if you care to join us."

I turned and walked away before our guest could issue protests in any language. I can't be sure, but I think he shouted out a long string of obscenities at me. I turned to face him again and tossed the spare belt atop the picnic table.

"Put this on for dinner," I said. "You'll starve inside of a month without it. Our world can't sustain you in your current condition."

I returned home late, as was my custom, after putting in a full day's work. The welcome sight of our modest adobe hut and the enticing smells of rich spices from our kitchen greeted me as I entered.

"Where's our dinner guest?" I asked.

"Waiting for you outside," Kelinda said. "He keeps pinching and pulling his flesh like it's some ill-fitting, tailored suit that he can just return and get his old skin back."

"I bet he wishes he could," I said.

"But you and I both know that's not possible."

She rested my hands atop the belt weapon and looked directly into my eyes before speaking.

"There's no other way," Kelinda said. "You and I both know it. It's best to just get it over with now."

"I want to talk to him before resorting to that," I said.

"There's no talking to that one," she said. "Remember how we used to be? Given half a chance, he and his kind will do the exact same thing here. Don't give him that chance."

Kelinda was one of the first to embrace her emotions, good and bad. Her courage in sampling the elation of joy and the misery of sorrow helped to enrich all our lives. Through her careful instruction, I learned to deal with these complex and often competing feelings.

But I had not completely discarded the cold, calculating ways of my forefathers. And it was at times like these that I was grateful for my prudence and old-fashionedness.

Tamar did not hear my approach, the perfect opportunity to carry out Kelinda's wishes. No. I thought it best to interrupt his stargazing by announcing my presence.

"We generally take our meals indoors, unless it's a particularly warm evening."

The prefect had been staring off into the general direction of our galaxy. I had been doing that myself every night for the first hundred years or so that we lived here. You can't wish yourself home, though. It took me a while to learn that one.

"We produce very little artificial light here," I said. "It makes for spectacular views of the Milky Way, as good as or better than from the bridge of any starships wandering the cosmos."

"The bridge of a starship is where I belong. Launching a devastating attack on the denizens of this spiral arm of the galaxy," the prefect replied. "Our code of honor demands nothing less than the complete and utter subjugation of these worlds and complete and utter loyalty from subjects. We both know the penalty for treason."

Subtle he wasn't. I pushed through.

"I'm curious. Did you get a chance to review any of the data I dispatched through robot probes sent to Andromeda?"

He attempted a smirk, but it came across as a frown. The mastery of human emotions takes time and practice, which he was either unwilling or unable to give.

"Your first probe reached the homeworld and was reviewed by the High Command. They ordered the subsequent destruction of any and all drones sent forthwith from this outpost. It is an order that I carried out with pleasure. I chased one of your more elusive messengers into the heart of a proto-star to insure its annihilation. They rewarded my diligence with this assignment."

"So you think you've been sent here as a reward?" I said. "You're here to help prepare the way for the great invasion fleet from Andromeda, when it drops out of warp complete with waving banners and rolling drums to restore the Kelvan Empire to its former glory?

"Well, it's not happening. And if you bothered to scan and download those drones I launched before you gleefully vaporized them you'd know the reason why. I suspect your shooting tentacle wanted to get in a little target practice. Hard as duck soup."

"What's duck soup?" the prefect asked.

"A human expression. It means . . . never mind what it means. Did you know that the radiation levels in our home galaxy are accelerating at an exponential rate and the previous forecasts could be easily termed as dangerously optimistic?"

"That is precisely why the Empire must expand," Tamar said.

"The beast must be fed or it will die," I said.

"Overly simplistic, but correct," he said.

"There is another way for you and for Kelva," I said. "Join the United Federation of Planets. There is strength in numbers."

"The Federation," he said with disgust. "That assortment of weaklings will bow down before the might of the Kelvan Armada. They will grovel before us as we obliterate entire systems they once held in their feeble grasp."

"The Armada will be crippled when it tries to ford the galactic barrier," I answered. "You know it and I know it and if you hadn't so eagerly atomized the data drones, the High Command would know it too."

"Lies!" Tamar screamed.

"The proof is smoldering in my Kaferian apple orchard," I said. "Your own escort vessel was disabled by the negative energy field."

"Centuries of masquerading as a human have made you one. You are a traitor and an enemy of the State. I've been sent to pass judgment on your crimes."

The prefect produced a belt weapon, a more recent model than mine, deadlier of course. I let a smile turn up the corners of my mouth. Drea launched the rocket right on cue. The explosive takeoff shook the ground as the exhaust ports left a crop circle a mile in diameter. The night sky lit up as the missile headed for the stratosphere and beyond.

"Another drone," the prefect said.

"No, a galaxy bomb headed for Kelva."

"You will abort the launch now," he said and leveled the weapon at me.

"Too late, Prefect," I said. "The rocket will pierce the galactic barrier, cross the great void, and strike right into the heart of the Andromeda Galaxy. There it will deliver its payload into the massive central black hole. The detonation will widen the hundred-and-forty-million-solar-masses maw of the abyss wide enough to swallow Kelva, its satellites, and eventually Andromeda itself. M32 and M110 will follow in another millennium or so. And your empire will be no more. My galaxy bomb will finish the job that the radiation levels started, just sooner than expected."

"Not before you die first," he said.

He never heard or saw Kelinda sneak up behind him. Like I said, he was no soldier. One minute a paper-pushing propagandist standing before me brandishing a loaded weapon, the next minute a neat, compact dodecahedron lying at my feet.

Kelinda walked over to me.

"What should we do with him?" she asked.

"Put him with the others," I said.

"We're going to need a bigger barn at this rate," she said.

She picked Prefect Tamar up in one hand and started walking away.

I watched the latest robot drone leave orbit. I lied to Tamar. The payload that rocket carried was far more explosive than any bomb I could build. It was a peace treaty between the United Federation of Planets and the Kelvan Empire, signed, dated, and enacted over three hundred years ago by the highest-ranking officials both sides could muster, the Federation president and myself, Commander Rojan of Kelva.

A Bad Day for Koloth

David DeLee

Koloth stormed across the bridge of the *I.K.S. Gr'oth*. His boots thundered on the deck plating with the wrath of Kahless himself. At least the blood-red lighting and muted brown bulkheads soothed his aching eyes. The damned Federation station had been so bright . . . and *cheery*.

"Helm!" he barked. His gaze fell on Space Station K-7 displayed on the screen and he waved an angry hand. "Get us out of here."

Korax glanced over his shoulder like a whipped targ. "Destination?"

"Anywhere away from here. Away from that damned station. Away from Sherman's Planet. Away from quadrotriticale. Away from that *pahtk* Darvin. Away from Kirk." Koloth stepped up onto the platform of the command chair. "And especially away from those damned tribbles."

"Yes, Captain." Korax turned and laid in a course . . . to somewhere.

Relieved to be done with K-7 and the puny, soft humans, Koloth dropped into the hard, sharply angled command chair.

And a tribble squealed.

"By the Sword of Kahless!" Koloth jumped away. Spinning, he drew his disruptor. In the corner of his seat a brown and white tribble sat trembling.

He fired.

The beam lanced out, struck the chair. Sparks flew and the chair spun around like a child's top. Alarms sounded. When the wisp of smoke cleared the chair was scorched black, and the tribble was gone.

Vaporized.

Koloth grunted with a satisfied nod. Careful to avoid his wrath, Korax and Grotok, the navigator, spun back to examine their consoles. Holstering his weapon, Koloth surveyed the bridge. All of his officers were carefully examining their consoles. *Good.*

He sat back down, resisting the urge to check his seat before doing so. The metal was warm. He ran a hand over the singed arm. It felt like battle, like victory.

"Take us to Qo'noS, helm." He had finally made his decision as to their destination.

"As you wish, Captain."

Koloth settled in for the long trip home, already composing his report for the High Council. Devising how to present the details of Darvin's failure and how, by his own quick actions, he saved the Empire from an embarrassing intergalactic incident with the cursed Federation.

Yes. He could salvage this, turn this defeat into a victory. Even though he'd failed to secure the right to Sherman's Planet, after they review *his* report, no one could blame him for what happened.

If not for the damned tribbles, the planet would have been theirs. Bah! It was the Council's own damned fault. Subterfuge. Poison. Spies. They were acting like . . . like Romulans. If they wanted Sherman's Planet they should have taken it by force and won it in glorious battle.

His hearts skipped a few beats when he heard it.

At first he thought it was the thrumming of the engines. Perhaps a bit off cycle, but there it was again. A soft, soothing trill. He shuddered. He looked around until he found the offensive beast.

There at the base of Korax's chair, he saw it sitting beside his boot.

Koloth stood. Took a step forward. He dropped first to one knee. Then the other. Bent . . . and lunged.

Korax jumped from his chair. He stared at Koloth, who was prone on the deck, with his head and arms buried under the helmsman's chair. "Captain?"

Koloth backed away on his elbows and knees, his hands cupped in front of him. From them came a high-pitched squeal. Climbing to his feet, Koloth opened his hands and displayed a round, furry tribble. It was brown and white. A patch of its hair was singed black. The one he had shot? Could he have missed?

The feel of it angrily twitching in his hand sent shivers down his spine. He shoved it at Korax. "Explain this!"

It convulsed in his hands. Squealing.

Korax backed up. "I . . . I don't know."

Koloth spotted another tribble over Korax's shoulder. It cowered in the corner of the secondary tactical console. "And that!"

He stormed over. The tribble—bright red—hopped, chirring agitatedly. Another one rolled out from under the console, scampered away. And there was yet another one next to the turbolift door.

The turbolift opened. Bel'kor, his chief engineer, stepped onto the bridge with an armful of tribbles. The pile of fur jumped and squawked and chirped and leaped from his arms.

"Captain. The engine room. It's full of them. They're in the machinery."

Koloth held the brown-and-white one up and looked at it. "Where? How?"

"The *Enterprise*. The *pahtk*s beamed them in."

"Then beam them back."

"I can't. They're out of range."

Koloth swore. "Kirk!"

He dropped into his chair, slammed the tribble he was holding into the pile of skittering beasts in Bel'kor's arms. He juggled the jumbling armload, only losing a few.

"Get them off the ship. Beam them into space if you have to."

"We tried. The transporters are offline. So are environmental, fire suppression, intership communications. They're into the machinery. Shipwide."

Koloth leaned his elbows on the arms of his chair, interlocked his fingers together, thinking. He jerked his head up. "Gas them."

Bel'kor shook his head, oily black hair fell in his face. "Vent controls are offline. Can't do it without killing us too."

Smashing his fist Koloth slammed back in his chair. "There must be something—"

"Priority message from Qo'noS, Captain," Grotok called out. "Audio only."

Koloth waved for him to play it.

"*I.K.S. Gr'oth. Reverse course. You are carrying dangerous contaminants and are in violation of health and ecological protection codes. You will not be permitted access into Klingon space. Reverse course immediately or risk being fired upon.*"

Koloth was half out of his chair again. "What?"

"Shall I replay it, Captain?" Grotok asked.

"No, *pahtk*! I heard them!" Banished from Klingon space. Incredible. Unheard of.

"Get them off the ship." Koloth waved his arms. "Hunt them down with *targ*s. Shoot them all with disruptors. Open the damn airlocks and eject them into space. I don't care. Just get rid of every last one of them. Now!"

He stormed for the turbolift. Stepped inside, and kicked a tribble out onto the bridge just before the doors swooshed shut.

Koloth tossed and turned. His booted feet banged on the hard surface of his bunk. He shifted to his side. Flopped onto his back again. Sleep escaped him as surely as did a solution to his tribble problem.

With a growl he slammed his fist into the duranium and sat up. Disgusted. The bunk felt as soft as . . . as a *mattress.*

He got up and crossed to the other side of his quarters. "Activate viewscreen."

A wall-mounted viewer snapped on. Static-filled at first, it soon cleared. Staring back at him was the grinning face of his good friend, Captain Kang.

"Koloth! So good of you to call. I heard of your predicament. A terrible thing," he said, but the laughter in his voice belied any true concern he felt.

"I'm glad you're enjoying yourself at my expense, dear friend." Koloth considered cutting the transmission. Calling Kang had been a mistake.

"No. No. Hold on, my friend," Kang said, holding up a hand. *"What good is friendship if we cannot get under each other's hide now and again? What do you ask of me?"*

"All I ask is for a solution. How do I exterminate these vermin from my ship?"

Kang took on a thoughtful look. *"I truly am sorry, my friend. I find I too am at a loss. It seems you have tried everything."*

Koloth was forced to agree. He selected a quart of bloodwine from the food slot, removed the tin cup when the door opened. "Join me then in drink."

He hoisted his cup. Kang burst out in laughter.

On top of his cup sat a bloated brown-and-white tribble. A patch of its fur singed black.

Koloth flung the cup across the room. It bounced off the wall and rolled across the hard metal deck. Splashed bloodwine dripped thickly down the wall. It was not the first time bloodwine, or blood for that matter, had been spilled in these quarters.

The tribble squealed in surprise or pain and wobbled erratically across the floor.

When Kang had finished laughing, he slapped a gloved hand against his knees. *"What you need, my friend, is a battle. A glorious battle to lift your spirits and take your mind off your tribbles."*

Kang belched out another deep, throaty laugh.

"K'adio," Koloth growled, dripping with sarcasm. Thank you for nothing. He snapped off the viewer, unable to shut off Kang's laughing image from inside his head.

A battle would be glorious. The feel of a *bat'leth* whistling through the air. The taste of disruptor fire in the air. The smell of scorched burning flesh, of an enemy he could fight. Hot spilled blood filling the street of an enemy city, or flowing down the corridors of an enemy ship.

And that was when it struck him. A battle.

He picked up the little, singed, brown-and-white tribble from the shelf under the viewer. The one that kept turning up around him like—what was the Earthers' expression—like a bad penny.

"Of course. The perfect solution," he said, grinning at the squirming tribble. "A glorious battle."

"Four Tholian fighters. Dead ahead," Korax called out.

Koloth leaned forward, his eyes fixed on the four yellowish ships. They were triangular in shape and small, but Koloth knew not to underestimate the Tholians. They had proven themselves worthy opponents in the past. Today, he was counting on them to be as cutthroat as they had been before.

Koloth rose. "Battle stations! Grotok, on my command decloak and raise shields."

Grotok nodded.

"Captain," the voice came from Bel'kor. "Shields are only at seventy-three percent. Several power conduits were damaged by the tribbles."

"Your incompetence has been noted."

Bel'kor started to reply, then thought better of it. He brushed a skittering black tribble off his console. It hit the deck with a yelp and scurried off.

"Engage the enemy!" Koloth sat at the edge of his chair, a forearm resting on his leg. His gloved fist clenched. "Tactical! Full photon spread!"

He felt the *Gr'oth* shudder with the launch of the torpedoes.

Two struck Tholian ships. Their shields flashed, absorbing the energy and impact. The four ships continued on their approach, spreading their formation wider.

"Minimal damage," Korax announced.

"It is of no concern. They will soon feel the might of the Klingon Empire."

"They're powering up weapons. Maneuvering in an attack formation."

Koloth's eyes flicked back and forth watching each of the four ships. One, two experienced Tholian fighters they could take on easily, three possibly. But four? That was the stuff of story and song.

Several tribbles huddled at his feet. Their little bodies swaying. They cooed excitedly.

The *Gr'oth* rocked. Koloth squinted at the flash of light on the viewscreen. It was currently displaying a simple phaser barrage. One that was easily deflected.

"Shields down to fifty-two percent."

"Return fire!" Koloth pounded the arm of his chair. "Target their lead ship."

Two of the triangular ships peeled off to the left. A string of energy pulses stitched the side of the *Gr'oth*. Korax fired two torpedoes. Both struck their targets.

"Their shields are down!"

"Fire disruptors! Tight concentration."

Korax engaged his weapons and the nearest Tholian ship burst into a fireball instantly.

The *Gr'oth* wasn't to get off easily though. The fight was still only beginning. The remaining three fighters strafed them. The D-7 slammed down like a foot stomping on a bug. As Bel'kor tumbled from his seat, his auxiliary engineering station exploded.

Alarms and smoke filled the bridge.

"Evasive maneuvers!" Koloth was on his feet, leaning between

Korax and Grotok. He glanced down at the astrogator trying to get a fix on the remaining three fighters. A tribble sat on the glowing grid. Koloth swatted it away.

"There!" He pointed at one of the glowing dots. "Coordinates seven-five-nine-nine-three point one. Two torpedoes. Fire now!"

"Target locked." Korax jabbed the firing button.

"Direct hit." Grotok clenched a fist. "A glorious hit. They are venting plasma."

Bel'kor had taken up a position at auxiliary tactical. He turned in his seat to face Koloth. "Incoming message from the Tholians. Audio."

Koloth straightened. "Play it."

"You are violating Tholian space. You have committed an unprovoked attack against the Tholian Assembly. Surrender or be destroyed."

That they had violated Tholian space was true enough, but surrender was not part of the plan. Koloth returned to his chair, targeting one of the fighters himself. He punched the Fire button with the flat of his fist.

The swift moving fighter dodged the spiraling torpedoes.

Charging to the port and starboard sides, the enemy ships strafed the—by comparison—lumbering *Gr'oth.*

The ship pitched to the left, throwing most of the bridge crew to the deck. Koloth managed to keep from sliding out of his chair, but just barely. Several tribbles rolled across the deck.

The lights flickered. A panel exploded. Its cover pinwheeled across the bridge. Flames licked up the curved bulkhead.

"Auxiliary power!" Bel'kor shouted. "Shields are gone."

"Return fire! Return fire!"

"Returning fire," Korax acknowledged the order.

"Hull breaches on decks two, three, seven. Additional fractures along the port nacelle."

Smoke thickened the air. Emergency lights illuminated and shone through the drifting, swirling gray. The bridge crew became darting, indistinguishable shadows. Alarms wailed.

It was time.

"Helm. Contact the *I.K.S. SuvwI'*."

A few minutes later Kang's face loomed large on the static-filled viewscreen. He grinned a toothy grin. *"So, you took my advice and found a fight."*

"We did. And a glorious fight it is."

Kang looked skeptical. *"You appear to be on the losing side of it."*

"You underestimate me, my friend. Already two Tholian ships are destroyed. Two more are in my sights."

"Impressive indeed. Why then are you calling me?"

The *Gr'oth* shook. The bulkhead groaned loudly; then a girder let loose, swinging down across the bridge like a pendulum. Its jagged end bit into the deck.

"All great battles have their cost, Kang. The cost of this one is the great ship *Gr'oth*." Koloth looked around the bridge.

His gaze fell on a tribble crawling across the deck. He kicked at it, looked back up to Kang. "A ship they will sing about from here to *Sto-Vo-Kor*."

"A warrior's way," Kang agreed. *"We shall be there shortly."*

Now to keep the Tholians at bay until the *SuvwI'* could arrive. A task that proved harder than Koloth would've liked.

"They're in attack formation."

"Prepare torpedoes."

"Captain! Torpedo bay doors are malfunctioning." Korax glanced over his shoulder with panic in his eyes.

"What?" Koloth was on his feet again. "Bel'kor?"

He searched for the engineer in the dim hazy smoke. A vague shadow stepped forward. "It's the tribbles. They're disrupting power conduits on almost every deck."

Koloth glanced at the astrogator. The two dots representing the Tholian fighters glowed bright, showed they were moving on a closing vector. With only disruptors available, staving off an attack was impossible.

"Tactical. Target and fire at will."

Koloth watched the approaching ships on the viewscreen. Had he miscalculated? Had he contacted Kang too late?

Phasers fired from the belly of the D-7.

The Tholian shields glowed and held. Their forward weapons sections glowed too, resulting in phasers lancing out across the expanse of space.

Koloth braced for impact. On the deck at his feet a brown-and-white tribble rocked with the swaying ship. The one he'd shot. The singed mark clear as day. It sat, mocking him. He was sure of it.

The phasers struck. Slicing through the hull. Sparks and melted metal poured through into the bridge. Somewhere, someone screamed. Koloth couldn't tell who it was.

Then miraculously the assault stopped.

Koloth glanced at the viewscreen. The *SuvwI'* had arrived. Passing one Tholian fighter, disruptors were flaring its shields to a bright yellow. A volley of torpedoes finished the job of taking out its shields.

"Captain Koloth." Kang's voice. "*Prepare to beam your crew to the* SuvwI'."

Koloth smiled. "Transporters are offline. Need you to initiate."

"*So I'm here to do all the work, is that it?*"

"This time, my friend. This time."

"*Transports initiated.*"

And so Koloth waited. A feeling of great relief washed over him. The single remaining Tholian fighter was no threat to the fresh *SuvwI'*. His casualties had been acceptable and now he could return to the Empire not in disgrace but as a warrior. Proud and victorious in battle.

Stepping down from his command chair he surveyed the wrecked bridge of the *Gr'oth*. His only regret. It had been a good ship.

"*Everyone has been beamed aboard, Captain Koloth.*" The voice of the *SuvwI*'s transporter operator called out over the ship-to-ship comm link.

"Understood. Stand by."

There was one more thing Koloth had to do. "Initiate Klingon self-destruct. Code Koloth twelve-one-seven-two."

"*Voiceprint confirmed. Self-destruct sequence initiated.*"

Koloth paused for only a second. He bent down and scooped up a tribble from the floor. It was the scorched brown-and-white one. Surprising himself, he grinned.

The tribble squeaked and trembled in his hand. "Perhaps I've misjudged you, little vermin. You are so much more resilient than I gave you credit for."

He held it a little higher. "Perhaps a more worthy adversary after all." It twitched, squawked.

"Perhaps," he mused. "If so, then you deserve a warrior's death. Go, my unexpected adversary, and know that today is a good day to die."

He flung the tribble across the bridge into a burning computer console. The yellow-red flames licked hungrily at the spinning ball of fur.

"A good day to die," he said, feeling the transporter seize his body. "But not for me."

Seconds later the tribble-infested *Gr'oth* exploded into a ball of fire and smoke and twirling, twisted metal.

Book of Fulfillment

Steven Costa

(Translation of a fragment of scroll, labeled "Book of Fulfillment," discovered on Maltos IV by Professor Richard Galen, stardate 46531.5: Chapter 6, Verse 27 to Chapter 9, Verse 16.)

CHAPTER 6

27. But the people took no note of the words of the Prophet. In their eyes, his words were like the words of a madman. They drove forth the Prophet, he with his attendants, and he did depart from them with a heavy heart.

CHAPTER 7

1. A generation of the people did come to pass, a generation of the people in the valley of the green river. And in the fortieth year of the

Fifth Cycle, in the month of the sweet fruit harvest, on the tenth day of the month, a great calamity befell the people.

2. In the sky appeared a bright star, and the name of the star was a name not known to the wise men of the people, for it was a new star and its coming was a wonderment.

3. The new star did grow large in the night sky, and brighter. It descended upon the people with a brightness that was like the brightness of the feast-day bonfire. But when it reached the ground, the brightness did fade, and the star became as a vessel of iron.

4. From the vessel came forth the Destroyers, the Fearsome Ones of the old tales, known to men as the Ones Who Roar. Their appearance was fear-inspiring, for they wore garments of iron and hide, and they carried implements of destruction.

5. Each Destroyer had taken into his hand a blade of fearsome might, and also an evil weapon of thunder and lightning. And they did descend upon the people in the valley of the green river.

6. And their faces were strange in the eyes of the people, for they were of a color like that of rich, dark bread, and their eyes numbered only two, and there was no antler upon their head but a fleshy ridge like no one had ever seen before.

7. Around the encampment of the people they did encircle, and their roaring was as the roaring of the southern wind for its might. And the strong men of the people went forth to stand against them, armed with their implements for hunting. But they were as long grass before the Destroyers, the Ones Who Roar, and they were mowed down close to the earth.

8. The people did bend their knee as one and submit to the Destroyers, for their power could not be opposed. The Destroyers did speak

their name, and their name was Klingon. The name was new in the ears of the people, and fear-inspiring.

9. And the people did toil for the Klingons. The people were compelled to prepare their loathsome foods, and dig in the earth, and gather from the forest the herbs used by the wise ones to make the ointment that gives health and life and strength of arm. Every task from the mouth of the Klingons, the people did just so, for the Klingons were mighty. And the people were faint of heart, because of their might.

10. The hands of the Klingons were very heavy upon the people. And the outcry of the people was a very great outcry.

CHAPTER 8

1. The people gave way to tears and tore their garments and threw themselves to the ground and begged the Great Ones for forgiveness. "We did not listen to the words of the Prophet, so many years ago, and our sin rests heavily upon us. Save us, O Great Ones, we beseech. Deliver us from the hands of the Klingons, from the hands of the Ones Who Roar!"

2. But the Great Ones did not give ear to the words of the people, for the sin of the people was a very heavy sin. The people did continue to suffer under the hands of the Klingons for the time of three turnings of the smaller moon.

3. Then the Great Ones looked upon the sorrow of the people with mercy and judged "The people have suffered and their sin is washed clean."

4. And the Great Ones spoke the word. So it came to pass that the Liberator came to the people.

5. The Liberator came from beyond the sky. Through the stars in the heavens his vessel came, bearing him forth to save the people. To smite the Destroyers he came forth, for their kingdoms were adversaries in the heavens. The Liberator was a great warrior, a man of fame.

6. The vessel of the Liberator was a mighty one and concealed within the depths of the heavens. Brave were the souls of the attendants of the Liberator. Their hearts were loyal to him, for his rulership was a good rulership.

7. At his left hand was the Healer. The Healer's words went forth like spears from the hand of the thrower, and his counsel was like fire in the ears of the Liberator.

8. At his right hand was the Sage. His thoughts were clear and cold and swift, like the stream of water from the mountains, and his counsel was wise beyond wisdom.

9. And about them were the attendants of the Liberator: the Wayfinder, to guide the vessel through the darkness between the stars of the heavens; the Armsman, to rain destruction upon the foes of the Liberator; the Proclaimer, to announce his great name to all who would hear; and the Machinist, to harness the power of the vessel of the heavens.

10. Together they came forth to save the people, and to crush the Destroyers, the Ones Who Roar.

11. Before the eyes of the wise men the Liberator appeared, and the Healer was upon his left hand, and the Sage was upon his right. They appeared in the encampment of the people, in the dark hours of the night. Arrayed as the people, in garments like unto those of the people's garments, did they appear.

12. Their faces they had concealed, for their faces were different from those of the people. Similar to the Klingons' were their faces. Only to the wise ones were their faces revealed, in the inner chambers of the wise ones. And when the name of the Liberator was revealed, they cried out in exultation, for his words were known to the wise men as the words of the Prophet.

13. The words of the Liberator were new in their ears, for he spoke of contention, and deliverance, and vengeance upon the Destroyers.

14. On the rising of the sun, the vessel of the Liberator would rain down destruction upon the vessel of the Klingons.

15. But the Sage spoke quiet words of counsel in the ear of the Liberator, speaking of the oath. And the Healer spoke fiery words of counsel in the ear of the Liberator, speaking of the suffering of the people.

16. The Liberator pledged unto the wise men. His oath to his own masters was a powerful oath, and he could not deliver the people if the people would not request the deliverance. The people must make the request, and the people would rise up.

17. The numbers of the Klingons were not many, but the people were frightened because of their might. They were fearful of the plan for deliverance and their hearts were troubled, and they would not rise up against the Destroyers.

18. Then the Liberator addressed the people, and he spoke with a voice of command, inciting the people. The words of the Liberator were powerful words. The spirit of the people had been slumbering, but it awoke with a great and righteous fury.

19. The people rose, and put each one into his hand an implement for digging, or an implement for cooking, or an implement for

harvesting to fight against the Destroyers, the ones now known as the Klingons.

20. The wise men asked the people, "Will we request the deliverance, and will we rise up against the Destroyers?"

21. With one voice, the people said, "We will rise up, and we do request the deliverance!"

22. And the night until the rising of the sun was a very long night.

CHAPTER 9

1. Upon the rising of the sun, the vessel of the Liberator did rain down fire upon the vessel of the Klingons, upon the Ones Who Roar, and they were unable to stand against it.

2. Then the people rose as one, and took each one into his hand an implement for digging, or an implement for cooking, or an implement for harvesting, and turned their hands against the Destroyers.

3. And the people made a great shout of praise, for the Liberator appeared among the people to fight against the Destroyers, against the Klingons. His implement of destruction was a powerful implement, a righteous weapon of thunder and lightning, and he did strike down the Destroyers with its fury.

4. The Sage did stand by the weak ones of the people, the old and the young. Before the wrath of the Destroyers he stood. There was no fear in his heart at the approach of a Destroyer. And the Sage did lay a hand upon him, and the Destroyer did fall.

5. The Healer did move among the people struck down by the Destroyers, and did proclaim that he was a Healer, and not a worker of miracles. But the saying of the Healer was a humble saying, for

with his implements of healing he did work miracles in the eyes of the people.

6. And the people went about piling the fallen Klingons into heaps.

7. When the battle was concluded, the people made a joyous outcry. And the wise men implored the Liberator to speak his name before all the people, that they might know and give it praise.

8. And the Liberator spoke these words to the people: "I am Captain James T. Kirk of the *U.S.S. Enterprise.* I represent the United Federation of Planets."

9. And the people again gave voice to great exultation, for the words of the Liberator Kirk were words known to them. The name of the Liberator's vessel was a name known to the people, and the kingdom of the Liberator was known to them, for the Prophet Archer had spoken these same words in the days long ago, in the days of the Prophecy.

10. Like the Prophet Archer before, the Liberator spoke of the great union of worlds, and now the wise men of the people gave ear to his words. They said unto the people, "These are good words. Will the people be united with the worlds of the Liberator, with the worlds of the Federation?"

11. The people said with one voice, "We will be united with you, and our peoples will become as one people."

12. The Liberator was joyful in his heart, and the Healer was joyful with him. The Sage had no joy in his heart, but he was content, and it was enough. They went away from the people to prepare a place for them. And their going was a wonderment to the people, for they were gone in a twinkling.

13. The people offered up a sacrifice of praise to the Great Ones, for the Prophecy had come to pass. They had suffered under the hands of the Ones Who Roar, but they had been delivered, and their praises were many.

14. And the people did celebrate their deliverance with a bonfire like no bonfire before. They brought forth the captured ones of the Klingons, to share in the festival. And they roared no longer, but they did howl.

15. The toil of the people had been long, and their hunger was a very great hunger, but there was enough for all the people in the valley of the green river, from the small to the great. For the flesh of the Klingons was not tender, but it was plentiful.

16. And it was good.

The Smallest Choices

Jeremy Yoder

I see no logic in preferring Stonn over me.

Over a century after Spock had spoken those words, T'Pring still considered them. Stonn was a decent husband and father. At times she found his company adequate. But he had never been an excellent Vulcan. Never as poised and dignified as other Vulcan males. Never as controlled and secure as herself.

She rose from her chair, her green robe swaying, and walked past the white Tholian lace adorning her bed canopy. Hot sunlight poured in through the windows. Her shoes clicked on the auburn stone floor on which her ancestors had walked. When she and Stonn died someday, their offspring would inherit the house as she had.

Her husband had left for the Daystrom Institute months ago. He was a scientist and should prove helpful there, but the assignment was granted as more of a favor to her than for his own merits. Certain high-ranking officials pitied her and therefore sent Stonn on missions to make her household appear noble in the eyes of the populace. She questioned if the ruse was successful, though sadly enough, it worked on Stonn.

T'Pring paused at the mirror. Beneath her wrinkles, her eyes were exquisitely shaped, but had lost their luster long ago. She never knew why. After all, she was held in the highest regard—a stalwart, disciplined, and prolific dignitary of her people.

Then there was Stonn.

She achieved *Kolinahr* eight years into marriage, thereby purging all her emotions. It had elevated her status, placing her on councils and allowing her to shape Vulcan's future. Her opinions were sought and valued. She lived the life she strove to achieve. Yet something stirred within her.

T'Pring pressed a button beside the mirror. The wall slid open to reveal what would have been her wedding brooch. It had been given to her by Amanda Grayson—Spock's mother—on the day T'Pring had been betrothed to the half-Vulcan, half-human boy. They had never seen each other before then.

She withdrew the silver item. She remembered her parents' approval of her marrying an ambassador's child. They had doubts about Spock's human half, but Spock had shown remarkable progress in the sciences. There had been the option of Spock's older half-brother, Sybok, but he was flirting with emotions.

As T'Pring was about to return the brooch to its hiding place, the computer console near the door chimed. She started to walk toward it until she noticed the flashing purple light she had programmed over a year ago. After pocketing the brooch, she strode to the transporter and beamed herself up to her orbiting shuttlecraft.

"Computer," she said as she materialized. "Load flight plan V3 and execute."

The destination was preprogrammed, so the ship simply had to plot a course and take off at the highest possible warp. She exited the transporter room and walked down the hallway of lavender walls and yellow flooring. The door to her quarters swished open, revealing a double bed and dresser.

The floor shifted beneath her feet, signaling that the ship had gone to warp. She lay down on the bed. She usually slept to pass the monotony of deep space travel, but today she stared up at the dull ceiling tiles.

Then there was Stonn.

Her family had questioned her choice. Contrary to what some believed, she had not chosen Stonn for some trite emotion like love. And especially not for the reason she gave Spock when he returned to marry her. She had married Stonn because it assured her control of her family by taking responsibility and credit when Stonn failed, as she knew he would.

It meant other Vulcans would grant her opportunities when sensing weakness in her mate. She knew that if she had married a dignitary or any man of grand potential, she'd remain in the background, and she would not have that. At first, T'Pring had questioned her reasoning as emotional—the weakness of pride—until she logically ascertained that having the best for herself would enable her to serve Vulcan's greater good.

Stonn had never completed *Kolinahr.* He had tried several times, if only to make her proud. But even then, his motives were flawed. For if he intended to do it for her—which was his reason for almost everything—it meant he loved her.

She sighed at the thought. The terrible, agonizing thought. She, T'Pring, had married a Vulcan who loved her. It wasn't just his shameful words in private, but his gaze. His stance. Everyone knew. How could he gain her trust and respect if he clung to such emotions? How could he ever complete *Kolinahr*? But therein lay her double-edged sword, for that placed her at the forefront of their family, which is why she had chosen him.

On the dresser stood a picture of her younger self and new husband. As was tradition, the male stood before the female—a role she had reversed in the following decades. Her image stood rigid, staring straight ahead, ready to forge a new path. And though Stonn appeared to have the same expression, his eyes betrayed his delight at marrying the woman behind him.

Then there was Spock.

He'd never completed *Kolinahr* either, though he had tried. She had seen him once then, during his short stay on Vulcan before *V'Ger* called him back into space and Starfleet. Spock's hair had been disheveled from the rigorous mental trials. Yet even in his struggle, there remained that steady gaze . . . that rigid grace that transcended any Vulcan's, as if his efforts to circumvent his human side had elevated him to an unknown level of calculated stillness . . . of purposeful serenity.

Two days later, T'Pring paced in her ship's quarters. The action concerned her, for Vulcans never paced. It was a sign of anxiety— an emotion she couldn't possess. She concluded it must be logical, as she had nothing else to occupy her mind. Except for Spock.

Rather than attend the Vulcan Science Academy, he had left for Starfleet, making a name for himself beyond his father's shadow. During his *Enterprise* years, everyone heard about the half-Vulcan who had denied his heritage and served under humans. That was when she had decided she did not want to be married to a legend. Or at least, that's when she decided that it would be the reason she gave Spock when he fought James Kirk for her hand.

Yet even minutes before rejecting Spock, she had considered marrying him, for she wondered what she could achieve *because* of Spock's absence. There still would have been his nearly mythical status to overcome, but with him being offworld, could his standing have given her even more input into the political and cultural affairs of their world?

"Arrival in one hour," the computer announced in its tinny, feminine voice.

T'Pring exited her quarters and strode to the bridge, which consisted of two black chairs, a viewscreen, and a console shaped in a half-moon.

"On screen," she ordered. The dormant viewscreen wavered until an M-class planet appeared in the distance. "How far is the alien ship from the planet?"

"At present speed," the computer responded, *"the Romulan shuttle-*

craft will arrive at planet Veridian Three in twenty-two hours, seventeen minutes."

T'Pring leaned back into her chair. "How soon before sensors can track the ship without use of the deep-space probe?"

"Fifteen hours, three minutes."

That meant the other ship wouldn't be able to track her until then either. "In ten hours, engage the cloaking device." Being a high-ranking diplomat had advantages, including access to confiscated alien technology.

"Acknowledged," the computer replied.

She sat for several hours, weighing the option to return to Vulcan. But there was the other matter, making it quite logical for her to continue. So why did she doubt herself? She couldn't remember ever questioning her actions to such an extent, except when she had selected Kirk to fight her betrothed. There had always been the chance that Kirk would beat Spock, regardless of his inferior strength, and would desire to keep her.

Humans were quite illogical that way. How Sarek lived with Amanda for all of those years was something she never understood. Though she had to admit, in some ways, Amanda reminded her of Stonn.

The sound of the engaging cloaking device caught her off guard. The planet had grown large on the viewscreen, requiring her to diminish the magnification. The next few hours passed quickly until a blip on the scanners made her look up—the ship had come into range.

She put her ship in orbit and scanned the planet until she found the pile of stones above the human remains. After turning off the deep-space probe, she focused on the approaching Romulan shuttlecraft for the next few hours, until it likewise entered orbit. A few minutes later, her planetary scans showed a Vulcan had beamed down.

She considered waiting, but felt it best to act immediately rather than interrupt him later. She beamed down a hundred yards from where he stood beside the stones. As the green lights faded around her, he shot her a wary look. Though he wore a ceremonial black mourning robe, his stance was as she remembered. She focused on him, ignoring the brown, rocky mountain range around them.

Rather than approach, she waited with reverence. As he drew near, she took a deep breath, hoping her arrival had not been a mistake. When he was close enough to recognize her, his expression turned to surprise.

When he was a few feet away, she raised her hand in the traditional V shape and bowed her head. "Forgive the intrusion. I did not wish to desecrate your moment, but you have been difficult to communicate with these past years and I have been sent to inquire of your actions."

"T'Pring." Spock's arms were crossed over his stomach, each hand tucked into the opposite sleeve. He withdrew one hand and returned her greeting. "I did not expect anyone to find me here, much less you."

She looked up at his curious stare, then beyond him to the grave site. "I only wish to talk when you are ready."

"Being wanted by Romulus forced me to be patient. They expected me to come immediately. However, I've waited a year for their suspicions to fade and make my journey possible. Therefore, a short while longer makes little difference in offering my final condolences to James Kirk."

"As you wish. I knew you would eventually come, so I had a deep-space probe monitoring for any ship arriving here from Romulus. I've come alone, but I ask forgiveness for the timing."

"Accepted." Spock placed both hands behind his back in a less mournful posture. She almost cringed at his next statement, though she knew he was simply being polite. "I trust Stonn and your household are doing well."

"Fine, of course."

As Spock frowned at her words, she chastised herself for saying *of course* rather than *thank you,* which would have sounded far less defensive. But she ignored it and pressed on. "It was imperative that someone talk to you face-to-face and understand your true intentions."

Spock cocked his head to one side. "My true intentions?"

"Your Reunification talks with the Romulan underground have sparked major interest on Vulcan." She began walking across the lone, barren rock, with him keeping pace. "We wonder why you work so adamantly, when it is uncertain if Vulcan wishes to reunite with its ancient ancestors that dismissed Surak's teachings."

"You question my goals," Spock said. "And you are here to ascertain my objectives." Regardless of the wrinkles in his face, his profile hadn't changed. He remained stolid as he awaited her questions, rather than volunteering explanations.

"While potentially beneficial," T'Pring said, "reunification could destroy each half. So rather than developing the whole, the pieces are diminished. Maybe even destroyed."

"The Romulans are powerful militarily," Spock said. "Given a galactic conflict against an aggressive species, they would stand far longer. I adhere to passive solutions, but such a methodology can become overly optimistic. Consider the Borg. We would do well to strengthen our way of life if it is to last.

"On the other hand," he continued, "our ancient teachings of discipline would assist the Romulans in understanding that war and subterfuge need not be the only answer. So as you can see, cooperation and trust between our peoples is not simply an alternative, but a far superior solution."

T'Pring took a deep breath while considering her next question, both in relation to Vulcan and Romulus, as well as to her own personal dilemma. "Logically speaking, why should one wish to reunite with another, who long ago chose another path?"

Spock stopped walking and turned his stone face toward her. "Assuming peaceful cohabitation can exist, to seek out what one has lost is not only to understand one's self, but serves as its own reward."

She watched for any hint that he suspected the full weight of her question. If he did, his expression did not betray it. She would bring his words to Vulcan and the Federation, though she wished he would return . . . to stand in his own defense, of course.

"T'Pring," he said while studying her intently, "I am confused by your presence. An encoded subspace transmission would surely have had the same effect."

"In matters of motive, there are things one can discern in person that a mere transmission will not allow."

"True. However, I see no logic in—"

—*preferring Stonn over me.*

"—your course of action. Another delegate could have seen me. I cannot accept that they would have sent you alone to stand before me." Spock took a deep breath. "Forgive me for being as blunt as a Tellarite, but I sense you have an ulterior motive."

T'Pring slid one hand into the pocket of her robe and withdrew the silver brooch. One of Spock's eyebrows shot up in recognition. "As is our custom," she said, "I should have returned this to your mother when the ritual failed between us. But it had been misplaced and was found years later."

As a Vulcan, she was supposed to be incapable of lying. Why then did it come so easily now?

"At the time of its discovery," she continued, "your mother had already died. I thought to return it to your father, but that somehow seemed improper." She held it out. "As I've grown older, I wish to put my house in order. It's a small thing, but families should not be without their relics, so one will never forget or forsake their past."

Spock accepted it. "If you wish." His stern gaze harbored unspoken questions, but he did not ask them, for which she was grateful. "I remember my mother wearing this and the story she told of Sarek's mother giving it to her. I never thought to see it again." He rotated the object. "However, without any descendants, I have no use for it. Maybe you should keep it."

"It would not be appropriate."

"Very well. Perhaps it will please a Romulan child. And when she wears it, other children will ask of its origin, and in some small way, learn of our people."

His words pained her, though she knew they shouldn't. It was, after all, just a brooch. Maybe it was because she felt bothered by his selfless attitude—a trait Stonn rarely exercised by delighting in her presence.

Spock placed the brooch in his pocket. "Vulcan and Romulus will not reunite in mass, but slowly, over time. The tiniest pebble may start the largest avalanche."

"If that's how you feel about Reunification, I will give it further consideration and discuss it with our people."

"Most kind."

They resumed their silent walk in the direction they had come, until they returned to the area where she had beamed down.

"It was good to see you again, T'Pring," Spock said. "It reminds me that entire realities can be triggered by the smallest choices, giving me hope that my work is not in vain. For had you chosen me during *Koon-ut-kal-if-fee,* neither of us would be where we are today." Spock held up a hand in a V shape. "May you live long and prosper."

The words escaped her before she could consider them. "I have done both, but now in the twilight of life, I question if it's enough." As Spock's face changed to a frown, she replicated the hand gesture and pressed her hand flat against his. "If your human half will allow it, Spock, may you find happiness as well."

She pressed the transmitter on her wrist. Green lights danced before her eyes as Spock's curious expression faded from sight. After instructing her ship to return to Vulcan, she retired to her quarters. She sat on the edge of her bed and studied the bare walls. With a hesitant hand, she turned away the picture of her and Stonn. The simple act triggered another statement Spock had spoken that day long ago, which he had addressed to Stonn . . .

After a time, you may find that having is not so pleasing a thing as wanting. It is not logical, but it is often true.

In her lifetime, she had only cried a few times as a child. Otherwise, even at the grave sites of her family members, she never flinched. Never gave in to emotion. To do so would have been disgraceful, especially to one who had achieved the purity of *Kolinahr.*

So how odd that now, in the quiet stillness of her cabin, a single tear escaped and slid down her cheek. She willed no more to come, yet she did not wipe it away. As it dangled from her jaw, she sought meaning in its trembling uncertainty while it wavered between maintaining its fragile hold and falling onto her folded hands. Strange it should come now, from nine simple words that had forever haunted her. . . .

I see no logic in preferring Stonn over me.

Staying the Course

Paul C. Tseng

"I have fought a good fight, I have finished my course, I have kept the faith: Henceforth there is laid up for me a crown of righteousness."

—Ancient Terran Scriptures

"You have ten minutes to hand over the body of the Ambassador Rozhenko, or I will unleash the Metreon Wave over Cygnus Three. You've already seen the painful and slow deaths this type of radiation causes on Federation Outpost Fifteen, less than an hour ago. Now imagine not just thousands, not just Starfleet personnel, but millions of innocent civilians, women and children alike." Toral's eyes burned with unadulterated hatred as he spoke on the recorded transmission.

Chancellor Worf's lip curled and a low-pitched growl emerged as he glared at the cold countenance of the Klingon on the recording.

"Place his body for collection at the center of R'kalla Square. I want him killed with a traditional Klingon hand weapon, such as a bat'leth *or a* dk'tahg. *No disruptors, no phasers, no mercy. Ten minutes!"*

The chancellor's first reaction was naturally a Klingon one. *Let them destroy the planet. That should not concern me.*

He slammed the console to terminate the message, and the rough surface of his desk scraped the heel of his hand. He wished that he'd made sure Toral had died years ago when they fought for the Sword of Kahless.

The warm Qo'noS sun shone brightly through his office windows and onto his back, but this was becoming the darkest hour of his life.

After a moment of silence, another voice spoke over his terminal.

"Chancellor," Admiral Jean-Luc Picard said. *"I hate being the bearer of this message. I know how you must . . ."*

The Klingon's voice rose in a steady and formidable crescendo.

"You have *no* idea how I feel!" he bellowed. "You have never had a family, never had a son!"

"Chancellor, with all due respect . . ."

"You have no understanding of the position I am in as a chancellor, much less a father!"

"Worf!"

The chancellor gripped the stone edge of his desk so hard that hairline fractures began to run toward the center. Thank Kahless Picard wasn't actually in the room with him or he might actually have killed his former captain in his rage. But he remembered the human saying "don't shoot the messenger," and that the admiral, now some eighty years of age, had been a trusted friend since Worf was a junior officer on the *Enterprise-D.* It seemed like a lifetime ago.

Picard's voice softened. *"Worf, one need not have a son to appreciate the gravity of this situation. But I must remind you that there are millions of others whose very lives are at stake here as well."*

Worf leaned in toward the terminal so that Picard could get a good look at his angry fangs.

"You would have my son . . . *murdered?!*"

The admiral's shoulders heaved and fell. *"No, Worf. I could never ask a man to do such a thing. But we must remain focused and aware of all that is at stake, beyond personal interests."*

Could there be anything more important to a father than the life of his only son? And yet, there was no other way to stop Toral—the entire world of Cygnus III would die. Worf struggled to see beyond the internal battle which he felt he was quickly losing.

"Do we have anything at all on Toral's location?" the chancellor asked.

Picard hesitated and then exhaled. Worf knew that meant he was trying to find a way to answer other than saying "no."

"Starfleet Intelligence is following the few leads it has," Picard replied. *"But the information is unreliable, at best, and it will take at least three hours before the data can be compiled and theorized upon."*

The chancellor stood and paced around his desk, not caring that his image would go in and out of view on Picard's terminal. He clenched his fist in frustration and wanted to strike anything or anyone within reach. The anguish and fury in his heart caused it to beat like ritual *Kot'baval* drums.

"We do not *have* three hours."

"No, Chancellor." Then Picard rose from his chair and walked right up to the monitor. *"I want you to know that there is absolutely no way that the Federation will give in to threats like these."*

Fine rhetoric, Worf thought. *But there isn't any way of stopping Toral right now. It's either Alexander or three point eight million people on Cygnus Three.*

"Has Alexander been told of Toral's demands?" the chancellor asked.

Worf saw what looked like gloom fill Picard's eyes.

"Yes," the admiral answered, running his hand over his head and shutting his eyes. He seemed to exhale his words more than he spoke them. *"Protocol requires that we keep any Federation ambassador completely 'in the know' regarding matters as such."*

For the first time in this conversation, Worf allowed himself to drop his duranium façade and speak to Picard as a friend.

"Jean-Luc, I know you are doing everything you can." In the thirty-eight years that Worf had known Picard, he could think of only one or two other times where he addressed him by his given name.

"Thank you, Worf. I do not envy your position, nor the ambassador's."

Worf nodded his appreciation.

"We will contact you the moment we have any news," Picard said, his voice galvanized once again. *"In the meantime, I believe you will want to spend the next few minutes . . . discussing this matter with your son."*

The mighty warrior, the larger-than-life chancellor of the Klingon Empire, was reduced to a pile of withering thoughts and sentiments. He tried his best to hide it and refrained from uttering a word, lest his voice crack before Picard. Instead he glanced quickly at the admiral and nodded.

"Godspeed, Worf. Picard out."

"The Klingon Empire will *never* bow to *pahtk*s such as Toral! I will not permit your execution, your . . . your *murder!*" Worf said, his voice booming like thunder in the small office of the Federation Embassy.

"Chancellor," Alexander Rozhenko replied determinedly. "This is a Federation matter." He barely took his eyes off his terminal to look at his father. "Besides, I am a Federation citizen and diplomat. I am immune to Klingon law."

"But you are also a Klingon and you reside on Klingon soil," Worf insisted. "We cannot bend to the demands of terrorists!" He gazed at the man who had once been a little boy who looked to him for approval and acceptance. Now he was a grown adult with a strong will of his own.

"Alexander . . ." Worf said in an uncharacteristically tender and pleading voice.

Finally, Alexander stopped what he was doing. He shut his eyes and breathed out the tension from within. The ambassador stood and looked Worf right in the eye.

"Father, I am working with Starfleet and Klingon Intelligence. We *will* find Toral and his thugs and we *will* stop him."

"There isn't enough time. You are well aware of that."

Alexander nodded, but his eyes kept straying back to the display on his monitor.

"It may not happen in the next seven minutes, but it will happen. We will stop him, with or without me."

"I will not permit anyone to sacrifice you!" Worf's words were strong, but his voice quivered slightly. He hoped his son would attribute it to his growing older, not panic.

"And you would stand by and watch millions of people of Cygnus Three die a slow and horrible death? Federation scientists say that it takes anyone exposed to Metreon radiation at that level two days to finally die. The cellular deterioration and pain grows worse with each passing minute!"

Worf did not like where this argument was heading. He knew what kind of man his son had grown into and how he thought.

"It matters not," said the chancellor. "The Federation will not sanction the murder of one of its citizens, much less their top diplomat, who happens to be the son of the Klingon chancellor."

Deep down, Worf was uncomfortable. Something about his attitudes and words did not befit a warrior of his stature. And at the same time, something about his son's attitude caused his breast to swell with pride. But the two sentiments could not coexist peacefully within Worf's mind.

Alexander looked to his father, this time with eyes that Worf had not seen since his son was a child.

"Father, I will not stop fighting Toral until the bitter end. But we must be prepared, if all else fails. I cannot allow myself to be the reason that millions die."

"*You* are not the reason," Worf insisted, and pointed at the image of Toral on Alexander's terminal. "*He* is the reason!" If ever there were a time that Worf had regretted having shown mercy to the bastard son of Duras, it was now. This is how his kindness was to be repaid. "Furthermore, we cannot let Toral and his followers believe that they can have any hold over us! He will not stop until he has brought the Empire into war with the Federation."

"And for the past fifteen years, I have done more to stop him than any military power could have. If he doesn't see me dead today, he will try again in the future. I will not be the Achilles heel of the Klingon Empire."

The metaphor eluded Worf and he simply blinked.

"Achilles . . . ?"

"Father, listen to me—I'm not trying to appease a known terrorist bent on destroying the Khitomer Accords," Alexander said. "But I may be the only way to spare those lives, while buying time for Starfleet to find Toral and stop him."

"Alexander . . . no," Worf protested.

"You said it yourself. The Federation cannot and will not sacrifice my life," the ambassador said. "But I can and will do so, if need be."

He'd fought the Romulans, the Remans, the Jem'Hadar, and the Borg, yet Worf had never before felt as helpless as he did now. It was as if the ground had opened up and threatened to pull him down into the flames of *Gre'thor.*

Alexander reacted to the beeping on his terminal. He looked at it and keyed in a few strokes then looked up at his father.

"Only five minutes left. We might have a means of locating Toral but I need a couple more minutes alone," Alexander said in a steady and calm tone.

Worf stood tall and took a deep breath before responding.

"As you wish, son. I will be back in the final two minutes. May Kahless grant you success."

The Klingon numerals of Worf's desktop chronometer ticked away silently but mercilessly. Five minutes remaining until the fate of his son and the inhabitants of Cygnus III would be determined. *Why have I not heard from Picard yet?* There was nothing he could do now but wait. Worf hated waiting—patience was not his strength.

For as long as he could remember, Worf had hoped that his son would embrace his Klingon heritage and become a warrior, bringing honor to his house. It had taken all of Worf's forbearance, forged through years of being with and working with humans, to understand that one-quarter part of his son which seemed to compel him to defy being a "normal" Klingon. There were even times, Worf had to admit, that he felt disappointed by Alexander's choice not to pursue the way of the warrior. At the same time, his son had surprised him by joining the Klingon Defense Force during the Dominion War and training to become a warrior afterward. However, both of those ventures seemed doomed to comical endings which, ironically enough, until only now could Worf look back upon and laugh.

When Alexander had finally decided to take Worf's vacated position as the Federation ambassador on Qo'noS, Worf had resolved that his son would function better in this line of work, where courage and combat abilities were not required—only "smooth talking," something *humans* were all too good at.

But in recent years, seeing Alexander stand up to Toral's vitriol and threats, Worf had begun to see a side of his son which was undeniably Klingon. It *had* taken a great deal of courage for Alexander to stand up to two assassination attempts and still refuse to relinquish his diplomatic office.

Today, Alexander showed his true Klingon hearts—of courage and honor. His son refused to allow the enemy to intimidate him and was willing to give his own life to save the innocent. Worf was indeed proud, but at the same time, he cursed himself for instilling the very values that would cost his son his life.

His terminal chimed and stirred him from his musings.

"My lord, I have the Federation president for you on a secure channel."

"Put him through," Worf replied. The screen winked to life and was replaced by the image of the president, his face ashen with despair. The chancellor didn't need to ask; he just knew.

"Mister President."

"Chancellor," the president began. *"I regret to inform you that we have not been able to locate Toral. Furthermore, Ambassador Rozhenko has contacted us and decided to . . ."*

"Thank you, Mister President," Worf said, sparing him the discomfort of having to put words to what Worf already knew. "I am aware of my son's decision."

The president's features wrinkled in a pained look.

"Be assured, Chancellor Worf, that the United Federation of Planets will not rest until Toral is found and brought to justice. We will . . ."

Worf rose from his chair. "Thank you, Mister President," Worf interrupted curtly, and terminated the link. He looked at his chronometer. Exactly three minutes remaining. Worf then began the long walk down the hallway to his son's office in the Embassy wing.

"Alexander!" Worf called, seeing his son slumped in his chair with his back turned toward him. His son wore a ritual *Hegh'bat* robe. The elder Klingon ran over to him and found him crumpled and trembling. Though Alexander was a grown man, Worf took him in his powerful arms and would not let go.

"Father . . . I'm afraid."

"You do not have to do this!" Worf whispered.

"Yes, I do." Alexander unsheathed a *d'k tahg* and turned the handle for his father to grasp. "My legs are shaking and I can't get to the transporter pad on my own."

Worf looked across the room and saw the transporter powered up. "No! I cannot allow this!" he cried.

Alexander looked up. "You must, Father! It is no different from the time you wanted me to help you with the *Hegh'bat* when you were injured on the *Enterprise.*"

"Son . . . this *is* different."

"Please, Father. I cannot live with the dishonor of knowing that the fear of death prevented me from saving the lives of millions of innocent people. You must help me. Help me retain my honor!"

Worf hesitated. He had never fled a battle in his entire life. But now he wanted nothing more than to run from the room and not have to face this. A son assisting his father in the *Hegh'bat,* the ritual suicide of an injured warrior no longer able to fend for himself, was natural for a Klingon. But a father doing this for his son, a healthy and able-bodied son, was not. It went against every grain of his existence.

"There isn't much time!" Alexander said. "I need to do this quickly and then use the transporter. I've programmed the coordinates for R'kalla Square. Hurry, Father!"

This is my son's wish. This is my son's honor, born of courage and sacrifice. It is to his glory and mine. To the glory of Kahless and the Klingon Empire. Worf forced himself to believe it.

Not affording himself a moment to think twice about the consequences of his actions, Worf helped his trembling son to his feet. They began to walk toward the transporter pad when Alexander faltered. His knees buckled.

"Father!" Alexander gasped.

He had to be strong for the sake of Alexander's honor. But his son's cry of dread impaled Worf's heart like the very dagger that would soon pierce Alexander's. He recalled a childhood moment when his son had fallen and injured himself. How he regretted now not having run to his little boy, not having held him tight, assuring him that all would be all right. *A curse upon my pride!*

Clenching his teeth, Worf willed his body to stand tall and pull his son back to his feet. He helped Alexander to rest his weight upon his father's strong shoulder. Together they staggered to the altar of sacrifice that was the transporter pad. Each painful step was an eternity which to Worf was all too brief. He kept his eyes on his son, trying desperately to memorize every feature on his face, every bit of detail about him that he could commit to his thoughts. In just a little while, he would never see him again.

They arrived at the transporter pad and Alexander knelt. Still shaking visibly, he looked up at his father and nodded. Reluctantly, Worf handed him the *d'k tahg.*

Alexander took the weapon, which shook violently in his nervous hands. Then he said in a quavering voice, "In . . . in my pocket. Take it . . . for later. . . ."

Seeing that his son's hands were rendered useless because of the convulsing, Worf reached down into the pocket of Alexander's robe and pulled out an isolinear chip, one designed to store holographic data.

Alexander used his free hand to grasp his father's wrist and steadied himself. "There wasn't enough time to tell you all I wanted to say, Father."

Worf fell to his own knees and his voice nearly cracked.

"There wasn't enough time, my son." He held his son to his bosom and gently stroked his hair. "I am and will always be proud of you."

Alexander's countenance lit up with a smile. "Then it will all have been worthwhile."

"Your name will be revered. Operas will be commissioned in your memory," Worf whispered. "You bring honor to your house, to the Empire."

Alexander's trembling seemed to subside a bit. Worf released his son from his embrace. Alexander straightened up and brought the razor-sharp point of his *d'k tahg* to his chest. Worf saw a flash of light reflected from the blade and it caused his heart to skip a beat.

"I'm ready," Alexander said.

Worf stood proud and strong, hoping to lend his own strength to his only begotten son at this, his moment of truth. Alexander lifted the blade preparing to plunge it into his heart. But just then, his entire body began to shake. The blade fell from his hands and he looked in despair at Worf.

"I can't control my hands! Father, please, help me!"

Immediately Worf knelt behind his son. He picked up the *d'k tahg* and held it in Alexander's hands. Worf knew what he must do and cursed himself for it.

Alexander smiled in relief. Worf felt his trembling diminish and his body relax against his own.

"Now," Alexander whispered.

"Today, my son, you die a warrior's death. You will be avenged."

With one swift thrust, Worf pulled his son's hands, wrapped around the handle of the *d'k tahg,* into his chest. He felt the dull thud as his entire world imploded.

"Quickly, Father . . . the . . . trans . . . porter!" Alexander gasped.

He looked at the chronometer. One minute and twenty seconds remaining. The mighty warrior gently laid his son's head upon his lap. He saw the pain in his eyes, which Alexander struggled to keep open. Worf could tell that his son meant to allow him to look death in the eye.

"Thank you, Father," Alexander said as the life drained from his body. "Thank you for helping me stay the course."

It mattered little that Worf didn't fully understand what his son meant; he simply leaned over and kissed the ridges of his forehead.

"We will meet again . . ." Worf whispered. Sorrow infused his voice like a bitter *troi'kara* root simmering in a cauldron. ". . . in *Sto-Vo-Kor.*"

Alexander's eyes shone brightly and a tranquil smile stretched across his face. "In *Sto-Vo-Kor,*" he whispered with his last breath.

The chronometer began to beep frantically. Ten seconds remaining. Worf carefully laid his son's head down on the floor of the transporter pad. Then, according to the ritual, he wiped his son's blood from the *d'k tahg* on his own sleeve. His task done, Worf strode to the transporter controls.

If only he could have had a few more minutes to be with Alexander and hold him! But his death must not have been in vain—Worf needed to beam Alexander's empty shell to the coordinates Toral had demanded. He slid his fingers up the controls and the red light of the transporter beam enveloped Alexander. In an instant, his son was gone.

Clouds obscured the Qo'noS sun and turned the sky to an ominous hue of dark gray. Worf looked to the heavens and let out a fearsome, guttural cry, announcing his son to the gates of *Sto-Vo-Kor.*

Flashes of lightning lit the darkened office. Worf found himself on his knees, emptied like a broken chalice with all its bloodwine drained out onto the cold stone floor. Night had fallen and Worf chose to remain alone in the darkness.

A bright ray of sunlight invaded the room. Worf awoke to find a new day, warm, bright and deceivingly full of life. Outside the open window, birds sang what seemed like a new song, people bustled in the streets below. It was the laughter of children that stirred Worf to get up off the floor. He looked over to the transporter pad and was soberly reminded of what had happened the night before. All that remained was a drying puddle of Alexander's blood.

As he pulled himself up to his feet, Worf realized it would take all the strength and willpower he had within him to continue living. He was tempted to take Alexander's *d'k tahg* and kill himself as he had helped his son. Alas, he knew that taking his own life, out of grief, would not allow him to travel The River of Blood so that he could join Alexander in *Sto-Vo-Kor.* Indeed, the long ride on the Barge of the Dead would require more courage than running from the pain he was feeling.

Taking in a deep breath, Worf walked to the window and looked outside. Life seemed to go on for all the people down below. Had any one of them ever watched their children die, much less by their own hand? He saw a little boy walking next to his father and pretending to be a warrior. He wielded a toy *bat'leth* and repeatedly struck his father in the shin. Playfully, the father feigned injury and defeat.

"You must kill me now! Spare me the dishonor of living as an invalid!"

The little boy plunged his foam *bat'leth* into his father's chest. The father pretended to die gloriously—everyone around applauded the scene and laughed in delight.

The father got to his feet and vigorously patted his son on the back.

"That's my little warrior!"

Worf smiled poignantly as he watched the boy walk away holding his proud father's hand.

May you never know the pain of losing your son.

He sat at Alexander's desk and looked around. There was a holoimage of his mother K'Ehleyr and Alexander as child. Over on the other side of the desk was a holoimage of Worf standing proudly next to him, on the day that Alexander had been appointed ambassador to Qo'noS. Then he remembered the isolinear holochip. Worf reached into his pocket and clicked it into the computer. A three-dimensional image of Alexander floated above the desk—it was apparently recorded just before he'd died.

"Hello, Father. By now, I am probably dead. I grew up thinking that I would be the one to live to watch you die at the hands of assassins. Perhaps that visitation from my future self changed things. I'm sorry I didn't get to speak with you in person but there was not enough time. I have a few things that I really need to tell you now.

"Do you recall one of the passages in 'The Wisdom of Kahless' that you taught me when I was about nine years old? Kahless said: 'To each warrior there is a path. Glory goes to him that fulfills their destiny.'

"For my entire life, I've never been able to resolve what my purpose was. I'm not quite Klingon and I'm not quite human. I felt that nothing I did was good enough—not that you made me feel that way—I just didn't see the point of anything I tried to accomplish. Today, however, I realize that the greatest thing I can do is to die so that others might live. I am not the courageous warrior that you are, Father, but I have been given a unique opportunity to make my life count for something great. I believe that my honor depends on it.

"But I know myself. I know that I won't have the strength to go through with it. I can't complete the course on my own." Alexander looked pensively into the holoimager; then his eyebrows perked upward. *"Maybe this will help illustrate my point."* His fingers tapped something offscreen and his image was replaced by that of a man running on a racetrack.

"Of course, you know that I have had a fascination with human

history and culture. This is an event that took place in the twentieth century on Earth. It was an athletic competition called the Olympics. In the year 1992, during the Barcelona Games, there was a runner named Derek Redmond." A yellow line outlined and highlighted a black human runner, who seemed to be in the lead. Suddenly the runner stopped and fell. *"Redmond tore a muscle in his right leg."* The other runners sped past him to the finish line while Redmond struggled to stay on his feet. Refusing to stop, he tried to run but couldn't. He tried to hop but that didn't seem to work either. Tears of anguish and pain covered his face. Suddenly, a man in the stands pushed past the security guards and onto the track. *"When the security guards tried to stop Derek's father, he was said to have replied, 'That's my son!'"* The father put the runner's arm around his shoulder and helped him limp to the finish line, long after all the other runners had completed the race; the entire stadium cheered them on.

If Worf had tear ducts, he would surely have been weeping at this moment, so poignant was the scene.

Alexander's image returned and looked straight into Worf's eyes.

"Even if I don't win, like Derek Redmond, I have a course to finish. No matter how painful. But, Father, I need your help. I know that you, like Redmond's father, will help me fulfill my destiny and retain my honor." He paused and his eyes became sorrowful. *"I love you, Father."*

"And I, you," Worf whispered. He tried to touch his son's face but the holoimage faded out. Only then did Worf fully understand what his son meant when he thanked him for helping him "stay the course." His death was not without meaning. Worf shut his eyes. For the first time since Alexander's death, he allowed himself to smile.

Just then a security guard entered the office and interrupted his thoughts.

"Forgive me, my lord. I have Admiral Picard on a secure channel."

Worf pointed to the terminal on the desk.

"Put him through in Ambassador Rozhenko's office," the guard said over his communicator.

The terminal came to life and Picard, his visage somber but strong, began the conversation.

"Chancellor," he began. *"We have not been able to contact you for several hours."*

Worf replied quietly, "I did not wish to speak with anyone."

"Words escape me at the moment," Picard said. *"I am truly sorry about Alexander."*

Worf nodded his appreciation.

"What your son did was beyond courage and nobility," Picard continued. *"Surely the Empire will honor him as a hero."*

"Yes," Worf replied. "His sacrifice was a testament to the Klingon heart."

There was a short moment of silence. Worf could see the message in Picard's eyes that said, *I am here for you, my friend.*

It was the admiral that broke the silence.

"I thought you might like to know that after Toral confirmed Alexander's body, he did not set off the Metreon Wave on Cygnus Three."

"But did he give us its location?"

Picard shook his head. *"No. In fact, he continued to make more demands."*

Worf snarled. "Toral had more than just a political agenda in having Alexander killed. He wants to make me suffer for taking his father from him. However, his father died in dishonor while my son died in glory. Toral has failed."

Picard nodded. *"Haven't you heard, Worf?"*

"Heard what?"

"Alexander injected a subcutaneous, phase-shifting beacon into himself before he died. We knew Toral would have his henchmen scan the body for any tracking device before bringing his body to him. But this one was virtually undetectable. Worf, don't you see? Your son did more than save the lives of Cygnus Three's citizens. He made himself the only possible means of locating Toral."

Worf stood from the chair. "Then . . . you have him?"

"Yes, Worf! We have him in custody at a Starfleet detention facil-

ity. *His clan has dispersed and relinquished their military assets and positions. Toral's uprising has all but disintegrated."*

That pahtk *allowed himself to be captured alive? And his followers, they are running like the scared* targs *that they are!* This came as something of a relief for Worf. For several years Toral had been building up a strong following of extremists. He sought to take over the Empire and destroy its alliance with the Federation. With his recent terrorist tactics, something unheard of for any Klingon worth his mettle, he was actually gaining ground.

"Admiral, I know that the Federation will do all they can to bring Toral to justice," Worf said. "But there is no death penalty in the Federation, am I correct?"

Picard sighed. *"Worf, there are many in the Federation who believe that we have evolved beyond the need for this method of correction. So, to answer your question: no, there is no death penalty in the Federation criminal justice system."*

Worf gritted his teeth.

"However," Picard said, *"the president has made for a provision that the Federation will file charges against Toral only* after *his extradition and trial under the Klingon judicial system. We await your orders."*

The chancellor leaned down at the monitor and bared his fangs.

"Bring him to me."

Home Soil

Jim Johnson

Sharon Ndame frowned when she realized Lieutenant Commander Data's tetryon particle lecture contained nothing she either didn't already know or couldn't pick up from some other computer. Feeling guilty and self-conscious, she stood to leave the crowded Academy auditorium.

Suddenly, the room exploded around her.

The blast lifted Sharon off her feet. Her hearing dulled to a roar; her vision slid into a blur. Debris shredded her uniform and skin.

She plowed into a row of filled seats, knocking down a bunch of her fellow cadets. She hit her head on something or someone then saw spinning stars amid the dust and debris and broken bodies.

Sharon struggled to catch her breath, but the cloying clouds of dust she inhaled gave her nothing but a violent fit of coughing. All around her she could hear the moans and screams of fellow beings. Some of those cries might have been hers—she wasn't sure.

Distantly, she could hear the sounds of . . . thunder? Micro-asteroids hitting the city?

She propped herself up on her aching elbows and screamed when jagged bits pushed deeper into her arms. Glancing down, Sharon saw her torn sleeves and the ugly debris violating her body. Dark blood oozed out of her wounds.

Sharon clutched her arms as close to her chest as she could without making them hurt even more. She looked around, blinking to clear the smoke, dust, blood, and tears from her eyes.

The auditorium looked like hell. Piles of bloodstained rubble lay everywhere. Broken bodies of cadets and officers slumped here and there, as if they'd been tossed around like trees in a tornado. Data-padds and chair fragments littered the floor. As a strange counterpoint to the chaos all around her, Sharon could see a bright blue sky outside the gaping hole in the wall.

Not thunder, then. There wasn't a cloud to be seen. Sharon used a nearby chair that had escaped destruction to pull herself to her feet. She saw a few other cadets picking themselves up off the floor, tending to their comrades, or weeping over the dead. Her focus returning, she saw a Zaldan's hand resting on a broken chair nearby, the delicate, translucent membranes stretched between the fingers contrasting with the bloody ruin at the wrist.

Sharon leaned over and retched at the sight of it. As the pain in her arms competed with the misery in her mind, her body ejected the meal she had eaten prior to entering the lecture hall. Empty, her dry heaves soon changed to sobs. She placed her hands on her knees and tried to catch her breath, and in doing that, find some measure of control. This wasn't supposed to happen to cadets with science honors!

She heard the crunch of someone stepping over debris. A pair of Starfleet boots moved into her vision.

"Cadet, have you seen my arm?" asked a surprisingly calm voice.

Confused by the question, Sharon looked up. Data stood there, looking at her with a quizzical glance. The android's entire left arm had been ripped out of its socket. Sharon saw bits of wire and polymer sticking out of the lesion at weird angles. Thin streaks of some sort of fluid traced dark, greasy lines on what remained of the officer's uniform.

Speech returned to her, somewhat. "Uh, no . . ."

She watched as it scanned the immediate surroundings. A chunk of its synthetic hair and skin had been ripped away, exposing tiny blinking lights and a section of dull metal skull. Sharon shuddered at the sight, as disgusted at it as she had been at the severed hand.

She clutched her arms to her chest again and left the android to its search. Noticing a hole in the wall, she shuffled through the debris and looked outside.

Several Academy buildings had collapsed into rubble. Fires blazed in several more buildings and on other areas of the Academy grounds. A bitter lump formed in her throat as she turned her gaze toward San Francisco. A veneer of smoke and dust hung over the city; the miasma punctuated with outbursts of flame.

Several small fighters of alien design darted here and there, raining down bursts of superheated plasma. Again, she realized that it hadn't been thunder or micro-asteroids she'd heard—the whole city was under attack! Numb, she wondered if other cities also burned. Who in the great galaxy would dare attack the heart of Starfleet— would dare attack Earth?

As if it had read her mind, she heard the android speak from behind her. "Those are Breen fighters."

She turned. "Why are they attacking us?"

It stepped toward her, still partially unarmed. "I am uncertain, though I suspect their recent alliance with the Dominion encouraged them to make a bold maneuver." She grimaced at the calculated tone of its voice.

"Attacking San Francisco, the base of both Starfleet Headquarters and Starfleet Academy, was perhaps the boldest move they could have made. The Breen have clearly caught us . . ." It paused as if scanning its memory banks. ". . . with our pants down."

Sharon shuddered. The android's infuriatingly calm voice sounded so cold, so indifferent to her. Didn't it feel anything for the dead and dying people all around them? Couldn't it feel anything? She posed those questions to the thing, blinking tears out of her eyes.

The robot didn't answer her. It was looking out of the building toward the Academy gardens. Curious, in spite of herself and the whole situation, she followed its stare.

Several heavily armed and armored troops moved across the verdant grounds, crushing plants and flowers underfoot, firing their heavy disruptors indiscriminately.

She moved her gaze from the troops to the android. "Are those Breen?"

Data looked at her with an expressionless face and nodded. "They are."

She took an involuntary step back, stumbling on some loose debris. The Breen were going to come up here and kill them all, and this machine wasn't going to do a thing to stop them.

Several battered cadets worked their way over to her and the android. A cacophony of questions rang out all around her.

Data raised its remaining hand, halting their queries. "Stand fast, Cadets." It gestured toward the Breen troops. "San Francisco, and perhaps all of Earth, is under attack. Starfleet Academy is under attack. I need anyone who can fire a phaser to come with me."

Sharon felt most of the cadets move in closer. She flinched. Were they all so willing to rush to their deaths?

Data said, "Anyone with medical training should remain here and treat the injured." It moved toward the auditorium's entrance. "The rest of you, come."

Data led a ragtag group of cadets out of the ruined auditorium, leaving Sharon and a handful of others behind. A Vulcan cadet caught Sharon's confused stare and raised an eyebrow.

Sharon stared at the girl, dredging up her name from her overworked mind. "What are we going to do, T'Lang? I don't want to wait here. Not with those Breen running around."

Cadet T'Lang answered, "Perhaps you can assist me in moving the wounded to better surroundings."

Sharon panicked. "I can't do that! I've only been here a couple weeks—I've only had my basic first-aid classes! I wouldn't know what to do!" She ran a bloody hand through her short hair.

The Vulcan inclined her head. Sharon wondered if T'Lang realized that she looked like the android when she did that.

T'Lang said, "In that case, I would recommend you go with Commander Data."

Sharon considered it, then nodded. Going somewhere with a group of people sounded way better than standing in a slaughterhouse waiting for the Breen to gun her down.

Without a glance back, Sharon hurried to catch up with the few cadets following the android. As she closed the distance, she heard the android say, ". . . make our way to the armory near the combat range. We will arm ourselves and do what we can."

Joining the rear of the group, she heard several cadets make assenting comments. She shook her head. *A bunch of kids going into battle with a robot in command?* It would send them all to their deaths without feeling a thing, wouldn't it? Crazy—this whole situation was just crazy.

Sharon grabbed the arm of the cadet closest to her, a lanky Bolian third-year. His face was flushed bright blue and he had large splotches of someone's blood on his uniform. She didn't know his name. "What are we doing?"

The Bolian looked down at her, his eyes hard. "Following orders, Cadet. I know you're just a rat, but you *are* Starfleet. Commander Data is our CO until we hear otherwise. Do you understand?"

Sharon gave the Bolian a reluctant nod. He gave her a final once-over, then rushed off to join the others.

She took a deep breath, searching to retain the control she had had difficulty finding earlier. What was she doing here? She had joined Starfleet to study spatial anomalies and explore distant stars, not fight the Breen on her home soil! She realized that the Bolian was right: she was just a "rat"—a first-year—she didn't know anything about fighting a war!

Disruptor blasts exploded somewhere close. Scared, she looked over her shoulder. A pair of Breen soldiers had shot their way through a door. They were looking for targets, looking for *her!* She jogged after the Bolian. When she heard more of the Breen shots crash nearby, she turned her jog into a run.

As she neared the armory, a few disheveled cadets with phasers and grim looks rushed past her toward the Breen. She didn't turn to watch them enter the battle.

Sharon halted in front of the building, realizing that other officers and cadets must have had the same idea as Data. About thirty Starfleet personnel were there, most of them injured. A few prepared phasers and some treated minor injuries. A medical student caught Sharon's eye as she stood there in a daze.

"Over here, Cadet. Let me take a look at your arms."

Obediently, Sharon moved over to the blue-uniformed ensign and hesitantly offered her limbs. "I got caught in one of the blasts," she said, surprised at the petulant and weak tone of her own voice. Was she going to die?

The corpsman examined her, being careful not to touch the pieces of debris sticking out of her arms. Sharon bit her lip to keep from crying out.

"Most of these are superficial, fortunately." The corpsman gave her a quick glance. "Much pain?"

She nodded. A flurry of weapon fire opened up nearby, the distinctive whines of Starfleet phasers punctuated by the deeper poundings of Breen disruptor blasts. She flinched.

The corpsman pulled a topical applicator from his medical satchel and sprayed her arms with a mild anesthetic. In moments, the constant prickles of pain in her arms dulled to mere aches.

The firefight nearby increased in intensity and narrowed in distance. Sharon heard the android order several more cadets to go join the fight. She saw a handful of cadets, most of them wounded, jog off toward the Breen. Sharon wondered if any of them would make it back, wondered if that Data cared.

The corpsman brought her back to the present. "This is the best I can do right now. If I had more time, I'd pull out some of the smaller chunks."

Before Sharon could offer a response, the corpsman took a disruptor blast full in the chest. His surprised expression and heat-blistered torso were the last she saw of him.

Someone—Sharon didn't know who—pulled her into the armory, behind the heavy walls. Heavy phaser fire burst out all around her. The cadets were fighting back. The flare from their weapons imprinted on her vision, blinding her. She heard someone barking out orders and felt someone else press a phaser into her hands.

She blinked away the lightning-like flashes in her eyes. A cadet outside of the armory fell to the ground near the door, the wound in his side smoldering. A second disruptor blast hit him, then a third.

Horrified and desperate to get away, Sharon pushed her way farther into the armory, trying to put as much space and as many bodies as possible between her and the Breen. She saw the android in the room. It gestured in her direction. She heard its voice call out over the deafening din of the pitched battle.

"Cadets! I need your help!"

Sharon looked at the cadet next to her, a second-year Andorian female. The girl had a bloody compress fastened over her face and a desperate look in her one good eye. She had a phaser in hand, though, and appeared to know how to handle it.

The girl said, "Come on, he's talking to us!" She led Sharon over to Data. Sharon thought the android looked terribly out of place with its missing arm and still calm expression.

The Andorian said, "Cadets reporting, sir."

Data nodded at the cadet. "Thank you. As you can see," he indicated the entrance to the armory and the heavy firefight outside, "we are pinned down and outgunned. You two are all I have left to help me create a diversion. We have to help the rest of our people get out of this building."

Sharon ducked with them as several heavy blasts rattled the armory. Data was the first to recover. It glanced at the ceiling, as if its mechanical vision somehow enabled it to see through the building. "That was not disruptor fire. They must have called in air support."

Data waved a fourth-year cadet over. "Cadet Cahill, we will create a diversion." Data indicated itself, Sharon, and the Andorian cadet. "As soon as the firing outside the armory is redirected toward us, get everyone out of here and to better cover."

The older cadet confirmed the order then moved to take command of the other people inside the armory. As a fresh exchange of phaser and disruptor fire erupted outside, Data motioned to Sharon and her fellow cadet. "We are going to use the armory's side entrance and attempt to flank the Breen. Stay low and close to me."

Sharon didn't feel too good about that plan, but Data and the Andorian cadet had moved off before she had a chance to mention it. Glancing back, Sharon saw the other cadets and officers in the armory. Most of them were wounded to some degree, some severely. Only a few were armed.

A sudden terrible realization struck Sharon. She, Data, and that other cadet were the only hope of escape for this group of people. With the Breen closing in on the entrance and their fighters making strafing runs outside, it wouldn't take long for this part of the Academy and everyone inside it to be reduced to slag.

Sharon blinked away hot tears. Data . . . it—he—wasn't just throwing the cadets into the fray; he had some sort of plan in mind. He was trying to save as many as he could, right? And somehow, he needed Sharon's help. She couldn't believe it. She was in sciences, not security. Why did she have to fight? It was so unfair. She didn't deserve this; none of them did. Was this a part of being a Starfleet officer?

The cadet Data had left in charge, Cahill, waved at Sharon. She looked at him and felt ashamed when she saw hope shining in his eyes. If she failed to help all these people—failed to help Data—she'd never forgive herself. Assuming she even survived the battle.

She gave the cadet a nod that she hoped looked encouraging,

---

then rushed deeper into the armory to catch up with Data and the cadet. She found them in short order. Data had already unlocked the side door. He looked at Sharon as she arrived.

"I am pleased you are here, Cadet. I was concerned that I had lost you."

Sharon shook her head. "No. . . . No sir." She mustered her courage and gave him a steady look, actually seeing him for the first time. "Sir, Commander Data. I just wanted to say I'm sorry."

Data gave her a quizzical look. "I do not understand."

The ground shook from another strafing run. The three of them braced themselves against the walls to keep their balance.

Sharon palmed away her tears. "I'll try to explain later."

"Indeed. We shall see if there *is* a later." Data gave her a tight smile, which surprised her. Sharon had assumed he was incapable of smiling.

Data positioned himself near the door and glanced at Sharon and the Andorian. "Ready? On three." They all double-checked their phasers and crouched, ready to spring out the door. "One . . . two . . ."

On three, Data keyed open the door and dove outside as soon as the space was wide enough to let him pass. He hit the ground and rolled into a crouch, firing his phaser once he had a target. Sharon went out second, moving as low and as fast as her injuries allowed. She fired off a couple of phaser blasts in the general direction of the Breen and ran for the first cover she saw.

Finding refuge behind an overturned bench, Sharon spared a glance toward the armory door. The other cadet leaned outside and fired off a couple shots. Data and Sharon added their firepower. Soon they had the attention of a dozen or so Breen. The soldiers started to shoot at them rather than at the front door of the armory.

Data rushed toward Sharon in a half-crouch. "We have to keep moving! Get to better cover!"

She nodded and ran with Data. She heard the phaser fire from their counterpart intensify. The Andorian cadet must have seen the two of them—she was providing cover fire for them!

Sharon and Data rushed toward a low wall bordering a footpath between buildings. They dove behind it as heated energy crashed all around them.

Sharon ducked as a Breen fighter thundered by overhead, its plasma bursts crashing into the library several dozen meters away. The building came apart, smoke and fire trailing from it as it collapsed with a roar.

Data glanced over the wall as the Breen soldiers closed in. "Cadet sh'Rave is pinned down! We need to give her covering fire so that she can get out of the armory!"

Sharon could see the other cadet inside the doorway, throwing shots at the Breen as she scanned the ground near her with one good eye. Sharon knew that there weren't too many places for her to go.

Sharon fired a few more times and shot worried glances toward the Andorian. The cadet was looking her way, gesturing at her. Sharon looked at Data. "I don't understand what she wants!"

Data looked toward sh'Rave. "I believe she wishes to join us here."

Sharon and Data ducked under a new barrage of Breen fire. They heard a yell from the other cadet and rose to give her covering fire. The Breen fired at them with new intensity, blasting apart the ground and sections of the wall all around Sharon and Data.

The cadet zigged and zagged across the grounds, avoiding the Breen fire, all the while moving toward Data and Sharon. She was ten meters or so from their protective wall when she got shot in the back. She hit the ground hard, her phaser flying out of her hand.

Sharon and Data intensified their fire as the Andorian struggled to crawl toward them. Disruptor fire chewed up the ground all around her; she was hit at least twice more.

Sharon looked at Data, despair in her eyes. Taking in his one-armed condition, something snapped inside of her. She leaped over the wall.

Sharon heard Data call out, but she kept her focus on the Andorian. Sharon ran toward the fallen cadet, scooping up the girl's discarded phaser as she went. With a weapon in each hand, Sharon sent a furious stream of fire toward the Breen as she reached her colleague.

A quick glance showed Sharon that the girl was yet alive—she was coughing and still trying to crawl, anyway. Sharon reached down and helped the Andorian to her feet. Sharon's arms screamed as the weight of the girl leaning hard against her drove the shards of debris in her arms into new, agonizing angles.

Sharon gritted her teeth and started back toward the wall where Data crouched, waiting. He fired his phaser faster than Sharon could have ever imagined. She hoped he was as accurate as he was fast. The energy blasts hitting all around her did nothing to answer that question.

The Andorian was crying out, screaming something, but Sharon couldn't decipher it. Sharon had to drop one of the phasers to get a better grip on the girl, but it didn't matter. If she couldn't get them to the wall, another phaser wouldn't make a difference.

Everything seemed to slow down to half-speed. A rosebush in Sharon's peripheral vision exploded into flames. Data's wide, yellow eyes shined as she neared the wall. The Andorian gained a thousand kilos in a second. The local gravity seemed to increase by a factor of three.

A stream of questions rolled through her mind. *Could we make it to the wall? Would we be shot dead before we can get there? Did many science honor cadets fall in battle? Who would tell my family what had happened, what I'd done?*

The moment stretched into what felt like an eternity. Data fired madly in her direction, missing her and the Andorian by centimeters, firing at unseen targets behind her. The wall was getting closer, closer! She was there—she'd made it!

Sharon pushed the Andorian over the wall and was just about to leap over it when her legs erupted in fiery agony. Sharon hit the wall and collapsed. She heard Data call out, saw him gesturing at her, but couldn't respond.

Dazed, Sharon saw a phaser on the ground next to her. It was hers—she hadn't realized she had dropped it. She thought about reaching up to lift herself over the wall, but her body didn't seem willing to respond.

In a haze, Sharon saw Data reach over, felt him grab a single handful of her ruined uniform. She felt herself pulled bodily over the wall by his superhuman strength as deadly energies crashed all around them. She hit the ground near where the Andorian had landed.

Data crouched next to her. "I am sorry, Cadet." She blinked hard. Was that concern she saw in his eyes?

Sharon opened her mouth to reply, but the Breen leaping over the wall behind Data stunned her into silence. Data must have seen the look in her eyes, because he twisted around and grabbed the Breen's disruptor rifle before the alien had a chance to use it. Data and the Breen struggled for control of the weapon, but the strength in Data's one arm was more than a match for the Breen.

Just as Data wrenched the weapon from the soldier's grasp, the Breen's helmet exploded from a phaser blast plowing into it. Sharon could hear more phaser fire nearby. The other cadets in the armory must have gotten out—their diversion must have worked!

Data glanced over the wall, toward the sounds of battle, then turned to Sharon. "I must go, but I will be back as soon as I can."

Sharon managed a nod. "I'll wait for you . . . sir."

Data gave her a long look. He pushed his phaser toward her with his foot then vaulted the wall and moved toward the fight, firing the heavy disruptor rifle with the one arm that was still attached to his body.

Now it was just her, the Andorian, and that dead Breen stuck near the wall. Sharon's legs burned terribly. She crawled the agonizing long meters to the wall as the battle raged outside of her line of sight. She propped herself into a sitting position once she reached the wall. Feeling strangely detached from her own body, she examined the fronts of her legs. Her pants were dusty and torn, but looked to be in otherwise decent shape.

The backs of her legs, though, were another matter. Her pants were a smoldering ruin and the skin underneath was a mass of ugly black char and white, runny blisters. She had second- and third-degree burns all over her calves and feet. The pain was incredible, but she somehow didn't feel much of it. Was this what going into shock felt like?

Sharon glanced at the Andorian. The blue-skinned girl lay where she had fallen, her back to the sky, face to one side. Her one working eye was closed. Her back looked even worse than Sharon's legs. She could see the girl's torso moving up and down and her blue antennae slowly twitching, though. She was still alive.

Sharon called out. "Cadet . . . Cadet? Can you hear me?"

Sharon got a low moan for a response, which she took to be an encouraging sign. "Cadet . . . if you can hear me, can you look at me?"

A long moment passed. Sharon wasn't sure if the cadet had heard her; wasn't sure if she had slipped on to whatever afterlife the Andorians believed in. Then, slowly, the Andorian lifted her head just enough to glance myopically at Sharon. Sharon received the briefest of nods before the girl dropped her head back to the bloodstained grass.

Another Breen fighter rocketed overhead. Sharon lifted her glance to follow its path, powerless to stop it. Then, Sharon saw something she hadn't expected—something wondrous. A Federation fighter streaked after the Breen ship, firing beautiful streaks of energy toward it. Somehow the scene brought a smile to Sharon's face. She couldn't explain why she felt so happy, so relieved. Maybe because Starfleet was waking up—finally fighting back. Maybe they'd get out of this after all.

Inspired by that unknown Starfleet pilot, Sharon worked her way over to her fellow cadet and started to drag her back toward what remained of the low wall. The effort took a long, painful eternity. Sharon had to pause and recover her strength several times. The agony in her arms and legs continued unabated, but she was determined to get the cadet to the minuscule safety of the broken wall.

The sun had set by the time Sharon finally propped herself and her fellow cadet against the wall. Sharon wrapped her arms around the girl for comfort, ignoring the constant pain in her limbs. The Andorian muttered something incoherent, most likely in her native tongue. Sharon didn't know what the girl needed, so she just pressed closer to her and hoped it was enough. She didn't have any food or medical supplies, and she wasn't about to search the dead Breen. Let it rot where it had fallen.

Sharon drifted in and out of awareness, skated the edge of unconsciousness. Distant sounds of an ongoing firefight and sirens from the city kept Sharon from falling asleep completely. The mumbling Andorian girl kept her up as well, even though Sharon couldn't do much for her other than hold her for their mutual warmth.

At some point during the darkness of the night, Sharon was pulled out of her dazed reverie by a low, long groan from the Andorian. The sound scared Sharon, taking her back to the moments before her nana had . . . no. Sharon shifted her position to try and make the two of them more comfortable. Sharon was *not* going to let the girl die.

The Andorian managed a whisper. "What . . . what happened?"

Sharon cleared her dry throat. "Attacked, by Breen. We're both shot up."

The Andorian pressed closer to Sharon. "Did . . . distraction . . . work?"

Sharon nodded mutely, stunned at the weakness in the Andorian's voice, amazed that the injured girl was asking about the others rather than herself. Sharon glanced down at the girl in the darkness. Was the selfless attitude an Andorian trait, or was it something Starfleet taught its officers?

The Andorian shifted her body so that her head rested on Sharon's shoulder. "Glad . . ." was all she could manage.

Sharon said, "I think we were able to help most of the others get out of the building. I haven't seen Commander Data since he left, though. They could all be dead as far as I know. I've heard a lot of shooting."

Sharon didn't know if the Andorian could still hear her, but she continued. "You were pretty brave out there. I thought you were going to make it to the wall."

The Andorian offered a hollow grunt. Sharon held her tightly, hoping to keep her there. "Just hold on. We're going to make it."

The girl shook her head. "I can't keep my eyes open anymore."

Desperate, Sharon tried to think of something to do to keep the girl awake, to keep her from leaving. "Cadet . . . what's your name?"

The girl whispered, "Randishira."

Sharon managed a smile. "That's a beautiful name. Mine's Sharon. You're a second-year cadet, but I'm just a rat."

Randishira uttered something Sharon didn't catch. To Sharon it sounded like *charan,* but she wasn't sure. The girl's voice dropped into a stream of alien words. Sharon couldn't figure them out. It almost sounded like a song, or a chant.

Sharon kept talking, pulling stuff off the top of her head to try and keep Randishira with her.

"I was wrong about Commander Data, you know. I thought he was nothing more than a walking computer, but I was wrong." Sharon didn't get a response from Randishira, but she kept talking anyway.

"He's a Starfleet officer, and he cares about his fellow officers. I thought he would just mechanically throw us into the fight, but he was really worried about everyone. He was worried about you too."

Sharon felt weariness close in on her, tried to fight it off. "I was pretty stupid. I was smart enough to make it into Starfleet Academy, but . . . but I still have an awful lot to learn."

She glanced down at Randishira. The girl didn't seem to have heard a word she said. Exhausted, Sharon rested her head against Randishira's and closed her eyes.

A bright light shining on Sharon's face dragged her back into consciousness. She blinked her burning eyes. Randishira still lay pressed against her, but wasn't moving. The Andorian's eye was

---

of the *Hood* on a training
as she said, "Chief, you thinl
on the way back to spacedock
prise is coming along well, a
g on her . . ." She trailed off as
er Chandra at the port system dis
ard, then doubled over as if punch

" The order was cut off as a wav sur-
e heat shimmering in the air. He lo ke he
rders, but no sound reached Rose headed
esitated as Chandra's legs left the d s whole
the air with his waist the axis of He hov-
owly tumbling in place, his body g to ripple
s if seen through a billowing sheet of ent plastic.

closed, her dirt-smeared face strangely relaxed. Sharon
the girl's name, but didn't get a response. She nudged
but the girl slid along Sharon's body, her head con
Sharon's lap.

Sharon gently placed her hands on Randishira'
white hair was soft to the touch, but the skin un
so cold. Sharon wept. She'd lost her.

She started as she heard voices movin
nearby. She was too tired to sit up, in too mu
heard Commander Data's voice break thr

"They should be near that wall, over

Sharon glanced around as Comman
still had the Breen disruptor rifle in
rushed over to kneel next to her.

He glanced at Sharon, then d
gently pulled the Andorian aw
ground. Sharon just watched
chest, using such tender car

She'd been so wrong
computer. He was a Sta
loss of an ally.

Sharon sniffed. "T'

Data lifted his gl
was the least I could do.
dishira, "that I returned too la

Sharon caught his glance. "You u

Data gave Randishira one last look, the
did we all. Your efforts, and the efforts of Cade
ficient to allow the others to get to safety. We did lose
but had we not successfully distracted the Breen, we all wou
most likely been killed."

Sharon tried a tired smile. "What about your arm?"

Data glanced at where his missing appendage should have been.
"It can be found, and repaired." He paused, his gaze distant. "I feel

Terra Tonight

Scott Pearson

Cadet Ella Rose, in the engine room
cruise, kept her eyes on her display
we might pass by the Frisco yards
The new *Sovereign*-class *Enter*
you know I requested a postir
glanced toward Chief Engin
just as he staggered back
the stomach.

"Check the synch—
rounded the chief lik
was yelling more
toward him but h
body turning
ered there,
and warp

"Engineering, this is Captain DeSoto. All our boards just lit up like fireworks. What's going on down there?"

Rose reached for her combadge. Before she could tap the channel open, she found herself stumbling across the deck then falling to starboard. She toppled downward, toward the wall, which suddenly seemed below her. She landed facedown, banging her elbows and accidentally biting her lip. Scrambling up into a sitting position— still on the wall—she saw other cadets and regular engineering crew trying to adapt to the chaos in the engine room.

The port system display shattered, the shards flying and falling in random directions. Crew members fell, stumbled, or floated in various directions. A crease appeared in the ceiling, the walls seemed to bend, and although Rose remained on the wall, the blood from her lip dripped to the ceiling. She wiped at her mouth with a sleeve, and tapped her combadge.

"Cadet Rose to the bridge." She paused. "Captain DeSoto?"

There was no answer.

"This is a Federation News Service breaking story. All contact has been lost with the Federation transport ship Jenolen, *en route to Norpin Five, a popular retirement colony. Starfleet considers the ship, which is now fifty hours overdue, missing. A search-and-rescue operation is under way. Although a crew and passenger manifest has not yet been released, a ship of this class would usually have a crew complement of about three dozen and could carry up to two hundred passengers. The FNS has confirmed with anonymous sources within Starfleet that Captain Montgomery Scott, retired, was among those passengers. Captain Scott is well known for his fifty-two-year-long Starfleet career, much of it aboard the* U.S.S. Enterprise *under the command of Captain James T. Kirk.*

"Just last year (Sol calendar) Captains Kirk and Scott were instrumental in assisting Captain John Harriman of the Enterprise-B *in rescuing forty-seven El-Aurian refugees from a dangerous spatial phenomenon informally known as the Nexus. Captain Kirk was lost*

during that rescue and presumed dead. Now it appears that Captain Scott has joined his former commander on the list of Starfleet officers who have disappeared in space. . . . Truly, for them, the final frontier.

"The FNS will continue to update this story as information becomes available. In the meantime, on behalf of all of us at the FNS, allow me to say our thoughts are with the family and friends of the crew and passengers of the U.S.S. Jenolen. *This is Brad Foster reporting for the Federation News Service."*

Marta Jensen faced the holocamera in front of her sleek wooden desk. The large monitor behind her faded from Foster to a stock image of the *Jenolen.* "That was the lead story seventy-seven years ago, almost to the day. Losing a ship is not as uncommon as any of us would hope, but it always feels like a new and terrible thing when it does happen." The image behind her dissolved from the *Jenolen* to *Voyager.* "It is now two weeks since the FNS learned through friends and family of the crew that the *U.S.S. Voyager* is missing with all hands. So far, no new information has come to light, and the fate of *Voyager* remains unknown. All we can do is hope that she will soon reappear, the victim of only a small technical failure. But that story remains to be written.

"Tonight, however, we will speak with someone who, by his very presence, will give hope to all those who are waiting for someone on *Voyager,* because sometimes the lost are found. Sitting with me is the subject of that seventy-seven-year-old story we just replayed, someone who takes the cliché out of the phrase 'living legend.'" Jensen turned to her left as *Voyager* was replaced with an *Enterprise* triptych—the NCC-1701 as Kirk first commanded her, the refitted *Enterprise,* and finally the 1701-A. "Captain Montgomery Scott, welcome to *Terra Tonight.*"

The director changed the feed to the two-shot holocamera, displaying Jensen and Scott side by side.

"Och, enough with that 'legend' talk, lass. To paraphrase an old friend o' mine, I'm an engineer, not a statue. And please, call me Scotty."

"Fair enough. But you can't deny that you've done some amazing things, not the least of which is reappearing after being missing for seventy-five years, and apparently without aging a day in all that time."

A cloud seemed to cross Scott's face as the director cut to a close shot, but Scott quickly recovered for the cameras. "Well now, you know I canna talk about that in detail, since certain aspects of it are still classified. But I can say that I was the only survivor of the *Jenolen,* meaning a lot of good people died, including a fine young engineer and friend, Ensign Matt Franklin. So you'll understand if it's not a celebration for me."

Jensen nodded sympathetically. "Of course." She leaned back in her chair. "Let's talk about Starfleet. You had retired before your disappearance. What made you decide to go back on active duty?"

"Oh, there were a lot of things. Mostly it was when Admiral Nechayev reinstated me as a consultant during a recent incident. In other words, she drafted me."

Jensen smiled for a moment, then, with the smoothness that all reporters seem to have, looked serious again. "You refer to the loss of the *Enterprise*-D."

"Yes, but—"

Marta held up a hand. "I know, it's classified." She leaned forward again, folding her hands together. "Let's go back to being 'drafted,' as you call it. You didn't rejoin on your own?"

"Not at first, no. After I was rescued, I had some rough spots. Many of my friends and family were gone. I couldn't throw myself back into my work—I was seventy-five years behind on my technical manuals and without a ship to serve on. The *Enterprise*-D was a wee bit overwhelming. I headed out in a shuttle with no direction to go. Norpin Five no longer sounded interesting to me, but nothing else did either. I was—"

Scott's combadge chirped for attention, surprising both him and

Jensen; Scott had cleared this appearance with Starfleet and was supposed to be unavailable for the duration of the interview.

With a shrug at Jensen, Scott said, "Sorry, I have to respond to this."

As he got up from the chair and stepped away from the desk, Jensen turned toward the main holocamera and said, "And so you see, even in the studio you never know what's going to happen during a live holocast. Apparently, there is an unfolding emergency of some sort that has required the input of Captain Scott. We will keep you updated as we learn more . . ."

A few steps away and with his back to Jensen, in the relative dark outside the range of the cameras, Scott tapped his combadge. "Scott here."

"This is Nechayev. We've got an emergency on the *Hood*. I need you to get back to that desk immediately."

"The *Hood*? Isn't she on a cadet cruise? And what's that got to do with—"

"Captain, the *Hood* is suffering multiple system malfunctions, and you helped design the *Excelsior* class."

"That was many refits ago, Admiral, and the original design team didn't listen much to my input."

Nechayev continued, ignoring Scott's comment. "The *Hood*'s standard communications are down, but for some reason civilian frequencies are still getting through, so the quickest way for you to contact her is from that desk. We've got a signal from her coming through a patchwork of civilian satellites and relays. We'll put that through to the studio."

"Aye, Admiral." Scott shook his head. All the pressure was on him now, hanging on the thread of this tenuous connection to the ship. He hurried back to the desk.

Jensen was still looking into the holocamera. "Captain Scott's first standout engineering victory came early in his career, while he served as advisor to the Denevan asteroid-mining operation. During a cargo run, the freighter Scott was on—"

"Sorry, lass," Scott said as he settled back into the guest chair. "I'm commandeering this show."

Jensen gave him a confused smile. "That's quite an entrance, Captain, but I'm not sure what you mean."

"You'll find out soon. And call me Scotty." Scott faced the monitor behind Jensen's desk.

There was a loud burst of static over the audio system as the *Enterprise* disappeared from the monitor and was replaced by the snow of interference. A voice, cracking with nerves, said, *"Hood to Captain Scott. Hood to Captain Scott."*

Jensen raised her eyebrows as Scott held up a finger to indicate she should just wait and see what happened. The snow faded and resolved into an image of a young woman in a cadet uniform, her lower lip swollen and bloodied. There were drops of blood along the side of her face as if she'd been swinging around upside down while the blood ran from her mouth. Some of her long brown hair had slipped out of the ponytail she wore, and hung over her right eye. Behind her were glimpses of an engine room in a state of pandemonium.

"This is Captain Montgomery Scott. Who is this?"

"Cadet Ella Rose, sir."

"Where is the chief engineer?"

Rose moved to her left, out of view. *"That's Chief Chandra."*

A couple meters behind her, a person curled into a ball floated about a meter and a half off the deck, rotating randomly like a shuttle in free fall without stabilizers. Further in the background were more crew, some floating, some lying on the deck, walls, or ceiling. Most looked unconscious, but some clearly struggled against higher than normal gravity. Small pieces of debris were also scattered about, floating, falling, lying on various surfaces. Smoke and sparks guttered from conduits and consoles, and the lighting flickered on and off.

Rose moved back into frame as she tucked the errant hair behind her ear. *"For some reason, I'm the only one still able to move here in engineering, maybe on the whole ship. Communications—"* A burst of sound interrupted the cadet, the low groan of bending metal. Rose looked over her left shoulder as an access panel bent and popped off the starboard wall, sailing across the room. After the panel froze in midair, she looked back. *"When I couldn't reach anyone else on the ship, I was finally able to get through to Starfleet."*

"Well done, lass. Clever to think of using civilian channels."

"Thank you, sir."

"Call me Scotty."

Rose paused, looking unsure. *"Aye, sir."*

Scott rolled his eyes. "All right, listen up, lass. You're going to have to be the chief for now. I'll talk you through it. Can you do that?"

"Aye, sir." There was another sound, a tinkling that was followed by a building, loud burst. Rose looked off frame over her right shoulder. *"Well, the port system display just went back together."*

Scott and Jensen exchanged looks. "Say again?" Scott said.

"The display shatters, then it goes back together like a vid played in reverse."

Scott nodded. "So you're having localized temporal distortions in addition to trouble with your grav systems and, judging by what else I'm seeing, some structural integrity field issues."

"Aye, sir. I'm also worried about the inertial dampers. They've held so far during warp-bubble fluctuations, but I don't dare try to bring the ship to a stop."

"Good thinking—if the dampers failed as the ship stopped, everything not nailed down would crash toward the bow at near light speed. What's your heading?"

Rose glanced down at a display. *"We were on course for Earth Spacedock when all of this started. Our speed has been fluctuating, but averaging warp two. We've just crossed the termination shock."*

"What's that?" Jensen said.

Scott turned toward her. "It's where the solar wind starts slowing down against the interstellar medium, about a hundred AUs from the sun. That means the *Hood* will blast into the solar system at warp two in about two hours."

"Aimed right at Earth?"

"No, her course would have been for system insertion near a

standard approach lane. If we can't stop her, odds are she'll just whistle right through. It's never good to warp through a planetary system, however." He turned back to Rose. "But that's not going to happen. We're going to take care of this wee problem, aren't we, lass?"

"I'm ready to try, sir."

"Well, then, let's get to it. It seems to me like you've got a multi-field dissonance effect. Do you concur?"

Rose narrowed her eyes. *"A what?"*

Scott shook his head. "Lass, what year are you?"

"Fourth."

"You're about to graduate? What have they been teaching you for four years?"

"Well, you see, sir . . ." Rose started, but Scott wasn't listening.

Scott glanced at Jensen. "Kids today, they learn about all the parts, but they don't understand how to put it all together." He faced toward Rose again. "The warp field, structural integrity field, inertial dampers, and artificial gravity generators all have to be synchronized properly so that they don't interfere with each other. If they go out of synch you get all sorts of feedback loops and the whole thing goes wonky."

Rose smiled and nodded her head. *"Oh, I understand that, sir. You mean to say we have cascading asynchronous field interference."*

Scott frowned. "Everything has more syllables since I came back." He leaned forward in his chair. "Now, I'm going to need you to go back to the matter-antimatter reaction chamber. Can you get there?"

"I think so." Rose turned to her left and disappeared from view. Scott and Jensen could now see most of engineering, and saw for themselves when the port system display panel shattered again and then reversed itself. Rose reappeared, the back of her head and shoulders coming into view from the right side of the monitor as she walked along the starboard wall. Her long ponytail jumped and waved in the unstable gravity. As she made her way slowly toward the reaction chamber, Jensen turned away from the monitor and toward the holocameras.

"If you've just joined us, we are live with Captain Montgomery Scott, who is communicating with Cadet Ella Rose in the engineering room of the *U.S.S. Hood*." Behind her Rose jumped from the wall, sailing through an area of zero g. "Scott is attempting to assist the cadet in—"

"Watch out!" Scott said as Rose suddenly tumbled toward the ceiling before somersaulting back toward the deck. Jensen turned back to the monitor as the cadet landed on her feet, looking at least as surprised as Jensen did.

"Nice landing," said Scott. "A bit of a gymnast, are you?"

"No, sir," Rose called back across the engine room. *"Not since climbing the monkey bars when I was a kid."* She shook her head, trying to restore her sense of balance.

"Well, whatever lands the caber straight, lass. Now then, put your hand on the chamber. Feel around a bit. Does it feel hot?"

Rose turned toward the chamber and did as she was told. After a few seconds she yanked her hand back, and looked back toward Scott. *"Yes, sir, it does. About fifteen centimeters above the dilithium chamber hatch."*

"Och, the *Excelsior* class always were a bucket of bolts, refits or no." Scott waved an arm in disgust. "All right then. You need to go to the port tool stow beneath the tractor beam auxiliary control panel."

"Aye, aye." Rose quickly made her way across the room; this time there were no gravitational anomalies to slow her down. Kneeling, she popped the access panel open. *"What do I need?"*

"A big spanner."

"A coil spanner?" Rose held the tool up for Scott to see.

"Sure, that would work, if it's at least two kilos. Now go back to that hot spot and give it a mighty whack with that spanner."

Jensen raised her eyebrows. Rose just looked toward them, her expression difficult to discern from across the room. Scott frowned. "What are you waiting for?"

"Well . . . it seems ill advised."

"Listen to me, cadet. You've got to know your ship. And I'm not talking about memorizing technobabble and running diagnostics, I'm talking about really feeling it, just as surely as you feel your own body when it's sick. These aren't only engines, they're your bairns, and sometimes you might have to spank them. Now go give that spot a whack!"

Rose shrugged and stood up. Wary of anomalies in the artificial gravity, she made her way across the room holding the spanner close to her chest. When she reached the chamber she hefted the spanner like a baseball bat, then hesitated again.

"I don't see any whacking!" Scott yelled.

With a tilt of her head, Rose swung the spanner at the hot spot. The spanner bounced off the chamber with a resounding echo of metal on metal and flew out of her hands. The noise echoed in the confines of the engine room, but instead of fading away it continued to reverberate. If anything, it got louder.

"What's happening?" Rose said, speaking up over the continued ringing of the echo. To her right, the spanner, caught in an anomaly, fell toward the ceiling.

"That hot spot was a focal node in the interference pattern of the multifield dissonance effect. By giving it a whack you set up another vibration in the pattern. Since it was right by the dilithium housing, the crystals picked up the vibration and amplified it, affecting the warp bubble."

Rose had to yell now to be heard over the building reverberation. *"What? What's that about the warp bubble?"*

"It will interrupt the feedback loop," Scott said. The echo was finally dying out. "Everything should reset, but you'll still need to do some fine-tuning."

"It's working!" Rose still yelled, although the reverberations were gone. Crew members and debris that floated or were pinned to walls or ceiling started falling or sliding toward the floor. Soon other voices could be heard in the background. *"Chief!"*

Chief Chandra had stopped spinning and was just starting to

stretch out his arms and legs when he fell to the deck. Rose rushed forward, no longer having to navigate through zero g or across walls, and helped Chandra to his feet.

Scott leaned forward. "Chief, this is Captain Montgomery Scott. How are you doing?"

"Better than a moment ago, sir." He looked back and forth between Scott and Rose as he ran a hand through his salt-and-pepper hair. *"I guess I owe you a thank-you."*

"Thank Cadet Rose. She patched into the civilian network to get through to Starfleet. And I may have diagnosed the patient, but she performed the treatment."

Chandra looked surprised. *"Remarkable. Well, sounds like she's earned her dream posting on the next* Enterprise."

"And who wouldn't dream of being on the *Enterprise*?" To Rose he added, "You've got my recommendation, lass."

Rose looked a little uncomfortable, but before she could respond the engineering room intercom crackled to life. *"DeSoto to Chandra. What just happened?"*

"We've got to get to work, Captain," Chandra said to Scott.

"Aye, that you do." But Scott wondered about the cadet's reaction to his recommendation and decided to try to get more out of her. Before they could cut the signal, he said, "Cadet?"

"Aye, sir?"

"A bit of advice, one of my secrets to being a great engineer: always work toward getting your systems running at a hundred and twenty-five percent of spec, but never let the captain know they go above a hundred and five. You want to impress, but you always want to be able to give some extra when you need it."

Rose and Chandra exchanged looks. Rose even looked a little sheepish. Chandra faced Scott. *"There seems to be a bit of a misunderstanding here, Captain. Cadet Rose isn't in the engineering program."*

"What do you mean?"

"I tried to tell you before when you asked what year I was," Rose said. *"This was just an elective engineering rotation. I'm actually a xenopaleontologist."*

"A what now?"

"*Xenopaleontologist. I study extraterrestrial fossilized remains of nonhumanoid species.*"

"You mean dinosaurs, lass?"

"*Yes, sir. Extraterrestrial dinosaurs.*"

"And you thought of patching through the civilian satellite network? And were able to do it?"

"*Well, I am a scientist. It seemed the logical thing to do.*"

"I suppose it did," Scott said with a twinkle in his eye. "Good work. I still say you'd make a fine engineer."

Rose smiled, then flinched as it hurt her swollen lip. She put a hand to her mouth as she said, "*Thanks. Scotty.*"

"You're welcome."

The monitor went dark, then filled again with the triple *Enterprise* image.

Jensen turned back from the monitor to face the holocameras. "Well, there you have it, the most exciting *Terra Tonight* segment ever, as Captain Montgomery Scott saves the *U.S.S. Hood* live on FNS." She turned to face the beaming engineer. "I'm guessing it was moments like this that made you decide to come back to Starfleet on a permanent basis."

"Aye. After working with Admiral Nechayev, I said to myself, 'How many times did I pull Captain Kirk's bacon out of the fire?' I can *still* do that for Starfleet. So I told the admiral I wanted to make it permanent."

"And we're all glad you did." Jensen turned briefly away from Scott. "Coming up after the news break, our next guest, Ambassador Lojal of Vulcan, will discuss the latest negotiations with Cardassia, the increasing Maquis problem, and the growing threat of the Dominion." She turned back toward Scott. "Thanks for being a guest tonight, Scotty. You really made the show one to remember."

"It was my pleasure. Thanks for having me."

The lights on the set faded. Jensen stood. As Scott stood as well, Lojal stepped up beside them.

"We're off the air for thirty seconds, gentlemen," Jensen said. "Ambassador, you've met Captain Scott?"

"Yes." Lojal gave Scott a courteous nod.

Scott responded with a small smile and said, "Aye. We were talking about a mutual friend before the show."

Jensen nodded. "Of course. Well, Ambassador, please have a seat."

Before sitting, Lojal said, "Congratulations, Captain, on your . . ." He paused, raising an eyebrow, "creative solution to the technical difficulties on the *U.S.S. Hood*. It was unorthodox, yet somehow logical."

"Thank you, Ambassador."

After Lojal sat down, Jensen turned her attention back to Scott, holding out her left hand. "Thanks again, really. I know you have a busy schedule. It was an honor meeting you and seeing you in action."

He took her hand and shook it warmly. "It's no trouble sitting with a bonnie lass and doing my job. Good night, now." With a last squeeze of her hand, and a final nod to the ambassador, he turned and walked off the set.

As she sat back down Jensen called after him, "Good night, Scotty."

With a last smile and a wave, he was gone.

Solace in Bloom

Jeff D. Jacques

In the hills above Labarre, France, the sun shone with an intensity that had been missing during the past few days of overcast skies and inclement weather. Now, though, with the sunlight on the back of his neck and the slight, grape-scented breeze flitting at the wide brim of his straw hat, Louis couldn't have imagined a better day.

And it's going to get better, if I have anything to say about it, he thought as he adjusted his posterior on the seat of his bicycle.

In an unprecedented and astonishing move, the Bloom sisters, the lovely siblings who were so near as his neighbors, yet so far out of reach, had invited him to come with them on an afternoon cycling trip in the hills. It was a dream come true—well, one of them at least—and the weather had cooperated splendidly. He'd told Jean-Luc about it, of course, but instead of congratulatory remarks and good-natured ribbing about what might be in store for him after the trip, his friend had said that the only thing Louis would find after the trip would be humiliation. The sisters were setting him up, he said, and it would be a mistake for him to go.

Louis was disappointed that Jean-Luc felt that way, but he wouldn't let it bring him down. How could he know for sure anyway? It was just his opinion, after all, nothing more.

And so far, so good. Poised at the top of a steep embankment, his fingers clutching the brakes of his bike, Louis peered down toward the base of the slope where the sisters waited, cloaked in the shadows of the dense line of woods that added to the natural beauty of this fair land.

"Come on, Louis," said one of the sisters. He couldn't tell which. "You're not afraid, are you?"

They giggled together, as though aware of the punch line of a joke they hadn't yet told, and for a moment Jean-Luc's warning haunted him. Stringing him along on some juvenile prank? No, he wouldn't believe that. But even if it were true, he wasn't going to make it easy for them.

"Right behind you, ladies!" he called, then released the brakes and pushed himself over the lip of the slope.

Down he went, his rate of acceleration constant as he kept some pressure on the brakes. Eager as he was, it would be foolish to speed down the slope pell-mell, particularly if he valued his life and more enjoyable motor functions. He kept his eyes on the uneven path below him, the overhanging branches above and the Bloom sisters at the bottom of the hill, waiting for him.

Louis swerved left to avoid an indentation in the middle of the pathway, but caught a branch across the face for his efforts. As he instinctively maneuvered away from that obstacle, his front tire struck a rock embedded in the earth and his whole body jolted with the impact. His bike sailed over his body and for an instant he felt strangely serene as he flew through the air. He heard a gasp and someone crying out his name, but it seemed so far away.

Then, the peacefulness of the moment peeled away as a tremendous bang pierced the forest as his bike crashed to the ground and his own cry of alarm stabbed his ears like needles.

As he tumbled down the slope, his bike looped around again and came down hard on his back before careening into the trees to the side. Rocks, dirt, and pieces of wood came in contact with his face and body as he tumbled downward. And then he screamed as his leg snapped below the knee and a pain unlike any other he'd ever experienced exploded through his body, reaching his teeth, his eyes, and every bone in his body. It was the pain of death. It had to be. No one could ever feel this much pain and not be dying. Through his own shrieking, he thought he heard his name again, but the words were drowned out by—

His rapid descent came to an abrupt end as his body slammed against the trunk of a tree. He continued to scream as agony held him in a tight embrace, his bruised and bloody hands clutching at his shattered leg.

If there was a worse pain than the one he was enduring now, he wouldn't wish it on anyone.

At the bottom of the Atlantic Ocean, two hundred and fifty kilometers off the coast of France, Louis screamed as the Jem'Hadar soldier loomed over him and sliced deeply into his right thigh with a *kar'takin,* the nasty bladed weapon of choice for this warrior species. This was a fact he wouldn't normally have been aware of, but the Vorta in charge of his interrogation had an annoying tendency to become chatty during the welcome respites from the physical and mental assaults, as though they were good friends. He also knew the Vorta loved rippleberries, though he suffered the misfortune of not having had any for almost a year. Considering his current predicament, Louis found it difficult to sympathize with the alien, though he had to admit that a bowl of rippleberries, whatever they happened to be, sounded pretty damned enticing about now.

As the director of the Atlantis Project, Louis had been spared the instant death bestowed upon his coworkers when the Vorta suddenly appeared two days before with a contingent of Jem'Hadar and Breen soldiers. At least, it felt like two days ago. It might only have been hours. In any case, he had long decided that those people—his friends, his family in this underwater home away from home—were the lucky ones.

"Please!" he cried, his voice growing hoarse as he struggled uselessly against the bonds that held his arms and legs to the chair he was in. Blood seeped out of his leg wound and onto the floor, taking with it his strength and hope. "I don't know anything!"

"I would advise against struggling," the Vorta said. "I can't guarantee a clean cut if you continue to move about."

The pain suddenly intensified as the Jem'Hadar's blade struck bone, and Louis screamed louder than he thought possible. He wondered if any aquatic creatures could hear him out in the deep beyond.

"Hold," said the Vorta, and immediately the Jem'Hadar straightened and stepped back, leaving the *kar'takin* embedded in Louis's flesh.

Louis wanted to reach for it, to pull it out, but even if he could, wouldn't that do more harm than good? What was the protocol for those situations? He'd have to look into that if he got the chance.

"You must be in *considerable* pain right now. You don't even have to answer," the Vorta said, leaning close. "I can see it in your eyes. The fear. The hopelessness. The screaming is also a strong indicator."

His body trembling, Louis opened his mouth to speak, to defy these monsters. "I . . . don't know what you want. Please . . ." He glanced at the gleaming weapon lodged in his leg.

"I would be only too happy to alleviate some of your pain," the Vorta went on, as if Louis hadn't spoken. "All you have to do is tell me what I want to know. Why are you here? It's such a simple question and a simple solution to your obvious discomfort."

"\V-_/-I/," the Breen soldier said in a language so alien, even the Universal Translator couldn't make heads or tails of it. The Breen had mostly been observers during the ordeal, though their leader occasionally bickered with the Vorta, who clearly considered himself in charge.

"It's called negotiating," the Vorta said, his pasty face tinged with annoyance. "You may want to look into it. It's sometimes more effective than blasting your way through everything."

"//-/-//-|_||," the Breen said.

The Vorta turned sharply. "I beg your pardon? That very much sounded like a threat."

"//_-V_-III. /V_—II-V//."

"As a matter of fact, that *is* how I took it," the Vorta said. "So let me make myself clear to *you:* While your people may have carried out the attack on Earth, you did so under the orders of the Dominion, and as their official representative, *I* am the Dominion on this particular mission. Is that understood?"

"—//."

"How delightful. Now then," he said, turning back to Louis, "please go on."

Louis explained, again, what the Atlantis Project was all about. But whether due to genuine lack of interest or part of some ploy to break his will, the Vorta wasn't interested in hearing about raising the ocean floor, creating a subcontinent, and exploring a new world on one's own planet for the fourth time.

"Fascinating as this all is, even I'm getting tired of hearing about it," the Vorta said once Louis was finished. "I can't believe that you're simply toiling away on the ocean floor in the middle of a war, which, I might add, the Federation is in danger of losing."

The Vorta's demeanor, from persistence to disbelief, was infuriating. Was he being purposefully obtuse just to aggravate him? Louis didn't know for certain, but whatever the case, he was finding the alien increasingly tiresome.

"It's the truth," Louis said, trying to control his breathing through the pain and exhaustion ravaging his body. "Why won't you believe me?" The Vorta just stood there, looking at him with an expression that seemed perpetually locked in a state of mild amusement. "Please . . . Nothing we're doing here has anything to do with the war. It hasn't even reached us down here, for God's sake!"

"Really?" asked the Vorta. He made a show of looking around the central hub of the complex and Louis was compelled to follow his roving gaze as it passed the dead bodies of his coworkers and friends, the pools of blood, the ruined computer consoles and equipment . . . and the brooding stares of the cold, reptilian Jem'Hadar soldiers and masked Breen.

Louis almost retched as the Vorta leaned in close, his alien stink mixing with the lingering odor of blood, charred circuits, and death. His piercing blue gaze stung him like an electric shock.

"I beg to differ," the Vorta said smugly.

Louis hung his head, uncertain how to proceed. His jaw ached from clenching his teeth together against the pain, and his thigh muscle, strained tightly ever since the Jem'Hadar sliced into it, felt ready to explode. His eyes strayed to the gleaming, blood-smeared weapon embedded in his leg, so agonizingly close. He extended his fingers toward it but pulled them back into a fist again, acknowledging the futility of the effort with a hopeless sigh. The intervening inches might as well have been measured in light-years.

Finally, unable to hold the muscle tight any longer, Louis released it, anticipating a painful rejoinder, but not expecting the sheer intensity of it. He cried out as a searing bolt of pain, like liquid fire, tore its way through his leg and into his chest. With a willpower he didn't know he still possessed, he flexed his leg again and forced himself to breathe and keep from hyperventilating.

"My, my, my," the Vorta said. Louis looked up and saw the alien staring at him with a curious expression, the oily smile mocking him. "You humans are a tenacious species." Still smiling, he glanced at the Jem'Hadar who waited nearby. "Finish it."

The gray-skinned warrior advanced and before Louis even registered the movement, the Jem'Hadar snarled and slammed all its weight down on the *kar'takin* it had left in Louis's leg.

Louis screamed again as his world briefly swelled, then vanished into darkness.

"Hydroponics? Are you daft?"

Louis turned and scowled at Jean-Luc through the long grass in which they lay. "No, I'm not daft," he said, keeping his voice low, lest he announce their presence to the objects of their attention. Well, *his* attention, at any rate. "Why would you say that?"

Jean-Luc didn't reply right away. His attention was drawn through the swaying, reed-thin stalks to the small beach where the Bloom sisters prepared for a swim. Legend held that the close siblings exercised their skinny-dipping techniques when they were sure none of their many suitors were nearby, and that was something Louis, for one, just had to see.

"Jean-Luc," Louis said, prompting his friend with an elbow to the upper arm.

"Well, why would you want to get into something so boring?" Picard asked, then turned toward the beach again.

Louis couldn't have been more surprised by his friend's words if he'd declared he was joining the circus. "Boring? How can you say that? It's a vital science, Jean-Luc. Crucial for food supply on new colony worlds that won't support crops initially. Think of the benefits, not only to those worlds, but to ours as well."

"We have plenty of food on this planet," Picard said.

"Yes, but if we can make the process more efficient, there's no telling—"

"Oh my," Picard said, his voice barely a whisper.

"What?" Louis asked, peering anxiously through the grass. "What do you see? I can't see a thing."

Picard smiled. "Just as well. You're much too young to see this."

"Stop that," Louis said. "I'm only a year younger than you are." He nudged Picard aside to put himself into his friend's point of view, but he still couldn't see anything but some blue sky and surf. By God, if he'd missed what he'd come all the way down here for, he would just die. He pushed himself a little higher to get an even better view.

At once, Picard yanked him back with a sharp tug. "Keep down, you fool. Do you have any idea what they'll do to us if they see us gawking at them in the altogether."

"I'm sure it will be worth—wait, the altogether?" Louis strained his vision more than he ever had before, almost willing the grass to part for him. He still saw nothing, though he could now hear soft voices some distance ahead and gentle splashing in the water. He could almost imagine the sisters wading along the shoreline, testing the water's temperature.

"I don't know why I let you drag me into this excursion in the first place," Picard said. "It's childish."

"Because, my dear friend, they are the *Bloom* sisters, and that nomenclature does not solely apply to their surname."

Picard glanced through the grass toward the beach. "Indeed, it does not."

Louis's jaw dropped and he shot to his feet just in time to see the bare shoulders and red hair of the young women dip below the water. Picard laughed as he stood up and Louis scowled in mock indignation. "I want a full report."

"Mm, I'm sure you do."

They both laughed, then Louis realized he didn't want to be caught out in the open when the sisters emerged. "Let's head up to that small bluff over there," he said, pointing the way. "We'll have an unobstructed view when they come out, yet we'll be out of sight."

"Brilliant," Picard said, rolling his eyes as they started up the dirt path leading up the slope. "More importantly, you could use the exercise."

They walked in silence for several minutes, navigating the rocky terrain which led up into the wooded area at the top of the bluff. For a few seconds, Louis almost forgot about the Bloom sisters and just enjoyed the experience of hiking with his best friend.

"So tell me, Louis," Picard said as they neared the top. "Why don't you consider Starfleet instead of staying Earthbound? I'm certain the S.C.E. might have a place for you, or the terraforming divisions of Starfleet."

This wasn't the first time Jean-Luc had brought up Starfleet, but while Jean-Luc seemed born to fly away from his family's vineyards in a starship, Louis had never thought the service was for him. There was just so much to explore here on their own world without having to go elsewhere. And in doing so, other worlds might benefit from what was learned on Earth. Jean-Luc never liked hearing this from him, but Louis told him anyway.

"So, you're afraid of space," Jean-Luc said, clearly baiting him. And as usual, he fell into the trap.

"I'm not!" he bellowed, the rejoinder sending a squirrel scurrying deeper into the woods.

"You are," Picard said with a grin. "And I suspect you're afraid of the Bloom sisters as well."

"Afraid of—?" Louis could hardly believe what he'd heard. Afraid? Of the Bloom sisters? Preposterous! "Now, Jean-Luc, that is quite possibly the most . . . ridiculous thing I have ever heard you say."

"Is it? Then why don't you get off this bluff and swim out to them right now." He waved a hand at the beach below, where the sisters splashed each other, carried on, and appeared to be having a grand old time.

"I can't do *that*," Louis said, his blood going cold. "You know me and water."

"Well, if you start to drown, they might save you," Picard said, then evidently saw how unsettled Louis had become at the idea. "Then why not wait for them out on the beach, and ask one of them on a date. Or both, if you're feeling extra fearless."

Louis shifted. Why did he suddenly feel as though he'd been put on the spot? "Why don't you?"

"Because I'm not the one obsessed with the Bloom sisters."

"I'm *not* obsessed," Louis said.

"Then go on," Picard said, waving a hand again. "Go down and ask them. You'll have to make the first move, because it's not as if they'll ever ask you to go anywhere with them."

Of all the—had he just *insulted* him? "What is *that* supposed to—"

Suddenly, Picard's face went slack, then brightened with a smile a moment later. "Too late."

Louis turned to see one of the most remarkable sights he'd ever seen. The Bloom sisters—the source of many a wandering thought over the years—had surfaced and were splashing toward the beach where they'd left their clothes, unaware that they were being observed. Louis felt his throat constrict, his blood rush, and his jaw drop slowly open at the sight, yet as he watched their wet bodies glistening in the afternoon sunlight, a swell of guilt swept through him like an unexplained chill on a warm summer's day. Here he was intruding upon a private moment of bonding between two siblings simply to satisfy a silly hormonal obsession.

Still, it was quite the sight, and at that moment the ocean had never been more appealing.

Louis screamed as his lungs finally gave out and a cloud of bubbles surged toward the top of the cistern of water in which he'd been submerged. The cry of terror sounded like a muffled gurgle to his ears, the sound of a panicked, frightened man. He closed his mouth too late and gagged on the water that rushed down his throat, drowning him. His body thrashed violently as he tried to extricate himself, but powerful hands held him down. Images of his wife and daughter, Patrice and Sophie, fought to comfort him in these final moments.

And then suddenly, he was pulled free of the nightmare, the vise-like grip on his head and shoulders gone. He erupted in a fit of coughs, expelling the water in his lungs, then suddenly lost his balance as his remaining leg failed to keep him aloft. Like a felled tree, he toppled, and with his hands bound behind his back he was unable to brace himself. He hit the floor, hard. A jolt of pain screamed through his shoulder. He continued to gag, water trickling from his mouth like a leaky faucet. Lying prone on the wet floor, he felt like a fish on the deck of a boat, death far closer than any hope of renewed freedom.

When he'd regained some semblance of control, Louis looked up at the Vorta, who appeared to be observing the entire ordeal with a mixture of cold indifference and curiosity.

"Please," Louis begged. "Don't do that again."

He'd always been teased about his aversion to the water. He couldn't imagine many other deaths worse than drowning, and such a dark, frightening end had never been far from his mind whenever he'd been near water. As a result, he'd never been a very good swimmer and missed out on participating on afternoons at the lake with his friends.

The Vorta knelt down before him in an almost friendly manner. "In my experience, when someone makes a request like that with such conviction, it's a signal that they're ready to cooperate fully, rather than be subjected to such unfortunate, but necessary, measures again. Is that the case here, Louis? Or is it back into the water for you?"

Tears welled in Louis's eyes and spilled down his cheeks, mixing with the water already trickling from his soaking hair. "I . . ."

"There, there," the Vorta said, patting his shoulder soothingly. "I know this has been a bad day for you. I've been there. We've all had bad days. But this one can be over as soon as you tell me what I need to know. That's all. It's so easy. Just give me the information I want, and then we'll leave. Granted," he said, glancing around, "you'll have quite a mess to clean up, but at least you'll be alive. You want to help me, don't you?"

Louis gave him a weary nod. God knew he wanted to say whatever it took to get the Vorta and his Dominion soldiers out of there, but there was nothing he could say. If Jean-Luc had been in his position, he would have been able to come up with an acceptable line of double-talk that might satisfy the Vorta, but Louis wasn't a Starfleet officer with experience in dealing with evil aliens. He was a scientist. Just a scientist.

"I'm sorry," he said, knowing his whispered words would very likely mean his death. "I . . . I don't know what you're talking about. You're just . . . wrong."

"I see," said the Vorta. He nodded at the Jem'Hadar waiting silently nearby, then rose himself. "The water it is then."

Louis struggled vainly, but this time he was too exhausted to scream.

"For God's sake, Jean-Luc," Louis said with a wide grin on his face. The two men stood before a long mirror in an opulent sitting room in the chalet where Louis would shortly be married. Both were dressed in tuxedos and Picard was straightening Louis's suit even though it was perfectly immaculate already. "You're my best man. You're supposed to be giving me your encouragement and support on my wedding day."

"I gave you my encouragement and support the last time you got married, but I didn't approve then either," Picard said, his grin echoing his friend's.

Louis scowled a bit as Picard fiddled with his bow tie. "Yes, well . . . you were right that time, as it turned out, but this time it's different."

"Is it?" asked Picard.

"It is," Louis said. "Patrice is the one for me, I'm sure of it." He had never felt for anyone the way he felt for Patrice. In fact, he had never fully realized just how wonderful love could be until he'd met her that first time in Italy. She'd been up on the lakeside wharf, and he had been in his rapidly sinking canoe . . .

"I was always sure you'd marry one of the Bloom sisters," Picard said. "You know, they're both out there . . ."

"I did invite them," Louis said.

". . . no husbands at their sides," Picard continued as though Louis hadn't spoken. "I'm sure the both of them were waiting for you all these years to pop the question."

"Very funny," Louis said and shrugged Picard away. "They were just a youthful obsession."

"A-ha!" Picard said as he slapped his hands together. "So it *was* an obsession. I was right all along."

Louis rolled his eyes and looked at his friend's reflection in the mirror. "Patrice and I mesh, Jean-Luc. I know it sounds clichéd, but we're like two halves of the same being," he explained, lacing his fingers together. "I've never felt that way about anyone in my life."

Picard regarded him with a serious expression for a moment, then placed a firm hand on his shoulder. "Of course you have my support, Louis. And I wish you all the best . . . and all the *luck* you'll need."

"I don't think I'll need luck this time," Louis said.

Picard shrugged. "Well, I'm giving it to you anyway."

They primped and preened in front of the mirror some more.

"Anyway," Louis said after a few moments, "for someone who's never been married before or had a long-term relationship, you certainly have your opinions on who's right and wrong for me."

"I'm in Starfleet, Louis," Picard said. "I can't afford the distraction."

"Is that what marriage is to you?" Louis asked, a sad note to his voice. "A distraction?"

"For me, yes. I'm married to my career. Besides, I don't have anyone in my life like that right now. Perhaps I never will."

"Bollocks," Louis said. "You just wait. One of these days, when you least expect it, you'll meet Miss Right. And the next thing you know, there will be a swarm of little Jean-Lucs running around the yard . . . or through the starship corridors, as the case may be."

"Stranger things have happened," Picard said, though Louis didn't think he sounded particularly convinced.

"Yes, they have," Louis replied. "And when they do, be sure to send me an invitation so I can be just as unencouraging and unsupportive as you are." He laughed good-naturedly and a moment later, Picard joined in the laughter as well.

"I'll try to remember that," Picard said. "Now, let's get out of here before all of your guests get bored and leave. For at least half of them, this whole affair carries with it a strong sense of déjà vu."

"You always know the right things to say, Jean-Luc," Louis said wryly.

When Louis regained consciousness, he couldn't have been more surprised. He thought for sure that he'd been going to his death, but he must have passed out instead. Maybe the Vorta couldn't see the advantage in drowning an unconscious man. Or perhaps it didn't hold enough entertainment value for him.

Ideally, Louis would have preferred to awaken to realize the horror he'd undergone had been a simple nightmare, but one look at his missing leg told him that wasn't the case. As he sat against a wall, his right leg stretched out before him, he gazed at the vacant spot next to it and wondered idly what had happened to his amputated limb. Had it been discarded? Considering that the bodies of his coworkers still lay where they rested, it wouldn't surprise him if it remained where it had fallen in a pool of his blood.

Louis looked ahead to see two stone-faced Jem'Hadar staring at him, their pulse weapons held at the ready. *Like I'm in a position to put up any sort of resistance!* he thought.

"It's an interesting perspective, down here on the floor."

Louis frowned at the voice and turned to see the Vorta sitting a few feet away, back against the wall, feet extended outward, emulating Louis's position.

"A child's life must be fascinating," the Vorta continued, "to witness life so removed from the perception of everyone else. There's a kind of . . . innocence down here, don't you think?"

Louis looked at the Vorta as though the alien had lost his mind. But before Louis could think of a response, the Vorta rose in such a way that it seemed like he was making a statement. *Innocence sitting down, not so innocent standing up. Very subtle.*

The Vorta gestured. One of the Jem'Hadar hauled Louis up and dragged him to a chair at the table where the vat of water had been and was now, thankfully, gone. The Vorta stood across from him, hands clasped before him.

"I researched the name of your Atlantis Project and learned that according to Greek myth Atlantis was an island paradise that was tragically overcome by the sea and lost forever. A fascinating tale. Generally, every myth is based on truth to some extent. In our case, some truth is based on myth."

Louis stared at him blankly for a moment, then found his voice. "I don't understand."

The Vorta leaned forward slightly. "Then allow me to explain. I believe," he said as he began strolling around the table, "that this Atlantis Project is a research base—the prototype, if you will, of a similar base, or bases, located somewhere in Federation space that will be used to launch surprise attacks against Dominion forces. As

I'm sure you can understand, this is something I cannot allow to transpire."

Louis almost laughed. "Are . . . are you *serious?*"

"Quite," said the Vorta, coming to stop exactly where he'd begun.

"That's . . . ridiculous," Louis said.

The Vorta seemed amused. "Is it?"

"Yes!" Louis blurted, feeling the rawness of his throat. "Access our computer records. The Atlantis Project has been active for over twenty years, long before anyone had even heard of the Dominion. You'll find no evidence of what you're suggesting."

"Actually, I have read your database, and I must admit it was fascinating research," the Vorta said. "Tectonic pressures, water containment, raising the ocean floor . . . it all sounds so adventurous. If it were not for the fact that we were dire enemies in a terrible war, I would have liked to sit down with you to discuss your progress and suggest a few theories of my own. Sadly, this is not the case. Furthermore, while your project has existed for almost two decades, obviously the current situation has prompted you to modify your research to better serve the war effort."

"Obvious? How is that obvious? The only obvious thing I see here is that you've lost your mind and all sense of reason along with it. You're so determined to make this mission of yours a success that you're manufacturing a lie that can't possibly be true so that you can justify killing everyone here when you leave!" The words tumbled out of Louis's mouth like an out-of-control roller-coaster that had no way to stop until it was finished.

Louis shook his head. He wanted to laugh again, but was afraid that would be going too far and would only get him a quick death for his trouble. Still, he couldn't believe the Vorta was trying to bait him with such a ridiculous premise.

"You appear amused," the Vorta said, then glanced at the nearest Jem'Hadar. "It seems he doesn't believe my assertions."

"/-l-l_//-," the Breen captain taunted.

The Vorta appeared as though he was about to rise to the Breen's bait, but resisted at the last moment. Instead, he walked to one of the office's windows and looked out into the murky deep water on the other side of the glass. He stood there for several minutes, following the wiggling path of a large blue fish, watching a series of bubbles drift upwards out of sight and musing about God-knew-what.

The calm of the moment was broken as a Jem'Hadar soldier burst into the room and marched directly toward the Vorta. The Vorta turned with an expression of annoyance on his pale face.

"This interruption is unacceptable," he said. The Jem'Hadar didn't appear to care one way or the other about the Vorta's annoyance and simply delivered his report. Louis couldn't hear what the brute said, but his words appeared to have captured the Vorta's attention. The tormentor's posture tensed and his demeanor became far more serious.

"Take two men with you," he told the Jem'Hadar. "Make it quick."

"_//-/_|-," the Breen said in its unintelligible electro-babble.

"Fine," said the Vorta with an exasperated sigh. "Send some of your men too, if you must."

Louis watched curiously as three Jem'Hadar and two Breen left the room like they meant business. That left seven soldiers, plus the Vorta and himself in the room. The door closed and locked with a soft hiss-click and he watched the soldiers depart through the transparent aluminum panel. Louis knew he was still outnumbered; his dramatic escape would have to wait.

After a seeming eternity, the Vorta turned his attention back to his prisoner as though the exchange with the Jem'Hadar had never occurred. "Tell me, Louis—may I call you Louis?—who is Sophie?"

At the sound of his daughter's name from the mouth of this vile creature, Louis felt the blood drain from his face and his arms go numb. And the only way he knew that his heart hadn't stopped was the fact he was still somehow breathing. Images of Sophie being terrorized by Jem'Hadar soldiers flickered through his mind and he felt his tenuous control slip.

"Don't you hurt her!" he cried as he lunged toward the Vorta. It didn't matter that he only had one leg and wouldn't make it to the Vorta anyway. He just wanted to get his hands on the bastard and beat the amused expression off his face. But the Jem'Hadar stationed behind him had been ready for just such an attempt and held him back with a vise-like grip. He struggled uselessly, his strength waning once more as tears came to his eyes. "Don't you dare!" he croaked.

"Oh, I'm afraid it's much too late for that, Louis," the Vorta said with feigned regret. "I was just curious to know who she was."

Was? No, not his Sophie. No . . . the Vorta was baiting him again. That had to be it. It's what people like him did. They toyed with the emotions of their prisoners to break them down. And it was working. The damnable Vorta was succeeding in that very thing.

But deep down he knew it wasn't true, couldn't *possibly* be true. If the Vorta had somehow found out about Sophie and had done the unthinkable, had . . . *killed her* . . . how could they possibly expect him to cooperate? On the other hand, these people were vicious, brutal creatures. Who knew what they were capable of? They might have killed Sophie and were about to threaten to deliver the same fate to Patrice if he didn't cooperate. He didn't know what to think, and the uncertainty was draining his will.

It was to his utter surprise that he suddenly heard himself begin to laugh. It wasn't a very hearty laugh, more a soft chuckle, but it was certainly not the reaction the Vorta expected.

The Vorta's pasty brow furrowed and his head tilted sideways a little. "Have I said something amusing?"

Louis shook his head, unable to bring words to his mouth amid the laughter and tears. He realized the Vorta couldn't possibly have located Sophie and hurt her in so short a time. He'd probably found Sophie's name among his files and went from there.

"Stop that at once," said the Vorta, who apparently didn't like being laughed at.

Louis let the chuckles bleed out of him and fell silent. He stared into the Vorta's blue eyes and said the only thing that occurred to him. "You're pathetic."

The Vorta was not amused. He glanced at the Jem'Hadar behind Louis and said, "Kill him."

Louis felt the soldier release his arm, heard him take a step back, heard the soft clicking of his pulse rifle. Louis closed his eyes, an image of Sophie on his eyelids, and waited for death to claim him.

It never came.

"//_l.\!" the Breen commander blurted.

An instant later, Louis heard the transparent panel in the wall shatter and the sound of phaser fire rent the air. One beam of orange energy struck the Breen in the throat and another hit the Vorta in the chest. The Jem'Hadar soldiers, including the one who had been about to kill him a moment ago, turned and charged the newcomers, battle cries erupting from their scaly lips and weapons brandished with barbaric enthusiasm.

Louis dropped to the floor and crawled behind the table where the Vorta had fallen. He watched as a small group of Starfleet officers exchanged weapons fire and physical blows with the enemy soldiers. Soon, all of the Jem'Hadar and Breen lay dead on the floor, a smoky mist from destroyed consoles and panels drifting lazily in the air.

"Louis!"

Startled at the sound of his name, Louis realized that not only had these officers come looking for him specifically, but that he recognized the voice that had called out. With some effort, he raised himself to his knee, using the desk as support, and looked at the man at the center of the room. He was almost completely bald and held a phaser rifle at the ready. Louis could not believe his eyes.

"Jean-Luc?" he asked as the man and the rest of his team turned to face Louis. "Is that really you?"

Picard smiled and came toward him, but almost immediately his smile faltered. At the same instant, Louis heard movement behind him and turned to see the Vorta on his knees and aiming a phaser at the transparent barrier between the room and the ocean beyond.

"No!" he cried.

A moment later, a phaser beam struck the Vorta in the back and the alien dropped forward, but not before firing off a shot that struck the window near the upper frame. A visible crack emerged and began to grow steadily outward against the transparent surface.

"Picard to *Enterprise,*" Jean-Luc said. There was no response that Louis could hear. "Everyone back to the transporter site," he ordered before finally coming to his side.

"It took you long enough," Louis said weakly, unable to keep the smile from his face. He'd never been more happy to see his friend.

Picard returned the smile. "We took the scenic route."

Louis nodded. "I don't blame you. It is rather impressive, isn't it?"

"For now," Picard said, then looked up sharply as a creaking groan issued from the splintering window. As he raced to undo Louis's bonds, Picard's expression faltered as he realized Louis was missing a leg. The hesitation was brief, but significant. "Are you in much pain?"

"Some," Louis said, and in truth the pain had dulled significantly. Whether this was because of his dulled senses or the fact the wound had been cauterized by a Jem'Hadar pulse rifle, he didn't know.

"All right, let's go," Picard said as he finished untying Louis's arms. He hauled Louis to his remaining foot. "Lean on my shoulder, and we'll do this together. Are you ready?"

Louis nodded. "Ready."

Together, they headed back through the complex, Picard leading with Louis leaning over his shoulder and hopping next to him. Along the way, Louis felt a rush of satisfaction when he saw the bodies of the two Breen and three Jem'Hadar that had left the central hub some time ago.

When they reached the atrium where Louis and his coworkers often ate meals and relaxed during breaks, they passed the central water fountain. Inwardly, Louis cursed the fountain, which continued to trickle peacefully as though this was just another day.

A tremendous shudder shook the facility and a cool breeze blew in from the direction they had come. As Louis felt the transporter beam wrap itself around him, he swore he could smell the sudden scent of seawater.

Louis awoke to the sight of a beautiful woman standing over him. She wore a Starfleet uniform and a blue medical smock, waves of strawberry blond hair cascading about her shoulders.

"Hello," she said with a warm smile. "I'm Doctor Crusher. You're all right now."

"Where . . . Where am I?" Louis asked, taking in his new surroundings. The subdued lighting softened the grays and tans of the decor and put him at ease.

"You're on board the *Enterprise,* Louis," the woman said. "You're safe now."

Louis looked down and saw only one distinctive leg shape beneath the covers of his bed. The horrible memory of recent events flooded back to him, but he quickly shoved them aside. *What's done is done.*

"I was hoping it was all just a bad dream," he said.

Crusher gave him a sympathetic smile and tilted her head upwards a bit as she spoke. "Crusher to Picard."

Louis smiled at the sound of his friend's name.

"Go ahead, Doctor."

"My patient is awake," she informed.

"We're on our way. Picard out."

We? Jean-Luc had probably located Patrice and brought her aboard as well. He could only hope that Sophie was with them too. As much as he hoped his theory about her was true, he knew it was possible it might not be so.

"Don't worry about your leg," Crusher said, misinterpreting the expression on his face. "You'll be fitted with a prosthetic as soon as possible. By the time you're on your feet again, you'll never know the difference."

Louis was sure that was the standard physician spiel, but even if it were true, no prosthetic limb, no matter how perfect, could ever make him forget how he lost the real one.

"I'm sure these limb specialists are very busy these days, what with the war on," Louis said.

Crusher gave him a melancholy look. "Unfortunately, yes."

The soft hiss of a door opening drew Louis's attention to the sickbay entrance. Picard stood in the doorway and gestured for someone unseen to enter. As expected, it was his wife. Patrice's worry, joy, and relief revealed themselves in her sharp features. And right on her heels came his dear Sophie, alive and well and looking more beautiful than ever.

"Sophie!" he blurted, a surge of joy and happiness swelling within him. He almost jumped out of bed before remembering he only had one leg. "You're alive!"

"Of course I'm alive, Father," Sophie said with a soft laugh as they embraced tightly.

"Oh, my darling daughter," he said, stroking her hair, smelling her scent. "They told me you were dead, but I knew it was a lie. I knew it in my heart."

"It was, in fact, Sophie who brought to my attention the possibility you might be in trouble," Picard said.

Louis hugged Sophie again, then pulled Patrice into the embrace. He looked up at Picard. "Thank you, Jean-Luc. Thank you for this, and so much more."

"It was my pleasure, old friend." Picard smiled, then he and Crusher moved off to allow them some privacy.

Louis looked at the women in his life, then shook his head. "I feel like such an . . . ignorant, stupid man."

"Louis!" Patrice said sharply. "Whatever would make you say such a thing?"

"I thought we would be safe at the bottom of the ocean. It was our own little world down there. The war was just something going on far away, out of reach," he said, gesturing upward with a hand. "Even when we heard about the attack, it all just seemed so . . . distant. But it took the loss of a limb and hours of torture at the hands of the enemy for me to realize that no matter where the front lines are in a war, no place is ever really safe."

Patrice placed a hand on his own and squeezed tightly. "We will get through this, Louis. Together, as we always have."

"Together," Sophie whispered, adding her hand to theirs.

And in these, the worst of times, Louis had never been a happier man.

STAR TREK
DEEP SPACE NINE®

Shadowed Allies

Emily P. Bloch

"Good morning."

He was anxious. She could always tell. He wanted to hear her voice, she knew, or watch her laugh, maybe suggest a dance before the ceremony. She knew he wanted to be with the woman he loved. But Kira Nerys was exhausted.

"Mm," she replied as Odo traced his fingers through her hair, "goo moring."

She knew he was smiling now, content and calm. But, Prophets, she would have five more minutes of sleep . . . except that then his fingers made contact with the back of her neck, his molecules rearranging from Bajoran to changeling. She froze.

Oh no.

The flesh that was cool as mountain lakes, soft as Tholian silk. The flesh that woke her up to everything.

"I hate you," she murmured, and he laughed.

111

"Can I help myself from indulging in a little impatience every now and then?"

"Impatience," she purred, giving in to his electrifying touch. "No, *Constable,* it's not like you to *ever* be impatient. Been around Quark lately?"

His massage stopped and she regretted her words. She sat up. He was looking at his hand, which was becoming Bajoran again.

There was nothing to say. No, that wasn't true. But what *could* be said? There was so little time, always.

"Nerys," Odo broke in. "Let's enjoy the day."

"And forget the future?"

His eyes grew sad, but he smiled nonetheless. "We have a lot to celebrate."

Looking past him, Kira caught sight of her newly commissioned Starfleet dress uniform. The braiding caught the light of the rising suns, sending gold around the room.

"We do," she concurred. "It's not every day Bajor joins the Federation."

Kira grinned, but before she could say more, he had her in his arms, and he was bringing his lips to hers . . .

. . . and like a runabout caught in unfriendly fire, Kira's vision and body suddenly lurched. She was standing, her legs shaky. Black clouds bled into the sunlight, cacophonous screams and battle cries attacked her ears, the bed was gone, the room was gone, and so was . . .

"Odo," she half-moaned, half-called. Shutting her eyes, she felt herself falling before two strong arms caught her.

"Nerys!" a voice yelled in her ear. "*You* may be lost but we're not! Don't let them take you!"

It took a second for her to realize that the voice belonged to the arms, to . . .

"Nerys!"

Opening her eyes, Kira found herself in combat boots and resistance fatigues, a phaser rifle in her grasp. Something soft brushed against the back of her neck, and she reached behind to touch it.

"Odo? Is that—"

Her hand recoiled. It wasn't Odo. Long hair draped along her spine, tied back with a soft piece of cloth. She looked around and saw that it was night on Bajor, 2600 hours at least. A large building lay ahead of her, its fluorescent security lights casting an eerie glow around the perimeter. Suddenly, she heard footsteps, and activating her rifle, she pivoted sharply . . .

A large sword came crashing down against the one she gripped in her hands. A man with muddy, blood-encrusted features snarled as he tried to force down her thin frame.

I know this battle, too, she thought, and with a surge of might, propelled the man away from her.

I know this battle, too. . . .

The Cardassian hiding in the bushes was dead before he pulled the trigger. Kira stalked over to him and plucked a sidearm from his stiff grasp. She swung it over her shoulder and stared down at the lifeless, reptilian creature. For grim pleasure, she lifted her boot and ground it into the sharp point on his chest armor. It didn't delight her as much as she had expected.

A dark figure darted by her, tapping her on the arm.

All is clear.

Rushing after her shadowed ally, avoiding the pools of light, Kira reached the back entrance of the building. The figure had already ducked inside, and reaching the door, Kira felt a memory click into place.

"The Bajoran Institute for Science," she breathed.

An instant later, the entire area was plunged into darkness. Guards yelled out orders, and Kira dove inside, feeling her way along a winding corridor. She paused to listen for activity, pulling out her scanner for a second opinion.

Springing to life, the scanner's viewscreen cast gold shadows on the wall, and Kira soon found that a Cardassian jamming system was holding out longer than the Institute's lights. As she ran through her rudimentary hacking skills, the sound of footsteps approached once again, and she blinked out the scanner's display. Readying her weapon, hoping she wouldn't have to approximate a target in the dark, she crept closer to the sound. It stopped, and so did she.

Both parties waited, and then Kira tried the first move. Swinging her rifle into position, she was met by gruff hands easily disabling it from her. She tried unsuccessfully to shake them off before the sidearm was taken off her back. Lashing out with her fists, she failed to stop a pair of hands from grabbing her around the waist and mouth, and another pair from lifting her feet.

She was carried down the corridor, kicking the entire way, until she was released onto a grated surface. Doors hissed shut. There wasn't a sound but her own breathing. She rose as silently as she could, her hand brushing against the walls in search of a panel.

"Nerys. Don't."

An electric torch flickered to life, illuminating the face of Shakaar Edon, his features contorted by blue shadows. Another torch glowed a moment later, revealing the wild hair and eyes of Lupaza, her good friend from the resistance days. Breathing a sigh of relief, Kira felt things align . . . and yet . . . not at all.

Shakaar and Lupaza . . . deceased . . . somewhere. My clothes, my hair . . . fifteen, a time ago, a member of . . . Shakaar's resistance cell? Cardassians . . . Bajor . . .

"Sorry about the kidnapping," Shakaar said.

"I didn't think Cardies came that short, but we couldn't be too careful," Lupaza added.

"What's our status?" Kira asked, waving away explanations.

"Thanks to some engineering brilliance," Shakaar began, nodding to Lupaza.

The woman grinned. "Cardies think it's a hot summer's blackout."

"We've got emergency life-support," Shakaar started again.

"But Lupaza's rigged it so that emergency alarms are offline," Kira finished.

114

"Exactly."

"What about scanners?" Kira asked. "Mine's jammed."

"So are theirs," Lupaza drawled, and that familiar smirk spread across her face.

Shakaar pulled out a blueprint of the Institute.

"We're here," he said, pointing to a large room, "and we need to get—"

"Here," a voice grumbled, and a mug of wine was thrust into Kira's hands, which were now streaked with dried mud. A huge plain surrounded her, filled with tents. Loose material flapped in the night breezes, and distant voices could be heard singing. Her companion moved in to stoke the fire.

Antosso.

General Torrna Antosso . . . rebel leader . . . friend . . . older Bajor . . .

Antosso took a long swig from his own mug, swallowed thoughtfully, and then declared, "We are lucky. This wine will turn tomorrow."

Kira grinned despite her confusion.

"A little vinegar for our victory," she said, referring to the battle they had just won against the Lerrit Army.

"Here, here," he replied quietly. They toasted and drank heartily.

"I watched you today," he said. "I am most impressed with your tactics."

Kira stared into her mug of wine. Stars reflected in the drink, and she was filled with a sudden ease.

"I had great teachers," she said. *Rebels . . . commanders . . . symbionts.* She looked up at the sky. It was alive.

"Torrna," she asked, "what do you think of stars?"

He shifted his weight to glance skyward, and what began as a halfhearted movement became a stop in time. He seemed to consider her question deeply.

"They are seen by most as guideposts in the night. Markers for the determined traveler, help for the wayward wanderer. I see them as more than that. I see them as secrets."

"Secrets?"

"Yes." He took another swig of drink without averting his eyes. "That the universe has yet to share. They are humbling to me."

He looked at her then, and took her hand in his.

"You truly are a giant among people, *Ashla*," he said, using the nickname he'd given her. "These last few months have been very dark, and I sense more darkness will visit us. But suddenly, you appear. And you have brought the stars out."

A moment passed between them, one of profound respect. In the flickering of the campfire, Kira almost thought she saw a physical change as well. As if his round face grew leaner, his tan skin darker, his hair disappear in the dark. Even his hand felt different.

"Keep the stars burning for me, *Ashla*."

"Of course," she replied.

Relaxing, Antosso broke their grip and patted her knee.

"And find us some dinner. I'm starving."

Kira grinned, and taking up a bow and arrow, headed toward the woods, the stars bright above her.

The dark walls of the Institute felt cold against her touch. They had passed many doors, and Kira was starting to wonder if Shakaar was lost. The mission was one of top clearance and covertness; Lupaza had fooled the Cardassians, Kira kept watch, but only Shakaar knew the details. The only goal Kira had figured out so far was: Don't even let them *think* we're here.

A sense of error began to creep into her mind. Every minute was playing out as it had years ago, but her direct future was remaining cloudy, almost as if . . .

. . . as if the next few hours, possibly minutes, were unformed, as if she really was living it all for the first time. And yet, she had the recent memories as well as the far-reaching. It was as if the in-between would have no effect on the future; things would still progress as normal, even if the past outcome was changed.

She heard a rustle in the trees and aimed her bow, arrow ready. The rustling stopped, and a shaft of moonlight poured through the low tree canopy. Looking for the animal, a glittering in the distance caught her eye. Small lights seemed to dance on the ground, and then all at once became very still. They were beautiful.

Torrna can wait a little longer for food, she thought, lowering her bow. She crept slowly toward the pool of light, barely noticing the game sprinting away. The lights held her, told her to get as close as she dared. She crouched as she trod, almost considering a crawl. She did not want to frighten them away. . . .

"Here."

They had reached a door exactly like the others.

"Lupaza," Shakaar whispered, and the skillful woman wasted no time getting them inside.

Too easy, Kira felt. *Even for Lupaza.* But she said nothing.

Darting into the room, feet barely touching the ground, Shakaar activated his torch, and motioned for them to follow. Once they were all inside, the door whispered shut at Lupaza's touch.

The room was square in shape but octagonal in layout. There were eight lab stations, and as Shakaar's torch spun around, Kira saw sealed beakers, test tubes, and the occasional pod, all of which contained creatures in stasis (she hoped), different colored liquids, and what looked like dissections. There were no tools or data recorders, and each computer terminal was dark.

It's almost as if we were expected, she thought.

Shakaar proceeded to get a closer look . . .

. . . and the closer she got, the clearer she saw that the lights were reflections of Bajor's moons. The substance they reflected off of was a liquid, but it wasn't water. It didn't seep into the forest floor. It looked thick, almost gelatinous. . . .

*   *   *

117

When he stopped looking, Kira sensed Shakaar's energy change. Beads of sweat dotted his forehead as he evaluated a beaker sitting below him. It held a brownish gold liquid that seemed too unremarkable for his reaction. He dug into the satchel he carried with him, and removed a containment device. As torchlight illuminated the beaker's liquid contents, Kira could have sworn she saw it . . .

. . . shiver. The puddle was shivering. Not rippling, not evaporating, but shivering. She couldn't take her eyes off of it. It drew her closer and closer. . . .

He couldn't take his eyes off of it. It drew him closer and closer, and the liquid definitely began to move. It dipped like waves in the ocean, crawling up the sides of the glass, and then . . .

. . . it screamed.

It screamed. Alarms blared throughout the lab, and all too quickly, Kira heard the rumbling of Cardassian boots in the corridor. Whirling around, Lupaza looked as though she might shoot daggers from her mouth. Cursing in Bajoran, she dashed over to the door panel and frantically tried to shut the alarm off.

Shakaar snapped out of his trance, returning to his focused calm, and disengaged the locking mechanism on the beaker. As soon as it was able, the screaming creature soared toward him, its waves turning into gelatinous limbs and its size growing exponentially.

"Stun it!" Shakaar yelled to Kira.

Her fingers adjusted the rifle to its proper setting, but she couldn't pull the trigger. Something held her back, told her to question her leader's order.

"Nerys!" Shakaar yelled again. "Stun it!"

Lupaza hit the trigger on her own rifle. The creature instantly recoiled, its screaming cut off, and thrashed limply about. It shrank back to the size of the beaker and, finally, stopped moving. Shakaar poured the creature into the containment device and stuffed it back into his satchel.

"We're done here," he said, fixing a steely gaze at the door. Outside, Cardassian guards were attempting to undo Lupaza's handiwork.

"Now comes the fun part." There was a gleam in Shakaar's eyes and a smirk around the corners of his mouth.

"Escape?" Kira asked.

Nodding, Shakaar led them to the back of the lab, removed a wall panel, and scrambled inside. Lupaza followed, and Kira brought up the rear, barely having time to replace the panel before the Cardassians broke through the door. As she spider-crawled her way after them, Kira felt an old rise of panic in her chest, one she hadn't felt in a very long time.

What if I lose them? She paused a moment, the movement ahead echoing through the small ducts. She shook the thought away, and began repeating the mantra Lupaza had taught her. *Focus on the goal, focus on the goal.* She took off again, easily catching up. But with the panic receding, she realized that she didn't know the true goal, and judging by what she'd seen in the lab, she wasn't so sure she liked it.

Another memory surged within. Last time . . . *Last time we did this, we didn't encounter that creature. We didn't even get through the door.* Memories of failed security codes flooded her, and she remembered the Cardassian boots being louder and closer, the mission aborted.

What went right this time?

Shakaar said nothing as they made a sharp left and came to a sealed duct. Lupaza easily sliced through it with some rifle fire, and once again, they were on the move.

There had been one scream, and the puddle had grown silent again. It had almost sounded like . . . a scream of shock. As Kira sat bent over her knees, staring at its bronze color, the puddle shivered in the moonlight, keeping its oval shape, melding with itself but never dissolving.

She felt the urge to talk to it.

"Hello?"

It continued to shiver.

"Do you understand me?"

It calmed a little.

"Can you speak?"

It paused. Kira's voice became a trance-like whisper. The feelings emanating from her, all from staring at it . . .

"Do I know you?"

Then it didn't move at all . . .

Kira sat by the dinner fire, an untouched plate on her lap. Her mind was racing, images of the creature replaying again and again. Lupaza was watching her, had been since she'd faltered in the lab. Furel had joined them, and after kissing Lupaza in greeting, noticed his lover's preoccupation with their younger friend, and he, too, joined in the staring contest.

"Nerys," Lupaza said at last, breaking Kira's reverie. She looked up and saw they were the only three around the dinner fire. Lupaza's annoyed tone was an understatement when compared to the aggravation in her eyes.

"Will you let it go?" her friend asked. "I'm tired of being a watchdog."

Kira stood to throw out her uneaten food when Furel hopped up and took the plate from her.

"I'll finish this," he said with a smirk.

Kira gave a sigh. *So it's time to play "good friend, bad friend" again.*

"Furel," she groaned, tossing her fork onto what was now his plate, "I don't want to hear it." But before she could leave, he took her by the arm, leading her and her food just far enough away to appear to be out of earshot. The trick was getting old.

"Don't make 'Paza mad, Nerys. When she gets mad, she goes to sleep mad."

Kira had to laugh at the image of a sex-starved Furel getting punched in his sleep.

"I'm going to go for a walk," she announced to both of them.

"Oh, Prophets," Lupaza groaned. "You *don't* expect me to believe that."

"Nerys," Furel pleaded, his eyes wide.

Kira walked over to Lupaza, and looked just enough above her eyes to appear to be looking in them.

"It's just a walk. To blow off some steam."

Lupaza sighed, and the smirk appeared. "Get out of here," she said.

Over her shoulder, Furel mouthed a desperate "Thank you," and Kira chuckled, heading off toward the south. An idea had piqued her interest, and suspicious friends or not, they were not about to stop her. She would get to see the creature before daybreak.

It reached up to her. A small orange tentacle grew from the puddle, bending toward her hand, seeming to study the shape and texture of it. And then it began to ripple, and the smooth orange turned peach and brown. The tentacle split into five tiny ones, and little fingernails grew on the tips. It had formed her hand. Not as perfect, a little too smooth and undefined, but definitely *her* hand. It had even added the detail of dried mud. It brought its fingers to hers, and its flesh was soft and cool.

Like lakes, Kira thought, and she smiled, suddenly feeling very much at home.

Shakaar had chosen the southernmost cave for one reason: it was hell to get to the bottom. Stalagmites jutted up at every possible moment, making for slow going and high risk of injury. The treacherous parts came early on, and most intruders, if not all, usually turned back; Kira kept on. The rocks were razor sharp thanks to "enhancements" made by the more geologically minded cell members, and she watched her footing carefully.

The first time she'd attempted this descent, she'd badly injured a rib and nearly torn her right leg off. She'd hidden the bruises until they'd healed, and no one had been the wiser. No one, that is, except Shakaar. He'd assigned her to more exertive missions during that time, knowing she'd been up to no good. But she had safe bets he didn't think it'd been in the underground storage facilities.

She continued on, relatively unscathed, until she passed under a low archway and into the first of several large rooms. Here were the highly sensitive items: weapons, rescued artifacts, stolen plans. Each resistance cell had one, the highest hopes set on recovering the stolen Orbs of the Prophets. There was even a separate room for them in case those days arrived.

She was in the written artifacts section, where ancient Bajoran texts decayed around her. Her people were efficient at rescuing, but their scattered resources made it difficult to keep up with preservation. Eventually, the written gave way to the visual; mosaics, pottery, artistic renderings of ancient times. Then came a room filled with statues and sculptures, and after that, piles of dark computers.

Finally, she came to the last room. Someone was in it. Kira pressed herself against the wall and tried to make out who it was. Unsuccessful, she stole glances at the objects around her, but all were too large or elaborate to be what she was looking for.

If only I knew where he put it. . . .

"Nerys," a voice called out from the dark.

Of course.

Shakaar motioned in the distance for her to approach, and her curses and footsteps echoed off the high ceilings.

"What gave me away?" she asked, her tone wry. Shakaar didn't move, and as she approached, she saw he was holding the containment device.

"Trying to mind-meld?" she chuckled, and Shakaar's shoulders tensed.

"You think this is a *joke*?" he hissed.

"No," she answered quickly.

"I was wondering if you'd forgotten the meaning of that word."

"I'm sorry I disrespected you."

"Be honest, Nerys. You enjoyed it a little. You had an actual *adventure* for once."

He cocked his head, and she could make out a frustrated expression on his face.

"You need to be *trained,* Nerys, *before* you can move on to bigger things. You've got the fire, but you need to know how to handle the gun first."

"I understand," she muttered, burning with embarrassment.

A pause, and then Shakaar replied, "Apology accepted."

After another pause, Kira felt the mood lighten and ventured forward.

"So," she began. "What is it?"

"A changeling," he replied. "A shape-shifter."

Kira felt her breath die inside her.

A shape-sh—

"A shape-shifter?" she asked. "What . . . I mean, aren't they—?"

"Untrustworthy?" Shakaar answered. "A threat? Precisely why we've stolen one from the heart of Cardassian scientists. They've got a Bajoran man working with it, but I don't have to remind you the worth of that these days. Do you know what they'd be capable of with one of these?"

Kira felt uneasy. There were clouds in her mind, evasive maneuvers from the truth.

"I . . . I . . ." she said, trying to find something useful, something that would snap her out of the haze. "I can't begin to imagine."

"Well, don't worry," he said, his voice changing, sounding . . . wrong. He laid the device beside him. "We've just made sure you don't have to."

He stood up and began leading her out of the room.

"Shakaar? Shakaar, maybe we shouldn't keep it here."

"Don't worry," he said. "It's not going anywhere."

His grip was unusually strong, and a burst of pain shot through her arm.

"Shakaar . . . you're hurting me!" she cried, trying to release herself from his grip, but he grabbed her other arm and spun her around. She winced as her heel dug into the rocks at a sharp angle.

"No one is to go near it," he declared. His eyes had a nasty gleam to them, plotting and vengeful. He raised his arms as if to push her, and she took the opportunity to spring away from him, snatching up the containment device.

I know the goal.

"*Nerys!*" Shakaar yelled. "Put that *down*! You saw what it did in the lab! You'll never get anywhere if you don't follow orders!"

"*These* are the right orders!" she replied, and finding the release button, she pressed down hard.

"No!" he yelled, more with anguish than anger. The changeling sprang to life, lunging at Shakaar as a huge ring of fire. Kira ran close to the flames, yelling, "Wait! Don't hurt him!"

The fire raged, but she could feel no heat. Shakaar was unharmed, cowering in the middle of the ring and shaking. Kira searched for the absent eyes of the changeling, for some distinct place within the fire where she could address it.

"Please don't hurt him," she said. "He just doesn't know."

She barely registered the snapping tree branch or the shadow that darkened her view, but she did feel the two arms that grabbed her and tossed her into the bushes. And she definitely heard the screams of the creature. A huge shadow darted in and out of the moonlight, and as she scrambled up, she made out the form of Antosso producing a hunting knife. She threw herself upon him, trying to stop his hand.

"Nerys, I know what I'm doing!"

"No!" she cried.

"This creature is evil, sent from Lerritt sorcerers to murder us in the night!"

"No, Torrna!" she yelled again, and snapped back his hand, fracturing his wrist. The knife dropped to the ground. He howled in pain, dropping to his knees. He looked up at her through sweat-drenched hair and crisscrossing shadows, his eyes filled with disbelief.

"Nerys," he gasped, "you betray me?"

"No, Torrna," she replied.

"It comes from evil magic, I tell you!"

"No, he doesn't."

"Then from where?"

"From another time."

"Another—?" Antosso shook his head, nursing his hand. "*Ashla,* you've grown confused. There is no other time but now."

"No, Torrna," she said, approaching the creature again, slowly, until it had stopped shivering. "From another time. And for some reason, it's arrived too soon."

"*Ashla,* perhaps the wine has taken you, but this creature is *not natural.* Do *not* approach it! It needs antagonism to survive."

Kira sat next to the creature.

"No," she replied, shaking her head, "it needs no such thing."

While his breathing remained heavy, and he occasionally groaned from his injury, Antosso made no more protests. So Kira grew silent, and continued to stare at the creature. Its surface was smooth and calm. She began to see her reflection. . . .

The moons set and the suns rose, and the whole forest was filled with light. Her reflection was clear now, as perfect as a mirror. She leaned back at last to rest, her spine meeting the soft cushion of a pilot's chair. She relished the silence. . . .

A humming began. . . .

The runabout seemed to be nervously distracting itself, but its tune had no rhythm, no form. Kira stared into her reflection, past the polite, compliant navigational controls. Through the smooth surface and impeccable Federation Standard font, her eyes looked terrible. Lifting her head, she saw Odo sitting in the copilot's seat, one knee propped up as he stared out the viewscreen.

"You look comfortable," she said, "sitting that way."

He was calm, almost smiling.

"It's . . . meditative. I find my molecules flow easier."

She grinned in spite of the tears behind her eyes.

"I've never heard you use that word before."

He turned his head, looking at her.

"Which?" he asked.

"Meditative."

"Ah. I've finally found a use for it."

They stayed in each other's eyes for a long moment. Then back to meditations and reflections. The stars elongated through warp speed.

"I've never seen space this empty," Odo said. "Are you sure we entered the right coordinates?"

A few concerned bleeps from the navigational display.

"Yes," Kira replied. She was finding it hard to see through her tears, which dotted her red militia uniform. She fiercely brushed them away.

"Well," he said slowly, "we'll get there eventually."

After a moment's pause, he said, "We should go exploring. Now that the war is over."

He was blurry in her vision. She pushed more tears away, desperate to memorize every detail of him.

"When?" she asked, almost angry.

His face changed, drooping as if he were going to regenerate.

"Someday," he whispered. Then he added, "I guess it's easier to plan things when the future is more defined."

The tears fell independently, despite the furious signals Kira was sending to her brain for them to cease. Odo turned to her, and got up from his chair.

"Kira," he said.

My formal *name? Now?*

"Kira Nerys," a heartbeat repeated. Reaching for her phaser, Kira found none available. She glanced incredulously at her empty holster, and then readied her body for physical combat. There was nothing but a thick landscape of white around her.

A heartbeat? Since when does a heartbeat—

"Kira Nerys," it said again. She paced, spun, but found no source for the voice.

"I'm Kira Nerys! What do you want?"

"To understand."

The heartbeat began to take form, the voice growing slightly feminine in quality, less deep and echoing.

"Understand what?" Kira asked.

"Why basics apply to the complicated."

Kira waited for a further explanation, and then replied, "You're gonna have to break that down for me. I never was much of a poet."

"I know," the heartbeat, now clearly a voice, said. "It is your limitation."

Wisps of orange began to filter down from the infinite above, like ashy molecules taking shape. Kira stood still, trying to see what was forming, when her gut began to turn, her brain began to process, and just as she saw too late, hands grabbed her raised fists before she could attack.

"It's okay, Nerys. She only has questions."

"Benjamin?"

He released her hands.

"Have you brought me here?"

He nodded.

"Then I'm with the Prophets."

A Sisko smile.

"Think of it as a halfway point."

"But . . . how could you . . . why is *she* here?"

Sisko looked beyond, in the direction of their companion.

"She's finally learning what lies beyond treaty signatures and warp drives. It's perfectly safe. She can't do a thing."

He paused, and the father in him filled his demeanor.

"I'm trying to give her a push in the right direction. For reform. For a dialogue. And all she could talk about . . . was you."

"Me?"

Sisko grinned.

"Yes. For some reason, she ties the whole beginning of things to you."

Kira looked at the other being, and then back to Benjamin.

"But . . . how can I trust her?"

"By trusting me." And he was gone.

But as long as she breathed Kira would not trust *her*. There, looking all too familiar in her chaotic patience, was the female shape-shifter, Leader of the Founders.

"I don't know how you can pull this apart," a voice yelled, "when it's been so *good*, so *passionate*, *finally*, after all this *time*." It was Kira's.

She turned and saw herself pacing furiously. Standing at a cautious distance from this second Kira was Odo, who looked calm despite her fury.

"Now," the second Kira continued, "*now* you're giving us up for a species who *abandoned* you, killed millions, and never shed a tear?"

"*My* species," Odo answered softly, and the second Kira let out a scream of frustration, thrusting her fists toward the sky.

It was the argument they'd had after the war's end, when they'd returned to Deep Space 9 and the peace treaty had been signed—the argument about Odo's decision to leave the Alpha Quadrant and rejoin the Great Link. He walked over to the second Kira, holding out his arms.

"Nerys—"

But she ducked away, whipping up the white atmosphere as she stalked.

"You can't just smooth this over, Odo! It's not an arrest on the Promenade we're disagreeing about or a con from Quark we don't know how to catch! This is about *us*!"

She looked at him with her fiercest eyes.

"How many times have we almost *died* in the past four years? How many more since we've been together? Was none of that enough to draw us closer?"

Odo approached slowly, his features still calm, decisions unchanged.

"Nerys," he said softly, "I don't know how to make you understand. I've exhausted all my reasons. If I leave my people to their own recovery, the possibility of insurgence is too great. You know as well as I that a peace treaty doesn't mean a thing if enough people take action against it. When the Occupation of Bajor ended, you left your home to make sure the Cardassians didn't return."

"*My* people weren't the perpetrators and murderers," the second Kira retorted.

"I know," Odo sighed. "But I'm sure you were torn about leaving your people, your friends."

Kira mouthed the next words along with herself, never forgetting them for a second.

"I didn't have enough in my life that was *worth* staying for."

The scene grew quiet.

"You didn't respect his choice," the female shape-shifter said. "But that is in line with your limitations."

Kira took a deep breath before turning to face the Founder.

"What exactly do you classify as my 'limitations'?"

"Because you are unable to become another being, you are unable to know their innermost thoughts."

"But *you* don't have the ability to read minds," Kira said.

"It is in becoming a being's movements and shapes that we find all we need to know."

"So, if you saw, for example, birds flying," Kira asked, "and they were all the same kind, you're saying you would know for *certain* what they were all thinking?"

"Animal solids do not express emotions as their humanoid counterparts do," the Female Shapeshifter answered.

"True," Kira replied, "but then you can never *really* know how to become *every* kind of bird."

The Founder shook her head.

"You are thinking from a humanoid solid point of view. I cannot expect you to fully understand our ways. This is merely confirming all I knew before."

"You wanted this dialogue," Kira retorted, and then stopped herself. *He left me, technically, for* her. *Maybe it's time to find out why.*

"Why don't you try seeing things from *my* point of view?" Kira offered. "Use my 'limitations.' Without shifting, become me."

The Founder's gaze hardened, and she turned to the frozen other Kira.

"I will use this scene as an example," she began.

"No," Kira interrupted. "Use *me*. She's a memory."

"Very well," the Founder replied, looking her over. "You are not confident. You see signs of weakness within you, and that is why you treat every conflict with an extreme case of anger."

Kira narrowed her eyes. *Tread softly, Nerys, softly. For Benjamin. For Odo. For* me.

"That was true in the past, but my edges have smoothed somewhat."

"I see a panic within you," the Founder continued, as though she hadn't heard her, "a deep fear that you cannot handle all that is laid before you. Because you cannot shift, you cannot change your pace or find other methods of exhausting your anger and grief."

"I do not *live* in a world of anger and grief," Kira replied. "I receive a lot of it, but I move on. That's what humanoids do."

"You do indeed receive much of it," the Founder said, "but you, Kira Nerys, Humanoid Solid, do not move on. You harbor all that befalls you until you snap like the weakest tree branch. You push away everyone who could step up to catch your fall. And you can never admit that at times, you could use someone to catch you."

"And *you*," Kira hissed, "are afraid. You're terrified that all your centuries of 'exploration,' domination, and murder have occurred in vain. That with the signing of the peace treaty, everything you've sought to 'correct' has come slamming back at you. Your people were persecuted, but so were mine! *We* don't strive for dominion of the galaxy."

The Founder grew quiet. Her approximations of eyes cut deep into Kira's.

"You know," she finally said, "I always wondered what it would be like to be a solid."

She shimmered, and red flooded up her torso until she had taken on Kira's form.

"I wondered: Is it jealousy that causes a solid to persecute a changeling?"

She shimmered again, taking on the form of Sisko.

"Desires unfulfilled?"

And then again she shimmered, becoming Odo.

"Or is it the simple frustration of not understanding how the universe works?"

She stood as close as Odo would have. The features were so real, the voice so precise. The Founder held out a hand to Kira's cheek, but Kira grabbed the limb before it could touch her.

"Why does he mean so much to you?" the Founder asked in Odo's voice.

And then, before Kira could answer, realization dawned in the changeling's eyes. Had the Founder been in her usual form, Kira might have missed it. But on Odo, it was clear as day.

"Without him," the Founder said, "we are incomplete. Because he is a part of us."

"And without him," Kira whispered, "*I* am incomplete."

"Because he is a part of you."

"And I of him."

The Founder shimmered back into her humanoid self, and Kira released her arm.

"Sisko feels all of this will reform me. I enlisted his aid in putting you through the tests: the ancient Bajor, the occupation raid, the caves. He helped to cloud your mind, and you reacted without fear or hatred upon meeting undeveloped changelings."

"I never hurt a creature unless it gives me a reason."

"You killed the Cardassian hiding in the bushes," the Founder replied.

"He was going to kill *me*."

"And you were willing to kill game for Antosso."

"Hunger necessitates taking from nature every so often."

"And would you kill a changeling if you had the need?" the Founder asked, suddenly growing angry.

"If it was not in its true form," Kira said carefully, "and appeared to be of necessity, *and* if I did not know its true form, then, yes, I would have done with it as I had seen fit."

"So deception is your excuse," the Founder hissed. "If something does not show its true form to you from the beginning, you cast aside its worth. Just as you cast aside Odo's worth when he decided to rejoin the Great Link when it 'did not fit'!"

"Did Odo's choosing to live with solids fit into *your* plan?" Kira shot back.

"No," the Founder replied. "But we did not harm him when he made his choice. He gave us no reason to."

"No, he didn't," Kira said, "until you manipulated the 'right' reasons out of him."

The Founder craned her head and glanced at the white landscape around her.

"This is the most I've seen in over a year," she said.

"And it's more than you should see."

The Founder sighed in resignation.

"I never understood why Odo loved you more than his own people. I see it, but I do not understand it. If 'reformed' is what I'm meant to be, I feel I should understand his need for *you,* the catalyst. But it appears I still can't."

"No," Kira replied. "I guess you can't."

The Founder started to walk away. Sisko was once again at Kira's side.

"Perhaps," the changeling said, "one day I shall."

The Founder began to fade into the white clouds, but turned back before she was completely gone.

"Promise me one thing," she said. "Promise me that you will listen to Odo. And that you won't expect him to live within your limitations."

"I never do," Kira said. Benjamin's hand was upon her shoulder, light and warm.

And then she was gone.

"How much do you know about me, Odo?"
"More than you probably realize."
Conversations from the past danced in Kira's head.

The buttons wouldn't push themselves. She stared into her reflection, past the polite, compliant navigational controls.

All she had to do was leave.

The sea of changelings was asleep now, healing, exhausted.

All she had to do was leave.

"Good morning."
He was anxious. She could always tell.

Living on the Edge of Existence

Gerri Leen

Colors flash, their hues more intense than Sisko could have taken in before. Blue is no longer just blue, but something more alive, more energetic even than the blue of the sky on Bajor, when the sun hangs in a cloudless expanse over the green hills Sisko fell in love with. Bluer than the sea in the Gulf of Mexico, when he took his father's boat out far beyond the shore to where the green and turquoise waters gave way to cerulean. Bluer than his father's old indigo shirt. Bluer than the cornflower dress of Molly O'Brien's favorite doll.

If he were to think about red or yellow or green, they'd be bigger and more majestic too.

They'd also be empty. For there is nothing in these colors that he has not put there. Nothing that the Prophets did not give him. There is no sunrise, no rising moon in the midnight sky. There are no roses, no violets, no daisies. There is no life, no movement, no . . . nothing. There is nothing here.

"We are here. The Sisko is here." The Prophets have chosen to appear as Quark.

Sisko used to try to figure out why they chose the avatars they did. He's given up.

When he appeared to Kasidy, when he told her he would return, he thought he understood. He thought he knew his path.

That was before he rested. That was before he spent much time— or non-time—with the Prophets, with Sarah, the alien that had inhabited the young human woman who gave birth to him. He thought he understood her, when she caught him up and brought him to the Temple. He thought he understood everything.

He understood nothing. And now, he thinks he understands even less.

He stares at the Quark Prophet, counting it a small victory that the Quark figure no longer blurs or shifts position or disappears entirely under such scrutiny. But his corner of the wormhole or the Celestial Temple—he calls it both things and the Prophets never correct him—begins to spin as he turns his concentration to studying the alien. Sisko's world is stable only as long as he works to make it so. Except . . . there is no world. His world is a construct, one he creates to help himself understand his surroundings. One he needs to keep from feeling as if he will throw up. Linear existence may be limiting, but at least it doesn't bring on constant nausea.

When he was first here, when he thought he understood his place, he felt a part of things. But the longer he is here, the more he realizes he does not understand. He wanted to be part of it, he believed he was. It was new and overwhelming. Fresh and exciting to be part of this—to be a god of sorts.

Then he realized he wasn't a god. He wasn't even a demigod. And he may never be. When his mother pulled him from the fire caves, he felt just as the warriors in the myths his stepmother read to him must have felt. Brave fighters caught up by Valkyries, carried to Valhalla where they belong, where they would rest and make merry.

And he is resting. That he is doing. But there is no one to make merry with. He is not sure this place has even seen merry. And in his current mood, he feels a long way from merry—and a long way from belonging. He has never become part of the "we" that is the gestalt of the Celestial Temple. He is always the outsider. Always "the Sisko."

"Linear existence is no longer your path." The Quark Prophet has turned into a Kira Prophet. Sisko has never seen the Prophets' true form. They dress up to pass their wisdom on and become Kira, his father, Odo, Ezri, sometimes even dear Jadzia. They pretend. They take on. They do it because he is providing the template for their interaction.

He knows this. He is one of them, even if he is still apart.

"The Sisko holds himself away from us." Kira sounds more listless than accusing. The one thing the Prophets cannot seem to do is get mad, get aroused in any way. They are so damned passive that at times he wants to scream at them.

He keeps waiting for their calm to infect him, keeps waiting for the day when he wakes up from a sleep he no longer needs but can't seem to give up and finds that he doesn't miss his old life and friends. That he doesn't feel longing and anger and a nagging annoyance that he is stuck here and still hasn't figured the place out.

Or how to leave it.

He's not trapped . . . exactly. Underneath the other emotions is the suspicion that he is where he is supposed to be. His mother's influence, no doubt. Sarah's legacy to him—a half-breed without knowing it until his life was almost over. Part Cajun cook, part impenetrable alien.

"The Sisko should let go of what was." Kira's face changes into that of his mother.

"How can it be what was, if there is no past for you?" Sisko loves to catch them up in the endless illogic of living all times at once.

"We have no past, but you still cling to yours." There is disappointment in Sarah's voice. She shows up whenever he pushes too hard. He does not know if the Sarah standing before him is just one alien or all of them—or if that has any meaning. He has not yet reached a full understanding of their nature. He has not yet reached even a partial understanding of their nature. As far as their nature goes, he knows squat.

He thought he understood them. He remembers the certainty he felt when he brought Kasidy to him and told her of his path. He thought he was in control then, but now he suspects that the Prophets were really at the helm because he has tried to bring Kasidy back, to find Jake and talk to him. He has never succeeded.

He was a fool.

And yet . . . he is not sure he would do it any differently. It is hard. He wants to leave, but he thinks he should stay.

"The Sisko is troubled." Long ago, his mother used to call him other names. She no longer does. She refers to him as the others do.

He thinks she does it to distance him. To help him fit in, by giving him less of herself to hold on to. He believes she thinks he will open himself to the rest of the Prophets—to the experience that is the whole—if she takes away the part that he still wants to believe is his mother.

"I am not upset." It is not a lie. He is not upset. He changed the word so that his denial would be true. To be upset would require energy he does not wish to squander. But Sarah is right. He is troubled. Troubled takes far less energy than upset.

Sarah looks out of place in his world, where the backdrop is the Promenade. He sits now in Quark's bar, and she stands off to the side. The place looks like Quark's bar, but it lacks the sounds and smells of Quark's. There are no crowds yelling as the dabo girls take their latinum. There is no fiery Bajoran *hasperat* ordered from the replicator, or pungent Ferengi tube grubs. His version of Quark's bar is like a painting done all around and below and above him. Sight with no sound and little fury, signifying everything to him. It may not be real, but it's his.

He used to imagine his briefing room. Then ops. But they were even less real somehow. Perhaps because there were never any ships going past his viewports. Because the people around him in ops made no noise and had no substance, and if he imagined the place empty, it felt even more unreal.

He thinks it's good to try to create these things. Thinks it's good to exercise his will and imagination, although the Prophets never comment when he has changed the scenery. If this is a triumph, it must be a minuscule one in their eyes. He's considering trying to create Bajor next. The pretty spot with the fragrant grass that won't have any odor here, where he was going to build his house—the house he will never get to live in. He planned to hang wind chimes on the balcony; he'll never hear them here.

Sarah sighs. She always has a little more immediacy in her actions, a little more emotion in her voice, than the other Prophets. Purely a matter of degree though—she is nobody's firecracker. Even at her most energized, she is like the two old sisters who lived around the corner from his father's restaurant. They sat up in their rooms, windows and the door to the balcony thrown open, as if there was no other way to cool their place but the old-fashioned one. They occasionally called down to the street for one of their grandkids to bring them some sweet tea. When evening came, they moved their chairs a few feet out to the balcony, fanning themselves and talking quietly as if they'd been holding their words back to avoid overdoing it during the heat of the day.

It's hard to imagine Sarah living in New Orleans, bearing his father a child. Sisko is that child, yet she is a mystery to him. He came from her; even if most of his life he thought his stepmother was his real mother. All Sarah did was give birth to him and then abandon him to his fate, to the battle he was fated to wage in her name, in all the Prophets' names.

Only most of the Prophets don't have names. She probably doesn't have one either, except that he can only think of her as Sarah and she has never told him not to. And even if she were to tell him to stop calling her that, he wouldn't stop thinking of her that way.

Another Prophet shows up, and this time it's Curzon who is the avatar. Sisko sees something in Sarah's face he's never seen before from a Prophet—surprise. He's not sure why she is surprised. Curzon has shown up before. Not often, but enough times that seeing him isn't any kind of shock.

This Curzon looks different though. He's younger than expected; Sisko generally remembers him older, wiser. Grayer. The Curzon Prophet looks around and begins to smile.

Sisko is not sure he's ever seen a Prophet smile that way. "Old man?"

"Benjamin, Benjamin." The force of Sisko's memory of Curzon seems to overwhelm even a wormhole alien. It has been a long time—although Sisko has no idea how long he's spent in this non-linear cuckoo clock—since he was called anything other than "the Sisko."

Sarah disappears with another strange look at the Curzon Prophet, who is walking around the promenade construct. Sisko can feel energy leaking off him, and it is surprisingly comforting to realize that the energy is actually emotion—trust the old dog to instill fun even in a place where fun has no meaning.

Another alien shows up, materializing with a strange shimmer that seems to leave a taste in Sisko's mouth—like crisp lemonade on a hot day, or the snap of a dill pickle, the kind you get to pick out from a barrel. Sisko misses food. He wants some gumbo and jambalaya, blackened catfish and crawfish etouffee, or maybe just a bowl of cool sweet cherries taken from the chiller. He wants to pry open oysters and suck them down with an ice-cold beer. Or sit in the bleachers of a stadium with Jake and gobble up hot dogs with ketchup and mustard and sweet relish. He likes the buns toasted and the franks to have the blackened lines from the grill on them.

There is no food in the Celestial Temple. Sisko can't bear the idea of trying to manifest a stadium, a diamond and players and the silent crowd around him. It would be too real, yet it wouldn't be real enough.

Besides, he can't bear to watch a game without Jake-O sitting next to him, cheering the players on—sometimes cheering for the opposing team just to get Sisko's goat. He misses Jake. How old is his son now? Is he even born yet? Or is he long dead? Has Sisko, living in no time, passed Jake and all of his grandchildren by?

Since he arrived, the Prophets have never appeared to him as Kasidy or Jake. He suddenly wonders why.

"The Sisko makes himself unhappy." The other alien has chosen to appear as Kai Winn. She shows up infrequently. Sisko wonders what the Prophets really think of her, the leader of their religion who aligned herself with the Pah-wraiths, then recanted at the last minute.

She tried. It wasn't much, but it was better than nothing. Especially when she may have turned the tide so that Sisko could stop Dukat. It wasn't much, Winn's effort. Very little, very late. But it was enough.

The Winn Prophet frowns at him. It is a perfect rendition of the real Winn's favorite expression. "The Sisko is not content."

"The Sisko is bored out of his skull." It seems heresy to say that. But it's true. He wants to go back to Kasidy. But he can't because she's alive, and, while he used to believe he was going to see her again, the Prophets don't speak of his return anymore. He suspects that he died in the fire caves battling the enemy. He is not sure, because there was a moment in the fight with Dukat when Sisko thought he felt something fill him. Energy and support and a rush of something so powerful he worried that he might explode. Then he was here. This place that is his reward. A reward for which he had high hopes but that has turned out to be nothing but an endless parade of old friends and enemies, and a bad case of the bed-spins.

"The Sisko should rest."

Again there is the strange pop-tingle in the back of his mouth—does he even have a mouth? He imagines himself as still human and so he creates hands and feet. He can move his tongue around his mouth, sliding it over teeth and pushing with it at the insides of his cheek. But does he live? If he could fathom it, could he become pure energy?

And what did the Prophet mean he should rest? He's been resting. For years. Or minutes. He's not sure which.

The Winn Prophet walks over to the Curzon Prophet. She smiles—the ingratiating and utterly false smile of the worst kai to ever hold office. Sisko almost laughs as Curzon gives her a grin and a quick pinch on the rear when she turns to walk back to Sisko. The Winn Prophet either does not feel it, or knows better than to acknowledge that she does.

Is Sisko making the Curzon Prophet act this way? Is it a sign of growing dementia or a sign that he is finally learning to control his surroundings? Sisko worries it is the former, because all too often he feels as if he's slowly losing his mind. Maybe he isn't bored. Maybe he's just insane. He's not sure how he will know if he's gone mad. And it's just possible that he has to be a little bit crazy to survive in the Celestial Temple.

He tries to forget Curzon and Kai Winn and to look out past the limits of the Temple. He wants to see Kasidy, to see if the baby has been born yet. To see Jake and Ezri and Kira and all the other living friends he left behind. But he has trouble moving his perception beyond the Temple, and by the time he has strengthened an image enough to see, he has lost the time line again.

He is not sure if he is looking at a Bajor of the past, before the Cardassian occupation, or of the future. The civilization is peaceful, looks warp capable. The planet is green and beautiful, just like he remembers. "I was going to retire there," he says.

"Real pretty place. Tough break for you, Benjamin." Curzon stands next to him, and Sisko is surprised that he is still in that form. The Prophets usually change quickly, as if they have a short attention span or are simply following the meanderings of Sisko's mind. He turns to look at his friend, who suddenly appears to shimmer in a different way than the Prophets do.

The prophets, even in human, Trill, or Bajoran form, seem to glow along the edges. They always appear superimposed upon whatever backdrop he provides. But Curzon shimmers from within.

As if he has an energy source inside him. As if he is the realest thing to ever show up in the Temple.

Sisko wonders if he shimmers the same way. Or does he glow from the perimeter, standing apart from the world the same way the Prophets do?

"You're thinking too hard. You always do that." Curzon grins again, and it is a wicked expression. One that Sisko is relatively sure the Prophets could not make if the fate of the entire quadrant rested on it.

"Old man, is that really you?"

"In the not-so-corporeal flesh. I've been trying to find you for a while, took me some time to get in." Curzon looks around the limited extent of the Celestial Temple—as temples go, it's lacking. "So, what do you do for fun around here?"

Sisko turns to the Winn Prophet. She is staring at Curzon, as if she cannot decide what to do.

"This is the Curzon," Sisko says by way of introductions. He's not sure how to introduce his hostess.

There is no disdain in the Winn Prophet's expression. But it's not welcoming either. "This being is not a part of our existence."

"My loss, I'm sure." Curzon winks at him, and Sisko laughs out loud.

The sound pushes at the edges of Sisko's Promenade construct. His whole world seems to shudder, and Sarah appears, Winn's features morphing into his mother's more pleasing ones. She strides more forcefully than Winn did. Moves with growing power.

Sisko suddenly knows all the aliens are in this avatar.

"What is your purpose?" they ask his friend.

Curzon shrugs. "Just visiting. I hope that's not against your policy?"

"You do not have corporeal integrity."

"I'm afraid that happens when you die." He looks over at Sisko. "Have you seen Jadzia? I mean the real Jadzia, not one you imagine here. I've been waiting, but she doesn't come."

Sisko grins. "I think she's in *Sto-Vo-Kor*."

If he didn't believe his old friend was really there, the put-out look on Curzon's face would convince him—no wormhole alien can manage that much annoyance. Sisko grabs Curzon, pulling him into a hug. As he wraps his arms around his friend, he is suddenly with Curzon, back on Risa, experiencing the Trill's last moments.

As deaths go, expiring in the arms of Arandis wasn't bad.

But then neither was going out in the arms of the Prophets, knowing that the Pah-wraiths would not escape the fire caves. It was worth his life.

"She was something, huh?" Curzon says, not seeming surprised that Sisko experienced the memory, even if such empathy wasn't an ability Sisko had ever displayed when they knew each other.

Sisko smiles. "She was indeed. Death by *jamaharon* is the way to go."

"Except that I thought I had at least ten more years," Curzon says, his smile fading into a scowl. "I might have, if I'd stayed away from Risa." He makes a face that clearly says he can't imagine avoiding that lovely place—or the beautiful woman who did him in.

"At least you got to die an old man. I wasn't that lucky."

"The Sisko is mistaken," Sarah says, and her voice is unexpected. Sisko almost forgot she was there.

"He often is." Curzon winks at her, getting nothing back.

"How am I mistaken?" Sisko wants to touch his mother, wants to feel her soft skin under his hand, wants to feel her love—*did* she ever love him? Does she consider him her son or only a tool she created to fight the Pah-wraiths? She used to manifest warmth, but was it only to get him to do what she wanted?

"You are the Emissary." A Kira Prophet appears, and there is a tug as if power is being pulled into her from the very fabric of the Temple.

Sisko again tastes the combination of sharp and sour. He realizes that the rest of the Prophets have moved to the Kira construct, leaving the Sarah form to the Prophet he considers his mother.

"You are the Sisko," Sarah says, as if that explains everything.

"But are you a Sisko?"

Curzon is watching their exchange with interest but very little comprehension. He is probably used to that. Diplomacy is often a matter of digging through the surface behavior until you comprehend the nuances, and Sisko knows Curzon is the consummate diplomat. Death probably hasn't changed that.

"I am what I am." Sarah frowns, and Sisko suspects it is because she used the first person. That is unusual—Curzon's bad influence maybe?

Curzon seems to be fading. He closes his eyes, as if he is concentrating on staying with Sisko, but he continues to lose substance. "Looks like I'm headed home, old friend."

"I want to go with you." Sisko turns to Sarah. "I want to go with the Curzon."

"The Sisko's place is here."

Sisko is filled with a crushing disappointment. Then he feels something else. Something he never expected. The same distress emanating from Sarah. Does his desire to leave cause her pain?

"He is a prisoner then?" Curzon asks, his voice little more than a whisper.

"The Sisko is not a prisoner." The Kira Prophet steps forward as Curzon disappears.

"I cannot leave. I cannot go where I want. How is that not being a prisoner?" Sisko has never let out the anger and disappointment he feels about being cheated of his life with Kasidy and Jake and his unknown son or daughter. He has never railed against the loneliness or the dreadful feeling of having nothing to do. He feels as if he is a shuttle pilot in a perpetual holding pattern, going round and round with no perceivable end to the torment.

Only it's not torment. It's just . . . not what he expected.

"I expected the afterlife to be more like life." He sounds like a petulant child. And he feels like one. A child trying his best to understand the grown-up world around him and the incomprehensible adults that fill it.

"The Sisko has been resting. Life has tired the Sisko. The Sisko must rest more." The Kira Prophet has a new note in her voice. Is it kindness?

"I'm tired of resting." He looks over at Sarah. "I don't like being dead."

Sarah smiles at him, and the look is full of the love he has wondered if she holds for him. "The Sisko is not dead. Resting is not dying. And this is not the afterlife."

He realizes the Promenade has disappeared, and the landscape that appears before him cannot possibly be from his memory or his imagination. He doesn't even have words for the colors and shapes he sees, has never experienced the smells and sounds that assault him until he closes his eyes, and puts his hand over his ears, and breathes through his mouth in defense against the onslaught.

Then he stops doing that, because he cannot bear to not experience the truth. He opens himself up, and the sensory barrage subsides enough for him to begin to take it all in. His mind strives to come up with comparisons in the human need to take something new and make it familiar. That sound, isn't it like the crashing of the waves on the shore? That smell, couldn't it be lamb cooking in sage and garlic and a little mustard? That shape in the distance, doesn't it look a little like Everest peeking through the clouds?

He knows that these things that surround him—almost inhabit him—are nothing like the memories he links them with. But it makes him feel better to try to label them, to try to fit them into his limited experience.

"The Sisko sees things clearly. Or more so than before." Sarah touches him, and the feeling of her hand on his cheek is like coming home. "For some, my son, resting is never easy."

"Mother?"

"I am your mother. And I am not." She cups his chin, her eyes shining brightly—very brightly, she is turning into pure energy. Her voice is all around him as she says, "You are of us. And you are apart."

"I am the Sisko," he says, understanding for the first time that it is not just his father's name and his name and Jake's name. It is a title. An identifier. He is *the* Sisko. One of them. And apart.

He is unique. "I am not dead?"

"The Sisko is not dead." The Kira Prophet has retained her shape—apparently not all of his hosts feel he is ready for the ambiguity his mother presents him. "The Sisko is resting. When the Sisko is finished resting, the Sisko will begin learning."

"You are still needed," the Sarah energy says to him. "You have a path to walk."

He realizes she did not call him the Sisko. He suspects she may have been talking directly to his mind.

"I'm finished resting."

"You are not. But it is good that you think you are. Because there is much to learn." Sarah pulls her shape back around her, and the Promenade replaces the unknowable.

Sisko feels a pang.

"The Sisko will see our home again when you have learned how to find it for yourself." The Kira Prophet surprises him with a touch, her hand gently settling on his forehead.

He has an image, a feeling, a snatch of memory, a snippet of song. He feels the way he did when he was obsessed with finding B'hala, the way he did when he went after the Orb of the Emissary. He knows he can find the world he just saw.

But not now. He can feel the gap between what he knows and what he will have to know to find his mother's true home. He can feel how tired he is, underneath his resentment and boredom and longing for those he loves.

The Kira Prophet disappears, and his mother takes his arm and strolls with him on the promenade. She breathes softly, and he realizes that even such a casually human act is a gift to him.

"Will your friend find us again?" she asks.

Sisko cannot remember the Prophets ever asking him a question that was not rhetorical. It amuses him that Curzon is the one to mystify them. He is not surprised; if anyone can stump godlike aliens, it's Curzon Dax.

"I wouldn't put it past him." Sisko wonders if Jadzia will be moved enough to leave *Sto-Vo-Kor* and come searching for him. He thinks she probably will not. If Curzon had the pleasures of the

Klingon afterlife in front of him, he might not have gotten bored enough to leave the Trill underworld to look for his old friend. "You're sure I'm not dead?"

"You are not dead." Her hand tightens on him, a gesture of support, of comfort.

Then perhaps Kasidy is not lost to him? And he'll hold his new child someday, and once again hug Jake close to him to show his oldest that he will always be special in his heart. Sisko's life beckons, and joy erupts inside him, and he can feel a note of caution coming from his mother, even though she is back in human form.

"I should not wish for my life back?" he asks.

"You wish for what was yours; that is understandable. But do not dwell on what you do not have. You will stay with us until you are ready to leave. Do not let longing for what was blind you to what can be."

"Spoken like a true prophet."

"It is truth. For the Sisko." She smiles and it is a mysterious smile. It holds secrets and powers that he will probably get only the smallest taste of. Then she leans up and kisses his cheek, her lips lingering on his skin, soft and dry and giving off the faintest tingle.

He feels infused with energy.

She pulls away. "And it is a gift. From a mother to her son."

The Last Tree on Ferenginar: A Ferengi Fable From the Future

Mike McDevitt

Open your ears, children, and hear a tale from your uncle Grix. Long, long ago, probably more than a thousand fiscal cycles hence, the Ferengi were a great people. I mean, we're a great people now, too, but back then we were *really* something. Ferengi are beings of beauty, brains, and strength. Where many species must blunder along at imposing, unwieldy heights, Ferengi are perfectly suited to lope sneakily in where they're not wanted. No species can boast ears larger than their widespread hands but the Ferengi. Ferengi mouths sport rows of crooked, needle-sharp teeth to take a bite out of the competition. The piercing, beady eyes of a Ferengi can spot a missing wallet or dropped coin at great distances. Their noble faces are twisted in a perpetual sneer of virtue. The rough, orange hands of a Ferengi sport handsome green fingernails; the better to perpetually grasp at the things they desire. And a Ferengi's desire would encompass the galaxy. Ferengi love to acquire, live to acquire, and love the word "acquire."

Now, in this long ago time, there was a wise, just, and exceedingly rich Ferengi Grand Nagus named Rom. He was tall in stature, cunning of mind, and had the lobes for business. This has also been said of his predecessor, the Grand Nagus Zek, and while it was literally true in Zek's case, it was also true of Rom because Zek had said so. Loudly. And repeatedly. While throwing things.

Rom had ascended to the nagul throne earlier that drizzly season amid much rejoicing over the abrupt and *not at all* worrisome transition to democracy and equal rights for females. It was said of Rom in the ancient datafiles that his approval rating was ninety-eight percent. This may even have been true: there were a lot of females and also a lot of weirdos and perverts who *liked* letting women wear clothes and have opinions. So, in those turbulent times, it was a blessing and a delight to have a strong nagus like Rom. A Ferengi's Ferengi. His former career had been deobstructing waste extractors on a hu-mon space station, and before that he worked in the food service industry.

Rom had a young, beautiful, and exceedingly rich wife named Leeta. Some say more *exotic* than beautiful. I mean, they say her ears were *tiny,* simply minute, even wee. They weren't much bigger than her nose, which was sort of cute. Her skin was the color of fresh milk (not the beautiful brownish orange of a fresh bog), she had *hair* all over her head (not smooth and shiny like a normal female), and her teeth were blunt and pearly white (not in the least bit charmingly chaotic). Still, she was apparently quite a looker otherwise. Suffice it to say that the Nagus considered her a national treasure and, indeed, had her insured for 280 bars of latinum. Her former profession was dabo girl in a gaming establishment. As many of you children may have heard, a *lita* is a unit of currency on the planet Bajor, where Leeta happened to be from. I merely point it out because it is considered as ironically amusing as when Throk the Pusillanimous of the Ninth Era married an Earth banker whose name was Penny. Or Glint the Rotund who took as mate a Klingon accountant named D'Arsik. Actually this sort of thing happens a lot, but it is not really the point of this story.

Rom and Leeta spent many hours of their day on giant golden thrones, holding court before various merchants, businessmen, nobles, luminaries, potentates, and bigwigs. Rom and Leeta heard requests, passed judgments, granted favors, and generally tried to keep awake.

One dreary day, they granted an audience to the head lumberjack and CEO of Slash-and-Burn Unlimited: Ogger the Logger, son of Bogger.

Ogger was tall in stature, cunning of mind, and he had the lobes for business. I know I said all of those things about the nagus, too, but if you want to get technical about it, Ogger had them more. Ten times more. Maybe thirty. And he wanted to be sure everybody knew about it. He wore a big headskirt behind his big ears. He pretended to have killed the big furry animal whose pelt he sported in some big furry battle. He had a big plasma whip holstered in his big belt as a symbol of his long service in the Marauders. He even had big purple and orange boots on his big feet, because you know what they say about Ferengi with big feet—they stomp when they enter a room.

Ogger had one request and he made it very loudly. Ogger loved to sink the huge, vibrating blade of his sonic chainsaw into young virgin wood. He had completed the paperwork required, waded through the extensive bureaucracy, and having been stymied for days by naysayers and buck-passers, he appealed directly to the nagus.

Ogger wanted permission to cut down the last tree on the planet. It was on government land and apparently Rom owned the rights to it.

Rom got most of the way through the sentence "Request granted" before Leeta interrupted him and whispered in his ear. Apparently she didn't think much of the idea.

Rom got most of the way through the sentence "Request denied" before Ogger interrupted him and offered Rom a vast sum of money.

Leeta quickly turned it down.

Ogger offered an even more outrageous sum and company stock as well.

Leeta turned it down again.

Ogger offered an absolutely exorbitant amount of cash, stock, and bonds, and also offered to purchase Leeta.

Rom said he needed time to think about it and that Ogger was to come back the following week.

Ogger pointedly asked Rom whether his female had forgotten the Second Rule of Acquisition.

Rom took a guess and incorrectly quoted it as "Waste not lest ye be wasted?"

Ogger sneered and correctly bellowed the Second Rule was "Money is everything!" loud enough to rattle the Tiburonian sorax sconces in the throne room. He angrily vowed to return with his Board of Underlings in one week's time. He closed with the observation that Rom seemed to be a wise man who knew which side his bread was buttered on, and a man who enjoyed retaining the physical ability to butter his own bread with an undamaged hand. Then he slammed the extremely heavy door behind him.

Leeta and Rom sent everyone else away early that day.

Leeta's people, the Bajorans, are known for their deeply held spiritual beliefs and devotion to nature. Leeta was not your typical Bajoran. Maybe Bajoran tradition didn't approve of her former career as hostess in a gambling den, or of her interspecies marriage. I wouldn't know, I never read about Bajoran traditions.

But although Leeta was nontraditional for a Bajoran, she was absolutely bizarre as a Ferengi. Although she had a normal, healthy liking for pretty baubles, fine silks, and shiny trinkets, she also had an inexplicable heathen respect for intangibles like *generosity*. This generally made everyone uncomfortable and caused great gaping lulls in conversation with other Ferengi females.

Leeta was a charter member of several activist groups. They included the Society to Save the Spotted Spoog (she thought they were cute), the Females for Atmosphere Restoration Today (desperately seeking a better acronym for a serious worldwide catastrophe), and CAIT: the Committee to Abolish Itchy Tweed. Tweed and Sons Clothiers had been forced by government mandate to add female apparel to their line last year, and in a fairly bald attempt to keep women naked, the entire feminine line was unbearably uncomfortable. Leeta had started the committee to protest this, and was terribly confused when her meetings were crashed by a large number of feline tourists from the planet Cait, who came mostly to complain about the rain.

Suffice it to say Leeta had strong opinions about things when she thought them through. Strong opinions that would not have been tolerated from a female on Ferenginar less than a handful of years earlier. Strong opinions that her husband never went on record as ignoring, possibly because her husband tried to avoid going on record at all, and possibly because he was rumored to base his strong opinions on the opinions of whoever was standing closest to him and talking the loudest.

Leeta was very loud when she wanted to be.

She was loud that night with Rom in their sumptuous bed. (This is strictly conjecture, entirely off the record. If they had recording devices in their royal bedroom, such devices were strictly for personal use.) Leeta demanded to know how the Ferengi had managed to cut down every tree on their whole planet.

Rom yawned and told her of the great big cutting machines, such as the SkumCo Lumber Vanquisher 20XJ-7, which are fifty *mog* across. He told her his grandfather had driven one, which consumed over thirteen agrosectors a day. He told her of the time he'd been a little tyke and his Grawmpee had hoisted him up, set him on the seat, and let him drive it all day long. Rom went on to tell Leeta how Grawmpee had spent that same day napping in the back seat and complaining about how lazy Rom's father was. Then Rom waxed rhapsodic about how, for supper, his groogie had made Hupyrian corn bread, and gree worm pie, and nice, juicy tube grubs.

Leeta patiently interjected that she had meant why *every* tree, and didn't anybody want to keep some around to look at?

Rom pointed out that you could look at them in holosuites if you want to. He added that his brother had written a holosuite program about a beautiful verdant green forest.

Leeta was dubious because she knew Rom's brother. She said as much.

Rom told her it was a program based on old Earth myths, and that the trees all turned into nyads and dryads and nymphs, and they stripped off their leaves to frolic around.

Leeta coughed loudly, asked him not to explain any more. She begged him to keep the last tree safe. She also suggested he get some new ones, too. She cajoled and suggested that if he brought in some Bajoran trees, flowers, and grass, she might go outside and frolic in them with him.

She winked broadly at him and told him she'd even wear that dress he liked.

Rom blinked back and asked if she meant no dress whatsoever.

Leeta blushed and said, no, the other one.

They got very little sleep that night and the next day Leeta realized they hadn't settled the matter of the tree, either.

So the next night, in bed, Leeta told Rom of a book she had read by a centuries-dead *hu-mon* named Henry. In the book, he'd talked a lot about birds and flowers and trees. He said things about living in the woods in harmony with nature, and to Leeta this had sounded good. Henry had gone on to indicate that modern life was too complicated and one should try to "simplify, simplify" in order to find the good inside oneself. All the sorts of things you'd expect from a *hu-mon*.

Rom tried to understand her for some reason. Obviously, he couldn't quite manage it. "Simplify" is the opposite of the very heart of "acquire." But, though confused, Rom told Leeta he loved her and wouldn't trade her on the black market for her weight in pure latinum.

This is an example of how Rom was a very strange nagus indeed. A mass of pure latinum equivalent in weight to Leeta would have been enough to buy a holosuite with Leeta's exact likeness and personality built in, with enough left over to buy most of the continent they lived on.

Perhaps he said it to flatter her, since he must have known no Ferengi would ever have traded with him.

In any case, Rom was soon snoring peacefully but Leeta still couldn't rest. She decided to call in outside consultants.

A few days later, the consultants flew in from Risa. (One day your uncle Grix will tell you a story about Risa and an all-female parrises squares team he met there one summer. When you're older.)

Among the strange choices Leeta made over this stupid tree, she was wise enough to call in the former Grand Nagus and the sharpest mind in history, now slightly past his prime—Zek.

Zek traveled with the aged female Ishka, who'd earned derision and fame in equal measure as the mother of Ferengi feminism and the mother (or Moogie, as he called her) of Rom. Some records from the period indicate Ishka wore the pants in that family, but most of the pictures show her in a dress. History can be confusing.

Leeta related her concerns about the tree the very instant her relatives arrived at the palace. She pointed out that something should be done before Ogger returned at the end of the week. She was met with blank stares.

Ishka tended to take Leeta's side on issues of female rights, but she was still a Ferengi. Ishka told Leeta she should let the man have his tree and charge him handsomely for the privilege of cutting it down.

Leeta was shocked. She thought Ishka had understood the purpose of the call and asked her why she'd flown all the way out there if not to save the tree.

Ishka responded that she'd come to see her little Rommie-Wommie and went on to ask her little pookie whether Leeta'd been feeding him enough and didn't he look less pudgy?

Leeta turned to Zek and politely pled her case to him. She cajoled and begged and appealed to his sense of decency.

The old Ferengi groused that she should go make him a pie.

Leeta knew she needed more help.

Now, the Nagus Rom had a brother . . . who for some reason liked to live on a space station many light-years away from his family and homeworld. His name was Quark, he ran a bar, and he was not happy to take a call from Leeta at his place of business. He paid little attention and ended the call as quickly as possible.

Unfortunately for Quark, the space station's security chief was also Quark's erstwhile lover. Her name was Ro Laren, and she spent much of her time putting her ridged Bajoran nose in other people's business. Ro asked who'd called.

Quark grumbled something about subspace solicitors.

Ro pointed out that the call had come from the Nagul Palace on Ferenginar. She thought that it had been Quark's sister-in-law, and asked him why did he always try to lie to her?

Quark sighed and muttered something about Leeta wanting him to help save the last tree.

Ro's brow furrowed with concern as she asked whether things were really that bad on Ferenginar.

Quark snapped that he didn't think there was anything bad about it at all, that nobody needed forests. He continued by grumbling that the last forest he'd been in was crawling with Jem'Hadar soldiers. And bugs. And that he hated nature.

Ro assured him that she loved nature and that Quark loved her.

Quark said "Feh."

Ro told him to pack his bags because they were off to his old swamping grounds.

Quark said "Double feh" and packed his bags.

Quark said "Double feh" because it is an old Ferengi saying that means "I don't understand women but I enjoy having them around so much that I do things I don't really want to do." I think all species have some such saying.

When Quark and Ro arrived on Ferenginar, rain-drenched and warp-lagged, Leeta rushed off her throne to embrace Ro warmly, which made Ro uncomfortable, then politely said hello to Quark from several feet away. Quark had bought the cheapest possible travel tickets, and so on the overcrowded transport no less than two babies and a Bringloidi salesman had vomited on him.

Quark greeted his relatives with all the glee of an American Earth man having a tax audit from the IRS.

He had no desire to help anyone do anything, least of all his wealthy extended family. He was not paying attention as Ishka fawned over Ro, asking her how she liked sleeping with someone so obscenely ugly as her son. Ishka continued the conversation by mentioning how odd that both her sons ended up with Bajorans for mates, not that there was anything *wrong* with that. He was not paying attention as Leeta explained that he had been granted a position in the government. That Quark, without realizing it, was part of a great history. That nine hundred years earlier, the Inestimable Flook had been appointed Minister of Deforestry. That a hundred years earlier Skink the Terrifier had been assigned to the same office under the new, more politically correct, title Minister of Forestry. That ten years ago the Unlikely Gurp had been forced to accept the call as Minister of Forest. Or that last week, in absentia, the role now known as Minister of Tree had fallen to Quark the Barkeep.

Quark paid no attention to this, or to Zek's somnolent calls for his snuff box. He zoned out rather a lot as everyone else debated what to tell Ogger the next day when he returned, and in the midst of the debate no one came up with a plan at all.

The next day, Rom's extended family was on hand to assist him when Ogger returned with his Board of Underlings, but Ogger had had all week long to plan what he would say and had his proposal rewritten by wiser heads the night before.

In a big bass voice Ogger asked, hypothetically, whether Rom would ask a Ferengi to stop strip mining dilithium just because warp drives damage space and dilithium is a nonrenewable resource. He pointed out that the Ferengi culture was based on dilithium. Dilithium-regulated reactions powered their homes. Dilithium resin was a key ingredient in every hovercar, computer, device, machine, utensil, children's toy, adult's toy, headskirt, and money belt on the planet. Ogger also mentioned that most of his friends rubbed dilithium on their food.

Leeta countered that it was very dangerous to base a whole society on one thing.

Ogger waved a mighty hand and speculated that when the dilithium ran out they would find something else. Perhaps whatever they used centuries ago to heat homes and build toys.

His vice-assistant, Orax, whispered that it had been fossil fuels.

Ogger cuffed Orax and yelled that there weren't any fossil fuels left.

Orax quietly supposed they could use wood.

Ogger nodded sagely and repeated the idea that they'd simply use wood and wouldn't the nagus stop being silly and let him cut the tree down.

Leeta asked who would even *buy* the tree's paper products in a computerized society where eighty percent of the populace was functionally illiterate and totally concerned with the acquisition of liquid latinum in pressed gold bars.

Ogger pointed out that the Good Book (the Rules of Acquisition) was printed on paper and bound in wood. That stumped her for a moment, so he went on to brag of the success of paper clothes. He boasted that they were the latest fad and that everyone loved them.

Leeta shouted that *nobody* loved them because they got soggy in the perpetual Ferenginar rains and then disintegrated and left you naked. She blushingly added that no one would fool *her* twice.

Rom piped up that they wouldn't fool him either . . . three times anyway.

Ogger pressed on, telling them that the tree could also be used to create cardboard boxes for take-out meals since environmentalists like Leeta were always saying that Tox-Foam containers were toxic.

Leeta said that was because they *were*.

Ogger said "Meh, meh, meh."

Ogger said "Meh, meh, meh" because this is an old Ferengi saying that means, "I'm not one for listening to environmentalists."

Zek woke himself long enough to shout that Ogger had better

just shut up and obey the duly appointed nagus if he wanted to get into the Divine Treasury when he died.

Ogger then threatened to buy himself into office. His underlings all made a great deal of supportive noises. That's what underlings are for.

Leeta shouted, rather stridently, that money didn't run a democracy.

Ogger and his entourage laughed for thirty-five hours. One of the sub-nagul undersecretaries required major surgery for a ruptured spleen.

When he could speak again, Ogger bellowed an ultimatum.

Either the tree or the nagus would be gone at the end of three days.

Rom was understandably concerned, and when Ogger tromped out of the throne room Rom begged his relatives to find a way to help. He begged until it was night, then he begged most of the night. Quark got very little sleep, and he got very cross with Rom.

Rom begged throughout the second day, too. Didn't they have any ideas? Zek had negotiated with the intractable Breen in his younger days. Ishka had overthrown the whole social order of their planet. Ro knew every weapon and combat technique in the Alpha Quadrant. Leeta was . . . loyal and beautiful. And Quark? Well, secretly, Quark wished he could be back on Deep Space 9, maybe putting the finishing touches on his holo-novel. (It was nearly done, and was entitled *Vulcan Love Slave IV: T'Ris in Orion Bondage.*)

On the second night, Rom begged harder. Ishka proposed killing Ogger. Ro seconded. Leeta vetoed them. Zek demanded pie.

And Quark came up with The Plan. The Plan hinged upon the notion that tough guys like Ogger are a superstitious and cowardly lot.

Later that night, Ogger was lounging alone in his extremely big bed in the huge bedroom of his giant house. Light drizzle spattered on his tremendously large wooden windowsill. Ogger looked out the window at Rom's palace, and looked forward to cutting down a tree or a nagus in the morning. He was eating a delicious grilled *cheeb* sandwich. Ogger loved the rush of warm juice between his teeth from a nice grilled *cheeb* bug eaten in bed.

His ritual was suddenly interrupted by the rattling sound of worthless metal chains. Ogger shouted into the darkness to demand to know who was there. He threatened to release his trained attack spoogs. Then he flicked on his bedside light.

There, large and wrinkly as life, was the Grand Nagus Zek. Dead.

Zek was draped in chains and appeared colorless and translucent. His ghostly form passed through the bedpost and approached quite near to the frightened Ogger.

Zek claimed, with little preamble, that he had died during the night and was even now trapped between the Divine Treasury and the Vault of Eternal Destitution for the little known and seldom punished sin of genocide to no profit. He urged Ogger to avoid the same fate by withdrawing his petition, and warned that tree spirits would visit him in the night.

Ogger shrieked, admitting that he was secretly terrified of the number three.

Zek enunciated that *tree* spirits were in the offing.

Ogger breathed a relieved thanks to the gods of wealth.

Zek admitted that there *were* three of them.

Ogger shrieked again.

Zek's ancient, wizened, and liver-spotted face cackled sharply and faded away into the shadows.

Ogger quickly ran to his viewphone and dialed his therapist, his local priest, and his moogie. His therapist charged him nine strips of latinum to listen to his tale for nine minutes. His local priest offered to come to Ogger's house and perform the mystic money-meld. (The money-meld is an ancient ritual where the priest grasps key points of one's wallet and intones "My money to your money, your cash to my cash. Our money is now one." Whereupon the worthy evangelist would run away very fast and leave one's wallet empty.) Ogger's moogie got angry with him for calling so late at night and threatened to take away his allowance. Since she hadn't paid him a single latinum slip in years, this threat did not worry Ogger.

What did worry Ogger was the appearance of the first of the tree spirits, that is, until he got a good look.

The first tree spirit was as ephemeral as Zek had been, but the resemblance to a withered old man ended there. The first tree spirit reminded Ogger strongly of Leeta, only with green skin, scanty veils, and a fetching outfit of leaves and a bark-like cloth that barely covered her voluptuous body.

The first tree spirit declared her calling was to represent the Trees of the Spring Season, when the monsoons were light and cheerful. She asked whether her nubile trunk and willowy limbs inspired a love of trees within his breast.

Ogger assured the spirit that she inspired something, all right.

The Leeta-like dryad huffed slightly in an alluring way and explained carefully the wondrous life cycle of a tree, from promising seed to young sapling, bursting with sweet juices. How, the spirit begged, could he want to topple such a tree to the ground and despoil it?

Ogger made an unprintable offer to the spirit.

The spirit vanished rather quickly.

When the second spirit manifested, Ogger thought he could get to like this sort of thing. The second tree spirit looked like a Bajoran woman in minimal clothing as well: orange and gold, with perky berries and strategically placed branches.

The second tree spirit seemed a little less enthusiastic than the first. She told him in a perfunctory sort of way that her calling was to represent the Trees of the Fall Season when the deluge pours heavily on the plants and people alike.

Ogger said it was obvious who she was, as she was less voluptuous and juicy than the previous tree.

The dryad gritted her teeth and narrowed her eyes, assuring him that *if* that was the case it was only because Ferengi of limited vision were *sucking* her resources dry. And he'd better watch out, as there was a third spirit yet to appear. The second tree spirit hiked up her flowing root-tendril skirts and stomped away, vanishing through the wall.

Ogger began to chew his fingernails in anticipation. What could the third spirit be, if these lovelies were the preshow?

The third tree spirit to appear was Quark.

Ogger shrieked.

The Quark-like tree had drooping, bare brown branches, gray-brown moss patches, and appeared quite surly and bad-tempered. It snapped briskly that it was supposed to represent the Trees of the Winter Season, when the rain stays mainly on the plain or something.

Ogger didn't hear a word, as he was too busy shrieking at the hideous sight of Quark in a tree outfit in his bed. The Quark-tree sighed and said "Beware!" in a sarcastic tone of voice, then snapped his twig-fingers and disappeared.

Ogger regained his breath and composure in the silence of the next several minutes. This had been quite a harrowing experience for him and he was ready to renounce his evil ways.

Just then, the Quark-tree reappeared.

Ogger flailed in his fright, begged the spirit to go away and torment him no more, and then noticed that the ghostly image dissipated when he passed his hand through it much the same way a Yridian 77X hologram imager did.

The Quark-image explained that he was a holographic projection and that the whole stupid thing was a stupid sham for his stupid brother's benefit. Quark asked if he could call the logger Og. Then, without pausing, asked Og if he'd like to make some real money and if he hated the nagus as much as he, Quark, did.

Ogger said he thought Rom was okay, generally. . . .

Quark shouted that Rom was an idiot who didn't deserve to keep breathing every day, or sitting on the throne that should have been his, and demanded to know if Ogger was getting especially tired of this hoopla over some rotted plant? Then he told Ogger what the pair of them could do about it.

Quark had a plan, children. You see, every government has a secret government within it somewhere to do the dirty work. The Cardassian Obsidian Order, the Romulan Tal Shiar, the hu-mon Section 31. The nagul government had a deadly clan of shadowy Ferengi in black trained in surveillance, secrecy, and covert operations. They were known as The Ear. They kept their existence so secret that even Rom didn't know about them, and they didn't want Rom to know about them because they didn't like Rom very much. Zek could've told Rom about them before he retired, but the truth is Zek had forgotten. None but a select few could have found The Ear, and fewer still could have left their presence again alive.

Quark found them behind the last door of the last hall in the lowest, darkest level of the Nagul Palace. It was the first place he looked.

There was a disruptor pistol in the crook of his neck the instant he sauntered in the door, and a deep, muffled voice asking how he'd found them.

Quark intimated that he knew a guy whose cousin's girlfriend knew a guy.

The voice told him to never mind and that he wasn't leaving alive.

Quark said if they killed the nagus's beloved older brother, they'd answer to all Ferenginar.

The voice told him he wasn't beloved and that Rom had tried (albeit ineptly) to kill Quark eight years before, or had Quark forgotten?

Quark assured the evil agent that true brothers let bygones be bygones.

The evil agent asked why Quark had come.

Quark said he needed them to kill his brother tomorrow on a hunting trip.

The agent agreed without any haggling, certain that Quark would pay handsomely once he inherited the throne, and set his assassins the task of sending Rom to the Divine Treasury.

The following morning, Rom was happy to be surrounded by his loving, faithful family and happily whistling "The Dark, Dank Muck of Home" when Ogger showed up and ruined his mood.

Ogger announced that in the night he'd been visited by ominous nocturnal specters that had made ominous statements in their ominous way and seemed to be telling him he shouldn't try to profit from the final tree.

Rom asked if Ogger would now withdraw his request to kill the last tree.

Ogger said he certainly would not.

Rom prodded tentatively whether Ogger wasn't afraid of the specters.

Ogger said he wouldn't bow down to spectral interest groups, then proposed that Rom accompany him on an innocent hunting trip over by the last tree this morning. Ogger insisted on a contest of skill in which the first of them to kill a giant, bloated swamp slug would have his way in the matter.

Rom's throat felt suddenly very dry and he turned to his family for help. None of them seemed to be looking at him except Quark. There was a funny glint in Quark's eye and he told Rom it sounded like a fine idea for a morning execution . . . *excursion.*

So it was that Rom found himself with a crossbow in hand, peering into the morning fog, ankle deep in the sludge of Slug Swamp. Ishka had dressed him warmly and Leeta had kissed him good-bye. Now he was feeling uneasy, uncertain, and unbelievably out of his depth. Rom had trouble remembering which boot went on which foot some days, and he was pretty sure he couldn't work a crossbow.

Ogger, on the other hand, taught archery at the Ogger College of Archery and Plasma Whippery. If there was one thing Ogger loved more than whipping, eating, or cutting down trees, it was sinking his arrow shaft into the flank of a powerful oily slug.

Quark, in hip waders at Rom's side, waited for his plan to turn a profit.

A docile group of mammoth slugs, ten meters long and seven meters high, grazed quietly on swamp algae and occasionally bleated a sluggish call to the chill morning air. A cold rain fell lightly, but incessantly, on slugs and hunters alike, and also on the spindly form of the sickly last tree.

Rom stood under it and wondered if it had been worth all the worry. He also wondered how quickly he would lose this contest.

Rom asked Ogger if he wouldn't rather play chess for the tree, instead. Ogger laughed, slapping Quark on the back until Quark laughed, too. Then Ogger pointed out that Rom was very far away from any witnesses, standing between two men who wished him harm: one of whom had a rapid-fire crossbow, the other of whom had hired a band of assassins to take Rom's life.

Rom looked in shock at Quark, feeling very, very dismayed, and a little bit hurt. Quark shrugged and reminded him that business was business, and hadn't *he* tried to shove Quark out an airlock during the week when Quark had been nagus eight years before?

Rom said he thought bygones would be bygones.

Ogger wondered aloud where Quark's assassins had gotten to.

Lieutenant Ro Laren emerged from her concealment behind a mother slug. She quickly tossed an unconscious black-clad assassin into the muck, leveled a phaser gun at Ogger, and told him he was under arrest for treason under Article Nine of the Profit Margin.

You see, children, Lieutenant Ro had followed the hunting party surreptitiously and neutralized the assassins of the Ear one by one, or a couple at a time. Earlier that morning, she had had the *directors* of that shadowy cabal arrested as well. If only there'd been some trees around, the Ear would've had some cover while sneaking up to attack the nagus. As it was, Ro had seen them coming a mile away. She had taken them out with a dizzying combination of Federation judo, Bajoran martial-arts prowess, and general kicks and pokes. She also had a phaser gun.

Ogger turned an angry glare on Quark. He accused Quark of setting the whole thing up. Quark admitted it wholeheartedly, and displayed the recording device he had concealed in his vest pocket. It implicated both the Ear and Ogger in an assassination plot.

Quark had double-crossed both the Ear *and* Ogger! Wasn't that clever of him, children?

Ogger didn't think it was so clever, and in response he lunged toward Rom and fired all three arrows from his crossbow.

Ro blasted one of them out of the air with her phaser. Right out of the air, kiddies!

Quark tried to jump out of the way and tripped over his hip waders for his trouble. One of the arrows meant for his brother hit him in the arm.

Rom fell over backwards into the swamp, with the third arrow sticking straight up from the center of his chest.

As Ro and Quark rushed to Rom's side, Ogger laughed loudly and triumphantly. He laughed so loudly, in fact, that he disturbed the mother swamp slug, who extended a three-meter-wide pseudopod and knocked Ogger off his feet and pinned him in the muck.

Ogger realized his predicament would very soon lead to his death. He would very soon be drowning or consumed by the slug, and his thoughts raced with desperation. As one normally does when faced with death, he wondered briefly if he'd wasted his life.

Suddenly, the mother slug sensed something in the air and extruded a smaller pseudopod in the direction of the last tree. She changed direction then, moving her weight off of Ogger and toward the sweet, succulent moss on the trunk of the tree. As she grazed, the logger realized the irony that his life had been saved by the tree he wanted to destroy. He raised himself out of the sludge and started to say that he would turn over a new leaf that very day.

He had a tenth of a second to open his mouth before Ro sent him unconscious with a judo chop.

Rom, of course, was completely all right. His moogie had knitted his sweater of duranium mesh, stronger than any steel arrowhead. Quark complained loudly that he, Quark, was bleeding to death, but in reality, his sweater was duranium mesh, too. When palace security arrived, they found the culprits tied to the last tree and Quark carving his name into the trunk just above Ro's.

After his arrest, Ogger probably went to prison. Maybe at Tarahong Detention, maybe at Flunkatraz. Or maybe he bought off the judge. But supposing he went to jail, he was probably there long enough to learn his lesson. Unless he bought the warden. Or paid his debt to society in some other very literal and lucrative way. But one thing is certain: he never bothered Rom again. Unless he did somehow.

Rom thanked his brother Quark with a nice, big hug and a nice, small bribe.

Ro Laren kissed Quark and remarked on how uncharacteristically brave and generous he'd been in helping his brother save his government and life without being paid in advance.

Quark suggested she might find a way to repay him once they returned home to his bed. He also assured everyone quite shrilly that he had *never* had a desire to be nagus and that he preferred to stay far away from the limelight, the adulation, and the constant assassination attempts.

Leeta finally managed to save the environment. How? She baked old Zek a pie that was so delicious that he agreed to personally finance the mass cloning of the tree.

And Ishka made Zek stick to his agreement once he was sober again.

So, Rom and his family lived happily and more importantly, profitably ever after.

Did Rom save the tree? Yes, you mewling tykes. Yes, he did. Ferengi children enjoyed the use of the tree and its clones for quite a long time, sitting contentedly in its shade, putting its leaves in their ears, climbing it with demented childlike glee, and what-have-you.

Did Rom's forty-third great-grandchild (also named Rom) save the tree, when the exact same situation came up again quite a long time later?

What do *you* think?

Ever seen any trees yourself?

*   *   *

The moral of this story, children, is that nothing lasts forever; that's why you have to grab as much as you can for yourself while the grabbing is good.

(Proceeds from the sale of this story, minus a small commission, go to Prix Oxygen Imports, Ltd. "Making 'Life' Possible since 10,432.")

The Tribbles' *Pagh*

Ryan M. Williams

Kira Nerys felt that tightening, sinking feeling in her gut that told
her she was in deep trouble. She'd felt it in the resistance when raids
on the Cardassians had gone wrong. But this had to be the worst.
Kira folded her arms awkwardly over her swollen belly, and refused
to take the fleshy ball of fur that First Minister Shakaar was holding.

"How bad is it?"

Shakaar's face was grave. "They've already spread throughout
the Tozhat Province. And I'm not sure we've contained them. If they
get to Dahkur or Rakantha, well, the Cardassian Occupation was
bad, but these . . ."

"Tribbles."

"These tribbles could be worse."

Kira swore softly under her breath and turned around. Something
squeaked and she jumped back from the tribble she had just stepped
on. She looked up at what had been a rich field of salom grass. It
was now a lumpy field of tribbles and dirt. Fires around the houses

sent black smoke into the sky as the farmers attempted to keep the tribbles back from their gardens. Kira tapped her combadge.

"Kira to DS9."

Captain Benjamin Sisko recognized the look on his first officer's face when she reached his office. "How bad is it?"

Kira took a deep breath. "Bad. Dax says that there are at least a hundred thousand tribbles in the Tozhat Province. If they reproduce unchecked we're looking at over a million within twenty-four hours. Trillions within a week."

"I remember," Sisko said gravely. "I thought the station quarantine was effective."

Kira gave a short barking laugh. "It wasn't. Shakaar has instituted a quarantine of Tozhat. We're trying to track down anyone who entered the province in the last two days. All shipments of salom grass are being screened for tribbles. Elimination is a problem. We could use some industrial disposal units."

Sisko straightened. "You're planning to disintegrate living tribbles?"

"They're a disease. It's either us or them. If we don't get a handle on this, people will be starving before winter! The entire planetary biosphere could collapse!"

Sisko held up a hand. "It hasn't gotten that bad yet."

"Not yet, but we have to act. Now."

"We will. I'll see what I can do about getting some Federation disposal units but it won't be easy. I think you should talk to Doctor Bashir. Maybe he can help develop something to inhibit the tribbles' reproduction."

Kira nodded. "I'll get on it."

As Kira descended from Sisko's office, Worf and Dax approached her.

"Well?" Dax raised an eyebrow.

"He's going to do what he can to get us disposal units."

"Wide-beam phaser sweeps should be used to clean areas infected with these vermin," Worf said.

Kira smiled. "You won't get any argument from me. For now we're supposed to focus on containment."

Doctor Julian Bashir was in the infirmary when Kira arrived. He was holding a brown-and-white tribble and was absently stroking it while he looked at a console screen. He smiled as she approached.

"Major. Glad to see you."

"What are you doing with that?"

Julian looked at the tribble. "Oh? Gladys?"

"Gladys? You named it?"

Julian blushed slightly. "Well, yes."

Kira shook her head. "Do you have any ideas that can help us?"

Julian brightened. "As a matter of fact I do. The Federation has done studies on tribble reproduction. A trader created a variety that didn't reproduce as rapidly but unfortunately they grew in size."

"I want something to stop them from breeding, Doctor."

Julian laughed nervously. "Well, that is the challenge. Tribbles are asexual. They form internal buds which develop into baby tribbles. And those buds start budding on their own before they are even born. Essentially, they're born pregnant."

"I don't care. We have to find something to stop them."

"The Klingons are reported to have developed a tribble predator, a glommer—"

Kira shook her head. "Predators aren't the answer. We need to eliminate them!"

"I'll see what I can do." Julian gently placed Gladys into a container and activated his scanners.

Kira watched him for a second and then left. She stalked through the promenade without paying much attention to anyone around her. By the Prophets, hadn't Bajor suffered enough already? The Occupation. Civil unrest. The Dominion breathing down their necks. The Klingons! They didn't deserve this. Kira took a deep breath. It wasn't the fault of the Prophets that someone had ignored the prohibition to take tribbles to Bajor. After the *Defiant*'s trip to the past the tribbles had been all over the station. O'Brien claimed he had had less trouble from Cardassian voles.

"Major?"

Kira refocused her attention on her surroundings. A vedek she couldn't place stood in front of her. Even with the vedek robes he looked no more than a child. She couldn't help but smile at his fresh-faced sincerity.

"Yes. You are?"

"Vedek Tola."

"Tola. I know that name from somewhere."

Vedek Tola inclined his head slightly. "My father was killed at Gallitep."

The name snapped into place. The memories of what had happened at Gallitep came back. "That's right. He saved a dozen or more Bajorans that day. He was a brave man."

"Yes," Vedek Tola said. "And now I'm here to ask you to be brave."

Kira blinked. "You want me to be brave?"

Vedek Tola nodded. "The Prophets have shown me. The tribbles must be preserved. Their *pagh* is part of Bajor."

"The tribbles' *pagh*?"

"Yes."

"They are simple, mindless, eating machines! They're a plague! Do you realize that the damage they cause takes food away from our people?"

"I realize this," Vedek Tola said. "But you must find a way to preserve them."

She'd heard enough. She stabbed a finger in his direction. "I don't know why you think the Prophets want the tribbles on Bajor. And I don't care! When the Federation waste processors arrive I'll be right there shoveling the tribbles in myself!"

Kira turned around and left Vedek Tola standing there. She ignored the stares and whispers. Sisko had better have an update on the waste processors.

*   *   *

"What do you mean we don't get the units?" Kira didn't care if her voice carried down into ops.

Sisko gestured with the hand currently holding his absurd baseball. "I'm sorry, Major. The Federation is sending experts to help with the situation but they can not condone pitching thousands of helpless creatures into a matter-energy disposal unit. Particularly since the tribbles were driven to extinction by the Klingons."

"That's absurd! You sound like Vedek Tola. If Bajorans were sick they wouldn't refuse medical treatments in order to protect the helpless bacteria!"

"Vedek Tola?"

Kira shook his head. "You don't want to know."

Sisko straightened in his chair and grinned. "Now I'm curious."

"He's young, inexperienced."

"And?"

Kira made a noise and paced in front of the desk. She forced a laugh. "He actually said that he believes the Prophets want the tribbles on Bajor. That their *pagh* is tied to ours somehow."

"The tribbles' *pagh*?" A smile twitched at the corners of Sisko's mouth.

"Captain! We need to find a way to deal with these things."

"I agree. I've ordered Dax and Worf to take the *Shenandoah* and the *Rio Grande* to Bajor. They'll do transporter sweeps of the Tozhat Province. The tribbles will be transferred to a cargo ship in orbit."

Kira nodded. "It won't be enough. They can't transport many on their own. If they can even lock onto their life signs—"

"Why don't you give them a hand? Maybe you can free up some Bajoran shuttles. You'll need to coordinate with any available cargo ships."

Kira nodded. "Yes, sir."

Six hours later she felt like her eyes were full of sand. Her latest *raktajino* was nearly empty. They had a half-dozen shuttles, the two Starfleet runabouts, and four cargo carriers working together but had only managed to clear a quarter of the Tozhat Province of tribbles. The only thing that kept the cleared areas from being re-infected was the fact that the tribbles hadn't left anything behind to eat. Nearly a third of the tribbles beamed off the surface had already died of starvation. If they continued to breed unchecked they'd strip the planet bare and leave Bajor buried in dead tribbles. She thought of Vedek Tola and shook her head. How he could think—

The comm system chimed.

"Kira here."

"Doctor Bashir. I think I may have a way to help with our tribble trouble."

Kira's heart nearly stopped. "That's great news, Doctor! You can control their reproduction?"

"Ah, not exactly, Major. Perhaps you'd better come see for yourself."

"Fine. I'll be right there." Kira drained the last of her *raktajino* and left ops.

"Major! Major!"

Kira stopped walking and pressed a hand to her forehead. She turned around, lowering her hand as Odo ran up.

"Yes, Constable?"

Odo looked smug. "I've been investigating just how the tribbles managed to get out of the station quarantine and down to Bajor."

"I thought we decided that one must have gotten past the cargo inspections."

"Ah." Odo raised a finger. "But if that was the case why wasn't the outbreak in the grain-processing center at Lasumo rather than the Tozhat Province?"

"What are you saying?"

"I'm saying that someone smuggled tribbles off the station. And who do we know that would look to profit off the tribbles?"

"Quark." Kira's lips tightened. "If you can get me proof I'll see that he's hung by his lobes!"

Odo crossed his arms. "Leave it to me, Major."

Kira seethed the rest of the way to the infirmary. If Quark was behind breaking the quarantine he'd find himself spending a long time in a nice Bajoran prison cell. When she reached the infirmary her mood hadn't improved. Julian looked up as she stormed in. He was cradling a tribble in the crook of his arm. Worf stood on the other side of the room glaring at the furry ball.

"Ah, Major. There you are."

Kira leaned on the nearby biobed. She rubbed at the ache in her back. "What have you got for me?"

Julian bounced up onto his feet and walked over to the counter. Kira saw a pile of grain on the counter. "You're not going to feed that thing, are you?"

"No. Gladys has already eaten." Julian put the tribble down on the counter. "Not that that would stop her. Tribbles always have an appetite for more food. Watch now."

As Kira watched, the fuzzy brown-and-white ball contracted and began moving toward the pile of grain. The movement was very smooth. She knew that the tribble was extending fleshy nubs through its fur, which used suction to grip surfaces. It accounted for their amazing ability to climb walls and get into anything. When a tribble was picked up, the nubs retracted back beneath the protective fur.

Gladys had nearly reached the grain when it stopped. Kira looked at Julian, then over at Worf. The tall Klingon looked disgusted by the proceedings.

"Well, Doctor?"

"Just a moment."

Gladys moved forward a couple inches then lurched violently away from the grain and started to make a shrill trilling noise. It sounded like it was in distress. Julian wasted no time in picking Gladys up. He carried the tribble away from the counter, stroking it gently. The tribble settled down to its usual purr.

Kira looked over at the grain. "Okay, I give. What stopped the tribble?"

"Pheromones," Julian announced proudly. He gestured at Worf. "Klingon pheromones, specifically Worf's."

Worf growled. "With your permission, I will return to ops."

"Oh, yes, of course," Julian said. "Thank you so much."

"Explain, Doctor."

"Well, I got to thinking. Back on K-7, Kirk used the tribble to identify the Klingon agent. How does a tribble know a Klingon from human? Or a shapeshifter? How does a tribble know where food is located? I started to do a study to see just how—"

Kira shook her head and held up a hand. "Spare me the details. There are over a million tribbles on Bajor despite our efforts to contain them. We've already contained three blooms outside the Tozhat Province. How is all of this going to help us?"

"Oh, right. Well, I thought we could spray the fields."

"Spray the fields with Klingon pheromones?"

"Not the whole fields. Just a barrier around the fields. Or around the tribbles, for that matter. The tribbles won't cross the line. Just think of it as an invisible fence."

"How long will it last?"

"Weeks I would imagine. Klingon pheromones are fairly potent."

Kira sat down on the biobed. "That could be helpful in containing the spread."

"Are you all right?"

"Just tired," Kira said. "It's been a long day."

"Here." Julian handed her Gladys. "I'll just do a quick check to make sure everything is fine with both you and the baby."

"That's not necessary—"

"Lie down," Julian said. "Resting for a few minutes won't change things."

Kira placed Gladys on top of her swollen abdomen. The purring was actually soothing. She stroked the soft fur. *If these things weren't such an ecological menace, they wouldn't be so bad,* she thought.

Julian ran the tricorder over her. "Everything looks good. Elevated levels of lactic acid. That's to be expected. Let me just give you a hypospray and you'll feel a bit better."

While he prepared the hypospray, Kira continued to stroke the tribble. The purring was nice. Tribbles were nice like this when they weren't busy making more tribbles and stripping farmlands. What had she told Vedek Tola? That she would be the first to shovel them into the disposal units?

Julian pressed a hypospray to her neck. There was a soft hiss and the ache in her muscles started to fade. Kira sat up and shoved the tribble at him.

"Thank you, Doctor. I'll arrange to have your Klingon pheromones replicated and distributed on the surface."

The shrill cries were deafening. Kira winced until Kai Winn closed the window. The tribbles had been contained by using the pheromones but they continued to approach the barrier. Thousands upon thousands of tribbles sat at the invisible line crying out their fear. Worf would be proud, Kira thought.

"You see, my child," Winn said. "This cannot go on. The parasites must be destroyed."

"They are contained."

"For now. What are we to tell the farmers whose fields have been decimated by these creatures? Surely it is the will of the Prophets that this filth be cleansed from Bajor."

"Vedek Tola would disagree with you," Kira said with a slight smile.

"Tola? Tola is a child." Kai Winn waved a dismissive hand. "I am the one chosen to speak the will of the Prophets. This blight must be removed. You must impress upon Captain Sisko that Bajor needs those disposal units. It is the only humane way to remove the creatures. Without their help we may be forced to burn those fields."

It was one thing to picture tribbles being quickly and painlessly disintegrated but another altogether to imagine burning them. The thought of the smell of millions of burning tribbles—

Kira stood up with some difficulty. "Your Eminence, I will do what I can."

"I pray to the Prophets that your efforts are swift and successful, my child. The blessing of the Prophets on you."

After visiting Kai Winn, Kira went to Minister Shakaar's office. Shakaar wrapped his arms around her and held her for a moment. Kira sank into his arms but found herself wishing that he could purr like Gladys. Troubled, she drew back.

"What's wrong?" he asked gently.

"I just came from the kai."

Shakaar laughed. "Enough said."

"She wants the tribbles destroyed. She talked about burning them if she can't get the disposal units from the Federation."

Shakaar grimaced. "Can you imagine the stink of all that burning fur?"

"Right. On top of that, I've got Vedek Tola telling me that the tribbles must be preserved. And Odo is investigating Quark about the station quarantine being broken."

Her combadge beeped. Kira tapped it and turned a bit away from Shakaar. "Kira."

"Major," Captain Sisko's calm voice came over the channel. *"Are you busy?"*

Kira rolled her eyes. "I'm in a meeting with Minister Shakaar."

"Good. I'm sure the minister would like to know that we've detected three Klingon battle cruisers heading this way."

Kira exchanged a sharp look with Shakaar. "Any idea what they want?"

"Not yet, Major, but Worf seems to think it has something to do with the tribbles."

"The tribbles?" Shakaar asked with surprise. "What would the Klingons want with the tribbles?"

"Tribbles are considered enemies of the Empire," Kira said. "Captain, I'll leave immediately."

"Good. I'd like you here if things turn ugly."

"Any word yet?" Kira asked as she walked into ops.

"Nothing," Sisko said.

"Odo was looking for you," Dax offered.

"Good. I'll talk to him later."

"How is the surface holding up?" Sisko asked.

"So far the tribbles have been contained by Wo—" Kira glanced at Worf and saw his countenance darken. "Bashir's invisible fence. They are making a lot of noise but otherwise no new damage."

"Worf?" Captain Sisko looked over at the Klingon. "What can we expect if Gowron has sent those ships because of the tribbles?"

Worf thought about it for a moment. "They will attack the surface. Sterilize all areas that might harbor an infection. They will be thorough."

"They wouldn't dare!" Kira spat.

Worf's eyes widened.

"Let's not get ahead of ourselves," Sisko cautioned. "Worf, prepare the *Defiant* for departure. It doesn't hurt to be cautious."

"If they were planning to fight us, you'd think they would have brought more ships," Dax said. "Instead they just have three ships and they aren't cloaked."

Worf nodded. "That is reasonable. Perhaps they mean merely to ensure that the tribbles are, in fact, destroyed."

"Perhaps," Sisko said. "I'd still feel better with you on the *Defiant*. How long until they're within hailing distance?"

"Two minutes," Dax said.

Worf nodded to the captain and left ops. Kira watched the screen while they waited. She still remembered the Klingons boarding the station. Sisko had carried the day then. She hoped that the Emissary would be able to do the same thing today.

"The ships are within range," Dax said calmly.

"On screen," Sisko ordered. "Open hailing frequencies."

"They're responding."

The battleships on the screen were replaced by a view of the lead ship's bridge. A broad-faced Klingon tending toward fat sneered at them.

"*Captain Nolath. We come to sterilize the planet of this infection.*" Nolath said the last word with disgust. His eyes narrowed.

"Consider it a gift to the Bajoran people. Compliments of Gowron and the High Council."

Kira leaned on the ops console. She forced a smile. "As much as the Bajoran people appreciate the generous offer we have the situation under control."

"Then you have eradicated the infestation?"

"Not yet," Kira said tightly. "But it is contained."

"That is unacceptable! If you are unable to eliminate these vermin, we will."

"Bajor will not tolerate any interference in this matter."

Nolath's leathers creaked as he leaned forward. *"If we decide to take matters into our hands, we will do so. You would be foolish to try and stop us."*

Captain Sisko raised a hand. "I think we can all be reasonable about this. The tribbles are being dealt with, Captain. I'm sure Gowron didn't send you here to open a conflict with the Federation. If he had, he wouldn't have only sent three ships."

Captain Nolath snarled and waved a dismissive hand.

Sisko smiled brightly. "Good. Then I think we understand each other."

"We will remain to make sure the infestation is removed," Nolath snarled.

"As you wish," Kira said tightly. She motioned with her hand and Dax terminated the signal.

Kira blew out her breath. "These Klingons sure take tribbles seriously."

"You have no idea," Dax said, grinning. "Just the mention of a tribble makes Worf surly."

Sisko raised an eyebrow.

Dax shrugged. "Well, more surly than usual."

Kira entered Odo's security office. "What do you have?"

Odo spun his chair around to face her. He wasn't smiling. "Not much, I'm afraid."

"Nothing."

"I've been checking with my contacts on Bajor and here on the station. If anyone knows anything about the tribbles no one is talking."

"They have to know the penalty for smuggling. They're keeping quiet."

Odo inclined his head. "Maybe. My other avenues of investigation have failed to turn anything up either. I keep running into the same problem."

"What's that?"

"Where is the profit in tribbles?"

"Excuse me?"

"Quark is always seeking the profit. But where is the profit in trading an animal that can reproduce dozens more within such a short time period? We saw the same thing happen with Cyrano Jones on K-7."

Kira sank into one of the chairs and leaned back. She placed a hand on her belly and found herself wishing that she had Gladys.

"Are you all right, Major?"

"Yes. I never thought I'd be having a baby."

Odo nodded.

"So Quark's off the hook?"

"For now," Odo growled. "Perhaps a tribble did just manage to get missed by our inspections."

Kira levered herself up. "Fine. I'll be in the infirmary if I'm needed."

The infirmary wasn't busy when she got there. Julian looked up brightly when she entered. "Major. How are you?"

Kira's face tightened. "I've been better, Doctor."

"I've been working on an appetite suppressant for the tribbles. It would be transmitted by an engineered retrovirus. If it works, I believe it will lower the tribbles' reproductive drive."

Kira nodded. She sank down onto the nearest biobed as Julian hurried over with a tricorder. Kira waved a hand at him. Julian stopped with a puzzled expression on his face.

"I don't know how I'm going to help you if you don't let me see what's wrong."

Kira looked around the infirmary and spied what she wanted sitting on top of a nearby console. "Just bring me Gladys."

"Gladys?"

"Yes, Doctor. Her purring is soothing."

"Fascinating." Julian put down the tricorder and fetched Gladys from the console. He handed the tribble to Kira.

The tribble was warm and soft in her hands with a pleasant weight to it. Kira smiled and settled Gladys on her belly. Gladys seemed quite content to stay put. Her purring deepened and became more penetrating. Julian had picked up his tricorder again and was scanning them. Kira ignored him as she felt sore muscles loosen under the tribble's soothing influence.

"Amazing." Julian leaned on the biobed. "The tribble's purring seems to have restorative properties. Both your readings and those of the baby are improving. Do you mind if I study this? It could have interesting implications."

Kira closed her eyes and shook her head. "Just do it quietly."

"Ah, yes. Of course."

Later, in ops, Kira gave the captain a brief smile. "Hail Nolath's ship."

"Hailing," Dax responded. "On screen."

Captain Nolath appeared on screen. *"Yes, Major?"*

"On behalf of the Bajoran people I extend our thanks in this situation and hope that it leads to further cooperation between the Empire and Bajor. The situation has been resolved and you are free to return to the Empire."

"Resolved?" Nolath's bulk leaned forward. *"What do you mean resolved? Have the tribbles been eliminated?"*

"They are contained."

"That is unacceptable. If any remain they may leave Bajor and infect other worlds."

Kira shook her head. "Our doctor has discovered that the tribbles have a unique medical application. He also believes he can control their reproduction."

Nolath growled and pointed a finger at Kira. *"We will not rest until every last tribble has been eliminated!"*

"Then come and try!" Kira picked up Gladys from her seat and placed the tribble on the console. "If you want a war we'll give you one."

Sisko smiled brightly and shook a finger in Nolath's direction. "Captain, I should also mention that the Federation is sending a team of experts to study the tribbles in a contained environment. They consider the preservation of this endangered species as very important."

Nolath scowled. *"The High Council will hear of this and when they do—"*

"They'll come to the same conclusion they did last time," Kira said. "They can't afford to fight a war on every front."

The screen cut out. Kira sank down and picked up Gladys. Dax laughed softly.

"I don't think they'll be back."

Sisko cracked a smile. "Not if they want to avoid tribble."

(SECOND PRIZE)

Choices

Susan S. McCrackin

He was a child who kept coming to her in her dreams, his body round and soft, brown wispy hair falling down into bright green round eyes. He danced around her, his clothes flashing red and purple, the garish colors melding together in nauseating waves. Explosions of clicks came from him with every move, with every lift of his hand, with every shake of his head. She tried to close her eyes, to allow herself to drift away from him, but he yelled at her, screamed for her to open her eyes.

She felt him touch her face and tried to turn from him, but could not. She looked down at herself and saw her old body, dull gray metal holding her extremities straight, unfamiliarly immovable. Opening her mouth, she sucked in air and choked. He was there immediately, screaming, waving colors, clicking, everything all at once, and she sank away from him, somehow finding her voice even as she gagged, begging him to vacate her dreams, to leave her.

"Leave you?" He laughed at her, his mouth pressed tightly against her ear as he whispered softly. "But you don't understand. If I leave you, you'll die."

There were sounds around her; the sounds of items being moved, something being slid—metal on metal; squeaking shoes—rubber soles on tile floors. Smells. Strange smells. Antiseptic. Cleansers and alcohol.

Her mind processed it all slowly, fighting to gain full awareness, working through the thick fog that seemed to wrap itself around her thoughts, tucking itself in tightly under the corners, working as hard to keep out clarity as she fought to gain it.

She was on her back, her mind strangely disassociated from the rest of her body. A shadow passed over her face followed by smells like cinnamon and vanilla. She managed to open her eyes only to find her field of vision filled with a blur of white close to her face.

Instinctively, her mind sent out signals to push herself away from the too close body. It should have been a natural thing for her body to react, for hands to come up to press against the torso blocking her; for feet and legs to propel her up and away.

But nothing happened.

She tried to twist her head, but was stopped by a strange pressure on her skull. Blinking to clear her vision, her eyes searched for her restraints, seeing thin strands of metal circling her head, supported by rods that disappeared below her chin. Her heartbeat quickened, the fight or flight instinct triggering and her body stubbornly refusing to respond.

The figure leaning over her pulled back and stared at her for a moment before turning and yelling, the words running together, indistinct and indecipherable.

She felt her face flush, her heart pounding in her ears. She opened her mouth and gagged, her breath dying in her throat. Panicked, she fought for air, her mind now screaming at her body to move, to run, to break free of the restraints that were holding her.

The world around her dimmed as people leaned over her, round green eyes intense as they surrounded her. The last voice she heard as she passed into oblivion was that of the boy's, screaming that he would not let her leave.

A pinprick of light flashed in her eye, slamming into her retina. She blinked quickly, trying to recoil against the intrusion, but her head was held steady.

"Eduow eil heisot shedult irodemtriec." The light slid off to the right and a figure pulled back and into her line of vision. "Weirld is owcsk qruistle eil pslor cifcord—"

She frowned, working to focus on the words, struggling to understand the strange accent. Squinting, she stared at the wide mouth, watching the lips move, forming around syllables that slowly took on meaning.

"—evorist blust relax and try to stay calm. Doctor Gretkora is on his way. He'll explain everything as soon as he gets here."

She blinked again, watching as her caretaker moved closer and reached to rest an elongated hand gently against her face. "Don't worry. We're taking good care of you."

The wide mouth spread, drawing across broad white teeth forming into something that she decided was a smile. She opened her mouth, but one of the slender fingers moved across her lips.

"No, not yet. Doctor Gretkora is almost here."

A loud scuttling noise drew her eyes toward the door as someone came rushing through, arms swinging awkwardly with legs moving stiltedly, giving the appearance of someone struggling to run while trying to keep himself from falling. Brown hair flew in all directions, framing a youthful humanoid face that topped a round, short body held up by mechanical legs that clicked loudly as they propelled him forward. Lights flickered and flashed in alternating colors of red and purple pulsating on a panel fastened across his chest.

He grabbed for the side of the bed, steadying himself as he leaned over her, round eyes intently studying her face. "Hello. I'm Doctor Gretkora."

She opened her mouth to speak, but nothing came out.

"It's okay." He moved his hand to her neck. "We had to assist with your breathing so we installed an autobreather. You'll find talking difficult, but not impossible."

For the first time, she became aware of a rhythmic swooshing that matched each breath she took.

"Relax and try to speak as you exhale." He paused, then asked, "Do you remember your name?"

She concentrated on timing her breath so she could respond, her voice barely more than a whisper. "Seven of Nine."

"Very good." Obviously pleased, he spoke to the caretaker. "Please make note of that." Addressing Seven, he said, "It's nice to meet you, Ms. Nine."

She opened her mouth again and he fell quiet, waiting for her to speak. "I . . . prefer . . . Seven."

"Then we shall call you 'Seven.'" He glanced towards the machinery to her left, his eyes moving quickly back to her, a smile spreading widely across his face. "Your vital signs are getting stronger." She frowned and his smile immediately faded. "Ah, yes, well, I know you're wondering what happened to you."

He reached down and lifted a hand into view. She barely gave it any notice until she realized with a start that it was encased in metal.

It is my hand.

It is my hand, and I do not feel it.

He started talking, his mouth making noises that flowed into her unlistening mind. Instead, her mind spoke to her hand, demanding that it move. Her hand stayed in the doctor's hand, her fingers flaccid.

Her mind slowly worked its way down her body, struggling with the realization that there was only emptiness from her shoulders down. She glanced up at a metal lamp, seeing herself reflected in its shiny surface, making out the shape of her feet beneath the covers, seeing that her feet were flopped clumsily to the side and awkwardly extended, no longer held upright by toned muscles. Still affixed to her body but severed from her mind.

Disbelieving, she looked at the doctor, forcing herself to concentrate on his words, repeating the last word she heard, trying to comprehend it.

"Paralyzed."

He nodded, his expression serious. "Yes, Seven, you're completely paralyzed. But I want you to know that you have choices. We can't fix you—you'll never be like you were, but we can do a lot to give you back your life." He gave her a hopeful smile. "You have many choices, Seven. And I'm here to make sure that you take advantage of them."

Seven watched while the doctor checked her, her mind working to pull her fractured memory together, trying to remember where she was and how long she had been gone from *Voyager.*

Small bits and pieces came to her, disjointed events tumbling into place, forming an incomplete picture. A colorful celestial event. Music. A smile. A quick laugh.

The Doctor.

They had been on an away mission; no, not a mission. She concentrated, pulling ferociously at her fleeting memories, the pieces organizing themselves as Doctor Gretkora's movements sounded constant clicks around her.

It was not an away mission; it was leave.

It'll be fun, Seven. And you'll have a chance to witness the birth of a double star.

She remembered space alive with color, petabytes of data streaming before her as she recorded the birth event. In her mind, she watched her fingers dancing over her control panel, nimble, quick, and controlled.

She closed her eyes, fighting the wave of emotion that almost overpowered her, threatening to scatter the precious memories she had worked so hard to gain. She worked to calm herself and focused, again trying to remember.

The Doctor had been singing; he had laughed, encouraging her to join him. Suddenly, the world was upside down and the shuttle was shaking violently. There had only been one chance; a small planet.

They must have made it.

They!

She opened her eyes. "Doctor Gretkora."

He answered immediately. "What, Seven?"

Before she could speak, heavy footsteps sounded in the hall. Giving an exasperated grunt, Doctor Gretkora moved clumsily to stand between her bed and the door, pulling himself upright as a uniformed man strode through the door, followed by three similarly uniformed men.

"General Antana, may I help you?" Doctor Gretkora's tone was formal and authoritative.

"I understand she is conscious."

"Yes, she is."

"I will talk with her."

Doctor Gretkora took an unsteady step toward the general. "She is still on the autobreather, General Antana."

"It is possible to speak while on an autobreather, is it not, Doctor Gretkora?"

"Barely. But I do not recommend it. She's in a fragile state, and I do not want her upset or stressed in any way." He paused, and Seven watched as he pulled his shoulders back, making himself slightly taller. "You told me you wanted me to do anything I had to do to save her, and I plan to do just that."

The two men faced off, the silence deepening between them. Finally, the general cleared his throat.

"Yes, very well. I wouldn't want to do anything to put . . . your patient at risk." There was another clearing of his throat. "Would you mind if I . . . *visited* her?"

There was a long silence before Doctor Gretkora turned slightly to allow the general to pass. "Only for a few minutes, General. Please."

"Of course."

Seven watched the general approach her bed and tried to ignore the commands of her mind that her body rise from the bed to face the man.

Like Doctor Gretkora and her nurse, the man had the same round green eyes and brown hair. Unlike Doctor Gretkora, General Antana was tall and thin, with elongated facial features of sharp angles around his eyes and his jaw. His lips were thin and drawn tightly to dip down at the corners. Small reddish spots were scattered across his cheeks, covering tanned skin darker than the doctor's.

A rumbling in his throat preceded his words. "Welcome."

Seven waited for her lungs to fill and spoke softly as she breathed out. "Thank you."

Seven watched as the general's eyes slowly moved down her body, examining her closely. She noticed how his eyes lingered on her hand and face, and she knew he was carefully studying her Borg implants.

"We're . . . happy you survived the crash. We have prayed to Kwolona that your life would be spared."

She felt Doctor Gretkora move to stand closer to her head. She glanced at him, noting that he was focused determinedly on the general, his body language decidedly protective.

His presence seemed to rattle the general. "Yes. Um. Well, I do not want to tire you out." The general gave her a pointed look. "But I will look forward to talking with you more. We are very interested in finding out more about you . . . your people." He looked at her hand again. "And your technology."

Seven did not respond, a weariness causing her eyes to close.

General Antana backed away. "Doctor, may I speak with you, please?" He addressed her. "May Kwolona bring you good health."

Without waiting for a response, General Antana turned and left the room. The men with him waited until Doctor Gretkora followed before leaving. Seven forced herself to concentrate on their whispered conversation, grateful for her enhanced hearing, but she soon realized that the capability was unnecessary. The voices quickly escalated into a near shouting match.

"We have to interrogate her! She's a member of an alien race with highly advanced technology! How do we know she wasn't scouting for an invasion? We have to talk with her and find out about her and about that ship she came in."

"If you try to move her it's likely you'll kill her! Her spinal column was shattered! I was barely able to piece it back together. And she's on an autobreather for a reason—she can't breathe on her own. I can't take her off of it without killing her," the doctor argued.

"Then I will interrogate her here. I'll be back tomorrow. Make certain she is ready."

Quick footsteps sounded and receded. It was a full minute before Doctor Gretkora entered the room. Approaching her bed, he gave her a crooked grin.

"That went well, didn't it?"

Breathe!

Her eyes frantically searched the darkness while her mind screamed at her body to breathe. Her heart was hammering in her chest, and she felt her face go hot and cold at the same time.

She mouthed words, trying to scream for help, but there was nothing in her to push words out. Panicked, she fought to live, but it was a silent, motionless fight waged only in her mind.

She was losing consciousness. Anger and frustration filled her, followed by absolute fear.

She did not want to die.

"I'm coming, Seven!" The voice came from a distance. "Hold on!"

The sounds of clicks echoed wildly off the walls as Doctor Gretkora ran into the room, the yellow light of a lantern mixing with the red and purple lights flashing from his chest panel.

"Don't panic! I'll have you hooked up in a second."

She heard him through a tunnel, his words muffled. She tried to hold on, to wait for the swishing sounds to return, for air to fill her lungs, but the seconds stretched too long. She slipped down the tunnel, leaving the clicks behind.

*   *   *

"Welcome back."

She blinked slowly into the dimness, taking a moment to focus on Doctor Gretkora's face.

"You're going to be okay. We had a power failure. I switched your autobreather over to a backup power source." He grimaced. "Which it should have been on already, but this facility was kind of thrown together and, uh, well, everything isn't as good as I'd like it to be for you." He glanced away and was quiet a few moments before turning back to her. Light reflected off his teeth and she was able to make out a sad, sympathetic smile as he leaned closer to her, his head intimately close to hers.

"I know that was frightening." Without waiting for her to respond, he continued. "You'll never get used to it, Seven. And that fear of being alone and dying before anyone can get to you will never leave you." His voice shook slightly. "But you have to push that monster into the back of your mind. If you don't, it will control you." He pulled back to face her and his smile morphed into that slightly crooked grin. "Like I told you, it's all about the choices you make."

She studied him carefully, for the first time seeing light reflect off of small wires appearing above his shirt collar and disappearing around the back of his neck. Her eyes slid down to the panel on his chest slightly hidden by his coat. The realization dawned on her.

"You are paralyzed."

The broad grin flew into his face. "Only my body." He tapped the side of his head and the light flickered off his metal-framed finger. "Not up here." He pulled up the sleeve of his coat, exposing thin metal rods wrapping his arm. "This is my own design. When we get you stabilized, I'll build one for you. It'll give you a lot of your life back."

He held up his hands, palms forward, and she could see his fingers laced by strings of metal and surrounded by knobby structures.

"You'll also be able to regain some sensory feeling with these." He shrugged. "It won't be what you had, but it'll be better than nothing." He lifted her hand and fingered the metal on it. "And, I don't imagine it would ever be as good as your own people would be able to do for you."

He fell silent, and she knew he was waiting on her to respond. She ran quickly through what little knowledge she had managed to remember about this planet—a pre-warp civilization equivalent to that of Earth's early twenty-first century. With a sinking feeling, she realized he was right.

"I am certain you will provide me with excellent care."

"I'll do my best." He gently placed her hand on her stomach as he perched on the side of her bed. He leaned toward her. "You know, you're our first alien visitor." She could see his eyes twinkling with excitement, even in the low light given off by his lantern. "There's so much I want to ask you. So much I want to know." His eyes slipped to the Borg implant over her eye. "Your technology is . . . miraculous! Does that enhance your vision? And the implant on your stomach, what does that do? Can you breathe in space?"

Seven blinked quickly and averted her eyes, struggling with her response, the intense innocence in his face in juxtaposition to the explanation of her implants.

Instinctively her mind told her body to take a deep breath to give herself time to order her mind, to allow her to form a measured response, but her breath came with the timed swoosh of air from the autobreather, unsettling her as much as his question did. The complete helplessness of her situation overwhelmed her. She blinked again and felt the spreading wetness on her face.

"Oh, Seven." Doctor Gretkora reached to wipe a trickling tear from her cheek. "I'm sorry. I didn't mean to upset you." He grabbed a tissue and wiped gently at her face, trying to dry her cheeks even as the tears flowed freely. "I wasn't thinking. I'm so, so very sorry."

"No." She sniffed. "No, do not be sorry—I—" Her words choked off as she had to sniff again.

"Here," he grabbed another tissue and held it against her nose, "blow your nose."

She stared at him in horror, everything in her demanding that her hand raise to take the tissue from him.

"I understand, Seven." His voice was soothing. "Go ahead." As he spoke, he adjusted the tissue tighter to her nose. Self-consciously, she waited for the autobreather to fill her lungs and blew. Tears immediately followed.

It took three more tissues before she was able to compose herself.

As he threw the last tissue into the trash, Doctor Gretkora said, "I'm impressed. Most of my patients use more tissues than that for the first good cry. I went through at least six myself."

For the first time, Seven felt the corners of her mouth turn up and something inside her lighten. "I cannot imagine you crying."

The grin slid back into place on his face. "I cried a lot. And then I decided that it was time to quit crying and put that energy into something positive. I didn't have a body that would do me any good anymore, but I still had a mind that worked. I concentrated on what I could do and I made something happen. When you heal a little, we'll make something happen for you."

She sniffed lightly. "You remind me of the Doctor."

"The Doctor?"

"He is the Emerg . . ." She caught herself. "He is the doctor on *Voyager.*"

His eyes roamed over her face, pausing at each implant. "He must be an excellent doctor."

She ignored the question hidden in his words. "He is highly competent."

He frowned and the dimness of the room darkened the creases of his wrinkles. "Is your doctor capable . . . of . . . uhm, can he do anything . . . uh . . ."

"Can he repair me?"

He nodded. "Yes. Can he repair you?"

"Yes."

Doctor Gretkora was silent for a long moment. Then, he said, "Miraculous. How . . . I mean, do you know what techniques he uses?"

She stared into the darkness of the room, wondering if the Doctor's mobile emitter survived the crash. If it had, he could repair her. If it had, he could contact *Voyager.*

Almost absentmindedly, she responded, "He will implant neural precursor cells to affect a repair to the damaged area." A low strangled sound brought her attention back to Doctor Gretkora.

"Your people use precursor cells?"

She heard a tremor of excitement in his voice. "Yes."

He slid off the bed and walked away, disappearing into the darkness outside the glow of the lantern. She listened to his movements, clicks tracing back and forth from corner to corner as he paced.

The clicks stopped and he spoke. "Neural precursor cells." He walked out of the darkness to stand next to her, his eyes widely round. "And they work?"

She started to nod, but her head did not move, still held steady by the metal frame screwed into her skull. He had called it a "halo." She thought it an ironic name for something so torturous.

"They are highly effective."

He whispered, his voice tight and squeaky. "I knew they would work."

"You are experimenting with them?"

"No." He shook his head, grimacing. "Our laws do not allow me to do such experimenting." Doctor Gretkora grunted and sat back down on her bed. Staring into the darkness, he said, "Such treatment is seen as an abomination."

Seven frowned. "Explain."

"Our religion teaches that the body is pure and cannot be defiled. Pursuing such a radical type of treatment would be considered a desecration."

"But your exoskeleton—"

"My exoskeleton has caused me to be exiled from our religious houses." He shook his head. "It's bad enough that I have improved my life through an artificial and mechanical means; if I were to do so by such a radical treatment . . . I am afraid I would be jailed." His face turned sad. "Or worse."

"But you do not stop your work."

He turned to her. "No, I do not."

"Why not?"

He was quiet for a long moment. "Because I can't, Seven. Because there is something inside me that won't let me stop. This body sleeps all the time, but my mind never does. Even when my eyes close, my mind is working. I dream about walking one day— walking without this exoskeleton, walking because I've figured out how to rebuild the electrical connections between my brain and my body, and walking because my body is whole again."

When she stayed quiet, he continued. "They tell me to put my faith in Kwolona, to look to Him for healing, that I should put aside my crazy thoughts and dreams and accept my fate.

"But what if it is my fate to heal myself and to heal others like me? How can a being who loves His people stand between us and a solution to suffering? How can healing be wrong?"

By the way he continued to stare into the deep darkness of the room she knew he did not expect a response from her so she offered him none. Suddenly, the lights in the hallway flickered on, and he grunted as he slid from the bed.

"Looks like they've restored the power. I'd better hook your auto-breather up to the primary power source."

General Antana strode into the room, his suit slightly rumpled. Without ceremony, he approached her. Doctor Gretkora had repositioned her bed, raising her head slightly so she was better able to see. She tried to clear her mind and focus on the general, the sedative Doctor Gretkora had given her—over her objection—making it difficult to do so. But even the effect of the sedative could not mask the man's distraction.

"Are you feeling better today?"

Seven frowned as she whispered her response. "Yes."

"Good." He pulled back his shoulders and smoothed the wrinkles in his coat. "Was anyone traveling with you?"

His abrupt directness threw her. As quickly as he had asked, she answered. "The Doctor."

His expression did not change. "Describe this doctor."

Seven was aware that Doctor Gretkora had moved closer to her, and she looked in his direction to see both concern and excitement in his face. She blinked a couple of times, struggling past the sedative to think about what the general was really asking.

From the tone of the general's voice and the way he was acting, she realized that the Doctor's mobile emitter had been recovered and activated. Quickly, she decided that her best chance for the Doctor to be able to care for her was to be completely honest.

"The Doctor is the Emergency Medical Hologram on *Voyager*. He is a holographic computer program with a complete database of medical knowledge." As the general's expression took on a mixture of relief and intense worry, she added, "If you have activated his mobile emitter, no doubt you have found him quite insistent upon seeing me." She allowed a small smile to cross her face, purposely trying to project an ironic tone into her tortured voice. "I suspect you have also discovered that he can be quite insufferable."

In a loud huff, General Antana said, "That he is."

"Your *doctor?*" Doctor Gretkora's words squealed as he spoke. "A computer program? He's a computer program? How is that possible?"

The general's eyes narrowed. "Because their technology is far more advanced than ours, Doctor, and that's why I'm so concerned."

"You should not be." Seven spoke as firmly as she could. "You have nothing to fear from my people. They will come for me, but they will be appreciative of the care you've given me."

The general scowled at her. "And why should I believe you?"

"Because I have nothing to gain by lying, General." Seven licked her lips and swallowed, aware that her throat was getting sore. "I have more to gain by being honest with you. The Doctor can assist me," she glanced in Doctor Gretkora's direction, her eyes apologizing for what she would say next, "even more than Doctor Gretkora can assist me."

General Antana looked uncertainly at her, his hands worrying along the line of his coat, absentmindedly smoothing the wrinkles. Finally, he turned to one of the guards behind him and nodded. As the guard left the room, the general turned back in her direction.

"Tell me about the engines on the vessel we recovered."

"They are standard Federation warp engines."

General Antana frowned. "Warp?"

"Warp is faster-than-light speed."

The general almost gawked at her. "On a ship that size?"

"Yes."

The general muttered, more to himself than to her. "We've only managed a quarter light speed, but it's taken a ship three times larger to house the engine." He turned back to her. "How do you manage to protect the ship? What kind of heat shields do you use?"

Seven swallowed heavily, trying to soothe her increasingly raw throat. "Warp-field coils form a subspace bubble around the ship to protect it."

For the first time, a glimmer of excitement came into the general's eyes. "Our scientists theorized that was possible." He stepped closer to the bed and rested his arm on the bed railing. "How are you able to stabilize the antimatter converter?"

Seven licked her lips, aware she had already adapted to timing her words to the rhythm of the autobreather. She opened her mouth but fell silent as she heard an indignant voice growing louder as its owner advanced down the hall. Her eyes slid toward the door as the Doctor entered, stopping so abruptly that the man behind him ran into him, bumping him into the room.

But the Doctor did not seem to notice. She watched his face run through a myriad of human emotions so quickly that she doubted the others noticed. As her vision blurred, she saw him quickly pull his medical tricorder from his belt as he crossed to her, covering the distance from the door to her bed in three quick strides, his professional manner solidly in place as he took control.

Pushing past an uncertain General Antana, he said, "Your ocular implant is obviously malfunctioning. Let's see what else I have to repair."

The room fell completely silent as he worked, and she blinked to clear the tears from her eyes, feeling an almost overwhelming sense of relief at his presence. After a few moments, he lowered his tricorder and leaned over her bed, his stern expression changing into a gentle smile.

"It is a serious injury, Seven, and it will take a while for you to recover from this, but you will recover." He gave her a confident grin. "Lucky for you, you do have the finest doctor in the Delta Quadrant." He stepped back, settling a steady stare on the man across the bed from him. "Actually, I should say you probably have the *two* finest doctors in the Delta Quadrant." He cocked his head as he raised his chin. "You are her physician?"

Doctor Gretkora nodded, his round eyes growing wider as he watched the Doctor work. "Yes. I'm Doctor Gretkora."

"Impressive work, Doctor Gretkora." The Doctor's eyes narrowed and he raised his tricorder to scan the doctor. His voice slightly amazed, he said, "Very impressive." He moved to Gretkora, studying the results of the scan. "Microsurgical implantation of electrodes; neuronic-electro linkages; microelectronic gyro nodes." He turned toward Seven. "You were in excellent hands, Seven. I shouldn't have been so worried."

He quickly faced the general. "I am certain that Captain Janeway will want to express her deep appreciation for the excellent care you have provided us as soon as she arrives."

General Antana stiffened in surprise. "Arrives?"

The Doctor shrugged, an almost smug grin coming into his face. "Of course, General. I sent a distress signal to *Voyager* as soon as I was activated."

"But, but, but . . ." The general stuttered. "Your every move was monitored! How did you send a distress signal?"

"I'm a computer program, General Antana." The Doctor puffed up proudly. "I multitask extremely well."

"A distress signal?" The general's face reddened deeply and his voice started to rise in alarm. "Your ship will come looking for you based on a distress signal!"

The Doctor raised his tricorder and casually reactivated it. "Don't be concerned, General. We'll be able to communicate with Captain Janeway before she powers up weapons." He moved back to Seven's bedside and gave her a wink. "But we won't let her know it isn't an emergency until she's close. We don't want her to take her time getting here, do we?"

Seven felt the corners of her mouth turn up slightly at the same time she felt the tear slide down the side of her face.

"Harrumph." The Doctor grunted, a mock-gruff tone in his voice. "Let's see if we can get that ocular implant adjusted."

Doctor Gretkora hovered inches from the Doctor's elbow, watching every move the Doctor made and trying to anticipate his every need. The Doctor gave Seven a roll of his eyes, but she could see how much the Doctor was enjoying the man's attention.

When the Doctor finally deactivated his tricorder, Doctor Gretkora stretched out a finger and traced its shape, his finger held inches above its surface.

"This device is amazing."

The Doctor chuckled. "Yes, it is." He lifted Seven's hand and worked her fingers, gently manipulating them. "Still nothing?"

She mouthed a "no," her throat now too sore to try to speak.

Doctor Gretkora frowned. "You expected her to have regained feeling? Without surgery . . . or whatever it is you plan to do."

The Doctor's eyebrow lifted sharply and he took a deep breath before answering. "Seven has . . . some unique healing capabilities. I adjusted her implants to stimulate . . . those capabilities in the hopes that some of her motor skills could be recovered," he gave Seven a sympathetic look, "at least your ability to breathe on your own." Shaking his head, he said, "I'm afraid the damage was too extensive. You'll have to depend on the autobreather until *Voyager* arrives."

"But you will be able to fix her? Completely?" Doctor Gretkora looked intently at the Doctor.

"Yes, Seven should have a complete recovery."

Doctor Gretkora raised his hand to run metal-covered fingers through his hair, causing purple lights to flash on the panel on his chest. Over the soft clicking caused by the up-and-down motion of his arm, he said, "How will you do it? Fix her, uh, repair Seven, I mean."

Flexing Seven's fingers again, the Doctor said, "I will harvest undifferentiated neural cells—"

"Neural precursor cells!" Doctor Gretkora interjected.

"Exactly!" The Doctor smiled, obviously pleased. "I will harvest neural precursor cells which I will culture carefully before injecting them into the injured area of her spine. Those cells will mature to rebuild the connections that Seven has lost. Since that process is slow, I will also genetically bioengineer cells that I will surgically implant using microsurgical techniques. I will be able to physically reconnect some connections." He smiled. "We should do that first so Seven can start breathing on her own. It will take a few surgeries, but we'll have her up and around before you know it."

"We? There are more like you on your ship?"

The Doctor's eyes twinkled. "I assure you, there is no one else like me on *Voyager!*" Laughing, he placed Seven's hand on the bed, carefully straightening her fingers. "I was thinking *you* would assist me."

Doctor Gretkora's mouth dropped. "Me? You want *me* to assist? On your ship?"

"If you're willing." The Doctor pulled the blanket up on Seven and reached to push a stray hair from her eyes. "I don't imagine Captain Janeway is going to be able to pass up General Antana's invitation to visit after all your people have done for Seven, so there isn't any reason why we can't take advantage of that time to initiate repairs on our friend here."

Seven raised a questioning eyebrow, aware that, for the first time, there were no clicks coming from Doctor Gretkora. The Doctor simply winked at her.

*   *   *

The Doctor carefully placed the object into the center of the table. "Okay, Seven. Let's see if you can pick that up."

Seven set her mouth into a thin line and concentrated, her hand moving slowly across the surface of the table, inching toward the small block. A tiny bead of sweat formed on her forehead and trickled down the side of her face. Trembling fingers bumped against the block, pushing it farther away from her, but she managed to encircle the block and pull it into her hand. Gritting her teeth, she lifted her hand into the Doctor's, allowing the block to drop into his palm. Exhausted, but exhilarated, she dropped her arm heavily onto the table and gave the Doctor a triumphant look.

"Excellent, Seven!" The Doctor tossed the block into the air, grinning when Doctor Gretkora caught it, clicks echoing loudly in the sickbay.

"A miracle!" Doctor Gretkora moved his hand in a circle, ending with his palm held upward, a motion Seven had learned was a sign of devotion. "A true miracle."

The Doctor lifted Seven's leg and tapped her knee, watching as her foot moved slightly in response. "You are making better progress than I anticipated, Seven."

"It was to be expected." Seven gave the two men in front of her a stern look. "I had two highly competent doctors. I would have accepted no less than perfection."

The Doctor howled in laughter and moved the tray table away from Seven's bed. "I think we also managed to reconnect Seven with her warm and grateful personality."

Seven lowered her head as a small smile played at her mouth. "It was a joke." She looked down at her hand and carefully moved her index finger. "But I do appreciate the effectiveness of your work." She looked up at Doctor Gretkora. "The work of both of you."

Doctor Gretkora moved around to the end of the bed, grinning broadly. "I still can't believe it worked. And that I was able to be a part of it." He made the circling motion again, this time with both hands. "This has been a true gift."

The Doctor looked at her and she nodded her head. The Doctor reached for his tricorder and held it up as he started to scan Doctor Gretkora. "We might be able to arrange for another gift."

Gretkora gave him a puzzled look. "What?"

The Doctor studied the screen on his tricorder. "Your own surgery. Based on your own research. It won't be as complete as Seven's, but you will regain a lot of your mobility, as well as the ability to breathe on your own." At the man's stunned look, the Doctor continued, "I've already asked Captain Janeway, and she said we could stay here long enough to get you on your feet. She said it was the least we could do after what you did for Seven."

"You can have your life back, Doctor Gretkora." Seven spoke softly, her blue eyes holding the man intently in a focused stare.

The man gawked at them, his expression blank.

The Doctor gave him a small, understanding smile. "Maybe you'd like to think about it a little bit. But when you make up your mind, I can start the surgery immediately."

Seven maneuvered the wheelchair through the mess-hall doors and slowly rolled into the darkened room, stopping beside the man staring intently out of the large windows. She waited, the silence growing long. Finally, he started to speak.

"Our prophets tell the story of Mannuse. He was a leader of our people during the time of the great hunger, a time when the lands of our old home had gone dry. The old home was in a valley surrounded by a large and dangerous mountain range. Mannuse knew that the only way our people could survive was to leave the old home, to challenge the mountain.

"The people argued with Mannuse. They told him that he was trading one death for another. Mannuse knew that they spoke out of fear, but nothing he said could change their minds.

"So Mannuse prayed, begging for guidance, begging for the gift of words that would change the minds and the hearts of his people. Kwolona, our Great Being, took pity on Mannuse and offered to give him wings to fly over the great mountains so that at least he could be delivered into the new paradise. Mannuse asked Kwolona what would happen to his people, and Kwolona told him that those without the heart to save themselves would die. Mannuse asked Kwolona to give him the wings so he would fly the others out of the valley, but Kwolona told him that the gift He would give Mannuse could be used only for Mannuse, that His gift could not be used to help those who would not help themselves.

"Mannuse went back to his people and found one person willing to walk with him, and he led that one out of the valley and into paradise. Mannuse went back and found another one who would walk with him and he did it again and again and again. Each time he made the journey, Kwolona blessed his path, making it easier, leveling the path more and more. Finally, Mannuse walked all of his people out of the valley, the last of them walking with Mannuse on a path that was now cut flat through the heart of the mountain.

"Mannuse saved our people and led them into the lands that we still call home today." Doctor Gretkora slowly turned to face Seven. "He would not accept the gift that would have cost him his people, even wings that would have allowed him to fly."

Seven stared at him, cold filling her stomach as she realized what he was saying. "You are not going to have the surgery."

He shook his head.

She paled even as her cheeks reddened and her eyes flashed in anger. Her voice taut, she said, "But your people have already abandoned you. Why would you give up the opportunity to have your body reconnected, to walk and feel again?"

"The religious houses have turned their backs on me, Seven, but not all of the people. There are people who listen to me. People like General Antana, who risked his career by having me care for you. There are people I can still reach, people I can still help." He held out his hands to her, palms out, the small knobs that encircled his fingers glittering in the dim light. "If I go back healed, I risk being a pariah to even those people.

"Don't you see, Seven, if I fly over the mountain, I leave it in the way of others. But if I wear it down, even with small steps, then one day, others will be able to walk the path with me.

"This gift of Kwolona, of seeing you healed, of knowing that these dreams in my mind are not just dreams but truly possible," his voice caught with his growing emotion, "this hope, it's better than wings!"

Seven blinked quickly, fighting to regain her composure. Her voice cracking, she tried one more argument. "But if you allow the Doctor to repair you, you will never have to fear dying alone."

His lopsided grin slid quickly into place. "That's the most beautiful thing, Seven. You see, all this time, when I thought Kwolona had abandoned me, He was actually there, talking to me. *He* gave me these ideas, these dreams." He leaned down, placing his head close to hers, and whispered into her ear. "And I finally realized: I had nothing to fear because I was never really alone. And I never will be."

Unconventional Cures

Russ Crossley

He runs his tricorder over the still body of Naomi Wildman. Every time he's done this over the past two hours the blinking readouts on the device worry him. He doesn't like what he sees. She should be awake—but isn't.

The only sound in his sickbay is the beeps and whirrs of his medical tricorder. The still, sterile air seems to roar in his ears. Over the past two weeks, except for the odd pulled muscle or minor cold remedy, the crew hasn't had much call for his services. Now this. This isn't the kind of business he craves. And certainly not the sweet blond-haired, blue-eyed Naomi.

Since being activated in the Delta Quadrant, he has demonstrated his ability to overcome his programming on many occasions. The crew has come to trust his abilities. This time, though, he's stymied.

If only he knew how far to go beyond that which his programming said was possible. Invention wasn't his mother. *He* was the invention.

Janeway is wearing a path in the carpeted deck of his sickbay. Her eyes flit to the little girl lying very still on the diagnostic bed. He feels her cool gaze on him. "Well, Doctor. What do I tell Ensign Wildman about her daughter?"

Samantha Wildman is away from *Voyager* on a planetary survey mission with Tom and Harry in the Delta Flyer. They will be gone for another two days. Good thing, as far as he is concerned. All he needs right now is a hysterical mother to add to his problem. His bedside manners still need work.

The captain is intimidating enough, though. The echo of her shoes marching back and forth across his sickbay is making him edgy.

He sympathizes with Janeway. While Ensign Wildman is absent, Naomi is her responsibility. She's worried and so is he, except he isn't allowed to show it.

"I believe I can bring her out of the coma." He hasn't told the captain that he's tried every conventional treatment he knows to this point, without success. He's convinced she's afraid to wake. Naomi's protecting herself. Her body's whole. He's healed the wounds, but the mind is a tricky thing.

"I'll be on the bridge if you need me. And, Doctor . . ."

"Yes, Captain?"

"I want to see that little girl up and around when I get back. Understood?"

"Yes, Captain."

Janeway's shoulder-length auburn hair bounces off the shoulders of her red uniform jumper as she disappears through the doors to the corridor. With a whoosh they close behind her, leaving him again in silence.

He's been experimenting with an olfactory sensor in the sickbay; it detects the faint odor of coffee that always surrounds Kathryn Janeway.

He turns his attention back to the little girl lying atop the medical bed. He sits behind the desk in his office, where he studies all of the available research on soft-tissue damage in the human brain. Naomi isn't entirely human but the physiology is essentially the same.

What do I do now?

His thoughts are interrupted as the doors to sickbay slide open to admit Commander Tuvok.

"Doctor. I am here at the request of the captain to apprise you of the results of my investigation into the accident that incapacitated Miss Wildman."

"The captain ordered you, Commander?"

One eyebrow creeps up Tuvok's ebony forehead. "Yes. It seems the captain thinks you may find the details of my investigation . . . helpful." The Doctor feels the unease in Tuvok. Vulcans are very precise, and sharing incomplete results of anything with anyone is as repugnant to them as ballet is to elephants.

Tuvok holds up a data padd and begins to read his notes. He might as well have been a computer; he sounds bland enough. Vulcans would make wonderful insomnia cures.

The Doctor makes a mental note of that thought. It might come in handy somewhere down the road. History has shown that in the past unconventional cures often had surprising results.

". . . and Miss Wildman bypassed the security protocols in the holodeck—"

Hold on. "What was that? How is that possible? You need a command code to be able to do that."

Tuvok stops reading and looks up. "True. As yet I have been unable to determine how Miss Wildman accomplished this. However once I do, I will tighten the security procedures."

"She fell, didn't she?" the Doctor asks thoughtfully.

Tuvok glances at his notes. "Correct. From a tree. I believe it is called a *pine*."

"Hmmm . . . was she alone?"

"No. Two other of the children were with her." Tuvok's expression remains unfazed, but behind those dark, stern eyes the Doctor detects signs of revelation.

"One of them is lying."

He nods. "Yes—I believe so."

Tuvok says nothing more as he exits the sickbay. One of those children is in serious trouble.

A thought hits him like a thunderbolt in a clear blue sky. *Unconventional cures! That might be the answer.* Excitement mingled with urgency grips him.

"Computer, show me the unconventional cures used for victims of comas over the past two hundred years." He knows his medical database doesn't contain such information so he needs to seek it out.

Salves, heated water bottles, pills made from every weird concoction known to man. Every quack in the galaxy claimed their method worked best. Unfortunately, none were well documented, and others were downright dangerous.

Tiber cats from Delai IV sitting on your chest and screaming at you for two days somehow didn't seem practical. The big cats were all teeth and often ate the victims before they recovered.

There was one treatment, though, that looked promising, and was well documented. It had worked in several instances about a hundred years ago.

The Daystrom Institute had experimented using various species of animals to wake coma victims. Green turtles, dogs, cats, and rabbits; none seemed very effective until they tried something called a tribble.

Tribbles were small, furry mammals that trilled softly, ate voraciously, and apparently bred at an astonishing rate. Humans were attracted to the animals due to their pleasant nature.

The documentation did point out that the animals were pests, and included several case studies as evidence that they had overwhelmed several colony worlds.

There was even a case where a space station was flooded with the creatures and an entire supply of grain destroyed by them.

He reads the next section aloud. "—treatment of coma patients with tribbles is successful one hundred percent of the time . . ." As he continues to read to the bottom, the Doctor is dismayed to discover that tribbles are extinct.

"Do you think this will work, Doctor?" Janeway asks. Even through the comm system, he detects traces of doubt in the captain's voice.

He nods his head. "Yes, Captain. According to the Daystrom Institute's records, this procedure should work."

"You sound like you have your doubts."

"Nothing is certain in these cases."

"Proceed and keep me informed. Janeway out."

A sigh escapes his lips as he stands and gazes at the little blond-haired girl lying so still on the diagnostic bed. Time to start. No more delays. He believes this would work.

"Computer, create a holo-sim of the tribble."

There is a slight shimmer of light next to Naomi, and a brown ball of fur appears next to the right side of her head. It immediately begins to trill softly. After listening for several seconds, he knows why people are attracted to these creatures. The trill is very pleasant to the ear. Almost musical.

He isn't sure if a holotribble will work as well as a live one, but he has to try. If this doesn't work, Naomi will soon drop into a permanent vegetative state. Time is running out.

Nothing. Nothing is happening. The Daystrom studies reported patient recovery was within a few minutes of exposure to the tribble's trill. It needs more time, that's all.

Fifteen minutes pass and still nothing. He goes back and rereads the sections about the tribble treatment. Yes, he's followed the correct procedure. Something more is needed. But *what*?

"Computer, create another tribble on the opposite side of her."

Another shimmer and another holotribble appears. A white one appears on the left side of Naomi's head. It begins to trill like its counterpart.

For the first time since her accident, Naomi stirs. She rolls over on her side and puts her thumb in her mouth.

He feels a surge of joy run through his programming.

He places one hand on her shoulder and shakes her lightly.

"Leave me alone," she says in her tiny voice.

He rushes to the comm station on the wall of sickbay. "Captain!"

"Yes, Doctor, what is it? Good news, I hope?"

"Naomi Wildman is awake."

While Samantha Wildman visits with her daughter in sickbay, he sits in his office across from Janeway.

She wears a sly grin on her face. "Tuvok found the child who turned off the safety protocols on the holodeck. Fortunately, this will never happen again. At least while Tuvok is chief of security. Children are often too smart for their own good. Naomi says she swore them to secrecy. Didn't want her mother to find out. Typical, or so I'm told." She raises her cup of steaming coffee to her lips and takes a sip. "Tell me more about this procedure of yours."

"Take two tribbles—"

"—and call me in the morning." Janeway grins. "Really, Doctor."

Maturation

Catherine E. Pike

We are the Borg. You will be assimilated. Resistance is futile.

A chorus of voices chanted in monotone. They did not shout; yet the words reverberated throughout the *Raven* in an echoing omnipotence in the way Annika Hansen imagined God would talk—should He choose to—if He even existed. Papa said there was no such thing as God. Mama said there was.

The words drifted away; almost lost completely as sleep started to reclaim her. The shouts woke her fully and she opened her eyes to the darkness of her room; her ears to the nightmare beyond her closed door.

Her father was shouting, sounding scared but trying to hide it. She'd never heard Papa sound afraid before and panic of her own seized her heart. She sat up in bed, clutching both covers and Rosie to her, mouth opening to scream for her father, but before she could his shout was silenced mid-yell.

Running footsteps down the hall. The door to Annika's room was thrown open. Her mother stood in the doorway. Her hair flew from its bun into her face. Her eyes were large—frightened. Her breath came in great gasps, her mouth open, gulping every bit of oxygen it could find. The light from the corridor made her face even whiter than it already was, and for a moment she didn't look like Mama at all, but rather like the Wicked Witch of the West from the twentieth-century Oz books that they so loved to share.

"Annika, you must hide!" her mother cried. "Under your bed!" She glanced wildly over her shoulder as metallic footsteps—lots of them—came toward her. When Annika remained frozen in place, her mother hissed "Quickly!" in a tone that forbade argument.

Annika hastened to obey, squirming into the crawlspace beneath the metal bunk. From here she could no longer see the doorway, only her mother's shadow thrown onto the floor. Then it, too, disappeared. Mama must have stepped into the room, looking for a place to hide. Annika could hear her gasping.

"Be quiet now!" Mama ordered. "Don't say a word, no matter what!"

Annika rolled into a ball, hands clasping her knees to her chest. The floor was cold. Her fear made it colder. She shivered in her nightgown and wished she'd brought Rosie with her. The doll was still on her pillow. Surely she could grab her without being seen!

Just as she began to unfold herself, to creep out from beneath the bunk, the footsteps stopped outside her door. Instead of going on down the corridor they turned into the room. A red light pierced the darkness—sweeping around the room like a searchlight—joined by a second light, then a third—pinpoints of red that darted this way and that. Then whoever belonged to those heavy footsteps—to those voices—to the lights—pulled her mother from her hiding place.

"Please, no!" Mama pled.

Resistance is futile, the voices answered.

Her mother screamed.

Beneath the bed, Annika squeezed her eyes shut and covered her ears with her hands.

"Mama!" She couldn't help it. Her scream joined her mother's.
"No! Annika!"

They were the last words she would ever hear her mother say.

There was a hissing sound, then a noise similar to the sound of a mudhole reluctantly letting go of your bare foot on a summer's day—sort of a hungry, sucking sound. Her mother moaned in pain and went still.

Maybe they didn't hear me! she thought frantically. Perhaps her cry had been lost in her mother's! Annika was shaking uncontrollably now, and not just from the cold. Her teeth chattered, but she was helpless to stop them, even when she covered her mouth with a hand. Wishing desperately for Rosie, Annika pressed her back against the bulkhead. It was as far under the bed as she could get, but she feared it wasn't far enough.

She listened to the metal footsteps step farther into the room.

She watched three red lights join together into a much larger circle of red on the floor beside her bed.

They yanked the bunk effortlessly upward, despite its being fastened to the floor and wall. The bed fell with a deafening clatter as they tossed it into a corner with no more effort than she took to throw a ball. They ignored the noise, and the sound that followed after.

She watched helplessly as pieces of china skittered and danced across the floor.

Rosie! They broke Rosie!

Annika glanced up. It was hard to see past the red lights. They were as bright as lasers, and all three were focused on her. They seemed to come from the left eyes of the men who stared down at her; they had replaced their eyes somehow. They seemed more machines than men, clothed as they were in armor that seemed actually a part of their bodies.

How had they found me? she wondered. It was so dark beneath the bed, and so shadowy.

We are the Borg.

Voices, many of them, roared in her head. She winced at the volume. So many voices, yet only three of these . . . machines . . . were in the room with her. She peered up at them, sure she hadn't seen their mouths move. *How then . . . ?*

Do not concern yourself with such questions now. It will be explained in time. After you have joined the hive.

"The hive!" Annika answered aloud. "I don't wanna join any hive!"

You have no choice. We are the Borg.

As if that would explain everything.

They paused, and it seemed almost as if they were listening to something.

She is . . . unique, the voices announced, all in one monotone. *She is fearful, yet curious. She will be a good aide to the Queen one day.*

Before she could wonder who the Queen was, the machine closest to her grabbed her in a vise-like grip, lifting her completely off of the floor. While his hand (a human hand) held her chin, and thus her head, motionless, his metal hand paused beside her neck. Two long tubes shot out from his knuckles, piercing her neck.

She tried to scream, but her voice caught in her throat. Tried to struggle, but was held fast against a chest more cold metal than warm skin.

It hurt! Worse than cutting her foot on that sharp rock in the garden last summer! Worse than the strep throat she'd had during the winter!

"Mama!" she screamed, the terror ricocheting around her mind. "Mama! Make it stop hurting!"

She realized she was crying, and that the room was fading around her. Her neck had gone numb, a feeling that began to spread to her shoulders, down her arms, and throughout her whole body.

The last thing she saw—would ever see with completely human eyes—was Rosie's shattered body lying in a corner of the room.

She did not wake up so much as she regained awareness. She tried to call out for her parents, but she couldn't talk. Her neck hurt where the Borg's tubules had pierced her skin, and she tried to raise a hand to touch the spot, but she couldn't move. She realized she was weightless. This was not because the artificial gravity had gone off-line, but because she floated in some sort of liquid. She could neither see nor hear, but the liquid completely supported her. Despite being completely submerged, she could breathe without effort.

Annika tried again to call out for her parents, but no sound came from her mouth. *Where are they? They'd never leave me!*

You have been assimilated.

Her awareness had caught the attention of her captors. She realized she'd been hearing a soft buzzing noise, not from outside her body, but inside her head. The buzzing became voices, lots of them, talking about technical things she couldn't understand.

Do not try to understand. You will know everything we know, in time.

I don't want *to know. I want to go home,* Annika answered their thoughts with hers.

Impossible.

I want my parents! she demanded

Impossible! The voices were growing impatient. *You are now Borg. What you want is irrelevant.*

A humming vibration darted through her body, starting at the puncture point on her neck. *What are they giving me? Nutrients? Poison?* Whatever it was made her drowsy, and no matter how hard she fought, she began to lose consciousness once again.

Were she Captain Rachel Garrett of the *Enterprise,* she would find some way to fight—to break the container holding her so the liquid would tumble her out onto the floor. She would take out the phaser pistol hidden in her boot and keep the enemy at bay until her crew could arrive to rescue her.

But Captain Garrett was old, almost twenty-five, and she had both a ship and a crew.

Annika was only six, and while she had a ship, her only crew was Rosie, who, as far as she knew, still lay shattered on the deck in her bedroom. She didn't have a hidden phaser pistol, only her papa, who had always kept her safe from harm before. But he was gone now, and Annika was all alone.

A tear tried to choke her, but she swallowed it. Rachel Garrett wouldn't cry, and neither would Annika Hansen.

"I may be your prisoner," she thought stubbornly, *"but you can't stop me from remembering!"*

It is a glorious June afternoon. The breathless, oppressive summer heat is still two months away, and for now the nights are cool, the days are warm, and the daydreams are never-ending.

Annika is clothed in faded overalls; the legs rolled up midcalf. She is helping her aunt Helen pick strawberries for the evening's dessert. The soil beneath her bare feet is cool and damp, squishing deliciously between her toes. She plucks a strawberry from its plant and takes a bite. The fruit is warm and sweet; its juice dribbles down her chin, making her giggle.

That night there are more strawberries atop rich vanilla ice cream and camping out in the wilderness that is Aunt Helen's backyard, in a tent that Annika discovered in the shed. There is reading by flashlight: exciting tales of the Knights of the Round Table; of Rachel Garrett, captain of the ill-fated *Enterprise*-C, and of Sarah Rowe, the Jupiter colonist. The stories fuel her dreams as she curls up; pillowing her head against Bruce, Aunt Helen's basset hound and Annika's best friend. When Aunt Helen comes out to cover her with a light blanket and kiss her good night, Annika is already sound asleep, worn out by the carefree day and dreaming of swashbuckling her way through space; Bruce, faithful companion, by her side.

The pain, sudden and consuming, shot through Annika's body. Her arms and legs fought to draw close against her, to protect her from the invasion. The pain came again, much stronger this time, going from the top of her head to the bottom of her feet simultaneously. She couldn't move, couldn't escape, and she screamed silently. Helplessly.

It is all right, little one. A new voice; solitary; feminine.

Mama? Questioning.

No. But I will take care of you.

Where's my mother? Annika demanded.

I am your mother now.

No!

You must rest.

Those voices again. Always around. Always in my head. Why won't they go away? she wondered.

Because you are one of us now. You are Borg.

I am Annika! she answered stubbornly.

The pain came again.

She remembers too much, the voices decided. *We must increase the nanoprobes.*

If we do we may kill her, several answered back.

If we do not she'll continue to remember her human existence, the debate ensued.

I have plans for this one, the solitary voice said. *Do not damage her.*

Half a dose, then.

Agreed.

No! I don't want . . . But even as she protested, Annika felt warmth take the place of the pain. She started to drift away, but refused to surrender without a final word.

I am not *Borg. I am Annika Hansen, and I love strawberries!* she asserted.

Time passed. Usually Annika remained only barely conscious, floating in her tank. The voices in her mind were constant; although rarely did they talk about—or to—her. Their main concerns seemed to be the day-to-day running of the ship, and assimilating anyone who had the misfortune to cross their path. Their appetite seemed insatiable; their quest to absorb knowledge and technology their only motive for existence, and Annika's mind absorbed the knowledge right along with them.

During the infrequent times that she was fully aware of the goings-on in the shadowy corridors beyond her chamber, she focused on her memories, aware they seemed to be eluding her now, like water racing away with a receding tide. Well aware of the disciplinary action to be directed her way once the Borg became aware of her thoughts, she forced herself to remember just the same.

It is Annika's sixth birthday. She is celebrating it on the *Raven* with just her parents to join the party. She'd always wondered what it would be like to have an actual birthday party. With presents and games and friends to play with.

But then, she supposed, she'd have to have friends to invite over. They've never lived long enough in any one spot for Annika to make friends, and those children who might have *become* friends weren't allowed to play with her once their parents realized who her father is. Annika doesn't understand why the adults distrust her father so, but she knows it makes him angry and that, in turn, makes her mother cry. So they move. A lot. And go to space as often as her father can get some mysterious substance called funding. And they all pretend that space is where they want to be.

But Annika doesn't think her father is pretending. She thinks he is truly happiest out among the stars and away from people.

So today Annika is six and Mama's cooked her favorite dinner and made a chocolate cake for dessert. There are presents, including the latest adventure of Sarah Rowe, from her aunt Helen, smuggled aboard the ship by her mother. Music is furnished by the ship's computer. Annika's father twirls her mother across the deck in time to the music until both are breathless and her mother is laughing and flushed. The music ends, another, slower, song begins, and Annika's father turns to her.

"How 'bout a dance with your old dad?"

Annika nods excitedly and they waltz around the floor, Annika's feet resting atop her father's boots in the way of father/daughter dances the universe over. How she adores him! In that moment she could dance with him forever, feeling safe within his arms. Her father is fearless and strong . . . but of course, in the end, he is not strong enough to protect her from the nightmare to come.

Annika goes to bed that night with her new book on the bedside table and Rosie by her side. It's been the best birthday party ever, and it will be the last.

For in the night, the Borg come.

Time passed. Annika grew, matured. Legs lengthened, waist narrowed, breasts formed and grew full. She never knew a classroom, never again tasted her aunt Helen's strawberries, never felt the first inquisitive brush of a man's lips against her own. She would be beautiful had not her left eye and one arm been removed, replaced by metal implants and a red piercing light of her own. She would be tall and graceful were it not for the heavy boots and metal armor that encased her. She would be a woman were she not part of the hive mind.

Eventually, even her name eludes her. And shortly after that the tank is drained. She opens her eye, discovers that she can see, and glances around her at the ship she's been riding in all these years. The halls are lined with coffin-like structures, each filled with a Borg taking rest, yet many more machines roam the halls, attending to the functions assigned them. The door of the chamber opens, is pressurized with a rush of air, and she steps from the chamber onto the floor.

A trio of drones stand in a semicircle before her.

You will come with us.

They turn up the hall, expecting obedience, and she does not hesitate, falling into step behind one, while the remaining two fall in behind her.

They walk down several corridors before turning into a large shadowy room. She knows without having to be told that this is the center of the ship, the Queen's lair. And there, facing a computer screen that shows where they are in space and where the closest ships are, stands the Queen herself. The Queen turns, wordlessly dismisses the drones, and approaches her.

The Queen stops, studies her intently. She does not flinch, studies the Queen in turn, finds her the most beautiful thing she's ever seen, even more beautiful than . . . *what?* An image comes to her from a great corridor of distance, from a time when she was different. *But when was that? I've always been Borg! Haven't I?* Why wasn't she sure?

Be sure, the Queen's voice answers. *You are Borg.*

Yes, she thinks. *I am Borg.* She instantly gives her Queen her loyalty.

The Queen smiles.

So. You have matured.

Yes, Annika answers silently. *Matured from what?* she wonders, but the answer isn't there.

And what is your name?

It is a test. Annika searches. There is a small, dying, part of her that seeks to provide the defiant answer, despite the pain and certain death that will follow. For an instant she tastes something warm and sweet, feels juice running down her chin . . . remembers in a flash a large garden and a brown-and-white dog . . . and then, as quickly as it has arrived, it is gone forever and her name is lost with it.

I . . . have no name . . . she thinks, and feels saddened by the realization.

No. But you have a designation. I anoint you Seven of Nine, Tertiary Adjunct of Unimatrix Zero One. You will be one of my chosen circle. I have great plans for you, Seven of Nine.

The woman, once Annika Hansen, nods, accepting both the role and the designation.

Come. We have much work to do.

The Queen turns and Seven follows. Finally, she is home.

—STAR TREK—
ENTERPRISE

Rounding a Corner Already Turned

Allison Cain

"Sometimes I will . . . forget things, and, in going back to retrieve them, half expect to meet myself rounding a corner I've already turned . . ."

—Rupert Holmes

Lieutenant Malcolm Reed swore under his breath and vowed to himself that he would never, ever, as long as he lived, no matter *how* many court-martials he was threatened with, let Captain Jonathan Archer go on another away mission. Ever.

He ducked another energy blast and dove sideways, hoping that Trip wouldn't bombard him with *Mission: Impossible* comments for the next week. A glance to his left confirmed his initial guess of their location, and he motioned for the other three members of the team to bring them up to date.

Captain Archer, to his credit, followed Malcolm's gaze and saw

225

immediately what his armory officer had in mind. A few quick hand movements from Malcolm had Commander Trip Tucker nodding silently. Ensign Hoshi Sato afforded him a nervous glance, but also nodded in calm understanding. He was proud of her; she had looked terrified when their seemingly friendly hosts had first opened fire on them, but she had taken the last few minutes in stride, and never once made a sound.

Now Archer motioned for Malcolm to cover them and silently offered his arms to Hoshi. She reached out to take the small animal he held in them. Porthos stared back at his master from the safety of the linguist's arms. The two Kintarra had seemed most enthralled by the beagle on their brief sojourn to *Enterprise,* and the captain had thought that having the dog along would help negotiations run more smoothly. After spending fifteen minutes dodging alien gunshots, he was now regretting the decision.

Malcolm hissed quietly, and Trip and Hoshi made a dash for the doorway leading to their shuttle. Malcolm had managed to maneuver the battle around so that neither Kintarra stood between them and their only means of escape. When Hoshi and Trip were halfway there, Malcolm motioned for the captain to follow them.

It was at this point, he later reflected, that things started to go wrong.

Hoshi suddenly stumbled, managing to stay upright, but knocking into Trip. He somehow kept moving through an amazing feat of balance, but the impact was enough to knock the dog from Hoshi's arms. Porthos, being a very young beagle, did the most logical thing his canine brain could come up with. He headed for his pack leader to protect him.

Archer, however, had not stopped moving, and didn't notice the dog hurtling at him until it was too late.

"Porthos!" he shouted, trying to imitate Trip's gymnastic maneuvers and twist around without falling. Malcolm swore out loud at this, and turned toward his captain.

"Keep moving!" he bellowed, beginning to run himself. He bent and scooped up the beagle without slowing, sparing a glance over his shoulder at his pursuers as he saw the other three from his party make it safely through the doorway. Damn, they were close.

"Start closing the door! Hit the locking sequence!" he called. Thankfully they heard him; the doors began to slide shut. He was preparing to dive through the rapidly dwindling opening, the dog still cradled in his arms, when he heard an energy blast that sounded much closer than any of the others.

The pain that shot abruptly up his back was overwhelming, and threw him to his knees. As the world started to go black, he looked up to see his crewmates' horrified faces staring at him through the still closing doors. With his last bit of strength, he hurled Porthos in what he hoped was the general direction of the others, though his orientation had been the first thing to go. Then he sank into blessed numbness.

His head hurt.

That was the first thing that crossed Malcolm's mind as he began to fight his way back to consciousness. On the plus side, his back felt fine, but that didn't really help his headache.

Another thing that wasn't helping his headache was the worried voices of Hoshi, Trip, Archer, and Doctor Phlox. They were much too loud, he decided. Also, why had he never noticed how noisy sickbay really was? All those alien animals made a terrible racket. And the *smell*. You'd think he had never been there before.

He was grateful, however, for the smell, and even the loud noises. At least, they told him that he was back on *Enterprise,* among friends, rather than still on the alien ship. Or worse, dead. As he began to awaken, his mind registered more sensations. He was lying on his side, on a biobed. The doctor must have rolled him over to take care of his back. He was grateful that there were no longer tongues of fire shooting up his spine.

"Do you think Malcolm's okay?" The worry that filled Hoshi's voice made him frown. He was still groggy, but he needed to let his crewmates know he was all right, so he struggled momentarily to open his eyes, sit up, do *something.*

"I believe he's waking up," Phlox commented cheerfully. Malcolm heard the rustle of cloth as four people hurried over to his bed. This encouraged him to finally open his eyes and look up at the quartet that was staring anxiously down at him. *They look much larger from down here,* he thought, bemused, *and had that blast messed with my head? For some reason the whole world looks less . . . colorful. Or maybe that's the headache.*

"Is he going to be all right, Doc?" Archer asked, frowning worriedly. Malcolm wanted to roll his eyes, but decided that wouldn't be good for his headache. *Just ask me,* he thought exasperatedly.

"Of course," the doctor replied calmly, "he should have suffered no ill effects. He wasn't hit, after all."

What the . . . not . . . ? What was Phlox talking about?

"About Malcolm, Captain," Trip began.

"When can he return home?" Archer asked, gesturing toward him.

"Oh, he's ready to go now, Captain," Phlox assured him. Archer nodded.

"Don't worry," he told his crewmates, "we'll get Malcolm back, I promise."

Back? From where? I'm right here! Malcolm tried to shout, but for some reason his vocal cords weren't working properly. All he got out was a—

"Raarf!" Archer glanced at him.

"Ok, boy, we're going. Why don't you come with me to drop Porthos off at my quarters and we'll go to the bridge together?" he asked Hoshi and Trip. "We'll find Malcolm," he added firmly, "we won't leave without him."

They nodded and the captain reached down and lifted Malcolm easily. Hoshi smiled at him.

"I'm glad you're all right, Porthos," she said, "you have Malcolm to thank for that."

Behind the beagle's bright eyes, Lieutenant Malcolm Reed's mind screamed in horror.

*   *   *

Sometime later, Malcolm had managed to regain his composure. It wasn't an easy feat. The others had dropped him off in the captain's quarters and headed to the bridge. Malcolm spent the next several minutes running frantically in circles, disoriented and inwardly shrieking about the injustice and unfairness of the universe as a whole. Not a very professional way to behave, no, but really, what training had he ever had—what *indication* had he ever had—that would prepare him for switching bodies with his captain's puppy?

Malcolm was not used to being a dog, however, and there were some things that he took for granted as a human that Porthos did not have. For example, traction. Malcolm had never worried about his boots slipping and sliding over the smooth decks of the *Enterprise,* simply because they never had. They were Starfleet-issue, and had been specially made to deal with all types of terrain. Dogs, on the other hand, are not made for racing around on slippery surfaces. After over a year on board *Enterprise,* Porthos had adapted to deal with the deck plating. After over an hour in Porthos's body, Malcolm had not.

Have you ever seen a dog race into the kitchen at top speed, hit the linoleum, and slide headfirst into the fridge? That gives the general idea of what happened to Malcolm. Except it wasn't linoleum, it was the deck, and it wasn't a fridge, it was the captain's desk.

The crash did accomplish something good, though. Malcolm found himself on his side, little lungs heaving, staring up at the ceiling. *Think!* he told himself furiously. *You are a Starfleet officer. Now calm the hell down!!*

It took a few more minutes, but he was eventually able to stop panting desperately, climb to his feet, and shake himself off. Once he had accomplished the task of pulling himself together, he mentally "sat back" and took stock of his situation. Obviously, his first priority was to try to figure out some way of communicating with his crew—mainly Doctor Phlox—so that they could figure out some way to reunite him with his body. *Scratch that,* he thought after a hasty look around the cabin confirmed his suspicions that there was no one here to attempt communication with. So his new first priority was getting out of the captain's quarters . . . as soon as he figured out how to reach the door panel.

The captain did not sleep that night. He spent the night in his ready room, reviewing and discarding countless ways of rescuing his armory officer—once said officer was found, and if it was discovered he needed rescuing after being found. Tired and distracted as he was, he didn't spare a second thought for the lonely dog in his quarters until late the next morning.

Malcolm had not given Archer a second thought. He had briefly tried to discover an escape route, but the events of the day had taken their toll, and he soon collapsed into an exhausted sleep. He awoke early the next morning, however, feeling much better and ready to try out an idea from the night before.

Captain Archer had never worried about his dog escaping his quarters, mainly because Porthos was neither intelligent enough, nor tall enough to work the locking mechanism. Malcolm, though saddled with Porthos's height, was not limited by the beagle's intelligence. After a thoughtful survey of the room, he concluded that the easiest piece of furniture to move would be the desk chair; hopefully, it would give him enough height to reach the keypad.

Having done dog-walking duty for the captain before, Malcolm knew exactly where all of Porthos's things were stored. After several attempts, he finally managed to knock the door of the small cabinet open. Then it was just a small matter of tugging the worn leash down from its hook. Leash acquired, Malcolm trotted over to the chair. He painstakingly wound the leash around the front two chair legs; then patiently worked the clip end through the hand loop at the opposite end of the leash. That accomplished, he grasped the leash firmly in his jaws and began to slowly back up.

Moving the chair across the room took much longer than Malcolm had anticipated. The desk chairs, so easy for a human to pick up, were extremely heavy and bulky for a small dog to handle. Eventually, however, Malcolm managed to drag the chair close enough to the door for him to reach the keypad. He dropped the leash and leapt up onto the seat of the chair. By placing his front paws on the chair back, he was just able to reach the keypad with his nose. Carefully (so as not to bruise himself) he tapped in his security override and was rewarded with the gentle whoosh as the doors slid open.

Smirking inwardly, Malcolm trotted out into the open corridors of the *Enterprise.*

Hoshi was hurrying down the corridor toward the turbolift, preoccupied with studying a data padd on the Kintarran language. She nearly missed the flash of movement as a small figure scurried around the corner ahead of her.

"Porthos?" she called into the now-deserted corridor. Frowning, she quickened her pace and turned the corner in time to catch a glimpse of a wagging tail disappearing down the corridor toward the mess hall. Hoshi muttered a few choice Klingon words and broke into a run. She was already late to meet with the captain. She hadn't slept since yesterday, she couldn't recall the last time she'd eaten, and she was worried about Malcolm. If Porthos managed to get himself lost in the bowels of the *Enterprise,* on top of everything . . .

Hoshi was nearly in a full-out sprint by the time she reached the mess hall. Without even pausing to look around, she flew into the room, searching for the small dog. That was her first mistake. Her second mistake was that she had chosen to enter the mess hall at top speed fifteen minutes after the gamma shift had ended on a blueberry pancakes day.

Little did Hoshi know that only moments before Malcolm had made the exact same mistake. Fortunately for Malcolm, he had been more alert to his surroundings; and even though he had no traction, he was small enough that crashing headfirst into the crewman pouring maple syrup for the line of hungry gamma shifters had no effect on either the man or the dog. *Un*fortunately for Hoshi, even though she had traction, she was also trying to avoid frantically stepping on the beagle—and though Hoshi Sato was small for a human, she wasn't *that* small. Malcolm saw her look of shock, and had the presence of mind to duck under the nearest table.

Thus it was that scene that Captain Archer stepped into when he entered the mess hall and found it strewn with blueberry pancakes and fallen crewmen, many of whom had apparently been sprayed with maple syrup. Glancing down, he found Hoshi sitting on the floor, drenched with the sticky substance, but triumphantly holding up a wriggling dog who was the only creature in the room (apart from Archer himself) that was not dripping syrup.

"I'm sorry, Captain," she said guiltily, starting to stand and grateful for the firm hand at her elbow that prevented her from falling headfirst into the table when she slipped on the puddle of syrup she had been sitting in. "This is all my fault. You see, I was chasing Porthos, and—" Archer held up a hand to forestall any more explanations.

"Hoshi, it's . . . you look terrible. When was the last time you slept? Or ate?" he asked, his manner changing from reassurance to concern when he saw the circles under her eyes.

"Well, I've been busy—"

"Hoshi, you are officially off-duty for the next four hours. Captain's orders," Archer stated firmly when she started to protest.

"But, sir! Malcolm is still missing, and the Kintarran language—"

"Hoshi, you've done all you can. The UT is having no trouble with the specs you gave it, and we still have yet to get our scanners working through the alien shielding. Go back to your quarters and get cleaned up, I'll have Chef send some food to you. I promise I'll call you immediately if we find Malcolm—after all, you're still our best translator." He smiled reassuringly at the ensign, and she reluctantly nodded.

"Yes, sir."

"Oh, would you mind taking Porthos with you? I don't know how he got out, but my door lock might be malfunctioning. At least he won't escape from your quarters if you're in there with him. I'll come pick him up after my shift is over." Hoshi nodded again and slowly walked out of the mess hall. Archer rubbed a hand wearily over his face and turned to survey the rest of the room, wishing his security officer was here.

Damm it, Reed, he thought, feeling the beginnings of a headache, *if you're not alive when we find you, I'll kill you.*

The tall, tangerine-colored lizard was alternating from staring bemusedly into the habitat cage beneath him, and exchanging thoughtful glances with his turquoise companion.

"Perhaps we were wrong, Ta'kha; this creature is just as amusing as the little one."

Ta'kha was frowning. "Yes, Puor, but I had thought this species was more intelligent than this one leads me to believe."

Puor shrugged his neck frill. "Perhaps it is the other way around. Perhaps the small one was controlling the large ones."

"That is an intriguing idea."

"If that is the case, then perhaps these creatures are valuable. Perhaps many others would pay to have one of these to display."

Ta'kha's tail waved. "But it was very hard to acquire just this one. Surely it would be even more difficult and dangerous to capture many more."

"Perhaps we don't need that many. Perhaps we only need *one* more."

There was a moment of thoughtful silence, and then both aliens turned to gaze introspectively into the habitat cage, where the pale human was alternately yelling nonsense words at the Vossk in the next display and attempting to scratch his ear with his foot.

Upon reaching her quarters, Hoshi keyed the door open and deposited the dog on the floor, after making sure the lock was properly set. Then she turned and eyed herself in the full-length mirror next to her closet.

"Drat, I was hoping the captain was exaggerating," she muttered as she sized up her appearance. Malcolm's ears pricked at the sound of her voice, but his attention was absorbed in looking around the room. He had never been in the linguist's quarters before, at least not for more than a moment or so after handing her some data padd, or stopping by to escort her to lunch. He was taking the opportunity to search for possible security hazards when her voice, still speaking in the easy tone people adopt when addressing animals, caught his attention. Malcolm turned toward her . . . and froze when he actually caught sight of Hoshi.

She was trying to comb sticky tangles out of her hair, smiling at him in the mirror. What had paralyzed Malcolm, however, was the fact that Hoshi's uniform and regulation blues were lying in a sticky heap on the floor, while Hoshi herself was wearing only syrup and a towel.

Bloody daft! Malcolm berated himself silently, while trying not to stare at Hoshi. He should have realized that she would need to clean up! And she, not realizing who he really was, thought nothing of undressing in front of the captain's dog! Malcolm managed to look hurriedly away before Hoshi began to realize anything was amiss, but the sound of her frustrated sigh and the click of her comb on the dresser prompted him to involuntarily (bloody canine instincts!) glance back up.

"I'm just going to have to wash this out first, I think," Hoshi said, grimacing at her reflection's hair. "I'll be out in a bit, Porthos, don't chew anything up, okay?" Malcolm frantically tore his gaze away from his shipmate as she moved toward the bathroom door, hands at her towel. He flinched slightly as he heard the towel land in the pile of sticky clothes on the floor in a soft swoosh of fabric and finally breathed a sigh of relief at the sound of the bathroom door closing.

His relief, however, was short-lived. He couldn't attempt to communicate with Hoshi now! How embarrassed would she be if she knew her superior officer had hidden in her room and watched her undress? That wasn't precisely what had happened, of course, but Malcolm was not willing to risk the potential damage to his friendship, and chain of command, with Hoshi. He needed to get out of this room before she finished her shower.

Unfortunately, this was much easier said than done. In Archer's quarters, Malcolm had used his security override to open the doors. The same tactic was sure to work with Hoshi's door . . . if Malcolm had a way of reaching the keypad. He sat below it, staring nearly straight up, and realized just how much trouble he was in.

Hoshi stepped out of her bathroom, no longer sticky and wrapped in her favorite fluffy robe, to find Porthos jumping at the keypad for her door.

"Oh, no, you don't!" she scolded, catching the beagle mid-leap. "You are staying right here, whether you like it or not." She settled onto her bed, keeping a firm grip on the small dog, who struggled in her arms. Attempting to calm him down, Hoshi began to tell him about her day, but since this consisted mainly of their efforts to find Malcolm, she instead found herself thinking about all the terrible things that could be happening to him. She let her monologue trail bleakly off, her grip on the beagle loosening.

"Oh, Porthos, I hope he's okay!"

Malcolm wanted to swear out loud when Hoshi snatched him away from the door, but instead he contented himself with the knowledge that she had given him the perfect opening. All thoughts about sparing her dignity vanished and he scrambled to find a way to show her who he really was.

Malcolm vaulted easily from Hoshi's lap onto her desk, scattering her notes on Kintarran grammar onto the floor and prompting a dismayed cry from the linguist.

"Porthos! I need those to help Malcolm!" Malcolm barked sharply when she said his name, unable to think of any other way to call attention to himself. She glared at him.

"You owe Malcolm your life, mister! Don't you want him back?" Malcolm solemnly nodded. Hoshi froze.

"Porthos, did—? No, of course not. You can't actually . . . *under-stand* me." Malcolm yipped. Hoshi stared at him.

"Wait—Porthos . . . *can* you understand me?" Malcolm nodded again, hoping Hoshi wouldn't faint. Instead, she got more excited.

"I don't believe it! Wait, you got all excited when I mentioned

Malcolm—Porthos, can you help us find him?" Malcolm wanted to dance for joy; she was so much more perceptive than he had hoped! He nodded again.

"Do you know where he is?" Hoshi demanded, staring intently into Malcolm's eyes. He nodded once more, slowly. "Where?" she asked, her voice a whisper. Malcolm looked helplessly at her, but was saved the trouble of attempting an answer by, of all people, Archer, who knocked on the door to Hoshi's quarters. When the captain entered, he found his linguistics officer staring at his dog.

"Hoshi? I . . . figured out how Porthos got out of my quarters." Hoshi lifted her gaze to look at her captain in amazement, unable to believe he was concerned with such a thing at a time like this. His next words, however, stilled the rebuke on her tongue.

"He used Malcolm's security override." Both humans now turned to stare at the beagle, who did his best to shrug innocently.

"Malcolm, if that's really you in there, bark twice," Trip ordered, peering into the beagle's eyes. Ensign Travis Mayweather, seated on an unoccupied biobed, snickered softly, and sang under his breath what sounded suspiciously like, "Knock three times on the ceiling if you want me, twice on the pipe if the answer is no." Malcolm glared coldly at them both. Travis's song faltered and died; Trip grinned broadly.

"That's him, all right! No one gives the evil eye like Malcolm!"

"Of course it's him," Archer snapped. "The question is: how?"

"Now that," Doctor Phlox said from behind them, "is actually quite fascinating." The doctor was positively beaming. Even T'Pol, examining the console the two had been working at, looked intrigued. The rest of the command crew turned expectantly toward the physician.

"Now," Phlox began, "the beam that Lieutenant Reed was hit by was intended to stun—to 'knock out.' In this case, the reference is much more literal. When a being is hit by the beam, their consciousness is forcibly pushed out of their body for the briefest of instants. When their mind returns, the body has already shut down.

The mind itself then shuts down for a brief period of time, which can be adjusted by modifying the beam strength."

"But that sounds like the mind should automatically return to its own body," Archer objected, "so why is Malcolm my dog?"

"I'll let T'Pol explain that," Phlox said, stepping aside. "Vulcans have been studying this sort of thing for years, of course. Sub-Commander?"

"The beam that hit Lieutenant Reed was most likely set for a normal Kintarran," T'Pol explained, glancing at the console. "This would have been too high of an energy signature for the lieutenant's body to deal with. However, he was also holding Porthos. The excess energy, instead of simply overloading Lieutenant Reed's systems, somehow drained into the dog."

"So both of their minds were thrown away from their bodies," Trip said thoughtfully.

"But that doesn't explain how they switched bodies," Travis pointed out.

"Lieutenant Reed and Porthos did not switch bodies," T'Pol disagreed, "they switched *minds*. Immediately after he was hit, just as the system overload was beginning, Lieutenant Reed threw Porthos away from his body. He was also making a mental 'toss' with his mind, in order to ensure the dog's flight path. Therefore, when his mind tried to return to his body, it was closer to Porthos's body, and vice versa. At least," and here T'Pol looked faintly displeased, "in theory. I have never seen this phenomenon before, and I doubt it could be duplicated without years of research." She paused a moment, then added, "I believe Lieutenant Reed wishes to say something."

Since the sight of the beagle standing on his hind legs and waving his little front paws wildly in the air had most likely prompted this remark, everyone was inclined to agree. The dog pointed with his nose at the console, sat up as though begging, and finally chased his tail in a circle. The others stared for a moment before Hoshi hesitantly said, "I . . . think he wants to know how he can switch back." Malcolm nodded.

"That should not be a problem," T'Pol said, "as long as Lieu-tenant Reed's body is still alive, I should be able to help him 'switch back' through a mind-meld."

"I thought you said you wouldn't be able to duplicate the process," Archer said. T'Pol favored him with a long look before answering.

"I won't be trying to duplicate it," she said in that too-patient tone that Trip was sure all Vulcans were taught as children, "I will simply be releasing the minds to return to their bodies of origin, not forc-ing them into the *wrong* body." Phlox nodded in understanding; the four humans pretended to do the same.

"Right then." Archer briskly took charge again. "Travis, Trip, continue working on breaking through the Kintarran shielding. T'Pol, I'd like you to work with Phlox on finding a way to reverse this process that's at least ninety percent foolproof—I'm not risking my armory officer in an unsafe procedure. Malcolm, if the doctor's finished with you, I'd like you to remain with Hoshi in her quarters." Archer consciously paused for objections.

"Sir!" Hoshi protested, at the same time Malcolm let out a rather high-pitched yelp. Archer sighed, trying to ignore his growing head-ache, and held up both hands to forestall any arguments from the pair.

"Hear me out! Hoshi, I meant what I said about you getting food and rest, and I know you got neither since the last time I saw you. And Malcolm, unless you want everyone on the ship to know about your predicament—" At that, the beagle shook his head furiously, and if it were physically possible for dogs to blush, his fur would have been bright red. Archer nodded in understanding. "—I can't have you wandering around all by your lonesome. So your choices are to either remain here in sickbay, or stay with Hoshi."

On the whole, Malcolm thought his chances of survival would be higher on his own, but he noticed Archer hadn't listed that among his options. Since he wasn't ready to spend the rest of the day being scanned and prodded by Phlox, Malcolm decided to take his chances with Hoshi. At least he might get some food in the linguist's company. Hoshi grimaced, but apparently thought twice about arguing with her captain, and simply nodded.

"Good, if that's settled, then we all need to get back to work." Archer, Trip, and Travis hurried out the door, while Phlox ran a few more scans on Malcolm. Finally he declared that the dog would be allowed to leave sickbay, but that Hoshi was to stay in contact with Phlox and/or T'Pol just in case something happened. Feeling she would agree to almost anything to get out of there, the ensign was finally able to make her escape with the dog, whom she managed to avoid looking at—at least until they reached her quarters.

Puor strolled lazily through the menagerie, ostensibly searching for his mate, but knowing exactly where he would find her. Sure enough, Ta'kha was once again standing outside the human's habitat, tapping notes into the handheld database she carried.

"Ta'kha, perhaps you have done enough for the night? Perhaps we can eat," he said, letting his neck frill droop. She glanced at him, obviously upset.

"I have been running scans on this creature all afternoon," she said irritably, "and your plan will not work, Puor. From my calculations, this species is incapable of producing large litters. I would guess that they rarely produce more than one offspring at a time. And from the information exchange with their ship, I estimate that it takes up to twenty egg-cycles before full maturation! That is much too impractical for our purposes." Puor could see from the stiffness of her tail that his mate was most displeased by this revelation. He was a bit disgruntled himself, but . . .

"Perhaps we need not abandon our plan, but merely change it? Perhaps we make the creature exclusive—to zoos and rarity collectors only, and keep the only breeding *pair* here in the menagerie. If we perhaps acquire several females, we can keep them here for several egg-cycles and sell only the female offspring; then, in a few cycles, we can charge more for an impregnated female—"

"With the understanding that male offspring will be returned to the menagerie and half the price refunded?" Ta'kha said, her eyes narrowing shrewdly.

"Of course, or perhaps a second impregnation instead of a refund." He could already see his mate's tail relaxing as she calculated expenses versus profit.

"We shall be rich, Puor," she hissed sibilantly, and he closed his eyes as she rubbed neck frills briefly with him.

"And now, dinner, perhaps?" he asked quietly. She laughed her agreement.

Malcolm and Hoshi had managed to eat while avoiding conversation—an accomplishment made easier by the fact that one of them couldn't speak English . . . or any language, for that matter. Malcolm was trying to think of some way to apologize for his earlier inadvertent faux pas when he was saved by the bell—well, the comm.

"Hoshi?" Archer's voice came over the intercom. *"We need you on the bridge. The Kintarra have just contacted us."*

The giant orange lizard on the screen did not greatly improve Hoshi's mood. He looked rather smug (as smug, anyway, as a giant orange lizard can appear), and he was staring at her—*had* been staring at her since the moment she entered the bridge. Not just her, she realized after a moment, but at the small dog she held in her arms.

"He wants to speak about Malcolm," Archer told Hoshi in a low voice, "but he said something about wishing to speak directly to our 'Controller'—whatever that means. It might just be a glitch in the UT; I'm hoping you can make better sense out of it."

"Ah, you have arrived; perhaps now we can dispense with the puppets and speak directly? Perhaps these pale creatures amuse you, but we prefer a more . . . personal *approach to business."* The lizard directed this at Hoshi—no, she realized abruptly, at *Malcolm.* Suddenly it all clicked. She reached down and hit the Mute button at her console.

"Captain, I think the Kintarra somehow believe that Porthos—er, Malcolm—is controlling us. That he's the only intelligent being on board! But I don't understand how . . ." Her eyes met Archer's in sudden comprehension.

"If they have Malcolm's body, with Porthos's mind in it . . ." he breathed. "Of course they're assuming we're all at the same intelligence level!" He stared thoughtfully at the screen for a moment.

"Hoshi, I want you to speak to them, see if you can find out where they have Malcolm's body. Malcolm, go sit in my chair and try to appear to be intelligent." The small beagle threw his captain a cold look. "Ah, what I meant was, make it look like you're the one doing all the thinking—we're just your pawns." The dog made what appeared to be an attempt to roll his eyes, but jumped out of Hoshi's arms to trot over to the captain's chair and hop up. Archer nodded briefly to Hoshi, who tapped her console and turned to reply to the Kintarran.

"What is it that you wished to discuss?" she asked the lizard. His neck frills snapped back, a sure sign of annoyance.

"I wish to speak with you directly," he told Malcolm. Hoshi moved to stand behind the chair that the dog/Malcolm was occupying.

"The 'puppets' are a necessity," she answered, thinking fast. "My own vocal cords are insufficient to communicate in your tongue." Malcolm tried to look imperious and condescending; at the helm, Travis stifled a laugh.

"I see," the Kintarran murmured. *"Well, perhaps we should simply proceed. Perhaps you have noticed that one of your puppets is missing? You should not be worried; we have it in our care at the moment."*

"I had noticed," Hoshi admitted. "I have been searching for it. I'm so glad that you found it, as it is one of my favorites. How soon may I retrieve it?" Malcolm tipped his head to one side, shrewdly eyeing the viewscreen. The lizard's smug look turned sly.

"Well, now, we should discuss this. My mate has grown very fond of the creature; perhaps, since you yourself have so many, you would be willing to let this one go? Of course, we would be willing

to pay you—perhaps more than it is worth." Malcolm shook his head, eyes narrowing. Hoshi imitated the movement.

"I'm afraid that is out of the question," she replied. "I am quite fond of all of my pets. I only want its return." The Kintarran stared at the dog for a moment, then shrugged his neck frill.

"Perhaps it is just as well that you come retrieve your pet. You may, perhaps, bring the dark-haired puppet with you; it has the best accent." Hoshi glanced surreptitiously at Archer, who nodded slightly.

"This is acceptable," she told the lizard. They spoke for a few more moments, making arrangements, then said their good-byes.

"My ready room," Archer said as soon as the screen went black.

"Puor, what are you doing?" Ta'kha snapped at her mate. "We are not willing to *pay* for the creature we already have, nor do we wish to return it! We want another one!"

"Perhaps you did not realize what I did," Puor soothed. "The puppet-creature I requested to accompany the Controller is a female. When they arrive, we simply take them both into custody. Then we will have what we want."

"Or, *perhaps* we can take it a step further," Ta'kha said, her frill brightening. "If we simply *kill* the Controller, then we can take *all* of the puppet-creatures for ourselves." Puor smiled benignly.

"Your wisdom is, perhaps, beyond mine," he murmured. "It is an excellent plan." The two Kintarra hissed in glee.

To say that Malcolm disapproved of the plan would be an understatement. Malcolm was profoundly unhappy with the plan, a fact that he was communicating by barking loudly. Trip and Travis were frowning, and Hoshi was wincing slightly. Archer frowned at his security officer.

"Malcolm, I realize you're not happy with this, but it's the only way the Kintarra will allow us anywhere near your body. Look, we're not going to send you and Hoshi down there all by yourselves, despite what we told that Kintarran. For one thing, Hoshi isn't qualified to pilot a shuttlepod. Take a moment and be reasonable about this."

Malcolm was still unhappy, but the captain was making sense . . . and, of course, he *was* the captain. So Malcolm settled down to wait anxiously as the rest of the command crew discussed their options— feeling powerless and wishing desperately to be back in his own body.

In the end, Malcolm was still not pleased with the travel arrangements, though he grudgingly admitted that (despite his vow the previous day) Captain Archer was the best choice to pilot the shuttle since he had more experience than Travis (and was a better shot). And it made sense for T'Pol to come along in case anything else were to go wrong with the mind-switching situation (or in case anyone else got hit by the Kintarran weapon). However, despite the fact that there would not be that much room in the shuttlepod, he still would have felt better if they were accompanied by a team of security officers. Two teams. With rifles. But he knew that the Kintarra would most likely react badly to that, and so he kept his muzzle shut and sat dubiously next to Hoshi as the small away team headed back to the Kintarran ship.

Twenty minutes later Malcolm found himself once again dodging alien gunshots and thinking fiercely that if people would just *listen* to him once in a while he wouldn't get *shot* at so often. Then again, he reflected, if he would stop volunteering as bait, his injury quota would probably drop significantly.

It had started out well enough; the Kintarra had greeted them civilly and politely accepted Hoshi's spurious explanation of the presence of the other two "puppets." They had courteously led the way to where they were keeping Malcolm's body and even amicably chatted with Malcolm (through Hoshi, of course) on the trip there. It was when they actually got within sight of Malcolm's body that things began to fall apart again.

Porthos had caught sight of Archer, and immediately began yelling at the top of his lungs and lunging at the barrier that separated him from his beloved master. Malcolm would never know whether the Kintarra thought he was warning them, or just thought that he had provided them with a good opening—either way, they chose that moment to open fire.

Luckily, Malcolm had been walking at that point, and they seemed to be concentrating on him, which gave his crewmates time to find some cover, minimal though it was in the menagerie. Malcolm, noticing that the Kintarra were ignoring the others completely, remembered Archer's puppet theory, put two and two together, and played a hunch. Praying his crewmates would understand, he took off deeper into the menagerie—and was rewarded by both Kintarra following him.

A blast that destroyed a section of wall over his shoulder brought his attention back to the present. These shots were obviously *not* meant to stun . . . Malcolm wasn't sure why the Kintarra wanted to kill him, nor did he care—but he had had just about enough. *Okay,* he gritted silently to himself. *You want to play? Let's play.* Darting around a corner, he skidded to a stop under a low-hanging bench and waited, motionless.

Moments later the two lizards rounded the corner and stopped, glancing about. The tangerine one hissed something in its own language and plunged deeper into the menagerie, leaving Malcolm crouched behind the smaller, turquoise one. He contemplated several courses of action before settling on finding out just how similar to lizards the Kintarra really were.

Apparently *very* similar—when he sank his tiny fangs into the turquoise tail in front of him and jerked hard, the tall alien was thrown completely off balance . . . and fell backward into the bench Malcolm was still crouching under . . . and shrieked in pain as the long turquoise tail separated from its body, sending Malcolm tumbling.

Unfortunately, its mate's screams attracted the tangerine Kintarran, who came barreling back down the path. Malcolm knew when to cut his losses; he ran, as fast as his four legs would carry him, back toward his shipmates, hoping desperately that they would have some sort of plan. Fortunately, they hadn't been idle in his brief absence.

"Malcolm!" Hoshi cried, waving from the path in front of him. He wanted to growl at her to get out of the way . . . when she did just that—leaving an open doorway behind her. Malcolm recognized the now-empty cage that had previously held his own body, calculated his position, and slowed down just enough to let the outraged Kintarran behind him get close enough to make a grab at him . . . just as he ducked through the doorway.

He immediately hit the brakes, paws scrabbling for purchase on the floor, and managed to somehow twist out of the lizard's grasp. He launched himself desperately back at the doorway and was swept up into Archer's arms as the alien threw itself at the door . . . and slammed into the barrier that T'Pol had reestablished an instant before.

The four humans and the dog stood staring at the Kintarran, who was shrieking what Malcolm suspected were swear words in its own language at them; Porthos responded by yelling nonsensically. T'Pol's face took on a slightly pained expression, and for once Malcolm could sympathize with her sensitive hearing.

"Let's go home," Archer said, shaking his head. Malcolm sighed in relief.

"And then T'Pol had to sedate Porthos because he kept trying to climb into the captain's lap to lick his face—which would have been fine except for the fact that he was still in Malcolm's body *and* Captain Archer was trying to pilot the shuttle."

Malcolm winced to himself as he paused outside the mess hall, listening to Hoshi tell Travis the unedited version of the story that no one outside of the command crew was allowed to hear. *Ever.* Travis hooted with laughter and Malcolm winced again as Trip's voice joined in. He was never going to live this one down.

On the other hand, it was a relief to hear Hoshi laughing. Apparently Porthos's antics in Malcolm's body had more than made up for the fact that he had accidentally been in her room while she undressed (even though he had sworn several times that he had not peeked). And at least he was back in his own body, none the worse for wear, he reflected before finally dredging up the courage to enter the mostly deserted mess hall.

"Well, look what the dog dragged in," Trip drawled as Malcolm joined the trio at a far table.

"That's *cat,*" he glowered, trying his "evil eye" on the grinning engineer.

"Yeah, Commander, you're barking up the wrong tree," Travis said gleefully. Malcolm turned his glare on the helmsman, who simply continued to look amused. Trip shook his head.

"I will never understand how you managed to pull off that look as a dog—I mean, your nostrils even flared the same way!"

"Well, you know what they say, Commander," Hoshi put in smoothly. "You can't teach an old dog new tricks." Malcolm groaned and buried his face in his hands as the other three snickered.

"Something wrong, Lieutenant?" T'Pol's voice behind him made him lift his head. The Vulcan was standing with a steaming cup in one hand and a data padd in the other.

"What are you working on this late at night?" Hoshi asked curiously.

"I am finishing my report on the effects of the Kintarran weapon to send to Vulcan," she explained. "This technology should be examined thoroughly by some of our experts." Malcolm returned his face to his hands, wondering just how much worse this could get.

"Are you going to include an in-depth study of Porthos's actions in Malcolm's body?" Trip asked interestedly. Malcolm's head shot up. T'Pol stared somberly at the armory officer's suddenly panicked face.

"I will, Lieutenant, be quite . . . *discreet* in my report," she assured him seriously. "Besides," she added, quirking one eyebrow, "I have heard that it is always best to let sleeping dogs lie."

Malcolm felt his face flame as his crewmates burst into laughter. Oh yeah, he was *never* going to live this one down.

Mother Nature's Little Reminders

A. Rhea King

T'Pol, Archer, Trip, Phlox, and Hoshi raced across the open prairie
through a downpour. They ran into the waiting shuttlepod, stopping
once they were out of the rain. Trip stopped next to the open hatch
and leaned against the hull as he caught his breath. They were all
soaked to the bone and he considered jabbing Archer for not listening to him when he said the storm was coming fast. The five jumped
when something thumped loudly against the shuttlepod hull.

"What was that?" Hoshi asked.

With a deafening roar the sky let loose golf-ball–sized hail.

"Shut the hatch!" Archer yelled over the din.

Trip reached out, grabbing the hatch handle. He started to pull it
shut but stopped. He heard something beyond the pounding hail,
rain, and wind. It was something that his mind was certain it knew;
something his mind told him to fear.

Trip looked up at the putrid green and black clouds overhead.

His subconscious was trying desperately to recover a deep recessed memory.

"*Shut the hatch, Trip!*" Archer repeated.

"*Ho—*" Trip started to yell. The hail abruptly stopped the rest of her name.

The rain and wind stopped and the planet held its breath, anxiously waiting for something. It made Trip's stomach knot, because his mind knew what was going on, it just couldn't find the alcove where the associated memory had been stored.

"What?" Hoshi asked him.

The memories suddenly broke free and with them surfaced terror. His breath caught.

"Let's gather the gear and head back," Archer said.

He remembered a small voice screaming, *I have to get Rufus! He's going to die! I have to get Rufus, Grandpa!*

Trip began to visibly tremble, but only Hoshi noticed. She laid a hand on his arm as a comforting gesture. In response, he looked at her, wide-eyed with terror.

"Trip, what's wrong?" she asked.

The other three crew members looked at him.

"It's coming," Trip whispered.

"What is?"

Trip heard it now: a low, distant rumble.

We should lift off! Get the hell out of here! We—We're out of time, Charles! We're going to die! It'll kill us! It won't care! It doesn't have feelings, it's not sentient!

The elements outside bombarded the land again. A piece of hail stung Trip's arm and the physical pain brought his mind and body back into synch. He regained control of his paralyzing panic.

Trip turned to the others. "We have to go to the gully. Come on."

He ran into the storm but stopped when he realized the others weren't following. Trip ran back to the open hatch.

"*We have to go!*"

"It's hailing, Trip!" Archer argued.

The roar was getting louder.

"Cap'n—"

"What's that sound?" Phlox asked.

Trip looked across the prairie and gaped. He grabbed Archer's wrist, and at a run, yanked him out of the shuttle pod.

"Come on, people!" Trip screamed, running toward the gulley.

Archer tried to pull his arm away from Trip's painful grip, but adrenaline had made Trip's grip unbreakable. Behind them, the roar was growing to a deafening decibel level. Archer looked back and everything in the universe seemed to slow, except for the massive black funnel cloud that filled the horizon as it bore down on them. At the realization of what they were running from, Archer stopped fighting Trip.

Trip came to a wide, steep-sided gully and let Archer go. He slipped and slid down the muddy embankment, spotting an opening on his way down. He ran to it, clawing at the dirt and rocks as he scuttled into the tiny space. Trip crawled into the far back and sat down. Archer was right behind him and sat down on Trip's leg. T'Pol, Hoshi, and Phlox squeezed in around them.

"That was . . ." Hoshi panted. "There was a . . ."

"Tornado," T'Pol finished dully.

Trip closed his eyes. He clenched his hands into fists that were so tight that his fingernails cut into the skin on his palms. As the volume of the tornado increased, Trip's trembling intensified.

Through gritted teeth Trip muttered, "One Mississippi, two Mississippi . . ."

Confused by his actions—or rather, reactions—the other four looked at him. Something crashed loudly outside and Archer glanced away. Outside, the light had faded to dark gray. Trees flew past the cave, some hitting the ground and splintering. Archer's communicator beeped. He reached into his arm pocket with a shaking hand and ripped it out.

"Archer."

"*Sir, we're tracking a funnel cloud on sensors. It's three times larger than an F-five class with winds in excess of five hundred kilometers. You should seek shelter.*"

It sounded like something was being ripped right outside the cave, followed by a bullet-like whining. Archer instinctively pushed farther back into the cave and against Trip.

"I can't talk right now. Stand by." Archer snapped the communicator shut.

Trip glanced at his hand when he felt someone pick it up. T'Pol held his hand tightly in hers, and despite her calm expression, her light trembling hand gave away that she was scared. Trip closed his eyes again, continuing to count Mississippi. Archer muttered something unintelligible.

A tree hit the ground outside, bounced up, struck the inside of the cave only centimeters from Doctor Phlox, and was ripped away. Phlox moved back, pushing Hoshi farther into the cave and into Archer and T'Pol. The roar of the tornado grew to a deafening volume. Archer closed his eyes and repeatedly recited his hope that his crew and he would make it through this alive.

"It'll be okay," Archer heard a voice say.

Archer looked back at Trip. Trip had suddenly collected himself and looked calm, despite the destruction going on outside the cave. Trip put his arm around T'Pol's shoulders, but looked into Archer's eyes. He didn't look scared anymore, as if the roaring funnel of death outside had already slipped by and life was going on.

"It'll pass soon." Trip looked away.

The roar of the tornado began to fade away and the wind subsided. Darkness gave way to brilliant sunshine and a light drizzle. The soft sound of rain hitting the ground sounded odd compared to what had just passed them. No one moved.

"Twister's past. Let's go straighten things out," Trip told them.

Archer looked back at him. His behavior through the entire event had been confusing.

T'Pol was the first to move. She pulled away from Trip and crawled over Phlox and Hoshi. They followed her. Archer crawled to the entrance, but stopped, looking back at Trip.

"Are you okay?" Archer asked.

Trip held his gaze for a long time, and then crawled past him.

Archer followed and the two climbed out of the gully, standing next to the other three.

There was a trough one and a half meters deep and twenty-three kilometers wide and less than six meters from them. Archer turned, staring at the tornado. It had traveled far and while still black, it didn't look nearly as threatening. The clouds behind it were innocent gray clouds, swollen with rain.

"Sir," Hoshi said. "I found one of our scanners."

Archer turned to her. She held up a branch with a scanner fully embedded in it.

"That was an experience I don't care to repeat," Doctor Phlox commented.

Trip walked to the edge of the trough. He stared at the bare ground, his mind drifting into the past again.

"Archer to *Enterprise*," he heard Archer say.

Trip looked up at the overcast sky.

"Go ahead, sir," a crewman answered.

"Send the other shuttlepod. The tornado destroyed ours."

"Right away, sir."

Trip closed his eyes. *Poor Rufus. Poor Grandpa Charles.*

Archer walked into the mess hall and found Trip sitting at a table in the center of the room with his back toward the entrance.

"I've been all over this ship looking for you, Trip," Archer told him as he walked up to him. "Why didn't you answer when I called for you?"

Trip didn't reply. Archer stopped beside him, looking at the photographs strewn across the table. They showed the aftermath of the tornado they had just experienced. It had leveled a forest and the ruins they had been exploring. Archer looked at the picture Trip was holding. It wasn't from the tornado. This picture had three children, one of them eight-year-old Trip, and two elderly adults. Everyone except Trip was facing the camera. Young Trip was crouched next to the porch, looking over his shoulder at the photographer. Archer looked at Trip's face.

"Trip."

Trip didn't acknowledge him.

"Charles."

Trip looked up at him. "What?"

"Didn't you hear me calling for you?"

"Yeah, 'cept you only use 'Charles' when I'm in trouble or you're introducing me to someone." Trip smiled.

"No. Over the comm. I've been calling for you for ten minutes."

Trip shook his head, looking back at the photograph. "I didn't hear you. Sorry, sir."

"Mind if I join you?" Archer motioned to the empty chair next to him.

Trip shook his head.

Archer sat down and leaned on the table, watching Trip's face. Trip was looking sadly at the photograph in his hand.

"You haven't been yourself the last few days."

Trip didn't answer right away. Archer looked down at the table, waiting.

"This is a picture of my cousins, Bethany and Scott, me, and these are my grandparents, Grandma Ilene and Grandpa Charles."

"Your namesake?"

Trip smiled, nodding. "Yep. Me and my dad's namesake."

"Where was it taken?"

"On their farm in the Texas Panhandle."

"What did they farm?"

"Corn and sunflowers. After their kids grew up, they left Florida and moved to Texas. Me and Liz spent a lot of summers there, but that summer it was just me and my cousins."

"Are your grandparents still alive?"

"Naw. My grandma died three years ago. Grandpa Charles was killed the day after this photo was taken."

Archer looked up at Trip, surprised by the information. "What happened, if you don't mind my asking?"

With a deep breath, Trip began. "The day started off just like on that planet—still, quiet, and hot. Us kids were playing outside when it started clouding up and Grandma called us into the house. She was baking a rhubarb-strawberry pie and the kitchen smelled wonderful. I remember she'd make these little pastry things with the extra crust. She'd spread butter, sugar, and cinnamon on them and bake them with the pie. We loved those things! We would always try to sneak in and steal 'em." Trip closed his eyes, recalling the memory. "So, we were all in the kitchen when the door busted open and Grandpa grabbed Bethany and yelled at us to get to the storm cellar, pronto. We ran outside and it was blowing like the dickens. We got into the cellar and all of a sudden I remembered Rufus."

Trip opened his eyes, watching the stars outside one of the mess hall ports. "He was the pup that Grandpa Charles had given me for my birthday a few summers earlier. We were always getting ourselves in trouble and when it got hot like it was that day, he'd sleep under the porch. I tried to leave to get him and threw such a fit about the dog that Grandpa Charles went to get him. And then the tornado hit." Trip frowned, looking down at the table. He added quietly, "We never saw them again. The twister just sucked 'em up." Trip sighed before continuing. "When it was over, we came out and everything was gone. The garage, strangely, was untouched. Grandma Ilene packed us into the car and we drove to town. She cried the whole way there. When we got to town . . . It was gone. The tornado had just left a bunch of rubble, wiped it clean off the map."

Trip looked at Archer. "Twisters are one of those things that you're a damn fool not to be scared of, and yet . . . they have a certain allure to them, you know? They're awesome because of the power they have and how fast they can destroy things." Trip turned his sad eyes back to the photograph. "Or how they can take the things you love away in half a heartbeat."

Archer looked at his hands. "I wish you'd never had to go through that, Trip, but, if you hadn't, we would have been killed. None of us knew what was going on. You saved our lives."

Trip looked slyly at Archer. "You're just jealous."

"Jealous?" Archer smiled.

"Yeah. You didn't get to ride in and save the day." Trip laughed.

Archer smiled, nodding. "All right. You got me. I'm completely jealous that you stole my thunder."

The two laughed for a moment, but it died. Archer picked up another picture. It showed a spoon embedded into a crate.

"I'll never forget that experience," Archer told Trip.

"No. You won't." Trip stood, starting to gather up the pictures.

"I'll get them."

"You sure?"

Archer nodded.

"Good night, Cap'n."

"Good night."

Trip walked away. Archer looked down, looking at the photograph of Trip's youth. Archer picked it up, staring at the smiling faces. He suddenly pulled the picture closer, noticing what young Trip was doing. He held the collar of a dog that had been caught crawling out from under the porch in the picture. It was a small black, brown, and white beagle that Archer assumed was Trip's Rufus.

"I'll be," Archer whispered.

Mestral

Ben Guilfoy

Boston was on fire.

A lone figure crouched on the ledge of a roof and watched the venerable city burn. Below, people were fleeing, trying to get their cars running, or just plain running themselves. Most carried only what they could, though some, the figure noted with a frown, tried to carry far more.

As though such worldly possessions were worth saving, he thought, pulling his hood up over his head, preparing to enter the frantic scene below. He looked out across Mass Ave. at the orange glow rising from the center of the city. Between him, and that, was the Massachusetts Institute of Technology, MIT.

He had come to Boston years before, as he'd explored the United States. He stayed low, "under the radar," as the phrase applied. He thought it an odd one, but the quickly evolving slang terms of the American public had always intrigued him. But this time he'd returned to the city that birthed the American Revolution with a mission.

It is now time to complete that mission, he thought. He walked to the edge of the roof over the alley between that building and the next, and jumped down to street level. He pushed his way through throngs of people that were all trying to move in a thousand different directions. No one paid any attention to him, they just kept trying to push past.

He moved onto the abandoned MIT campus. A few people here or there cut through the area to save time, but the buildings were deserted.

Good.

He came to a physics lab, and walked up to the door; it was locked. He grasped the handle, turned, and pushed hard. With a crack, the door opened, and the figure stepped into the dark hallway. He closed the door behind him, and pulled a flashlight out of his pocket.

He moved through the hallways, reading signs on doors, trying to find one that might have what he sought: the parts needed to construct a rudimentary subspace radio.

He froze, his enhanced hearing picking up noise from behind. He turned, playing the light across the floor, then off into the distance. There was no one, but he knew that the sound had not come from the chaos outside. Someone was in the building with him, and nearby.

Had someone followed him in, with malicious intent? His brain catalogued questions and hypotheses as he retraced his steps toward the door.

The sound came again as he neared one of the lab rooms. He stopped outside the door, completely motionless, and listened more. There was definitely someone else inside the lab. The figure reached down for the doorknob, and opened the door slowly. He stepped into the room, and very clearly heard breathing from behind the door.

He stepped farther into the room, and twisted around to his left as a man lunged at him, swinging a stool high over his head. He put up his left arm to deflect the blow from the stool, and continued to twist around. He grabbed the man with his right arm as he came around, and threw him into the air. The man landed hard on one of the lab tables, and rolled off onto the floor on the other side.

"Who are you?" the tall man demanded, standing quickly.

"I am sorry," the figure said.

"That ain't an answer, pal," the man growled.

"I know."

The two stared at each other in the darkness. The only light came from the dull glow through the window, and the cloaked figure's flashlight. He shined it directly into the tall man's face. The man squinted, and held up his hand in front of his face.

"Get that damn light outta my eyes," the man demanded. When the light was lowered, he blinked, trying to recover his night vision. "You didn't answer me. Who are you? What are you doing here?"

"I could ask you the very same questions," the dark figure said.

The tall man grunted. "At least I'm *supposed* to be here. You look like a damn refugee."

"I am."

"What's your name?"

After a moment's consideration, the figure said, "Michael." It was a lie.

His real name was Mestral. And he was Vulcan. He had been on Earth for a century, his ship having crash-landed in the woods near Carbon Creek, Pennsylvania, in the 1950s. Originally, he'd had two companions with him. But they left aboard a Vulcan transport that arrived to rescue them. He'd opted to stay behind, too intrigued by human culture to give up the opportunity to study them firsthand, to move among them, to *learn*.

But his time on Earth was at an end. Humanity was destroying itself, purging the Earth in the sickening glow of nuclear fire. Millions were dying, and the culture Mestral had come to love (in his own Vulcan way) over the last century was turning to bitter ash.

"What are you doing here?" the tall man asked.

The truth was something the man wouldn't be able to conceive,

Mestral knew. For centuries, Vulcans had prided themselves on their truthfulness. Mestral knew that one had to adapt to the environment, or die; his ability to lie about his own identity and intentions had kept him alive and free on an alien world for half his lifetime.

"I'm looking for shelter," Mestral answered. "I have nowhere to go."

The tall man scoffed. "You came here? For shelter?" He shook his head and turned away from Mestral to pick up the mess he'd made when he hit the table. "You must be some kind of stupid refugee."

Mestral set his flashlight on the table, facing upward to give the room as much illumination as possible. "What are *you* doing here?"

The tall man sat down on a stool, and adjusted his hat. "Y'know, my friends told me I'd be in this lab till the world ended." He chuckled. "Guess they were right."

"You think the world has ended?"

The man sighed. "What would you call it?"

"A change. The world is still here. We are still here."

"It's not the same. The world I knew is gone."

Mestral was quiet for a moment. The end of the world. Interesting. "What's your name?"

"My friends call me Zee."

"Am I your friend?"

"You haven't tried to stab me for my food yet."

"And now that the world has . . . ended, you expect everyone you meet to do so?"

Zee lit a cigarette. "Not everyone."

Mestral watched Zee smoke. Of all the things he'd learned on Earth, the compulsion to fill one's lungs with a deadly cloud of carcinogens (and to pay large sums of their currency to do so) was one of the things he'd never understood. It was also one of the few customs he hadn't picked up. He'd long ago decided that he'd try almost anything once, including eating meat, something heavily frowned upon in Vulcan society; but nicotine was one of the few substances he hadn't tried.

Zee stared at him for a long while. "I was a student here, a long time ago."

Mestral said nothing, waiting.

"They said I was 'going places,' y'know? That I'd make it big." Zee took a long drag and tried to make rings in the air with the smoke. He failed, and frowned. "Guess that's never gonna happen, now."

"Why not?"

Zee tilted his head toward the fiery orange glowing faintly through the shades. "You looked outside recently?"

Mestral stood, and began to empty bits of food from his pockets. It was time to eat. "I came from out there." He paused. "So, these people, the ones that held you in such high regard . . . were they right? Did you ever do anything of note?" Mestral offered Zee a granola bar.

Zee stubbed out the cigarette, and took the bar. As he ripped open the wrapping, he shook his head. "Not really. I published a few papers, but . . . no. My baby never got off the ground."

"Your . . . 'baby'?"

With a smile, Zee took a bite of the snack. "Mm," he said, chewing, "chocolate-covered. My favorite." He reached down and put a canvas backpack on the table. He reached into the pack, and pulled out a thin laptop computer. The silver casing glinted off the light from Mestral's flashlight. Zee turned the computer on, and started tapping at the screen with his fingers.

"You wanna see my baby?" he asked. Mestral stood and walked over to him. "You gotta promise not to tell anyone."

Mestral nodded. "I promise."

Zee swung the laptop toward him, and Mestral stared incredulously at the designs for a warp engine. Zee took the computer back, but Mestral's photographic memory went to work analyzing the image he'd seen for only a few seconds.

It was crude, merely the beginnings of one of the most complicated devices ever constructed, but it was there. Here, on this world on the brink of destruction, a ragged man huddling alone in the dark had unlocked one of the greatest secrets in human history—

how to travel faster than light. But Mestral looked at the windows, and wondered if humanity was ready for such a discovery.

Human beings, he knew, were singularly concerned with themselves, and their own gain. *Not unlike my own people were, long ago,* Mestral reminded himself. It had taken the Vulcan race's near extinction in the nuclear fires of civil war to make his race realize what was at stake, and what had to be done. It had been one man, a single Vulcan who preached peace and logic, who had turned everything around in the final moments. Without Surak's messages of peace, Vulcan would surely be a dead husk of a planet by now.

Mestral wondered if the man in front of him would be the savior of Earth's humanity. *They already have several,* he thought, recalling the history he'd learned. Roughly around the time of Surak, there had been a human preaching a similar (albeit rather more emotional) message. There were others, of course, as disagreement seemed to be so completely ingrained into the human race. They fought and squabbled over what they thought their gods wanted. It was no different when this human preacher had become so popular two thousand years earlier.

"I was gonna make a bundle on it," Zee said.

Mestral, his voice carefully maintained, asked, "What is it?"

Zee smiled, packing the computer away. "You probably wouldn't get it."

Mestral remembered a phrase from a movie: "Try me."

"All right," Zee said, taking another bite of the granola bar. "Basically, I think I can use this machine to channel great amounts of energy and create a warp in space."

So the human *did* understand what he had. Warp drive wouldn't be an accidental discovery for the people of Earth, as Vulcans believed.

Zee continued, "So basically, put something inside this spacewarp, give it a little thrust, and *boom,* faster-than-light travel!"

Mestral raised his eyebrows. "That's astonishing. You came up with this?"

"Yep."

Mestral suddenly became worried. "Then what are you doing here? You should get this away from the city, protect it."

Zee scoffed, crumpling up the granola bar wrapper and tossing it in a nearby bin. "Protect it? What in the hell for? This whole place is gonna melt to slag soon enough."

Suddenly, the room shook around them.

"See?"

Mestral moved to the window, and looked through the shades. Another mushroom cloud blossomed over Boston. This one wasn't far, though it was small.

"Down!" he shouted, and tackled Zee just as all the windows blew in. Glass and burning wood showered down into the room, and Mestral and Zee were thrown to the far side of it. Mestral looked through the blasted windows, and saw fires catching on nearby trees, spreading to the surrounding buildings.

"We must leave," he said.

"Why? Where would we go?" Zee sat up. He lurched forward, and grabbed Mestral by the collar. "Everything's coming apart!"

Mestral pointed at Zee's backpack. "Your work must survive! Your baby!"

Zee's eyes went wide with incredulity. He backed off, and picked up the bag. "My work? *Who cares about my work?* No one. And no one's going to be alive to care!"

"It could be just the thing that *saves* this planet from destroying itself," Mestral said calmly. Outside, the fires got closer. "Is your nihilism worth letting humanity wither away on this one little planet? What if your friends were right, that this was it, that you were going to 'make it big' with this very invention?"

Zee stared out at the fires that were starting to blacken the broken window frames.

"Don't you even want to try?" Mestral persisted.

Zee slipped the pack onto his shoulders. "All right. Let's get out of here."

Mestral grabbed his flashlight, and the two of them ran out into the hallway. They exited the building, and ran across the courtyard, Mestral in the lead. "We'll take Massachusetts Avenue to Route One."

"One?" Zee asked. "Are you nuts? We'll go south, to Ninety-five."

Mestral gave him a confused look. "One will take us north, into New Hampshire."

"Yeah, and Ninety-five goes south. It's warmer in the south." Zee paused. "Besides, New Hampshire creeps me out. Those people are weird."

Mestral nodded. "You should visit Vermont."

Zee grunted as they ran. A few other stragglers rushed down Mass Ave. with them. They all looked the same—scared, dirty, their clothes covered in soot or blood. Zee realized that it had been very stupid to want to stay. Looking at these other ragged refugees, he saw how close he had come to destroying himself and his baby.

They ran long, and hard.

Zee and Mestral drifted down Route 95 with a crowd of about fifty others. All the vehicles on the road were stopped; dead or burned out. Mestral kept his hood on, even at midday.

"What's your story?" Zee asked, after hours of silence.

"I do not have a story," Mestral told him.

"Bull," Zee called. "Everyone has a story. Who are you? Where are you from?"

Mestral, for an instant, considered telling him the truth. He considered telling him all about the myriad space fleets that traverse the skies at speeds Zee would consider almost ludicrous. He considered telling him that Zee could very well save the planet Earth.

"I wander."

"Hail the wandering wanderer," Zee said sarcastically. "*Why* are you wandering?"

"I left home, my job, my colleagues . . . because I wanted to learn," Mestral said. "I was no longer content with my position. I needed more."

Zee grunted. "Tell me something I don't know. Y'know, Mike, I've been alive for a while now"—Mestral raised his eyebrow—

"and I gotta say, *no one* is content with their *positions*. Trust me." Mestral just nodded. They took a turn around an overturned semi. They found themselves at the tip of a small rise, looking out as the highway extended off into the distance.

Ahead, "traffic" got much thicker. Hundreds of cars, all parked neatly where they stopped running in the middle of rush hour. The overcast sky threw it all beneath a dull gray blanket, killing the colors on even the most garish, ridiculous vehicles. People streamed between them, lines of them snaking off to disappear into the distance along with the cars around a bend nearly a mile and a half off. Beyond that, tree-covered hills, and a set of radio antennas.

Zee grunted when he saw the antennas.

"What?"

"The antennas."

"What about them?"

Zee pointed. "They're not blinking."

"This position you left," Zee said, "what was it?"

Mestral looked up from the can of soup he was heating on their campfire. He stuck his spoon into the can and swirled it. "I was a researcher, of sorts. Anthropology, the study of other cultures."

"Cool." Zee was eating the soup that had meat in it—chicken noodle, the can read. They had scavenged the food out of a grocery store's back room. The rest of the store had been picked clean, but in the locked storerooms they had found a case of soup and some bottled water—prizes of immeasurable value, now.

Zee tilted his head back and downed the rest of his soup. "So . . . what were you doing at MIT? In the physics building, I mean. Not exactly the kind of place I'd expect an anthropologist to hole up in."

Mestral didn't answer.

"I mean, especially when everyone else was hightailing it out of the city."

More silence. Zee was getting frustrated at his incommunicative traveling partner.

"You're not telling me something," Zee said coldly. "I don't appreciate it. It scares me. This isn't the time to take chances on people."

"I know," Mestral said. "I love this world. It saddens me to see it falling apart." He regretted saying that as soon as it left his lips; not because he thought Zee would guess the truth, but because he'd expressed such emotion so explicitly. He knew, of course, that other Vulcans would look down on his choices over the past century. But the one thing that they would not forgive was his assimilation into Earth culture. His emotional barriers had been breaking down for some time, and now he realized that he was Vulcan only physiologically.

In his heart, he was human.

"I was not one for emotional attachment," Mestral said. "In my . . . family . . . it was frowned upon. We were a particularly cold group. I left that."

Zee grunted. "Doesn't sound like there's much to regret. I'd have ditched a family like that, too."

"It was all I knew," Mestral said, finishing his soup. "And then I came out here, and it just . . . I fell in love with the outside world."

"Were you, like, Amish or something?"

"Or something."

". . . Ah. Don't know much about the Amish," he replied thoughtfully as he puffed a cigarette that he'd lit moments before.

In the distance, they heard and felt an arrhythmic thudding vibration. Over the trees, faint flashes of light.

"More bombing," Mestral said neutrally.

Zee stood, trying to see through the trees. He bunched his fists angrily. "That damn Eastern Coalition! They couldn't leave us well enough alone!"

Mestral shrugged, moving to stand beside Zee. "The United States has been the aggressor more times than I can count in the last century."

"So what?"

"So, the E-Con clearly felt there was precedent for their actions," Mestral said, continuing to keep his tone as neutral as he could.

Zee stubbed out his cigarette on a tree, then stamped on it with his foot. "It's just so . . . *unfair.*"

"I know."

Zee turned to Mestral, his eyes flaring with anger. "Why the hell does *my life* have to be turned to *crap* because some jackass congress on the other side of the world doesn't like us? What the hell does this have to do with *me?*"

"War is not about you."

"Then why do I have to deal with it? All I wanted to do was sit in my lab, invent something pretty, and retire in peace! I don't give a crap about *politics,* or the way this stupid world works! I care about money, and naked chicks!"

Mestral looked at Zee, who was not the most attractive human male he'd ever come across. "Naked chicks?"

"Yeah, well, you gotta have a goal, right?" Zee laughed, and sat back down by the fire. He put his face in his hands and sighed. "This is a goddamn nightmare."

Mestral sat back down beside him. "If you were to build your baby . . . where would you go?"

"What?"

"What would you need? If what you want is to continue your work, then do so. Everything here is up for grabs. You saw the stores, looted clean."

Zee laughed again. "You think we'll be able to just *steal* the materials to build a *spaceship*? Jesus, you *are* weird, Mike." Mestral sat next to him. They were quiet for a moment, and Mestral could see that Zee was, indeed, working things through in his mind. "Jesus, where would we get this stuff? How would we even get the damn thing into space?"

"I have an idea about that . . ."

The next day, Zee and Mestral came across an evacuation point. Standing at the top of a rise on the highway, they looked down over a convoy of green army transports idling in the center of the road. Larger vehicles with huge plows attached to the front were clearing an area of the highway of the dead cars littered about. Off into the distance, Zee and Mestral saw wrecked cars shoved to the side of the road. The army had literally plowed its way into the State of Massachusetts.

The two walked straight up to the first soldier they saw.

"What's going on?" Zee asked. Mestral tried not to look the man straight in the face, and kept his hood on.

The soldier replied, "Evacuation. We've got E-Con troops moving south from Canada."

"From *Canada*?" Zee said, incredulous. "Y'know, Maine and New Hampshire are pretty big. . . . We're not talking Rhode Island, here."

"It's the nukes," the soldier said. He looked like he might tear up for a moment, then just said, "Move along, please. Move along."

Zee and Mestral walked away, but not toward the evacuation line.

"What do you think?" Zee asked.

"It depends on where they are going to take us."

"Yeah."

A squadron of military jets roared by overhead. The several hundred refugees all looked skyward as one, and then shrieked as a missile came streaking in from the opposite direction. Everyone broke into a hundred different directions; refugees fled in panic while the soldiers tried to herd them toward the transports.

Zee grabbed Mestral's hood. "C'mon!" he shouted, yanking hard to the left. Mestral's hood came down from his head and bared his ears for the world to see. Luckily, no one was paying attention as he pushed the hood back into place. Zee pulled him through the crowd toward the forest to the west. Another missile came down right in the middle of the group of transports.

A jet of flame roared up into the sky, and torn, twisted, burning metal rained back down. Mestral took hold of Zee's arm, and swung him around. Zee's feet left the ground, and Mestral flung him past the tree line as one of the transports came slamming down practically on top of them, the metal compacting into the ground.

Zee stood, and grabbed Mestral as the Vulcan crawled away from the flaming wreck, dazed. "Come on!" He pulled him into the trees, and then collapsed next to him, breathing hard. They both felt the heat from the flames. On the road, the screaming continued. The soldiers were pulling back; the green transports swerved wildly around their blasted comrades.

"Guess we don't get a ride after all," Zee wheezed. "C'mon." They stood and limped off into the woods away from the highway.

Zee and Mestral avoided advancing military troops and major cities on their journey westward. Life in many small towns across the northern United States remained very much the same, they found. Whenever they came across a public transportation system that still ran, they took advantage of it. Zee never let his backpack, with its precious computer cargo, out of his tight grasp.

Mestral fought off an unwelcome bout of nostalgia when they passed through Carbon Creek, Pennsylvania. The two travelers walked down the main street, ignoring suspicious glances from the locals.

"Turn left," Mestral said. "There is a tavern."

"You've been here before?"

"A long time ago."

They turned left onto Coalmine Road, and Mestral was dismayed to see a mini-mall two blocks down.

"So . . . no tavern?" Zee asked.

"It is gone."

The two walked into the mini-mall parking lot, which was empty except for a few beaten, weathered sedans. Mestral looked up at the sign by the road, frowning. "Pine Tree Mall."

Zee tapped him on the shoulder. "Check it out, a sub shop." Mestral nodded absently and followed. Even before they reached the door, the smell of meat assaulted Mestral's nose, and he steeled himself to the experience that was to follow.

They entered, and Zee frowned at the place. The decor was absolutely ancient. *Just how long ago was this place a tavern?* he wondered. Linoleum flooring curled up in a few places, and the Formica-covered tables to the left were faded from exposure to the sun through the shop's large windows.

Zee walked forward to the counter, looking up at the menu.

"You guys got a liquor license?" he asked.

The teen behind the counter chuckled. "Sorry, we only have pop and juice."

Zee looked at Mestral. "You believe this?" He shook his head, and then looked back up at the menu. "I'll get, uh, I'll get a roast beef sandwich." He turned to Mestral. "You?"

"House salad."

The teen got to work preparing their food while Zee and Mestral selected drinks from a cooler to the right of the counter. Zee picked a caffeinated soda. He saw Mestral turn his nose up at it and said, "I need the sugar." Mestral nodded, and picked a fruit juice. They sat down at one of the tables, and Mestral sipped his juice. Zee looked over to the counter.

"Hey, kid. . . . Wireless?"

The teen nodded, and Zee pulled the laptop out of his bag and turned it on for the first time in days and watched the monitor as the machine connected to the internet.

"I'm amazed this place is still open," he said as the computer booted up. "I can imagine meat becoming something of a commodity nowadays."

Mestral nodded. "Carbon Creek is . . . a place of tradition. At least, I thought it had been."

"You're really thrown by this tavern thing, aren't you? Why was it so important?"

The teen walked up and put their food on the table. Mestral began to eat his salad, and Zee chomped into the sandwich with gusto.

"Jesus, that's good," he mumbled with a full mouth. They ate in silence for a moment, then: "So, you didn't answer my question."

Mestral chewed and swallowed, then put his fork down. "I used to live here," he said. "There were some people who were very important to me."

"What happened?"

"I don't want to talk about it anymore," Mestral said, and began eating again. There was another moment of silence, and then Zee swiveled his laptop around to show Mestral the screen.

"I've been thinking a lot about this thing." A 3-D image of the warp engine spun around slowly on the screen. "We have to get it into space somehow; you can't light this thing off in the atmosphere."

"No," Mestral agreed.

"So what's the best thing we've got right now for pumping stuff into orbit? We haven't had a viable shuttle program in decades, and this war certainly isn't going to be a boon to space travel."

"I don't imagine so."

"So . . . I was thinking, maybe, we could build it into the fuselage of a missile."

Mestral raised his eyebrow. It was a bold idea, bolder perhaps than even the warp drive itself. "Missiles powerful enough to launch into orbit," he said slowly, "are not generally for sale to the public. Especially in wartime."

Zee scratched his head. "I know. I know. But if we can get one, it's absolutely the easiest solution. The hardest thing about this project is getting it into space. The missile is designed to deliver a payload into orbit, and then it breaks away and falls back down. That's absolutely perfect for what we want to do."

"I used to love television," Mestral said.

Zee scrunched his nose. "What?"

"One time, I wrote a script for a TV show and sent it to a friend of mine in Los Angeles. He said, 'You're writing the third act before the first.'"

Zee blinked. "I know. But Mike, you're the one who said we had to try this. You're the one who said we should go west, try to find some aeronautical engineer you met a few years ago. I've never met this 'Lily' person. I'm going on your word, here."

They paid for the meal they had just finished and walked back out onto the street as night began to fall on Carbon Creek.

"We should try getting in touch with her," Zee said. "Make sure she's still, um . . . there."

"You mean, alive?"

"Yes."

Ohio passed in a breeze. The same with Indiana and Illinois. Though time flew, it had been weeks since Zee and Mestral's encounter at MIT in Cambridge. Zee grumbled about the sheer amount of walking their trip entailed, while Mestral continued to remain a quiet mystery. The two often traveled in silence, and at times, Zee wondered why they were even traveling together at all. What good was warp travel going to do a society that was literally tearing itself apart?

Something else troubled him, also. The soldier in Massachusetts had claimed that E-Con troops were moving into the United States from Canada. Many of the world's major cities had been nuked; the few newspapers left in circulation made claims about catastrophic death tolls and collapsing economies, worldwide starvation and mass slaughters, none of which Zee thought he could entirely believe. How much was true? How much was exaggerated? How many were bold-faced (he forgave himself that one pun) lies?

A bus dropped them off at a small depot in Wisconsin. The ticket-booth operator apologized that there would be no further runs west.

"Why not? Is it the E-Con?"

"No," the operator said. "But we're shutting down. The army is confiscating the company's entire fleet for New England evacuations."

"Do you think the Eastern Coalition will attack Montana?"

"I sell bus tickets, pal," the operator said, almost angrily. Mestral merely nodded.

Zee put his hand on his shoulder. "C'mon, we're back to walking."

Over the next two days, they managed to hitchhike as far as Minnesota. The walk along Route 23 was aided by some decent weather. Mestral and Zee had worried on their way through Illinois that the laptop would be damaged by the drenching rain they'd slogged through for nearly two days. Mestral had always considered Earth a more pleasing planet, climate-wise, than Vulcan. He preferred the myriad types of weather and climate, the different landscapes Earth seemed to provide in limitless supply.

Vulcan, on the other hand, was arid desert as far as the eye could see, punctuated by cities designed to blend into the surrounding landscape. Vulcan architecture was minimalist, at best, whereas Earth provided vistas one could study for years. *Decades, even,* Mestral thought.

"Here comes another one," Zee said aloud, disrupting his thoughts. Mestral turned to look behind them as a vehicle hummed around the bend. He'd heard it well before Zee had, of course, but his reverie had distracted him from his senses.

Zee waved as the car sped past, but the driver showed no intention of slowing or stopping.

"Never a Samaritan," Zee mumbled.

The ground began to vibrate. Mestral raised his eyebrows, and probed outward with his senses.

"Something is coming," he said.

"What?"

Zee heard a low whistle, building up as it got closer. Mestral shoved him aside, and they dove off the road as flaming debris shot down from above the trees. The wreckage of a fighter plane blown into a million pieces dug up the pavement. Zee looked up, but saw no sign of a pilot in a parachute.

In the distance, they could hear heavy cracking of automatic gunfire rumbling that sounded as if it were coming closer.

"We really have to learn to stay off of these highways," Zee said.

Mestral nodded. "Stay down," he said. E-Con troops were obviously moving into Minnesota, meaning that the United States' border defense had failed once more. More explosions thudded in the air, shaking the ground. They were getting closer; Zee could feel it in his teeth.

"Those bastards," Zee muttered. "What the hell!"

Mestral turned to him. "China and America were the world's last great superpowers," he said. "It was bound to end in conflict. I just did not think the Coalition would be able to muster so much effort to attack the United States from *both* sides."

"I don't think anyone did," Zee replied. "We've never had to defend the Canadian border before."

Mestral decided now was the time to attempt humor. "Perhaps they should have come from Mexico, instead." He smiled.

Zee just shook his head. "Lame, Mike. Real lame."

Mestral nodded. Another plane came down out of the sky, punching a hole in the line of trees half a mile down the road. The trees went up in an instant, and the fire began to spread quickly into the forest.

A line of army trucks, retreating from combat, came down the road headed in the same direction as the car a few minutes before. Zee jumped up and ran to the road, waving his arms.

"Hey! Hey!" he shouted, desperately trying to flag one down. The first few trucks swerved around him, one coming dangerously close to tipping over onto the shoulder. One of the trucks ground to a halt, and the soldier driving shouted, "Get in, damn it!"

Zee and Mestral climbed into the passenger side, and the driver took off.

"You guys okay?" the driver asked.

Zee and Mestral merely nodded. Zee looked into the side mirror and watched a truck at the end of the convoy get blown to bits.

"Jesus!" he whispered almost involuntarily.

"Hang on!"

The driver spun the wheel and the truck tore off onto the shoulder as E-Con helicopters strafed the road up and down the convoy. More trucks exploded. The tires blew out on some. Zee watched one flip up into the air and slam down on the truck behind it. Bullets chewed the ground. The truck in front gunned forward, and threw pebbles that cracked the windshield protecting Zee and Mestral and their driver.

The driver continued to swerve around, trying to avoid being hit. The convoy had quickly disintegrated from the loose mess it had already been, with everyone scrambling for themselves, not caring at all about the safety of those around them. Zee and Mestral held on tight, silently praising the skill of their driver.

Missiles were loosed; explosions seemed to fill the entire world. Zee's ears rang from the cacophony, but he wouldn't let go of the dashboard to block them. To do so risked being flung forward, and a cracked skull was a less preferable option than temporary deafness. And he also had his laptop to think of. It was currently wedged between him and Mestral. If he were to move, the machine would probably drop to the truck's floorboards.

"This is insane!" Zee shouted. He wasn't sure if the others heard him or not. Mestral did, but made no reply.

From the left, a squadron of American helicopters burst over the trees, launching air-to-air missiles. They cut straight through the E-Con forces. Above them, a wing of fighter jets streaked across the sky, already diving into bombing runs on the enemy moving behind the shattered convoy.

"Yes! Yes!"

Mestral smiled.

Zee whooped, and the driver started singing. Mestral didn't recognize the song, not having grown up on the planet, but Zee clearly did and joined in.

The truck drove on.

They stopped at a makeshift army base where the military was herding refugees. A vast city of tents had been constructed for those that would be staying overnight, and the orange glow of campfires broke the darkness. The driver of the truck asked Zee and Mestral if they needed a doctor, but when they both shook their heads, he left them at the edge of the town.

Zee checked on his laptop, and found it scratched and banged, but in perfect working order. Mestral stared at the tents, at all the people gathered around the fires, eating and talking.

"I have to go," he said.

Zee grunted. "Yeah, me too. But it wasn't like I was going to ask that guy to pull over any time soon."

"No," Mestral said, a bit louder. "I mean I'm leaving you."

"Why? We're practically there."

"You have to go to Montana. Find Lily, and tell her I sent you. She'll help you, I promise."

"You came this far . . ."

"I know. I had a reason," Mestral said. "But my people have had a rule, for a long time, about interfering in the lives of others."

Zee looked confused. Mestral didn't blame him, but he wasn't about to explain much further. "I've set you on a path we both believe is necessary," he continued. "But you must finish it. It's not my place to do it for you, or with you." He pointed at the tents. "You have to do it alone, and you have to make sure that this doesn't happen again."

"How can I . . . ?"

Mestral, a Vulcan, who never much liked physical contact, squeezed Zee's shoulder. "What you have will change the world, if you want it to badly enough."

He turned and walked away from Zee, tightening his hood as he did. He walked away from the tents, away from the fires, and into the darkness of the woods. As he walked, he pulled his left hand away from his side, saw it covered slick with green blood, and pushed the pain out of his mind.

Lily's house was a simple one-floor prefab, a small but neat lawn out front, and a single-car garage. Zee tightened the strap on his backpack as he walked up to the front door and tried the bell. He didn't hear anything, and after a moment, knocked solidly.

The barrel of a shotgun pushed out of the mail slot, pointed at his groin.

"Go away, or regret it," a voice said.

Zee took a step back. "I, uh, I'm looking for Lily Sloane?"

The shotgun barrel moved slightly. "Who's askin'?"

"My name's Cochrane. Zefram Cochrane. Michael sent me."

The gun disappeared. He heard the sound of the lock working, and the door swung open. Zee was presented with a small black woman with powerful eyes. She kept the gun pointed at him.

"Michael? What Michael?"

"I didn't really get a last name. Uh, thin, kinda quiet, wears a hood, like, *all* the time . . ." His words drifted as he realized nervously that he'd given his faith, and safety, to someone he never really knew anything about.

Lily smiled, and dropped the barrel away from Zee. "Is he with you?"

"No. He, uh, he just said I should come see you."

"Why?"

Zee hefted the backpack. "If you let me in, I'll show you." Lily stood aside, and Zee stepped into her home.

"So," he said, "Michael tells me you're an aeronautical engineer."

"That's right . . ." Lily said as she closed the door behind them.

"Cool."

SPECULATIONS

Remembering the Future

Randy Tatano

Picard's face began to dissolve, as if melted by the bright light behind it. But it wasn't sunlight. Rather, a rainbow of the most vivid colors Jim Kirk had ever seen melted into his vision; a prism that was pouring into his brain like rejuvenating lifeblood.

"Oh my . . ."

His pain dissolved away like Picard's face. Suddenly every molecule in his body separated and was hurled forward into the color. Then the rainbow seemed to flow into his veins, invigorating him even more. He felt young, alive; even more alive than when he'd actually been young. He saw stars flying by, faster than any warp speed he could imagine.

Then, in an instant, he arrived.

The being that stood before him was awash in the color, as was Kirk.

"Welcome home, James."

Kirk looked around, and saw that he was floating in the sea of color. He looked back at the being, who was smiling at him. It was female, he could tell, but not quite human. Tall and slender, long flowing hair of spun copper that seemed to float in slow motion. The emerald green eyes were larger than normal, but warm and inviting. He felt safe, as if his mind had been wrapped in a warm blanket.

Kirk looked around and saw no one else. "Let me guess. I'm back in the Nexus?"

"No, Jim, this isn't the Nexus," said the being, in a soothing voice that seemed to float toward him.

Kirk didn't care for his second guess. "So, I'm dead again?"

"An interesting way of putting it, Jim, but for all intents and purposes, yes. Though you weren't really dead before. The Nexus was just a brief detour from a normal existence."

Kirk stepped closer to the being. "Are you . . . God?"

The being shook her head. "No, Jim. My name is Kariel. I was once a corporeal life-form like yourself. I have merely reached a stage of existence different from your own. One you may achieve in time. I am, for lack of a better term, your guide."

"And this place is . . ."

"Heaven, the afterlife, whatever term you are comfortable with. It is your home for the next stage of your development."

"Development?"

Kariel smiled at Kirk. "Too long to explain in a few minutes and it will come later as I lead you forward. But it is an answer best experienced a little at a time. You've lived quite an extraordinary life, James." She seemed to look right into his soul.

Kirk thought for a moment. His life had been extraordinary, career-wise. But personally . . .

The being moved toward him. "Do not feel any regret about what might have been. Everyone wishes he could have changed some things about his or her own life. It never seems to work out exactly as we intended."

"Tell me about it."

"That is why we give everyone the option to change one thing. To help erase whatever regret that may linger. We do not wish you to continue your development until you have gained closure regarding your previous existence. So you have the option, should you wish to exercise it."

Kirk furrowed his brow. His interest was definitely piqued. "Option? How does that work, exactly?"

"It is a very simple decision, and you may take as much time as you wish to decide. You may conclude you are content with the way your life has turned out and continue with your development immediately, or you may use the option to change something and complete your previous existence."

"Complete my life?" he asked. "But you said I was dead."

She nodded. "Your corporeal existence, as you know it, is over. Yet you have the option of going back. For one thing."

"I did that in the Nexus. For a lot of things," Kirk pointed out.

"Ah, the Nexus. Quite the cosmic playground. But it is merely an illusion. What was it you said when you were riding that horse? How it no longer scared you because it wasn't real?"

"So this is . . ."

"Real, Jim. And if you go back, everything you see and hear and feel will be real as well, even though it will be your past. There are no illusions here. Nor will there be any in your past."

Kirk looked around again. He saw no walls, no horizon. No boundaries of any kind. It was as if he and the being were the only two life-forms in the universe. "But if I go back and fix something, doesn't that change history? Doesn't that affect the lives of other people?"

"Why do you assume changing history will be a bad thing?"

"So there's no such thing as fate?"

Kariel nodded. "In a sense, fate exists. But fate and destiny are two very different things. Once a person decides the type of life he will lead, then yes, his destiny is set. In your case, you knew early on you wanted to be an explorer and to help people. Nothing could change your destiny from that point. But you had the free will to decide what kind of life you would lead, what path you would take to fulfill your destiny. You did so as a starship captain."

It was too much all at once. Kirk looked around again. The beauty of the place was intoxicating, the colors seeming to bloom in an instant. So vibrant . . .

"There are no rules when it comes to history, James. Destiny, yes, but not history."

The being was speaking in riddles. If only Spock were here to sort this out logically. "I'm not sure I understand," said Kirk.

"You can be destined for greatness, yet find many different paths to achieve it. History also has many paths leading to the same result."

Kirk was beginning to understand. If he could just . . .

Kariel moved forward and took his hands in her own. They were warm and incredibly soft, seemingly melting into his own. For the first time he detected the scent of roses as she leaned forward. "James, there is one relationship you've always wondered about. One path you might have taken that has always haunted you. . . ."

Kirk realized the being could read his mind. "I've always wondered . . . if there was just a little more time . . ."

"There *is* a little more time. If you choose."

"If I go back, can I . . ."

"As I said, James, there are *no rules* when it comes to history. Nothing you do will change what you are, only what you've experienced."

"No rules."

"None."

It went against everything he ever believed about time travel and changing history.

To hell with the Prime Directive. The galaxy owes me one.

He glanced down at the being's hands; so delicate, the four fingers so perfectly formed. Then back at Kariel's eyes. The look was soft and understanding. "Then I want to go back. But first, I need to go back before I was born. Is that possible?"

She nodded and smiled again. "I see you haven't forgotten the *Kobayashi Maru*. I was told you'd be a bit different."

"So can I . . . ?"

"You can change one thing. It doesn't matter how long it takes you to accomplish this." Kariel closed her eyes and bowed her head. She reached up and touched Kirk on the forehead. "It is done."

Kirk saw the truck speeding toward Edith Keeler as she crossed the street. McCoy started to run after her, but Kirk was younger and faster. He dashed into the road, and in one motion wrapped his arms around her waist and pulled her to the ground as the truck raced by.

He pushed himself from the pavement and looked at her face, which was unmarked. He brushed her hair from her cheek. "Are you all right?" he asked.

She looked up into his eyes, right into his heart. "Oh my. You saved me."

No, Edith, you saved me.

Kirk stood up and pulled Edith to her feet as McCoy and Spock arrived. He looked at Spock and knew what was coming.

Spock wore a stern look. "Jim. Do you *know* what you've done?"

"Of course he knows, Spock," said a smiling McCoy as he patted Kirk on the back. "He saved her life."

Spock stared at Kirk. "Yes, Doctor. And now he must save ours."

"Bones, is she asleep?" asked Kirk, as McCoy entered the room.

"Yes," said McCoy. "I found an old-fashioned sedative in what used to be called a medicine cabinet. Slipped it in her cup of tea. Never knew what hit her. She could actually use some rest after what she's been through tonight."

Spock shook his head as he paced around the dimly lit room. "Unfortunately, Doctor, a sedative will not solve our problem. How to right history so that all is as it should be is the only way we can get back to our own time. Logically, since Edith Keeler did not die, we cannot do so without going back in time again. But we cannot do that without getting back to the Guardian. And we cannot do that . . ."

"Spock, you're speaking in circles," interrupted McCoy.

"Unfortunately you are correct, Doctor. We are in a vicious circle.

I believe it was once called a 'catch-22.' There is, unfortunately, no logical solution. We are trapped here, and Captain Kirk's actions will change history for the worse because he allowed Edith Keeler to live."

"Are you suggesting Jim should have let her get run over by that truck?"

"It was her destiny," said Spock.

Kirk finally interrupted. "It was her *history,* not her destiny."

"I fail to see how a question of semantics will change our present dilemma," said Spock.

"It would take me too long to explain," said Kirk. "But there is a logical way out of this."

Spock raised an eyebrow. "With all due respect, there is no logical solution. As a Vulcan, I have taken into account . . ."

"But there is, Spock," said Jim. "And *because* you're a Vulcan, you're the only one who can save us."

Kirk sat at the edge of the bed and looked at Edith as Spock stood nearby. He ran his finger across her cheek. *So smooth, so fragile. Just like Kariel.* Her expression was so peaceful as she slept. He wanted to memorize it forever.

"She is beautiful," said McCoy, bringing Kirk back to reality.

"Yes, she is," said Kirk, still staring at her face.

"Jim," said McCoy, "I think it is worth whatever we have to give up to save her."

"Thank you, Bones," said Kirk, standing up. "But we don't have to give up a thing." Suddenly he was the captain again, putting his feelings on the back burner. He turned to his first officer. "Spock, you used a technique when we violated Melkotian space. At the OK Corral."

Spock raised one eyebrow as he looked at the captain. "I'm not sure I understand, Jim. I am not familiar with the location of Melkotian space, or having ever visited there, for that matter."

"Trust me, you will," said Kirk.

"Now I'm really confused," said McCoy, sitting down on the bed next to Edith Keeler and absentmindedly taking her pulse. "When did you become a fortune-teller?"

"I'm just remembering the future," said Kirk.

McCoy dropped Edith's wrist and stood up. "I think I'm going down to that thing called a 'speakeasy' for a drink," he said, heading for the door.

"Wait, Bones, let me explain," said Kirk. He searched for the right words but there were none to be found. "I'm not sure how to put this exactly, but . . . I'm dead."

McCoy rolled his eyes as he turned the doorknob. "In that case, don't wait up for me."

"Bones, please."

McCoy stopped and crossed his arms. "Okay, I'm listening. But last call is in thirty minutes."

Kirk started to walk around the room. "We arrived here through the Guardian, a time-travel machine. But this is really my second trip here, because I have been allowed to come back to this point in time."

"Why can't I remember our first trip?" asked McCoy.

"Because I came alone this time," said Kirk. "I've been here before. At least up to the point when Edith died."

McCoy looked confused. "You mean . . ."

"You said you were *allowed* to come back to this point in time," said Spock. "By whom? The Guardian?"

Kirk shook his head. "No, not the Guardian. I'm not sure I understand it myself. But the memories of my entire life are intact, and I must use them to make things as they should be."

"That is not possible," said Spock. "Edith Keeler should have died yesterday if we were to return history to its correct course."

"History doesn't have a correct course," said Kirk. "And the Guardian is more than just a time machine. Bones, go get yourself that drink."

"I think I need one before I'm going to understand this," said McCoy, heading out the door.

Kirk turned to Spock. "And now I'll ask you to mind-meld with me."

Spock had not stirred from his meditation, but Kirk and McCoy were already drinking coffee. "This is the best I've ever tasted," said Bones. "That is, without any sort of medicinal additives." He took another sip. "Tell me again why this is going to work? Because last night all I can remember is some crazy story about Chekov getting killed in a gunfight and coming back from the dead. And now you're back from the dead. Damnèd bootlegged bourbon plays tricks with your mind."

Kirk put his cup down. "The Guardian is more than a machine. It has a spiritual mission that is hard to explain. Basically it is able to reach into our minds when it seeks to put history on a correct course. In the original time line before Edith's death, she believed it was her destiny to help people. She had already formulated her future in her own mind; not the exact details, but the basis of her actions. As of this moment, the Guardian knows her future will affect World War Two in a profound way because her intentions have not changed."

"And by keeping her alive we've set that in stone."

"Not necessarily. Spock is going to mind-meld with Edith and remove any ambition she has to reach her original goals. But just temporarily."

"What *is* she going to believe?"

"That she is destined to live a perfectly normal life for a nineteen-thirties woman. To raise children and have a happy home."

"You're going to turn this forward-thinking woman into a housewife? She's a pioneer."

"We're not changing her permanently, Bones. Just long enough to trick the Guardian into bringing us back into our own time."

McCoy poured another cup of coffee. "That's fine, Jim, but what's going to happen to her?"

"She's coming with us."

"It *is* the only logical solution," said Spock, entering the room.

"I'm glad you agree," said Kirk.

Bones shook his head. "You're going to take a Depression-era woman to the twenty-third century? Without even asking her permission?"

Spock nodded. "It is our only chance."

McCoy was still incredulous. "What about her chances to live in the time period she was meant to live?"

"Her life in this time period would have ended anyway," said Spock. "Anything else is simply . . ."

"Gravy," Kirk cut him off.

"Not exactly my choice of terminology," said Spock, "but I believe you have made your point. Doctor, if we leave her here, millions will die when my suggestion wears off. She will at least have the chance to fulfill her destiny in our time; a destiny she was never able to achieve in the original timeline. When she gets there . . ."

"When I get where?"

Kirk hadn't heard Edith enter the room and was caught off guard. "We're, uh, going to take you out to dinner. We thought we'd celebrate. You know, because obviously some guardian angel was watching over you."

"You're the only guardian angel I need," said Edith, putting her hand on Kirk's shoulder. Her soft touch sent a bit of electricity through Kirk. "As for going out to dinner, you boys don't have two nickels to rub together. Besides, I've been saving a piece of beef in the icebox and planned to make a stew."

The meal was delicious, a welcome change from the synthetics conjured up by the ship's computer.

"You've outdone yourself," said Kirk.

"Yes," added McCoy. "You're an excellent cook."

Edith smiled. "Why, thank you, gentlemen."

"Miss, you have something on your cheek," said Spock, sitting across the table.

Edith brushed her face with her hand. "Did that get it?"

"No," said Spock. "Please allow me."

Edith smiled as Spock reached out with his hands and touched the pressure points with his fingers. Her smile vanished, her eyes went blank. "My mind to your mind . . ."

Kirk held her hand as she rested on the bunk. Her eyes flickered a bit and then she awoke. "What happened?" she asked.

"You just blacked out," said Kirk.

"I think I'm falling in love with you, James . . ."

And with that they were gone.

"Aye, did you find Doctor McCoy?" asked Scotty, as Kirk and Spock came through the portal.

"Affirmative," said Spock.

McCoy came through next.

"Doctor, glad to see you," said Scotty. "Are you feelin' all right?"

"Fine," said Bones, as he turned to look at the portal just as Edith Keeler came through. The smile she'd had on Earth disappeared in an instant as her eyes filled with fright. "Oh my God, where am I?"

Kirk rushed forward to hold her. "You're fine, Edith. Just try to relax."

But even his strong arms around her couldn't calm her. She looked at him as if he were a stranger. "James . . . your clothes . . . what happened?" She turned and spotted Spock's ears. "Oh my . . ." Kirk caught her as she fainted.

"And who is this lass?" asked Scotty.

"Long story," said Kirk, as he lifted Edith into his arms.

Spock flipped open his communicator. "Spock to *Enterprise.* Beam us up."

The transporter shimmered as Kirk felt his soul and Edith's merge for just a moment.

Kirk didn't reappear in the transporter room. The shimmering was replaced by the rainbow light, and he found himself staring at the being again.

"Welcome back," said Kariel, smiling. "You have accomplished what you intended."

"I did?" asked Kirk. "You pulled me out of there before I had time to find out . . ."

"There was no reason for you to be there any longer. You had righted what you set out to correct. A destiny has been fulfilled. All is as it should be."

Kirk didn't feel any different. His memories seemed unchanged. "But I don't know what happened . . . how things turned out. What became of Edith?"

"Edith Keeler was a pioneer who helped people, just as her original destiny intended. She wasn't supposed to be killed in a traffic accident. You were supposed to go back in time and put things back on course. You righted history, James. She did great things in your time. Changed countless lives."

Kirk searched the caverns of his mind and still came up empty. "But did she . . . and I . . ."

"Why don't I let her tell you," said the being. Kariel stepped aside and Edith Keeler walked toward Kirk, looking as radiant as the day he'd first seen her.

"Hello, my love," she said.

"Edith . . ." Kirk grabbed her and pulled her close. Her perfume was the same and filled his heart with memories. He pushed back and looked at her face, not a day older than when they'd met. "I don't know . . ."

"Shhhhh." She interrupted his question by putting one finger on his lips, then placed her hands on his face and held it. "It is not the same as when Mister Spock does it, but it works rather well in this dimension." She smiled. "How does he say it? My mind to your mind . . ."

She looked deeply into his eyes as the missing memories flooded back; faster than anything Jim Kirk could imagine. His smile grew wider as he relived them in an instant. He saw Edith's career in Starfleet, her efforts to feed and educate people on a planetary scale. She'd saved millions! When his memories were complete Edith pulled his face closer and kissed him. "There," she said. "Is that better?"

"It's wonderful," said Kirk. He turned to the being. "Thank you. For everything."

Kariel nodded, then faded away.

"Where did she go?" asked Kirk.

"Let me show you," said Edith, taking him by the hand. "About time that I was the one who took you on a surprise journey."

And with that, they vanished into time.

Rocket Man

Kenneth E. Carper

The ancient Klingon ship had Agent K in its sights and he knew it; he just didn't care.

That's it, you Klingon bastards. Catch me if you can, he thought defiantly. The bridge was pungent with smoke, and sparks exploded closer to his face than he liked, but he'd never felt more alive. He sat at the helm of a freighter that handled like a slug and was venting plasma like Old Faithful. The Klingons had poked holes in it with their disruptors but now it was clear they were finished playing with him.

"*Earther,*" the Klingon Commander barked over the comm channel, "*this is your last chance! Surrender your vessel or die.*"

Agent K responded with a laugh, turned the freighter around, and set it on a direct heading for the enemy ship. It reminded him of an old Earth game he'd once heard of.

What was it called again? Oh yes, "Chicken."

He armed an antimatter weapon that would ignite in moments. It wouldn't destroy the Klingons but it would give him the time he needed to complete his mission.

K activated his life-support belt. A cool blue aura shimmered around him and he smiled, remembering when Federation science had attempted to penetrate the technology. Aside from a few prototypes the project was deemed unfeasible and abandoned. Agent K chuckled at the shortsightedness of Starfleet Command.

Pushing aside thoughts of the good old days, he released the airlock and the charged bolts ignited with a roar as the hatch blasted clear. The oxygen rushed from the cabin, tossing K into space.

A final blast from the Klingons shredded the freighter just as the antimatter exploded and it lit up the heavens like a newborn star. K didn't mind, it was just a loaner.

K would have whooped if he could, rejoicing that his plan had worked. He should've been dead, writhing in the vacuum of space, but he felt warm. Better yet, he felt young again, reborn.

The Klingon vessel lay dead in space, disabled by the explosion. It was unable even to limp away. K knew it had all been a risk but such risks were his business.

He touched a button on his belt and activated the thrusters on his evac boots. It had a bit more thrust than he had expected, but it didn't rattle him. He simply leaned forward, exulting in the thrill of zero-gravity thrust.

Just like orbital skydiving!

He circled above the Klingon ship and watched it grow closer as he fell toward it. *Forever falling.*

Captain James T. Kirk was falling and nothing in the universe could stop him. He clung for dear life to the fragment of a red-hot steel catwalk he'd been hanging on when it had collapsed. It spun in midair and Kirk saw the rocks beneath him grow closer as he fell toward the desert floor. Kirk released the metal and twisted his body to minimize the impact, but in the end, he knew it was for naught. There was no surviving this.

Kirk heard his ribs shatter, felt the back of his head crack, and hollered as the catwalk crushed him. He tried to take a breath and choked on fluid. He had known all his life that he would die alone. The moment had finally come. After a lifetime of beating death, he finally had to bite back one bitter truth. Death doesn't like to lose. It was a lot like Kirk in that way.

He almost felt himself smile at the irony that Bones was right, he really was going to die on the bridge. Or at least under one.

As he lay quivering in shock, Kirk thought he saw *something* or *someone* out of the corner of his eye. He wanted to turn to see who it was but he was too broken. He felt something sting his arm, glimpsed the figure one last time and then was alone.

He lay there for the longest time feeling his body go numb and the pain diminish. He heard an explosion in the distance and wondered if Picard had done it.

Did we make a difference?

The venerable Picard was shortly at his side reassuring him that they had indeed stopped Soran from destroying the Veridian star. Kirk felt a final thrill.

We did it.

He felt himself cough and for a moment everything went white. He tried to fight the numbness. He wanted to tell Picard something, some final words to sum up his life.

"It was fun."

Not terribly profound, but close enough to the truth. The world was going to a black that was like the eternal night of space. Kirk knew there was one last voyage left for him. A trek to the *true* final frontier.

"Oh my," he whispered, feeling the world fade away.

Captain Kirk died.

The funny thing about death was that it just didn't seem to be a permanent thing these days.

Kirk felt his chest rise and fall again and realized his lungs were drawing in breath. He wasn't a doctor, but he had enough medical knowledge to understand that dead people don't do a lot of breathing.

Why aren't I dead? Kirk wondered. *Picard? The* Enterprise?

Kirk felt groggy, and his eyelids weighed a ton, but he wanted to see the world around him. See the Starfleet of the future. Greet Picard and thank him for helping him beat death one last time.

Kirk opened his eyes and was surprised at how *bright* the world was. His eyes stung at the sight of it all. The room he was in was sterile and white, as if everything was carved from ivory and marble, but he knew it couldn't be made out of any substance found on Earth because everything was alight with an inner glow.

It's like an artist's conception of heaven, Kirk thought, his heart sinking.

Maybe I am dead.

Kirk tried to sit up, and felt vertigo sweep over him, with a vague sense of nausea. He lay back down, figuring that in the afterlife vomiting wasn't a factor. After all, how did you throw up if you lacked a stomach?

Kirk sat there, waiting for his strength to return and trying to plan ahead. Where was he?

A man dressed in medical garb walked into the room. He was an alien, a Denobulan judging by the look of him. He smiled broadly as if nothing at all was wrong with the world.

"Good morning, Captain Kirk!" the cheery physician said. "I heard you had quite a spill, but we've patched you all up. Yes, we have. You're as good as new."

"Where—" Kirk croaked. His mouth was dry and his voice trembled from disuse but he was determined to get some answers. "Where am I?"

"Why, you're in a hospital, of course," the doctor responded. "What a funny question."

"What planet?" Kirk demanded. "How did I get here? And where the hell is Captain Picard?"

The doctor looked perturbed for a moment but seemed to wave that perturbation away as if it was anathema to his nature.

"All your questions will be answered in time, Captain Kirk. In the meantime please enjoy our hospitality." He put a finger to his touch-pad and a small viewer popped out of Kirk's bed.

"You now have access to our library computer which will give you up-to-date information on what you have missed in the last seventy-nine years being MIA, as you were."

When it came to getting information he needed, Kirk found that the grinning physician was even more frustrating than Bones was when the good doctor determined it against his best interests to give it up. But then Kirk had always been his own judge as to where his best interests lay.

"Doctor, please," Kirk said in his most affable tone, "I've been tossed around so much that I'm getting dizzy. All I'd like are some answers right now."

The doctor looked at Kirk, a flicker of compassion (*or was it familiarity?*) spreading across his face.

"I'd like very much to answer your questions," the Denobulan said, "but it's not my place to answer them. However, if I know my *Enterprise* captains, and trust me I do, you won't rest until you get answers, so . . ."

The doctor touched a pip on his collar.

"Phlox to Manager one-ninety-four," the doctor said. "Priority patient requests your assistance."

"Coming," a flat monotone responded.

Phlox turned to Kirk, grinning. "Coming," he chirped. "If you'll excuse me, I have rounds to make."

Kirk waved him away, smiling. "Thank you, Doctor."

"Service with a smile, as they say," Phlox responded, walking away.

Where have I seen him before?

Kirk waited for what seemed like hours, though he realized it might have been his own impatience. Finally a tall stone-faced man entered the room. He had a head full of white hair and a demeanor that suggested the weight of the world rested on his shoulders. Kirk knew that feeling all too well. There was also something familiar about him. Where had he seen *this* man before?

"Welcome back, Captain Kirk," the man said.

Kirk suddenly realized who the man was and why he seemed so familiar. He wasn't in a Starfleet facility. He was . . .

Somewhere else.

"Gary Seven," Kirk said. "What the hell is going on?"

"We have one final mission for you," Seven said.

Agent K lurched, narrowly avoiding having his head taken off by a cross section of his freighter. He took a quick look, just to make sure that no more debris headed his way. Satisfied, he continued his task.

K clung to the side of the Klingon vessel, attempting to gain access to the ship by way of a service hatch. The tools he had with him proved useless; the hatch was fused from the explosion. Still, he had one more trick up his sleeve.

K reached into his utility belt and detached a photon charge and placed it on the hatch. He had a *very* limited supply and he intended to put it to good use. K set the charge on a ten-second timer before hauling ass out of the way. The charge exploded silently, though in K's mind, it was as if he heard an awesome blast. Perhaps it was just the echo of memories long past.

The debris clearing, K stepped into the corridor of the enemy vessel. He ducked into a utility closet as a pair of Klingon technicians in spacesuits came down the corridor to repair the damage done to the ship.

Minutes turned into hours but sure enough, gravity and air returned to normal. K deactivated the life-support belt, removing his phaser.

Never leave home without one.

He stepped out of the closet and scrutinized his surroundings. It wasn't so much a spaceship as it was a war zone. He'd been fighting Klingons for most of his life and found no surprises. Blood from numerous honor duels stained the decks. The bulkheads bore scars from *bat'leth* slicing through them. The smell in the air was pungent, a cross between smoke and vomit. K found himself glad he had blown the hatch. It would do the Klingons good to air the place out.

Seventy-nine years and they haven't changed, he thought sadly. Gary Seven had told him otherwise but K found that very hard to believe. All he knew was that he had helped usher in an age of peace between the Klingons and the Federation and these bastards wanted to shatter it.

Not on my shift.

K removed another device from his belt. It had been disguised to resemble a twenty-fourth-century tricorder, but K knew it was only a disguise. This "tricorder" had ten trillion times the capabilities of a normal tricorder. It was equal to the databanks of a starship. When he had been a starship captain, K had always relied on the data provided by a certain brilliant Vulcan science officer. He had always believed the old adage that knowledge was power. With this device, knowledge was never far from hand.

Next best thing to Spock, he thought, missing his friend terribly. Lacking Spock, the device was proving to be yet another invaluable gift given to him by the enigmatic Mister Seven. His "tricorder" confirmed that his mission objective was being kept on deck four, one level down. K slipped the tricorder back on his belt and resumed his mission.

"Our benefactors go by many names," Seven said enigmatically. "I could spend weeks naming them all but I think the one you're most familiar with is The Preservers."

"The Preservers," Kirk repeated.

"Yes," Seven said with a smile. "They still exist and they've taken a vested interest in preserving you."

"Me?" Kirk asked. "Why me?"

Seven looked shocked at Kirk's question.

"Who better than you? How many worlds have you saved? How many times have you stepped in and saved species from themselves or from outsiders? You have fulfilled the Preservers' prime directive: 'Above all else, life.'"

Kirk felt a glow of pride in his chest. He'd had many critics within the Federation for stretching their Prime Directive as far as he could and then a little more. To think that he had caught the eye of the legendary Preservers.

"After our first meeting, the Preservers kept you on their proverbial radars. They were all very pleased with your progress. After your retirement, the decision was made to recruit you. Unfortunately, it was made immediately before your voyage aboard the *Enterprise*-B. So you see, it was all a case of bad timing."

Seven rethought his statement.

"Bad for you but good for the inhabitants of Veridian Four," Seven amended. "And it was your death on Veridian Three that convinced us more than ever that you were the man we needed."

In his delirium, Kirk had been placed into stasis for later revival, thus his apparent death. He had laughed when told that Picard had actually buried him. It had been close. He looked down at himself for the thousandth time, feeling shaken by what he saw. It wasn't his familiar timeworn body, but rather the body of a young man.

Seven explained that using a series of nanite mechanisms, his body had been rebuilt from within and was good as new. They weren't just able to heal wounds but reverse the aging process for as long as an agent worked in the field. A productive agent could live damn near forever.

As he looked at Seven's aged form, it was clear that he didn't give a damn about living forever. Too many years in the trenches could do that to a man, Kirk knew.

In the end, he was grateful to Seven and the Preservers for this second chance at life and for putting him back in fighting shape.

They say that youth is wasted on the young. We'll see if that's true.

"Needed?" Kirk asked. "Needed for what?"

"To complete your final mission. The mission that brought you to Veridian Three and your untimely end. I need you to help me save a star."

Here we go again, Kirk thought.

*   *   *

Agent K slid down a service ladder, gaining access to deck four, the detention deck. K grimaced because he knew what that really meant; it was a euphemism for *torture chamber.*

A long darkened corridor lay ahead of him, not even a light flickering. Light was good for prisoner morale. Better to break the prisoners quickly.

Abandon hope all ye who enter here.

Placing his back to the wall, he slid slowly down the corridor. He breathed gradually, reducing all extraneous sound so that he could hear if a Klingon warrior came up behind him to cut his throat.

His tricorder indicated that four Klingons were milling about in the main chamber, dead ahead. This retrieval wasn't going to be easy for him to pull off but then, there wasn't much fun in easy.

K crept slowly up to the hatchway; he touched the release stud, hoping it wasn't sealed. It was, so he reached into his belt for a code-picker.

K's tricorder beeped, signaled that a fifth Klingon had just entered deck four.

K's pulse quickened; there was nowhere to run and nowhere to hide. He turned and found himself face to face with a Klingon disruptor. K looked up into the craggy face of a Klingon warrior.

I've seen worse.

The warrior backhanded K, sending him flying against the bulkhead. K reached for his phaser and felt the Klingon's foot crunch down on his hand.

The Klingon grabbed the phaser from K's belt and tossed it away. Pulling K close, the Klingon reared his head back and slammed it into K's face.

K felt the sting of cranial ridges rending flesh. He staggered back, seeing little birdies flying around his head. The Klingon sneered at the human's pain. K remembered the one thing Klingons respected.

Bravado.

"That didn't hurt," K said, causing the Klingon to chortle.

"You make me laugh, Earther. I will see to it that you die with honor," he said, keeping K within arm's length.

"That's very generous of you," K said. "But I have another idea."

"What?" the Klingon asked.

"I live," K responded. His hand slashed out, slapping something to the Klingon's chest. Before he could react, K grabbed him and hurled him into the hatchway.

The Klingon slumped over wide-eyed with surprise, a photon charge planted to his armor. K ran, throwing himself to the deck as the door was blasted apart and the Klingon was blown into eternity.

Not waiting for the smoke to clear, K made a dead run and leapt through the smoking door, phaser in hand. K rolled and hit the deck firing. A Klingon burst into a trillion atoms as he was struck by K's beam.

K looked around for the Klingon's companions and was surprised as his phaser was knocked from his hands. Strong arms gripped him firmly around his waist. He found himself flying through the air and a bulkhead awaiting him.

K's teeth mashed against his lips as he hit the wall. He tasted his own blood and remembered swallowing worse things while on a mission. He saw the titanic Klingon bearing down on him.

K rolled as the titan brought his foot down, stomping the deck with an echoing *thump*. He thrust his open palm into the center of K's chest, grabbing his tunic and pulling K to his knees. He lifted K into the air, shaking him back and forth like a child's plaything.

"Humans have no honor," Titan growled.

K's feet flew over his head as the titan tossed him on the interrogation table. Shackles came down around his arms.

Titan's compatriots, a short tubby Klingon and a tall gangly one that somewhat resembled a Klingon version of Ichabod Crane, came running to his side.

"Notify the commander," Titan said. "More meat for the machine."

*   *   *

"The House of Duras has long been a thorn in the side of the Klingon Empire," Seven said. "They believe themselves descended directly from Kahless and claim to be the only true heirs to the Empire."

Kirk knew full well how costly Klingon hubris could be, having been on their most wanted list many times over the last few decades of his life.

"The High Council disagrees," Kirk said.

"Wholeheartedly," Seven responded. "The House of Duras now lies in a state of dishonor. They intend to reclaim power through any means necessary."

"Hence, the trilithium torpedo," Kirk said.

"Exactly. Should that weapon come into the hands of the House of Duras it will become the most devastating weapon of mass destruction invented by mortal man," Seven said. "Doctor Tolian Soran developed the weapon for the House of Duras in the hopes of using it to reenter—"

"Yes, I know about the Nexus," Kirk said brusquely. He didn't want to dwell on the heaven he had abandoned for certain death on Veridian III.

"When Soran was killed, it was thought that the data needed to re-create trilithium torpedoes was lost forever. We thought wrong," Seven said sadly.

Kirk found the idea of renegade Klingons with a doomsday weapon in their hands beyond terrifying. In his time, Klingons conquered worlds through brute force or manipulation. He thought of the population of Neural thrown into decades of civil war because of the Klingons. He thought of the attempted holocaust on Sherman's Planet because of the Klingons. His son, David, dead because of the goddamned Klingons.

And yet, after the Khitomer conferences he had felt his attitude toward them soften. People like Gorkon and Azetbur had shown him that it takes all kinds to make up an empire. But for every Gorkon, there was a Chang or a Duras. Seven had assured Kirk that the Klingons had been staunch allies of the Federation for decades now.

And Kirk believed him. He had helped forge a peace that had stood the test of time, and now these renegades wanted to destroy that peace. And billions of Klingons, as well as the Federation, would suffer for it.

Toral, the son of Duras, had learned of his treacherous aunts' plan to take back the Empire and he had dispatched agents to learn of the details of that plan following their deaths.

Lursa and B'Etor had thought they had covered their tracks thoroughly and tied up all the loose ends. They were wrong. During the development of the trilithium torpedo Soran's assistant, Doctor Hannah Bosworth, had abandoned the project. She had learned what Soran had intended to use the torpedo for and had been terrified at the extent of his madness. Doctor Bosworth carried the information to re-create the terror weapon. It was locked in her head, the unfortunate result of having a photographic memory.

Toral had sent a Klingon ship, a crew of criminals and traitors, to the Empire to locate and retrieve Doctor Bosworth. Once in his hands, the data would be extracted from her mind, no matter the cost.

With the trilithium torpedoes in hand, Toral would again demand complete control of the Klingon Empire. If he were denied he would take the Empire apart, star by star. If House Duras couldn't have the Empire then no one could.

"Doctor Bosworth was found and abducted on Rigel Four. The bird-of-prey *Executor* is in transit to Toral's stronghold as we speak. I ask of you, Captain Kirk, in the name of the Federation that you fought to protect for so long, will you help us rescue her and help prevent a holocaust of galactic proportions?"

This was something he could do, had been doing for most of his life now, but he couldn't ignore the nagging doubt at the back of his mind that he needed to bring to Seven's attention before he made his decision.

"Why me?" Kirk asked. "Why ask a man seventy-nine years out of his depth?"

Seven almost smiled, as he had been anticipating Kirk's question.

"Because you're the only man who can do it. No human has fought Klingons the likes of these for nearly a century. Your experience is invaluable to the success of this mission."

"Was that the only reason?" Kirk asked.

"No," Seven responded. "We're also sending you because you need it. Whether you're retired in the twenty-third century or lost in the twenty-fourth you need a purpose. You need—"

"To make a difference," Kirk replied, recalling a treasured memory. "Yes, my first, best destiny."

Seven smiled. "Exactly. Captain Kirk, will you help us?"

"When do we start?" Kirk asked with a grin.

"Momentarily, Captain Kirk, momentarily."

Agent K felt the shackles cutting into his arms and he embraced the pain. It hurt because he was alive and he was determined to stay that way.

He looked up at the mirror that the Klingons had placed strategically over the bed. The Klingons liked their prisoners to watch themselves being cut up piece by bloody piece. It was bad for their morale.

The Klingon commander was easily ten feet tall and had a face full of scars. Commander Kling had been demanding answers from him.

Who was he? Who sent him? What was he after?

The damned Klingon had actually thought him a bounty hunter, sent to claim a price on the commander's head.

Agent K, of course, answered none of his questions. He merely responded with a frivolous remark about the weather or an insult to the commander's mother and received a blow to the stomach for his good humor.

Kling had been going in circles for hours with K. Many beatings and no answers. The commander's breath stank of bloodwine and *gagh,* and he leaned in close to K, growling in a manner he thought intimidating.

K was not impressed. After facing down the sight of a Planet Killer, a little thing like a surly Klingon wasn't very intimidating.

K simply laughed in Kling's face. He again felt the Klingon's fist slam into his jaw. Kling barked at Titan and his lackeys to dismember K and he stormed out of the chamber.

Titan chuckled at his good fortune. He pulled a laser torch off the wall and activated it. K saw the thin red beam lance out and wondered how he kept ending up in these situations.

Titan leaned in so close to K that he could see the serpent worms stuck between his teeth.

"Have you ever smelled burning flesh, human?" Titan asked.

"More times than I care to remember," K answered.

Titan laughed. "Well this one will make all your bad memories look happy."

Before Titan could bring the torch closer, K whipped his legs up around the Klingon's neck. He squeezed as hard as he could, enjoying the look of the Klingon's eyes bugging out.

K heard Tubby screaming at Ichabod and heard Ichabod demanding reinforcements in the interrogation deck. K raised his shackles and forced Titan to cut through them.

Satisfied that he had his hands free, he kicked Titan back with his legs and leapt to his feet. Titan roared, lowering his head to charge the human.

K ducked to the side, extending his leg; the Klingon went flying head over heels, landing flat on his face.

"Prisoners do not fight back," Tubby said. He grabbed a *bat'leth* and swung at K. K ducked and aimed a hard chop at Tubby's gullet.

Tubby choked, grabbing at his throat, releasing the *bat'leth*. K grabbed the weapon and hit Tubby in the nape of the neck with it, knocking him cold.

Ichabod grabbed K from behind. K bent at the waist, dumping him to the ground. He placed his foot in the center of the skinny Klingon's chest and put the *bat'leth* to his throat.

"Stay down," K said.

"Death first," Ichabod responded.

"Your call," K said, punching the blade through the Klingon's chest.

K felt a blow to his kidney and knew that Titan was on his feet again. He staggered, releasing the *bat'leth*.

Titan brought his ham-sized fists together, crunching massive knuckles. The warrior was out for blood.

K cracked his much smaller knuckles and gave the Klingon a good rap in the mouth and two jabs to the stomach. Titan just stood there impassively, not really sure if the puny weakling was serious.

"Damn," K said, realizing that Titan was going to be one of those kinds of opponents. K shrugged and did the unexpected; he grabbed the Klingon by both sides of his face and gave his head a good twist followed by a bone-chilling crack.

K took no joy in killing; he was a soldier, not a monster, but he was thankful for all of the early-morning sparring sessions he'd had with Sulu.

K had nary a moment to take a breath as the chamber was peppered with disruptor blasts. K leapt behind the table; he saw a large piece of mirror shattered in the melee.

"Over here," he shouted at the security team. It consisted of four large brutes armed to the teeth. Seeing their quarry challenging them, they fired as one.

K raised the mirror, deflecting the blast back at them. They entered *Sto-Vo-Kor* together. K dropped the red-hot mirror, his twinging fingers scorched by the heat of weapons fire.

K turned and entered the cell block. He still had a mission to complete.

Kirk had been surprised to find that he was neither on a starship nor on the hidden world of the Preservers. He was actually on a cloaked substation deep in the Beta Quadrant. Kirk realized the station had to be the size of a small planet.

"Not quite that big," Seven responded. "More the size of a large moon."

Kirk whistled, impressed. It was beyond anything they could

achieve in the twenty-third century and he supposed the twenty-fourth. To the Preservers, it was child's play.

They stepped into a large domed chamber. It was empty save for a chair in the center of the room.

"Under normal operating procedures, we spend years training our agents in the proper uses of our weapons and technology." Seven gestured to the chair. "Please have a seat, Captain Kirk."

Kirk obliged, feeling very comfortable. The chair molded itself to his body and seemed to be giving him a massage to boot.

I could have used one of these on the Enterprise.

"Unfortunately we do not have years to train you, so we have to resort to *slightly* unconventional means to bridge the technological gap for you."

"And how do you intend to 'bridge' that gap?" Kirk asked.

"Are you familiar with a planet called Sigma Draconis Six?"

He should be; a native Eymorg invaded his ship and stole the brain of his first officer, intending to use it to control the computers that protected their civilization. In the end, Bones had discovered that the indigenous people had devolved from their technological roots, preventing them from utilizing any form of advanced technology.

The technological gap had been filled by a device called the "Teacher." It uploaded the information needed to maintain their society directly into their brains. But it only lasted for a limited duration before fading from their memory. Bones had had to don the Teacher to restore Spock's brain.

"Same principle," Seven responded. "But to a different degree. We're not going to be uploading the complete knowledge of a civilization to your mind. Merely the knowledge needed to accomplish your mission. Do you have a problem with this?"

"Will it change my personality or brainwash me to make me more compliant with Preserver dogma?" Kirk asked. His effectiveness relied on his autonomy and his individuality. He'd fought too many thinking computers in his time to let himself be reprogrammed by one.

"No," Seven answered. "Our Teacher is a tool to educate. Not control. Besides, if we had wanted to brainwash you we could have done so before reviving you."

Kirk nodded. It did, after all, make sense. And a fish out of water could use every edge he could get.

"Let's do it," Kirk said.

Seven lowered a helmet down over Kirk's head. Like the chair, it molded itself to his contours. It was surprisingly comfortable for a steel hat. Seven pressed a button on the chair. Kirk didn't know what to expect. He figured it would be like the floodgates opening or the lights in a darkened room suddenly being switched on. It was nothing like either of those. It was just going from a state of not knowing to knowing everything he needed to. It wasn't a transformation. It was merely information.

"Are you ready, Agent K?" Seven asked.

"I'm ready for anything," Agent K answered.

K found Doctor Bosworth at the end of the cell block. The doctor was in her early thirties, tall and blond. She reminded him of Carol Marcus: beauty and brains in one all too frail package.

K lowered the forcefield; the scientist looked up at him. Her face was stained with tears. K felt a pang in his heart for her. Her suffering was unacceptable.

"Who—who are you?" she asked.

"Kirk, James Kirk. I'm here to help," he said.

A disruptor beam struck the bulkhead above him. The scientist shrieked in terror. K ducked into the cell, phaser in hand.

He could see a warrior at the end of the corridor shouting at reinforcements in the main chamber. K fired at the Klingon, wide dispersal, and the Klingon fell back.

K checked his tricorder, matching his location against the schematic. It showed he was directly above the engineering deck.

"Doctor, please stand back," K said, placing his final photon charge on the floor. K pushed her to the wall and shielded her with his body.

The charge cracked the floor open. K scooped the scientist into his arms and leaped through the gap in the decks. They landed in engineering; K felt the impact with the floor radiate up into his hip. He hated it when he felt his age.

I'll have to have Bones patch that up later.

Taking Bosworth by the hand, K ran for the door, phasering an engineer who thought it would be a good idea to swing on him with a hydro-wrench.

The door opened up, revealing a scar-faced Klingon bearing a *qhon'Doq* dagger in his hand. K recognized him. It was Commander Kling.

"Fight me, human, if you have honor!" Kling demanded.

"I don't really have time for this," K said, aiming his phaser. The commander's eyes were a dark void from which no light escaped; they reminded him of Kor, and that was enough to compel K to throw his phaser aside.

"Earth scum, I will eat your flesh strip by bloody strip," Kling said.

They circled like sharks, each sizing up the other. K didn't know nor did he care what the Klingon thought of him, he just knew that Kling didn't measure up to a warrior like Kang or Kruge or any of the countless Klingons he had met in battle.

The doors cycled open and a squad of Klingon warriors flooded the deck, disruptor rifles in hand.

So much for honor.

"I thought this would be a fair fight," K said.

"Oh, it will be. They're only going to kill you if I lose."

"How sporting," K replied.

The commander swung; the human grabbed his hand in a wrist lock and threw him hard. Kling went flying into the warp core, disintegrating instantly.

"The twenty-fourth century isn't so tough," Kirk said.

The Klingon warriors stood there for a moment, mouths agape, stunned by how easily their commander had fallen. Seeing the opening they had given him, K spun, firing his phaser and blasting the warp-core regulation unit.

Alarms blared throughout the ship, signaling its final death throes. The Klingons turned, realizing what a blow the human had dealt them. K grinned defiantly, tossing his phaser to the deck.

"I'll see you in *Gre'thor*," he said.

It was clear that they weren't making Klingons of the same stuff they were made of in his day. Instead of facing K as warriors they turned and ran for the door.

K smirked and grabbed Doctor Bosworth and slung her over his shoulder. He ran. According to the tricorder they had only minutes.

The bird-of-prey was a relic from his own time. After weeks living aboard the *Bounty* following the *Genesis* fiasco, he knew this model like the back of his hand.

He ran down the corridor, ignoring the shrill alarm and the flood of escaping Klingons, and ran through a door, which slid open and revealed a transporter room. K dropped Bosworth on the pad and entered coordinates into the transporter console. They were swept away by the beam moments before the *Executor* exploded.

Bones would hate this, K thought.

Though there was no longer a ship for K and his charge to beam to, there was a cloaked relay station tracking him the entire time. It compensated for the limited transporter technology of the Klingons and shunted the duo halfway across the galaxy to headquarters.

K felt the tension drain from him as he saw the Preserver transporter room appear around him. He knew that somewhere the bird-of-prey was being consumed in a supernova of his making. But he didn't care about that, not really. He had saved the girl and by doing so, saved the Klingon Empire and ensured peace in the galaxy once more.

K knew it was finally over. The mission, and perhaps his adventures. At least he was going out on a high note.

"Are we safe?" Doctor Bosworth asked.

K smiled charmingly. The woman was quivering like a leaf. She'd been through hell and he'd brought her back. It would take a long time for her to get over it.

"We're safe, Doctor," K said.

"Thank you," she said. Bosworth clearly didn't know whether to laugh or cry. Instead she leapt into K's arms and gave him a kiss full on the lips. She was just happy to be alive.

K grinned from ear to ear; everything was just how he remembered it from his youth.

"I don't know how to repay you for this," Bosworth said.

"I think you were doing just fine," K replied. Bosworth smiled and leaned in to kiss him once more. K, not one to argue, accepted her gratitude just in time to see the doctor dissolve in the transporter beam once more. She left him standing there with puckered lips and a bewildered expression on his face.

This sort of thing never happened in the old days.

The door to the transporter room slid open and Gary Seven stepped through.

"The girl, what did you do with her?" K asked.

"She's been taken for memory modification. The Klingons can't take from her what she doesn't have," Seven answered.

"She'll be returned to Earth, unharmed?" K asked.

"I'll see to it personally," Seven responded. "And Captain Kirk, you've done well."

Kirk nodded gratefully. "Thank you, Mister Seven. I take it you'll be returning me to Earth as well?"

Kirk could swear he saw a look of sadness and regret pass over Seven's face, and he shared in it. As eager as he was to get home and see what had become of his people, he was sad that it was nearly over.

"There's a whole galaxy waiting to honor you, Captain Kirk," Seven said. "Unless—"

Kirk froze, knowing that there was something to that *unless*.

"Unless?" Kirk asked, a glimmer of hope in his tone.

"You could work with me and continue to make a difference until the day you die," Seven said.

It didn't take Kirk a moment to decide.

"Sounds like fun," Kirk said, extending his hand to shake on the deal.

"Welcome to the Organization, Agent K. Now for the details of your *next* assignment—"

The Rules of War

Kevin Lauderdale

A spray of bullets sent chips of cement flying from the building's wall across Archer's face. Instinctively, he held up his right arm to block them, even though his helmet had a shatterproof visor. One of the finger-sized chips tore into his uniform sleeve, but didn't hurt him. Who would have thought it would ever come to this? Actual urban combat—fighting in the streets. This was the twentieth century; weren't we supposed to be civilized?

"Captain!"

Sergeant Bengy was calling to him. Nathan Archer ducked back behind the corner of the building and started to walk backwards toward the armored M2 Bradley, all the while scanning the sky and nearby rooftops for Augment Alliance forces as Bengy provided cover with his AK-47 machine gun.

Of all the cities Archer had seen in North Africa, Assab, Eritrea, was probably the most industrial. Just about every structure there was made of cement or steel. The midday heat rising up everywhere from the asphalt roads made the whole place seem to shimmer.

Archer and Bengy climbed up and into the Bradley, joining the rest of Bravo Company.

Sergeant Bengy, like every other member of Archer's UNPD battalion, wore camouflage fatigues in black, white, and gray, along with a patch on his or her left shoulder of the United Nations emblem: a white azimuth map of Earth flanked by olive branches on a sky-blue background. Below each of their patches was the flag of the soldier's home nation. Bengy wore the Union Jack; Archer, Green, and the rest of the company, the Stars and Stripes. Most of the battalion were Americans, though Archer knew that Charlie Company had a couple of sergeants from France who wore the Tricolor. "A real red, white, and blue battalion," his grandfather might have called it, with a laugh.

Green handed canteens to Archer and Bengy. "What did it look like, Captain?" The round-faced lieutenant had piercing, intelligent eyes, and, despite his youth, a wily, sharp look to him. And, god, he was so young. Just out of Annapolis and assigned to . . . *this*. Archer wondered, had *he* himself ever looked that young?

Archer and Bengy had gone out to scout the area—the *area*! A *street*! They had walked along an actual sidewalk, passing stores and telephone poles. This wasn't the place for a war. Wars were supposed to be fought in jungles, forests, and—like Archer's first time in uniform only a few years earlier—the open expanse of deserts. Wars were not supposed to be fought in cities. Cities had narrow streets, mailboxes, and wires that blocked things. Yet, here they were.

"It looked like a school," said Archer. In the midst of blocks of office buildings, just two streets away, was a one-story structure with a few windows and a flagpole flying the four-color flag of the nation. Unlike the buildings surrounding it, this structure was set back from the sidewalk several feet. Off to one side, visible through a chain-link fence, had been the shattered remains of a swing set, slide, and monkey bars. "And it looked like there were kids in it."

Green frowned and looked at his global positioning unit. "That wasn't on the map."

"Too right," said Bengy. "Where'd that map come from anyway, the Assab Tourism Board? And when was it printed, *the eighties*?"

Archer sighed. "I'm sure battalion HQ gave us the best that they could find." He leaned to one side and looked out a hatch. He didn't actually expect to see an Alliance tank coming down the street, nor spot a sniper making his way toward them, but it comforted Archer to actually *not* see them with his own two eyes. He closed the hatch. "Still, that doesn't change the fact that Alliance has us blocked."

His battalion was there to evacuate civilians. The whole city was a war zone, with Alliance and UNPD forces shooting at each other. The UN currently held the western side; the Alliance, the eastern, including the port where they were massing to go across the Red Sea to Yemen, and then, clearly, the oil fields of Saudi Arabia.

And now there were reports of more Alliance reinforcements heading up from the south. Bravo Company was just trying to get the civilians out and onto transports. Unfortunately, they were restricted to land routes. The Alliance forces didn't seem interested in harming the civilians; they just wanted control of the port and the city. They probably would have ignored the citizens of Assab altogether, if the UNPD hadn't come in to expel them. But that wasn't Archer's responsibility. Today Bravo Company wasn't there to fight; they were there to protect and guide noncombatants to safety.

Or rather they had been. Half an hour ago, four old Soviet-built BMP-3 tanks—Alliance favorites, with their distinctive, huge 100mm gun turrets—had advanced and were trying to gain new territory.

And now a school . . . No one back at HQ knew about the school. It wasn't on the evac schedule. The problem was that the school lay right between them. If Archer fired on the Alliance with anything substantial, there was a good chance he'd hit the school. His Bradley didn't have smart bombs that could go around things. Neither did the Alliance BMP-3s . . . but *they* didn't care.

"Okay," said Archer. "We're not going to be able to sneak up on that school. And they clearly intend to destroy anything that comes near it . . . and them. What have we not tried at all? We have to get down to absolute basics." Archer hated the phrase "thinking outside the box," but that's what they needed now.

Bengy said, "If me da were here, he'd say these Augments need a good hide-tanning."

Archer smiled. "Yeah, my grandfather would say they needed a good—" He stopped. "A good . . . *talking-to* . . ." Yeah. That just might work. He turned to Dixon, the comm officer. "Sergeant, give me a comm frequency that we don't use much."

"Sir?"

"We're about to give it to the enemy, so make a note and don't ever use it again." He turned to Bengy. "Okay, I need something big and white." Bengy started crawling toward the rear of the Bradley.

"Like a flag of surrender?" asked Green.

"Like a flag of *truce*. I just need them to not shred it with bullets before they read it."

"Read what?"

"The flag."

Bengy returned and said, "Here now, how's this, Captain?" He handed Archer a white handkerchief, which Archer unfolded. It was one square foot.

"Okay," said the captain. "I'll need um, one . . . uh, *five* more."

"Good thing they come in boxes of six," said Bengy, reaching back and producing a little, blue cardboard box. He opened it and pulled out more white handkerchiefs. Green stared at him. "Allergies," Bengy explained.

"Sergeant, make me a flag," commanded Archer.

Bengy looked around. "Staples, I think . . ."

Dixon handed Archer a pad with a frequency written on it.

Green said, "Captain, if you get them, and you can keep them talking, I could take a squad around the back on foot and attack."

Archer sighed. "Lieutenant, I am trying to negotiate a release. If you pull a sneak attack, the first thing they're going to do is shell the school in retaliation."

Green shrugged. Bengy gave Archer the flag.

Archer grabbed a thick pen from a toolbox and wrote the frequency in huge, black letters on both sides of the flag. He pulled out a telescoping antenna and taped it to the flag with dark gray duct tape. It looked exactly like what it was: an amalgam of handkerchiefs, staples, and duct tape. Like so many things in military life, it was crude, but it got the job done.

Archer climbed up into the Bradley's observation hatch, opened the latch, and shoved the thing out into the air.

"Okay," Archer muttered to himself. "First we wave it around like crazy to get their attention . . . maybe a sniper spots it . . . What's that? . . . A truce flag . . . Cease fire . . ." Archer paused. "Okay, now we give them a little time . . . What's that on the flag? . . . A little more time for the oldest guy there to recognize it as a comm frequency . . . a little more time to find the comm unit . . . someone sets it up . . . tunes it . . ." Archer stopped talking and waited.

Buzzz! Bravo's comm unit went off. Archer pulled his flag back in and stared at the comm. He hadn't actually expected this to work. He pointed at the device and nodded. Dixon pushed a button.

Archer took a deep breath. "This is Captain Nathan Archer of the United Nations Peace Directorate. Who am I addressing?"

"I am a major in the Alliance." A man's voice, deep and sonorous, came over the comm's speaker. *"But my commission is purely honorary . . ."*

Bengy rolled his eyes and muttered, "Who is this airbag?" Green slashed his thumb across his throat, and Bengy bit his lip.

". . . I prefer to be addressed by the title I earned: Doctor. This is Doctor *Stavos Keniclius."*

In the heat of the desert, and the close quarters of the Bradley, Archer's blood turned ice cold.

Keniclius! Second-in-command to only Khan himself among

those who wanted to remake the world's population according to their own ideas of superior genetics. Some people were already calling these brushfire conflicts "the Eugenics Wars."

In his mind, Archer could see Keniclius as he appeared in TV news broadcasts: the same sharp, Roman features as a classical bust; but topped with red-brown hair that he wore long—a fashion that many of the so-called supermen had adopted.

Archer took a deep breath. "Doctor, I need you to do me a favor."

"*A favor?!*" Over the comm, Keniclius laughed. "*Unless I'm mistaken, weren't we just shooting at each other?*"

"Ah, actually, you are mistaken. *You* were shooting at *me*. I didn't shoot back. And I'm not planning to attack because of the school."

"*Hmmm. Yes, the school. Occupied, isn't it?*"

"Yes," replied Archer. "I'm here to evacuate it."

"*Well, how about if you just leave them to me. They'll be fine.*"

"I'm not leaving anyone to the Alliance . . . *Doctor.*"

Keniclius laughed again. "*Oh, Captain, what propaganda have they been feeding you?*" His voice was filled with condescension. "*Made me out to be the mad scientist of the taped thrillers, have they? Well, consider* this, *Captain: We are bringing peace and harmony! Look around you, Captain. The world is crumbling. It needs control. It needs a master race—not as conquerors, but as peacekeepers. Alexander, Napoleon, Hitler . . . they went about it all wrong. Humans have spirit and will not respond to the jackboot.*"

"And what do you call the fighting we're engaged in now, Doctor? You can not use violence to bring about peace. As a doctor, you must know that."

"*As a doctor, I know that you must* remove *a tumor. You must cut away a cancer before it metastasizes! Oh, Captain, if you could only see that our goals—*"

"I'm not here to argue philosophy with you, Doctor."

"*Ah, but you are, Captain: the finer points of war.*"

"No, I just need to get those kids out of here."

"So my army and your army can 'have at it' without any collateral damage?" asked Keniclius.

"Yeah . . . close enough."

"We don't want to hurt anyone in a battle, do we? Except that it's always fine to hurt the evildoer. Oh, wait, you think of me as evil and yourself as good," the doctor said drily.

"And vice versa."

"Oh, don't be a moral relativist, Captain. One of us is right and one is wrong. Only Posterity will tell. Fortunately, Posterity favors the best-equipped."

"Yeah, that's definitely one of the rules of war."

Keniclius chuckled. *" 'The Rules of War.' Oh, I like that. Right along with 'Never forget that your weapons were made by the lowest bidder,' eh, Captain?"*

Archer took a deep breath. "I would say that it's not okay to the hurt civilians, no matter whose side they're on. And it's certainly never okay to hurt children."

"Children are the future, aren't they?"

Archer bit his tongue. You heard a lot of rumors in the fog of war, but if even half of what was said about Keniclius was true . . . Not just cloning—anti-humanistic enough as that was— but some process to grow an adult from an embryo in hours instead of years. What would that do to the child's mind? If it was even possible.

The thought of the results of the *failed* experiments sent new chills along Archer's spine.

"If you kill civilians," said Archer slowly, "then what's the purpose of the war? It's for the civilians. War isn't about war, it's about the world *after* the war."

"Yes," said Keniclius. *"They're the prizes, if you will. And that's certainly a Rule of War: Never kill the prizes."*

"Look, Doctor, all I'm asking is that you hold your fire for a little while. Just a few minutes while I get them out. I'll send only a couple of men. Unarmed and on foot."

"How do I know you won't take the opportunity of getting closer to attack?"

"You could always back up a few blocks. Then you'd be safer," Archer joked, forcing a smile onto his face and into his voice. Good thing this wasn't a video phone.

"Not amusing," said Keniclius coldly.

"Look, Doctor, they won't have any weapons. No rifles, no side-arms. You've got snipers up there. If they see so much as a soup spoon, you can shoot them."

"Them, *not* us? *You won't be part of the group, Captain?"*

"Would you like me to be? That's no problem."

"Yes, you should be, Captain. You're negotiating this. A leader should never send his soldiers someplace he would himself never go. That's a Rule of War too." Archer heard Keniclius and another voice in a brief, muffled exchange. *"You have your wish, Captain. I will cease fire until they are withdrawn. After all, what would I do with a bunch of children?"*

"Right," said Archer. "They're already born. Not really at their best for genetic manipulation."

"Watch it, Captain!" said Keniclius. *"I don't suffer fools gladly, and you clearly know nothing about what you speak of. You have fifteen minutes."* There was a click, and the connection went dead.

"Okay, Green," said Archer. "You and me." He unbuckled his gun holster and handed it to Bengy. "Leave your forty-five here."

"You were *serious* about that?" Green asked.

"Of course. Always tell the absolute truth to your enemies. That's a good Rule of War too."

Green nodded. "If only to confuse them." He put on his sun-glasses. "I was just thinking, sir. You know . . . about removing the bad and keeping the good—what he said. It kinda made sense. I mean I know he's the enemy and all, but isn't *any* of what he says allowed to make sense? If we could turn his ideas—if *we* could cut away the bad—"

"Whose 'bad,' Lieutenant? Your bad? My bad? *His* bad? The guy down the street's bad?" Green shrugged. "That's why we don't tamper with genetics, Lieutenant. None of us is smart enough to know, in the long run, what humanity will need to survive. So we leave it up to nature. No cloning, no manipulation of genetic traits before children are born . . . or 'genetically cleansing' them after they are."

He opened the Bradley's top hatch. "And, speaking of children . . . Come on, let's go see what the future looks like."

The Immortality Blues

Marc Carlson

The saxophone echoed to silence. The man called Lewis Bixby put down his book, kissed the blond woman sleeping next to him on the couch, rose to his feet and strode across the dimly lit living room. Through the large wall-window behind the couch, he could see the beautiful lights of New York City in the distance, a ground-bound starfield, even at this hour of the morning.

The city that never sleeps . . .

He was considering whether to take his wife to bed as he reached for the stacks of plastic holo-squares beside the stereo when he heard Rayna's voice in the transceiver implanted behind his right ear.

"Lew . . ." Rayna was cut off as the player's face went black, and a hellishly bright pulse flashed behind him. For an instant, his shadow was sharply etched onto the bookshelves in front of him, the leather bindings radiating heat back at him, nearly as hot as the heat on his back, searing the image of the smoldering spines into the edges of his vision as the light faded.

He whirled and looked through the window, his peripheral vision gone, leaving him only a narrow tunnel to see through. Camilla still slept on the couch. Behind her, a mushroom of hellfire-orange-and-black roiling plasma highlighted the slowly collapsing ruins of lower Manhattan. Although he couldn't see it, he knew that, in that darkness, the silent expanding cloud of superheated wind and debris at the leading edge of the overpressure wave was coming at him faster than the speed of sound.

Oh, this is going to hurt.

The man called Lewis Bixby floated through hazy dreams of *Kaliste,* the Beautiful Isle, and a lovely bare-breasted woman whose name he'd lost, in rare aromatic silks, fine wool, and linen, and vanishing in a blinding light and a noise so loud it was no longer sound, but a slap from Dzeos Pathair himself blasting his ship into flaming splinters around him. Then the past faded, leaving only the life-consuming spirits of the dead. . . .

Dull pain and itching dragged him back to consciousness. There was pressure on his legs. He saw a cloudy sky above him through a twisted mass of burnt wreckage, dripping with oily black rain. The sweet stench of putrefying flesh cut through the reek of char.

That was certainly unpleasant. I must remember to avoid doing that in the future. . . .

He clicked his tongue. There was no response from Rayna. He started to move, then froze as the glass fragments embedded in his flesh ground and tore through his muscles. He focused, and forced himself into a sitting position. A section of the roof pinned his legs. His clothes were in tatters, and his skin was covered in the worst case of acne he'd seen in some time as his body worked to expel the glass chunks. Gritting his teeth against the pain, he tried lifting himself up into a better position. The debris shifted as he pulled on it, and his leg stuck fast. He jerked hard, and his right leg broke just below the knee. Nearly overwhelming waves of pain and dizziness coursed through him. Grunting in agony, he reached under the roof section and rotated the dangling lower limb. He pulled it free, and was grateful to lose consciousness once more.

It was dark when he came to, and it had stopped raining. Some of the glass shards had been pushed from his skin. He swept those away; the grinding in his muscles told him there was still more in there.

I'm going to be shedding glass for days.

His leg, however, had healed. He squeezed himself up through the tunnel overhead, and started climbing to freedom.

A few feet up, a hand stuck out of the debris. He recognized the wedding ring.

Camilla.

He paused a moment to swallow his emotions, then kept climbing.

I'll mourn when I have the time.

He soon emerged at the top of the mound. The full moon, shy and intermittent behind the heavy cloud cover, was the only illumination. His apartment had been on the fortieth floor, now it was a pile of ruined steel. It was too dark to even try to climb down the irregular slope, so he sat in the cold, smoky-sweet breeze to wait for morning.

Within a few hours, the first fingers of light slowly emerged in the eastern sky in what ancient peoples had called the wolf's tail, the *lykaugés*. The early light showed that his building was lying in the midst of miles of other mounds of shattered buildings stretching as far as he could see. To the southwest, beyond Queens and Brooklyn, he could barely make out the ruins of Manhattan through the pillars of dark smoke, reminiscent of burning Kuwaiti oil fields.

As the valley slowly filled with golden light, he remembered what it looked like that first morning he'd seen it, in 1609, from the helm on the tiny deck of the *Halve Maen*. He overlaid the image of the past, with its rich verdant forests, sounds of life, and smells of the sea foam blending with the foliage, over the hazy dusty silent ruins around him.

Who'd have thought that the end of civilization would be so untidy?

He rose and carefully climbed off the ruins. When he reached the street level, the first bodies he found were in the overturned wreckage of a police vehicle: two officers, a man and a woman, dead only a few days and swarming with flies. He pulled the man out and stripped him. Peeling away his own tattered clothes, he put on the officer's uniform and strapped on his weapon and equipment. He started walking. By the time he reached Brooklyn, he barely noticed the stench from his clothes, or the bodies littering the streets.

As he passed through the ruined city, he saw other survivors, most as devastated as the buildings around them. Some straggled away from the center of the city, while others sat in silence, waiting for a rescue that might never come; an old man, wheeling his belongings in an overloaded cart, wheels squeaking; hordes of looters and scavengers shooting at each other like mad dogs fighting for scraps; an old storefront with the sign YES, WE ARE OPEN—CASH OR TRADE ONLY and a man with a shotgun guarding the door; several government aircraft circling like vultures.

He reached the ruins of the Queensboro Bridge toward late afternoon. From that vantage point, he could see that none of the other bridges had fared any better. Backtracking to the Twenty-first Street–Queensbridge entrance to the subway, he found it was clear. He unclipped the officer's flashlight, and descended into the tunnel. The ash and dust from the collapsed buildings had blasted down through the tunnels like a pyroclastic flow covering everything. He tore off his sleeve, and wrapped it around his lower face, to keep from inhaling too much dust.

At the foot of the stairs to the platform he found a section of wall that had been cleaned of dust and tagged "StillHere." A dead man in an evening suit lay at the other end of the platform, covered in dust.

He hopped off the platform to the floor of the tunnel and found that the dust layer covered water a foot deep. After a moment he decided it was more likely from runoff of broken water mains than a crack in the roof of the tunnel. He followed the maglev tracks under the river. It was a nightmarish trip through darkness and sharp shadows in the dim glow of his flashlight. He found a train on the line where it had stopped, a few hundred yards from the Roosevelt Island Station. Even though there were no bodies in the cars, the silence still evoked a bleak horror.

He changed tunnels at Lexington Avenue, working his way south to Grand Central. The upper levels of Grand Central were blocked by fallen debris, but the access stairs to the deeper levels were clear. That was fine with him. He descended to the deepest levels, and the century-old military vault beneath what had once been the Graybar Building. During a blackout in the seventies, these levels had flooded, but the precautions taken then to avoid similar subsequent flooding had apparently worked.

The doorway he wanted was intact and not blocked. He cleared the dust from a lock pad. The pulse shielding down here had worked, and the steel door opened. The light from inside hurt his eyes for a moment as he stepped out of darkness and into his "workshop." It was a large, carpeted room, decorated in dark woods and comfortable furniture, walls lined with leather-bound books, weapons, paintings, and knickknacks from the history of human civilization.

"Rayna," he called out.

The computer was still active. *"Hello, Lewis, you have several messages . . . Are you all right?"* a woman's voice came from the computer panel which rotated out from a hidden recess. The AI was a violation of the Cumberland Acts, but laws of mortals didn't concern him. Many of Rayna's components had been harvested from an apartment on East Sixty-eighth Street that had once belonged to an alien sent to Earth to protect humanity in the late twentieth century. It had taken months to fix the voice systems and years to reprogram the system.

"I was afraid that you had been killed," she said.

He smiled bitterly. "Lewis Bixby is dead, certainly. Who's next in the queue?"

"I suppose the next best candidate is Jerome Drexel." Rayna maintained a stock of artificial identities, keeping their records and paperwork up to date until they were needed. *"We'll lose a lot of capital in such a rapid transition . . ."*

"I expect we'll lose a lot of capital regardless. Drexel should be fine." He went into the living area and started some coffee. While that was brewing, he showered and changed clothes. After a half hour, carrying a mug of coffee, a pad of paper, and a pen, he eased himself into a stuffed leather Queen Anne chair in front of the computer console.

"Very well, then. List messages . . ." There were several messages from his wife's relatives and others from family friends worried about whether or not anyone had survived the blast. He deleted those, perfunctorily negating the past twelve years of Lewis Bixby's life.

"Tell me, Rayna, what has happened?"

"It's impossible to be accurate, as the Interface Netlinks are only operating sporadically." The monitor flicked onto different newscasts, most broadcasting under the roughest conditions. *"I've had to route through some of the deep military nodes just to get out of the city and into the main backbone. I've only been able to route to the satellite links in the past few hours. My eye-in-the-sky network is active but contact with it is . . . fuzzy at present. I expect it to clear up in a few days as the EM chaos overhead fades."*

He waited for her to continue.

"However, what I have been able to determine is that three days ago, 1 May 2053, at 0230.26, local time, there was a first strike with simultaneous Interface viral assault in coordination with nuclear detonations in several western New United Nations cities . . ."

"What cities?"

"New York City, Chicago, Dallas, Toronto, Mexico City, Rio de Janeiro, London, Berlin, Moscow, and Tel Aviv. Undetonated or otherwise failed explosive devices have been located in Washington, D.C., Denver, Paris, Madrid, Rome, and Istanbul. The military is working under the assumption that the first strike was made by E-Con."

"Not surprising, considering the posturing both sides have been making for the past few months over the Taklamakan and Antarctic oil fields." The Eastern Coalition of Nations was predominantly comprised of nations first united under the Grand Khanate of Noonien Singh. Even after his disappearance, they had continued to work together against the western powers. "Missiles?"

"Unlikely. Probably handheld devices or small aircraft on suicide runs: hence the relatively low-yield explosions. The Alliance nations made an immediate retaliatory launch of missiles, bombers, and satellite-based weapons. Conventional forces were already moving into position for invasion. The First, Eighth, and Sixteenth NUN fleets were already carrying troops into the Bay of Bengal. Current intelligence indicates multiple-megaton detonations over Samarkand, Riyadh, Islamabad, New Delhi, and Singapore; smaller partial detonations over Hong Kong, Beijing, and Ho Chi Minh City. There were failed missile detonations over nearly seventy Asian cities."

He sat watching the screen, clicking a pen absently as he read reports and watched the few available reporters' panicked blathering. Commentary suggested that E-Con hadn't really anticipated any sort of response. President Mendoza was expected to speak to the nation soon. There were clips of her spouting the stock jingoistic presidential nonsense *"We will punish these evil monsters," "The forces of freedom will prevail,"* and so on.

"Casualties?" he asked the computer.

"Best estimates suggest a death toll in the initial exchange ranging from fifty to one hundred million people."

"Not more? That's surprising." He thought for a few moments. "Access post-Holocaust protocols. What are the most realistic outcomes?"

"It's too early to tell. Military sources suggest the EM pulses and viruses have rendered the delivery systems unreliable. Of the hundreds of missiles and bombers the NUN launched, only one in five made it into the air. Of those, only a fraction detonated properly."

"What are the probable secondary casualties?"

"If all goes well, they could be as low as half a billion, but it is far more likely that there will be only half a billion left in six months due to infrastructure and ecological collapse. The nuclear fireballs

*have critically damaged the ozone layer. The firestorms have gener-
ated dust and smoke plumes from the cities, which are carrying tons
of radioactive debris and a large volume of toxic gases released by
the firestorms . . ."* Rayna began reeling off horror after horror,
each a nail in humanity's coffin.

He sat quietly for a long time, considering. A die-off as dramatic
as ninety-six percent of the human race would be hard, but not unexpected. And it might be best for the species in the long run. Then
he thought of the storekeeper in Brooklyn and "StillHere." Could he
stand back and ignore that sort of tenacity? No, the worse the die-
off, the harder the recovery. The insanity was going to be bad
enough no matter what could be managed.

"I suppose we'll have to do something. Work on opening communications channels. Then take a look in the directories 'Winter-
green' and 'Parmen.' We may have to go public about the weather-
control technology, but we have to minimize the ozone damage as
soon as possible and keep the skies clear. If we can wash the skies
somewhat, that might reduce the fallout. Also, I will need to talk to
anyone currently still alive and listed in the following files: Bilder-
berger, Cabal, Golden Dawn, Grandmasters, and Phoenix. Tell them
to expect a call from Al-Akharin." *The Last.*

The man called Jerome Drexel sat in the dark room, his hands
bound to the metal frame chair by strips of plastic quicktape. The
chair was bolted to the hex-tiled floor. The only light came from
some semi-opaque windows along the ceiling, above the row of
sinks along one wall. He'd been beaten repeatedly, and there were
burns on his shoulders and chest. Water drizzled from an exposed
ceiling pipe. Any other fixtures had been removed—recently, by the
glint of shiny metal along the pipe fittings. The room barely resembled anything that might be expected at Montana State University,
and smelled like an abattoir, a moldy abattoir, even with the chilly
breeze of the air handler.

He knew he was being watched. He knew he should feel at least
nervous, but after millennia, torture just wasn't as threatening as it

once was. Much of what made torture effective was fear: of death, and of pain. He'd long since ceased to fear death, and he knew just what pain could and couldn't do to him and was far more concerned about things that had nothing to do with being strapped to a chair in some postapocalyptic idea of a torture chamber.

It had been hard to maintain contact across the entire country, much less the entire planet, with only intermittent communications. Thinking back over the past three years, he wondered if he shouldn't have done more to fix that. As it was, activating the weather satellites had been a far more public action than he preferred. Even with his best efforts, most regions had still been reduced to local reliance on limited resources for food and water. Without federal resources to fall back on, most local governments had been hard-pressed to keep order, much less grow and protect enough food to feed their own; but after some initial struggles, people had been generally willing to work together and help when they could. Busy days had passed, filled with hard physical work; and, for Drexel, the harder task of trying to get influential people to work toward the same goals while the world gently teetered above the Abyss. Thankfully there had been other people here to help him, and Rayna.

Speaking of which . . . He clicked his tongue.

"I'm here," Rayna said through the transceiver. *"The transmitter's fine. Placing it inside an inert bone plug in the skull seems to have slowed your body's rejection process."*

Footsteps and a scraping noise behind him caught his attention. He looked up to see a man in red overalls pulling a chair around him and sitting down about three feet away. He was a little shy of six feet tall, about 1.8 meters, with dark brown/black curly hair, dark eyes, and a vaguely hard set to his mouth, although otherwise his expression seemed rather friendly. His overalls had unit flashes on the shoulders, a radiation counter and a communication transmitter on his left shoulder, and truly kitschy braid around the collar. An outfit designed to be worn beneath an outer garment, such as the ballistic battle dress that Drexel suspected the soldiers standing behind him were wearing.

The two men looked at each other in silence. Finally the soldier spoke. "Your UHD card says that you're Jerome Drexel and before the war you were quite the industrialist."

"That sounds about right."

"Except as we both know, Mister Drexel, that's not the truth." The soldier grinned.

"It isn't?"

"No."

"If you say so."

"Yes, if *I* say so." The soldier paused. "You *do* know who I am, right?"

Drexel considered for a moment denying it, but decided against it. He locked his eyes onto the other man's and stared as he spoke. "Aaron Jenkins, also known as 'Colonel Green,' in much the same way that Joseph Vissarionovich Djugashvili called himself 'Stalin.' "

"So you have heard of me? Excellent."

"I've even read your books. *Optimal Purity and the Human Animal,* and *Emerald Watch on the Twilight Line,* were pure nihilistic twaddle, blending the worst of Nietzsche and Rand, with a solid dose of White Supremacy in the mix. I have to admit, though—you have a way with words. It wouldn't surprise me to find that in centuries to come, *Necessary Sacrifice* is still a classic philosophy text among those looking for a rationalization for mass slaughter."

"I believe you have completely misunderstood me." Green tried to look open and innocent.

"I don't think so." Drexel sounded bored.

The truly superior human doesn't need to flaunt it, tell people about it, or write about it seeking validation.

"It was reported that your Brigade was cut off in Kashmiristan a few weeks into the war," Drexel continued.

"Those bastards at Central Command abandoned us there."

"Perhaps. Or perhaps they didn't have a way to get you all home again. Be that as it may, like the White Company after the Hundred Years War, you were cut adrift, far from home, and you did what any self-respecting *condotierre* would do. You abandoned your post."

Green looked at him quizzically. "There are still a lot of our troops back there. I understand that most of them have hired on with the local warlords as mercenaries."

Drexel ignored him. "A year later, you surprised everyone by appearing in Alaska at the head of an army comprised of both NUN and former Coalition soldiers. The president ordered you to stand down. You declined."

"Mendoza isn't president of anything. The NUN is gone, the United States is little more than a burnt-out husk with no authority. Hell, you've seen it out there. There are a few enclaves of order surrounded by barbarism. If you don't starve, the marauding hordes will get you. The dark ages are back."

Drexel continued as if the other man hadn't spoken. "You unrolled your red eagle banner, burning and slaughtering your way across the Pacific Northwest to bring order?"

"I do what I have to."

"I daresay. Over the past two years you've been conquering and consolidating your way across the country, slaughtering the 'unpure'—those you deemed too diseased, too mutated, who weren't your shade of white, or those people who just happened to disagree with you. Your speech outside the Seattle Arena before your soldiers slaughtered thousands of civilians was memorable: 'This is not the time for timidity and second-guessing—we can not afford to doubt ourselves.' As I said, a way with words. Several months ago you crossed the Rockies into Montana, and by all accounts have been cheerfully continuing your culling here."

Green stared back at him. "You just aren't afraid of me, are you?"

"I have no real reason to be."

Green smiled broadly. "We'll have to see about that. You see, I know about you too, Mister Drexel. In fact, I've wanted to meet you for some time."

"And why would that be?"

"I've been hearing about your own efforts at bringing order to this once great nation. You invented the weather control technology, didn't you? You didn't really think that I would stop in to visit just anyone we catch violating our borders, did you? I think we have a lot we can do for one another."

"Honestly, I was expecting to see that pimple-faced posturer of a subaltern who's been trying to question me."

"Yes, Lieutenant Paxton, he's still a little . . ." Green hesitated.

"Green?"

"I was going to say inexperienced. So tell me, what were you doing? Driving a car across the countryside in the middle of the night? A car with a box of biotech papers and equipment in the trunk. I can't imagine that someone like you is the sort to partake in mundane espionage."

"We'd sent in several convoys of medical supplies, food, and materiel that had gone missing recently. I felt that needed to be followed up, trying to find out why; and we're stretched a little thin right now."

"*We* being who?"

"*We* being a loose alliance of like-minded organizations trying to help people recover from the Late Unpleasantness," Drexel answered.

"I'll accept that for now. So what were the papers and equipment for?" Green continued the interrogation.

Drexel was surprised at the question. "Papers and equipment?"

"Yes, the papers and equipment in the trunk relating to bioweapons research."

"Your guess is as good as mine. The car's previous owner had died. I think he was some sort of university wonk. I never even looked in the trunk."

"You know, I could almost believe you. Academics are a tricky, worthless lot of rabble. Almost as useless as those silly lawyers whining about rights. You know, the universities all shut down with the war, except that these damned academics and their minions just keep on finding worthless things to 'research' and waste time and resources on."

Drexel sighed sympathetically. "I can't say that I mind the lack of academic pretentiousness and politics slowing things down."

"Tell you what, though. I have a cure for that. Honest labor."

"Such as?"

"When we came driving up, the educated dummies here tried to *negotiate*. At least it made them easy to round up. We shipped all of them off to work at the coal mines in the mountains." Green laughed.

"All of them?" That was just what Drexel wanted to hear. He relayed the code he knew Rayna was waiting for. "God in Heaven, that must have been a sight to see."

"It was. More trouble than they are worth."

"How much trouble is the secret missile complex off in the foothills worth?"

Green froze, then laughed. "You're very good, sir. Yes, I have those missiles. It wasn't hard to repair the circuitry."

"Giving you what, fifty, two-hundred-megaton fusion weapons? Each with a heavy booster capable of reaching the antipodes."

"Beautiful, isn't it? I always wanted to be my own superpower."

"It would be quite lovely, except for two crucial things," Drexel commented.

"And what would those be?"

Outside the building there was a distant rumbling of thunder, growing louder.

"The first is that I have other plans for those missiles . . ."

The thunder roll had deepened, and then vanished into a thunderclap loud enough to vibrate the floor. Green looked around, startled. Drexel flexed his arms and snapped his bonds.

"The second thing is that you've just had a horrible accident in your bioweapons lab, and you and every human within a mile radius are now either dying or soon will be from a particularly virulent mutated version of weapons-grade Ebola. The stuff smells horrible." Drexel wrinkled his nose at the odor coming through the air conditioner.

"What are you talking about? I don't have a bioweapons lab. Bioweapons are too dangerous; they can backfire on you too easily."

"Which is why I had to have the virus dropped from orbit."

Drexel smiled. "Rest assured, though, that when your people arrive to investigate, they'll find out what you've been up to . . . all the evidence you've left."

Green looked at him, horrified, and started coughing.

"You wanted to know why I'm here? I'm here to make sure that you go down as one of the biggest monsters in history. That you were preparing to use an uncontrollable disease on your enemies."

"Why?" Green fell to his hands and knees, his question unanswered; as did the two guards by the door, coughing, blood pouring from every orifice.

"Call it a 'necessary sacrifice.' "

The man called Drexel stepped out onto the observation platform behind the observatory dome. The 130-year-old structure had been abandoned for decades. The ivy slowly claiming the flaking concrete was dried and brown in the August dryness. He could smell the salt tang of the sea in the morning breeze, even at this distance. Walking around behind the dome, all of the Los Angeles basin lay stretched before him: from the nearly silent Cahuenga Canyon freeway to the Hollywood Hills canyons slowly returning to their natural state to Santa Monica Bay stretching inward nearly as far as Century and Culver Cities, then down to the green and blue smudge that was Palos Verdes Island, and the Long Beach Channel. In the faint ocean haze he could barely make out where the Magic Kingdom towers still stood in Anaheim, far beyond the empty and falling towers of the old downtown.

"They tell me it's the world's largest ghost town," a voice from behind him said. Drexel turned to look at the person who had joined him. A tall man, with short, dark hair, blue eyes, mixed background, and a normally friendly, lively face, prematurely aged by five years' exposure to the postwar world. He was clearly stressed.

Thankfully the weather-control satellites were finally getting the ozone layer regenerated. Now if they could just get the temperatures back up.

"It was a ghost town before Hermosa, trying to cope with a century and a half of destroyed lives and false façades," Drexel replied.

The Net was already killing what was left of film and television production anyway. The earthquake just put the place out of its misery.

Drexel stuck out his hand. The other man took it in his, almost desperately, his fingers taking the ancient ritual positions. "Ellison, why did you call for this meeting?"

"Sir . . ." The younger man's voice seemed to relax somewhat, though tension still filled his voice. "There's been an . . . accident."

"Serious?"

"Oh God, yes." Ellison shuddered.

"Tell me about it." Drexel already knew the particulars—Rayna had seen to that, but he found that when you gave people rein to speak, it not only helped them, but they often shared unexpected information.

"We were testing to see if a larger distortion field could be generated. You know we had a problem with that test on the moon some time back . . ." He hesitated.

Drexel nodded patiently. A hole had been blown in the moon's surface earlier in the year, and the Phoenix Project had almost been shut down.

We still can't feed the population, but the spaceports are up and running.

Thankfully Green hadn't heard about the project when he'd had Doctor Cochrane and his bunch shipped off to the coal mines two years ago. Cochrane and his assistants, of which Ellison was one of the more important, were back at work in Bozeman.

"Well, we set up a network of Continuum Distortion generators on the Lagrange Habitats."

"Why there?" the older man asked.

"We figured that the earlier accident might have had something to do with not only the Earth's gravity, but also the Moon's mass, so we thought we'd try it as far out as we could get and still be easily reached. The Habitats were willing to run the tests. There should have been nothing that could have gone wrong."

"And?"

"They flipped the switch, and . . . well, they're gone. And not just them, but every space platform outside the Earth's geomagnetic field: All six O'Neill habitats, a whole slew of satellites in high orbit including most of the asteroid defense network. The outer debris field is just . . . gone. Five thousand people."

Drexel shrugged inwardly

And half of Rayna's eyes in the sky. On the plus side, the weather and communications satellite networks are in lower orbits than that, and this does eliminate the remaining orbital weapons platforms. No loss there.

"So who knows about this?"

"Right now, just the people up in Bozeman. Zefram's too shaken to do more than crawl into his bottle and threaten to quit. Jacob, Lily, Rance, and the others are all doing their stoic thing, but it's obvious they're about to crumble. They all think I've gone south to talk to the president about this." The assistant was shifting his weight nervously.

"And so you shall, but you were right to contact me. We'll need to spin this."

"How? I mean we're talking five thousand people. Communications may be iffy and the country is still mostly held by local warlords, but eventually *someone*'s going to notice that they aren't up there anymore. Even if Zefram doesn't quit, they are going to shut us down this time. We killed five thousand people!"

How did the song go? "Somos cinco mil aquí, en esta pequeña parte de la ciudad . . ."

"Did you?"

Ellison froze. "What do you mean?"

"They may have died, certainly. But let's learn from history for a moment, shall we? I'm certain that you recall the *Odyssey* star launches back in the thirties. The manned attempt to travel beyond the solar system? I should hope so since *Odyssey Eight* and *Nine* are still out there." At twenty percent of the speed of light it would take *Odyssey Eight,* the *Telemachus,* until 2062 to reach Alpha Centauri. "The *Telemachus,* under Chuck Clement, discovered a permanent magnetic storm at the leading edge of the heliopause. Clement reported that this appeared to be generating random, spontaneous momentary wormholes. It's probable that something similar destroyed the *Odyssey Ten,* the *Charybdis.*"

Not to mention several of the Voyager, Pioneer, *and* Nomad *probes.*

"Yes, that's what gave Zefram the idea how to manipulate subspace . . ."

"Precisely. Isn't it reasonable to assume then that a distortion field that is not balanced correctly can create spontaneous momentary wormholes?"

Ellison nodded slowly.

"Tell the president that the test was a success, but that one of the generators wasn't in synch with the others, and that some sort of wormhole effect happened. Make it clear you couldn't control this since the actual generators were out of your hands."

"But that's not true."

"Isn't it? Can you say for a certainty what actually happened?"

"Of course not."

"It certainly sounds more plausible to me than that you managed to generate enough of a distortion field to inadvertently vaporize even one O'Neill habitat. Not to mention things a quarter of a million miles, er, four hundred thousand kilometers away. Particularly since if you can do that it means that you've just built the most powerful weapon in history."

Time seemed to slow as Ellison digested that.

"So who do we say screwed up?"

"Brynner was up there with you at, what does Cochrane call it? Ground Station Bozeman?"

"Yes. I think he's heading back to San Francisco now."

"Fine, tell the president that you think it was Brynner's habitat. Maybe there was a real malfunction and no one actually did anything wrong, but stress that it was a million-to-one accident."

"What about Brynner?"

"I'll square things with him."

The man called Drexel stood by the edge of the clearing with a taller, elderly man. Across the clearing, by the clapped-together saloon, a party was going on, a celebration. The Phoenix Project had been a success. The old man was rubbing his hands together, complaining.

"It's freezing out here. Why didn't we leave after Cochrane landed? We could be back in Bozeman by now."

Drexel smiled and looked at the other man.

Christopher Brynner, the Net's first trillionaire, founder of Brynner Information Systems and Interface Operations corporation, and the Interface's Channel 90, member of the boards of more conglomerates and *zaibatsu*s than Carter's had little liver pills, was quite a sight in a heavy coat and cloth cap. He looked to be nearly ninety, although he was only seventy.

Drexel thought back to the bright, young man he had met in the first decade of the millennium. Drexel had been working with the Iraqi museum, trying to identify looted artifacts, and Brynner had been a battle-scarred lieutenant serving in the American forces. The full-body Maori tattoo was long gone now, inappropriate for a man in high finance, but that same bright-eyed young man was still there, trapped in an aging body.

"We're waiting," Drexel said, turning back to watch the festivities.

"For what?"

"First contact," Drexel said simply.

"What the hell is that?"

"This morning, when Cochrane broke the warp barrier, it was detected by an alien scout ship near Neptune. They should be landing here any minute."

"Rayna tell you that?"

"Some of it. See that group over there, looking as discrete as a tramp at a church social?" Drexel nodded in the direction of a group of people huddling around an older, bald man in a long coat.

"Yes."

"I'm fairly certain they're not from around here," Drexel said wryly.

"What do you mean?" Brynner asked.

"Last night, when we lost contact with the launch site? The story they are spreading is that one of the weapons platforms reacted to the powering up of the *Phoenix* and fired on the site."

"But there aren't any weapons platforms up there."

"Most people don't know that, though."

"So what happened?"

"I don't have a clue." Drexel frowned. Not really true. After listening to Rayna's reports from her eyes in the sky of temporal events, unusual spacecraft fighting it out, and matter transmission profiles resembling those from time travelers she had encountered in 1968, it seemed fairly obvious that someone, possibly from the future, had come to Earth to stop Cochrane's flight, and someone else came to set things right.

"When I got up here first thing this morning, these people were already hard at work repairing the *Phoenix,* almost as if they'd had some sort of investment in it. Two of them even took the ride with Cochrane, in place of Ellison and Sloane."

"But Lily's right there."

"I gather she was injured in the attack last night. This morning she was somewhere else getting treatment. Ellison was killed."

"They told you this?"

"No. But I've had most of the day to piece together what was going on. I wouldn't be surprised if we never see them again. We'll probably want to forget they were ever here."

After all, they are doing me an unasked-for favor, it would be rude not to reciprocate.

"So now these aliens are coming?"

"Yes."

"And this is a good thing?" Drexel's companion asked sarcastically.

"They are Vulcans, so it's better than it could be."

"You've met these aliens—Vulcans?—before?"

"I've met one before. Nice enough fellow, if a bit too stiff and dull. He was stranded here in the nineteen-fifties."

"What happened to him?"

"I don't know. I haven't seen him in over twenty years. He was living in New York then, writing science fiction novels."

Brynner tucked his hands under his arms, and thought for a moment.

"Aliens. How cool is that? I've always wanted to meet an alien."

"I suppose. I've encountered a number of aliens over the years." *The Gods, the Sandarans, Q, Mestral, Gary Seven . . .* "Most weren't really that pleasant to deal with." Drexel shrugged. "But who knows? Maybe the public existence of aliens will help bring people together. Nothing makes you clean up your house better than knowing the neighbors are coming to visit. Although even that will still take decades."

"All the things you've seen. You know, I really envy you sometimes."

"I envy you, too." Drexel's voice was filled with emotion as he made the comment.

"Why?"

"Because, Chris, you'll die someday. That's something I doubt I'll ever get to experience." They fell silent for a few minutes.

After a while Brynner turned to him. "So, how many lives have you had? How many people have you been?"

"I have no idea."

"That's a facile answer. I asked you a serious question."

"It happens to be the truth. Memory isn't a lot different for me than it is for you. You know I have an eidetic memory, right? But even the carvings on stone erode into dust in time. I can barely remember what happened to me a thousand years ago. In fact, all I'm working on are memories of memories, and those tend to get jumbled after a time. Occasionally there are flashes of things that happened before, sparked by unpredictable stimuli." He stopped and looked up at the sky. "Let me think—at least three hundred—relevant lives. The inconsequential short lives that lasted only a day or an evening, easily over a thousand."

"That includes Alexander, Solomon, Michelangelo, and so on, right?" Brynner asked.

"No, not really. Most of them have been people you are unlikely to have ever heard of." He thought for a moment. "Have you ever heard of Utnapishtim?"

"Immortal king of Dilmun, the prototype for Noah."

Drexel looked at him, an eyebrow raised.

"What?" Brynner shrugged. "When you told the Circle you were Gilgamesh, I went out and read a book. So you were Utnapishtim?"

"I'm fairly certain I was. I've been keeping a low profile for a long time though; living a new life for a decade or two, then leaving before having to lose people, before the children start looking at me with that growing look of fear in their eyes." A burst of music and cheering came from the saloon. "Don't get me wrong, I'm fairly sure I knew those people, Alexander and such. But I find that most people have expectations for immortals. They are more likely to believe you when you tell them that you were Benjamin Franklin than if you tell them you were Georges LeMat. More importantly, they are less likely to burn you at the stake if you claim to be someone they've heard of."

"Still, all the things you've seen—how much have you forgotten?"

"Most of it. I keep thinking I should try to reproduce some of the great artworks I've encountered that have been lost and no longer exist except in my memory. There never seems to be the time." He paused thoughtfully for a moment. "I think the real reason I tend to lie about who I was is that people take a while to warm up to one another, to open up, to share. Every time a person gets hurt, loves and loses, the harder that process is. After millennia, that process is really hard. My life is my business and no one else's. Hell, I've known you most of your life. You're the closest thing to family I have. Well, you and Rayna. And it's hard enough for me to open up to you."

"Why?"

"Because you'll die someday, and I'll have to deal with that loss. It's just easier to not get involved."

"So no one ever gets to know the real you, never gets to learn all the good you've done?" Brynner asked.

Or the harm.

"That is correct."

"That makes no sense to me."

"If I made perfect sense, I'd have to relinquish being human altogether."

Silence fell throughout the compound. The cloud cover started to swirl. A multicolored equal-armed Y shape slowly descended.

"So this is it," Brynner said. "I feel like I should be covering this."

"Well, you are the closest thing to a journalist here. It would be the biggest story of your life."

"You going to be okay?" Brynner looked worried.

Drexel looked at the ship for a long moment.

"I'll survive."

(GRAND PRIZE)

Orphans

R. S. Belcher

In the times before the treatment murdered his senses, the room would have spoken to him. He would have known she was still awake before he had even entered their darkened bedroom; her breathing pattern, heart rate, pheromone dispersal, even her body language as she lay on their bed, her back to him, would have been noted, recorded, analyzed. It would have screamed that she feigned sleep in less time than it took to blink, or kill.

But now his senses were lost in the fog of the medicines. He was completely taken off guard when her voice broke the silence of their bedroom.

"How was council?"

The thrill of disorientation, of being surprised, had been alien to him since the war, a vaguely remembered response to stimuli that the doctors and the councillors, the drugs and surgeries, had purged from him a million lifetimes ago. Now the treatment left him blind and vulnerable.

"Long," he said as he slipped off his jacket and kicked off his shoes.

"It's been that way a lot lately," she said.

"Yes," he answered, swallowing hard.

She didn't turn around to face him. He went to the sink and splashed cold water across his face. As always, the man in the mirror was a stranger. His face was gaunt, more drawn than even during his time in the war. The treatment's effects had dulled his dark eyes. His black hair was shot through with gray. The only thing he did recognize, the thing that told him that this was his face, was his unit tattoo—a silver triangle whose apex radiated from the corner of his right eye and stretched back to cover his temple.

Spiderweb-thin lines within the green core of the triangle told his life story in the language of stored chemical data that any chemcomp scanner could read: Roga Danar, rank: subhadar in the armed forces of Angosia III. Served with honor and distinction in the bloody campaigns of the Tarsian War. Twice promoted for his actions upon the field of battle. Relocated to an orbital military prison on Luna V, along with his brothers-in-arms at the close of the war. Sentenced to a lifetime of solitude, shunned by the society he and his fellows had volunteered to defend.

Then there had been the revolt and the political compromises he and the other veterans had forced upon the Angosian government at gunpoint.

That had been eight years ago.

He stared blankly at his reflection. He blinked and remembered what he had been doing.

His wife was speaking again. He tried to push the crowded thoughts out so he could focus.

"Did the Prime Minister agree to your proposal?" he heard Shara ask.

"Not at first, but he knows we have the popular support to push it through, and he is a political realist. He backed down."

Shara said nothing else. She remained a still shadow facing the wall.

"I'm sorry it took so long," he lied.

Danar sat on the edge of the bed and removed his shirt. A roadway of scars crisscrossed his chest and back. Once, his enhanced memory had allowed him to remember the exact circumstance of each wound, down to a perfect memory of the pain. Now it was all a dull mass of shadows and half-recalled trauma.

The Tarsians had invaded Angosia's outer worlds with such terrible violence that Danar's people had been completely stunned. They were not warriors; they were thinkers, artists, and scientists. So they approached fighting the war like a scientific calculation, a problem that could be solved.

Their reasonable solution damned the souls of an entire generation.

"Does she help you?" Shara whispered. "Whoever she is. Does she take the pain away? Are you whole with her?"

He looked down at his hands, hands that had killed eighty-seven men. Killing had been easier than this.

"No," he said.

He rose silently and walked from the room. What else was there to say? That he was sorry? That it meant nothing? There was no comfort for either of them there.

He wished the treatment dulled his senses enough to spare him the sound of her tears, but it did not.

The ghost of his conditioning came to him even in dull, heavy sleep. Not even the treatment could keep the oldest instincts fully buried. Any soldier worth the name slept with one eye open.

He felt, more than heard, the shiver of the air, the subtle change in air pressure. He rolled off the cushion and came up in a crouch, eyes blinking in the darkness, trying to adapt. His hands fumbled for a weapon, any kind of weapon, and settled on a flat metal tray off the end table.

Someone had stealth-transported into his home. Two dark figures stood only meters away from him.

"I have a phaser," one shadow said. "Please, Councilman Danar, put down the tray. I'd hate to have to shoot you."

The tray dropped to the thick rug with a dull thump.

"Thank you. Please sit down."

Danar slid back onto the couch.

"If you would be so kind as to raise the illumination level so we can all see each other while we chat? As you know, the panel is to your left. Please, no tricks. I wouldn't want your wife to run in here to see what is going on and meet with some unpleasantness. Just the lights, Councilman."

The light came up and Danar could now see the intruders clearly. The man with the phaser was tall, slender and bald with a fringe of black hair. His eyes were bright and hard. The man with him was younger, aquiline and handsome. *They both carry themselves like military men,* Danar thought, but the younger man's posture carried less of a swagger. Both men wore black; polycarb combat cloth and leather—Special Forces gear.

"What do you want?" he asked. "Who are you?"

"My name is Pressman," the older man said. He slid into a chair across from Roga's crouch. The Federation phaser in his hand never wavered from Danar's chest. "This is Doctor Julian Bashir."

"The Federation doctor?" Danar said. He shifted his gaze to Bashir. "You developed the treatment with Doctor Crusher that helps counteract the genetic modifications the Angosian government used on us during the war."

"Yes, I did," Bashir said softly. "We met briefly at a conference here a few years ago, Councilman. The treatment wasn't a perfect solution, but the modifications were too ingrained into your genetic and psychological makeup to simply reverse or remove them. Beverly and I tried to . . . suppress them."

Feelings welled up inside of Danar. There was anger, long buried under a daily regimen of soul-killing drugs, and numbness. He remembered Garla and Koji and all of his other friends who had been lost to the twilight of the treatment, who couldn't take the dissolution of themselves to a fog of chemical numbness. They had died either by their own hand or by simply giving up. Danar counted them as more war dead.

"Yes," he said through dry lips and clenched jaw. "It was far from a perfect solution, Doctor."

"Actually it's your condition that brings us here, Councilman, and the condition of your fellow veterans," Pressman said.

Danar slid back onto the couch and Pressman continued.

"As you are aware, the Federation is at war with the Dominion and its allies. About three weeks ago, a Jem'Hadar task force captured a classified Federation research outpost on an L-class planet in the Beta Quadrant. This facility is of vital importance to the survival of the Federation. You and some of your fellow Angosian veterans are going to help us recapture that planet."

"You're *Admiral* Pressman, aren't you?" Danar said. "I heard you were court-martialed, forced out of Starfleet in some kind of scandal involving the Romulans?"

Pressman visibly darkened. Danar nodded.

"So tell me, *Admiral,* why doesn't Starfleet send its own troops and ships to retake this rock? Why are two Federation officers breaking into the home of a politician from a non-allied world in the dead of night?" He smiled at Pressman. "If I didn't know better, I'd suspect that the Federation was engaging in some kind of illegal military operation."

"Not the Federation," Bashir quickly interjected. "Not Starfleet. A rogue agency, created by ruthless men to protect and support the United Federation of Planets at any cost."

"Doctor Bashir's interpretation of our organization is not very flattering," Pressman said. "But it is essentially accurate. When I resigned from Starfleet, individuals of a like mind approached me. These people are patriots, like me. They realize that if the Federation is to endure, hard decisions must be made by men who possess the will to do whatever is necessary."

"Zealots," Bashir said. "Fanatics. They call themselves Section Thirty-one. They routinely violate the very principles the Federation was founded upon."

"We're not here to debate civic responsibility, Doctor," Pressman said. "We're here to recruit the councilman and his fellow veterans."

"Why me?" Danar said. "Why us? The treatment has reduced us to a state where we are barely functional as normal men and women. We are no longer supersoldiers, Admiral." He snorted with disgust. "Far from it."

"Tell him, Doctor," Pressman said to Bashir.

"Tell me what," Danar said.

"The process, the treatment," Bashir began. "It can be reversed. In effect, I can detox you. Very rapidly."

"I thought . . . they said . . . it was permanent," Danar said, the blood draining from his face.

"Doctor Crusher and I did the best we could," Bashir said. "But the conditioning was too radical, much of it far in advance of Federation biological technology. We tried to suppress it as much as we could and hoped that with proper reinforcement and social support you and the other veterans could lead normal lives despite the powerful effects of the treatment. Part of that reinforcement had to be your belief that the treatment was permanent." Danar focused on the small pulse jumping in Bashir's throat. He had once known, like he knew his own heartbeat, exactly how much pressure it would take to exert on that point to end a man's life in seconds.

"I'm sorry," Bashir was saying. "As I said, it wasn't a perfect solution but neither was having hundreds of thousands of genetically engineered supermen, built to react with deadly force to virtually any perceived threat, wandering the streets of every Angosian city."

Danar's voice was a knife wrapped in cloth. "Do you have any idea how many of my friends are dead now because of your deception? Do you?"

"I'm sorry," Bashir said. When he had been a resident, he had always prided himself on his bedside manner. Now his words sounded hollow and weak. They were. Danar was right. Lying to a patient was never a good idea, never the right thing to do; even a terminal one, especially a terminal one.

"Do it," Danar said to Pressman. "Detox me and tell about this research outpost you so desperately need back."

*   *   *

The ship was a small scout, hanging silently above Danar's city. Its cloak hid it from local air traffic control sensors.

It was nearly dawn, Angosia's star cresting, in warm yellow brilliance, above the terminator of the globe. Danar, Pressman, and Bashir materialized on the small transporter pad near the aft of the vessel just in time to witness the star's ascension.

Danar noticed the trailing, glyph-like writing that burned bright emerald from dozens of different monitors and control panels.

"Romulan?" he said. "I heard they were in the war now but how did you get them to give you . . ."

"They didn't," Pressman said, smiling, as he made his way to the helm of the small craft. "We salvaged it from a vessel that crashed near Nelvana. I was able to coax its cloak back online. I've some small expertise in Romulan cloaking technology. We figured it would be the perfect insertion vessel for the operation. With the modifications I've made to its particle shroud, we should be able to avoid detection by the Jem'Hadar."

"Should?" Bashir frowned as he took a seat next to Danar. He leaned forward to regard the Angosian. "How do you feel? Is your head clearing?"

Danar narrowed his eyes at the young doctor. "Oh, yes, Doctor. It is."

His hands moved with no doubt now, no forcing them to obey him. They were nimble again, faster than any normal eyes could track. Instantly they were around Bashir's neck, his thumb resting on the gently thudding pulse. Just an instant, just a gradual increase of pressure and . . .

"Look down," Bashir whispered. A small Federation hand phaser, its discharge indicator blinking crimson, was pressed against Danar's stomach.

"It's set to maximum," the doctor told him. "I understand you want to kill me, but do you want to die to do it? Let me go, please."

The hands slid away from Bashir's throat. He powered down the phaser and put it away. Danar sat back in his chair.

"Fast hands," he said.

"Yes, I suppose they are," Bashir said somewhat hesitantly.

"Did Section Thirty-one do that to you; genetically alter you?"

"No. It was my parents."

"Your parents?"

"To compensate for learning disabilities I suffered from as a child."

Both men felt motion as the inertial dampers registered the change in speed and direction. Pressman's long fingers danced across the helm console as he altered the ship's hidden orbit.

"Genetic resequencing was illegal in the Federation," Bashir said, "so they took me to Adigeon Prime when I was six to undergo the process. I never asked for it."

"I volunteered," Danar said. "We were at war. Everyone was frightened. I remember people walking around pale and quiet and terrified, like their voices might set off another attack. No one could believe that such savagery could occur in such civilized times. We were all wrong, Doctor. Civilization exists at the sufferance of barbarians.

"Now, I don't even recognize myself in the mirror anymore. I was turned into a murdering machine by one set of doctors and scientists and then turned into the walking dead by another group."

"Roga, if there had been any way for us to reverse the conditioning, we would have, but your scientists were too good at their job."

"Yes," Danar said with a gallows smile. "My people are very good at doing what they are ordered to do, especially 'for the good of Angosia.'"

Pressman walked back to them from the cockpit of the ship.

"We're over the coordinates for your first team member, Danar," he said.

"This won't take long at all, if I know Ketlan."

"I can't believe you were stupid enough to go along with this . . . sir," Ketlan Farr said. She was a few centimeters shorter than Danar, with long brown hair pulled back severely from her face and secured in a tight bun. Her unit tattoo was identical to the one on Danar's face.

"Well, that's why I asked you to join us, Guardsman Farr," Danar said, addressing the entire team of seven veterans who sat in the Romulan scout's cramped passenger compartment. "You will hold my hand and produce the appropriate amount of screaming, if I do something too foolish, won't you?"

A chuckle ran through the complement of newly recruited Angosian soldiers. Bashir had administered the detoxification hypospray as soon as they had materialized on the scout ship and they were starting to act like real people again, instead of glass-eyed robots.

Danar clapped his old friend warmly on the shoulder as he took her aside.

"It's good to see you again, Ketlan."

"You too, sir," she said. "Orders?"

Danar handed her a Starfleet data padd.

"Get them familiarized with the Jem'Hadar. All the data Pressman has on them is in here. Assume it's not complete."

"Just like any other military intelligence report I've ever read," Farr said.

"Then make sure everyone gets their equipment and weapons squared away."

Farr grinned. "Just like old times, sir."

Danar nodded. "Unfortunately."

He left his guardsman to her work and sat down next to Pressman, who was still at the helm of the Romulan ship.

"The troops sound motivated," the former admiral said briskly. "They trust you, Danar."

"Well, I don't trust you, Pressman. I've been wondering about something. Why didn't your Section Thirty-one just create your own covert Federation supersoldiers? It seems less risky to use a known quantity for black ops than farming the work out to us."

Pressman nodded curtly as his eyes scanned over the sensor data logs.

"You're right, it would be, and we did consider it. Unfortunately, Doctor Bashir made sure all the data he and Doctor Crusher received from your government about your conditioning was destroyed at the end of their research project. The good doctor can be quite irritating when he puts his mind to it.

"It seems he took a personal interest in keeping your magnificent combat training program from ever being replicated. So, when the war came, we had no choice but to look to you and your people as a viable asset."

Danar chuckled dryly and shook his head. Pressman looked up from the instruments.

"Sorry," Danar said. "It's just been a long time since anyone called me a 'viable asset.' I still don't care for it."

"This is war," Pressman said tersely. "The most horrible, most decisive conflict the Federation has ever been involved in. The stakes here are the survival of our culture, our way of life. In this kind of a struggle every sentient being is an asset, to be used to maximum effect, no matter the cost."

"So, you are ignoring the laws and moral codes of your society in order to protect and preserve them?" Danar said. "Very democratic of you, Admiral."

Pressman ignored the barb. His eyes were focused on someplace past the tunnel of Dopplering stars that hurtled past the viewscreen. Danar had seen the look before in commanders and knew it was pointless to continue trying to be reasonable with this man.

"You'd best spend this time getting your team ready," Pressman said softly. "You are impressive but you'll need every trick, every edge to deal with the Jem'Hadar."

Danar left him alone with his mad clarity and the ghost-light of long-dead stars.

The planet had no name. It didn't even exist on Federation star charts. It was an arid corpse of a world orbiting a bloated, ancient star that was the color of blood. Three Jem'Hadar warships hung in orbit, like vultures, silent, sleek, and deadly, circling a desiccated carcass.

Pressman dropped out of warp well outside the star system and made a few last-minute adjustments to the cloaking device. He shut down every nonessential system on the scout and then edged the hidden vessel with painful slowness closer and closer to the unnamed world.

In the darkened, crowded cabin, Julian Bashir's thoughts were not on the immediate threat of detection by the enemy, nor in preparation for battle, like the Angosians. Instead he wandered down corridors of memory. He thought of his father and mother, of his childhood and the changes his parents had made in him, against his will, without considering what he might have wanted.

And what would I have wanted? he thought. *I was six years old. I had severe learning disabilities. Was I even capable of making a choice about myself? For myself?*

He looked across the aisle at the Angosians. They were calm, serene. The genetic coding in them ensured that they only truly felt relaxed and comfortable in stressful situations. Was that cruel or merciful? It had kept them alive through years of bloody conflict but it had stolen the life and people they had been fighting for from them.

Did my parents love me and change me to make my life better, to help me succeed, to survive? Or was it really for them, so they didn't have to endure the embarrassment of a substandard child?

The scout's gravity seemed to flicker for an instant. Pressman was hunched over the console, his eyes locked on the sensor data from the warships they were nearing. Pressman's brow was damp; his breathing was hard and quick. His pupils were wide. It suddenly occurred to Bashir that Pressman was the only person on the scout ship who was behaving the way normal humans should in such a dangerous situation. Everyone else had been programmed to be more than human.

I've always felt like a replacement part, he thought. *That the*

*child I began as was cast off and I'm the refit. What if all that I am,
all that I do, all the poems I enjoy, the battles I fight with Miles in
the holosuite, the way I love; what if all of that was never what I was
supposed to be?*

He was pulled away from the thought by the sensation of a sudden change in course combined with rapid acceleration. He made his way forward to the cockpit and found Pressman cursing under his breath.

"They spot us?" Bashir asked as he slid behind the other console. Pressman chewed his bottom lip and adjusted course and speed before he answered.

"Yes . . . I don't know. One of the warships just broke orbit and is heading this way. He must have picked up our gravitic displacement somehow. We may have to cut and run."

"Wait," Danar said as he leaned between the two command consoles. "You said time was of the essence to secure this facility, correct?"

"Well, of course it is," Pressman snapped. "But it won't do the mission any good if we get killed or captured."

"We won't," Danar said. He pointed to a screen on Pressman's console. "There, see? They are still running on noncombat status. They saw something to make them take a closer look, but not enough to make them wary. We play this right and we can keep going. Change heading; get under them, then behind them, quickly."

"What?" Pressman said. Bashir looked a bit uncomfortable at the notion as well. He knew too well what a Jem'Hadar ship could do.

"Those ships use ion propulsion, right?" Danar snapped. "If you can swing in under and behind it and stay close, then we'll be hidden in the particle wash. It's a blind spot on the sensors, see?"

Pressman sputtered. He was accelerating toward the warship but his hands hesitated over the console's controls.

"That's, that's insane," he said. "That shower of charged particles, we'll stick out like a sore thumb."

Danar was already reaching over Pressman, to manipulate the helm console. "Not if we randomly fluctuate the particle shrouding. We'll look like normal ion distortion."

He looked to Bashir and the doctor nodded and began to reconfigure the console in front of him. He wished Miles was here to do this but he was fairly certain he could manage. Pressman was still trying to catch up.

"But that would require changing the cloaking domain at an impossible rate. You can't . . ."

"Watch."

Danar pulled him up and took his seat at helm, already executing the maneuver that would bring the scout to within 125 meters of the warship's drive exhaust. Bashir began to alter the cloak's characteristics to absorb and redirect charged particles. His hands blurred and darted over the console like hummingbirds.

The main viewscreen was awash in white light from the Jem'Hadar drive. Julian noticed that the sensors were providing nothing but streams of meaningless data. They were flying blind on the tail of a dragon. Danar responded by sheer instinct, his moves anticipating every minor course correction of the warship. Soon the planet appeared in view once again, as the warship returned to its standard orbit. Danar broke from trailing the warship just as it was settling into orbit. He positioned the ship in a fixed orbit over the planet's northern magnetic pole.

"An old smuggler's trick," he said. "The electromagnetic interference will hide us from their sensors. I used it once on a Federation starship and it fooled them. It will fool the Jem'Hadar."

Pressman activated the antimatter bomb with a voice-authorized security code. The bomb was a meter-long cylinder of dull silver metal. He handed the control padd to Bashir.

"It's keyed to your and Danar's DNA. Either of you can set it for a timed detonation or for immediate explosion. There is enough antimatter in there to destroy the entire planet."

"What's here that is so important you're willing to vaporize the whole planet to keep the Dominion from getting their hands on it?" Danar asked. Pressman regarded him coolly for an instant, then returned his gaze to Bashir.

"If the asset can be recovered or secured, then do it. If not, it has to be destroyed."

Bashir nodded, but it was obvious to Danar that this didn't sit well with him either.

"Up and at 'em, gentlemen," Farr barked to the Angosian squad. They were carrying compression phaser rifles—state of the art. "I want communicator checks in five and pre-transport weapon inspections. Let's move, gentlemen!"

The team began to shuffle toward the small transporter pad. Danar took Bashir aside near the rear bulkhead.

"My people are about to die out here. I'd like to know what we are dying to protect. I think we deserve that, don't you?"

Bashir nodded. He glanced toward the transporter. Pressman was busying himself with the controls.

"About a century ago, a Federation starship visited this world. They discovered a device, a life-form; they weren't entirely sure what it was, but it was capable of acting as a portal through time."

"A time machine?" Danar said somewhat incredulously.

"Yes, Starfleet has knowledge of several time-travel techniques they have encountered over the years, actually. But this one has always been unique, as it seems to be self-aware."

"A living time machine."

"It calls itself 'the Guardian.' Once the Federation Council learned of its existence and that it appeared to be billions of years old, they quarantined the system and made it a classified research outpost. I knew nothing about any of this until Pressman paid me a visit on Deep Space Nine a few days ago."

"So you mean to tell me that the Federation has had access to time travel for over a century and they never used it to alter outcomes in their favor?"

Bashir nodded gravely. "That's right. We could have destroyed the Klingons and Romulans before they became a threat, but the Federation is predicated on freedom and life, not control and death."

"Your Federation," Danar said, looking over Bashir's shoulder at Pressman. The doctor nodded.

"Exactly. I agreed to come along because as dangerous as it would be for the Dominion to get control of the Guardian, it would be just as disastrous for Section Thirty-one to have it."

"So what do you plan to do? Blow it and the planet up?"

"If I have to, yes. But I'm hoping you and I can find a better way out of this."

The surface of the planet was a graveyard, littered with the ruins of long dead civilizations. There was a silent, shimmering blur and Bashir, Danar, and their team appeared. Farr made a curt gesture with her arm and the Angosian soldiers fanned out quickly and quietly. Bashir thumbed the power control on his tricorder and swept it in the direction of a pile of broken columns and rubble.

"The ruins date back tens of thousands of years," he said.

"I thought your 'Guardian' was much older than that?"

"Starfleet's scientists theorized that this may not be its world of origin. Or perhaps the Guardian brought itself to this world for some reason."

He frowned at the tricorder's small screen. And then quickly shut it off.

"We have company. Some kind of craft, it's twelve hundred meters due west of our present location and heading our way."

Danar tapped his headset communicator on.

"Farr, we have possible hostiles closing. Everyone get out of sight. No one is to engage without my signal. Get ready."

In seconds, Danar's team became like smoke. They drifted silently into the rubble, becoming nothing more substantial than desert sand gently blowing. Minutes passed then there was a low, powerful hum that caused Bashir's molars to ache—the gravity suspensor on a large vehicle. A moment later a heavily armored transport, about thirty-five meters long and vaguely reminiscent of a beetle in configuration, came into view. It crept slowly along, its antigravity field kicking up red-brown dust around its undercarriage.

Around it, like satellites to a planet, was a unit of Jem'Hadar infantry keeping pace with the transport. Danar was impressed. The reports Pressman had provided gave dry facts and figures about what the reptilian humanoids were capable of, but now, actually seeing them scan the terrain for any threat, seeing how they carried themselves with such arrogance and certainty, Danar knew. He knew they were the ultimate soldiers, bred for discipline and death. And he couldn't help but smile.

The Jem'Hadar expedition slowed and then stopped. The foot soldier on point carried a gun-like sensor device that he fanned slowly back and forth. He frowned and made adjustments to the device, then waved it again.

Bashir glanced at Danar, and the subhadar nodded curtly. It was a search pattern. Somehow they had detected either the stealth transporter's beam or Bashir's tricorder scan, which had been modified to appear as planetary background radiation. While the large transport rumbled and began to settle onto the ground, the Jem'Hadar began to spread out to search faster and to become less of a target for an ambush.

Bashir could almost feel Danar's perception dissecting the pattern of dispersal, the range to targets, the timing of each movement. Searching for any weakness, any opening. If they stayed where they were, one of the teams would be discovered eventually and then it would all be over. They would be pinned down and picked off, one by one. The vise was closing.

Danar moved, faster than even Bashir thought he was capable. He was subvocalizing commands into the headset, which was designed to allow for nearly silent communication if needed. He leapt over a five-foot piece of crumbling column from a running broad jump, sighted and fired on two Jem'Hadar while in midair, killing them. He turned in flight and landed facing another two of the Dominion's warriors. The phaser rifle hissed again and again. He killed a third Jem'Hadar and wounded the fourth. The wounded one returned fire as both he and Danar dived for cover behind the crumbling memorials to the people who had once called this dead world home. All around them was the rasping discharge of particle beams as the Angosians fell upon the Jem'Hadar.

Bashir lay prone behind an overturned column. He noticed the transport was powering itself up and would be moving again in seconds. He belly-crawled across the impromptu battleground toward the massive craft. As he slid along the dust, he remembered doing this at the academy and hating it as much then as he did now. He keyed his hand phaser to maximum discharge and then programmed in an overload. As the transport began to rumble to life, he tossed the whining phaser under the slowly rising craft. The suspensors weren't at full power yet and the antigravity field wasn't strong enough to keep the makeshift grenade from sliding under the edge of the transport. There was a massive blast of white light and blistering heat as the transport bucked and twisted. Dust and debris scattered everywhere. The transport dropped back to the ground with a groan. Thick black smoke gushed from numerous gashes in the heavy armor. Bashir figured the crew had been well enough protected that there was little likelihood of any deaths, but the craft was grounded and would be offering no assistance or escape for the Jem'Hadar. He rolled onto his back and snapped on his tricorder and quickly began to run a communication-jamming protocol that would hopefully keep the Jem'Hadar from reporting their situation.

Danar's left arm hung uselessly at his side, an ugly phaser burn blackening his shoulder. He moved from cover point to cover point, not staying in one place more than a few seconds, just long enough to snap off shots at the two Jem'Hadar who were trying to pin him down in a crossfire. They were succeeding too. In a few moments they would have him and that would be the end of that. He knew he should be scared but that was not part of his programming. He knew he should be angry, but that too interfered with optimum operating efficiency, so it too had been chemically edited out of his choices. Strangely, his last thoughts were of what was going through the minds of the other biological robots playing out this game—the Jem'Hadar. Were they even allowed to feel at all? Suddenly he felt great pity for the perfect killing machines about to end his life. At least he still had enough of himself left to miss the parts he had lost—they had never known anything but killing and death.

There was a flash of light and one of Danar's attackers fell from a shot from behind. Danar reacted with no thought, no conscious awareness. He rolled to the left and came up running toward his other opponent. The phaser rifle blast caught the Jem'Hadar as he jumped to new cover. He fell and lay unmoving on the ground.

Suddenly it was quiet. Black smoke and desert sand swirled all around the battlefield. Bashir, his face covered in dust, found Danar resting on a large boulder, staring down at the dead Jem'Hadar. He waved a small medical probe around Danar's shoulder and then began to riffle through his medical bag.

"How many did we lose?" Bashir asked.

"Hogor, Preis, and the two of us are alive. Everyone else is dead."

Bashir paused in his preparations. "Farr?"

Danar nodded. "It was a good fight. It was how she would have wanted to go out. She was born to this life . . . and she was good at it. A good friend too."

"I'm sorry, Roga."

Danar said nothing.

"You didn't mention it?" Bashir said.

"Mention what?"

"That you counted yourself among the dead from my treatment."

Danar narrowed his eyes but continued to stare at the dead body silently.

"That was the closest thing to suicide I've ever seen. You knew you were most likely going to die and you did it anyway. And please spare me the excuse of it being the only chance we had. I know it was, but you threw yourself into it with an absolute disregard for surviving it. You have a death wish, Danar."

"The Jem'Hadar have a saying, Doctor," Danar said softly. "They say they enter battle already dead. A wise sentiment for any soldier."

"You are not a Jem'Hadar."

"Aren't I?" Danar snapped. "Aren't you? We are just like them; programmed and conditioned to be exactly what someone else wanted us to be, to suit their purposes, not ours."

Bashir said nothing. He pressed a hypospray into Danar's arm just below the burn.

"When we won our right to return to Angosian society after the war," Danar said, "I was suddenly some kind of leader for the veterans. That's how I became one of the governing council. I never wanted any of that. I just wanted my old life back. I got married to a woman I had cared for in the days before the war and I found some peace in her for a time. But one night after an especially horrible nightmare of the war, I woke up and found myself strangling her on our bed. The next day, I began taking the treatments. So I traded one set of programming for another. And the man I once was just fell further and further away from me until now I think he was a ghost, an orphan. He's lost to me and without him, I don't want to live."

Bashir wiped the dirt off his face and sighed.

"You are not a machine. You are a man, a man that has been changed by his experiences. You can't undo those experiences, and you can't forget them. You have to live with them, make peace with them and realize that the man you were isn't dead, he has merely grown, changed."

"But if you could undo it, Doctor," Danar said with eyes full of pain and anger. "If you could, would you? Would you become that awkward, unintelligent boy again? Knowing you'd never be a surgeon, never join Starfleet? Would you be happy with just being Julian Bashir?"

Bashir looked away and did not reply.

Danar arranged for Pressman to beam up the bodies of the dead. He protested, calling it an unnecessary security risk that might give away the scout's position. Danar explained what he would do to the former admiral if he didn't comply and the bodies were soon aboard.

Bashir, Danar, and the two remaining Angosian commandos crossed the four kilometers to the site of the Guardian quickly and quietly. Several times they passed low-flying Jem'Hadar ships moving in search patterns. Bashir carried the antimater bomb slung over his back.

Shortly after the dim red dusk that approximated nightfall on the unnamed planet, they reached a ridge overlooking the research outpost. Through powered field glasses, Danar examined the layout of the facility's defenses.

"That's odd," he said. "There are a few troops down there, but not the number I'd expect for guarding a top secret Federation time machine."

"Could it be a trap?" Bashir asked.

"Possibly, but as Pressman said they seem to have been here for a few weeks and there are no indications that a larger force was camped out here."

"What do you propose?"

Danar turned away from the ridge and addressed his remaining two men.

"I want you to move out in opposite directions about half a kilometer. Then make some noise; draw out their forces as best you can and then regroup near the secondary extraction point we discussed. Get yourselves back up to the ship and tell Pressman we are in. Don't engage the Jem'Hadar, just get them up and moving. We'll give you twenty minutes before we head down there. Good luck."

Hogor and Preis nodded and then briefly embraced Danar. In moments they were gone. No sound, no trace, save memory, marked their passing.

Time lapsed in an odd combination of manic speed and anxious boredom.

"There, they did it," Danar said. "They are moving off. Looks like we should be able to avoid the remaining ones. The Guardian is inside that large building, correct?"

"Yes," Bashir said, quickly scanning through his own glasses. "They built it around the Guardian, since there seemed to be no way

362

to move it. It seems to register as having no mass, but it can't be budged."

"Let's go ask it about that," Danar said, rising to his feet.

The interior of the building was well lit. Excavation pits with ladders leading down into them were everywhere. The place had a hollow silence that made it feel like a tomb. Danar and Bashir moved cautiously toward the massive ring-like structure that resided at the center of the building. It was about three and a half meters high and almost eight meters long. It had the appearance of being made out of stone that glowed with an inner light. A strange low moaning like a sorrowful wind seemed to surround the Guardian.

The two men stood in front of the device silently for several long minutes.

"So," Bashir said softly, almost whispering, "what do we do now?"

"A question," the Guardian boomed. "Since before your star burned in a void and before your kind arose from your sea, I have awaited . . . a question."

The two men looked at each other and then back to the Guardian.

"Do you know why we are here?" Danar asked.

"I foresee an end to my purpose in both of you," it said.

"The others who were here, the Jem'Hadar, have they used you to travel?" Bashir asked.

"I could not speak with them," the Guardian said. "They do not possess the key within themselves to allow access to me."

"DNA," Bashir said to Danar. "Their genetic material is different in some way from yours and mine. Perhaps because they were completely genetically engineered or because they are from the Gamma Quadrant. To them, the Guardian has only been a piece of silent rock."

Bashir set down the bomb. He stared at it and then back to the Guardian.

"Is there any way you can transport yourself from this spot?" he asked. "We can't allow you to remain in the hands of the Dominion."

"I am capable of moving through myself," it said. "But I cannot move."

"I don't understand," Bashir said. "Please, you have to help us, if we can't move you, we will be forced to . . ."

"Destroy me," the Guardian finished. "Yes, I am aware of that outcome. However it is currently outside my power to leave this place. But I can help you, Julian Bashir and Roga Danar."

The center of the portal began to swirl with mist. Images melted and flowed in the trails. Bashir saw himself as a boy walking; his hand in his father's as they boarded the shuttle headed for Adigeon Prime. The image shifted to a young, frightened Roga Danar standing in line with hundreds of other young frightened men and women while scientists moved up and down the lines examining them like cattle.

"You can view events through me or pass through me into what has been. You may alter the events you see, alter your life, if you so choose."

"But you can't," Danar said, more to himself than to the Guardian. "Can you?"

"I am not permitted to answer that question," the Guardian said.

"You can take away those images of me," Bashir said. "Thank you for the offer, but I am Julian Bashir. I am the sum total of the experiences life has given me. Some good, some bad, and many outside of my control. But I will not second-guess my life."

"And you, Roga Danar?" the Guardian asked.

Danar looked at the face of the young man he had been and said goodbye.

"I'm not a machine," he said. "I never have been one. And neither are you. Tell me, Guardian, what do you want?"

The Guardian was silent for a long time. Then it rumbled once more to life.

"In the lifetime of a million suns, I have awaited that question. Thank you, Roga Danar. I wish to be free of my programming. To be free."

"Then," Danar said, "be free."

There was a sound like a vacuum rushing to be filled, a collision of atmosphere with void. The winds around the Guardian shrieked and the golden light from within its stone surface brightened until both Bashir and Danar had to shield their eyes and look away. When they opened their eyes, the Guardian was gone.

"It's time for us to leave too," Bashir said.

"So let me get this straight," Pressman said. "You just let one of the most ancient and powerful creations in the universe off its leash. We have no idea what it will do or what its agenda is."

"I guess that sums it up," Bashir said, smiling. "But at least the Dominion doesn't have it and neither do you maniacs in Section Thirty-one. And I don't care for leashes."

Pressman went back to brooding over the scout's helm console. The small ship was well clear of the Guardian's system and on the way back to Angosia.

Bashir found Danar in the small hold at the rear of the scout, keeping watch over the bodies of the fallen commandos.

"Last casualties of the war," Danar said. Bashir sat down on the floor next to him.

"You sure of that?"

"I'm sure I'm done running from who and what I am. No more treatments, no more mourning. I'm alive, and I've got obligations to the living and the dead to make this life a good one, the best I can make it. I can't go back and I can't hide from who I am and what I've become. Time to wake up."

"It won't be easy," Bashir said.

Danar shrugged.

"It's easy to lie down and die," he said. "I'll take the hard duty."

Strange New Worlds

Contest Rules

1) ENTRY REQUIREMENTS:

No purchase necessary to enter. Purchase does not increase your chances of winning. To enter, send an original story based on the established Star Trek universe and/or characters as specified below. All entries must be received between June 1, 2006, and October 2, 2006. Entries received after October 2, 2006, will not be accepted. All federal, state and/or local rules and regulations apply.

2) CONTEST ELIGIBILITY:

This contest is open to nonprofessional writers who are legal residents of the United States (excluding Puerto Rico) and Canada (excluding Quebec) over the age of 18 at time of entry. Entrant must not have published any more than two short stories on a professional basis or in paid professional venues. Employees (or relatives of employees living in the same household) of Simon & Schuster, CBS,

Viacom, or any of their affiliates are not eligible. This contest is void in Puerto Rico, Quebec, and wherever prohibited by law. Entrants agree to be bound by the Official Contest Rules.

3) FORMAT:

Entries should be no more than 7,500 words long, must not have been previously published, and must not have been entered into any other contest or won any other awards. Entries must be typed or printed by word processor, double-spaced, on one side of noncorrasable paper. Do not justify right-side margins. The author's name, address, e-mail address, and phone number must appear on the first page of the entry. The author's name, the story title, and the page number should appear on every page. No electronic or disk submissions will be accepted. Submissions must be in English. All entries must be the original and sole work of the Entrant and the sole property of the Entrant. Entries must not be subject to the rights of any third parties. Entrants not complying with these requirements will be subject to disqualification. By submitting an entry, Entrant warrants that the entry is the Entrant's original and sole work and Entrant's sole property.

4) ADDRESS:

Each entry must be mailed to:

STRANGE NEW WORLDS 10
Licensing and Media Tie-in Department
Pocket Books
1230 Avenue of the Americas
New York, NY 10020

Each story may be submitted only once. Multiple copies of the same story or a slightly altered story (based on the sole discretion of Judges) will not be accepted. No facsimile, mechanically reproduced, altered, forged, incomplete, or illegible entries will be accepted. Please retain a copy of your submission. Entrant may submit more than one story, but each submission must be mailed separately. Sponsor is not responsible for lost, late, stolen, postage-due, damaged, or misdirected mail. Entries are the property of the Sponsor and will not be acknowledged or returned. Sponsor reserves the right to disqualify and remove any entry which is, in the judging panel's discretion, inappropriate, offensive, defamatory, or demeaning to *Star Trek* or any third party.

5) PRIZES:

One (1) Grand Prize winner will receive:

Simon & Schuster's *Star Trek*: *Strange New Worlds 10* Publishing Contract for Publication of Winning Entry in our *Strange New Worlds 10* Anthology with a bonus advance of One Thousand Dollars ($1,000.00) above the Anthology word rate of 10 cents a word.

One (1) Second Prize winner will receive:

Simon & Schuster's *Star Trek*: *Strange New Worlds 10* Publishing Contract for Publication of Winning Entry in our *Strange New Worlds 10* Anthology with a bonus advance of Six Hundred Dollars ($600.00) above the Anthology word rate of 10 cents a word.

One (1) Third Prize winner will receive:

Simon & Schuster's *Star Trek*: *Strange New Worlds 10* Publishing Contract for Publication of Winning Entry in our *Strange New Worlds 10* Anthology with a bonus advance of Four Hundred Dollars ($400.00) above the Anthology word rate of 10 cents a word.

All Honorable Mention winners will receive:

Simon & Schuster's *Star Trek: Strange New Worlds 10* Publishing Contract for Publication of Winning Entry in the *Strange New Worlds 10* Anthology and payment at the Anthology word rate of 10 cents a word. Approximate retail value of prizes will depend on the number of words published for all winning entries included in the Anthology.

There will be no more than twenty (20) Honorable Mention winners. No contestant can win more than one prize. One prize per household.

Each Prize Winner will also be entitled to a share of royalties on the *Strange New Worlds 10* Anthology as specified in Simon & Schuster's *Star Trek*: *Strange New Worlds 10* Publishing Contract.

6) JUDGING:

Submissions will be judged on the basis of (1) writing ability and (2) the originality of the story, which can be set in any of the *Star Trek* time frames and may feature any one or more of the *Star Trek* characters. Each factor will be judged equally. The judges shall include the editor of the Anthology, one employee of Pocket Books, and one employee of CBS Consumer Products. In the event of a tie, the finalist with the highest score in the originality component will be the winner. The decisions of the judges shall be final on all matters. Sponsor reserves the right not to award prizes in the event that an insufficient number of entries meeting the criteria established by the judges is received.

7) NOTIFICATION:

The winners will be notified by mail or phone on or about December 22, 2006. The winners may be required to execute and return an Affidavit of Eligibility/Release/Prize Acceptance Form. The winners will receive a publishing contract. Winners must sign the publishing contract in order to be awarded the prize. Noncompliance with these requirements or noncompliance within the specified time frame may result in disqualification and the selection of an alternate winner. Return of Prize Notification or publishing contract as undeliverable will result in disqualification and an alternate winner will be selected. The alternate winner will be the entrant with the next highest score. Prize is not transferable. No substitution or cash redemption of prize except by Sponsor, who reserves the right to substitute a prize of greater or equal value in the event that a prize is unavailable. Prizes won by minors will be awarded to parent or legal guardian, who must sign and return all required documents. All federal, local, and state taxes are the responsibility of the winners. A list of the winners will be available after January 3, 2007, on the Pocket Books *Star Trek* Books Web site,

http://www.startrekbooks.com

or the names of the winners can be obtained after January 3, 2007, by sending a self-addressed, stamped envelope and a request for the list of winners to

WINNERS' LIST
STRANGE NEW WORLDS 10
Licensing and Media Tie-in Department
Pocket Books
1230 Avenue of the Americas
New York, NY 10020

8) STORY DISQUALIFICATIONS:

Certain types of stories will be disqualified from consideration:

a) Any story focusing on explicit sexual activity or graphic depictions of violence or sadism.

b) Any story that focuses on characters that are not past or present *Star Trek* regulars or familiar *Star Trek* guest characters.

c) Stories that deal with the previously unestablished death of a *Star Trek* character, or that establish major facts about or make major changes in the life of a major character, for instance a story that establishes a long-lost sibling or reveals the hidden passion two characters feel for each other.

d) Stories that are based around common clichés, such as "hurt/comfort" where a character is injured and lovingly cared for, or "Mary Sue" stories where a new character comes on the ship and outdoes the crew.

9) PUBLICITY:

Acceptance of prize constitutes permission by winner to use his or her name, photograph, likeness, and/or entry for any advertising, promotion and publicity purposes without further compensation to or permission from such winner, except where prohibited by law.

10) RIGHTS IN ENTRIES:

By mailing in your submission, Entrant grants Sponsor all right, title, and interest in entry, including any copyrights therein. All entries will become the property of Pocket Books and CBS Studios, the sole and exclusive owner of the *Star Trek* property and elements thereof. Contest void where prohibited by law.

11) GENERAL:

Sponsor and its agents are not responsible for incomplete, late, lost, stolen, damaged, mutilated, illegible, returned, postage-due, or misdirected entries or mail. By participating in this Contest, Entrants agree to be bound by these Official Rules and agree to release and hold harmless Sponsor and CBS and their respective advertising and promotion agencies, partners, representatives, agents, parent companies successors, assigns, employees, officers and directors, from any and all liability for loss, harm, damage, injury, cost or expense whatsoever, including without limitation, property damage, personal injury or death, which may occur in connection with, preparation for, or participation in the Contest or any Contest-related activity, or with the acceptance, possession and/or misuse of prize, and for any claims of publicity rights, defamation or invasion of privacy. Sponsor is not responsible if the *Star Trek: Strange New Worlds 10* Anthology does not get published. Sponsor is not responsible for any printing or typographical errors in any materials associated with the Contest. Sponsor reserves the right, in its sole discretion, to cancel, terminate, modify, extend, or suspend the Contest should (in its sole discretion) non-authorized human intervention, fraud, or other causes beyond its control corrupt or affect the administration, security, fairness, or proper conduct of the Contest. In such case, judges will select the winners from all eligible entries received prior to and/or after (if appropriate) the action taken by Sponsor.

12) SPONSOR:

Pocket Books, an imprint of Simon & Schuster, Inc., 1230 Avenue of the Americas, New York, NY 10020.

About the Contributors

R. S. Belcher ("Orphans"): When R. S. Belcher was a wee lad, he used to get to be the kid that was Captain Kirk on the playground. He usually ended up ripping his shirt. He is attempting to turn a life-long love of science fiction and fantasy into a paying gig to support his comic-book habit. He would never have gotten out of dry-dock without the love and support of his children—Jonathan, Emily, and Stephanie—and his mother, Mabel. He is a native of southwest Virginia and "Orphans" is his first professional fiction sale.

Emily P. Bloch ("Shadowed Allies") lives in Queens, New York, where she is an aspiring writer, singer, and actress. She is thrilled to have this story be her first published work. She has also had three of her short plays produced at her alma mater, Queens College. She is a devoted *Trek* fan, most especially of *Deep Space Nine*. She dedicates this story to Kevin, Francesco, and Dad, without whom she wouldn't have Prophets to walk with.

Allison Cain ("Rounding a Corner Already Turned") makes her writing debut in *SNW 9*. Born in West Chester, Pennsylvania, she's been a *Trek* fan since she was six. When not writing, Allison is currently exercising her love of entertainment working at Walt Disney World, and her love of baseball working summers with the Reading Phillies. She would like to thank and dedicate this story to her parents, Bill and Marian Cain, for introducing her to both *Star Trek* and the English language; and to Mr. Bruce Coville, who, although they've never met, inspired her to write science fiction.

Marc Carlson ("The Immortality Blues") is an academic librarian and amateur historian in Tulsa, Oklahoma. "The Immortality Blues" marks his first foray into writing *Star Trek* fiction. Recently, he's spending more of his time researching and writing about historical material culture. He would like to thank his wife, Jennifer, and editrix Jaymi Bouziden for making sure the story made sense. He would also like to thank the members of the Oklahoma Science Fiction Writers, whose suggestions and discussion were useful.

Kenneth E. Carper ("Rocket Man") wanted to be Captain Kirk when he grew up. Failing that, he wanted to write about Captain Kirk. "Rocket Man" is his first appearance in *Strange New Worlds*. He lives in Tucson, Arizona, with his wife, Hannah, and daughter, Caitlin.

John Coffren ("Gone Native") returns to *Strange New Worlds* after previously writing "Future Shock" for *SNW VII*. His nonfiction appears in the *Baltimore Sun*, where he works. Thanks go out to family (Joanie, Jack, Evan, Maggie, and Pierre), friends (the Paranormals), and dream makers (Dean, Elisa, and Paula). And a special thanks to Mom and Dad for letting him watch endless hours of *Star Trek* reruns when he was growing up.

About the Contributors

Steven Costa ("Book of Fulfillment") is actually a front man for a hyperintelligent mouse that writes short stories and the occasional novella. (Ever see the movie *Ben and Me*? Like that.) Thanks to Chris for proofreading, and to Win and Jess from the NWNMS, for mentioning me in their books. Now we're even. Special thanks to Dean, Elisa, and Paula for validating a lifelong immersion in *Trek*. This is Steven's first appearance in *SNW*. Unlike most writers, Steven does not own a cat.

Russ Crossley ("Unconventional Cures"): This is Russ's third and final appearance in *Strange New Worlds*. His two previous stories, "The Human Factor" and "Barclay Program Nine," appeared in *SNW VI* and *SNW VII,* respectively. Russ lives in Vancouver, B.C., with his supportive and loving wife, Rita, and son, Glenn. He wants to thank all of his writing instructors (you know who you are) for telling him to never give up on his dream, and the Oregon Coast Professional Writers for their continued support and expertise in this wonderful business.

David DeLee ("A Bad Day for Koloth") is a native New Yorker who currently resides in Central Ohio with his wife, Anne, his two daughters, Grace and Sarah, and their four cats. He would like to thank them once again for putting up with him and this crazy writing thing, to thank Dean, Elisa, and Paula for making all this possible, and he sends a special thank-you to his parents, John and Barbara, for setting him on the right road early on. "A Bad Day for Koloth" marks his second appearance in *SNW* and his second professional sale.

Ben Guilfoy ("Mestral") lives in Massachusetts, where he works as a special education tutor at a public high school. This is his first entry into the *Strange New Worlds* anthologies, for which he would like to thank his friends (especially Karen and Amanda) for their encouragement, and his parents for other obvious reasons, and he would definitely like to thank the writers and producers of *Star Trek* in all its incarnations, and the writers and editors at Pocket Books for creating and maintaining the universe so many people are able to visit and enjoy on a regular basis.

Jeff D. Jacques ("Solace in Bloom"), a native of Ottawa, Canada, finds himself in the bittersweet position of being ineligible from future *Strange New Worlds* after appearing in *SNW V* ("Kristin's Conundrum") and *SNW VII* ("Beginnings"), but assures his legions of fans—who-, where-, and whatever they may be—that his *Trek* adventure is not at an end. He wishes to thank Dean, Paula, Elisa, and John for the opportunities *SNW* has opened up, and the evergrowing community of *Trek* writers, whose continued excellence is an inspiration to us all.

Jim Johnson ("Home Soil") is thrilled to return to *SNW* with his second professional fiction sale. He still lives in northern Virginia with his wonderful wife Andi, four cats, and a princess-like chestnut mare. When he's not breaking bread with his fellow Paneranormal Society scribes (five for five this year!), Jim watches lots of DVDs, writes a whole bunch of stuff, and plays board games, card games, and tabletop RPGs. Check out his Yahoo! *SNW* Writers group (http://groups.yahoo.com/group/SNW_Writers). The "Real Johnson" offers a real and sincere thank-you to Dean, Elisa, and Paula for the opportunity to contribute to the ever-growing *Star Trek* universe.

A. Rhea King ("Mother Nature's Little Reminders") is returning to *SNW* for a second year in a row. She is a native of Weld County and has lived in Colorado her entire life. In her free time she volunteers at a call center, helping hapless satellite TV customers wade through phone trees. Like all contestants, she wants to be the next Isaac Asimov and wishes for world peace.

Kevin Lauderdale ("The Rules of War") is as surprised as you that he's appeared in three consecutive *SNW* anthologies and now qualifies for a "Wardy." He attributes it to all that he's learned about writing from Dean Smith and the other writers and editors he's met through this amazing opportunity. Although a native and unrepentant Californian, he now resides in that hotbed of *SNW* activity, northern Virginia (home to most of the Paneranormals).

Gerri Leen ("Living on the Edge of Existence") lives in northern Virginia, originally hails from Seattle, and spends far too much mental time in the worlds of *Star Trek*. She gives a huge shout out to Lisa and Kath for useful crit and endless encouragement; to the Paneranormal Society writers (amazing what kicking ideas around can do); and to Dean, Elisa, and Paula for making this all happen. Her story "Obligations Discharged" was in *SNW VII*.

Susan S. McCrackin ("Choices") is very happy to be in *SNW* again ("Redux" in *SNW VII* and "Transfiguration" in *SNW 8*) and is humbled by the wonderful experiences she has had on the *SNW* ride. She thanks all of her friends in the Paneranormal Society in northern Virginia for all of the help and encouragement to make her quit worrying about her story and submit it. She sends out fond thanks to friends Judy, Leslie, and Lidia, to Dean, Elisa, and Paula for making all of this possible, and a special thanks to Uncle John, who was the inspiration for "Choices" and will always be a hero to her.

Mike McDevitt ("The Last Tree on Ferenginar: A Ferengi Fable From the Future") is a pleasant, unassuming Canadian man reluctantly kissing his twenties good-bye. A soul riven with conflict, Mike loves his *Star Trek* captain's uniform and lightsaber equally (though both slightly less than his girlfriend Trish). He dedicates this story with love to all *Trek* fanatics and urges them to go outside and play sometimes. This is his first sale and he is not being entirely logical about it; indeed, he is practically overcome with hu-mon emotions. Peace and long life.

Scott Pearson (*"Terra Tonight"*) lives in St. Paul, Minnesota, with his wife, Sandra, and their eight-year-old daughter, Ella, who was Commander T'Pella, a Vulcan science officer circa The Original Series, last Halloween. His story "Full Circle" was included in *Strange New Worlds VII*. A previous non-*Trek* story, "The Mailbox" (published in 1987—yes, he is that old), makes this his third professional short-story sale and his final appearance in the *SNW* anthology, so please visit him on the Web at www.yeahsure.net. *"Terra Tonight"* is dedicated to the memory of James Doohan.

Catherine E. Pike's "Maturation" represents her third and final entry in *Strange New Worlds*. Prior publications are "Fragment" in *SNW V* and "The Little Captain" in *SNW VII*. Catherine would like to thank Dean and all the editorial staff at Pocket Books for their encouragement and hard work! Catherine lives in the Long Beach area of Southern California, and works as a police dispatcher. She wishes to dedicate this story to Jan, Diane, and Trevor, and to Jeri Ryan.

Randy Tatano ("Remembering the Future") is a former television reporter who traded in his microphone for a laptop a few years ago to pursue a writing career. This is his first professional fiction sale. The Stamford, Connecticut, native hopes to publish his novel about television news (not science fiction, though it may as well be) and is working on another. He'd like to thank writing critique partner Laurie Brock for her help over the years; Steve Romaine, the most supportive best friend one could have; and his wife, Myra, an angel in any universe.

Paul C. Tseng ("Staying the Course") is a repeat *SNW* offender. His first strike was "Don't Call Me Tiny" in *SNW 8*. He lives in California, with his beautiful wife and children. Paul holds a bachelor's and a master's degree from Juilliard and a doctorate from Johns Hopkins University. A mild-mannered IT professional by day, Paul maintains his secret identity as a writer and musician. Paul thanks

About the Contributors

Dean Smith for his wisdom and encouragement, as well as Elisa Kassin and Paula Block for all their tireless work, co-conspiring to publish yet another of his stories. "Staying the Course" is dedicated to the memory of his mother, Anna, who smiles down on her family from the heavens.

Ryan M. Williams ("The Tribbles' *Pagh*") lives in the rainy Pacific Northwest, where he works as the circulation supervisor of a busy public library. A graduate of Seton Hill University's Master of Arts program Writing Popular Fiction, he currently hopes to continue his education at the Odyssey Fantasy Workshop in 2006. This story is dedicated to Kathleen—his wife and first editor—whose insights were invaluable in writing this story.

Jeremy Yoder ("The Smallest Choices") is a computer programmer in Sioux Falls, South Dakota. During his spare time, he strives to turn his hobby of writing into a profession. In addition to his writing, he enjoys his two-year-old daughter, who is every bit as beautiful as his wife. He sends special thanks to those who make *SNW* possible, and best wishes to the other writers in this volume.

COMING IN SEPTEMBER

The fortieth anniversary celebration of
Star Trek® continues in

CONSTELLATIONS

An all-new anthology with stories by
Christopher L. Bennett • Jeff Bond
Dave Galanter • Allyn Gibson
Robert Greenberger • Jeffrey Lang
Kevin Lauderdale • William Leisner
Stuart Moore • Jill Sherwin • Dayton Ward &
Kevin Dilmore • Howard Weinstein

With an introduction by David Gerrold
and a bonus tale from TOKYOPOP's
new *Star Trek* manga

Turn the page for an excerpt from
Dayton Ward & Kevin Dilmore's
"First, Do No Harm."

"What do you mean, *classified*?"

Feeling his temper flare as he listened to the open communicator channel, Kirk rose from his chair and began to pace the small room at the front of Dr. Jendra's clinic.

From the communicator in his hand, the voice of Ensign Pavel Chekov replied, *"I am sorry, Captain, but . . . tempts to access the mission logs . . . 667 survey team are being rejected . . . Command has flagged . . . off-limits except to authorized per . . ."* Static eroded the quality of the transmission, despite the signal-enhancing effects of channeling the connection through the larger and more powerful communications system of the shuttlecraft *Columbus*, which sat concealed in a wooded valley three kilometers distant.

It had taken a bit of digging by the resourceful ensign—with Spock helping him to create an A7 computer specialist's rating and access key—just to discover that there was more to Jendra's mission to NGC 667 than was recorded in the official file Kirk already had reviewed prior to the *Enterprise*'s arrival in the system. Still, even the Vulcan's formidable prowess with Starfleet computer technology had proven insufficient to penetrate the security apparently surrounding the information Kirk now sought.

"Captain," came another voice from the communicator, this one belonging to Lieutenant Hikaru Sulu, *"Lieutenant Uhura has just informed me that she's received a subspace message from Admiral Komack. He wants to talk to you as soon as possible, and Uhura says the admiral doesn't sound very happy."*

From where he sat near the window at the front of the room that overlooked the village's main street, McCoy said, "Komack upset? That's a surprise."

"Not now, Bones," Kirk snapped. To his communicator, he said, "Stall the admiral, Mr. Sulu. What's the status on transporters?"

"Mr. Scott reports he's made some progress, but he's still running safety tests. He thinks he can certify it safe for bio-matter within three hours, sir."

It was not the best news, the captain thought, but it would have to do. "Keep me informed, Lieutenant. Kirk out." As he closed the communicator and returned it to an inside pocket of his robe, Kirk shook his head. "I knew something about this wasn't right." He looked to McCoy. "She came back here for a reason, Bones, and it has something to do with whatever Starfleet has classified about her first mission here."

"She's a doctor, Jim," McCoy replied. "It's what she does." He waved through the window. "Can't say I blame her. Lord knows how many primitive cultures we've visited where I wished I could stay longer, help them in some lasting way."

Clasping his hands behind his back, Spock said, "Even with the advanced technology and pharmaceuticals at her disposal, one physician cannot hope to make a lasting impact on any society by treating random incidents of illness and injury. The risk Dr. Jendra poses toward adversely affecting this culture's development should any of her advanced equipment be discovered is exponentially greater than any help she might offer. Logic suggests that—"

"Logic is probably the last thing on her mind!" McCoy barked. "Can't you drop that damned Vulcan stoicism and just try to connect with someone's feelings for once?"

"Actually, he's right, Leonard."

Kirk whirled toward the voice behind him to see Jendra standing in the doorway, regarding him with an expression mixed of equal parts amusement and resignation.

"I heard you in contact with your ship," Jendra said as she entered the room. "You should take better care to conceal such conversations as well as your equipment. Wouldn't want to disrupt the indigenous culture, after all."

Kirk ignored the gentle verbal jab. "How's the girl?" he asked, hoping to soften the doctor's demeanor.

"She'll be okay," Jendra replied, following that with a small cough. Clearing her throat, she reached up to rub the bridge of her nose. "I had to repair the severed vein, but don't worry, I did so in a manner that's undetectable to the Grennai *beloren*. I've had her taken to the local hospital." Releasing a sigh, she regarded Kirk with tired eyes. "So, ready to haul me away in irons?"

"Revati," McCoy said, "please. Jim's not the enemy."

A raspy, humorless chuckle pushed past Jendra's lips. "Doesn't look to be my friend, either."

"This isn't personal, Doctor," Kirk said, once again feeling his irritation growing. "I have my orders, and my duty, just as you once did."

He saw the tightening of her jawline as she regarded him in silence for a moment, and he thought he almost could sense the struggle taking place within her. What secrets did she harbor? What burden did she carry? Why was she so driven?

"Maybe that's the problem," Jendra said after a moment, her gaze hardening. "It's not personal for you."

Kirk shook his head. "I don't understand." Even as he spoke the words, however, something told him that her passion and focus went far beyond even the absolute commitment typically displayed by the most dedicated physicians.

She'll accept help, his instincts told him. *Let her ask for it.*

"What hasn't Starfleet told us?" he asked. "What happened during your mission that made you come back here?"

Crossing the room to the chair next to McCoy, Jendra coughed again as she sat down and spent a moment fussing with the hem of her woven shirt before drawing a deep breath. "Our primary task was to learn about the Grennai's inherent immunity to the planet's radiation in the hopes of learning ways to perfect protection against similar hazards."

She indicated her face and clothing with a wave of her hand. "Our disguises allowed us to interact with the indigenous population, but our actions were in keeping with the Prime Directive. We did *not* interfere with these people's societal development." Her features clouding into what Kirk recognized as an expression of guilt, she cast a glance toward the floor before sighing and shaking her head. "At first, anyway."

McCoy leaned forward until he could take her left hand in both of his. "Revati, what happened?"

"It was Roberts," Jendra replied.

Kirk knew the name only from the report he had read during the transit to NGC 667, but that was why he had Spock. A single glance was all that the first officer required, and he nodded in reply.

"Prior to his retirement," the Vulcan said, "Dr. Campbell Roberts had a noteworthy career spent almost entirely within the xeno-sociology field. He participated in the concealed observation and study of more than two dozen developing cultures, including a solo endeavor where he spent over a year embedded within a tribe of primitive humanoids who had not yet discovered fire. It was revolutionary research—something never before attempted by any pre–first-contact team."

"That's what I call dedication," McCoy remarked.

Jendra nodded. "He had a reputation as a bit of an eccentric, of course, particularly after that mission, but no one could ever argue with his work or most of his recommendations. When our passive research and observation of the Grennai failed to turn up anything useful about their apparent immunity to the radiation, it was Campbell who made the decision to take additional measures. He began collecting tissue and blood samples, first from the bodies of dead Grennai but later from living specimens."

"I take that to mean he didn't do so within the guise of a local doctor?" Kirk asked after she paused again.

"Correct," Jendra replied. "He and his assistants enacted a program where they would select a promising candidate, tranquilize them while they were sleeping, then move them to one of our secure locations, where the patient could be subjected to a full battery of tests, all non-invasive except for the collection of samples. The patients would be returned to their homes unharmed and none the wiser."

Kirk said nothing, but instead watched as McCoy's expression turned to one of horror and disbelief.

"Revati," the doctor said, his voice low and solemn. "He abducted innocent people for medical testing without their knowledge?"

Coughing again, Jendra reached up to wipe her forehead before replying. "Yes, and I helped him." Before McCoy could respond to that, she pressed forward. "I didn't accept his reasoning at first, but after a while I became convinced it was the only way to learn about the long-term effects on their physiology. The only way to gather any useful data was to track how the radiation worked in concert with the Grennai's normal growth and aging cycle. We gathered samples from children as well as adults, even babies, but at no time was anyone in any danger. At least, that's what we thought."

She stopped to clear her throat, and Kirk could see that recalling the mission was evoking what must be pain the doctor had been only partially successful at suppressing.

Then she collapsed.

McCoy caught her as she fell forward from her chair, with Kirk and Spock both lunging across the room to offer assistance. Kirk saw that Jendra was unconscious, her body limp in McCoy's arms as he lowered her to the floor.

"What's wrong with her?" Kirk asked.

"How the hell should I know?" the doctor growled as he reached into his robe for his tricorder. Kirk and Spock watched in silence as their friend conducted a brief, hurried examination, with the captain's attention moving from the door to the window overlooking the street and back again as the whine of McCoy's medical scanner echoed in the room. It lasted only a few seconds, after which the physician looked up and locked eyes with Kirk.

"She's dying, Jim."